Famous Trials in History

Famous Trials in History

Elisabeth A. Cawthon

Facts On File
An Infobase Learning Company

Facts On File, Inc.
An imprint of Infobase Learning
132 West 31st Street
New York NY 10001

Library of Congress Cataloging-in-Publication Data
Cawthon, Elisabeth A., 1957–
    Famous trials in history / Elisabeth A. Cawthon.
        p. cm.
    Includes bibliographical references and index.
    ISBN 978-0-8160-8167-7 (alk. paper)
1. Trials. I. Title.
    K540.C39 2011
    345'.02—dc22   2010047037

Facts On File books are available at special discounts when purchased in bulk quantities for businesses, associations, institutions, or sales promotions. Please call our Special Sales Department in New York at (212) 967-8800 or (800) 322-8755.

You can find Facts On File on the World Wide Web at http://www.infobaselearning.com

Excerpts included herewith have been reprinted by permission of the copyright holders; the author has made every effort to contact copyright holders. The publisher will be glad to rectify, in future editions, any errors or omissions brought to its notice.

Text design by Erik Lindstrom
Composition by Hermitage Publishing Services
Cover printed by Yurchak Printing, Landisville, Pa.
Book printed and bound by Yurchak Printing, Landisville, Pa.
Date printed: October 2011
Printed in the United States of America

10 9 8 7 6 5 4 3 2 1

This book is printed on acid-free paper.

We are always on the forge or on the anvil. By trials we are shaped for higher things.

—*Henry Ward Beecher*

CONTENTS

LIST OF TRIALS

ACKNOWLEDGMENTS

I am grateful to several individuals for contributing to my understanding of famous trials. Professors Calvin Woodard and Charles McCurdy were inspirational guides. Benita Campbell, Zainab Ezzi, James Grissom, Alex Hunnicutt, Aaron Johnson, and Christopher Johnson wrote papers on aspects of trials that I discuss here. In addition, persons in my "great trials" classes at three universities during the past 28 years have offered adept observations about some of these episodes. The comments of History 3319 students Miguel Villafana, Wahija Rizvi, and Justin Jones, for instance, honed my view of the John Brown trial. Jennifer Hudson Allen's reading of the Picton case during a graduate legal history seminar sharpened my appreciation for that episode in Atlantic history.

A number of libraries and repositories have been gracious in granting access to rare materials, particularly the W. A. C. Bennett Library at Simon Fraser University, the McFarlin Library at the University of Tulsa, the main library of Texas Tech University, the University of Waikato library, and the University of Michigan Law Library. Professor George Behlmer of the University of Washington, Captain Ann Sanborn of the U.S. Merchant Marine Academy, Dr. David Narrett and Dr. Steven Reinhardt of the University of Texas at Arlington, Reverend Phil Geleske, Dr. Phyllis Gee, Professor Richard Cosgrove of the University of Arizona, Professor Martin Wiener of Rice University, and Professor Caroline Cox of the Georgetown University School of Law made illuminating comments on various trials. Dru Richman came to the rescue in a computer crisis. Friends, including Samina Rashid, Michelle Hernandez, and Rupali Deshmuhk, and the entire 8:00 A.M. exercise class offered energy and encouragement during years of writing. Owen Lancer shepherded the manuscript through the editing process.

Despite any errors I have made, I hope that my continuing enthusiasm for legal history comes through. My children implore me not to write any books for a while. As I complete this one, I promise them and my wonderful husband more weekends at the park.

INTRODUCTION

The American abolitionist Henry Ward Beecher referred to trials as tests of the mettle of a society rather than simple determinations of guilt or innocence in a courtroom. His imagery is befitting the trials considered in this volume. While they may not all be well known to modern Anglo-American readers, the episodes spotlighted in this book are each of historical importance. These trials forged the people in whose midst they took place.

In the 21st century most societies hold trials. That is not to say that all trials are conducted under similar rules. One nation's trials may be only for show, to convince its citizens or the world that justice is being done. In other places trials are genuine contests in which the winners and losers are determined during the proceedings. Throughout history trials have been used less consistently than they are in more recent times, and they have differed from one another greatly in procedure and meaning. Trials sometimes have served as the crudest demonstrations of divine will, as when two champions engaged in a physical battle. In certain circumstances trials have been sophisticated and subtle, as when they have provided catharsis for a nation that is grieving the assassination of a beloved leader. As Beecher surely would have concurred, such was the case with the trial of the assassins of Abraham Lincoln after the United States Civil War.

Did a legal proceeding herald a great alteration in the course of future events, such as in the case of Thomas More? Or, was it a flash in the pan like the O. J. Simpson trial, intriguing contemporaries yet having no lasting impact? This collection of famous trials leans on the former type and mostly omits the latter. Despite great variation through time and across territory, trials often do have common characteristics. They are encompassed in finite episodes. They contain moments of joy, surprise, and drama. They have winners and losers. They involve stories that can be recalled long after the fact. They provide resolutions of disputes that have been intricate and longstanding.

Trials are not necessarily the same as cases. To follow a case from beginning to end means to probe the background of a legal controversy and study it through to its effects—sometimes long past a trial's conclusion. Even great cases do not always result in interesting trials. Cases of magnitude may be decided in dull hearings or on technical grounds while gaining little public notice. Sometimes it is only in looking back that scholars and the public realize a case was a watershed. Trials, on the other hand, attract attention when they occur. Indeed, some trials are deceptive; they seem galvanizing when in fact they are merely sensational. Certain trials are rallying points for great causes and can spur profound change.

Accounts of trials and collections of trial records in and of themselves can be of historical significance. As repositories of information about English history, for example, one thinks of the impact of Edward Coke's *Reports* as well as the State Trials compilations of the 17th through the 19th centuries. The Notable British Trials series of the modern era also is a rich offering for historians and the general public. While England has the most self-conscious tradition of legal historicism of any nation in the world, other countries also cherish writings about trials. The Islamic legal scholar

Nur al-Din Ali ibn Dawud al-Jawhari al-Sayrafi, for example, wrote a compendium of judicial decisions from 15th-century Egypt, and the Korean bureaucrats Hong In-ho and Ui-ho produced an exceptional record in the *Simnirok* of the 18th century. Such respected assemblages of material have shaped national conceptions of what law ought to be.

Trials and recollections of trials are of interest outside the ranks of scholars, lawyers, and politicians. Within the past few decades a number of books about trials have been published for both general and educational markets in the United States and the English-speaking world. In the 1990s, for example, Edward Knappman produced several books for Gale Press that focused on famous trials. Knappman's geographical coverage was broad, although he did concentrate somewhat on English and U.S. trials. At about the same time John Johnson edited *Historic U.S. Court Cases: An Encyclopedia* (Garland Publishing). Frank McLynn assembled an attractive single-volume collection for *Reader's Digest* called *Famous Trials, Cases That Made History.* Modern scholars have offered syntheses of certain classes of trials—state trials, for example, and human rights prosecutions—that go beyond the interpretive scope of this project. The present volume, for example, cannot approach the depth of analysis of Sadakat Kadri's *The Trial,* nor can it offer the links between cases that a more philosophical treatment features.

The Internet has enormously affected the availability of trial materials. Records and commentary that would have been obscure 20 years ago now are accessible for use by experts and casual readers. Several online sourcebooks were helpful in the preparation of this volume: Douglas Linder's famous trials online project, sponsored by the Law School of the University of Missouri–Kansas City; the Yale Law Library's Avalon Project; and Paul Halsall's Internet History Sourcebook at Fordham University. The Nuremberg Project at Harvard Law School and Yale's Genocide Studies Program provide superb collections of trial materials, as does the Law Library of Congress. Certain smaller Web projects, such as that of the

Chicago Historical Society and the Surratt House Museum, also offer beautiful presentations of annotated documents.

In addition to following trials online, the 21st-century public often learns of trials from the broadcast media. Television programs dramatize the operation of justice. There is a recent trend to depict real-life trials, as well, through news broadcasts and "reality shows." An older medium for describing trials is motion pictures. Several of the trials included here have been memorably treated on screen. A personal favorite for evocation of the physical aspects of one great trial is the film version of *A Man for All Seasons* with Paul Scofield in the role of Thomas More.

In the present summaries this author has made a conscious effort not to rely too heavily on commentary found on Internet sites, particularly Linder's valuable collection. In providing a fresh look at these episodes one does not want to be overinfluenced by other scholars' interpretations and selections of material. Instead, this author worked as much from documentary sources as possible, supplementing primary sources with recent monographs. Thus, summaries here rely about equally on other scholars' work and the raw material. About a quarter of these entries are grounded in this author's original research.

There are many provocative cases that are not included in this volume. Also, not every intriguing aspect of each trial is mentioned. A goal here has been to reflect mainstream scholarly opinion about the trials; some alternative interpretations, therefore, do not appear. Treatment here offers a general academic opinion of the trials but is not specifically geared to scholars. Rather, the focus is on presenting the facts of the trials and explaining their historical contexts for the general reader. The Further Reading section after each trial provides suggestions for analyses that are more detailed and that offer divergent viewpoints on the proceedings.

The entries in this volume come from every era in recorded history, but there is far more source material available from modern years than from medieval and ancient times. This study includes a range of different types of trials, such as those before military courts, inquisitions, tribunals, religious courts, and juries. In the choice of trials one sees more proceedings from western Europe and the New World than from other regions of the globe, such as Africa, for several reasons. First of all, the author's own training leads to a concentration on certain geographical areas. But, there is a substantive justification as well for a Western—even Anglo-American—bias in discussing great trials. England and the United States have as a cornerstone of their constitutional systems the guarantee of justice. The notion of a fair trial has been paramount in English and U.S. history. Thus, U.S. cases are dominant among the 20th century selections for this book, and English trials figure prominently in the 17th century.

What was the impact of a trial in a geographical sense? Certain proceedings may be little known to U.S. readers and yet quite familiar to persons in other nations. Trials that were famous in their localities, sometimes for many generations, often do not have any worldwide reputation. Such is true with the Ceylonese trial discussed here and each of the trials from Korea and Egypt, as well as the medieval French trials of Jacques Le Gris and the sow of Falaise. The handful of Canadian and Mexican cases included fit that description, testifying to the relative ignorance of U.S. citizens about important events concerning our northern and southern neighbors.

Particular themes are well represented among these trials. The religious controversies of the medieval and early modern Mediterranean and European regions are illustrated here. Rebellions against the state are prominent throughout written history. Other types of trials, such as those concerning domestic violence and private vengeance, proliferate among courts worldwide, but rarely do such controversies affect much more than their local communities. Besides, there is the key issue of sources. Most criminal offenses against individuals are not as well chronicled as crimes against the state, such as treason. The exception, of course, is when parties to cases are famous, as with the Lindbergh kidnapping and the Manson and Simpson murders.

The need for an accessible trial record biases this study toward sources that are available in the languages that this author can read and legal scholarship that she can understand. Her own inability to grasp the complexities of Jewish law, Confucian law, Islamic law, traditional African law, and southeastern Asian law means that those deep legal traditions are not treated extensively here. Instead of aiming for a definitive collection of trials, this author chose to make the selection of trials provocative and to spur further reading.

TRIALS

The trial of Socrates

Date: 399 B.C.E.

Key Issues

The trial of Socrates was as much about politics as philosophy. At the time that Socrates was accused of crimes, the Greek city-state of Athens only recently had emerged from a sobering military conflict and attendant civil strife. During the Peloponnesian War (431–404 B.C.E.), Athens endured the governance of persons loyal to the rival state of Sparta. Many Athenians regarded the rule of the so-called Thirty Tyrants as a kind of occupation. The self-described gadfly Socrates had influential pupils among the collaborators, although Socrates also was connected with persons such as Alcibiades who had the potential to overthrow the Thirty Tyrants.

Those who superseded the Spartan-connected government of Athens in 403 styled their government as a democracy. Like the heads of much later democratic governments, though, these new leaders were not above retribution against those who had made life miserable during the previous regime. With his critical attitude toward the deities and loyal group of disciples, as well as a former association with the Thirty Tyrants, Socrates was an obvious target for those who sought to signal a new order in Athens. Yet, it also was ironic that Socrates should be chosen for prosecution after the restoration of democracy as he had resisted pressure from the tyrants toward the end of their rule to take a larger role in that regime. He had declined to take part in their efforts, for example, to force the regime's opponents back to Athens from Sparta. Socrates took an apolitical stance, saying he was interested in logic and morality rather than statecraft.

The large public trial of Socrates nonetheless served as a demonstration of a renewed Athenian commitment to democracy. The mechanisms for dispensing justice in the city-state were centuries old by the time of Socrates. The *dikastery* was a court composed of Athenian citizens. Jury service was random, chosen by lot, and compulsory. Male citizens were paid for their service and might sit in various courts throughout their one-year term. The more important or high profile the case, the more jurors were required. They made decisions—how else?—by simple majority vote. Juries usually were composed of an odd number of members in order to avoid ties. For certain serious crimes, defendants might propose their own sentences in contrast to the penalties that prosecutors requested. Each jury determined which of the suggested penalties to apply.

Prosecutions were private, that is, not state sponsored. Still, powerful politicians clearly were behind certain cases. Decorum suggested that state leaders not go to court and argue their causes directly but rather send junior colleagues to do their bidding. The three men behind Socrates' legal troubles in 399 were of varying degrees of influence. The most powerful was the general Anytus, who worked through the younger accusers Meletus, a poet, and Lycon, an orator.

History of the Case

The case against Socrates began with a set of accusations presented to the city's chief executive, the archon. Such statement of charges was analogous to the modern indictment. The archon decided if the accusations had validity, calling a trial if they did. Socrates was a very well known—indeed, public—figure, though he held no office at the time. He was a fixture in the marketplace in Athens, a man who taught students in the art of reasoning. The substance of the charges against him was that he was too influential with the young people who seemed to flock to him. His detractors claimed that Socrates encouraged his eager students to question traditional religious values and perhaps take up new ones. The general charge was "corruption of youth," but the vehicle by which Socrates did so was religious unorthodoxy. In their indictment his three principal accusers sought the death penalty.

The Athenians had no system of court reporting, so it is fortunate that a record of the trial of Socrates was made. It came from the hand of one of Socrates' many pupils, a wealthy young man named Plato. His recollections of the episode were set down about 40 years after the fact in Plato's work the *Apology*. Several of Plato's works may be argued to reflect Socrates' philosophy, as do the writings of Plato's pupil Aristotle. The question of whether Socrates said and thought the things attributed to him by Plato is a major debate among classicists and philosophers. Most scholars, however, do not doubt that Socrates faced a trial and that it proceeded generally as Plato related the episode.

Much of the Athenian courts' focus was on oral argument, and persuasive speeches were key to winning one's case. In a trial such as this one, in which a large jury (more than 500 men) was mandated by the archon, it was vital to be able to appeal to a cross-section of Athenians. Though perhaps a galvanizing teacher and even an egalitarian thinker, Socrates did not have the ability to pander to a crowd. His defense was brilliant in thought but unwise as a self-advocacy.

SUMMARY OF ARGUMENTS

In addition to the large number of jurors present, many other Athenians gathered to watch the trial of the 70-year-old local fixture. The prosecution had to present its case—really a long argument—followed by the defense (spoken in this case by Socrates himself). Each side had equal time. According to custom, neither called witnesses, although each position could be supported by evidence that was generally well known by the citizenry. In other words, evidence was not subject to cross-examination, but rumor and hearsay were admissible.

Meletus, speaking for the accusers, critiqued Socrates' cynicism about the pantheon of gods. He also cited statements from Socrates that he believed himself the hearer of a divine voice. It was an inspiration that the old man claimed was apart from the traditional deities. That inner light (which Socrates called a *daimonion*) called him to question conventionalities personally and to instruct young people to be skeptical as well.

Meletus also hammered away at Socrates for leading young people astray. Part of the offense lay in separating children's affections from their families. Socrates, in questioning cherished ideals, had contributed to a more general rejection of authority on the part of young people. As Xenophon related it in his *Memoirs of Socrates* (probably composed ca. 380–350 B.C.E.), Meletus argued:

> Socrates taught his companions to abuse their parents by persuading them that he made them wiser than their parents and by claiming that according to the law it was possible for a son, if he proved his father insane, to imprison even his own father.
>
> Socrates, he said, also made the youth think that other men were of no account in comparison with himself, for he persuaded them that he was the wisest man and the most competent in making others wise.

Such a view of Socrates was recognized among Athenians, the prosecution stated. No less a playwright than Aristophanes had satirized Socrates' views in his play *The Clouds,* a work known in the city for a generation already.

Socrates brought out a full range of arguments to defend himself. His emphasis, he said, would be logic. He refused, for example, to play on the emotions of his jurors by asking children in his family to plead for his life:

> My friend, I am a man, and like other men, a creature of flesh and blood, and not of wood or stone, as Homer says; and I have a family, yes, and sons. O Athenians, three in number, one of whom is growing up, and the two others are still young; and yet I will not bring any of them hither in order to petition you for an acquittal. And why not? Not from any self-will or disregard of you. Whether I am or am not afraid of death is another question, of which I will not now speak. But my reason simply is that I feel such conduct to be discreditable to myself, and you, and the whole state. One who has reached my years, and who has a name for wisdom, whether deserved or not, ought not to debase himself.

Socrates ranged between ridicule for Meletus's main accusation (that Socrates had ruined Athens's young people), humility (he said he never had been the object of a court case and was not an important figure), and invincibility (his ideas, he claimed, would outlive his physical body). Socrates admitted, for example, that he was no orator; he called this speech—his defense—his "junior oration":

> For I am more than seventy years of age, and this is the first time that I have ever appeared in a court of law, and I am quite a stranger to the ways of the place; and therefore I would have you regard me as if I were really a stranger, whom you would excuse if he spoke in his native tongue, and after the fashion of his country;—that I think is not an unfair request. Never mind the manner, which may or may not be good; but think only of the justice of my cause, and give heed to that: let the judge decide justly and the speaker speak truly.

Shortly after that humble set of comments, Socrates launched into a devastating examination of the motives of his accusers. To the defendant these amounted to insecurity on the part of the prosecutors:

> . . . for they do not like to confess that their pretence of knowledge has been detected— which is the truth: and as they are numerous and ambitious and energetic, and are all in battle array and have persuasive tongues, they have filled your ears with their loud and inveterate calumnies. And this is the reason why my three accusers, Meletus and Anytus and Lycon, have set upon me; Meletus, who has a quarrel with me on behalf of the poets; Anytus, on behalf of the craftsmen; Lycon, on behalf of the rhetoricians: and as I said at the beginning, I cannot expect to get rid of this mass of calumny all in a moment.
>
> And this, O men of Athens, is the truth and the whole truth; I have concealed nothing, I have dissembled nothing. And yet I know that this plainness of speech makes them hate me, and what is their hatred but a proof that I am speaking the truth?—this is the occasion and reason of their slander of me, as you will find out either in this or in any future inquiry.

Did the prosecutors expect to quiet all dissent? Socrates argued that they certainly would fail:

> . . . but as I was saying before, I certainly have many enemies, and this is what will be my destruction if I am destroyed; of that I am certain;—not Meletus, nor yet Anytus, but the envy and detraction of the world, which has been the death of many good men, and will probably be the death of many more; there is no danger of my being the last of them.

Although certain contemporaries such as Xenophon opined that Socrates' ideas were not all that unconventional or upsetting, Socrates did not cite such evidence. It was as though he did not wish to disprove allegations that he was an irritation to conventional Athenians. Indeed, he argued quite the opposite: His best contribution to his society was shaking up the status quo. His most famous comment at trial was that "the unexamined life is not worth living."

Still, Socrates did attack the notion that he had poisoned the minds of young people. He asked the prosecution why not a single person in the crowd came forward to make a personal allegation of corruption in regard to a particular son or brother. Supposedly Socrates specifically spoke of Plato, as a favorite pupil, wondering why his influential family did not charge the elder man with corruption if he were such a bad influence on their son.

Another moment in his speech at which Socrates became more earnest than mocking was his refutations of the accusers' point that he had accepted money to teach. Exactly what Socrates had done to earn a living was not clear from his own words at trial. Plato and Xenophon give evidence that he had served honorably in the Athenian army, and some scholars believe him to have been a stonemason as well. Though he had learned from the Sophists, he did not emulate their practice of charging for instruction. By his own account Socrates was instructing the young out of a desire to increase knowledge and ethical behavior.

Socrates also took seriously the implicit charge that in working as a private individual he was denying his services to the state; surely, the prosecutors alleged, service to the community ought to be the first duty of a citizen with a keen mind. The defendant's answer once again was thoughtful but did not sound self-sacrificing enough to appeal to the jurors:

> Someone may wonder why I go about in private, giving advice and busying myself with the concerns of others, but do not venture to come forward in public and advise the state. I will tell you the reason of this. You have often heard me speak of an oracle or sign which comes to me, and is the divinity which Meletus ridicules in the indictment. This sign I have had ever since I was a child. The sign is a voice which comes to me and always forbids me to do something which I am going to do, but never commands me to do anything, and this is what stands in the way of my being a politician. And rightly, as I think.
>
> For I am certain, O men of Athens, that if I had engaged in politics, I should have perished long ago and done no good either to you or to myself. And don't be offended at my telling you the truth: for the truth is that no man who goes to war with you or any other multitude, honestly struggling against the commission of unrighteousness and wrong in the state, will save his life; he who will really fight for the right, if he would live even for a little while, must have a private station and not a public one.

Socrates' self-defense was an exhausting and in some ways off-putting verbal tour de force. Socrates seemed more interested in challenging his listeners to think than in saving his own life.

VERDICT

The jury answered his self-confidence and dispassion with a guilty verdict. It was by a narrow margin, however, which gave Socrates' defenders some hope that in the punishment phase of the trial he yet might have the chance to avoid the death penalty. Historians are not of one accord about the exact number of jurors, although most settle on 501, nor do they know the exact numbers of who voted for conviction.

The defendant was in no mood to trim his sails, despite conviction. Though several of his friends suggested to him that the jury very well might accept the opportunity to exile Socrates, the convicted man insisted on adopting a wry tone again when proposing his own sentence. He declared that he deserved a very large pension from Athens for the many contributions he already had made to the city-state. It was a suggestion that he must have known would provoke a severe reaction.

And it did bring down the jurors' wrath. By a larger margin than they had convicted Socrates, the jurors declared the death sentence as the accusers had proposed. A privileged group including Plato offered to contribute a large payment—a kind of fine—in exchange for Socrates' life. This the court rejected, probably at the behest of the prosecutors.

Due to the fact that a delegation of Athenians was making a yearly pilgrimage to Delos in honor of the god Apollo, the execution had to be put off for several weeks. Again, Socrates' admirers offered to help him avoid the capital sentence and leave Athens. He instructed them that it was his duty to the state to obey the law. He repeatedly insisted that he had no regrets. Just as he had said at trial, Socrates affirmed that if he could do things over again he would change nothing. On the appointed day of the execution, literally on his deathbed in his home, Socrates calmly accepted the dose of hemlock that the law prescribed. His last words, ostensibly concerning a debt owed to Asclepius, the god who cured disease, probably were meant to be an expression of Socrates' willingness to die to bring peace to Athens.

SIGNIFICANCE

Socrates' prosecution is one of the earliest trials for which there is a good historical record. Scholars have Plato's account as well as the corroborations of contemporaries relating to Socrates' reputation and his reception among political figures. It is a much-told story that appeals to many constituencies. Many schools of thought, particularly those coming from the classical tradition, have located their origins in Socrates' work.

Lately, historical scholars have emphasized the degree to which Socrates got into trouble for his unconventionality. In modern assessments of Socrates' condemnation it was not so much his philosophical rebellion or even religious irreverence that caused him difficulty. Rather, Socrates' insistence that he would teach every individual who came into his presence—slave and free, female and male, rich and poor—that shocked the supposed democrats of the new government of Athens. Adding to the legal troubles of Socrates was the old man's refusal to ally completely with either the tyrants or the democrats that cost him his life. He insisted, instead, that being a well-informed citizen and moral person was possible under many types of governments.

Further Reading

Brickhouse, Thomas, and Nicholas Smith. *Socrates on Trial*. Princeton, N.J.: Princeton University Press, 1989; Cartledge, Paul. *Ancient Greek Political Thought in Practice*. New York and Cambridge: Cambridge University Press, 2009; Nails, Debra. *The People of Plato: A Prosopography of Plato and Other Socratics*. Indianapolis, Ind.: Hackett Publishing, 2002; Ober, Josiah. *The Athenian Revolution: Essays on Ancient Greek Democracy and Political Theory*. Princeton, N.J.: Princeton University Press, 1996; Stone, I. F. *The Trial of Socrates*. Boston: Little, Brown, 1988; Taylor, C. C. W. *Socrates: A Very Short Introduction*. Oxford: Oxford University Press, 2001; Waterfield, Robin. *Why Socrates Died*. New York: Norton, 2009; Wilson, Emily. *The Death of Socrates*. Cambridge, Mass.: Harvard University Press, 2007.

The trial of Sextus Roscius

Also known as: *Pro Sexto Roscio*

Date: 80 B.C.E.

KEY ISSUES

Trials were entertainment for the citizens of the Roman Republic. Many criminal cases were heard in the Forum. They featured the talents of lawyers who hoped not only to win judgments for their wealthy clients but also to advance their own political fortunes. Skill in oral argument was much admired and could be a path to leadership in the state. Such a transition from court success to Republican authority is illustrated by the career of Rome's greatest advocate, Marcus Tullius Cicero.

Cicero is known among historians in these two respects: He was a superb orator who left excellent records of his own greatest speeches and later a successful politician. His account of this trial, a work entitled *Pro Roscio Amerino*, of course, emphasizes the author's cleverness. Classical scholars note that Cicero would have had time to embellish his recollection of oral arguments in the years between the trial and the writing of the memoir. Still, Cicero's own account of the case probably is accurate as a whole; there is corroboration of his skills and methods in other cases. Cicero's peak of political influence was during the years just before Julius Caesar's ascent; in 43 B.C.E. Cicero fell victim to the machinations of Caesar's even greater rival Mark Anthony.

HISTORY OF THE CASE

The case that first gave Cicero's legal reputation a great push was his defense of the accused murderer Sextus Roscius the Younger of Ameria. Cicero made the case much larger than an effort to acquit Sextus for killing his father (the offense of parricide or patricide). This defense attorney had the temerity not only to try to discredit the prosecution's allegations but also to provide an alternative solution for the crime. In explaining how the murder had really transpired, Cicero spoke to the highest levels of Roman politics. Cicero proposed to the panel of judges that Lucius Cornelius Chrysogonus, a powerful associate of the dictator Lucius Cornelius Sulla, had both arranged the murder and—in great effrontery—set up the prosecution.

Cicero's acceptance of the case represented a gamble. Sulla was attempting to convince the citizenry that the ruinous strife that had typified his earlier reign was under control and that the law had pride of place again in the Republic. It was a high-profile case—the first capital charge heard in Rome in several years—and as such, drew more than usual public interest. Cicero sought to impugn the honor of the chief henchman of Sulla, the Greek former slave Chrysogonus, without a direct attack on Sulla. Cicero dared those who would rule in the case to make a statement that (in effect) criticized Sulla's previous unchecked wielding of authority. Cicero claimed only to be inveighing against the civil disorder of the past few years, but he would come perilously close to attacking Sulla himself.

It was a dangerous trial for all involved. The defendant was on the line for his life. Parricide was a capital crime. The prescribed punishment was not unique to the Romans and remained in use in early modern Europe, for example, in Germany in the 1400s. In Rome, the convicted person was blindfolded, scourged, and then put into a sack called the *culeus*. Later refinements involved additions to the sack, such as a snake, a dog, an ape, and a rooster; all would be thrown into a river (*projectio in profluentem*). All that was required for conviction was a majority vote of the judges.

The men who sat in judgment of criminal cases (the judges, or *iudices*) were selected each year by a chief judicial official (the praetor, himself an appointee of Rome's consul. Usually the *iudices* came from among the senators. The judges were men of wealth and influence and were closely connected to what in modern times is known as the executive branch. In later western European law the jury was the descendant of the panel of Roman judges. Overseeing each criminal trial in Rome was a *quaesitor*. That presiding officer in subsequent parlance would have been known as the court's president.

There was no mechanism for state prosecutions. All criminal cases were private, so it took money to launch a formal case in court. Advocates were expensive and rare enough so that only Rome's wealthy could afford to mount such accusations. The crowd played a part. The public attended in large numbers; legal contests were especially suited for the open environment of the great city's forum. Lawyers stood to lose more than their reputations. If the judges believed that a prosecution lacked merit (that is, was without factual basis), then they could recommend that an unsuccessful prosecutor be branded on his forehead with the letter *k*, standing for *"kaluminator"* (one who bears false witness).

Despite the very real threat of injury and ignominy, lawyers who prosecuted within Rome's criminal court system (a system called the *quaestiones perpetuae*) had certain distinct advantages over defense counsel. For one thing, the standard for conviction in Roman law was fairly low. It sometimes was expressed as the principle of *fecisse videtur* (one who seems to have committed an act must have done so). Most courts accepted the right of the prosecutor to force witnesses to appear and testify; the defense had no parallel power. In Cicero's time it appeared as though there was no requirement that the prosecution should divulge all of the charges before everyone came to court. Defense lawyers, therefore, had to think quickly at trial in order to rebut charges that popped up.

SUMMARY OF ARGUMENTS

The prosecuting attorney in the case of Sextus Roscius, a man named Caius Erucius, was experienced and well connected. He had a reputation with the Roman crowds as a forceful, no-nonsense advocate; most histories describe Erucius as a professional lawyer. On the face of things Erucius's case looked solid. He introduced the murder as a simple instance of a son being unwilling to wait for his inheritance. The prosecutor called for the ultimate penalty, saying that a son who would turn on his father was near to a person assaulting a deity: Parricide was a "monstrous abomination against nature."

The victim in the case, Sextus Roscius the Elder, had been stabbed while visiting baths in Rome—a common enough activity among the citizenry. Although the era had seen numerous assassinations, for a time at least it seemed as though the elder Sextus had the protection of Sulla himself. The prosecution, however, introduced evidence to show that the victim actually had been placed on a "death list" maintained by Sulla. For the prosecution to make such a point initially seemed counterproductive, but Erucius had a point in mind. He wanted to demonstrate that the murdered man's property legally could be confiscated by the state and sold at auction. This was to become important within the case, for Erucius rightly anticipated that the defense would focus on the disposition of Sextus the Elder's estate.

In his work *On the Orator* Cicero maintained that a great speaker had to provide proof along with emotional engagement for his listeners. His defense of Sextus the Younger fulfilled both requirements. Cicero explained in his writing about the case, *Pro Roscio,* that his defense of the younger Sextus was a three-part affair. First, the defense counsel addressed Erucius's character attack on Sextus the son. Next, Cicero took on the witnesses that Erucius had summoned to relate that the deceased man had rejected the son and that Sextus the Younger knew it. Finally, he pulled together evidence of the larger plot in the case, which Cicero claimed emanated from Chrysogonus.

First, however, Cicero needed to justify his own appearance in the Forum. He was a comparative novice, and a little modesty would do him credit. He had to admit to the court that others had sensed peril in the cause; he received the brief not so much owing to his skill but his willingness to take on a case that seemed so cut and dried:

> I imagine that you, O judges, are marveling why it is that when so many most eminent orators and most noble men are sitting still, I above all others should get up, who neither for age, nor for ability, nor for influence, am to be compared to those who are sitting still. For all these men whom you see present at this trial think that a man ought to be defended against all injury contrived against him by unrivalled wickedness; but through the sad state of the times they do not dare to defend him themselves. So it comes to pass that they are present here because they are attending to their business, but they are silent because they are afraid of danger. What then? Am I the boldest of all these men? By no means.
> . . . On these accounts I have stood forward as the advocate in this cause, not as being the one selected who could plead with the greatest ability, but as the one left of the whole body who could do so with the least danger.

Cicero next acknowledged the political context: Rome had been in tumult, crime had been greatly on the rise, and that now, perhaps, a new era of calm would ensue. He spoke flattering words to the president of the court:

> You see how great a crowd of men has come to this trial. You are aware how great is the expectation of men, and how great their desire that the decisions of the courts of law should be severe and impartial. After a long interval, this is the first cause about matters of bloodshed which has been brought into court, though most shameful and important murders have been committed in that interval. All men hope that while you are praetor, these trials concerning manifest crimes, and the daily murders which take place, will be conducted with no less severity than this one.

Having set the scene and introduced himself, Cicero went to work on attacking the facts as presented by the prosecution. Whereas Erucius had painted the son as a profligate that the father did not trust with responsibility, a young man whom the elder was prepared to disinherit, Cicero drew an altogether different portrait. As was frequently his métier, Cicero made a much larger point besides.

The prosecutor had noted that Sextus the Elder lived in Rome, while he "relegated" the son to the countryside and the management of 13 large farms. Here, Erucius played to the crowd: This surely was proof that the father was ashamed of the son, for who would not want to reward a worthy heir by bringing him to Rome? Cicero had to address that contention without alienating a Roman crowd. He did so cleverly, reminding the court of the value of farmers in the Roman economy and their historical prominence as founders of the state. Living in the countryside, Cicero said, usually was associated with hard work and a rejection of pleasures. Also, surely, the father placing the son in charge of his valuable land demonstrated trust in his progeny. Far from being an ingrate and a murderer, Sextus the Younger was the *rusticus bonus*—the honest farmer—upon whom Rome's success depended.

Cicero went on to link the two main witnesses against Sextus the Younger, Roscius Magnus and Roscius Capito, with the purchase of the confiscated lands of the victim. It turned out that both had profited personally from the sale of the land to none other than Chrysogonus. The men were beginning to look now not so much like simple witnesses to a father-son feud but rather as persons whom Chrysogonus had employed to help him grab land. Here, Cicero used the most famous phrase of the speech: *"Cui bono?"* Under the guise of quoting a previous judge, Cicero was posing the not-very-hypothetical question "Who benefited?" It was a devastating refrain, inviting the jury (in more modern terminology) to "follow the money."

And that trail led, Cicero said, to Chrysogonus. The lawyer for the defense then took the extraordinary step of characterizing the favorite of Sulla in most unflattering terms. Chrysogonus, besides being a foreigner, was effeminate and a seeker of luxury. He had a special appetite for land. According to Cicero's theory of the crime, Chrysogonus not only ordered the murder but also contrived to add Sextus the Elder's name to the list of those proscribed under Sulla, a list that had ended in the previous year. When, Cicero asked, would he stop? Ambition and greed might not cease with the confiscation of this dead man's land and the persecution of Sextus the Elder's son. Cicero reminded the panel of privileged judges that they could be next to come within the grasp of Chrysogonus:

> But if, O judges, we cannot prevail with Chrysogonus to be content with our money, and not to aim at our life; if he cannot be induced, when he has taken from us everything which was our private property, not to wish to take away this light of life also which we have in common with all the world; if he does not consider it sufficient to glut his avarice with money, if he be not also dyed with blood cruelly shed—there is one refuge, O judges; there is one hope left to Sextus Roscius, the same which is left to the republic—your ancient kindness and mercy; and if that remain, we can even yet be saved.

VERDICT

The judges, probably both exhausted and impressed by Cicero's lengthy speech on his client's behalf, took a vote that the president of the court

announced. The letter that the *quaesitor* held up to the crowd signifying the decision was an *A*. It meant that Sextus Roscius the Younger had been absolved of the murder.

The long-term outcome was not as dramatic as it might have been for most of the participants. The younger Sextus never got his farms back, and the prosecutor Erucius somehow dodged a branding. The fate of Chrysogonus is unclear; he simply disappears from the historical record. Sulla retired from the dictatorship about a year after the trial. He died of natural causes in 78 B.C.E. and was honored with an enormous funeral in the Forum.

SIGNIFICANCE

Cicero's success in the case of Sextus Roscius the Younger helped raise his profile considerably. Cicero was not from one of Rome's patrician families. Despite his being of only upper-middle-class background, his oratorical skills and political courage came to notice during the defense of Sextus Roscius. In fairly quick succession Cicero gained successively higher offices. He became a kind of accounting administrator called a quaestor in 71 B.C.E. That led to his involvement in another famous case: a triumphant prosecution of the Sicilian governor Gaius Verres for corruption in 70 B.C.E. Within a decade Cicero himself gained the office of praetor and only three years later reached the pinnacle of power as Rome's elected consul.

Further Reading

Alexander, Michael C. *The Case for the Prosecution in the Ciceronian Era*. Ann Arbor: University of Michigan Press, 2003; Cicero, Marcus Tullius. *Murder Trials*. London: Penguin, 1975; Dyck, Andrew, ed. *Cicero: Pro Sexto Roscio*. Cambridge: Cambridge University Press, 2010; Husband, R. W. "The Prosecution of Sextus Roscius: A Case of Parricide, with a Plea of Alibi and Non-Motive." *Classical Weekly* 8 (1915): 98–100; May, J. M. *Trials of Character*. Chapel Hill: University of North Carolina Press, 1988; Metzger, Ernest. "Roman Judges, Case Law, and Principles of Procedure." *Law and History Review* 22 (2004): 243–275; Saylor, Steven. *Roman Blood: A Novel of Ancient Rome*. New York: Minotaur Books, 1991.

The trial of Jesus of Nazareth

Also known as: Christ before the Temple of Elders and Pontius Pilate

Date: 30 C.E.

KEY ISSUES

The first accusers of Jesus Christ demanded religious orthodoxy; the second, political obedience. Even that simple descriptive statement carries worlds of controversy. The story of Christ's trial is a central historical episode for those who call themselves Christians. It also is a great moment within other religious traditions, notably Judaism and Islam, although other belief systems contest the Christian view on key points about the trial.

In the first place, whole schools of historical and religious thought dispute that Christ was an individual at all. Some have argued that Christ was a composite figure, created among persons dissatisfied with Jewish law and restless under the Romans. In such a reading the image of Jesus in the Christian writings of the first century C.E. represented people who were of similar birthplace, social status, and religious tenets to the Jesus depicted in major Christian texts. But, in this interpretation Christ was not a particular person— indeed to some, *Jesus* was a generic term for "every person." Some interpreters of the historical record, such as persons within Orthodox Judaism, maintain that histories contemporary to the supposed events of Christ's life left no evidence of his activities, including his trial. Others, including certain writers within the Christian tradition, view accounts of Jesus' trial that came down through traditional Christian writers as so biased that they must be considered only general representations of those events rather than literal reports.

Muslims usually do not take issue with the idea that Christ was a single, identifiable person, nor do they object to his portrayal as an exceptionally ethical man. Indeed, many Muslims believe Jesus to have been a prophet who ran afoul of both religious and secular authority. Rather, the Islamic tradition diverges from the Christian one in how to depict the results of the trial of Jesus. According to Christianity, the trial resulted in Jesus' crucifixion and subsequent resurrection from the dead. Islam, on the other hand, believes that the Almighty would not have allowed a worthy messenger to suffer such an end. Thus, religious scholars within the Islamic tradition maintain that Jesus was removed to be with God, perhaps before execution. The followers of still other major religious traditions portray Jesus as a highly worthy person, a holy man or a prophet, but not the son of God.

At the heart of a discussion of Jesus' trial for many persons, both Christian believers and those outside that faith, is the question of whether the trial occurred at all or took place as it is commonly reported.

In addition, certain scholars ponder whether the result of the trial was the utter demise of the defendant or a miraculous resurrection. The present treatment is rooted in the Christian tradition that Jesus was an identifiable person who did live in Judaea when Rome governed much of the Mediterranean region. Further, this discussion assumes that the accounts of the trial and death of Jesus that appeared in the century or two following Christ's life were informed by eyewitness observations.

What are the major sources for information about Christ's trial? Scholars of Christianity recognize four major writers who lived contemporaneously and recounted Jesus' fate. These are the composers of the Gospels, known by the modern names in English of Matthew, Mark, Luke, and John. They all focus on events in and around Jerusalem during the year that modern scholars identify as 30 C.E. The Gospels probably were composed in a certain order, with Mark's and Luke's being closest in time to Jesus' life and Matthew's and John's appearing slightly later. Many religious scholars assume that Mark's version came through his connection with the biblical figure Peter (Simon Peter, also Saint Peter), who was said to be the founder of the Christian Church in Rome. Luke was an associate of the apostle Paul (Paul of Tarsus, or Saint Paul), who, like Peter, knew Jesus personally. In addition, scholars point to a noncanonical but tantalizing fragment that may be from Peter and that details the death of Jesus. If Peter's account is accepted as authentic, then it could have been written within about 15 years of Jesus' trial.

During the reign of Emperor Nero (perhaps 35 years after Jesus' death), the Roman writer Tacitus wrote briefly of Jesus as a known historical figure, locating Jesus' death during the reign of Tiberius. In addition, there is one major reference by a Jewish writer, Josephus, from approximately 50 or 60 years after Jesus' death. Josephus was well placed geographically to have known about the events in Judaea. Although Christian writers later amended Josephus extensively, certain basic elements of his history are widely accepted outside of Christianity. For example, Josephus was Jewish but critical of those who were in charge of the Jewish religious affairs in Jesus' time. Josephus argued that Jewish leaders' religious fervor brought down the wrath of the Romans and the consequent destruction of the Temple in Jerusalem in 70 C.E. In that conflagration priceless records were lost, including what may have been records about Jesus' case from the Jewish perspective.

HISTORY OF THE CASE

Each of the Gospel writers recounts the story of Jesus' trial and execution with something of a different emphasis and with varying details, but certain facets of the story are common to more than one account. It is possible to extract themes and a rough timeline of events from a reading of all four Gospels.

The first important element in all of the Gospel accounts concerning Jesus' legal treatment is that he committed acts that were offensive to the local rulers of the city of Jerusalem. Judaea was at that time a Roman possession, but Rome could not administer its far-flung territories with an all-Roman government. It had to rely on native leaders for everyday decision making, the collection of local revenues, and general control over the populace. In Jesus' day the de-facto mayor of Jerusalem was the Jewish high priest, Joseph Caiaphus. Caiaphus and the elders of the Temple employed Jewish law to run the city under ordinary circumstances. They certainly had charge of matters concerning the Jewish faith.

The Roman governor of Judaea was Pilate of the Pontii family (later called Pontius Pilate). The-oretically, Judaea had a native-born ruler even higher in rank than Pilate, Herod Antipas; he had inherited the throne from his father, who also was known as Herod. Although Pilate had the authority to refer controversies to Rome—for example, difficult legal cases—he usually preferred to handle matters without such recourse as a means to demonstrate that he was fully in control of the potentially troublesome region. For the most part Pilate kept out of daily oversight in Jerusalem. As long as Roman taxes were efficiently collected and there was order in the streets, the religious leaders at the Temple operated the city according to the precepts of Jewish law.

Jesus had come into the city at a time of the year when there occasionally was turmoil and at the very least a large influx of people: just before the feast of Passover. He entered Jerusalem in an unusual fashion: riding a donkey and accompanied by hundreds of followers who strew palm branches in his path. The Gospel of John notes that Jesus' admirers shouted to him their confidence in him as a leader: "Hosanna! Blessed is he who comes in the name of the Lord, even the King of Israel!" The Temple leaders and the civil authorities may have already heard of the man, but this was no doubt their first experience with Jesus at hand.

Those around Jesus spoke of him as a leader of the people, befriender of the poor, and worker of miracles. To those who sought to keep order during the lead-up to Passover, he was a nuisance at best and a blasphemer at worst. When Jesus and his admirers went into the Temple and physically upended the tables of those who exchanged local currency for Roman scrip (to pay taxes to Rome), the religious authorities sensed danger. Luke related vivid scenes at the Temple in his gospel:

> And he entered the temple and began to drive out those who sold, saying to them, "It is written, 'My house shall be a house of prayer'; but you have made it a den of robbers."
>
> And he was teaching daily in the temple. The chief priests and the scribes and the principal men of the people sought to destroy him; but they did not find anything they could do, for all the people hung upon his words (19:45–48, English Standard Version).

The Temple elders saw Jesus as critiquing their decision to allow such an exchange of money to go on within the confines of a religious site. They also may have sensed a larger attack on their political role as intermediaries between the local people and the Romans. Who was this man of humble origin to cast aspersions on them as the hereditary guardians of religious tradition? Would his actions cause the Romans to pay undue attention to Judaea? Such focus only could rebound to injure the Jews if local leaders failed to keep order.

Caiaphus and the Temple elders aimed to bring Jesus before the Sanhedrin, the court that heard religious cases, but they were anxious not to antagonize the many followers of Jesus. They especially did not want to cause a scene within the Temple itself, which might alert Roman officials to the situation before the Jewish leaders had sorted it out. The Temple located a person close to Jesus who was willing to lead them to him in a location less sacrosanct, a garden called Gethsemane just outside the city. For 30 silver shekels, Judas Iscariot offered up the man he supposedly admired to those who were prepared to examine Jesus' religious orthodoxy.

SUMMARY OF ARGUMENTS

The Sanhedrin was an authority charged with both judicial and political roles; like the English court of the Exchequer it heard appeals about taxes and sat in judgment in cases. The persons who served as judges numbered around 70; they were drawn from among the priests of the Temple and the families of the highest social orders in Jewish society. About 200 years after Jesus' trial, the procedures of the Sanhedrin became better documented than they were in 30 C.E. There is some indication, though, that certain rules of procedure held true even at the earlier time. For example, the Sanhedrin could not hand down death sentences at night. Also, for a conviction to be valid, the court had to establish the basic facts of the offense (for example, the crime of blasphemy). It was preferred that the judges themselves would "test" the evidence by inquiring sharply of witnesses to make certain that their accounts did not contradict one another.

It was not difficult for the Sanhedrin to point out instances when Jesus had offended against Jewish regulations. Not only had he caused disorder within the Temple and come into the city triumphantly—as though he fulfilled prophecies of the Messiah—he also had a long record of speaking and acting against the rules on ritual purity. Jesus walked about and took meals with persons who were ritually unclean, such as lepers. He stated that what went into the body was unimportant, a clear repudiation of the intricate prohibitions on food, cleansing, and personal association of which Temple leaders were guardians.

Jesus also seemed to go out of his way to state that persons of lesser status (such as prostitutes, children, and people with mental problems) were worthy of inclusion in what he called the "kingdom of heaven." He was reputed to be able to heal the sick and even bring persons back from the grave. He had the potential, that is, not only to challenge religious authority but to convince many people to accompany him spiritually.

The Gospel of Matthew conveys some of the discussion that went on between Jesus and the Temple leaders:

> Now the chief priests and the whole council sought false testimony against Jesus that they might put him to death, but they found none, though many false witnesses came forward. At last two came forward and said, "This fellow said, 'I am able to destroy the temple of God, and to build it in three days.'" And the high priest stood up and said, "Have you no answer to make? What is it that these men testify against you?" But Jesus was silent. And the high priest said to him, "I adjure you by the living God, tell us if you are the Christ, the Son of God." Jesus said to him, "You have said so. But I tell you, hereafter you will see the Son of man seated at the right hand of Power, and coming on the clouds of heaven." Then the high priest tore his robes, and said, "He has uttered blasphemy. Why do we still need witnesses? You have now heard his blasphemy. What is your judgment?" They answered, "He deserves death." Then they spat in his face, and struck him; and some slapped him, saying, "Prophesy to us, you Christ! Who is it that struck you?" (26:59–68, English Standard Version).

The Temple elders had a multipronged problem on their hands. They must have thought Jesus to be a heretic, and they probably imagined that he made them look ineffectual to the Romans. In Jewish law the proper punishment for such divergence from religious tradition was death by stoning. To impose that gruesome and public penalty at this time of the week and year, however, would have been risky: Such an execution might incite riots on Jesus' behalf, which could cause the Romans to lose confidence in their local representatives.

Caiaphus and the elders apparently decided to refer the case to Pilate, who happened to be in town for the holiday. They sent Jesus to the Roman prefect with the notation that Jesus claimed to be "the King of the Jews." It was an astute hand-off, for such a charge meant that Jesus had committed a political offense over which the Jewish authorities wanted the Romans to have cognizance. The Gospel accounts do not support the argument that Jesus had previously characterized himself in such a way. Indeed, he had repeatedly downplayed the political implications of his message, according to the Gospels, for example, advising his admirers to "render unto Caesar what is Caesar's" when they inquired whether they still had to pay their taxes if they were followers of his.

VERDICT

Pilate first deferred the case to his supposed superior, Herod, who was interested in the reputed miracle worker. Jesus refused to play that part before Herod, however, and Herod angrily sent him back to Pilate, dressed in "royal" robes and accompanied by Roman troops.

Pilate spent more time with Jesus, asking him a series of questions that indicated he saw through the device of the Sanhedrin. At the end of that conversation, which hardly could have been called a trial but rather was more of an interview, Pilate appeared to conclude that Jesus was no political threat to the Romans. John, in chapter 18 of his gospel, recounts a brief but intriguing philosophical debate between Jesus and Pilate:

> Pilate entered the praetorium again and called Jesus, and said to him, "Are you the King of the Jews?" Jesus answered, "Do you say this of your own accord, or did others say it to you about me?" Pilate answered, "Am I a Jew? Your own nation and the chief priests have handed you over to me; what have you done?" Jesus answered, "My kingship is not of this world; if my kingship were of this world, my servants would fight, that I might not be handed over to the Jews; but my kingship is not from the world." Pilate said to him, "So you are a king?" Jesus answered, "You say that I am a king. For this I was born, and for this I have come into the world, to bear witness to the truth. Every one who is of the truth hears my voice." Pilate said to him, "What is truth?" After he had said this, he went out to the Jews again, and told them, "I find no crime in him" (33–38, Revised Standard Edition).

When the prefect announced his decision that he did not believe Jesus guilty of an offense against the Roman state, the religious traditionalists were the loudest speakers in the assembled crowd. They called for Jesus to be executed.

Pilate seemed troubled by that prospect and instead proposed a bargain much in line with the yearly tradition of Roman authorities' releasing one political prisoner at Passover. If the crowd desired an execution, then they could choose between Jesus or a convicted insurrectionist and murderer, Barabbas. Barabbas was slated for execution by crucifixion.

Jesus' followers, besides being at that point very afraid, were outnumbered by the religiously orthodox. The Gospels recall the denials by Simon Peter, Jesus' close friend, that he even knew Jesus while Jesus was on trial before the Sanhedrin. As the situation worsened, more and more followers melted away. Jesus' critics called for Barabbas to be set free. Pilate literally washed his hands, signifying that he was free from blame in condemning to death a person he considered innocent of any crime.

Roman soldiers presided over the execution, which consisted of a brutal whipping (scourging), followed by a march to the place of execution. To ridicule the idea that Jesus was a leader of the Jews, he was made to wear a "crown," or hero's wreath, made of thorns. The executioners nailed the convicted man by his palms and feet to a wooden cross. He was suspended, arms open, until he strangled or bled to death. Jesus' demise was relatively quick; he spent six hours on the cross before drawing a last breath at about three o'clock in the afternoon. He was executed along with at least two other condemned men, one of whom mocked Jesus and asked why he did not save himself; the other seemed moved by Jesus' words of forgiveness to his tormenters. Most of his followers were too afraid to accompany him to the execution or to tend to his grave. Only a few brave souls—all women—took charge of washing his body and visiting his tomb, which was donated by a wealthy follower named Joseph of Arimathea.

SIGNIFICANCE

The Gospel writers emphasize that to them, as well as to Jesus himself, the trial and execution were the conclusion of Jewish prophecies. In the eyes of his contemporary critics Jesus knew Jewish religious history very well and simply tailored his actions to the words of persons who had predicted the coming of a messiah, or savior. He was, in other words, a false prophet and a manipulator of simple-minded folk who justifiably was crushed by the Romans with Jewish help.

Many of those who had placed confidence in Jesus were stunned by his death. They either were in hiding or beset by grief. Within days, weeks, and months, however, some of those former followers became convinced that Jesus had been awakened after death in accordance with his pledge to ascend to be with his father, God. Among persons who accepted the argument that Jesus was sent by the Almighty to atone for the sins of the world, recent events in Jerusalem became a fulfillment of sacred promises.

Those who had known Jesus split into two main groups after his death, with one faction (led by James, reputedly Jesus' brother) emphasizing Jesus' resistance to Roman rule. With James' own execution about 30 years after the crucifixion of Christ, that branch of Christianity suffered. Another group, headed by Jesus' associate Paul, put its efforts into conversion. The telling of the story of Jesus' trial, execution, and resurrection became the mission of that segment of Christians. Like Paul, who was Jewish, the other Gospel writ-

ers, who were Gentiles, had either known Jesus personally or talked to those who had. The Pauline writers, composing between the 60s and about 90 C.E., stressed the responsibility of the Temple leaders rather than of the Romans in Jesus' earthly end. As the Gospel writers' goal in part was to survive under Roman rule in order to convert others, they exonerated Roman authorities to a certain extent. The four Gospels' interpretations of Jesus' life and death indeed served as the theological foundation of the Christian Church, first as an underground movement, later a tolerated sect, and finally the official religion of the Roman Empire.

Further Reading

Catchpole, David R. *The Trial of Jesus: A Study in the Gospels and Jewish Historiography from 1770 to the Present Day.* Leiden, Netherlands: E. J. Brill, 1971; Evans, Craig, and Wright, N. T. *Jesus, the Final Days: What Really Happened.* Louisville, Ky.: Westminster John Knox, 2009; Porter, J. R. *Jesus Christ: The Jesus of History, the Christ of Faith.* Oxford: Oxford University Press, 1999; Sanders, E. P. *Jewish Law from Jesus to the Mishnah.* Philadelphia: Trinity Press, 1990; Sloyan, Gerald S. *Jesus on Trial: A Study of the Gospels.* Minneapolis, Minn.: Fortress Press, 2006; Watson, Alan. *The Trial of Jesus.* Athens: University of Georgia Press, 1995; Wroe, Ann. *Pontius Pilate: The Biography of an Invented Man.* New York: Modern Library, 2001.

The trial of Anatolius

Date: 580 C.E.

KEY ISSUES

Emperor Tiberius II, like his predecessors Justinian and Justin II, forced the conversion of so-called heathens. The two earlier emperors were especially repressive toward the remnants of the School of Athens in modern-day Greece and Turkey and worshippers of female deities such as Isis in Egypt. One of the toughest enforcers of imperial policies on religion was Bishop John of Ephesus, who in 542 C.E. embarked on an effort to tear down older religious sites and construct Christian buildings first near his home base in Turkey and then in the Bekaa Valley (modern Lebanon).

Although personally tolerant at the start of his emperorship, Tiberius became increasingly stern toward non-Christians throughout the Near East. He did show a certain amount of leniency toward persons within Christianity who deviated from his orthodoxy; for instance, he allowed Arianism to endure in the empire under certain circumstances. But the Christian populations of the region occasionally became alarmed at natural disasters and impatient with the pace of Christian conversion of "idol worshippers." Then, Tiberius lost control over not only his religious policy but also order. One such occasion was the case of Anatolius, a high-level imperial official accused of practicing sorcery and worshipping non-Christian deities.

HISTORY OF THE CASE

Scholars rely on two contemporary accounts for the trial of Anatolius: the writing of John of Ephesus, who was a highly partisan participant in the affair, and the chronicle of Evagrius Scholasticus that covers the years in question. Chapter 18 of Evagrius's *History* is titled "Commotion on Account of Anatolius."

Anatolius was a governor who represented Tiberius in the region around Antioch. Anatolius, who was of non-noble birth, was a tradesman who became well connected to Gregory, the prelate of the Theopolitans. Anatolius occupied an official position within the empire as well; he presided over the area near Edessa as both a governor and a deputy to the praetorian prefect of the east. Anatolius had a high public profile and a number of enemies who were jealous of his rapid rise to power from humble circumstances.

Anatolius was caught up in a wider scandal involving local leaders at Baalbek who had been accused of participating in non-Christian rituals, particularly sacrifices. Led by Theophilus, a representative of the emperor, a group of officials went to Edessa to investigate charges levied against a priest there, Rufinus. They found Rufinus at Anatolius's house. While they were in the process of apprehending those leaders and others who were engaged in an allegedly pagan ceremony within Anatolius's residence, Rufinus committed suicide. Anatolius was arrested. At this juncture Tiberius himself was made aware of the raid and ordered Anatolius brought to a more secure location, the capital city at which he presided.

While in prison, Anatolius tried to demonstrate that he was a pious Christian. He found an icon, either of Christ or the Virgin Mary, hanging from a cord in the jail. He began to pray before it, even clasping the image close to his body in a show of reverence. But several witnesses reported that the image turned its back to Anatolius, as if to reject him. This happened several times, despite Anatolius's efforts to control the icon's movement. Some observers reported that the icon was double sided; the section that had rotated toward Anatolius contained an image of Apollo. Several individuals also testified to having dreams in which the Mother of God (Mary) inveighed against Anatolius.

Though he made several efforts to use his political connections to secure bail, Anatolius eventually was transferred to the imperial capital, Constantinople. His ally Gregory narrowly escaped legal condemnation as a coworshipper of false deities and was threatened by mobs that attacked his home. Upon the confession of an official who worked for Anatolius, Gregory was rumored to have committed serious misdeeds, including the ritual sacrifice of a child at Daphne. Inhabitants perceived such heresy as precipitating the terrible earthquake of a few years earlier (577) that had destroyed a major portion of that city. Gregory was never charged with any offense, although he had to hide within his home and avoid public appearances for some time.

SUMMARY OF ARGUMENTS

The trial of Anatolius was shaped by mass violence that Tiberius was either unwilling or unable to control. At an early point in the investigation of Anatolius, Tiberius decamped for his country estate, simply leaving matters in the hands of a reactionary urban mob. Under the leadership of Eutychius, the esteemed and elderly patriarch of Constantinople, Anatolius was put on trial within the palace of Placidia at Constantinople. His fellow defendants also were accused of pagan practices.

As was customary, Anatolius was tortured with an eye toward his offering up the names of accomplices—in this case, others with whom he had engaged in non-Christian worship. He refused to implicate anyone else, including the priest Rufinus and his family. At this point in the proceedings crowds in the capital took matters into their own hands. They apparently were enraged that the trials were not open to public view and were not moving along quickly in establishing Anatolius's guilt.

Mobs raged throughout the city, menacing the imperial palace and the residence of Eutychius. An officer in the service of the absent emperor suggested to the crowd that he would journey to Tiberius's country place to "request" his attendance in the city; that promise bought him safety for a while. The citizens entered the judicial proceeding itself, dragging several codefendants of Anatolius from the palace courtroom and demanding that they be killed before the conclusion of the trial. The accused were placed into boats that then were set on fire. A court official narrowly escaped death when he was taken out with that set of defendants by mistake.

VERDICT

The verdict in the case did not come from a formal body but rather the crowds who called for death to the heathens. Chroniclers such as Evagrius saw the hand of the divine in such mob justice: "There was one of our number who, even before these things happened, said that he saw in dreams that the verdict against Anatolius and his associates had been granted to the populace."

As the city at that moment was not in the control of imperial authorities, the court had no choice but to offer up Anatolius to those who sought his blood. His death served as a spectacle: He was taken to an amphitheater—the circus at Constantinople—where he was attacked by wolves. His body then was impaled or crucified, and the animals consumed the corpse. Even in an age accustomed to the violent deaths of criminals, it was reckoned an unusually gruesome end.

SIGNIFICANCE

Did the horrifying fate of Anatolius help stamp out paganism in Antioch? Probably not. The region was too steeped in alternative religious practices to convert wholly, even under such intense pressure. Although commentators such as Evagrius would not admit it, pagans almost certainly retained some of their local influence after this episode. Still, the general direction of imperial policy was toward the elimination of religious minorities. Tiberius, who personally inclined away from extremism in religion, thought it politic to follow the execution of Anatolius with a roundup of suspected religious troublemakers. He punished the Jews and other non-Christians severely, sometimes even with death, but rumor had it that the Christians accused of lacking orthodoxy simply were let go, their backs painted red to simulate whippings.

Further Reading

Allen, Pauline. *Evagrius Scholasticus, the Church Historian.* Louvain, Belgium: Spicilegium sacrum Lovaniense, 1981; Bouchier, Edmund Spense. *A Short History of Antioch.* Oxford: Blackwell, 1921; Harvey, Susan Ashbrook. *Asceticism and Society in Crisis: John of Ephesus and the Lives of the Eastern Saints.* Berkeley: University of California Press, 1990; John of Ephesus. *Ecclesiastical History.* Available online. URL: http://www.ccel. org/ccel/pearse/morefathers/files/ephesus_1_ book1.htm/. Accessed January 1, 2009; Smith, William, and Henry Wace. *A Dictionary of Christian Biography.* London: John Murray, 1880; Turtledove, Harry Norman. *The Immediate Successors of Justinian: A Study of the Persian Problem and of Continuity and Change in Internal Secular Affairs in the Later Roman Period during the Reigns of Justin II and Tiberius II Constantine (A.D. 565–582).* Ph.D. diss. University of California, Los Angeles, 1977; Whitby, Michael, trans. *The Ecclesiastical History of Evagrius Scholasticus.* Liverpool, U.K.: Liverpool University Press, 2000.

The trial of Leo III

Date: 800 C.E.

KEY ISSUES

In the year 800 the legitimacy of Pope Leo III was in question. Challenges to his holding the papal see began upon Leo's election and installation in 795, largely due to the machinations of allies of the pontiff's predecessor, Adrian I. Those partisans of Adrian, who included two of his nephews, had themselves hoped to be named pope; they were members of noble families from the city of Rome. Leo, in spite of having risen to the offices of cardinal and pontifical treasurer, did not have the high social origins of his opponents. However, to Leo's rescue came Charlemagne, king of the Franks. The secular ruler presided over a trial at which Leo successfully defended himself against a variety of charges including embezzlement. Leo rewarded Charlemagne by crowning him as emperor—a symbolic gesture with grand ramifications for western Europe and Christianity.

The pope provided acknowledgement of Frankish superiority in western and central Europe and thus is credited by historians with having established the Holy Roman Empire. Charlemagne and his heirs returned the generosity of Roman church leaders by supporting the Roman church's claim to be the true heir of Peter, who himself was supposed to have been given the keys to the church by Christ. Coincidentally, another Leo III recently had contributed to the split between Roman and Byzantine Christianity: In the late 720s Emperor Leo III of Constantinople condemned icons, thereby exacerbating tensions with Roman church leaders. That rift within Christianity was a divide that King Charlemagne hoped to heal with his personal influence. Thus, his intervention in the troubles of Pope Leo was but a part of Charlemagne's much larger designs.

HISTORY OF THE CASE

The history of Pope Leo III's trial remains inextricable from the history of the Carolingian rulers such as Charlemagne, the story of the rift between Eastern and Western Christendom, and the alliance between Christian monarchs and the Christian Church. Such a link between church and secular authority was critical to the success of efforts by both religious and secular authorities to face down non-Christians in the Near East and southern Europe, particularly Spain.

Charlemagne's grandfather, Charles Martel, had burnished his military reputation when he halted Muslim expansion into Gaul at the Battle of Poitiers (Tours) in 732. Charlemagne went so far as to try to push back the Muslim armies to the Iberian Peninsula. Although he suffered a rare defeat in that effort, the Frankish forces secured a cultural victory. The pro-Christian account of that victory, *The Song of Roland,* enshrined in the memory of Europeans the heroism of many of Charlemagne's warriors.

There had been a working alliance in the intervening Frankish reign, between the son of Charles Martel, Pippin the Short (Charlemagne's father), and the papacy. Pippin had the prestige of a papal recognition of his kingship over the Franks in recompense for Pippin's having forced the Longobards, who lived at Ravenna and periodically threatened Rome, to support Pope Zacharias rather than the Byzantine church. Such assistance by the Frankish kings continued, with Charlemagne assisting Pope Adrian (sometimes called Hadrian). By all accounts the link between Adrian and Charlemagne was genuinely friendly; Charlemagne's epitaph for that pope survives on an engraved tablet in Rome.

Pope Leo expressed a kinship to Charlemagne immediately upon his own election to the papacy, which occurred a day after Pope Adrian's burial. The new pope and the longtime Frankish monarch engaged in a flattering correspondence, with Charlemagne sending funds for the mission of the church. The relationship between Charlemagne and Leo proved to be a wedge that Leo's enemies employed to argue that this pope (non-noble that he was) was subservient to a foreigner.

Leo's enemies physically attacked him—hoping to maim him so that he could no longer serve as pontiff. The assault took place on April 25, 799, as Leo was traveling along an established processional route from Rome to Lucina. As well as attempting to cut out the pope's tongue, the plotters tried to blind him. They may have taken their idea for the attack from another crime that was notorious in the day: the blinding of the son of Leo III of Constantinople by the elder ruler's widow, Irene, in 797. Pope Leo managed to survive the serious wounds, calling his own recovery miraculous. He noted that he actually saw more clearly after being injured than before, and he was not speaking rhetorically. It is possible that Magnus Forteman, a Frisian partisan of Charlemagne and commander of about 700 troops in Rome, aided in Leo's escape.

Still, the attackers achieved at least part of their objective: to remove Leo from office. The pope fled first to a monastery under the protection of Duke Winegis of Spoleto, a subject of Charlemagne. Then he made his way to see Charlemagne himself at Paderborn, in modern-day Germany. Charlemagne already had heard accounts of the incident from those who had organized resistance to Leo. He gathered information from those plotters. Though rebuffing their direct political overtures, the Frankish king granted Leo's critics the dignity of a full hearing in Rome.

Charlemagne first sent Leo back to St. Peter's. Protected by that safe conduct—meaning the avowed support of Charlemagne—and the control over Rome by the Frisians, the deposed pope returned and watched a commission convene under Frankish authority to investigate the actions of his enemies. That commission could neither clear Adrian's supporters nor Leo, so the partisans of Adrian were sent under arrest to the center of Frankish territories to await a fuller resolution of matters in Rome.

The Frankish monarch then journeyed to Rome, taking along a retinue that included several clerics, notably Arno of Salzburg, Theodulph of Orleans, Riculf of Mayence, and Witto and Fredugis of the Saxons. Although Charlemagne's learned adviser Alcuin of York could not attend on account of old age and infirmity, Alcuin offered a pretrial commentary on the situation in which he rehearsed several arguments in favor of Leo. For example, Alcuin argued that canonical authorities said the pontiff should not be liable to allegations against him unless at least 72 witnesses to serious misconduct could be located—probably an unat-

tainable standard of proof. Armed with Alcuin's writings (which Alcuin already had circulated among the clerics who did travel with the king), Charlemagne arrived at Rome on November 23, 800. Leo welcomed him at St. Peter's Basilica.

SUMMARY OF ARGUMENTS

In form, the body that met at Rome beginning on December 1, 800, at Charlemagne's behest was not a judicial panel at all. Rather it was a religious conference, a synod known as the Concilium Romanum (Roman Council). In practice, the meeting was called to sort out whether Leo was morally fit to be pope and, conversely, whether those who sought to unseat him could substantiate their accusations that he was unacceptable to hold the Holy See. In the course of such an inquiry it was quite plausible that the synod would hear about the attack that sent Leo into the safety of Frankish territory; thus, the attackers in effect would be under investigation. The synod, therefore, had the power to investigate and to direct punishment if it found fault with either Leo or his attackers. If Leo were exonerated, then he would continue to preside as pope; if his critics were vindicated, then Leo's power would be irreparably undermined.

Clearly it was a church gathering; each session ended with religious chanting, for example. The dozens of participants were arranged in the meeting hall by type of church office they held, with the higher categories of persons (king, pope, and bishops, for example) being allowed to sit down while mere laypeople and deacons had to remain standing. And yet, the meeting was not perfectly in line with religious tradition, either; for example, King Charlemagne obviously oversaw it. Certain scholars who have examined the relevant documentary sources on the synod have called it a "Frankish" rather than "Roman" synod, comparing the proceedings to a conference at Frankfurt in 794 at which Charlemagne also presided.

VERDICT

It took three weeks for the synod to conduct its business. The records of that inquiry have not been preserved but must have been lengthy if similar synods managed by Charlemagne are any guide. Among the matters heard must have been recitations, copies of correspondence between Rome and Charlemagne, the accounts of those who accused Leo of misconduct, and various witnesses' testimony. One key feature of the trial remains clear: According to principles of Roman law, the accusers—Pope Leo's critics—had the burden of proof. It was very important, therefore, that no accuser took the step of appearing at the synod to speak openly against Leo.

On either December 23 or 25, the synod wrapped up its work, proclaiming that they were prevented by canonical custom from pronouncing a verdict upon the pope:

> We dare not judge the Apostolic See which is the head of all the churches of God. For all of us are judged by it and its vicar; it however is judged by nobody as it is the custom from ancient times, but as the highest pontiff will have decided (in the case of the accusations leveled against himself) we shall obey canonically.

Leo, in other words, would have to judge his own case. The clerics would respect his decision. It was, of course, a decision in Leo's favor, but the beleaguered pontiff's reaction would determine whether he would earn the trust of his flock, the city of Rome, and his political patrons. Leo's response was to take a solemn oath declaring his innocence: "Since I have no knowledge of these untrue charges which the Romans, who unjustly persecute me, have laid on me, I acknowledge that I have not committed the like."

Alcuin had noted prior to his master's trip to Rome that previous popes had employed a similar method of clearing their names. Leo's oath could have been read as a partial victory for his accusers. He had felt obliged to clear himself, though the synod had not required that action of him. On the other hand, the synod also made clear—through a statement of Charlemagne at the trial—that there was insufficient evidence to support charges of adultery and graft against Pope Leo. And so, Leo rested his self-defense on a simple note: He did not know that he had done anything wrong. It hardly was a ringing declaration of innocence on the defendant's part, but to go into greater detail would have risked dignifying the accusations.

The synod did go further, though. It maintained that Leo's accusers had been motivated by malice. It was a short step for any observer to conclude that jealousy of Leo's position probably had inspired his enemies to attempt his assassination. The nephews of Adrian already had been sent into exile in Frankish lands by order of the commission that met in Rome in November 799. And so it was that about a year later the synod recommended that the Franks execute the plotters. Pope Leo asked the religious assembly to commute their sentence of death, and they disappeared into exile.

As Charlemagne prayed at St. Peter's on December 25, a surprising thing occurred. Pope Leo, now vindicated, put a crown on the head of Charles the Great. The crowd inside the basilica exclaimed: "To Charles, the most pious Augustus, crowned by God, to our great and pacific emperor life and victory!" Was Leo's crowning of his benefactor a spontaneous bit of generosity or a carefully calculated political action? Scholars cannot agree, nor can they decide whether Charlemagne orchestrated the entire affair in order to further his own designs of empire.

SIGNIFICANCE

Frankish control over a great sweep of territory in western Europe did not long survive Charlemagne's death in 814, but the working alliance between Rome and Christian kings in the region endured. Pope Leo III died in 816; his successor, Stephen IV, continued in the steps of Leo and Adrian by crowning Charlemagne's heir, Louis the Pious, as emperor. That act not only gave credence to the idea that there was a Holy Roman Empire close in league with the Holy See at Rome. The pope's bestowing of a secular crown underpinned the notion that religious leaders invested kings with their authority—an important idea for hundreds of years after Leo's pontificate. It was a theory that would provoke division, though, in cases such as the Becket controversy. Rulers and the see at Rome each contended that they ultimately represented the Almighty on earth.

Further Reading

Barbero, Alessandro, and Allan Cameron. *Charlemagne: Father of a Continent.* Berkeley: University of California Press. 2004; Browne, G. F. *Alcuin of York*. New York: E. S. Gorham, 1908; Duffy, Eamon. *Saints and Sinners: A History of the Popes*. New Haven, Conn.: Yale University Press, 1997; Noble, Thomas F. X. *The Republic of St. Peter*. Philadelphia: University of Pennsylvania Press, 1984; Wallach, Luitpold. "The Roman Synod of December 800 and the Alleged Trial of Leo III: A Theory and the Historical Facts." *Harvard Theological Review* 49 (1956): 123–142.

The trial of Flosi

Date: 1010

KEY ISSUES

Communities worldwide employed divine tests to help resolve disputes. Faced with a disagreement that involved the breaking of laws, a set of local people would assemble and then defer to wise persons among them (the judges), who would set procedural guidelines. First, a hearing was convened, at which judges sorted out facts and made an initial determination on what sort of evidence would suffice to demonstrate the truth. Only then would the "trial"—a proof of guilt—take place. In western Europe from about 500 C.E. until after the year 1200, courts allowed the truth to be revealed through an "ordeal." The ordeal was a chance for the Almighty (or multiple deities) to indicate the veracity of parties to a case. Ordeals usually involved physical pain or at least the threat of it. Sometimes that harm occurred to a guilty party or one who swore falsely, though on occasion even innocents had to suffer for justice to be done.

Which type of ordeal was applied was based on the customs of the area and the type of offense alleged. For instance, in certain places it was common for ordeals to involve contests between humans and animals. Other trials by ordeal involved an accused person being submerged in water or walking through or on top of fire. Perhaps the most common form of the ordeal was the

application of heat to a suspect's body in order to see if the flesh healed cleanly.

Certain tests appear bizarre by modern standards, such as in the case of Richardis of Swabia, wife of Holy Roman Emperor Charles the Fat. Richardis's ordeal in 887 involved wrapping the queen in a garment made of wax, which then was set afire as a test of her purity. (Having survived the trial, Richardis retired to a nunnery and later was celebrated as a saint.) Certain ordeals were opportunities to root out witnesses who were nervous; for example, the act of swearing an oath—compurgation—was a divine test. If one could not speak the words of the oath exactly or without stumbling, then the court declared that "the oath burst," exposing the oath taker as a liar.

The simplest form of the ordeal was that of trial by battle, also called trial by combat. The accuser and the defendant either fought personally against each other or chose others to represent them. The use of such "champions" was usual when one of the parties to a dispute was aged, infirm, a cleric, a woman, or young. Trial by battle as a way of resolving conflicts was popular in societies that were permeated with militarism. It was common among the Scandinavian and Germanic peoples in the years between the fall of Rome and the Norman Conquest. Among northern Europeans, trial by battle served as a direct substitution for the blood (or family) feuds that threatened to tear apart localities. Trial by battle was not sanctioned by ancient authorities; for instance it was mentioned neither in the Code of Hammurabi nor the laws of the Hebrews. It first appeared in the law codes of Germanic peoples in the years after the fall of Rome.

Western Christian authorities voiced religious objections to trial by battle. The church did not relish giving its blessing to such spectacles. Canon law in theory was opposed to the shedding of blood. As became apparent in the Becket controversy of the late 1100s, Rome's opposition to ordeals in church courts meant that religious authorities had to hand over repeat malefactors to secular courts for punishment. That in turn created complex interactions between religious and worldly justice. In 1215 the Fourth Lateran Council decreed that the church should discourage trial by battle—indeed, trial by ordeal in general. At that juncture, however, trial by ordeal was widespread in western Europe and the North Atlantic region, including England (where "judicial combat" was called "wager of battle") and Nordic lands.

Christian officials, especially those closely tied to Rome, increasingly tried to deemphasize ordeals and to play up the importance of alternative methods such as the use of juries. Still, trial by ordeal remained embedded in many places. Literary references to trial by combat as a form of the ordeal were famous in the medieval period: Such depictions appear in *Beowulf* among the people of the British Isles, for example, *The Song of Roland* of the Franks, and *Tristan und Isolde* from Germanic lands. Trial by battle remained most popular among castes (for example, warring noblemen) and in vicinities (for example, Iceland) most prone to internecine violence.

HISTORY OF THE CASE

Blood feuds were common among the agrarian and clannish residents of Iceland during the era of Christianization in that land, around 1000 C.E. Such conflict seemed endemic; one scholar remarked that all of medieval Icelandic literature could be summarized with the phrase "farmers came to blows." The *Saga of Burnt Njál* is preeminent among Icelandic legends, conveying the prevalence of feuding. Scholars assert that this tale is among the most important pieces of fiction in world literature. In addition to its compelling narrative, the saga describes legal approaches that Icelanders employed to curtail their tendency to kill one another. *The Saga of Burnt Njál*, or simply *Njála*, culminates in an effort to cease feuding by holding a trial.

The offense that gave rise to the case—the burning of a house and its owner, Njál—almost certainly was an actual occurrence. The story of Njál was written down 200 to 300 years after the crime, during a great age of saga composition. Based on internal references within *Njála*, scholars locate the factual cornerstone just after the year 1000. The saga's presentation of law in Iceland governing criminal trials is detailed, though not always set in the appropriate time period. Characters in the saga are adaptations for the purposes of

telling a compelling story, as are many of the episodes of violence depicted. For all of the qualifications that must surround taking *Njála* as fact, it is a vivid depiction of certain key elements in Icelandic culture and law.

First and most important, the saga presents a disastrous blood feud. As that warfare within clans unfolds, the reader discovers legal mechanisms that are available among Icelanders to try to manage the violence. For example, in one section of the saga two leading characters, Gunnar and Njál, find their friendship severely strained due to the plotting of Gunnar's new wife. This woman, Bergþóra, resents the fact that Njál has warned Gunnar about his wife's bad character. The wife arranges the killings of several of Njál's family members, and Njál's relatives retaliate.

The two old colleagues buy a lull in the hostilities by paying what among the Germanic peoples is called the wergild, a monetary compensation for the loss of a life according to the victim's social station and gender. The rules governing this "man-money" were set out in law codes throughout western Europe, such as in the code of Ethelbert of Kent from the early 600s.

Even with the presence of those rules governing wergilds, however, there was room for negotiation in individual cases. Thus, at certain points in the *Njála* persons who felt themselves particularly aggrieved resorted to arbitrators to determine if a wergild might be increased to indicate the enormity of an offense. At a pivotal moment in the *Njála* warring factions require such a high-level arbitration. They repair to a central area for a consultation with leading lawmakers. The delicate negotiations on the wergild are proceeding well until someone offers an insult. The arbitration falls apart, and the warring clans, including a character named Flosi, plot renewed violence.

It is at this moment in the saga that the decisive offense occurs: the besieging of Njál's house by his enemies. Njál and his family and friends are badly outnumbered, but they choose to defend their honor and their homestead to the death. After letting most of the women and children escape, the attackers, led by Flosi, set fire to the place. Only one person inside survives. Njál's nephew, Kari, makes a dramatic exit by running along a beam on the roof and jumping down, undetected amid the smoke. Kari now has the responsibility of exacting revenge for his kin's deaths.

SUMMARY OF ARGUMENTS

With Kari's survival, the Icelanders faced the question of what should be done with Flosi. This blood feud was longstanding and complex enough so that those who called for justice went straight to the highest levels for answers. Before an actual trial could take place, someone had to determine what form a trial should take. And prior to that, judgment was needed about a number of matters including who should sit in resolution, whether the lawyers retained on both sides were hired in an ethical fashion, and who was qualified to be a juror. Just as was true in other countries at this time, jurors were not supposed to determine guilt or innocence; they were there to monitor the legitimacy of the proceedings, for example, by affirming facts of which they had personal knowledge.

Flosi's case was heard by the order of the national assembly called the Althing, a body that served as the highest legislative and judicial authority in Iceland. In the year 1000 the speaker of the Althing ruled on difficult questions of procedure that might arise when one of the four courts (Quarter Courts) in Iceland could not reach a verdict and a decisive additional hearing was needed. Each of the four regular courts as well as the superior venue, the Fifth Court, had nine judges each. The speaker of the Althing was more than a judicial arbiter given that Iceland had followed the recent settlers of that land, Norwegian immigrants, in rejecting monarchy. He was a leader who through moral suasion and political influence might compel the enforcement of a verdict.

Flosi and his accusers, led by Kari, gathered their legal advisers and friends and went to the site of the Althing. It was an impressive open space surrounded by lava fields. They assembled, still in family groups, near a high rock called the Law Mount. The initial sparring in Flosi's case was about procedural matters. Did kinship with one of the legal counsel, for example, disqualify a juror? Were the lawyers themselves properly involved in the case?

The saga tells how each side, but particularly the defense, raised such questions so as to maneu-

ver to best advantage. Given the intricacies of the law, Flosi's advocates had some hope of getting the case thrown out on a technicality. Complicating the situation was the fact that one person who was keenly interested in effecting justice on behalf of Njál, a legal expert named Thorall Asgrimsson, was laid up at home with a badly infected leg. But, Thorall dispensed advice via couriers who ran back and forth to the Law Mount; in large part the Althing's speaker—really the chief judge in this case—accepted Thorall's wisdom. Finally, the advocates for Kari (the prosecution) made an error. They challenged the legality of the sitting of the judges who were hearing the case and requested that another panel be brought in. In asking for the wrong number of new judges, however, they placed their whole case in jeopardy because they had (in the eyes of the court) called the entire proceeding into question. It was as though the prosecution had shown a lack of respect and the case would be dismissed as a result.

VERDICT

The pace of the story quickened. Thorall, waiting anxiously in his sickbed, got news of the latest intricate argument before the speaker. He grasped that the prosecution had committed a fatal blunder and decided to intervene, no matter how painful it would be for him. He rose, lanced the swelling on his leg, and advanced to the Law Mount. He killed at least one member of the defense team on his way. The speaker attempted to maintain order, but the outdoor courtroom dissolved into a brouhaha. It did not take much to push the observers over the edge. At Flosi's trial, as in most other such judicial proceedings at the time, attendees came garbed with military apparel just in case they needed to resolve their differences extrajudicially.

Bystanders who were unwise enough to offer opinions on the courage of those in the fray found themselves drawn in, or worse. Those who were battle ready simply pitched in. Here, the saga offered intriguing commentary about the tenuous position of Christianity at the trial. The Althing had pronounced Christianity the official religion of Iceland in 999–1000, just a few years prior. The speaker asked a priest for assistance in calming the furor and was answered with the holy man taking up a sword himself.

SIGNIFICANCE

Flosi's case contained another message about the Christian religion that was more hopeful. Hallur, the father of one of the men killed in the melee at the trial—another kinsman of Njál—not only requested that the speaker arrange a truce but also declared that he would not press for a wergild for his son. Such an action was in line with the Christian notion of forgiveness rather than the older idea of retribution. That act of grace spurred the parties to agree to a cessation of violence. Those in attendance took up a collection to give to Hallur in recognition of the loss of his son, which amounted to a larger-than-usual wergild. The court then resumed its business. Those who were accused of the killing of Njál, Flosi chief among them, were exiled.

The resolution at trial did not end the saga, though. Kari pursued some of the "burners" who were not sent abroad, wreaking vengeance. Flosi used his exile as an opportunity to visit Rome; the religious implications of such a pilgrimage to the capital of Western Christianity were obvious. Though Kari followed him, still seeking revenge, in the end they were reconciled through shared misfortune and a marriage within their households. The storyteller thus suggested that while it was important to attempt legal solutions, the law sometimes could not bestow emotional satisfaction.

Further Reading

Bloomfield, Maxwell. "Beowulf, Byrhtnoth and the Judgment of God." *Speculum* (October 1969): 548–549; Cook, Robert, ed. *Njál's Saga*. New York: Penguin, 2002; Kadri, Sadakat. *The Trial*. New York: Random House, 2005; Friðrik Þór Friðriksson (dir.), *Angels of the Universe*. Icelandic Film/Peter Rommell Productions, 2000; Hollander, Lee, ed. *Njál's Saga*. Ware, U.K.: Wordsworth Editions, 1998; Online Medieval and Classical Library. *The Story of Burnt Njál*. Available online. URL: http://omacl.org/Njal/. Accessed February 1, 2009; Ziegler, Vickie L. *Trial by Fire and Battle in Medieval German Literature*. Rochester, N.Y.: Camden House, 2004.

The trial of John Italos

Date: 1082

KEY ISSUES

To what extent was philosophy reconcilable with the Christian religion? Did the study of ancient writers such as Aristotle and Plato lead the minds of the Christian faithful away from religious devotion? To some religious authorities in both the Eastern Orthodox and Roman Catholic traditions in the mid-11th century, "pagan" intellectualism was incompatible with piety. It might be expected that legal condemnation of ancient intellectual traditions would arise from within a Christian Church anxious to stamp out heresies. Such a formal condemnation of philosophy, especially the philosophy of the Greeks, however, occurred only in the East.

It is a further surprise that the prosecution of Byzantine cleric John Italos for his advocacy of "paganism" found impetus from secular leaders. Particularly with the rise to power of the Byzantine emperor Alexius I Comnenus, public discussion of classical texts clashed with the ruler's new push for orthodoxy in religion and a fresh determination to consolidate imperial authority. The trial of John Italos was ostensibly over heresy, but the proceedings were motivated as much by politics as belief.

HISTORY OF THE CASE

John Italos (Johannes Italus) was named for his native land. Like many others who sought intellectual attainment in his time, he was drawn to Constantinople. As a younger man, Italos studied philosophy with the well-known scholar Michael Psellus, who was the leading teacher of philosophy at the University of Constantinople. Psellus combined academic prowess with the ability to serve successive royal families. His most notable pupil was a young man who became the emperor Michael VII Doukas in 1071. Psellus's protégé Italos likewise was connected to both politics and the life of the mind.

When Michael VII needed someone with knowledge of Italy to assist in his effort to reconquer Byzantine holdings on the Italian peninsula, he sent Italos. The effort did not pan out; in fact, Italos for a while was suspected of being disloyal but worked his way back into the emperor's favor. He appeared to have been allowed to return to the empire upon a promise that he would confine himself to a monastery rather than working from a university setting. Italos's connection with the monastery at Pege helped burnish his reputation within the church, but Italos also began moving into a more prominent role as a teacher.

When Italos's mentor Psellus got into difficulty for his championing of Platonic philosophy and was forced to retire to a quieter setting, Italos became the leading teacher of philosophy in Constantinople. Somewhat brash and self-promoting but unquestionably interesting, Italos had a number of pupils. He also garnered the attention of those within and outside the church who thought his pursuit of philosophical inquiry objectionable. This was a complicated matter, for the church—and even conservative elements within it—did not automatically condemn those who taught ancient philosophy. The ancient Greeks might be instructive, as long as they did not conflict with Christianity. And so, for example, the church in Constantinople held that it was not necessarily wrong to teach logic with reference to Aristotle. But Plato was especially suspect, as were certain of his disciples, for promoting ideas such as preexistence. Platonic philosophy also was at odds with the idea of the resurrection of the body. To place students in contact with such dangerous views was to lead them into temptation.

Icons had been an issue of immense concern in Byzantine society for many years—certainly since the Iconoclastic Controversy of the eighth and ninth centuries. Iconoclasts condemned the use of human imagery for religious purposes. Conversely, iconodules (or iconophiles) argued that the incarnation of Christ meant that human images might be—perhaps even should be—associated with religious devotion. Iconoclasm tended to be strongest in the eastern portions of the Byzantine Empire, where contact with Muslim societies was most frequent. Muslim theology by this time condemned icons, and it was as if Christians in those areas absorbed Muslims' unease with human representation. Difference of opinion on icons helped fuel the slow split between Western and Eastern Christianity, which occurred definitively in 1054 (the Great Schism).

With the accession of a new secular leader in Constantinople—Emperor Alexius I—in 1081, Italos's influence came under scrutiny for several reasons. The most damaging criticism of Italos emerged, interestingly, not from within religious but political circles, specifically from the emperor and his family. Scholars disagree about why Alexius was behind the prosecution of Italos, although they concur that the campaign to discredit him was orchestrated by the emperor. Some refer to the famous writing of Alexius's daughter, Anna Comnena, to contend that the emperor's concern was with social order. In her contemporary history, *The Alexiad*, Anna Comnena states that the emperor feared Italos's influence among seditious persons.

Other learned sources maintain that Italos's connection with the previous emperor hurt him with the new regime. Alexius distanced himself from his predecessor by persecuting the philosophers who had found favor with Michael VII. Italos thought himself especially vulnerable because of his foreign origins. He also had a whiff of disloyalty because of his previous dealings with a Norman leader during Emperor Michael's Italian campaign. At the time of Alexius's accession the Normans were enemies of Constantinople.

The patriarch Eustratius Garidas was sympathetic to Italos, although there were more conservative members of the church who contended that Italos was not in line with the views of the patristic authorities, notably John of Damascus. John's iconodule writings, along with the statement of the Seventh Ecumenical Council of 787, were church dogma. Icon veneration, in other words, was not simply allowed within the church but rather highly respected. Thus, as some recent scholars argue, the newly seated emperor courted more conservative leaders of the church when Alexius directed that the church launch proceedings against Italos for lack of orthodoxy. It also was the case that as a person, Alexius was a traditionalist and a man of action, who leaned away from intellectualism and toward the established order in religion.

SUMMARY OF ARGUMENTS

Italos was the object of several proceedings designed to expose his ideas publicly and pressure him to renounce any notions that were at odds with the emperor's vision. In 1082 the emperor directed that his brother, Isaac Comnenus, undertake an investigation of Italos. This was in effect Italos's first trial.

As a followup to that inquiry, the church synod held its own trial of Italos within a meeting chamber at the great church of Saint Sophia (Hagia Sophia). That proceeding, however, was completely managed, and indeed often personally directed, by Alexius. Italos was fortunate to dodge the ire of a mob at an early point in the proceedings (reportedly, he hid on the roof of the sanctuary). The impingement of violence was not without precedent, for the city had seen such rioting on other occasions when heresy was being investigated. But, for an incursion to happen within the sanctity of the great church itself was less usual.

Still more remarkable was the fact that most observers agreed the mob was a tool of the emperor, whereas other unruly crowds had seemed to serve the church. Scholars note that the violence against Italos demonstrated the emperor's control over the city and domination of the church. Specifically, the emperor was firing a warning shot at the clergy associated with Saint Sophia itself. Patriarch Eustratius took the hint and moved the trial to the confines of the imperial palace. Italos, who had begun the examination with a certain confidence, flanked by several pupils and carrying his writings, no doubt was shaken.

Italos was charged with 10 or 11 (there is some obscurity in the trial records) types of unorthodox belief and teaching. The evidence against him was his own words, so the church trial might have been an opportunity for Italos to explain his views. Those presiding at trial were a mixture of church officials of several ranks plus some courtiers. With most of these persons, especially the sympathetic patriarch, Italos should have been able to hold his own in disputation, yet a key problem he had was that as the trial unfolded, the charges against Italos kept shifting.

Most of the evidence against Italos was a set of writings that he had been asked to present before a synod in 1076–77. This had been done supposedly under the cover of anonymity; at that time Italos quietly had rejected the ideas that the church had found objectionable and had been allowed to go on teaching. Italos, therefore, must have felt in 1082 that he was being reexamined on old issues. For example, Italos had to confront allegations that he had applied the errors of Arius to church teachings and was engaging in Neoplatonism. His accusers put it memorably: He had dabbled in "Hellenic ungodliness." Italos again stated that these had been mistakes that he was willing to abjure in future.

Apparently Italos acquitted himself reasonably well on the bulk of the charges but had trouble with one that appeared late in the proceedings—that he had physically desecrated an image of Christ. This he called an outright fabrication. Still, the allegation put him in an awkward spot. At that point in the proceedings he had to try to explain his views on iconography with a view toward extricating himself from the charge of iconoclasm. The record from the case is not much help in understanding what Italos argued in his own defense on this key point. Certain contemporary sources on the trial paint Italos as taking a position that was iconoclastic; others describe his views as supportive of a moderate skepticism about icons, and still others portray him as respectful (though perhaps not completely orthodox) with regard to sacred images. What seems apparent is that Italos's accusers—notably the emperor—wished to introduce an emotional element into the charges against Italos after he defended himself competently early on.

VERDICT

The church court found Italos guilty of all the heresies of which he was charged and forced him to recant his teachings in a very public setting. He was, in the language of the day, anathematized. At the basilica of Saint Sophia on March 13, 1082, Italos had to articulate his mistakes, renounce the beliefs that he had held, and listen to those present (including many of the church's leadership and the emperor) recite his errors. The date of this humiliation was carefully chosen; it was the anniversary of the ending of one episode in the Iconoclastic

Controversy more than two centuries earlier. In mid-April several clerics at Saint Sophia, as well as certain other of Italos's pupils, were compelled to defend themselves against the charge that they shared Italos's views. These men successfully argued they did not have similar views and renounced his influence. Among those caught in the net but released by the emperor was Patriarch Eustratius, who went on to become Alexius's main religious adviser.

Italos, like Psellus, was allowed to retreat to a monastery. There is some evidence that Italos later changed his mind about his retractions at trial and in Saint Sophia and suffered further as a result of that alteration, but his later life remains obscure. If he did renounce his own apology, the church would have viewed him—much as in the Western Christian tradition—as a lapsed heretic. His treatment by the church at that juncture would have been quite harsh.

SIGNIFICANCE

Italos's condemnation—whether or not it resulted in a death sentence after a relapse into heresy—certainly stilled his voice. The Italos trial also had a chilling effect on others who might too freely mix ancient ideas with the Christian religion in Constantinople. After the intellectual and religious retraction of the 11th century, church officials—rather than private instructors like Italos—increasingly controlled university education. Qualifications to teach religion grew more restrictive. It was no longer sufficient to be expert in ancient languages or philosophy; one also needed to be demonstrably orthodox to be an instructor who touched upon ancient texts.

The Byzantine state was under attack from external forces in the time of John Italos; most obviously Constantinople felt pressure from the Turks. But the capital of the empire also was nervous about encroachment from provincial leaders, of whom Alexius I was the most successful example. Alexius and the Comneni represented the triumph of provincial leadership against the urban aristocrats of his day. And, there were additional threats, for example, from the Normans. In the 11th century, then, Constantinople stepped back from the intellectual expansion that reached a high point during the lifetimes of Psellus and Italos. After the trial of Italos, to study ancient thought still was permissible, as long as that study did not intersect with Christian belief. But to undertake the consideration of philosophical topics was to run a real chance of being shut out of the church as a career, or worse. Delving into philosophy was tantamount to inviting the unsophisticated (such as Italos's pupils) to commit theological errors. When the barbarians were at the gates, errancy in religious matters was equivalent to courting disaster.

Further Reading

Angold, Michael. *Church and Society under the Comneni, 1081–1261.* Cambridge: Cambridge University Press, 1995; Clucas, Lowell. *The Trial of John Italos and the Crisis of Intellectual Values in Byzantium in the Eleventh Century.* Munich, Germany: Institut für Byzantinistik, Neugriechische Philologie und Byzantinische Kunstgeschichte der Universität München, 1981; Comnena, Anna. *The Alexiad.* London: Penguin Books, 1969; Duffy, John. "Hellenic Philosophy in the Byzantium and the Lonely Mission of Michael Psellus." *In Byzantine Philosophy and Its Ancient Sources,* edited by Katerina Ierodiakonou, 139–156. New York: Oxford University Press, 2002; Gazi, Effi. "Reading the Ancients: Remnants of Byzantine Controversies in the Greek National Narrative." *Historein* 6 (2006): 144–150; Hussey, J. M. *The Orthodox Church in the Byzantine Empire.* Oxford: Oxford University Press, 1990; Meyendorff, John. *Byzantine Theology: Historical Trends and Doctrinal Themes.* New York: Fordham University Press, 1974.

The trial of Pierre Barthélemy

Date: 1097

KEY ISSUES

Trial by ordeal was an ancient practice employed in a number of places such as India, Japan, Russia,

Africa, and Europe. It had regional variations, but the central idea was the same: The community appealed to divine power to demonstrate the validity of a claim or an accusation. The ordeal was a spectacle that persons would remember; written records were not necessary. Some ordeals also had the advantage of marking persons who had been accused through the infliction of either physical or emotional damage. Thus, those who had a propensity for crime might think twice before again misbehaving. Even if they did not reform, they probably would bear scars that alerted their neighbors to be watchful.

In Thailand one form of ordeal was to place the defendant and the accuser into an enclosure with a tiger. In theory the innocent party survived. It was not unheard of for the religious officials who administered ordeals to imbue the process with even greater meaning, or even to try to influence the outcome. Among the people of Madagascar an accused person had to ingest a drink made from the tangena plant, which is toxic in large quantities but only nauseating when diluted. Obviously, the outcome depended much on those who mixed the divine potion. Japanese priests made accused persons swallow paper printed with characters that would torment guilty individuals who did not confess.

There were certain types of ordeals that proved especially popular with Europeans, several of which involved the infliction of injury via heat, a bandaging of the injured portion of the body, and an examination of the wound within several days. Germanic peoples may have adopted the concept of trial by ordeal from India or the Near East. The Indian historic epic *Ramayana* includes a fire test undergone by the hero Sita in order to demonstrate her innocence. In Cappadocia, holy women employed techniques such as walking on red-hot farm tools to show that they had the confidence of the gods.

In Germanic and Frankish lands from at least the 700s onward, an individual accused of breaking a law who would not admit fault might be made to grasp a hot iron, recover an object from a boiling cauldron, walk on heated plowshares for a certain number of paces, or pass through a gauntlet of flames. For some years the Christian Church approved such methods of showing the state of

mind of a defendant. A church council at Mayence (Mainz) in 829 specified that pieces of metal that had been placed in a fire should be applied to persons who denied murdering priests and desired to prove their innocence. If the body of a person who had undergone the ordeal healed cleanly, then he or she was said to be pure of heart and had not sworn falsely.

Ordeal by water was another common method of assessing culpability, differing from trial by fire in that persons tested by water stood a smaller chance of surviving the procedure. The standard practice was for an accused person to be bound hand and foot and thrown into a deep vessel of water that clerics had blessed. If the holy water "accepted" the claimant, then he or she was innocent; if the individual floated, however, then guilt or sin was proven and the accused would be liable to punishment. The Christian Church taught that those who sank but could not be pulled out in time to save their earthly lives had died in a state of grace.

Authorities even accepted some more unusual ordeals as authentic, though their use was more sporadic. A common thread in ordeals was the use of a foreign object or element in order to test a suspect's truthfulness. Clerics who participated in trials by ordeal would imbue an object such as a hot iron with divine powers. Those powers would help reveal the suspect's veracity. Often, such tests were closely related to Christian theology. The swallowing of consecrated bread, for instance, was a method for showing one's body capable literally of accepting the Host. A famous application of that ordeal—a test sometimes called "cosned"—occurred just before the Norman conquest, when a member of the English king-making family the Godwins imposed such a test on himself at a great dinner. Within a matter of minutes Earl Harold Godwin had collapsed and died. Several years earlier Godwin had provided supposed proof through oath helpers that he had been declared not complicit in a murder. His contemporaries saw the ordeal of the sacred bread as a kind of second appeal to the Almighty, an appeal which Godwin lost.

Ordeals usually were employed to try criminals, but they also might demonstrate whether a person was telling the truth about an important matter. For example, in 876, when the German leader Louis was arguing with his uncle Charles the Bold about Louis's inheritance, Louis turned to an ordeal to illustrate the justness of his cause. Louis had 10 of his retainers undergo trial by boiling water; 10, ordeal of a hot iron; and 10, ordeal by cold water. All emerged unscathed, allowing Louis to advance successfully into territory that he had said was rightly his. Persons of high social rank like Louis often did not have to submit personally to the ordeal but could employ (or compel) others to do so for them. Defendants of lesser status were not so fortunate.

HISTORY OF THE CASE

In the case of Pierre Barthélemy, Western Christian crusaders relied on trial by ordeal to determine whether one of their faithful indeed was divinely inspired. In 1097 Barthélemy was part of a force that sought to capture the Muslim city of Antioch. The area was hotly contested, with Antioch having been captured from the Byzantines only about 10 years earlier. The Christian forces besieged and then finally overtook the city on June 2, 1098, and in turn Muslim forces laid siege to Antioch. In each case the defenders of the city were holed up, desperate for relief.

Conditions within Antioch deteriorated rapidly during June when the Europeans were inside. Barthélemy, an obscure monk, became famous within Antioch because he claimed to have had a revelation. He said that in a hole in a church building (that had served recently as a mosque) he had found a holy object: the spear that a Roman soldier had wielded to pierce the side of Christ when Jesus was hanging on the cross. Barthélemy swore that St. Andrew had appeared to him, telling him of the spear's existence and assuring him that the object was authentic. When word of the holy lance spread, it seemed to give hope to the besieged crusaders. One of the noblemen who had begun the crusade, Bohemund of Taranto, led a force out of the city gates to attack the besieging force. With disunity among the Turkish attackers, the siege was lifted.

SUMMARY OF ARGUMENTS

During the summer of 1098 when Antioch was nominally under Christian control, problems still raged within the city. Food still was not plentiful because Muslim producers in the countryside were reluctant to supply the crusaders. There was an outbreak of typhus. Both Rome and Constantinople demurred in sending reinforcements. The powerful nobles from Normandy, Provence, and the Frankish lands squabbled among themselves over who was in charge at Antioch and what direction the crusade ought to take next. A significant faction wished to forge ahead to besiege Jerusalem.

In the months that had elapsed after Barthélemy voiced his claim, both believers and skeptics of the holy lance discussed whether Barthélemy had actually made direct contact with God. Some critical of Barthélemy charged that he simply possessed a military motive and was in the pocket of Bohemund. The fullest account of the arguments concerning Barthélemy came from the chaplain Raymond of Aguiliers, who traveled with the bishop of Puy and the count of Toulouse on the First Crusade. The bishop was well connected; he had been papal legate to France on behalf of Pope Urban II. It was Pope Urban who in 1095 had urged Christians in his famous speech at Clermont to undertake the effort to wrest Christian holy sites from "infidel" control. Father Raymond was among those who supported Barthélemy, although subsequent historians have found him to be a quite biased reporter. Father Raymond led the crusaders out of Antioch in late June at the head of the troops that broke the siege. He had been carrying the holy lance.

The church took physical objects such as the holy lance seriously when an item's provenance was of long standing. But Christian authorities also looked dimly on the idea of relics being put forward by hucksters, an increasingly common problem on crusade. Some simply objected to the claim of this relic being real because of who had uncovered it. Barthélemy ran into trouble not only because he was linked to a particular noble faction within Antioch but because of his peasant background. Even Barthélemy's defender Father Raymond commented on the monk's lack of sophistication.

Barthélemy decided to silence his critics by volunteering to undergo a trial by fire. A crowd of 40,000 made up of the crusaders, their leaders, and a number of Christian church officials, gathered. The proceeding began in early morning. The large group of priests who supervised the ordeal went barefoot, though they wore vestments. The test that Barthélemy faced was walking through a fiery gauntlet. He had to pass between two 14-foot-long rows of olive branches, four feet high, placed one foot apart. The priests blessed the blaze after it was lit, and Barthélemy set out.

VERDICT

Some observers noted that when he got to the end of the walk of fire, Barthélemy obviously was badly injured, his body charred. Raymond of Aguiliers wrote that Barthélemy died in 12 days' time after suffering greatly. Others reported, though, that Barthélemy got through the flames safely but was mauled by his supporters in their overenthusiasm. Despite the deep conflict that existed in Antioch about him, the monk from Puy was remembered as the crusader who turned around the fortunes of the Europeans at Antioch. Not just in Raymond's chronicle of the First Crusade but also through the medieval *chanson du geste* (songs of great deeds) that recalled the long march from Europe to Jerusalem, Barthélemy was a hero.

SIGNIFICANCE

The participation of persons of noble status in the Crusades is well known. Less familiar are the experiences of individuals who were poor but still felt a calling to fight on behalf of Christianity in the Middle East. Pierre Barthélemy's story at Antioch is intriguing because it provides a brief glimpse at a crusader who in many respects was ordinary. Was Barthélemy simply delusional, perhaps from physical causes due to the privations of the siege? Did he do the bidding of a powerful politician in unifying the defenders behind a military push? In any event Barthélemy believed in himself enough to undergo a rigorous test of his veracity.

Long after Barthélemy's demise the Christian Church headquartered in Rome continued to struggle with the issue of how miracles should be authenticated. That divinely inspired events occurred, theologians and church administrators had no doubt. But, they remained uneasy about revelations to individuals, especially when visions occurred to persons of lower social and ecclesiastical status. Such was part of the reason why the church was ill at ease regarding how to proceed with Joan of Arc in the early 1400s.

A trial by ordeal, however, was a divine manifestation with which the church felt comfortable—at least up to a point. An ordeal could be employed by Christian clerics as a forum in which to demonstrate the power of the Almighty. It also was a large public gathering at which religion could be taught in small doses. Among the images that clerics frequently conveyed to the faithful was the notion of hellfire, a concept vividly gotten across when fire injured the bodies of the sinful.

An ordeal also was a spectacle that kept a community from engaging in more riotous forms of justice—particularly self-help in the form of blood feuds—that the church condemned. In time, ordeals would lose much of their religious meaning. Around the year 1400, for example, at the ordeal involving Girolamo Savonarola, the crowd simply wanted theater. Denied it, they took out their rage upon the party whom they held responsible for canceling the show. By that date the church, too, was more cynical. By the dawn of the Renaissance there were plenty of observers who argued that religious authorities were not above rigging the proceedings to rid themselves of an outspoken critic of the church.

Further Reading

Aguiliers, Raymond. *Historia Francorum qui ceperunt Iherusalem (History of the Franks Who Captured Jerusalem).* Philadelphia: American Philosophical Society, 1968; Aguiliers, Raymond. "The Discovery of the Holy Lance." In Krey, A. C., ed. *The First Crusade: The Accounts of Eyewitnesses and Participants,* edited by A. K. Krey. 1921. Available online. URL: http://www.fordham.edu/halsall/source/cde-antioch.html#raymond5. Accessed March 1, 2009; Bartlett, Robert. *Ordeal by Fire and Water.* Oxford, U.K.: Clarendon Press, 1986; Lea, Henry C. *Superstition and Force.* Philadelphia: Greenwood Press, 1870; "Ordeals." *The Friend* 43 (1870): 228–229; Paris, Matthew. *The Illustrated Chronicles of Matthew Paris: Observations of Thirteenth-Century Life.* Cambridge: Cambridge University Press, 1958; Truzzi, Marcelo. "A Bibliography on Fire-Walking." *Zetetic Scholar* 11 (1983): 105–107.

The trial of Thomas Becket

Date: 1164

KEY ISSUES

The trial of Thomas Becket in 1164 was the result of the clash of enormous egos, but it also fit within a much wider context. Several questions that bedeviled other church leaders, the monarchs they served, and the leadership of the Christian Church in Rome came to the fore in Becket's case. Who had ultimate say over church appointments within a particular country—the king or church officials? How much money could Rome expect monarchs to help them collect on behalf of the church? If a disagreement arose within the church locally, could church officials there take their case to Rome on appeal? What was to be done if a monarch outright disobeyed the instructions of the pope?

Such dilemmas had been the subject of bitter dispute all over Europe prior to the middle of the 12th century and would continue to affect relations between monarchs and Rome long after that time. In that sense the controversies involving Thomas Becket during the 1160s were only part of a succession of events. But the events that included Becket had a particular poignancy because of one aspect of Becket's situation: He had been the close companion of England's extraordinarily powerful king, Henry II, before his appointment as archbishop of Canterbury. Once he occupied the position at Canterbury, Becket was the spokesman for a position often critical of the king. The old friends had become ideological foes, lending a personal element to the dramatic debates over the roles of church and king.

HISTORY OF THE CASE

There was nothing to mark out Becket as an unusually dedicated churchman prior to about 1162. He was the son of wealthy Anglo-Norman parents. Like many other well connected young men, he made his way up the church hierarchy not necessarily because of spirituality but through administrative skill and social polish. He did a great favor for Count Henry of Anjou in 1154 while serving as an aide to Theobald, archbishop of Canterbury: Becket worked as a facilitator with the papacy, strengthening Henry's claim to the English throne while helping discredit the case of a key royal rival. As a reward for that service, the new monarch, Henry II, shortly thereafter appointed Becket as his chief legal adviser.

While lord chancellor, Becket distinguished himself as a policy hand to Henry. Henry, who was known for the expansive quality of his social life, soon found that Becket could match him expense for expense, quaff for quaff. The two men became companions, but that changed drastically when Archbishop Theobald died in 1162 and the king decided to make Becket head of the see at Canterbury. Becket began to behave very differently. He had a crisis of conscience and took up the role of defending the church against those critical of its authority. Becket was not immediately acclaimed within the church. Some clerics still distrusted him because of his association with the king; they envied his rapid rise to power. Among Becket's first signs of defiance to Henry was his support of a campaign to canonize Anselm, a previous archbishop of Canterbury who had admonished his royal patrons.

Becket soon clashed with the king on the issue of "criminous clerics." It was the long-held position of the church that the religious sphere ought to have the opportunity to discipline persons of clerical status who were accused of secular crimes. The church argued that clerics might be reformed if their religious superiors could reason with them. Further, spiritual authorities contended that they had earned first chance at the rehabilitation of their own: The church had educated clerics from an early age, therefore it had a long-term investment in helping sinful clerics see the error of their ways. Accused persons who pleaded "benefit of clergy" would not suffer corporal punishment at the hands of royal justice but rather would be delivered to a church court, which did not countenance the shedding of blood as punishment.

Henry II, on the other hand, maintained that the church was sheltering scoundrels under the guise of rehabilitation. He famously said "it takes two crimes to hang a priest," thus criticizing the church's prescription for handling a cleric convicted in church court for a crime. The church, at worst, would defrock a serious offender. Then if the former cleric committed a second felony, he would be subject to the secular authorities. Henry painted such a scenario as a scandal against law and order. The church replied that the king was less interested in justice than in grabbing power for his temporal courts.

For some months in 1163 church officials and those loyal to the king bandied such arguments about, for example, at the Council of Westminster. Becket was bolstered in his aim to stand up to the king by the support of Rome. Under Pope Gregory VII and subsequent pontiffs, the church had been reemphasizing the need for such important issues to be mediated by Rome. Becket initially resisted Henry's position stoutly but finally agreed to accept some reforms put forward by the monarch. Henry, typically, moved quickly to solidify his success. He convened a gathering at Clarendon in January 1164 and proposed a set of written reforms in the law. Becket at that point balked, and the simmering disagreements between the two old friends became very public. The Constitutions of Clarendon of 1164 were a statement of the royal agenda, promulgated over Becket's objections.

SUMMARY OF ARGUMENTS

As archbishop of Canterbury, Becket presided over the church court at Canterbury. In a suit filed by John FitzGilbert le Marshal in a royal court, Becket was accused of not administering justice properly in the church court. Did Henry II put Marshal up to the legal challenge of Becket, or did Marshal simply nurse a separate grudge against Becket? There is no way to be certain, but Marshal's suit certainly played well into Henry's agenda. Whether the origin of the case against Becket at Northampton was independent of the king or engineered by him, the effect was much the same. Becket was forced to defend himself in the king's court against the charge that he failed to work properly within a system of justice delicately balanced between temporal and spiritual authority.

At Northampton in October 1164 the king's advisers called Becket to appear before them. Sig-

nificantly, the king's councilors at Northampton who were to serve as Becket's judges included several ecclesiastical officials. Those individuals probably thought Becket too aggressive in his positions, resented him personally, or disagreed with his interpretation of the church's positions.

Henry aimed to force Becket to either back down or resign. The council at Northampton was an inquiry that had many elements of a trial. First, Becket had to answer the charge that he failed to give justice in the court at Canterbury and then had not appeared in court to answer that charge. In other words, he was accused of contempt of court for not defending himself initially. At Northampton Becket was fairly quickly found guilty of that transgression.

Next, the king's representatives came up with a new charge: Becket had misappropriated government funds while serving as chancellor. The king demanded an immediate accounting of all revenues over which Becket had control while he was chancellor. It was an impossible undertaking and a manifestly unfair request during a trial. Alternatively, perhaps Becket could repay the whole sum over which he had had cognizance. The bishop of Winchester intervened, proposing a sum in settlement, but Henry II declined to negotiate. It was a dramatic few days; Henry was at the fortress of Northampton while the trial proceeded, though not in the room itself. Messengers literally carried proposals back and forth between the hearing chamber and the royal apartments.

Among the statements that Becket made at Northampton that exacerbated his difficulties with Henry were two direct challenges to the Constitutions of Clarendon. Becket declared he would ask for a ruling about the present matter from the pope, and he denied the authority of the current tribunal to try him. Becket's contention that the papacy ought to review the case angered the English clerics who were participating as part of Henry's council, for Becket in effect was saying they were working counter to the interests of Rome in supporting the king of England.

When the judges called Becket in to hear their decision on October 13, they intended to rule that he was in violation of the Constitutions of Clarendon. Becket entered the chamber carrying a cross, which he called "his sword." He refused to accept the court's judgment. He declared that he had been summoned only on the charge concerning John le Marshal. He exited the room and the fortress at Northampton, eventually using disguises and the cover of night to leave the town and the country. His critics called the escape cowardly, while his defenders said it was miraculous. Among the many miracles later associated with Becket was one connected with his flight. Upon being recognized by a poor farmer, Becket supposedly struck the ground in surprise with his bishop's staff. The spot where his symbol of office touched the earth bubbled up with water; it was said that Becket had created a holy well.

VERDICT

The result of the hearing at Northampton was similar to that in a more formal trial: Becket suffered foreign exile. His flight removed him from office in effect if not through a sentence. The proceedings did not so much resolve cleanly as end dramatically. Becket journeyed abroad rather than stay to hear the judgment of the court. He had had a very narrow escape from Northampton, and his deportment at trial had been defiant. Clearly he and Henry were in open breach.

On the Continent, Becket stayed for much of the remainder of his life. He was disappointed with the lack of support he received from Pope Alexander III, who himself was in exile and dependent on the protection of the French king Louis VII. While first in France and then in Flanders, Becket increasingly adopted habits of contemplation and privation. He had to make do with a reduced staff. His small household was a contrast even to his less lavish days at Canterbury. Becket's lifestyle was so austere at times that remaining supporters feared for his life. They told of his standing for hours in a cold stream, for example, in an effort at self-denial.

Becket and Henry made two efforts at reconciliation beginning in 1169, but they fell out again when the king, who had grown impatient waiting for his son and heir Henry to be crowned prince by an archbishop, set up the ceremony not with Becket presiding but rather under the archbishop of York. Becket saw that action as a personal and religious snub. York traditionally was the less prestigious of the two English archbishoprics and the

one not as closely associated with the monarch. Becket first threatened and then excommunicated the church officials who had participated in the coronation.

The two also tried a face-to-face meeting in 1170. It was an emotional encounter but did not have lasting effect. Henry's furor at Becket's continuing "betrayal" of their friendship was testimony to Becket's effectiveness at gathering support in England, even while Becket was mostly abroad. Those around the king knew of his frustration, so it was unsurprising when four of the monarch's more hotheaded knights took it upon themselves to slaughter Becket in Canterbury Cathedral in December 1170.

SIGNIFICANCE

Those who profiled Becket in his own time—whatever their affiliation—tended to paint him during the years from 1163 until his death as stubborn to the point of ineffectiveness. They noted, though, Becket's growing and unquestionable religiosity. Among later biographers who assessed his movements in exile, Becket's actions took on a more saintly hue. Many of the eyewitness or near-contemporary reports of Becket's confrontations with his critics were modeled on biblical incidents. In the hands of his greatest admirers Becket's controversial stances after 1163 naturally led to his martyrdom. Any challenges he faced in those years were tests of his character in which he increasingly proved himself worthy of offering the ultimate sacrifice. Meanwhile, Henry II continued to be a powerful ruler, making lasting contributions to the administration of justice in England. The force of his reforms related to the church courts, however, had been blunted, and his overall popularity, seriously damaged.

Even those who took a more cynical view of Becket admitted his effect as a historical figure. He energized those who resisted the incursions of Henry II into church authority. In 1173 Pope Alexander III rewarded Becket's efforts with canonization. Becket became the greatest English saint, the inspiration for pilgrimages to the site of his death at Canterbury (the destination in *The Canterbury Tales*), a Europe-wide hero, and a reminder that the English church retained vital connections to Rome.

Further Reading

Anouilh, Jean. *Becket, or the Honor of God.* New York: Coward-McCann, 1960; Barlow, Frank. *Thomas Becket.* Berkeley: University of California Press, 1986; Butler, John. *The Quest for Becket's Bones: The Mystery of the Relics of St. Thomas Becket of Canterbury.* New Haven, Conn.: Yale University Press, 1995; Eliot, T. S. *Murder in the Cathedral.* New York: Harcourt and Brace, 1935; Hilliam, David. *Thomas Becket: English Saint and Martyr.* New York: Rosen Publishing, 2004; Staunton, Michael. *Thomas Becket and His Biographers.* Woodbridge, Conn.: Boydell Press, 2006; Duggan, Anne J., ed. and trans. *The Correspondence of Thomas Becket, Archbishop of Canterbury 1162–1170.* Oxford, U.K.: Clarendon Press, 2000; Wallis, Hal B. (dir.), *Becket.* Paramount, 1964.

The trial of Nahmanides

Also known as: The Disputation of Barcelona

Date: 1263

KEY ISSUES

Medieval disputations were intellectual showdowns over religion. At stake was not simply theological supremacy. Often, it was the safety of minority groups that was under discussion. In Muslim North Africa and Christian Spain, as well as at other locations in the Mediterranean region, Jews in particular defended their beliefs in public debates. Such opportunities for discourse amounted to trials—sometimes trials of the very right to exist within societies that considered Jews as interlopers and heretics.

The three most important disputations of this type between Jews and Christians in Europe in the premodern era were at Paris in 1240, Barcelona in 1263, and Tortosa in 1413–14. Scholars of history and religion count those meetings as influential due to the ample source material that survived concerning them, publicity about them among Jewish and Christian communities, and the large exposure generated by each confrontation. Observers at the time of the disputations and commentators ever since have disagreed about which side "won," even in terms of the quality of the argument presented. Also unclear are the results from the disputations. Did they lead to conversions to Christianity among Jews and inspire the missionary efforts of the papacy and local clerics? Or did they instead cause Jewish communities to draw closer together, bound by pride in the efforts of their esteemed intellectuals to defend their faith? Or were they perhaps not influential in the ordinary lives of the faithful but only an intellectual or political exercise?

HISTORY OF THE CASE

The Disputation of Barcelona and certain legal actions that were connected with it afford an opportunity to assess such questions. The debate that occurred in a public setting in 1263 was marked by the presence of several memorable personalities who lent color to the often-abstract arguments. In particular, one must keep in mind the influence at Barcelona of two well-known scholars of the Talmud: Rabbi Moses ben Nahman (Nahmanides) of Gerona, and Rabbi Moshe ben Maimon (Maimonides). Although Maimonides was not physically present at the disputation—he having lived in the previous century—his esteemed writings were very much under consideration there.

Nahmanides was a community leader within Catalonia (a region of Aragon) and the spokesperson for the Jewish viewpoint at the Disputation of Barcelona. He later published his own account of the debate that got him into difficulty with his adversaries. Prior to the disputation Nahmanides had laid stress on an understanding of scriptures and rabbinical writings, with special focus on the Midrash, or expositions on holy texts. Although defending Maimonides against Christian critics, Nahmanides argued against too much reliance on the philosophy that Maimonides treasured. Rabbi Nahman's writings examined mystical elements within the Jewish faith and, among modern scholars, are viewed as a basis for kabbalism.

Friar Paul Christian (Pablo Christiani) was a convert *(converso)* from Judaism and a member of the Dominican order. He developed a critique of his former faith and envisioned a mass conversion program for the Jews of Aragon. The disputation was Father Paul's opportunity to test his arguments; he expected that the skilled rejoinders of Nahmanides would allow him to hone his reasoning. Several colleagues from the Dominicans joined Father Paul at Barcelona, with Friar Raymond of Penyafort being especially active in support of the Christian position. Father Raymond was the confessor to the king of Aragon.

That ruler of Aragon, James I, had the task of administering a diverse kingdom. Himself a major force in the Reconquista (reconquest of the Iberian Peninsula from non-Christians), James the Conqueror clearly wished to keep Christian groups such as the activist Dominicans happy. James also did not want to incur the displeasure of the Christian Church in Rome. He made several attempts to demonstrate his piety in an international sense, including going on crusade in 1269. And yet this monarch personally may have been uncomfortable with repression of the Jews in his kingdom. James appeared genuinely interested in what venerated scholars within the Jewish tradition had to offer. He kept a full-time Hebrew translator at court and was conversant with Jewish texts. It bears noting that James was among the first Christian monarchs to compose prose extensively. He appeared to appreciate effective writing of the type that Nahmanides and Maimonides produced. James seemed to think that Jewish moralists had something to offer; he quoted them alongside Christian authorities in some of his own writings.

SUMMARY OF ARGUMENTS

The leading speakers for the Christian viewpoint at the disputation were Friars Raymond of Penyafort, Raymond Martini, and Arnold of Segarra, all Dominicans, as well as the leading Franciscan in Barcelona, Friar Peter de Janua. Rabbi Nahman was the only speaker for the Jewish side. The disputation took place at the royal court of Aragon. The public was admitted, and King James himself governed the sessions, often interjecting comments or questions. One should look at the disputation as

a trial. Although it was not in form a criminal proceeding, ideas as well as their proponents were being judged. The court convened on four separate days beginning on July 20, 1263.

The ground rules heavily favored the Christian disputants. They were allowed to frame the debate. Nahmanides was supposed only to reply to specific claims that the Christians made. Nahmanides later said that he had met with his adversaries prior to the public confrontation. He reported securing their promise that he could speak freely as long as he was not disrespectful of Christianity. Such a pledge, however, hardly was a carte blanche for the rabbi; the Christians got to determine when a remark of his indicated a lack of respect.

The Christian argument at Barcelona included the contention that the Talmud was not an authentic reflection of the Judaism that Christians knew from the Bible. Christian debaters at Barcelona also maintained that the Talmud included a number of statements that validated Christianity. In support of their interpretations of the Talmud the Christian scholars such as Father Paul used the Midrash. Among the specific claims that the anti-Jewish disputants put forward were that Jewish sources pointed to the appearance of a messiah who already had appeared on earth, that such a figure (who the Christians said was Jesus) had the character of the divine and the human, and that Jesus' death had absolved humanity of its sins.

A reconstruction of what exactly was said at the disputation is not possible based on extant sources. None of those records of the disputation was a transcript to begin with. It also is difficult to be accurate about the words used or even when they were spoken, because the two major contemporary accounts of the debate are so at variance in both tone and citation of specific examples. The Christian (Latin) account of the proceedings cites exchanges that make Father Paul look victorious. Nahmanides' version plays up his own astute ripostes. What is clear from the competing reports of the trial, though, is the nature of the discussion. For instance, a key point of disagreement was whether the Messiah was divine. Nahmanides' version of an exchange on the last day of the disputation concerns just that question. It begins with the Christian assertion that Psalm 110, verse 1, refers to a divine messiah: "The Lord said to my lord, 'Sit at my right hand, while I make your enemies your footstool'" and continues:

> Friar Paul: Who is it that King David would address as "my lord," except for the divinity? And how could a human being sit at the right hand of God?

> King James: He asks well. For if the messiah were totally human, actually from the seed of David, David would not address him as "my lord." If I had a son or grandson from my seed, even were he to rule over the entire world, I would not address him as "my lord." Rather, I would wish that he address me as "my lord" and that he kiss my hand.

> Nahmanides: Are you the wise Jew who discovered this insight and apostasized as a result? And are you the one who told the king to gather before you the sages of the Jews so that you could debate with them over these insights that you discovered? Have we not heard this claim heretofore? Indeed, there is neither a priest nor an infant who does not pose this difficulty to the Jews. This question is most antiquated.

In addition to Nahmanides' rejoinder that the Christians such as Friar Paul had employed Jewish sources simplistically or incorrectly, his answers to the Dominicans' contentions were broad ranging. In other words, the debate went much further than those who had arranged the disputation must have intended. Nahmanides at certain junctures observed that Christianity had not served the Roman Empire well: When the Romans became Christians their fortunes plummeted, "and now the servants of Muhammad have a greater realm than they." The remark hardly could have won Rabbi Nahman acclaim among his enemies, and yet he made many such trenchant observations.

VERDICT

Medieval disputations usually did not conclude with a formal declaration of victory for one side. Supremacy was decided in the aftermath of the discussions. The outcome became apparent over some time and then only according to public,

political, religious, or scholarly judgment. For the Christians at Barcelona the trial would have been a stunning success if many Jews had immediately or even eventually converted. Such an outcome was unlikely, and indeed, it did not occur. Among Jews the best possible outcome would have been for Christian leaders to admit in public that they had interpreted Jewish texts incorrectly. But, of course, Nahmanides and those who supported him did not realize their fondest hope, either.

The battle for public opinion at Barcelona was played out in several forums. First of all, there was a continuing intellectual debate that took the form of a pro-Christian versus pro-Jewish account of the disputation. In effect, these were as close as contemporaries came to transcripts of the proceedings. One recollection was composed in Latin, a terse recollection concentrating on the supposed superiority of the Christian position, and the other was a much longer treatment by Nahmanides, emphasizing his argumentative prowess.

The participants in the Disputation of Barcelona also continued their debate in less structured settings. Several of the principals in the disputation, including James I, in early August 1263 paid a visit to the synagogue at Barcelona to preach to the Jews. It was a sign of royal favor for the king to be a guest speaker at one's place of worship, thus signifying that Nahmanides indeed had made a name for himself at the public contest. And yet, the monarch brought a message that was antithetical to the rabbi's views. How should Nahmanides act in such a situation? What could be his reply to the monarch whom he thought wrong but yet a monarch who also felt some favor toward Nahmanides? Rabbi Nahman's response to the king's sermon was a clever acknowledgement of the ruler's authority and yet gainsaid the substance of the Christian position:

> The words of our lord the king are in my eyes noble, superior, and revered, for they proceed from the mouth of a noble man, a superior man, and a revered leader—indeed there is none like him in the world. However, I cannot praise these words as correct. For I have obvious proofs and counterclaims as clear as the sun that truth is not as he says. It is, however, not appropriate to

disagree with him. One thing only shall I say. I am most surprised at him. For the words that he speaks in our ears—that we should believe in Jesus as the messiah—Jesus himself was the one who brought this claim to our ancestors.

In the political and legal realm the royal court first followed up on the disputation by issuing a series of edicts. Those proclamations of James I, made in late August 1263, at first glance appeared to be an affirmation of the Christian perspective on the disputation, that the Dominicans had prevailed, and that Friar Raymond was welcome to pursue his agenda of conversion. Upon close inspection, however, the policies were not much more than a restatement of older rules for Christians to follow in engaging in their labors of conversion among the Jews of Aragon. Also, the 1263 policies showed the influence of James I and the impact of Nahmanides, for they included safeguards for Jews among the pro-Christian regulations.

The 1263 edicts did repeat statements from the 1240s that Jews had to listen (upon pain of fines) to sermons from those who sought to convert them. The 1263 policies did not mention Muslims as potential converts as certain earlier edicts had done. (The rules promulgated just after the Disputation of Barcelona were not broadly aimed at non-Christians but rather at one group of non-Christians.) Furthermore, Friar Paul was prominently mentioned in the 1263 regulations governing missionary work; it was his program that was to be pushed. The new rules specifically targeted a key writing of Maimonides. Persons who possessed copies of his *Sefer Shofetim* had to turn over that book to the authorities for burning, based on the Franciscan contention that Maimonides had committed blasphemy against Jesus.

But those strictures were mitigated in several other royal announcements, some coming only days after the initial statements of new policy on August 26, 1263. On August 30, for example, King James clarified that Jews did not have to leave their quarter of the city in order to hear the missionary sermons. He enforced segregation, to be sure, but also inserted language that seemed to undercut enforcement of the edicts. It was as though Jews did not have to listen to the proselytizing, though the king would support Friar Paul's missionary work. In addition, in 1264 the king of Aragon set up a process whereby those who objected to orders to turn over and burn books could appeal those orders. It allowed disagreement with the Christian interpretation of "banned books." That measure was sufficiently protective of Jewish writings that the papacy felt compelled to protest against it in 1267.

Nahmanides' elegantly written version of the disputation eventually caused him further trouble. In 1265 he was hauled before an ecclesiastical tribunal and criticized for producing and circulating his record of the episode. The complainants in church court were none other than Friar Paul and Raymond the Royal Confessor, along with Friar Arnold. The tribunal was not, however, solely a mouthpiece for Nahmanides' critics, for it had to act in concert with King James. The monarch put forward what he thought was an appropriate punishment for the rabbi's "offenses": two years in exile for Nahmanides. The sentence was in line with the treatment of other learned Jewish leaders in Spain. A century earlier Maimonides had chosen exile when Islamic rulers took over Cordoba. It was not only the Spanish disputants/complainants who took exception to such a comparatively mild sentence for Rabbi Nahman. The papacy also weighed in, calling the writings of Nahmanides summarizing the disputation an insult to Christianity. Somewhat in a pique over the Christians' grousing, King James declared that henceforth such complaints would be heard directly in his presence rather than before a tribunal. He also prorogued the sentence; Nahmanides could stay in Catalonia for the time being.

SIGNIFICANCE

Nahmanides finally followed his heart to the Middle East. That journey was less a push than a pull. He had long been of the opinion that Jews ought to return to the Holy Land. In the short term the situation of his community did not change much either as a result of his leaving or due to the Disputation of Barcelona. In the immediate wake of the public discourse the only element that altered for participants or observers was a refinement in the arguments that the Dominicans used to try to show why they were correct.

Read in long hindsight, of course, it looks as though the debate in 1263 heralded a new commitment by Christians to eliminate the Jewish minority in their midst. Within a couple of centuries the Reconquista was nearly complete. That such an effort did not succeed at an earlier date may have owed much to the spirited defense of his religion and his people by Nahmanides.

Further Reading

Baer, Yitzhak. *History of the Jews in Christian Spain,* vol. 1: *From the Age of Reconquest to the Fourteenth Century.* Philadelphia: Jewish Publications Society, 1993; Caputo, Nina. *Nahmanides in Medieval Catalonia: History, Community, and Messianism.* South Bend, Ind.: University of Notre Dame Press, 2008; Chazan, Robert. *Barcelona and Beyond: The Disputation of 1263 and Its Aftermath.* Berkeley: University of California Press, 1993; Kramer, Joel. *Maimonides: The Life and World of One of Civilization's Greatest Minds.* New York: Doubleday, 2008; Maccoby, Hyam, ed. *Judaism on Trial: Jewish-Christian Disputations in the Middle Ages.* London: Littman Library of Jewish Civilization, 1993; Smith, Damien, and Helen Buffery, eds. *The Book of Deeds of James I of Aragon.* Aldershot, U.K.: Ashgate Publishing, 2003.

The trial of Ariq Boke

Date: 1264

KEY ISSUES

The conquest of enormous areas of Asia by Chinggis (Ghengis) Khan and his Mongol troops involved a clash of cultures in addition to military confrontation. The Mongols' rule in China was momentous for Chinese history, but it also represented a challenge for Mongol society. Where would the Mongols make their capital? What type of govern-

ment would they institute in their new lands? Who would be the governors they trusted to administer their recent acquisitions? During the time of Chinggis Khan those issues were not settled, nor would they be for several more generations.

The descendants of the Great Khan were a fractious lot. They regularly fought to the death for political ascendancy over Chinggis Khan's legacy as well as in regard to less significant matters. No showdown among them was more of a watershed than the brother-vs.-brother battle between two grandsons of Chinggis Khan in the early 1260s.

On one side of the rift was Ariq (Arik) Boke, who eventually recognized his brother Khubilai's (Kublai) superior military position but still served as a symbol to certain groups within the Mongol homeland. Traditionalists among the victorious Mongolians thought that China ought to be a subject kingdom. It should be plundered for its riches while the Mongols remained rooted on the steppes of their native territory. Such factions chose Ariq Boke and, later, the Mongol Kaidu (Qaidu) as their head. Their great fear was that the Mongols in their homeland would become merely an outpost of a larger empire ruled by the Khans based in China and made up of peoples beyond the Chinese—Persians, Arabs, and the Muslims of Samarkand, for example, with whom Khubilai's troops had allied.

Opposing this conservative vision of Mongol rule were Khubilai, his subjugates in China such as the Song in the south, and others who fell under his control either willingly or grudgingly. The partisans of Khubilai appeared to enjoy warfare. When they were not killing, they were celebrating victories or drowning their sorrows. They were imperialists but at the same time multiculturalists who enjoyed urban life. By contrast, Mongols usually disliked straying from their horses and grazing lands.

The partisans of Khubilai adapted Chinese forms of government, art, and law to their own purposes. Khubilai chose the Chinese designation "Son of Heaven" when he was enthroned as emperor of China. His court preferred loyal Mongols in charge of key positions, however. Chinese officials who wanted to stay on had to prove their loyalty to the new regime. The old Mongol nobles—the Golden Family related to Chinggis Khan—were afraid of their influence being diluted within Khubilai's new order.

HISTORY OF THE CASE

The brothers Ariq Boke and Khubilai, along with other siblings, were fully engaged in hostilities in the late 1250s. For a while it looked as though each might maintain his area of influence. Ariq Boke held court in Mongol lands with a capital at Karakorum, and Khubilai, among the Chinese to the east. Each held his own assembly, a *khuriltai (kurultai)*, that proclaimed him to be the Great Khan. But, then the Mongols in Karakorum ran out of food, especially cattle; Khubilai was cutting off their supplies. The situation was made worse for Ariq Boke's supporters by a lack of grass for the animals caused by lower temperatures in the region.

In 1260 Ariq Boke realized that his brother Khubilai had the upper hand. Ariq Boke sent word that he was ready to call a truce, and Khubilai seemed ready to accept the offer. Ariq Boke, however, was not able to control the people who fought in his name. The old-style Mongols embarked on another series of confrontations, recapturing Karakorum after several losses of it and attempting to surprise Khubilai in another location. The brothers continued to campaign until 1264, when Ariq Boke and his adherents admitted defeat after an especially hard winter the year before. There was little for Ariq Boke to do but beg for mercy from Khubilai.

SUMMARY OF ARGUMENTS

Khubilai had integrated Mongol legal practices with those of China. He also was quite interested in alternative forms of law and queried Marco Polo and his father and uncle concerning legal systems in the West. A notable aspect of Khubilai's legal administration was his effort to temper the severity of court-ordered punishments. In particular, the ruler seemed to shy away from an over-reliance on executions. In the Song law code, for example, there were well over 200 capital offenses; under Mongol rule the number was 135. Some scholars attribute Khubilai's leniency to the influence of his wife Chabi, who was interested in many aspects of governance. Chabi interceded on behalf of many convicted criminals simply on grounds of mercy.

The Great Khan famously rebuked his judicial officials for bringing before him a large number of condemned persons at once, reminding the judges that the prisoners were not to be considered sheep. It also was typical of Khubilai and the Mongols that they allowed criminals to substitute monetary payment for physical chastisement. In terms of courtroom decisions the Mongol tenure in China was far less bloody than might have been expected in such a large geographical area, with only dozens of executions per year in the middle to late 1200s.

As the highest-profile case of his reign, the prosecution of Ariq Boke for treason demonstrated Khubilai's leaning toward moderation in such matters. Ariq Boke appeared before Khubilai in person at Shangdu (called Xanadu by Westerners, who were dazzled by its riches), which is located in what later was called Inner Mongolia. It was the summer, northern capital for Khubilai, the main capital being farther south at Dadu (modern Beijing). Although in a legal sense the meeting of the two men at Shangdu served as a preliminary step to a more formal proceeding, Khubilai's purpose was twofold. He wanted a public demonstration that Ariq Boke had surrendered, but Khubilai also appeared to desire a talk with his sibling about the reasons for the fracture.

The lengthiest contemporary discussion of that dramatic meeting between the brothers comes from the Persian historian Rashid-al-Din Hamadani. Rashid-al-Din emphasized what he thought was Ariq Boke's disloyalty to his brother. At the time that Rashid-al-Din wrote his history, Khubilai was Rashid-al-Din's ruler. The historian may have thought it impolitic to paint Ariq Boke in too favorable a light considering what happened later.

This much is certain about the face-to-face meeting: Khubilai insisted on questioning Ariq Boke personally. In reply to Khubilai's inquiry as to which side ought to have won the civil war, Ariq Boke was reported to have responded, "We were then, and you are today." Under the circumstances the defeated man showed fortitude, but he still had to bow low in obeisance to his brother before a crowd. Rashid-al-Din's point was that Ariq Boke was ungrateful for the opportunity to explain himself to his sibling. Subsequent scholars have read

Ariq Boke's reply as more diplomatic than un-brotherly.

It remained for a formal proceeding to determine Ariq Boke's fate. Khubilai envisioned that such a hearing would take a hybrid form. Trial would begin with an inquiry according to Chinese principles to examine Ariq Boke's actions against his brother—an investigation of alleged treason. But, what forum should hear such a case? Khubilai Khan already had summoned a *khuriltai* to announce his consolidation of power, but that convocation had taken place in Kaiping (in the far south of China) at the same time that supporters of Ariq Boke backed him through a similar assembly in their territory.

Politics suggested that the Mongols should demonstrate their acceptance of Khubilai's victory, so Khubilai called a meeting of the *khuriltai* on old Mongol lands. The trial of his brother was to have been akin to a condemnation of an English nobleman by his peers in the House of Lords. Khubilai's problem was that the traditional leaders among the Mongols, the heads of the Golden Family, did not appear for the proceedings. They understood that Khubilai had emerged victorious in battle, but they would not chance coming close enough to be implicated in Ariq Boke's resistance. Particularly worrisome were the absences of three regional khans: Berke of the Golden Horde (modern Russia, Kazakhstan, Ukraine, and Belarus), Hülegü of Persia (modern Iran, Turkey, and Georgia), and Alghu of Chaghatai (modern western China, Tibet, and Pakistan).

Khubilai could not hold the trial for Ariq Boke because of a rule that there had to be a majority of the *khuriltai* present in order for it to convene. Still worse, those among the Golden Family who were brothers of both Khubilai and Ariq Boke went so far as to rebuke Khubilai publicly for his embarrassment of the defeated sibling.

VERDICT

The episode demonstrates that even the Great Khan Khubilai subscribed to certain rules about how high-profile cases should be conducted. It is important, indeed, that Khubilai insisted on there being rules at all. The trial was aborted, but Khubilai now could say that the trial's suspension was not his fault. He declared that in the absence of a judicial determination of Ariq Boke's complicity, he would intervene personally. He banished his brother from court for a year. Remarkably to those who thought the Golden Family vengeful, the supposed traitor walked away with his life. Viewed in the larger context of Khubilai's aversion to the death penalty, though, the outcome seems consistent with the Great Khan's policies.

The resolution of the situation did not end there, however, unfortunately for both Ariq Boke and his backers. Apparently those close to Khubilai required a purge of Ariq Boke's supporters in order to demonstrate the solidity of Khubilai's position. Starting with Bolghai, a leading adviser to Ariq Boke's and Khubilai's brother Möngke (who had allied with Ariq Boke), 10 key associates of Ariq Boke were tried, found guilty of treachery against Khubilai Khan, and executed.

Less than two years after his military defeat and legal escape, Ariq Boke died under sudden and mysterious circumstances. Khubilai Khan certainly could have had him poisoned, but such an action could also have been undertaken by others who were jealous of Ariq Boke's survival. It probably was no accident that Ariq Boke's demise occurred in 1266, just after the deaths of the three khans who had blocked the effort to convene the *khuriltai* in 1264. Whether it was Khubilai Khan or those just under him in rank who wanted Ariq Boke dead may be impossible to determine.

SIGNIFICANCE

Despite his glittering reputation as an emperor among Westerners, Khubilai Khan was unable to hold together his grandfather's conquests. Under Khubilai, Chinggis Khan's empire was divided into four major parts. Khubilai controlled the area that in modern times is northern China, Korea, Tibet, and eastern Mongolia—certainly an impressive swath of territory. But, in effect, he had to leave other Mongol conquests to his fellow rulers of the Ilkanate and the Golden Horde in the west. The new Great Khan also had to admit that he needed the cooperation of the native rulers of southern China, the Song, in order to administer that region. Khubilai Khan could not even claim to enforce his will on the central steppes, from Siberia in the north to Afghanistan in the south. Khubilai's lack of control over the Chaghatai Khanate was a reminder that Ariq Boke represented serious resistance—a threat to Khubilai's power that came from the very center of the Mongol homeland.

Further Reading

Gumilev, Lev Nikolaevich. *Searches for an Imaginary Kingdom: The Legend of the Kingdom of Prester John.* Cambridge: Cambridge University Press, 1987; Man, John. *Kublai Khan.* New York: Bantam, 2007; Nicolle, David. *The Mongol Warlords.* Victoria, Australia: Firebird Press, 1990; Rossabi, Morris. *Khubilai Khan: His Life and Times.* Berkeley: University of California Press, 1989; Weatherford, Jack. *Genghis Khan and the Making of the Modern World.* New York: Three Rivers Press, 2005.

The trial of William Wallace

Date: 1305

KEY ISSUES

Over the course of hundreds of years as neighboring kingdoms, Scotland often chafed at England's efforts to be the dominant power. Scottish resistance to English overlordship ran deep by the later medieval era. In the late 1200s it was the Scots' misfortune to face a formidable leader on the English side: King Edward I, whose informal titles ("the English Justinian" and "Edward Longshanks") betokened his talent for lawmaking and strong leadership in general. The Scots particularly disliked an English nickname for Edward: "the Hammer of the Scots." That label made clear Edward's success in subduing even the most charismatic and militarily talented of his Scottish foes, William Wallace.

Little is known of Wallace's background before he emerged as a leader of military campaigns against England in 1297. His family's status is a matter of some dispute among scholars, but it is not unreasonable to infer that his kin had run-ins with the English. It is possible that Wallace himself was a cattle thief, much as the English were to allege later. The border areas between England and Scotland were rife with such activity. Precisely how much education Wallace had also is uncertain, but his admirers argued that he had been taught by priests and spoke his native tongue as well as English and French.

In May 1297 Wallace led a raid on Lanark with a force of 30 men. They took vengeance on the Englishman William Heselrig, who had been installed as sheriff to bring English justice to the area. The effort to kill Heselrig was precise and successful, and it quickly gained recruits to Wallace's cause. Wallace was part of a general uprising against the English presence in Scotland that included figures such as Andrew Murray and the earl of Carrick, Robert Bruce (later, King Robert I). With his unorthodox military style, Wallace gained his greatest support not from Scotland's mightiest nobles—many of whom were beholden to the English—but rather from lesser elites and poor folk, who perhaps identified with him as from a similar background.

The Scots initially were successful in the field, scoring an improbable victory at Stirling Bridge in September 1297. Wallace took the opportunity to make forays into England. He assumed the position of "guardian" of Scotland—presumably keeping the Scots safe until a more permanent government could be worked out. Bruce knighted Wallace in 1298.

Up to this point Edward I of England had been successful as a military leader, particularly in his overrunning of Wales. Although already engaged in a war with France, he turned his attention to the Scottish situation, meeting Wallace head-on at Falkirk in July 1298. The Scots fought bravely but were badly outnumbered. In addition, many Scottish nobles simply refused to fight. King Edward next worked hard in Scotland to reestablish English influence and confidence in his authority.

HISTORY OF THE CASE

After his retreat at Falkirk, Wallace turned from the battlefield to diplomacy. During several years on the Continent he focused on securing support from the papacy and France for the resistance in Scotland. He was unsuccessful with both foreign powers. He returned to Scotland and began a series of raids that were independent of the Scots' government. His peers officially had placed authority in the hands of John Balliol, who also was Edward I's choice for the Scottish throne. Balliol turned out to be far less tractable than Edward had planned, but that became apparent only a few years later.

During 1304 and the first half of 1305, Wallace was on the run from both the king of England and those in Scotland to whom Edward of England had offered palpable monetary inducements. Renegade Scots connected with Wallace managed to inflict damage in several skirmishes during that time, and yet, at least one English chronicle notes that Wallace also was making overtures to Edward for a truce. The Hammer of the Scots reportedly was enraged by the thought of such an arrangement to buy Wallace's quiescence and increased the reward for Wallace's capture. Sir John Menteith of Dumbarton ensnared Wallace and some of his companions on August 3, 1305, near Glasgow. Wallace's brother Geoffrey was apprehended with him, and they all were taken under close guard to London for trial.

SUMMARY OF ARGUMENTS

The captives first were paraded through the streets of London. Wallace went to court on August 23, 1305. The crimes with which he was charged included murder (in particular the killing of Sheriff William Heselrig of Lanark), robbery, setting fires, and miscellaneous offenses. The indictment listed a number of actions for which the English held Wallace accountable. To the modern reader the document appears as though Wallace was being charged with war crimes. But, at the heart of the case was the allegation that Wallace had led a revolt against King Edward, to whom he owed allegiance:

> And after this, joining to himself as great a number of armed men as he could, he attacked the houses, towns, and castles of that land, and caused his writs to run through the whole of Scotland as if they were the edicts of the overlord of that land . . . and he invaded the Kingdom of England and

especially the counties of Northumberland, Cumberland, and Westmorland, and all whom he found there loyal to the King of England he feloniously slew in different ways . . . and he spared no one who spoke the English tongue, but slew all in ways too terrible to be imagined, old and young, brides and widows, babes and their mothers. . . .

An indication of the seriousness with which the English government approached Wallace's prosecution was that it transpired in Westminster Hall, the very center of England's government. There were two major types of judicial proceedings carried out at Westminster during the later medieval and early modern eras: impeachments and trials of peers. Both occurred in the chamber where the House of Lords met regularly. In the early 1300s the physical separation of the two houses was not as clear as it later would be. Wallace's trial was in the portion of the hall where magnates tended to meet when they gathered officially. The lords did not preside over this state trial but rather a collection of officials: John Seagrave, who brought Wallace from Scotland; Peter Maluree (Mallore); R. de Sandwich; Johannes de Bakewell; and J. le Blound, mayor of London.

The hall at Westminster was very large—the biggest secular space in Britain at the time. When it was crowded with spectators, as it must have been in Wallace's case, hearing and seeing would have been difficult for those to the rear of the hall. According to historians connected with the houses of Parliament, Wallace's trial was the second state trial held under the auspices of the House of Lords at Westminster, the first being the trial of Thomas Turberville for spying for the French, 10 years prior to Wallace's prosecution.

Wallace's defense was that he had not sworn allegiance to Edward I. This was in contrast to many other Scottish leaders who had taken such formal oaths. It was a delicate matter to make such a contention, for Wallace thus was distancing himself from those who would have conciliated with the English king. Wallace's statement—described as a "shout" in some accounts of the trial—was his only known comment at the proceeding. That Wallace was unable to say much was characteristic of the stage-managed affair.

Some modern scholars find it ironic that Edward has become known in history as one of the great law givers among English monarchs. The English Justinian's commitment to due process—even by the standards of the time, which greatly favored those in power—was very limited. Wallace and his fellow defendants, who were charged with the gravest crime possible under English law, had no attorney and no opportunity to speak in their own defense, except as noted by interjection.

Edward and his supporters viewed Wallace as an outlaw because technically he had failed to appear on earlier charges in an English court. Their line of reasoning was that any trial was more than Wallace deserved: Those who did not avail themselves of the English judicial system placed themselves outside it and could be killed on sight. It is of no small consequence for legal historians that the English argued Wallace had committed atrocities against civilians. This makes Wallace's trial one of the earliest known examples of a prosecution for "war crimes."

VERDICT

The verdict was never in doubt. Wallace was to be accorded a traitor's death. The theory was that the law ought to distinguish between capital crimes that were more private in nature (though in most offenses the "king's peace" had been disturbed) and those that involved the security of the state. The more serious felonies were punished in more grisly and, therefore, more memorable ways. As the worst criminals of all, traitors had to endure "three or four deaths": hanging (either until one was unconscious or not), being pulled by the limbs until they were dislocated, being butchered like an animal (including beheading), and being denied a Christian burial. The court's verdict was formulaic in Wallace's case of treason. Hanging, drawing, and quartering were what was prescribed:

So resolved that the above-mentioned William . . . should be dragged from the Palace of Westminster to the Tower of London and from the Tower of London and thus through the middle of the city to the Elms (Smithfield) and as a punishment for the robberies, murders, and felonies which he had commit-

ted should there be hung and afterwards disemboweled.

And because he had been outlawed and had not been afterwards restored to the King's peace he should be beheaded.

And afterwards as a punishment for the great wickedness which he had practised towards God and His holy church by burning churches, vessels and reliquaries, his heart, liver, lungs, and all internal organs should be thrown into the fire and burned. . . .

Wallace's body parts were to be scattered so they could be displayed in various key locations in England and Scotland and in order to make it more difficult for his admirers to gather the body together to memorialize him. The site of Wallace's execution is near the modern St. Bartholomew's Hospital in London. A plaque at the hospital frequently sees donations of flowers in his memory.

SIGNIFICANCE

Wallace was remembered among the Scots for his patriotism. A composition by the blind balladeer Harry, in the 1400s, was widely circulated. It served as the basis for biographical information on Wallace that was more favorable to Wallace than the stories told in English histories. Harry's poem was the background to the screenplay of the 1995 film *Braveheart*. Among other authors who leaned on Harry for their own famous accounts of Scottish history was Walter Scott. Robert Burns's anthem "Scots Wa hae," also based on Harry's heroic portrayal, immortalized the blood sacrifice of William Wallace on the battlefield and in an English courtroom:

Scots wa hae wi' Wallace bled
Scots wham Bruce has aften led
Welcome tae your gory bed
Or tae victory. . . .

Further Reading

"Early State Trials." Parliament.uk. Available online. URL: http://www.parliament.uk/about/livingheritage/building/westminsterhall/government_and_administration/early_statetrials.cfm.

Accessed May 15, 2009; Fisher, Andrew. *William Wallace*. Edinburgh: J. Donald, 2002; Gibson, Mel (dir.), *Braveheart*. Icon Entertainment International, 1995; Gray, D. J. *William Wallace: The King's Enemy*. London: R. Hale, 1991; Henry the Minstrel. *Blind Harry's Wallace*. Edinburgh: Luath Press, 1998; Morton, Graeme. *William Wallace: Man and Myth*. Stroud, U.K.: Sutton Publishing, 2001; Power, William. "The Trial and Death of Wallace." Available online. URL: http://home pages.tesco.net/~scotlandweb/wallace/wallace trial103.html. Accessed May 1, 2009.

The trials of John Wycliffe

Date: 1377, 1378, 1382

KEY ISSUES

Medieval Europeans endured war, hunger, periodic famine, and chronic bad health. It hardly seemed possible for their lot to grow more dismal, but in the middle of the 14th century things took a turn for the worse. In 1348 bubonic plague struck many portions of western Europe. The misery was of epic scale over a widespread area.

The Christian Church usually could provide explanations for affliction. Individuals who saw hardship might look to the church for guidance and be told by a priest to examine their actions; perhaps one could atone for sinfulness by acts of penance or charity. The church might prescribe such remedies for whole communities or even nations. In fact, some of the first commentaries about plague before it reached European shores were from papal representatives who got wind of terrible outbreaks among the people of Asia Minor in early 1347. Churchmen declared that such loss of life obviously was a divine judgment against unbelievers.

But the plague then spread among the Christian populations of the West. Few communities were unaffected by the illness in 1349, and many saw population losses of one-third of their people.

This plague, called "the pestilence," "the great mortality," or "the Black Death" because of the dark swellings on the bodies of victims, seemed to exceed all previous outbreaks in virulence. What did the church have to say now to explain such a ravaging force?

The authorities argued among themselves. They held conferences and disputations on the topic, for example, at the University of Paris in 1349, but no clear answers emerged. Meanwhile, the Christian faithful were deeply disappointed in the lack of a coherent explanation. They also expressed disillusionment at the failings of individual clerics to minister to the sick and dying. Some priests fled to unaffected areas or refused to administer last rites to the afflicted for fear of contagion, although among the laity, nuns had the reputation of tending to the sick.

It was hardly surprising that some began to reason it was the church itself that was to blame for divine displeasure. Perhaps plague was a severe warning to a church that was out of touch with the needs of its flock, unwilling to divest itself of corrupt or unspiritual clergy, or divided within itself about governance. That last charge rang particularly true in the 1340s when the papacy had become a kind of political prize to be fought over by warring nations and rulers. Indeed, when plague appeared in western Europe, there actually were two persons who were making serious claim to be the pope: one based in Rome and the other in French-controlled territory, at Avignon. Each of these rival papacies had a bureaucracy and its particular defenders throughout Europe. Nations often hedged their bets, sending emissaries to both papal courts. It was a short step, logically, to accuse a church that was in schism of calling down God's disapproval.

HISTORY OF THE CASE

That the most influential critic of the church in the aftermath of the plague was John Wycliffe is surprising in certain respects. Wycliffe was not from well-known forebears, at least beyond his small community. Wycliffe's family history and early life are not well known, but he appears in the records of several Oxford colleges in the 1350s and 1360s as first a student and then a teacher of theology.

His presence as a faculty member made clear that Wycliffe was a man of scholarly talent, and his reputation as a lecturer grew. At the same time that Wycliffe was creating a name for himself in university circles, he also took positions as a clergyman, for example, holding multiple appointments in the vicinity of Lincoln and York. Wycliffe's abilities caught the attention of the English royal court. In 1374 the king dispatched him to Bruges as part of an English party charged with discussing (and protesting an excess of) clerical taxes with the papacy.

Wycliffe met John of Gaunt, the duke of Lancaster and a son of King Edward III. A master behind-the-scenes politician, Lancaster used Wycliffe in his quest to raise revenue for the Crown. Wycliffe inveighed against corruption in the church and overcollection of tithes from the poor. Lancaster and other members of the royal party saw such criticism as a means to recapture revenue that otherwise would have enriched the church in England or gone abroad to Rome rather than into their own coffers. Especially in a time when the church was marred by the Papal Schism, Lancaster had a fairly easy case to make that English leaders should be cautious in passing the collection plate.

That Wycliffe was a well-trained and highly regarded scholar with ties to elites in his country still made him unlikely as a critic of the church. Such persons could live comfortably as clerics, switching benefices through the help of political patrons. But, Wycliffe came to a set of conclusions that created unease in his mind and eventually caused him grave difficulty in continuing with an easy churchman's life. By what process he reached those views it is impossible to say, though he left no indication that his opinions were the result of a sudden revelation (a "road to Damascus" conversion). Easier to understand are the elements that made Wycliffe's theology objectionable to religious leaders, especially those connected with the papacy.

Wycliffe drew attention when he maintained that the best ministers were the itinerant friars. Wycliffe appreciated those who interacted most humbly with their flock rather than fleecing them. That emphasis on the mendicant, or "begging," friars of several different orders was in line with Wycliffe's core beliefs. To him, the center of

authority lay in Holy Scripture rather than in an ecclesiastical hierarchy. The church had long taught that its institutions were directly descended from Christ's giving the "keys to the Kingdom" to Peter; the church was thus endowed with authority directly from God. Wycliffe's treatise from 1378 or 1379, titled *De officio regis* (On the office of the king), was an assault on the papacy's claim to supersede kingly authority.

Also essential to Wycliffe's philosophy was his examination of the nature of the Eucharist, the portion of the Christian Mass that the church said was a transformation of the bread and water into Christ's body and blood. Wycliffe did not deny the mystical quality of the Eucharist but rather argued that such "transubstantiation" was a complex concept. This was best stated in his Scholastic treatise *Trialogus,* in the form of an imaginary disputation. Ordinary folk, he said, easily could be misled into thinking that transubstantiation was a kind of hocus-pocus.

Modern theologians have contended that Wycliffe's view of the sacrament was close to the Lutheran concept of "consubstantiation." To Wycliffe, the bread and wine did not change form, yet Christ's presence was real during the ceremony. He certainly did not fully accept the Catholic position that transubstantiation (a literal substitution of body and blood for bread and wine) occurred when a priest elevated the Host, though neither did Wycliffe contradict the statement of Christ that the bread and wine were Christ's body and blood.

Wycliffe made his concerns about theology too public for the church to allow him to continue. He became embroiled in debate that spilled from the confines of the academic community. Wycliffe associated himself with political leaders, such as the duke of Lancaster, who were critical of papal power—at least when it suited their political machinations. When he began preaching not in church Latin but in English in London, and lower-class rebels started citing him as an inspiration (as with the leaders of the Peasant's Revolt in England in 1381), Wycliffe stepped into real danger.

That social instability in 1381 forced church administrators to take a hard look at what was going on in England, even within the universities. Oxford and Cambridge traditionally had been left free to pursue somewhat liberal lines of discussion with the justification that such discourse would not confuse or corrupt the general populace. But in 1382 the archbishop of Canterbury cracked down on Oxford for not handling Wycliffe more firmly. Wycliffe and several of his friends were dismissed from their posts. Lancaster distanced himself from Wycliffe, saying that Wycliffe's views on the Eucharist had become too extreme. The likelihood, though, was that Lancaster simply saw it as politically expedient to drop his protection in view of Wycliffe's association with peasant rebellion.

There was a further element of Wycliffe's radicalism that made him highly suspect to the church: his insistence that the Bible should be available in the language of the nation. In the 1300s only persons trained by the Christian Church were supposed to read the Bible—and then only in Latin. This often worked out naturally, for in the medieval era the church educated almost everyone who was able to read and write, and then those literate folk became servants of their faith as monks, nuns, priests, or church administrators. Thus, there were multiple layers insulating the ordinary person from misinterpretation of Christian scripture: They could not read Latin, or even read at all in most instances; books were extremely expensive; and clerics were charged with explicating the word of the Almighty.

Wycliffe came to the extraordinary conclusion that the Bible ought to be translated into English. In about 1380 he set about producing an English version—a rather stilted word-by-word translation from the Latin Vulgate. Several of his faculty and students such as Nicholas of Hereford and John Purvey helped to bring out that version in English, with a more readable edition appearing in 1390 after Wycliffe's death. Wycliffe's contribution was a rendering in English of most of the Hebrew texts that Christians called the Old Testament, along with the four Gospels.

SUMMARY OF ARGUMENTS

Wycliffe's trials took place in 1377, 1378, and 1382. The trials were not full proceedings; indeed, two of the hearings did not get far at all before dissolving into violence or disorder. Still, they were real threats to Wycliffe, as the fates of others who were not so well connected demonstrated. He was one of the rare individuals suspected of heresy by the church in this era who escaped with his life.

When the archbishop of Canterbury summoned Wycliffe to appear before Bishop Courtnay of London in early 1377, the basis for the charge was Wycliffe's writing known as *De civil dominio* (On civil lordship), which he had delivered to students as lectures at Oxford the previous year. Within that treatise Wycliffe seemed to take political lessons from reign of Edward I, who in the previous century had engineered legislation that shunted money from the church to the monarchy. Wycliffe looked at the royal justifications for laws such as the Statute of Mortmain with respect to their incursions into clerical authority. He concluded that righteous kings could regulate impious clergy—clearly, an argument tailored to suit the needs of Lancaster and the young Richard II (Lancaster's charge).

Thus, although Wycliffe based much of his philosophy on the actions of a great king and his arguments were adopted by political figures, he was not spared the attention of religious leaders. The church found him a dangerous spokesperson for views it considered not simply promonarchy but also anticlerical. In his first run-in with a formal church court, Wycliffe's political connections were decisive. He entered St. Paul's Church in London on February 19, 1377, accompanied grandly by Lancaster, other dignitaries, and several representatives of different orders of friars. Immediately, a fight broke out between the politicos' retinue and the bishops' supporters. The proceedings had to disband completely when Londoners joined the fray; apparently, they were angry that Lancaster's men had dared to attack anyone within the sacred confines of St. Paul's.

Church authorities in England probably already had sent a dispatch against Wycliffe to Pope Gregory XI, who in May issued a condemnation of several of Wycliffe's arguments. It was a several-pronged attack: The university was to stop coddling Wycliffe, English ecclesiastics were to try him, and the civil authorities were to make sure Wycliffe was delivered into the hands of the church. The university balked at surrendering such a popular and respected individual, however, and stood its ground on traditional liberties.

VERDICT

Wycliffe remained free. In 1377 Parliament even asked for his opinion on a key matter. The legislature saw him as an honored expert with regard to sending funds outside England, that is, to the papacy. In 1378, however, he was in trouble again. The clerics who originally had summoned him to St. Paul's required him to appear, this time at Lambeth Palace. Once more the hearing was interrupted by the threat of force—this time, from Wycliffe's poorer admirers. Those supporters probably had heard him preach to memorable effect. As if on cue the wife of the heir to the throne provided an element of drama to this hearing. She sent a messenger offering her support of Wycliffe, practically daring his accusers to proceed. England's church authorities backed down temporarily, but they sent a record of their concerns to Rome. A fortunate set of events occurred for Wycliffe at this juncture: Gregory XI died, precipitating another fracture within the church concerning the choice of the pope's successor.

Wycliffe suffered yet a third inquisition into his writings in late 1381 into 1382. That inquiry was led by William Courtnay, who had become archbishop of Canterbury and remained determined to reel in Wycliffe. Courtnay began with those who defended Wycliffe at Oxford. In an inquiry at the Blackfriars' convent in London and some subsequent hearings, the officials of the university conceded the authority of the church to censure Wycliffe. The church declared some of Wycliffe's writings to be heretical and others in error. A chronicler of the period, Henry Knighton, described Wycliffe's being summoned to one more hearing beyond that at Blackfriars, this time at Oxford. But that proceeding probably was a mere formality, that is, simply a reading of the established opinions against Wycliffe, or else a misunderstanding on the chronicler's part. There is no evidence that Wycliffe was charged with anything new at a third trial.

Wycliffe remained a religious critic with powerful friends. The House of Commons went out of its way to underline its confidence in Wycliffe during the middle of 1382 by stating its support for the poor priests that Wycliffe had championed. Wycliffe lived his few remaining years in retirement away from Oxford and London, the intellectual and political centers of the nation. His quiescence was more certain once he had a series of strokes. He died peacefully at the end of 1384 in Lutterworth, Leicestershire.

SIGNIFICANCE

Wycliffe's admirers such as Jan Hus spread his ideas far afield, although it is not clear if Wycliffe knew of his own influence outside England. The church clearly recognized the staying power of Wycliffe's views. He was articulate and well connected, and he had appeal among ordinary folk as well as within an academic setting. The church made burning at the stake the official penalty for heresy in 1401. In 1415 at the Council of Constance (which tried Hus), Wycliffe's writings also were condemned. The church disinterred his bones and burned them in 1428 as a mark of his having been declared a heretic. Detractors of Wycliffe termed his admirers "Lollards," and Wycliffe's followers eventually embraced that designation.

Wycliffe's ideas were somewhat more cautious than his admirers later claimed. His was the voice of skepticism rather than disbelief about certain practices and views within the church. For example, Wycliffe came to the conclusion that Christians ought to look critically upon the veneration of images, but he did not outright reject iconography, nor did he decry the ornamentation of churches.

The most far-reaching argument that Wycliffe made was his contention that the Bible ought to be available in the vernacular and, by extension, accessible to the ordinary person. The English translation that he inspired but did not complete—the version put out by his colleagues in 1390—became known as the Wycliffe, or Lollard, Bible. It proved very influential, though only a few persons managed to purchase such an expensive work in the century before movable type. Even more far reaching was the concept behind the Wycliffe Bible that every person should read the Holy Scriptures and attain an individual understanding of them.

Scholars have had difficulty in constructing a portrait of Wycliffe the man; his writings can seem sterile, and his demeanor, aloof. Still, Wycliffe's ideas were undeniably important, in large part because he survived his trials and could spread those views among admirers and students. Writers from the late 1500s onward underlined Wycliffe's impact upon those who found flaws within the Roman Catholic Church. The 16th century martyrologist John Foxe, himself a key disseminator of religious history, characterized Wycliffe as "the Morning Star of Protestantism."

Further Reading

Butler, Donna, and David F. Lloyd. "John Wycliffe: Setting the Stage for Reform." Available online. URL: http://www.vision.org/visionmedia/article. aspx?id=613. Accessed June 15, 2009; Evans, G. R. *John Wyclif: Myth and Reality.* Downers Grove, Ill.: Intervarsity, 2005; Levy, Ian. *John Wyclif: Scriptural Logic, Real Presence and the Parameters of Orthodoxy.* Milwaukee, Wis.: Marquette University Press, 2003; Levy, Ian, ed. *A Companion to John Wyclif, Late Medieval Theologian.* Leiden, Netherlands: Brill Academic Publishers, 2006; Wilks, Michael, and Anne Hudson. *Wycliffe: Political Ideas and Practice.* Oxford, U.K.: Oxbow Books, 2002.

The trial of Jacques Le Gris

Date: 1386

KEY ISSUES

The use of judicial duels in western Europe dates to around 501 C.E., when the monarch of the Burgundians published a law code called the Lex Burgundiorum. That ruler, King Grundebald, seemed primarily interested in promoting trial by battle as an alternative to swearing in court. Apparently, when more gentle methods of ascertaining divine judgment were applied, there were many instances of perjured testimony. A "wager of battle" provided a decisive answer to an accuser, as well as entertainment for the community.

The Christian Church at first blessed duels, with some monasteries even specializing in hosting such events. By around the year 1000, however, church leaders grew concerned that dueling bred bloodlust among the general population and encouraged some people to become full-time champions-for-hire. The Council of Limoges of 994, for example, as part of a larger effort by the church to control lawlessness through its "truce of God," declared dueling to be an affront to Christianity, even if it was to a judicial purpose.

In late medieval France duels both with and without judicial sanction diverted a certain amount of quarrelsomeness among the nobility into well-worn channels. Although there was fighting to be had in the war against England in the late 1300s and although crusading was always an option, on occasion a disputant wished to obtain judicial redress through a duel. This was the case in particular when an accuser already had tried to get satisfaction through other legal means and had found ordinary processes lacking.

HISTORY OF THE CASE

The allegation against Jacques Le Gris was that he had raped Marguerite Carrouges, the wife of Le Gris's old friend Jean de Carrouges. This Jean de Carrouges sometimes was called Jean IV to distinguish him from his forebears. Jean IV was a squire, the lowest rank among French nobles. His family had been vassals to the greater nobles of Normandy, the counts of Perche and Alençon. Jean IV continued that relationship with the current Perche and then, after Perche's death, Count Pierre of Alençon.

At Alençon's court in Argentan, Carrouges and Le Gris had become comrades in 1377, both serving as they did the same overlord. The men both were mature by the standards of the age, in their 30s when they met. Carrouges had honored Le Gris by asking him to be godfather to his son. But, the two also had their differences. Le Gris, though of more humble family origin, was better educated than Carrouges. And Le Gris's star was on the rise with their patron, Alençon. From the count Le Gris got a large grant of land, a better command posting, and more access to the royal court in Paris.

Carrouges suffered another setback when his wife and young son died in quick succession, but he married a second wife, Marguerite Thibouville, in 1380. The bride was young, beautiful, and very wealthy; her only flaw, apparently, was that her father's loyalty to the French throne twice had been called into question. As the marriage was being celebrated, Carrouges became aware that the bride's father recently had sold a valuable piece of land to Count Pierre, who in turn had bestowed it on his new favorite courtier, Le Gris.

Though the funds from the sale had enriched Marguerite's dowry, the dowry was only a short-term infusion of cash for Carrouges. Jean IV wanted the land so he could reap continuing income and, therefore, set about petitioning for it. The better-connected Alençon secured a statement from the old king, Charles V, that ratified the count's right to dispose of the contested property. Carrouges was digging holes for himself: He had angered the king by marrying into a family accused of treachery, alienated Count Pierre by questioning his right to bestow property on his chamberlain Le Gris, and incurred Le Gris's enmity besides.

The political and social standing of Carrouges continued to deteriorate under the new boy-king Charles VI, in spite of the fact that Carrouges had performed valuable military service to the former king in the late 1370s. Carrouges initiated another lawsuit against his liege lord Alençon, this time over the captaincy of a fort that Jean III had held but which Alençon transferred to another man upon the death of Carrouges's father. In time the count settled yet a third quarrel over land in Le Gris's favor.

The rivals reconciled briefly in late 1384, at which time Carrouges introduced Marguerite to Le Gris at a social function. In May 1385 Carrouges departed on a campaign with Admiral Jean de Vienne to Scotland. Carrouges returned to France in late fall having lost some of his health and money. His only consolation was that he had gained promotion to a knighthood. He and Marguerite traveled to see Jean IV's mother at Capomesnil; Marguerite and her mother-in-law stayed there while Carrouges went to Paris to procure funds due from the royal treasury for his military service. En route he made the mistake of stopping at the count's court, where he encountered Le Gris.

Apparently, Le Gris asked one of his assistants, Adam Louvel, to keep Le Gris apprised of the whereabouts of Marguerite. In modern parlance Le Gris was stalking her. When Dame Nicole Carrouges was summoned to appear in court in a nearby town on January 18, 1386, she took along most of the household servants and left Marguerite in the house. Le Gris and Louvel appeared at the near-empty home. Le Gris tried seducing Marguerite with words and then offering her money in return for sexual favors. She refused. Assisted by Louvel, Le Gris then raped her.

SUMMARY OF ARGUMENTS

Marguerite told Carrouges of the assault a few days later. He immediately convened a council of close friends and family to offer advice on how to proceed. She repeated her story to them and seemed credible. Her believability was crucial in this time and place when women could not lodge felony charges without the support of their husbands or other legal protectors. The assembled friends also recommended that Carrouges approach his liege lord about the situation. Therein, of course, lay a problem for the aggrieved couple: Alençon was publicly partial to Le Gris.

Alençon, however, saw it as his duty to offer justice. After asking the opinion of two trusted noblemen who knew both Le Gris and Carrouges, the count summoned all of the key parties to a hearing. Marguerite and Carrouges did not appear. Although Alençon had Louvel arrested, he did not seem to question Louvel very closely. The count convened a session of his noble court and declared the charge of rape to be baseless.

Carrouges went over his lord's head, appealing directly to the king of France. Instead of asking for a traditional trial by the king *coram rege* (in person), Carrouges applied to the king to authorize a trial by battle. It had been the law in France since 1306 that monarchs had to authorize judicial combat. The option was available only in regard to certain serious crimes, including rape. In such a case the accuser and the accused had to battle personally; they could not have champions fighting for them.

There was grave danger in such a move—and not only in the obvious sense that Carrouges could die in battle. If he lost, the original accuser, Marguerite, would also be proven a perjurer and would be executed—burned alive—as a result.

Although Carrouges was an experienced military campaigner, Le Gris was the more powerful of the two men physically. It promised to be a fight to the death. Finally, the process of setting up a judicial duel was elaborately laid out, and any misstep could incur invalidation of the whole proceeding.

Trial by combat involved a number of steps, including an initial lodging of a complaint by the *appelant* (appealer or accuser), a formal challenge that necessitated a face-to-face meeting between *appelant* and *defendeur* (the accused or, in English usage, the defendant). The defendant and the accuser had to name persons to serve as pledges that each party would appear for trial. Such cases might involve pledges who were not much acquainted with the two parties but who wanted to be connected with a case because it was a cause célèbre. The formal challenge, which literally involved the throwing down of a gauntlet, or glove *(jeter le gage)*, took place before the members of the Parlement of Paris.

The 17-year-old king was more interested in seeing the spectacle of a judicial duel than in protecting Le Gris. Charles VI authorized Parlement to hear the formal challenge, in effect a rehearsal of the case in a traditional setting prior to the arduous physical trial.

Both Carrouges and Le Gris procured excellent legal advisers. The prosecution was led by Jean de Béthisy and included Pierre d'Orgement, who was an adviser to the bishop of Paris. Le Gris hired Jean Le Coq, who often had represented members of the royal family. Le Coq kept a diary in which he recorded interchanges with Le Gris. That recollection of the case made clear that Le Gris rejected one pivotal piece of wisdom from the attorney early on. Le Coq urged Le Gris to use a technicality in order to have the case heard in a church court instead of through wager of battle.

It was the old dodge of benefit of clergy. Not only clerics in formal orders but by this time almost anyone with a formal education could declare himself a clergyperson. This meant an accused person would be tried in a court that was forbidden to hand down sentences of death—an enormous advantage in a capital case. Probably motivated by pride, Le Gris disregarded the expert advice of his lawyer.

On July 9, 1386, the parties met in front of members of Parlement, the king, and a number of nobles at the Palais du Justice. The two principal men were in attendance, but the main victim perhaps was not. The record is unclear as to Marguerite's presence at that early stage, though she did appear at the next element of the proceedings.

It was quite apparent now, even to those outside her family, that the woman at the center of the controversy was pregnant. Given the fact that she and Carrouges had not conceived a child during the first five years of their marriage, her condition lent further drama to the case. Folk wisdom had it that pregnancy could not result from a rape; thus, to many observers Marguerite either had consented to sexual relations with Le Gris and was pregnant with his child or was carrying her husband's baby and may or may not have been raped.

After Carrouges threw down the gauntlet and Le Gris took it up, the Parlement convened an official *enquête* (inquiry) to determine whether a battle should be commenced. It was at that hearing that testimony of the type often heard in courtroom trials was taken. Testimony was written down by official court reporters. The original transcript in this case has survived into modern times. The record tells what both "the Lady Carrouges" and Jean Carrouges alleged. In Jean IV's account Le Gris was a profligate who conspired to either seduce or rape a rival's wife. Whether lust or jealousy was the primary motive, the accusers did not specify, though Carrouges alleged that Le Gris's actions in total amounted to a betrayal of their friendship.

Le Gris's picture of the situation was altogether different. He painted Jean Carrouges as difficult to get along with and an abusive spouse. According to Le Gris, there was not enough time in which Marguerite's mother-in-law was absent from her home on January 18 for an assault to have taken place. Le Gris flatly denied ever having seen Marguerite except in Paris in court and at the social gathering where Carrouges had introduced him to her. Le Gris provided an explanation of what had happened to inspire the accusation. He claimed that the knight had beaten his wife and then concocted the accusation of rape in order to cover his actions and avenge years of perceived wrongs. Finally, Le Gris and his counsel offered the defense that Le Gris could not have traveled to Capomesnil on any day during the week in question on account of distance and winter weather.

While Parlement was considering the case, Louvel answered a summons to appear in Paris. He had been released from the detention ordered by Alençon but now found himself challenged to a duel by one of Marguerite Carrouges's relatives. Louvel also had to undergo torture by order of the *enquête* to determine whether he had so far been truthful in his testimony about the episode. Louvel's questioning under duress yielded no new information.

VERDICT

On September 15, 1386, the Parlement's inquiry ended with a ruling that judicial combat should take place. It was more of a victory for Carrouges than for Le Gris, and was one of the rare instances in recent years when such a verdict had been rendered. The alternative judgment would have affirmed the opinion of Count Pierre of Alençon and likely would have stuck Carrouges with ruinous court costs. King Charles had gone off to war with England, so the chief judge, Arnold de Corbie, announced the decision. The duel was scheduled for late November.

The showdown on the field occurred a month later than planned. The French king wished to be present, so the contest was delayed to allow his return from the other theater of battle. The setting of the ordeal by combat was an old religious site previously dedicated to such exhibitions: the monastery of St.-Martin-des-Champs. The priory had a *champ clos* (enclosed field) and plenty of room for spectators.

On December 29 the duel took place. The two combatants required several attendants each to help them into plate armor and chain mail. Mounting their expensive, well-clad horses was also a chore. They were armed with lances to knock each other off of their animals, swords to engage in more direct combat, and axes and daggers for closer grappling. Marguerite Carrouges attended both as a spectator and another potential victim of the day. She wore black because if Jean de Carrouges lost, she would be turned over for immediate execution.

The spectators were forbidden by the king's order to interfere in any way. They were to remain seated and silent throughout the ordeal. Trials by battle customarily were marked by extraordinary obedience to that regulation even when the confrontations lasted many hours. To level the field in a social sense Le Gris on that day was made a knight like Carrouges.

The next phase of the trial by battle was a religious sanctification of the proceedings. Several priests reminded the assembly that the ordeal was designed to demonstrate divine judgment of guilt and innocence. Each combatant swore belief in the validity of his cause while touching a crucifix. Lady Marguerite also had to swear to the justice of her case; it was a dramatic moment in the tense recitation of formalities.

When a herald cried out for the warriors to enter the fray, the gates of the enclosure were closed. In the fight to the death there were no longer any regulations. After three charges both men remained on their horses, but their lances were shattered. Next they went after each other with axes. Le Gris struck a blow that killed Carrouges's horse, but Carrouges remained on his feet and held off the mounted attacker. Next Carrouges dealt a deathblow to Le Gris's mount. Le Gris regained his footing, though, and the men commenced fighting with swords and daggers.

Le Gris inflicted the first major human injury with a sword to Carrouges's leg. But he made the mistake of pulling out the weapon from the injured leg, giving Carrouges more mobility despite his bleeding wound. Carrouges lunged at Le Gris, throwing him to the ground. The standing man now had a temporary advantage, for rising from a prone position in a full suit of armor was difficult. The accuser Carrouges tackled him, desperately searching for an opening in the armor through which to thrust his knife. Le Gris fought for his life while Carrouges shouted, "Confess, confess!"

It took several minutes for Carrouges to pry loose Le Gris's face visor. When he did, Carrouges gave his enemy one more opportunity to declare the truth. Le Gris responded defiantly: "In the name of God, and on the peril and damnation of my soul, I am innocent of the crime!"

The accuser responded by stabbing Le Gris in the throat. Carrouges's moment of triumph had several components: a bow to the king, a meaningful look at Marguerite, and then a drawing in of the crowd. "Have I done my duty?" Carrouges inquired. The thousands of spectators finally got to speak, shouting affirmation.

After receiving honors and a considerable sum of money from King Charles, the accuser and his wife celebrated their victory at a service in the Cathedral of Notre-Dame. A public executioner dragged the body of Jacques Le Gris to the execution grounds at Montfaucon, where the corpse was placed in chains and eventually thrown into a common grave.

SIGNIFICANCE

The combat in which Jacques Le Gris lost his life sometimes is said to herald the demise of the judicial duel. Le Gris's trial did not end the use of wager of combat in courts in France or elsewhere in Europe, but the episode did encourage widespread scrutiny of the use of duels for judicial purposes. The Le Gris case proved contentious even after its principals had died, because rumors continued to circulate about the truth of the original charges. Some of Le Gris's family no doubt fueled those rumors.

Neither Parlement nor the Crown henceforth resorted to wager of battle as a method within the French judicial process. The Parlement of Paris officially banned duels in 1559, though the French king countermanded that prohibition shortly afterward. Extrajudicial duels nonetheless remained popular, especially in France. Historians claim that in the late 16th century enough French noblemen died in private duels to rival fatalities in a modern war. In the early modern age duels became a social rather than a legal mechanism.

Further Reading

Billacois, François. *The Duel: Its Rise and Fall in Early Modern France.* New Haven, Conn.: Yale University Press, 1990; Carroll, Stuart. *Blood and Violence in Early Modern France.* Oxford: Oxford University Press, 2006; Cohen, Richard. *By the Sword.* New York: Random House, 2002; Froissart, Jean. *The Chronicles of Jean Froissart.* London: Macmillan, 1895; Jager, Eric. *The Last Duel.* New York: Random House, 2004.

The trial of the sow of Falaise

Date: 1386

KEY ISSUES

Medieval Europeans cherished the idea of a divine order. One of the reasons that they punished crime so ferociously was that acts of violence threatened such a scheme. The law was especially fierce toward offenders who struck out against those of higher social, religious, economic, or sexual stature. Thus, the wife who killed her husband was subject to a worse punishment than the husband who killed his wife. The servant who murdered his or her master could expect a more gruesome sentence than that bestowed on a ruthless employer. Whole minority groups, such as Jews and Muslims, among medieval Christian communities could also anticipate that they would be handled with ferocity in court when they reacted against their supposed moral superiors.

There was a certain consistency to the logic. Medieval legal scholars argued that the law was concerned mostly with the harm that was done. Only secondarily did medieval courts aim at prevention of similar offenses in future, reform of individuals' behavior, or deterrence among potential criminals. Those would be the main goals of much later theorists and reformers, especially Enlightenment thinkers. No type of case better illustrates the premodern view of criminal trial and punishment as serving the maintenance of order than the trials of animals.

It was a rare individual in the medieval world who proffered a philosophy that animals ought to be accorded gentle treatment, even when the nonhumans "behaved." The Catholic saint Francis of Assisi was the most prominent example of what modern folk would call an animal rights activist. Most cases involving animals in European courts until the 1700s indicated that animals needed to be kept in their place within the natural realm and that animals' proper position was as subservient to humans.

The law was informed by Christian theology. A text from Exodus providing for the stoning of a murderous ox frequently was cited as justification for the trial and punishment of animals. Whether ancient Greeks or Romans conducted trials of animals is a matter of some debate among scholars. Evidence exists of procedures involving "murderous things" in classical Athens, for example; the question is whether those episodes should be termed judicial hearings, religious events, or some other type of occurrence.

When Western lawmakers provided for the punishment of animals, they sometimes made themselves intermediaries in the process. In England, for example, the monarch could seize an "object that moved to the death" of a person. The thing (animal, tree, house, etc.) was to be a "deodand" (god-gift), funding Christian prayers for the human victim. Such a confiscation, though, usually did not involve a full trial but rather a decision by a lower judicial authority such as a coroner's inquiry.

There were laws against bestiality among medieval Europeans, for it was an offense against the Almighty (who had created Adam in the divine image) for animals to be placed on the same sexual plane as humans. This era also saw prosecutions of animals for criminal offenses, including bestiality. Medieval thinkers did not argue that animals should be condemned because the creatures knew right from wrong—far from it, because animals were considered "dumb beasts" in the words of Thomas Aquinas. Instead, animals were tried and found guilty of crimes because not to recognize them as culpable when they harmed humans would allow animals' "rebellion" against the divine order to go unpunished.

It was no accident that in discussions of how and why animals ought to suffer for their "transgressions" the justifiers of such prosecutions made analogies between animals and non-Christians. In fact, it was not uncommon for religious minorities such as Protestants in early modern France or Jews in Germany to endure punishments that involved animals literally being bundled with them. A Jew convicted of a crime might be hanged upside down between two vicious dogs, for example, to demonstrate that both the animals and the despised group should remain servile.

HISTORY OF THE CASE

A surprising number of references to animal trials and punishments crop up in premodern legal and literary sources. In *The Merchant of Venice*, for example, William Shakespeare writes of "a wolf, hanged for human slaughter." The character speaking in that passage is, tellingly, referring to Shylock, a Jewish moneylender. The animals that proved physically dangerous among premodern Europeans were not only the ones that people in modern times still associate with injury, such as dogs, wolves, horses, and cattle, but also vermin, small cats, and insects.

Pigs in particular were a frequent threat to the safety of persons when animals resided in human habitations. Hogs roamed loose in both inhabited and wilder environments, within villages and near brush as well as in urban areas. Swine might feed on bodies unburied on battlefields, or worse, cause harm to the living. Young children were especially likely to be victims of pig attacks—even in the cradle—if they were left unattended.

Such fatal incidents were relatively common, especially in France and Germany, places that had a fairly high proportion of farmers who could afford their own livestock. Instances later were recorded in colonial America, Brazil, and other nations. Scholars who have examined judicial cases involving animal attacks note that although some prosecutions of animals clearly were based in the expectation that authorities would confiscate valuable "convicted" animals, there was something else at work: the need to demonstrate human mastery. That overriding motivation sometimes was tinged with an element of sadism.

SUMMARY OF ARGUMENTS

Not many detailed accounts remain of most animal trials, probably because the persons affected by animals' violence often were poor and did not command much notice among reporters or collectors of trial records. Often the researcher finds only a dry notation that prosecution of an animal occurred, with a listing of punishment appearing among accounts of municipal authorities that paid the public executioner. There are a few fuller stories of animal trials, though, and from them the historian can assemble a composite portrait of such proceedings.

In several instances in premodern France pests were accused of eating crops and therefore causing people in the vicinity to starve. Such cases were not unknown, as well, in the Near and Middle East. Modern readers of such accounts are struck by the courts' keen attention to the procedural niceties required when animals were prosecuted—supplying lawyers for the defense to appeal points of law, for example, and administering torture in prescribed ways.

In cases of rats accused of destroying crops in France during the early 1500s, an ambitious young attorney named Bartholomew Chassenée was appointed to argue for the vermin in court. Chassenée later rose to prominence and left a description of the proceedings in which he was involved as a novice lawyer. From his writings one can infer the types of arguments that lawyers employed in animal prosecutions in premodern France, although Chassenée was much more than usually successful in defending his clients. He managed to delay the rats' attendance in court and thus prevented their eradication.

Many animals accused of crimes, especially pigs, were cited for their violence not toward a community (as were Chassenée's rats) but rather one person. It often was a child or infant who had been harmed. In Falaise in 1386 a sow killed a baby by biting the child on the head and arms. The sow was imprisoned in a jail and kept alongside humans awaiting trial for their crimes. One cannot be certain, but it is quite likely that the animal in Falaise had counsel. Since few such attacks were witnessed (in which case they might have been prevented), the creature probably was tortured, with its cries serving as admissions of guilt. In this case the prosecution very well may have cited the biblical precept known as the *lex talionis*—"an eye for an eye and a tooth for a tooth,"—in arguing for an appropriate punishment.

VERDICT

Counsel on neither side maintained that the sow had meant to harm, for it was not the intent but rather the harm itself that was the basis for the crime. Besides, animals were not sentient beings. Since the animal in Falaise had attacked a child, the case provides a window into attitudes concerning youth in premodern society. Sometimes judges lectured the families of the victims, warning them not to leave children in spots where they could be harmed by livestock or else to tie up the animals. Although legal historians maintain that premodern laws generally exempted the very young from full personhood, animals that killed infants were judged quite harshly. In the case of the sow of Falaise the court seemed to place great value on the young human.

This particular animal was convicted and sentenced to die in much the same manner as it had killed the child: by being mauled about its head and upper body. Then the sow was strangled by hanging in the public square. Occasionally convicted animals, like people, were "shown mercy" by being strangled quickly before being either more slowly hanged or burned for their crimes. The sow of Falaise, like especially blameworthy human convicts, was hanged while alive.

The town's regular executioner meted out punishment with solemnity. The executioner of Falaise was listed as a "master of high works." The record seems to emphasize that he was a public official rather than a butcher who killed only animals. In Germany in 1576 an executioner hanged a pig accused of mauling a child rather than waiting for trial to take place. He had to leave his town of Schweinfurt in disgrace. The episode gave rise to an epithet for a person of low morals who would take the law into his own hands: a "Schweinfurt sow-hangman."

As in capital cases throughout Europe, even well into the early modern era, the executioner and judges wore new gloves when conferring the death penalty. To keep one's hands clean when announcing and administering justice was a representation that the law was ethically and procedurally correct.

At the sow's execution at Falaise the authorities used one bit of symbolism that was unusual: They dressed the animal in a man's clothes. Were they implying that human murderers could expect the same fate? Who decided to dress the sow? Did the judge or the hangman order such a thing, or was it an extralegal act by the crowd or the victim's family? The meaning of the farcical costuming remains obscure.

It is known, though, that this trial was considered important within its area of Normandy. The sow's punishment was featured in a fresco at the Church of the Holy Trinity in Falaise. The painting occupied a prominent place in the community for nearly 500 years.

SIGNIFICANCE

Scholars suggest that by the time the fresco at Falaise was painted over, animal trials were a relic and perhaps an embarrassingly crude one. The 1700s were a transitional age with regard to animal trials in the West. In the early modern age those who condemned animals in a judicial setting often acted out of personal rather than legal or religious motivation. Indeed, cultural historian Robert Darnton's famous example of the French apprentices who "prosecuted" cats was a private matter rather than an affair conducted in an official judicial setting.

Cases redolent of the sow of Falaise were not confined to the Mediterranean world, nor did the prosecution of animals die out completely in western Europe after the Age of Reason. Anthropologists note examples of crocodiles being tried for murder among early 20th-century peoples of Madagascar, for example. The crocodile trials consisted of a selection and punishment of one animal as having been the human-killer, the reasoning being that God would not allow the wrong animal to be punished. Historians point to such instances as a pig being tried for human mutilation in the 1800s in Slovenia and efforts to eradicate locusts from fields via the reading of sacred texts in Asia Minor in that same era.

By the 19th century the terms of the debate concerning criminal punishment were fundamentally different than they had been in premodern Europe. The focus was much more upon deterring future offenses than punishing the harm already done. For laws and penalties to prevent crime, potential criminals needed to be cognizant of the consequences of their actions. Such a debate often was cast as applying to considerations of mental illness or incapacity among defendants, but it also called into question whether animals should be tried and punished at all.

Further Reading

Beaumanoir, Philippe de. *The Coutumes de Beauvaisis of Philippe de Beaumanoir*. Philadelphia: University of Pennsylvania Press, 1992; Biernes, Piers. "The Law Is an Ass: Reading E. P. Evans' *The Criminal Prosecution and Capital Punishment of Animals.*" *Society and Animals: Journal of Human-Animal Studies* 2 (1994): 27–46; Cohen, Esther. "Law, Folklore, and Animal Lore." *Past and Present* 110 (1986): 6–37; Darnton, Robert. *The Great Cat Massacre*. New York: Vintage, 1985; Evans, Edward P. *The Criminal Prosecution and Capital Punishment of Animals*. London: W. Heinemann, 1906.

The trials of Jan Hus

Date: 1415

KEY ISSUES

Jan Hus wanted to become a priest because of the comparatively secure life that clerics led. Born to a relatively poor Czech family in the village of Husinec (hence his last name), in southern Bohemia around 1369, Hus showed neither spiritual nor scholarly gifts. Despite such an unprepossessing beginning, Hus's career in the church would be marked by conflict and, ultimately, martyrdom.

Through diligence Hus became a priest in the year 1400. He soon gained appointments at the University of Prague and Bethlehem Church in Prague. Hus became well known for preaching in the Czech language. Though not forbidden by Rome, such outreach was unusual. Hus's effort to speak in the vernacular made him more and more popular with ordinary folk. Initially, Hus's superiors, such as Archbishop Zbyn k Zajíc, regarded him as an asset.

Hus's theological views profoundly changed during the late 1390s and early 1400s when he and others in his country became aware of the writings of England's John Wycliffe. Knowledge of Wycliffe in central Europe was made possible through diplomacy. Anne, the sister of the king of Bohemia and Holy Roman Emperor Wenceslaus, married the English monarch Richard II in 1382. Along with the courtiers and administrators who began to travel between the two countries were ecclesiastical scholars such as Jerome of Prague, who while in England had admired Wycliffe.

After 1405 Hus found himself between two opposing political factions whose disagreements were tied to larger events involving the Papal Schism. Wenceslaus had expected support from the Roman pope Gregory XII in his bid for firmer control of Bohemia, but found the pontiff's backing to be lukewarm. Wenceslaus's response was to require church officials within his realm to show neutrality toward the opposing popes in Rome and Avignon, and Hus and many of the Czech faculty at the university concurred. Wenceslaus at first was drawn to Hus theologically because Hus reiterated Wycliffe's argument for "territorial churches" rather than strong governance from Rome.

Hus's immediate superior, the archbishop, continued to support Gregory. The rift split apart the University of Prague and led to the founding of the University of Leipzig by more German-oriented faculty and students. The archbishop Zajíc from that time onward nursed a grudge against Hus for having thrown in his lot with the secular authorities and was emboldened by the election of Alexander V as one of the reconciliatory popes in 1409. Alexander was supposed to help heal the church's schism by being an alternative to either a Roman or a French-controlled Holy See. Roman Christians then and in future referred to this third pope as "the antipope." Zajíc took the opportunity to demonstrate his clout by purging Bohemia of Wycliffite teachings. In return for local support the papacies of Alexander and his successor, John XXIII, stood ready to condemn Wycliffe's theology.

HISTORY OF THE CASE

In 1409 the papacy issued a formal statement, a papal bull, ordering the writings of Wycliffe to be burned. Priests and professors were to cease spreading Wycliffe's doctrines upon pain of excommunication. The king continued to protect Hus, who went on preaching to a loyal following among the ordinary citizens of Prague.

Hus ran into trouble, though, on the matter of indulgences. The early 1410s were a period when the papacy attempted to finance military actions through the selling of indulgences. In theory, indulgences simply were goodwill offerings to the church. But, many of the "campaigns" that indulgences financed were in effect battles among rival popes. Also, unscrupulous hawkers of indulgences sometimes presented them as remissions of sin or lessening of the time that a soul would spend in purgatory. The church often looked the other way in regard to such mischaracterizations. Hus relied on Wycliffe's reasoning that such practices were not based on the Bible. He publicly condemned indulgences in his sermons in Prague during 1412 and invited his fellows at the university to join him. Hus further argued that the church had no business promoting war in the first place. The church was alarmed at popular rioting in support of Hus's and Wycliffe's views and eventually executed three individuals of "no influence"—in other words, poor folk—as a warning to the intellectuals.

It was at this point that Hus lost the backing of the emperor. The political leader had been simmering ever since Hus had opposed indulgences because Wenceslaus received a portion of that revenue in return for his allowing their collection. Now Wenceslaus disapproved of the popular protests and ordered Hus to stop promoting 45 key principles that originally had been enunciated by Wycliffe—known as the "forty-five theses." Hus's position was that he would back down if his critics would show that Christian scripture did not support the theses.

SUMMARY OF ARGUMENTS

Wenceslaus hoped that removing Hus from Prague would ease tensions, but it did not. From his internal exile near the Austrian border Hus continued to voice opinions that proved disruptive, and his influence spread abroad. For example, Hus propounded the view that he could not accept condemnation from a church court alone but would submit only to a secular authority. He also repeated Wycliffe's charge that councils and the papacy did not represent the entire Christian Church. Rather, he maintained that individual believers, following their consciences, had a key role to play. Hus's popularity in Prague grew in his absence. The church in Rome (or at least that part of the church that remained in Rome) condemned Wycliffe's writings at a general council in early 1413.

The church was trying to heal itself of the great division that had occurred throughout most of Hus's lifetime. The Council of Constance began meeting in 1414 with the goal of eliminating the three alternative popes and establishing one line of papal succession based in Rome. The successor to Wenceslaus, his brother, Sigismund of Bohemia, pushed for the church gathering to take place within his lands. Sigismund gained Hus's trust and promised safe conduct to Hus if Hus would travel to Constance voluntarily. Hus's assumption probably was that the proceedings would not be completely managed by the papacy, which itself was in turmoil. And, even if an inquiry concerning Hus were to be directed by the pope, Hus had maintained a civil correspondence with John XXIII. Hus had some hope, in other words, that he could distinguish himself from Wycliffe in the eyes of this pope and that he would get protection from his critics.

Those hopes were not borne out, however; John had to abdicate his position in order to avoid being forced from the papacy. Hus was left to the tender mercies of local church leaders including the archbishop of Constance. There also were a number of Italian and French church officials in attendance at Constance. Many of them had a larger agenda of seeing the church reunified. Hus was a reminder and perhaps even a cause of discord, and his association with Wycliffe was too close to be tolerated.

In December 1414 Hus was taken to the archepiscopal castle and held, shackled and incommunicado, until the commencement of two interrelated trials on June 5, 1415. Chief among the charges against him were Hus's admiration for Wycliffe and his dissemination of Wycliffite views, most particularly the 45 theses. Most objectionable of all to Hus's accusers was Hus's failure to condemn Wycliffe's opinions on the Eucharist. Although Hus apparently did not share Wycliffe's ambiguity about the mystical nature of the consecrated bread and wine, he also did not sufficiently distinguish himself from Wycliffe concerning transubstantiation.

Hus's response was that he needed more time to defend himself properly. He also argued that in Prague he only had called for the review of Wycliffe's ideas; what he opposed was a summary condemnation of them. In that sense Hus was an early proponent of the marketplace of ideas, particularly in a university setting. He also wished that contrary views could be considered by the common person.

The emperor Sigismund had hoped to make Hus back down, whereas Hus increasingly saw himself as doomed and was willing to die for his principles. On July 6, 1415, the Council of Constance formally divested him of his priestly attire, destroyed his monk's haircut, and placed a mock crown on his head. Prostrating himself, Hus calmly said that he forgave those who were against him. Led by an Italian churchman, the authorities ordered Hus burned at the stake. The sentence was carried out the same day.

VERDICTS

Hus's admirer Peter of Mladenović had traveled to Constance with his mentor. Mladenović's account of how Hus behaved when faced with the stake emphasized Hus's resolve not to abjure his beliefs. Mladenović also noted that Hus said he had been falsely accused on several points. Composed in Latin, Mladenović's rendering was translated into Czech and soon became widely known. Mladenović's narration of Hus's last hours was self-consciously modeled on biblical versions of Christ's route to Calvary.

According to Mladenović, the church authorities turned Hus over to the local count Palatine, Clem, who enforced the sentence of death with his marshals. Hus had trouble finding anyone to hear his final confession (a key rite of the church), although a kindly priest at the archbishop's prison earlier had served as a confessor. A number of townspeople from Constance accompanied Hus on his way to the stake. Some of those citizens professed their admiration for the convict because of Hus's calm resolve. He behaved, they said, like a holy man. No one intervened, though, to prevent the execution or to make it less painful.

As the wood was piled around and the fire lit, Hus sang psalms. He declared that his own suffering was nothing compared to that of Christ. He turned down one last offer from Clem to save his life if he would recant. To witnesses, Hus's death seemed fairly quick and peaceful; the condemned man continued to move his lips in prayer as he suffocated. The executioners made sure that after Hus's skin had been burned, his bones and internal organs were incinerated, as were his shoes; they wanted to leave behind no relics for the local people to venerate. Hus's ashes were thrown into the Rhine as a further precaution.

SIGNIFICANCE

Jan Hus was not an original thinker, yet he amassed a dedicated following with his translations of Wycliffe's teachings for a Czech audience. His death only underscored the strength of his ideas, which already had spread to Germany, Austria, and Hungary. In Bohemia Hus's views became an inspiration for a group called the Taborites, who, like Hus, were deemed heretics and perhaps even political radicals. The Taborites were religious ancestors of the Moravians, a group of charismatic Christians who eventually settled in Pennsylvania and other areas of North America.

Hus had made clear his contempt for a church that did not condemn priests who required the faithful to pay for Christian ceremonies such as baptism and burial. In that respect Hus's populist tone was similar to the Englishman Wycliffe's and his sympathizers' such as the writer William Langland. Such empathy with the poor and anger at venality among clerics were shared with writers and preachers such as Erasmus of Rotterdam and Thomas More, who were moderate Catholic reformers. The late 15th-century writer Erasmus, for example, ridiculed church corruption yet never attacked the church on fundamental doctrinal points.

Besides linking Hus with Wycliffe, scholars often connect him to Martin Luther for several reasons. Clearly, Luther viewed Hus as an inspiration. The admirers of Luther used Hus's example overtly during the Reformation. Both men had considerable popular support that induced the church to worry about their influence. Although Hus labored under the confusion created by the Papal Schism, they both had to take account of the competing ambitions of political as well as church leaders. Hus lost vital protectors at key moments, while Luther's secular patrons proved decisively

more loyal. Luther also adapted several of Hus's arguments at his trial, emphasizing, for example, that he would accept his court's condemnation if he were convinced of its scriptural authenticity. Both Luther and Hus elevated their consciences— their personal understandings of scripture—above the traditional teachings of the church and the authority of courts that the church employed.

In Czech lands during the late 20th and early 21st centuries, Hus is highly regarded as a patriot somewhat apart from his religious role. His widely known writings, for example, greatly influenced the development of the Czech language and its standard notation. Furthermore, the position of the Roman Catholic Church in regard to Hus shifted in modern times, largely due to the efforts of Czech cardinal Miroslav Vik. In 1993 Vik appointed a commission to reconsider Hus's impact on the church and on Czechoslovakia. At a papal conference focused on Hus in 1999, Pope John Paul II declared that Hus had been a man of "moral courage who died in a cruel fashion." Those words from Rome were an ecumenical tribute to Hus. The Evangelical Lutheran Church in America—itself a child of the Taborites and Lutherans whom Hus had inspired—considers Hus a saint and offers prayers of thanksgiving for him each year on the day of his trial and execution.

Further Reading

Fudge, Thomas A. *The Magnificent Ride: The First Reformation in Hussite Bohemia.* Aldershot, U.K.: Ashgate, 2008; Haberkern, Phillip. "'After me there will come braver men': Jan Hus and Reformation Polemics in the 1530s." *German History* 27 (2009): 177–195; Hus, Jan. *Letters of John Huss Written During His Exile and Imprisonment, with a Preface by Martin Luther.* Edinburgh: William Whyte & Co., 1846; Peter of Mladenović. "How Jan Hus Was Executed." Available online. URL: http://www.columbia.edu/~js322/misc/hus-eng.html. Accessed July 1, 2009; Spinka, Matthew. *John Hus: A Biography.* Princeton, N.J.: Princeton University Press, 1968; VNTS. "Jan Hus." Available online. URL: http://www.vnts.nl/index.php/janhus. Accessed July 10, 2009.

The trial of Joan of Arc

Date: 1431

KEY ISSUES

It is rare in history for women to be military heroes and still rarer for them to change the course of a major war. The odds of an illiterate young woman from a small village achieving such a feat in the Middle Ages were remote, but France's Jeanne d'Arc (known in English as Joan of Arc) proved a great exception to the rule that medieval European women neither should lead men in battle nor direct politics. She accomplished the monumentally difficult tasks of unifying France behind a single leader and turning the tide of a long war back toward France. Ironically, the very men whom Joan of Arc had helped to victory abandoned her to misogyny and class prejudice.

The conflict that would come to be called the Hundred Years' War had already dragged on for nearly 70 years at the time of the birth of Joan in 1412. The military action had been intermittent; open warfare had been forestalled for certain periods of years by truces, political emergencies on both sides, and even the outbreak of plague during the late 1340s. There certainly had been no clear winner before the early 15th century. But, if a loser had been called in the 1410s, that title would have gone to France. The region where Joan lived, Champagne, and her village of Domrémy, had not been affected by the war as much as certain other portions of France, yet the area certainly saw upheaval that would have disturbed a child.

France was deeply divided from within. The French Crown, presided over by King Charles VI, was under challenge from several formidable regional aristocrats such as the dukes of Orleans, the count of Armagnac, and the duke of Burgundy. Another group clustered around the heir to the throne, the dauphin Charles, whose claim to the throne was pressing because of the precarious mental state of the old king. The situation was complicated further by occasional alliances by leading factions in France with the foe, England, in order to crush their domestic opponents. Thus, in the 1420s the Burgundians were fighting alongside the English. Meanwhile, the English had fresh momentum from their unexpected victory at Agincourt under the young monarch Henry V. Henry followed up that campaign with a treaty (the Treaty of Troyes in 1420) to marry the daughter of the king of France. Henry V hoped that their heir (later Henry VI of England) would occupy the English and French thrones jointly. Some of England's most powerful noblemen, such as the duke of Bedford, were dispatched to manage France on behalf of England.

HISTORY OF THE CASE

From about age 13 Joan claimed that angels appeared to her; she told of messages from Saints Catherine, Michael, and Margaret. Joan was a serious and dutiful young woman but not unusually pious. Her claims of divine visitation had a ring of truth about them because she was not perceived as being high strung. Eventually Joan said that the apparitions told her to act on behalf of the dauphin and specifically to lift an English siege at Orleans. In early 1429—after repeated visits—she argued persuasively to Robert de Baudricourt, a local official, to provide her with an escort to visit the dauphin at Chinon. Even the journey to Chinon was a hazardous undertaking, and convincing the jaded dauphin Charles to lend her troops would be an uphill battle. Remarkably, she succeeded on both counts. Charles decided to let the clergy question Joan to determine her sincerity; in a hearing at Poitiers they gave a favorable opinion of her piety, demeanor, and good reputation. Charles then agreed to lend Joan word of his support, though he did not proffer more tangible assistance.

Aware that being a woman put her at risk of assault in a vastly male military theater, Joan repeatedly reminded those around her that her "voices" had instructed her to remain a virgin. She sought to distance herself from female "camp followers," who sometimes had the reputation of being prostitutes. She also linked her personal safety with a divine sanction for her military cause. Almost everyone around Joan knew her, therefore, as "the Maid."

She and an army went to Orleans, arriving in late April 1429. By mid-May they had lifted the siege. Two months later Charles was on his way to be crowned king at the traditional site for such ceremonies, Rheims. Although again in name Charles supported an effort by Joan and her troops to assault Paris, then under English control, in September, he eventually ordered the force to withdraw. In the late fall and winter of 1429–30 Joan undertook a series of campaigns that were largely unsuccessful, including one engagement at which she sustained a serious injury. But, Joan was not only concerned with French affairs; she watched, for example, the clashes between Hussites and the church in central Europe with anxiety, even composing a letter warning the followers of Jan Hus to return to what she considered to be the true faith.

In May 1430 Joan was captured as her forces tried in vain to lift the Burgundian siege of Compiègne. She was held prisoner for four months before being formally transferred to English custody in exchange for monetary payment from the English to the Burgundians. Her trial took place at Rouen, the center of Burgundian and English influence in France. She was accused of various acts of heresy related to her visions and deportment. The official in charge of the proceedings was Pierre Cauchon, the bishop of Beauvais, whom the Burgundians had previously entrusted with delicate political tasks. Records of the English government provide overwhelming evidence of the English having financed Joan's prosecution. The tide in the war had turned—or at least the English momentum had been stopped—and England's frustration centered on the Maid of Orleans as the architect of that development.

SUMMARY OF ARGUMENTS

By what court was Joan to be tried? In England an ecclesiastical court would have heard her case if she had fallen under church jurisdiction. She would have been subject to a military proceeding if the English had tried her as a prisoner of war. Why was Joan not termed a military prisoner? English and Burgundian authorities avoided such a designation for several reasons: They were loath to publicly acknowledge her military importance; they were angry at a woman's battlefield success, and they did not want to make Joan available for a prisoner

swap. The court that did hear the case against Joan was not an ordinarily constituted body but rather a hybrid tribunal made up of officials of the Inquisition in France (represented by France's Vice-Inquisitor Jean le Maistre), plus Cauchon.

The court was under the nominal authority of Cauchon as the bishop of Beauvais, and as such it evaded the rules of the Inquisition. Despite its later reputation as cruel toward accused persons, in this instance the Inquisition would have provided more protection to a female defendant than the body directed by Cauchon. Early on, Joan criticized the proceedings as contrary to accepted practice during an inquisition. The court rejected that objection; technically the judges were correct because they were not running the inquiry strictly according to the Inquisition's rules, although it was an "inquisitorial" procedure. Subsequent historians have argued that the trial, therefore, was legally sound. But, several legal authorities in France during the trial—despite the political danger into which it put them—did object to certain occurrences at Rouen.

The church officials from the cathedral at Rouen were notably quiet during the trial. Cauchon tried to get their stamp of approval on several occasions, but they demurred. At one point they even objected to the prominent presence of theologians from the University of Paris at the proceedings. Cauchon excluded those objections in the official transcript of the trial. Cauchon asked one of France's most famous canon lawyers, Jean Lohier of Normandy, to appear at the trial. On February 24, 1431, Lohier did visit Rouen to look over what had been going on in the case. Probably to the chagrin of the bishop of Beauvais, Lohier expressed to Cauchon certain misgivings about the trial.

Lohier objected to the courtroom being "enclosed and private"; participants did not feel free to express their opinions. Worse, there seemed to be political pressure on the judges. Lohier reminded Cauchon that Joan had been instrumental in making the dauphin into King Charles VII. Now, due to Joan's trial, that ruler might feel that "his honor had been impugned." Lohier recommended that someone from the royal party should be allowed to testify concerning Joan's character. In addition, Lohier decried the lack of formal written charges being set down against the defendant, and he condemned her lack of representation by counsel. Although Cauchon demanded that Lohier stay to help lend legitimacy to the affair, Lohier left Rouen. Lohier told one reliable witness that he was certain that Cauchon simply intended to trick the unsophisticated young woman.

But, before one even considers the trial itself, it is critical to note that church law and practice were almost completely on the Maid of Orleans's side. Joan was terrified of being raped by her guards. She understood that church regulations said that if she were being tried on religious charges, then she should be held in a church facility. The church had its own jails for women; there, she would have nuns as custodians. Not being successful in that plea, Joan insisted on wearing her military clothes—pants and a belt that she literally could tie up tightly, making sexual assault more difficult. Not finding much else with which to charge her, Joan's accusers latched on to the alleged cross-dressing as proof of her heresy. There again, Joan had the law on her side. No less a contemporary theologian than Jean Gerson (former chancellor of the University of Paris) gave the opinion in 1429 that the church allowed women to dress in men's clothing in certain situations and that Joan's circumstances were within those guidelines.

As well as insisting that she be placed among female captors, Joan maintained that the judges at Rouen were biased against her and that she ought to be able to take her case to the pope. How she managed to know, still less to state succinctly, the correct theological positions with respect to such matters is one of the great mysteries attending her case. No matter how sophisticated Joan's understanding of what should have been done according to church practice and law, that knowledge availed her little.

The officials in charge of prosecuting her appeared bent on a swift verdict of guilty. The English soldiers were pleased to have custody of a person who was a key reason that the English were losing the war. Ample evidence exists of threats by English and Burgundian officials toward those taking part in the trial who dared impugn the integrity of the proceedings or speak well of the defendant.

Early in the trial there often were more than 60 persons at any given moment firing questions at Joan. Many of the lawyers and judges were very

well educated, having been trained in theology at the University of Paris. A large number of them had been dislocated by the war and were indebted to the Burgundian-English faction. France's vice-inquisitor, Jean le Maistre, was present at the trial, although he had tried to avoid participating in it at first. Troubled by aspects of the proceedings, he several times voiced his concerns to Cauchon, who brushed him off.

The trial record (officially called Joan of Arc's "trial of condemnation") was made available for the first time in 1435 as a transcription based on notes taken in court at Rouen. Of course, the court itself kept the trial record, yet an examination of even that heavily biased record establishes how effectively Joan answered her accusers. The proceedings began on February 21, 1431. Prison had been a trial in itself for the teenaged woman. Joan was kept in close confinement, usually shackled, frequently harassed about her male attire, and kept from attending mass. In other words, she was under great psychological and physical duress, yet she managed to give simple and effective answers before the court. Occasionally she actually took the offensive, for example, predicting (on March 1) that the English would lose Paris in seven years' time; it was a prophecy that came true in late 1437.

The inquisitors decided not to call witnesses against the accused in spite of the fact that taking such testimony was standard procedure in heresy cases. Rather, they pressed Joan about a number of details of her experience, hoping to catch the unlettered young woman in errors of fact or faith. That did occur, for example, when the court mentioned one church council to Joan and she seemed not to recognize the reference. Often, though, when Joan was confused about how to reply, she stated simply that she would not respond, thus indicating that she thought she was being directed—even in court—by her voices:

> Joan further said that she went to him whom she called her king without hindrance, and when she reached to town of Ste. Catharine de Fierbois she was sent to Chinon, where he whom she called her king was. She reached this place about noon and lodged in an inn; and after dinner she went to him whom she called her king who was

in the castle. She also said that when she entered his chamber she knew him from the rest by the revelation of her voice. And she told her king that she wished to go making war against the English.

Asked if when the voice disclosed the king, there was any light in the place: she answered: "Pass on." Asked whether she had seen an angel above her king: she answered: "Spare me, pass on." Still she said that before her king gave her a charge she had many beautiful visions and revelations. Asked how the king regarded the revelations and visions: she answered: "I shall not tell you this. This is not to be answered you; but send to the king himself and he will tell you."

It was not only her recollection that the voices advocated a French victory that caused Joan difficulty with the prosecution. Joan's contention that angelic figures spoke directly to her was itself problematic within the church at the time. It was rare for the church to acknowledge that persons outside the clergy might receive direct word from the Almighty. How likely was it, the theologians wondered, that divine revelation would come to humanity via an obscure peasant girl?

Cauchon may have sensed that Joan's answers were winning sympathy among the large assembly and on March 1 ordered that the trial would take place henceforth within a smaller chamber inside the prison. The defendant continued to answer well under questioning, even though the inquiries that the court made were designed to force confessions or at least contradictions from her:

On Saturday, March 17th, asked how she knows that St. Margaret and St. Catherine hate the English, she answered: "They love those whom God loves, and hate whom He hates." Asked if God hates the English, she answers that she knows nothing of God's love or hatred, or what God will do to their souls, but she is certain that with the exception of those who shall die there, they will be driven out of France, and that God will send victory to the French and against the English. Asked if God was for the English when they were prospering in France, she answered that she knew not whether God hated the French, but she believed it was His will to suffer them to be beaten for their sins, if they were in a state of sin.

The judges (who were called "assessors" in the trial notes) finally prepared a list of 70 articles that they presented to Joan on March 27, 1431. There was some disagreement as to how Joan should respond to these (for example, as individual counts or as a whole, by reference to previous statements or with new replies?), but eventually she was required to answer each charge in turn. Although early on in the trial Cauchon had toyed with the idea of charging Joan with witchcraft and indeed had taken testimony from her related to such matters as her alleged bewitching of children, those allegations do not appear in this later portion of the trial. Instead, the focus was on Joan's visions, their instructions to her to act against the English, and her adoption of male dress. Once again, Joan's replies were succinct and powerful, yet also clever and evasive. The transcript relates first the Article of Accusation (Article 16) and her rejoinder:

Previous to, and since her capture, at the Castle of Beaurevoir and at Arras, Joan had been many times advised with gentleness, by noble persons of both sexes, to give up her man's dress and resume suitable attire. She had absolutely refused, and to this day also she refuses with persistence; she disdains also to give herself up to feminine work, conducting herself in all things rather as a man than as a woman.

"What have you to say on this Article?"

"At Arras and Beaurevoir I was invited to take a woman's dress; then I refused, and I refuse still. As to the women's work of which you speak, there are plenty of other women to do it."

VERDICT

In early April 1431 the trial officials took Joan's answers to their 70 articles and, with the help of the Paris faculty present, condensed them into another document made up of 12 sections. When she was brought into court or approached in her cell at least four more times and asked to assent to the shorter articles, she refused. There is indication that within this time period Joan was taken to a place of execution and threatened with burning. The official record itself notes that her inquisitors discussed torture as a means of exacting compliance; they decided, however, that she would resist it successfully. On May 24, for whatever reason, she relented and signed (by making a mark) a brief abjuration. There is some evidence that Joan had been assured she would be released to the French if she provided an admission of guilt, but in fact, her judges condemned her to perpetual imprisonment in an English jail. On the same day they also supervised her donning of women's clothing.

The English and the Burgundians were furious at the outcome at that point, for they wanted Joan dead rather than permanently imprisoned. Cauchon, however, assured several persons at Rouen that he was not finished yet. On May 28 several officials of the court went to visit the prisoner and found her wearing male attire again. Her explanation (as listed in the official record) was that she never had promised to give up male attire permanently. Several scholars have suggested that between May 24 and May 28 her captors sexually assaulted Joan. This made her despair about future treatment and sealed her decision to embrace martyrdom.

It is likely that her jailers—perhaps on orders from Cauchon or someone else in the court— removed her women's clothing and substituted the men's garb, knowing that this would make Joan's position legally dire: If she went back on the terms of her recantation she would be judged a lapsed heretic and could be burned at the stake. In the strictest sense church authorities did not burn heretics; they simply declared that a heretic had lapsed and then turned the person over to the secular authorities for execution.

On May 30 the court at Rouen did exactly that: In the marketplace at Rouen they declared Joan an excommunicate and a lapsed heretic. She was to be "abandoned" to secular authority. She was tied to a stake, and the fire was lit. Witnesses said that she called out to the saints and to Christ in her last moments. Many of those in attendance, including some who previously had been in favor of the proceedings, expressed great discomfort at the execution. The executioner himself was chagrined at the fact that authorities prevented him from strangling Joan before the fire reached her, a common act of charity among executioners toward young, female, or especially sympathetic condemned persons. After Joan died, those presiding made certain that her body was displayed to the crowd to dispel rumors of her escape. Her ashes were thrown into the Seine.

SIGNIFICANCE

The role of Charles VII in Joan of Arc's condemnation is puzzling. Why did he not help her at the time of trial? In 1449, whether his motive was long-felt guilt or a wish to further legitimize his own presence on the throne, Charles asked for university specialists to inquire into Joan's trial. An even more thorough examination of the full records was possible a few years later when archives in Rouen came into French hands upon English withdrawal from France.

At about the same time Pope Calixtus III ordered an inquiry into the trial of Joan of Arc—a questioning of the legitimacy of that trial, which eventually was termed a *trial of nullification*. Among those who brought appeals for a reconsideration of Joan's case was her mother. During the nullification procedure Inquisitor Jean Bréhal heard a number of eyewitnesses and participants explain that in 1431, trial officials either had been bought off or pressured into unfavorable findings. The original verdict of heresy and the decision that Joan had relapsed both were vacated in a decision sanctioned by the papacy in 1456. Rome pointedly did not absolve Cauchon of his complicity in the faulty proceedings. Those nullifications were the basis for subsequent efforts to obtain petition for Joan's canonization, a process completed in 1920.

Joan of Arc remains a figure much discussed among not only historians and theologians but also the wider public. Her answers at trial provide some of the fullest details about her motivations— even filtered as those replies were through her detractors. The brevity of her answers helped her before the judges; she seemed to understand that the more she disputed with her tormentors, the better chance they would have to ensnare her in argument. And yet, her concision is frustrating to those historians who would know her better.

Was Joan politically astute—an early French nationalist? Was she, on the other hand, rather simpleminded, playing into the hands of wily politicians such as the duke of Bedford and Charles VII? Was she a protofeminist? Was she mentally unstable? All of these propositions have been advanced about her; Joan is a hero to a variety of causes. There is considerable agreement on her treatment, though, at the hands of the legal process. Scholars almost universally concur that Joan of Arc's trial was politically motivated and managed. The misgivings of the few officials in her own time who dared to impugn the proceedings were ignored. That she fared even as well as she did—managing to leave a record of her remarkable self-defense—was itself a miracle.

Further Reading

Barrett, W. P., trans. "The Trial of Jeanne D'Arc." Available online. URL: http://www.fordham.edu/halsall/basis/joanofarc-trial.html. Accessed August 3, 2009; Guiraud, Jean, and E. C. Messenger. *Medieval Inquisition.* New York: AMS Press, 1980; Hobbins, Daniel, trans. *The Trial of Joan of Arc.* Cambridge, Mass.: Harvard University Press, 2005; Pernoud, Regine, Katherine Anne Porter, and J. M. Cohen. *The Retrial of Joan of Arc: The Evidence for Her Vindication.* New York: Harcourt Brace, 1955; Pinzino, Jane Marie. "The Condemnation and Rehabilitation Trials of Joan of Arc." Available online. URL: http://smu.edu/ijas/pinzino.html. Accessed August 2, 2009; Shaw, George Bernard. *Saint Joan.* New York: Brentano's, 1924; Williamson, Allen. "Issues Concerning Joan of Arc's Trial." Available online. URL: http://archive.joan-of-arc.org/joanofarc_trial_issues.html. Accessed August 1, 2009.

The trial of the Mamluka bride

Date: 1470

KEY ISSUES

The case concerns a young woman in Egypt who was angry at treatment by her former husband.

Among Islamic sources, which use the Hijri calendar, the date is in the late 800s, corresponding to the late 1400s C.E. Although the unnamed petitioner in the case may not be of historical importance, she is representative of an influential group in Egyptian society—the military elite. Those military rulers, or Mamluks, held power during the period to which they gave their name, 1250–1517. The courts hearing this case, though attached to the ruler, made their decisions according to sharia (Islamic law). The episode provides an example of how courts in the region applied the religious rules concerning conjugal rights specifically and gender generally. It also shows the interlocking connections between Islam and the state in this portion of the world.

The most striking feature of the case to modern eyes is the age of the petitioner; she was 12 at the time of the trial and even younger when she was married. Sharia allowed the age of marital relations for females to be the age of puberty (which generally was reckoned to be around 12), although marriages could be contracted earlier. To present-day Western readers, her age may shock sensibilities both because such a young female was allowed to enter into marriage and because the law allowed sexual relations after age 12.

Among non-Western societies, however, marriages of young girls were historically and still remain more commonplace, although medical personnel now warn of the dangers connected with sexual intercourse and pregnancy among very young persons. When sharia has been applied in such instances, it often is and has been a protection for preteen girls against sexual activity, even within marriage, until the girls are more physically mature.

Another key element of the case in question was that it occurred in a region where connections with the ruling caste were key to securing legal and political rights. Military values predominated within Mamluk Egypt, just as they permeated other societies such as Norman France. Thus, this young bride appears to modern readers to have been at a distinct disadvantage: Not only was she young and female in a male-dominated, martial country, but in this instance, the Mamluka (the term for a female member of the Mamluk class) did not even have parents or a male relative stating her case. Rather, the Mamluka's spokesperson was her mother's sister, or *khala* (maternal aunt).

HISTORY OF THE CASE

The trial was set down in some detail by the legal chronicler Nur al-Din 'Ali ibn Dawud al-Jawharī al-Ṣayrafi at some point during the later 1400s. Like other aspirants to legal promotion—for example, England's Edward Coke about a century later—al-Ṣayrafi hoped to make a name for himself by chronicling notable trials. He chose, therefore, to detail cases that set precedents or illuminated thorny points of law. In this episode al-Ṣayrafi had a vital role, and not just as a legal historian. He also served as a local magistrate, and one of his decisions concerning the Mamluka petitioner came under scrutiny by a higher judicial authority, a leading officer of the sultan.

Although al-Ṣayrafi's account is brief and cannot be corroborated fully owing to the obscurity of the plaintiff, it does sketch out the facts of the situation. There already had been harm done by the time the case came to court. When the girl was about nine years old, her aunt affianced her in return for a marriage settlement. She was betrothed at a cost of eight dinars to a bondsman, a military attaché or assistant, who worked for a Mamluk named Faris. The bondsman-fiancé was unnamed but rather referred to by his rank—that of *ghulam*.

The aunt and the niece stated that they understood that the betrothal of a girl who had not reached puberty meant that conjugal relations could not yet take place. The person who presided over the original marriage contract was al-Ṣayrafi. He agreed, restating the prohibition on spousal intercourse according to his understanding of sharia. Al-Ṣayrafi allowed the marriage, and the Mamluka went home with the bridegroom. The *ghulam* and (the record hints) also his protector, Faris, raped the child. The Mamluka ran away to her aunt, who was outraged. When she protested to Faris and the *ghulam*, the groom divorced the girl and kept the dowry.

The Mamluka's parents had been absent from Cairo for several years at the time that the case came to the attention of judicial authorities. There were no male relatives ready to act on the petitioner's behalf or, presumably, to care for her at all. She had to resort to begging. Thus, the courts that had charge of Mamluk affairs accepted the argument that they should take the case, for the petitioner was of the Mamluk caste. The courts also let the maternal aunt act as the Mamluka's protector. The aunt was requesting a restoration of the Mamluka's dowry so that it could apply toward another match. She also wanted a public judgment so that the girl's reputation was untarnished though she was no longer a virgin. The case, therefore, did not begin as a criminal trial but instead as a civil hearing or investigation in which damages were requested. As it unfolded, though, criminal penalties were not out of order.

SUMMARY OF ARGUMENTS

The case came to the attention of a representative of Sultan al-Ashraf Qaytbay. Qaytbay's reign is known for restoring political order after a time of turmoil; the ruler embarked on a notable program of architecture and public works upon his accession in 1468. In legal matters the sultanate leaned upon the Hanafi, or Arabic school of law. Hanafi jurisprudence was based on the Qur'an and used certain other highly respected texts but also allowed jurists to apply reason when exact precedents could not be found in the sacred writings.

The right to dispense justice belonged to the sultan. Just as European rulers in this era occasionally exercised their prerogative to hold courts *coram rege*—that is, to preside personally over jurisprudence—so sultans throughout the Middle East could sit directly in judgment. In practice they delegated that responsibility to trusted lieutenants. The courts run by the sultan's representatives were called *mazalim* courts. In theory, Islamic law as administered by sultanates had no appeal process. In effect, though, the *mazalim* often acted as higher courts.

Such was what occurred in the Mamluka's case. The request of the petitioner and her aunt to receive protection from the court and redress for the wrongs they had suffered came to the attention of the second-ranking military official in the sultanate: Grand Majordomo Yashbak min Mahdi. Why did the majordomo agree to become involved in such a seemingly low-level case? On the surface it would seem beneath the notice of the major-domo. The young Mamluka's only real advocate was her aunt. Those who had wronged the child bride appeared to be much better connected. Also, it would not be an easy decision to make. The religious rules governing the case had to be elucidated through reason by the *mazalim* court; in other words, the case required some theoretical consideration.

The record from al-Ṣayrafi sheds light on the situation. It seems that three factors worked in the plaintiff's favor: her original class identification as a Mamluk; the fact that Faris, who now was retired as a military officer, was connected to the previous regime; and the poor local reputations of Faris and his aide the *ghulam*-groom. Al-Ṣayrafi mentions that the *ghulam* and his protector ran a local gang that controlled key markets and supplies, siphoning off a large percentage for themselves and intimidating poorer folk.

Another rationale for the sultan's taking notice of this controversy through a *mazalim* court was that the ruler was interested in how his local magistrates (the *qadi*)—in this instance, al-Ṣayrafi—were performing. The first set of actions that the majordomo undertook was to establish the Mamluka's social status and her legal status as an orphan. In other words, he had to satisfy himself that this court, which was concerned with the Mamluk class, had jurisdiction. The majordomo decided this court could hear the case simply on account of the petitioner's parentage, although perhaps an argument could have been made based on the Mamluk status of the groom's patron.

The sultan's representative next inquired into the validity of the original marriage contract, the document that al-Ṣayrafi had drawn up. In particular, the majordomo investigated whether the groom had been told of the sharia rule about abstaining from intercourse with underage girls. The majordomo took two lines of inquiry in that part of the case: First, he summoned all of the witnesses to the betrothal contract to give testimony as to whether that point had been discussed during the marriage negotiations, then he spoke with al-Ṣayrafi.

He examined the actions and words of al-Ṣayrafi, trying to assess whether that original magistrate (in Western terms, "the court of first instance" or the "original court") had applied sharia properly. The majordomo summoned al-Ṣayrafi and asked him why he had given permission for the marriage to take place at all, given the prospective bride's pre-reproductive status. According to his own account, al-Ṣayrafi had a good explanation: The Prophet himself had married his fourth spouse, Aisha, when she was but nine years of age. It was a risky argument, as the majordomo pointed out, for it implied that the magistrate was drawing a parallel between the revered figure and the *ghulam*—a sacrilege. The reply from al-Ṣayrafi, though, was acceptable: He did not mean to compare the Prophet or his esteemed wife and this prospective bride and groom, but rather, he sought wisdom from the Prophet as a lawgiver.

VERDICT

The case was resolved on several levels. The majordomo first ordered the *ghulam* to be whipped as a punishment for violating the terms of the marriage contract that had prohibited marital relations until the Mamluka entered puberty. It was a stern enough penalty: 100 lashes, although such a beating could vary greatly with the fervor of the administration. The patron Faris also came in for recrimination for his part in the rape, whether as a protector of the *ghulam* or perhaps as a participant. He had to carry the victim through the neighborhood on his shoulders. Such a humiliating act was supposed to lessen Faris's standing within the community in a literal sense. More obliquely, it indicated that Faris no longer had the political connections he enjoyed under the previous regime.

The majordomo asked that an even higher Hanafi authority, the leading justice Muhib al-Din ibn al-Shihna, should review the judgment. Although al-Ṣayrafi's account is inconclusive about that judge's ruling, it is a reasonable inference that the resolutions from the lower authorities were allowed to stand. Still, Faris at least had the satisfaction that he, a privileged person within Egyptian society, had been taken notice of at the highest judicial levels. He also could comfort himself in the fact that several of his peers had attended the hearings and had spoken strongly on his behalf.

SIGNIFICANCE

Besides seeing Faris cut down a notch, what did the Mamluka and her aunt receive through the verdict? The judgment of the highest (Hanafi) court was that the guilty parties should pay back four dinars to the aggrieved bride and her guardian aunt. The money would be used to help the Mamluka effect another marriage. It was exactly half the sum requested. Perhaps that amount was just enough to satisfy the plaintiffs but not to enrage the groom and his protector.

The various judicial authorities took pains to state that the bride was innocent of any wrongdoing and therefore fit for another respectable marriage, in spite of the loss of her virginity. It was a finding that has some parallels with religious authorities' rulings in modern instances when persons have been raped and still wish to claim that they enter marriage as chaste. In such scenarios (for example, the aftermath of the kidnapping and rape of Elizabeth Smart by a polygamist in 21st-century Utah), religious figures sometimes declare crime victims to be virgins in a religious if not a physical sense.

Whether the hearing of the case lessened the local influence of Faris and the groom is a matter of some conjecture. On one hand al-Ṣayrafi hoped that these local gangsters would find their influence curtailed as a result of their public humiliations. In another respect, though, al-Ṣayrafi ends his account of the Mamluka bride on a cynical note. The chronicler recalls that he ran into the *ghulam* walking around the neighborhood, the day after his lashing. The former groom appeared healthy and spoke loudly of his deliverance due to the grace of the Almighty.

Further Reading

Esposito, J. L. *Women in Muslim Family Law.* Syracuse, N.Y.: Syracuse University Press, 1982; Finer, S. E. *The History of Government II: The Intermediate Ages.* Oxford: Oxford University Press, 1997; Neilsen, Jorgen S. *Secular Justice in an Islamic State: Mazalim under the Bahri Mamluks, 662–789/1264–1387.* Leiden: Nederlands Institut voor het Nabije Oosten, 1985; Petry, Carl F. "Conjugal Rights versus Class Prerogative: A Divorce Case in Mamluk Cairo." In *Women in the Medi-* *eval Islamic World: Power, Patronage, and Piety,* edited by Gavin R. G. Hambly, 227–240. New York: St. Martin's Press, 1998; Vikor, Knut S. *Between God and the Sultan: A History of Islamic Law.* New York: Oxford University Press, 2005.

The trial of Peter von Hagenbach

Date: 1474

KEY ISSUES

The Nuremberg War Crimes Trials of the mid-1940s were a prime example of the difficulty of applying international standards to human rights offenses committed during declared wars. The Allies' prosecution of Nazi officials at Nuremberg was well planned and managed, yet in some quarters Nuremberg was criticized as an application of laws that did not exist at the time that the crimes were committed. Legal scholars have identified a foreshadowing of such controversies in a case from the early modern era in north central Europe: the trial of Peter von Hagenbach. Hagenbach was on trial for his leadership of a town in which soldiers and government officials committed various atrocities. Adding even greater interest to the case is Hagenbach's defense strategy: He leaned on the justification that he was "just following orders."

Hagenbach's case contained some of the dilemmas that confound modern prosecutions of alleged war criminals. Are atrocities that occur during war punishable once peace has been established? If so, to which laws should the prosecutors refer? Should a trial take place in the location of the crimes or within another jurisdiction? Should the court be local or have a broader scope? How does a multinational tribunal decide whether it is hearing a war crimes case rather than an instance of criminal misconduct?

HISTORY OF THE CASE

Breisach was situated on the Rhine River across from French lands and near the Swiss region—a three-cornered location that made the fortified town easy to reach. It was a favorite stopover for Swiss traders journeying to the Frankfurt fair. Breisach, however, had the misfortune of being in the crosshairs of several ambitious politicians. The area suited the territorial ambitions of Charles, duke of Burgundy, also known as Charles the Bold and (to his enemies) Charles the Terrible.

Like many regional lords, the duke of Burgundy hoped to gain more territory contiguous to his homeland. Charles's goals, though, went beyond mere expansion. He aimed to be Holy Roman Emperor. Eventually, Charles was thwarted; he died at the Battle of Nancy in 1477. But before that decisive military and personal defeat, Charles and the Burgundians inflicted a great deal of damage.

In the middle of the 1400s Breisach was under the control of Sigismund, the archduke of Austria. In 1469 the archduke ceded authority over certain of his territories on the Upper Rhine to Charles of Burgundy in exchange for 100,000 gold florins. Charles looked upon that granting of authority as an opportunity to demonstrate his control over the region. He expected his appointee as governor *(Landvogt)*, Peter von Hagenbach, to make an example of Breisach. It seems that the duke gave Hagenbach carte blanche to tighten Burgundy's grip on the town. Hagenbach engaged in a campaign of persecution in Breisach and the surrounding region. The part played by Hagenbach was recorded in the contemporary chronicle of Johannes Knebel and was described in the following century by Philip Melancthon.

The *Landvogt* sanctioned activities ranging from extortion and confiscation of private property to rape and murder. Reportedly, he gave orders to German mercenaries lodging in local homes to kill the men in the households so that soldiers would have no resistance when attacking women and children. So revolting were these acts of intimidation von Hagenbach finally faced a siege led by his external foes from towns in the Upper Rhine and Alsace regions and the area around Berne. He also was forced to counter a rebellion begun within the city walls. Hagenbach was captured and Charles of Burgundy put on the run from Breisach and environs. The powers allied against Charles the Terrible offered to repay the entire sum that Burgundy had loaned to the Austrian archduke, but Charles wanted the territory more than the money.

Those who held Hagenbach in custody refused to allow him to appeal to his employer, nor did they assent to the case being heard in a jurisdiction controlled by Charles. It was not that the captors were unanimous. Interestingly, the foes of Hagenbach who were from Breisach itself were in favor of turning him over to Burgundy, while his critics from Berne pressed for the trial to take place under their control. Berne's connection with the trial, along with the participation of another entity, Solothurn, is important because it points to Swiss influence on the tribunal. Swiss merchants said that their trade had been damaged and their lives imperiled by Hagenbach.

Under which law, and whose law, was Hagenbach tried? The record of the case leaves much room for doubt, although there are indications that the tribunal applied both the standards for knights (the law of arms) and the law of the Holy Roman Empire. The composition of the tribunal was unusual in its time and has caught the attention of legal scholars ever since. The court was a conglomeration of participants. Each of the towns that had suffered under either Charles of Burgundy generally or Hagenbach specifically sent at least one judge. Breisach named eight of the judges. The prosecutor and the main judge acted directly under the authority of Sigismund of Austria. These political units were so angered at the Burgundian campaign of terror that they managed to put aside their many differences in order to try Hagenbach.

SUMMARY OF ARGUMENTS

There were a few examples of regulations against war crimes within particular nations prior to the Hagenbach trial but nothing approaching international standards. King Richard II of England, for example, had published rules in 1388 that warned members of English armies not to attack unarmed priests or women; those injunctions also forbade the sacking of churches. King Charles VII of France issued an order in 1439 (the Ordinance of Orleans) that military commanders could not claim a lack of knowledge by subordinates as an excuse for avoiding command responsibility. Thus, individual rulers declared that their armies should observe rules of conduct, especially toward civilians. The English prosecutors of the Scot William Wallace tendered a charge against Wallace for what they said was Wallace's brutality toward women, children, and the elderly.

The court presented four specific charges against Hagenbach, including his beheading of four citizens of Thann (a city in the Alsace region) in November 1473. That charge, like the input of the Swiss, points to the multinational character of the prosecution. Hagenbach also was accused of changing the governance of Breisach although he had promised not to alter the local political situation. Specifically, charge number two against Hagenbach was that he had abolished guilds, fired judicial officials, and instituted new taxes, backing up such changes with foreign troops. Charge number three stated that Hagenbach had planned to kill Breisach citizens who resisted him along with their families and that he had plotted to hide their bodies. Perhaps most disturbing to his contemporaries were the rumors of sexual assaults perpetrated by Hagenbach and his soldiers as stated in charge four; apparently, his victims included nuns. Although the court records do not reflect it, other sources indicate that Hagenbach sexually assaulted his own wife.

Thus it was that Hagenbach had governed repressively within Breisach as well as ensnaring travelers in the cruelties and spreading destruction to the whole vicinity. Prosecutor Heinrich Iselin set out the litany of crimes that Hagenbach had either allowed or directly authorized. Iselin offered the memorable characterization that the defendant had "trampled underfoot the laws of God and man."

In contrast to many trials in this time and place, both sides had the services of competent counsel. Coincidentally, the lead defense and prosecution spokesmen both were from Basel. Hagenbach obviously profited from his association with Charles. While the duke of Burgundy could not save the governor from a trial, he at least could pay for Hagenbach's lawyer. The defense pursued two main lines of argument: The present court had no jurisdiction over the case because Charles had not sanctioned it, and the *Landvogt* had no choice but to follow the orders of his superior, the duke

of Burgundy. As Hans Irmy, the leader of the defense, phrased it, "Is it not known that soldiers owe absolute obedience to their superiors?" He further contended that Charles's military campaign through the region was proof of his support for Hagenbach's tactics.

Hagenbach's defense did not make a line of argument that modern scholars have suggested in similar cases: His actions should not be thought of as having occurred during wartime at all, since there was no formally declared conflict ongoing at the time of the acts alleged. There had been military campaigns in the region only as a result of Hagenbach's actions. Quite to the contrary, Irmy argued that Hagenbach had been acting in a military capacity when most contemporaries would have said he had not been within a theater of war at all.

The application of torture to the defendant prior to trial was fairly standard to force a confession, but contemporary commentators as well as modern scholars pointed out that it was without purpose in this instance. There already was plenty of proof of Hagenbach's crimes. The existence of coerced testimony prolonged the proceedings; during the trial Hagenbach retracted statements he had made under duress. To no one's surprise, some of the strongest criticism of the trial came from the court of Charles of Burgundy. Indeed, the duke's most modern biographer repeats the opinion of Charles that the trial was only for show.

VERDICT

Although Hagenbach argued that he was absolved of responsibility as he was carrying out the orders of his superior, Charles of Burgundy, the tribunal hearing his case disagreed. Quite the opposite, the court ruled. Hagenbach had a duty as a knight to prevent atrocities from occurring on his watch.

At his execution Hagenbach was deprived of his knightly garb. It was an evocation of the central tenet against him in the eyes of the court: He had done discredit to his rank. Ordinary folk also appeared satisfied with the trial's result. Even though they had seen many brutalities during war, Hagenbach's actions must have crossed the line into unacceptable violence. Several hundred citizens of Basel traveled to Breisach to witness Hagenbach's beheading.

SIGNIFICANCE

Was the court that tried Hagenbach an international body? It would be more accurate to describe it as multinational, for while the entities that participated certainly were united for the purpose of opposing Charles, they also had little in common in legal structure or principles. Their unity came from opposition to Burgundian ambition, though the prosecuting powers also indicated that they expected certain behavior from Hagenbach because of his social position.

Did Swiss participation in the trial make it international? Not in terms of the modern understanding of international law. The Swiss Confederation, although it gained independence from the Holy Roman Empire in this era, was not formally recognized during Hagenbach's lifetime. Thus, it would be inaccurate to conclude that Hagenbach's conviction and execution represented international law, yet the Hagenbach trial did signify an effort to enforce certain norms of behavior that transcended national boundaries.

Legal historians of the international tribunal at Nuremberg and the Bosnian war crimes trials of the late 20th century often cite the 1474 trial at Breisach. The International Red Cross also notes the unequivocal condemnation by Hagenbach's accusers of his use of rape and murder. In Hagenbach's hands those actions were tools to intimidate civilian populations. Whether there was a formal war going on was immaterial to Hagenbach's critics, just as it is somewhat beside the point to modern advocates for fundamental human rights.

Further Reading

Greppi, Edoardo. "The Evolution of Individual Criminal Responsibility under International Law." *International Review of the Red Cross* 835 (1999): 531–553; Johnson, Sterling. *Peace Without Justice: Hegemonic Instability or International Criminal Law?* Aldersgate, U.K.: Ashgate Publishing, 2003; Knebel, Johannes. *Hans Joh. Knebels des Kaplans am Münster zu Basel Tagebuch Juni 1476–Juli 1479.* Leipzig, Germany: S. Hirzel, 1887; Levine, Eugenia. "Command Responsibility: The Mens Rea Requirement." *Global Policy Forum* (February 2005). Available online. URL: http://www.globalpolicy.org/component/content/article/163/28306.html. Accessed September 14, 2009; Mitchell, Andrew. "Failure to Halt, Prevent, or Punish: The Doctrine of Command Responsibility for War Crimes." *Sydney Law Review* 22 (2000): 381–388; Schwarzenberger, Georg. "Breisach Revisited: The Hagenbach Trial of 1474." In *Grotian Society Papers, 1968,* edited by C. H. Alexandrowicz, 46–51. The Hague, Netherlands: Martinus Nijhoff, 1970; Vaughan, Richard. *Charles the Bold: the Last Valois Duke of Burgundy.* London: Longman, 1973.

The trials of Girolamo Savonarola

Date: 1498

KEY ISSUES

To advocate reform of the Roman church in the 1400s was to step into trouble. Pointing out that the leader of Western Christendom might be corrupt or overworldly was particularly fraught with danger the closer one was to Rome. No matter how well known the moral failings of pontiffs such as the Borgia popes, even controversial leaders of the church usually had enough clout to bring down their critics.

Girolamo Savonarola refused to temper his anger at several aspects of the papacy, although he also remained a loyal believer in key Catholic doctrines. Savonarola's location—the tumultuous city of Florence—proved another element of his undoing. Site of the machinations of the Medici family and a prime target for foreign intrigue, Florence was a place where someone of great talent could make himself famous. But, fame also might inspire jealousy, especially if a person overstepped his traditional role. When Savonarola succeeded not only as a religious leader but also a political and social figure, he engendered enormous rancor. That ill will was marshaled, in turn, when the papacy wished to quiet him.

HISTORY OF THE CASE

Born into a well-educated family at Ferrara in 1452, young Savonarola decided to follow a religious vocation. Savonarola thought that his family would be disappointed in his career choice for a couple of reasons: His grandfather was an eminent physician who hoped Girolamo would follow in that path, and the young man leaned toward strict religious observances such as were practiced under the Dominicans at Bologna, whereas his family was not particularly devout. He returned to university in Ferrara to round out his studies and then took a teaching position at a local priory.

Savonarola was a capable scholar. He had a thorough understanding of Aristotle's philosophy, which along with other ancient writers he ultimately rejected. To him, the Bible was the sole source of religious inspiration and truth. Savonarola's major writing was *The Triumph of the Cross,* a vivid effort to depict Christ's sacrifice using imagery comprehensible to ordinary people.

In 1482 Savonarola and his colleagues at the priory had to flee to Florence owing to military activity in the area—a contest for Ferrara between the duke of Ferrara and Pope Sixtus IV, who was supported by Venice. Florence was at the height of its fame at the time that Savonarola arrived, with much of its lavish display financed by the regional overlord Lorenzo de' Medici. Lorenzo "the Magnificent" at this time was bankrolling artists such as Leonardo da Vinci, Michelangelo, and Sandro Botticelli. The city looked splendid and had a distinctly secular air. Savonarola found the environment decadent, if not immoral. He set about preaching against the hedonistic atmosphere. His sermons were full of visions of the Apocalypse; he warned that divine judgment would come to Florence if its inhabitants did not cease the pleasures of the flesh. Lorenzo de' Medici did not appreciate the religious lectures.

Savonarola's Dominican superiors decided it would be politic to relocate him for a while, but in 1487 the Dominican official John Pico della Mirandola, who was deeply moved personally by Savonarola's sermons, interceded with Medici to allow Savonarola to return to Florence. Savonarola's growing influence and confidence can be shown through the well-known story about what transpired in 1492 when Lorenzo the Magnificent requested that Savonarola give him the last rites. Savonarola agreed to serve as confessor for Lorenzo, but on three conditions: Medici must repent of his sins, renounce ill-gotten wealth, and "restore the liberties of Firenze [Florence]." When Lorenzo refused to agree to the third demand—ceding his role as Florentine despot—Savonarola let him die unabsolved.

At the priory of San Marco in Florence, Savonarola drew ever-larger crowds with his fire-and-brimstone messages. Among his listeners were political leaders within the Medici family, notably Cosimo de' Medici and his son Piero. Piero had the difficult task of trying to defend Florence against a French assault in 1494; he had to run for his life upon a French victory. Savonarola had become such a force within the city that although it officially surrendered to King Charles VIII of France, the religious figure dictated that the French should allow Florence to govern itself.

Beginning in November 1494, Savonarola was in a unique position within Florence: Although neither an elected official nor a member of the social elite, he was the person to whom all looked for direction. He took the situation as an opportunity to found a Christian republic and remake the city's reputation. He reminded Florentines from his pulpit that Jesus was of humble origin and that Mary, his mother, never would have clothed herself in the ornate fashions of the day. Savonarola proposed that there be a much broader base of political power. A council of thousands should govern rather than a few dozen of the city's wealthiest. When an outbreak of disease hit Florence but spared most of its young people, Savonarola invited the youth of the city to be his most zealous disciples.

Among the other controversial actions that Savonarola undertook was directing his congregants to raid the houses of the wealthy, demanding that they surrender items that were frivolous or luxurious. These articles Savonarola's adherents consigned to the fire in notorious episodes during pre-Lenten periods in 1497 and 1498. Although such "bonfires of the vanities" consumed a number of personal possessions such as valuable clothing, the rumors that they destroyed many great paintings were exaggerated.

Savonarola faced opposition from several groups: Medici partisans who hoped for a return of that family from Venice and elsewhere; certain younger elements within the elite of Florence who found Savonarola too stern; anti-Medici oligarchs; and clerics who disagreed with Savonarola's theology or simply envied him. No less an observer than Niccolò Machiavelli thought Savonarola effective as a leader though personally distasteful. On a few occasions Savonarola's friends and fellow monks literally had to surround him to save him from foes. In the summer of 1497 Savonarola allowed five leaders of a pro-Medici plot to be executed without a full trial and appeal. At that point even some moderates within Florence began to say that Savonarola was too powerful.

Pope Alexander VI was increasingly angry at Savonarola's calls for international conferences concerning the governance of Rome. Savonarola wanted to examine not only the pontiff's election to office—widely thought to be the result of purchase—but also the Holy Father's religious orthodoxy. To some, the powerful priest made an effective case for the deposing of a heretic pope. But, the papacy also distrusted Savonarola as too radical in theology. Pope Alexander tried to coax him into higher office (a cardinalship) and away from direct contact with the common folk with whom he was so influential. Savonarola looked upon the idea of elevation to the College of Cardinals in a characteristically moralistic way: "A red hat?" he supposedly said. "I want a hat of blood." It was becoming clear that Savonarola had a taste for martyrdom. He was not inclined to compromise with either secular or religious authority. Pope Alexander excommunicated Savonarola in 1497 and ordered the leaders of Florence to surrender him upon pain of interdict.

SUMMARY OF ARGUMENTS

In the spring of 1498 a Franciscan monk named Francesco di Puglia lured the followers of Savonarola into an untenable situation. The monk challenged Savonarola to a trial by ordeal, a test of whether the holy man was literally protected from harm by the Almighty. The idea was to have the accused walk along a path surrounded by fire. (It was in a similar ordeal that the crusading monk

Pierre Barthélemy met his end.) If Savonarola was burned or overcome by the smoke, he would be shown as not divinely inspired. Savonarola's critics planned to rig the test against him.

Savonarola resisted the idea, apparently because he perceived the ordeal as a trap. One of his more zealous defenders, Father Domenico, however, jumped at the opportunity to demonstrate his mentor's saintliness and agreed to the display. There was great popular anticipation of the spectacle. The people of Florence had found Savonarola mesmerizing for a time, but it seemed they had adhered to austerity just about long enough.

On April 7, 1498, the trial was set up. Enormous piles of wood stood ready to be burned on either side of a walkway in the Piazza della Signoria. Before it could get under way, however, each side said that it would confirm how the test would be conducted. Savonarola's supporters, smelling a rat, wanted to ensure that their man had some chance of survival. The two main factions (pro-Savonarola Dominicans and anti-Savonarola Franciscans) argued for hours, until a thunderstorm interrupted their disagreement. The wood was wet and thus ruined. There would be no display that day.

The citizens of Florence were angry at the loss of the theatrics. Due to their objections Savonarola had difficulty leaving the scene. By the next morning Savonarola's enemies had whipped the ordinary folk into a riotous rage by contending that Savonarola had interceded with the Almighty to send rain. A mob surrounded the priory of San Marco. Most of Savonarola's clerical colleagues allowed him to be captured; Father Domenico and another brother, Father Silvestro, were hauled off with Savonarola.

VERDICTS

The three men were tortured before and during their civil trial. Domenico never turned on his hero; Silvestro repeatedly implicated Savonarola in whatever crimes the torturers wished. Savonarola broke under the physical duress, but as soon as the torture was stopped for a while, he recanted his "confessions." It made for a messy trial record. The authorities finally decided to have a transcript made up out of whole cloth so that it would appear that Savonarola and his colleagues had admitted being heretics.

By a terrible irony the French king Charles VII died on April 7, the same day as the abortive ordeal by fire. Charles was the only secular leader who would have had any motive to spare Savonarola's life or even campaign for fairer legal treatment. Savonarola's remaining defenders, all far less powerful individuals than the French king, wrote in desperation to Pope Alexander. The pontiff turned down their request for extradition to Rome but did send a panel to hear the case at Florence.

That hearing on May 22, 1498, was in theory a separate religious trial from the earlier proceeding at which the three Dominicans had been convicted of heresy. In effect, however, it was an appeals procedure; Savonarola's only chance at survival was papal intervention. The two-man ecclesiastical panel did include a leading Dominican representative, though even he seemed unwilling to argue for Savonarola. At this trial the defendants once more were tortured, but now Savonarola seemed better able to bear up under the physical pressure. He repeatedly asked divine pardon for having been weak before. The verdict, again, was that the three men should die as heretics.

His admirers, including a priest who sat with him on the night before execution, recorded Savonarola's anguished meditation entitled *Infelix ego*:

> Alas wretch that I am, destitute of all help, who have offended heaven and earth— where shall I go? Whither shall I turn myself? To whom shall I fly? Who will take pity on me? To heaven I dare not lift up my eyes, for I have deeply sinned against it; on earth I find no refuge, for I have been an offence to it. . . .

On April 23 the three men were taken to a central plaza in Florence, stripped of their clerical robes, and hanged; then their bodies were burned and the ashes scattered in the Arno River. Pope Alexander and Savonarola's secular enemies had won in the short term. Soon, though, underground support for Savonarola would surface, especially when calamities befell Florence shortly after his death.

SIGNIFICANCE

Savonarola's admirers have been a diverse lot, both immediately after his execution and in later centuries. Catholic saints from the 1500s and 1600s cited him as an inspiration, as did followers of Martin Luther. In modern times the church in Rome apologized for the severely flawed trial records but did not officially reverse the ecclesiastical courts' verdicts. Nor have efforts to canonize Savonarola found much support within the church hierarchy.

Savonarola condemned the carnality of Florence and "the Borgia pope" Alexander, winning him the admiration of those who sought to turn back the Renaissance, and yet Savonarola counted among his admirers some of the very artists whom the Medici patronized. (Botticelli, for example, may have included positive visual references to Savonarola in such work as his painting *The Mystical Nativity* of 1500). He had harsh words for the moral state of the church while never advocating structural reorganizations. He found supporters among many classes, especially the poor who benefited from the charity programs that he advocated. Ironically, many common people literally helped deliver Savonarola into the hands of the city elite who finally killed him.

Further Reading

Hibbert, Christopher. *The House of Medici, Its Rise and Fall*. New York: Morrow, 1975; Martinez, Lauro. *Fire in the City: Savonarola and the Struggle for the Soul of Renaissance Florence*. Oxford: Oxford University Press, 2007; Munoz, Antonio. *Virtuous Christian or Religious Fanatic: Girolamo Savonarola in Florence, 1494–1498*. Bayside, N.Y.: Europa Books, 2006; Pugliese, Olga Zorzi. "A Last Testimony by Savonarola and His Companions." *Renaissance Quarterly* 34 (1981): 1–10; Seward, Desmond. *The Burning of the Vanities: Savonarola and the Borgia Pope*. Stroud, U.K.: Sutton, 2006; Villari, Pasquale. *Life and Times of Girolamo Savonarola*, translated by Linda White Mazini. New York: Charles Scribner's Sons, 1888.

The trials of Richard Hunne

Date: 1514

KEY ISSUES

The controversy that cost Richard Hunne his life cannot be boiled down to a conflict between church and state. Such a dichotomy would have seemed foreign to people in 16th-century Europe. Still, when criticisms of the church emerged within a particular geographical area, it often was true that secular authorities clashed with powers in the Western Christian Church. For example, when persons who were not priests or monks inveighed against church practices or doctrines, were secular authorities supposed to address the reformers?

It was easy to say in the abstract that church courts should try "religious offenses" and that royal courts should hear crimes against the king. But, sorting out what constituted a religious offense was not always easy. Besides, the church was jealous of its privilege of defining exactly which persons were clerics and thus required judgment by religious authorities. Such questions concerning religious and secular authority were very much under discussion in several places in Europe in the late medieval and early modern eras, but nowhere were they more vigorously debated than in England.

By the early 1500s England had a long history of both anticlericalism and anti-Roman sentiment. Criticism of the clergy as venal, unspiritual, and perhaps even unnecessary had occurred to the English since at least John Wycliffe's time. The actions of Richard Hunne brought such expressions into the open. Eventually, the ideas that Hunne espoused found reinforcement among English political leaders with their own agendas, most particularly, Henry VIII.

Hunne's case also was historically important because it reminded the citizens of England that that nation had well-developed traditions involving trials. The populace took pride in recourse to trial by jury, for example. English citizens relied on the use of coroners' inquiries that decided which deaths involved crimes instead of mere accidents. When church courts threatened to undercut or devalue those long-established legal practices, English people struck back—perhaps less in favor of Hunne than in defense of the concept of a fair trial.

HISTORY OF THE CASE

Hunne was a merchant, often described as a tailor, who lived in London. He reputedly was active in the underground religious community that cherished the legacy of Wycliffe. Hunne had a life crisis that caused him to challenge the church in a public manner. That challenge struck a chord with many English people, appealing far beyond those who identified openly with Wycliffe's views.

When Hunne's infant son died in March 1511, Hunne spoke harshly to a parish priest in Whitechapel, Richard Dryffeld, who demanded that in order for the baby to receive a funeral Hunne had to pay a "mortuary fee" equal to the value of the child's funeral attire. The money itself was not the problem, for Hunne was very well off. The principle, however, seemed to rankle Hunne. His protest to Dryffeld was legalistic: The baby was dead and therefore could not own property. Hunne, in other words, was resting his argument on English common law rather than the customs of the church.

Although Hunne's own voice does not come through clearly in the historical record, scholars have pieced together his views from those around him who did speak more openly. Apparently, Hunne believed that such fees were yet another example of the clergy being callous toward their flock, caring more about lining their own pockets than seeing to spiritual needs. Wycliffe's followers had argued that mortuary fees placed a particular burden on the poor at a time when they already were grieving; therefore, the fees were not only unnecessary and unsupported by scripture but also cruel.

Hunne's argument with the priest resulted in his being called to explain himself in a spiritual court. There was some confusion about the venue in which the case should have been heard. Although a court under the jurisdiction of the archbishop of Canterbury ruled against him, in part because

Hunne failed to appear at the appointed location, the presiding official at that hearing, Cuthbert Tunstall, seemed willing to let Hunne simply pay the disputed amount. Since Hunne did not appear to hear that ruling, however, the church's case against him went formally unresolved for several months. In December 1512 Hunne tried to attend mass, and another priest named Henry Marshall recognized him as he entered the church. Marshall then took the drastic step of stopping the church service and calling out Hunne as an excommunicate. Hunne exited the sanctuary and consulted with a lawyer.

SUMMARY OF ARGUMENTS

Hunne argued that he had not been officially expelled from the church and, therefore, the priest's public denunciation of him was slander. He went forward with a suit for defamation in a royal court in January 1513, naming not only Marshall and Dryffeld but also Charles Joseph, the man who delivered the summons for Hunne to appear in church court, and Archbishop of Canterbury William Warham and his auditor, the hearing officer Tunstall. Hunne intended his legal action to involve issues much wider than his angry exchanges with the local clerics.

Hunne drew out the scope of the discussion considerably when in the course of his suit he mentioned *praemunire* (the refusal to have recourse to papal courts in preference to royal ones) and cited Warham in particular, for Warham was the papal representative (legate) to England. Hunne's evoking the principle of praemunire (established in statutory form in 1353) called into question the legitimacy of religious courts in England. Hunne maintained that the church in England had no right to try him because such a prosecution necessarily would involve an appeal to church authority outside England; thus, the church's action against him was contrary to the Statute of Praemunire.

Hunne was on dangerous ground in taking such an argument to the Court of King's Bench. Although they were secular figures, that court's judges were also employees of Warham, who wore another hat besides that of Canterbury. Warham also was lord chancellor of England, the king's key legal adviser. Thus, Hunne proposed to convince his judges that their secular superior, Warham, was

acting contrary to the Statute of Praemunire when he employed his legatine status. The royal judges delayed for months, hoping that Hunne might back down. They also had some expectation that Parliament—which was heatedly discussing limitations for clerical status in court—might act in a manner that somehow would remove them from their untenable position in Hunne's case.

The church reacted sternly to Hunne's suit. A raid authorized by the bishop of London in October supposedly turned up at Hunne's house a Bible in English translation with annotations clearly marking it as a banned book. The bishop of London charged Hunne with heresy in November of 1514 and detained him in a cell at St. Paul's Cathedral in a holding area that was nicknamed "the Lollards' Tower." Whether the Bible that the church produced at trial actually was found in Hunne's house is a matter of some debate among historians. On balance, though, it would not have been improbable for a person of Hunne's wealth and convictions to possess such a volume. That Bible became the key piece of evidence against Hunne. At trial he refused to give clear answers in court as to his views, but the Bible's introductory matter contained ideas that the church regarded as heretical. For instance, the Wycliffe Bible contained expressions of cynicism about transubstantiation.

The conditions of Hunne's incarceration were harsh. His jailors denied him contact with the outside, often shackled him, kept him on a short diet, and refused to let him change clothes. There is some evidence to indicate that at a hearing on December 2, 1414, Hunne was about to break down and admit he held heretical opinions. If he had done so, he might have expected to do penance and that that would suffice. The day of the hearing was a Saturday, however, and the court adjourned for the Sabbath before either Hunne or his accusers came to any final resolution of the case.

VERDICT

On Monday, December 4, Hunne was found dead in his cell. His jailors said he had committed suicide, but immediately rumors began to circulate that something else was amiss. On December 6 a jury under the direction of coroner Thomas Barnwell began to investigate the situation, going so far as to take a tour of the cell to examine the scene of Hunne's death. The jurors saw Hunne's body still hanging, suspended by a silk belt or girdle, but when they pushed the body slightly it came out of the noose easily. Hunne's hands appeared to have been bound recently, although they were not restricted as he hung in the air. A stool was too far away for him to have used it to elevate himself. A bloody shirt was crumpled in a corner. Persons who were hanged often bled from the nose and mouth and had loose bowels, but the clothes on Hunne's body were clean.

The church continued to hear testimony about Hunne after his demise. These religious proceedings, directed by Bishop of London Richard Fitzjames, were a continuation of the ongoing heresy case. The other members of the judicial panel (for there were no juries in church courts) also were bishops, Thomas Young and John Longland. To the other counts against Hunne, Bishop Fitzjames added the charge that Hunne had died through suicide. On December 10 Fitzjames warned anyone who might possess a Bible like Hunne's to immediately confess his or her sins or else risk prosecution for heresy.

Fitzjames engaged in a condemnation of Hunne after death for several reasons. If Hunne were officially declared a heretic not only would it serve as an example to other Lollards, but Hunne's considerable estate would be forfeited. Most of the evidence presented at the posthumous church trial strains credibility among modern scholars; more important, it seemed improbable at the time. When Londoners heard testimony, for example, that Hunne had related his views on the Bible to Bishop Young, that testimony must have convinced almost no one. Hunne, though opinionated, was far too savvy to have discoursed on a combustible subject with a bishop.

Even in an era when justice was heavily weighted on the side of authority, the religious condemnation of Hunne seemed unfair—if not illegal—to many observers. On December 20 Hunne's body was burned. According to the judgment of the church court, Hunne was a heretic, and his death, a suicide. Among ordinary persons' objections to the church's actions was their understanding that the usual church practice with regard to heresy had not been followed in this case. Had

Hunne been alive at the conclusion of the church trial, though technically a heretic, he would have been entitled to an opportunity to repent. Only as a lapsed heretic was he supposed to have been consigned to the flames. The net effect of the trial and especially the burning of Hunne's body were not at all as Fitzjames had intended. The episodes raised Londoners' ire and made them even more interested in what the coroner's court would find.

The public in London seemed to believe that Hunne was murdered on the orders of Fitzjames. The coroner's court heard a stream of witnesses that reconstructed events between the last time that Hunne appeared in court and the discovery of his body. The coroner's jury centered their attention on three individuals, all in the employ of the bishop of London: Dr. William Horsey, the bishop's chancellor; Charles Joseph, the summoner (process server for Horsey and Fitzjames); and the bell ringer–prison guard John Spalding. The coroner and jury heard testimony that was very damaging to the bishop's cause, including an account of Horsey's visiting Hunne on December 3 and offering him what seemed to be last rites. Several witnesses said that Joseph's behavior was suspicious during the weekend before Hunne's death. For instance, just prior to December 4 both Spalding and Joseph had seemed anxious to spread the word that Hunne looked suicidal to them.

In early February, while the coroner's inquest still was meeting, Parliament was considering legislation that would have abolished clerical status for persons whom the church traditionally had called clerics—individuals who were employees of the church but not ordained. In the midst of that debate Bishop Fitzjames made a lengthy and emotional statement against tightening up on benefit of clergy. It was an argument most relevant to the coroner's inquest, for two of the persons that the jury was investigating—Joseph and Spalding—were in that gray area of clerical status. Fitzjames's remarks to Parliament, in other words, may have been an effort to save his henchmen.

The coroner's court returned indictments against all three men: Spalding, Joseph, and Horsey. Now thoroughly alarmed at the situation, Fitzjames composed a letter (which survives) to Thomas Wolsey, begging for intervention from Henry VIII before the case for murder could be thoroughly adjudicated in the Court of King's Bench. It is almost certain that the monarch sent word to his judicial appointees to acquit the men. The royal judges obliged. The coroner's court continued its investigations, though, for at least several months and perhaps more than a year. The Hunne affair had become a grievance among not only Lollards but also anyone who was concerned that the church had engaged in criminal conduct. Worse, the actions of the bishop of London seemed to indicate an anxiety to move quickly, to avoid secular inquiries.

SIGNIFICANCE

Scholars point out that Henry VIII was greatly affected by the Hunne controversy in several ways. On the most mundane level the government received several petitions for a restoration of Hunne's estate to his family. The king, however, saw an opportunity to be perceived as dispensing justice in line with the coroner's investigation while enriching himself. In 1523 he declared Horsey to have been guilty of misconduct in the case. The monarch ordered Horsey to personally repay the money that had been forfeited—but to royal coffers rather than Hunne's heirs.

Hunne's argument about praemunire was a line of thought that the king resurrected in his struggles with Rome beginning in the late 1520s. In particular, the monarch seemed troubled by the conflict of interest that arose when one royal councilor served both the Crown (as lord chancellor) and Rome (as legate). This was in part what inspired Henry VIII to distrust Thomas Wolsey even after Wolsey's many years of service—the nagging fear that Wolsey would choose to put the church first in a crisis.

Perhaps an even greater legacy of the Hunne case was its lingering effect on Londoners. It underlined the fact that Lollardy had survived among diverse elements of the English population, despite the efforts of the church to stamp out such heresies. The English Protestant historian and activist John Foxe overestimated the existence of Lollardy among Londoners, therefore influencing future readers to believe that Hunne was more representative than he was. Still, it is clear that when Henry VIII and certain other English leaders

launched their critique of church corruption in the late 1520s, they found a receptive audience among some who recalled the Hunne affair. Hunne may have lashed out simply because of the loss of his son, but his trial resonated with many who already were or would yet become disillusioned with Rome.

Further Reading

Cooper, W. R. "Richard Hunne." Available online. URL: http://www.tyndale.org/Reformation/1/cooper.html. Accessed September 25, 2009; Dickens, A. G. *The English Reformation.* New York: Schocken Books, 1964; Marius, Richard. *Thomas More: A Biography.* New York: Knopf, 1984; McBride, Gordon K. "Once Again, the Case of Richard Hunne." *Albion* 1 (1969): 19–29; Ogle, Arthur. *The Tragedy of the Lollard's Tower.* Oxford, U.K.: Pen-in-Hand, 1949; Smart, S. J. "John Foxe and 'The Story of Richard Hun, Martyr.'" *Journal of Ecclesiastical History* 37 (1986): 1–14.

The trial of Martin Luther

Date: 1521

KEY ISSUES

In the history of Protestantism there is no more pivotal figure than Martin Luther. No point in Luther's life was more decisive than his trial at Worms. Redirecting or silencing Luther hardly would have stopped criticisms of the church at Rome. Such criticism was far too deep seated and widespread for officials in Rome to turn back. But, if Luther had recanted his beliefs and writings when formally challenged at Worms in a trial requested by Roman Catholic authorities, Protestantism might have taken a very different course.

The western Christian Church was the target of critics on many fronts long prior to the early 1500s. Among the more important lines of argument aimed at the church were that it did not stamp out immorality among clergy, and church personnel were vital figures because church doctrine emphasized the role of priests as intercessors with the Almighty. The church frowned upon laypeople's reading the Bible and thus on vernacular versions of Christian Scripture. It was important to church authorities that individuals not assert that they were in direct contact with the divine; that was one of the church's key condemnations of Joan of Arc. Rome insisted that supposedly divine revelations to individuals too easily could be the work of darker forces, so the church often punished persons who said that they had talked with the deity.

The church was an enormously wealthy institution at the dawn of the 16th century. Its most public face was Rome itself, which church leaders such as the Florentine popes rebuilt. Granted, the edifices and interiors of St. Peter's were executed by the finest talents of the days such as Michelangelo, but those masterpieces came at exorbitant expense. The church increasingly turned to unusual methods of finance, justified by the flimsiest theologies. Means of raising revenue such as the selling of indulgences (which the common folk often thought meant remission of time in Purgatory for departed souls) were targets for reformers.

Rome sought to quash actions and doctrines that it considered to be in error. Even private individuals who were accused of heresy faced inquisitors such as Spain's Tomás de Torquemada, named grand inquisitor by Pope Innocent VIII in 1487. Persons that spread allegedly heretical thoughts too widely, such as Jan Hus of Bohemia and John Wycliffe of England, found themselves prosecuted and their writings banned. Groups that the church opposed included the Cathars, the Waldensians, and the Lollards, which all of which Rome sternly suppressed.

Luther's insistence that he would continue writing and preaching doctrines that the Christian Church in Rome considered anathema was no doubt personally courageous. His comment, "Here I stand . . ." is one of the best-known assertions of conscience and religious protest in world history. What gave Luther the wherewithal to take on a 1,500-year-old institution? In part, Luther was spurred on by anguished, deeply personal reflec-tion, but he also was aided by the political situation in his homeland.

Specifically, the protection of the elector of Saxony and indecision of the Holy Roman Emperor kept Luther safe at key moments. Germany was too important to Rome for the church to write off, and so the church had to deal with Luther's patrons. The allure of Luther's ideas among more ordinary folk also was undeniable. His popularity, that is, pushed political leaders to consider carefully how they proceeded against him.

HISTORY OF THE CASE

Like many scholarly young men in the early modern era in Europe, Martin Luther considered a career in the church an attractive prospect. The church, after all, provided lifetime job security, the finest education, and plenty of opportunity for intellectual discourse. He was a dutiful son, however, so he heeded his father's wishes to study law. As an 18-year-old, Luther enrolled at the University of Erfurt in 1501. He literally received a jolt of consciousness, though, that intensified his desire to be a priest: He was hit by lightning and immediately decided to take orders as an Augustinian monk. A studious and self-reflective person, Luther in the monastery found himself troubled by what he saw as the free spending of the church and the licentiousness of its clerics.

Through his study and teaching about the Bible at the University of Wittenberg, Luther became focused on certain key portions of the Christian Scriptures, especially the letters of the apostle Paul. In Luther's mind Paul emphasized the role of grace in salvation. Luther went public in late October 1517 with a list of doctrines and practices of the Roman Catholic Church that he considered fallacious—a critique known as his Ninety-five Theses. The Ninety-five Theses may not actually have been nailed to the castle church door in Wittenberg on All Saints' Day (October 31) in 1517. The rumor that they had been posted, though, probably was as important as that event actually having occurred. Luther already had broadcast his views widely in sermons and pamphlets.

At this same time Luther put his arguments in a letter to the bishop of Mainz and Magdeburg—

an action at least as provocative as tacking them up. The Ninety-five Theses were inflammatory in a theological sense. They also were written in language not calculated to smooth over disagreements with Rome. According to Luther, priestly intercession was not necessary; believers could read the Bible for themselves. He maintained that the church placed too much emphasis on faith supplemented with good works. Luther would turn the focus to divine grace that made faith possible—his concept of "justification by faith." He also contended that a focus on papal authority led Christians away from the truth that was found in the Bible.

The papacy leaned on Luther's superiors, both ecclesiastical and political, to quiet him. In August 1518 Pope Leo X threatened to require Luther to travel to Rome to have his ideas examined. Luther's key German protector, Frederick of Saxony, negotiated for Luther to be questioned closer to home by Thomas Cardinal Cajetan, the papal legate (emissary) to the Holy Roman Emperor. Luther's words had excited concern of the highest order, but the pope wanted to placate powerful Germans, so Luther would undergo examination, but under German auspices.

Luther's appearance before Cajetan at Augsburg in October 1518 failed to cow the German monk. Indeed, it was the papacy that blinked first. In a bull of November 1518, Pope Leo permitted the sale of indulgences to continue, yet admitted that indulgences had been improperly employed by the clergy and misunderstood by the public. In another series of angry communications between Germany and Rome, Luther pressed for his concerns to be aired either at a debate presided over by a university or under the direction of a political authority, the newly elected Holy Roman Emperor Charles V.

In 1520 Rome had had enough. Through the papal bull *Exsurge Domine,* Luther was warned that he would be excommunicated unless he retracted key points of his theology. Most of those core criticisms by Luther were expressed in the Ninety-five Theses; he then had fleshed out his arguments in a series of writings in 1520. Luther's comparison of papal authority to the biblical description of the Babylonian captivity was especially polarizing. The argument in Luther's *The Babylonian Captivity* that the Bible would support the mystical nature of only two of the church's sacraments inspired a passionate "Defense of the Seven Sacraments" from England's Henry VIII and Thomas More. The papal bull and its follow-up—actual excommunication—did not quite equal a charge of heresy, but they could pave the way for it.

The rhetoric on both sides often was shockingly coarse. Luther called the majority of Catholic priests a "whole filthy pack of asses." He referred to Rome's doctrines as "the sludge of the harlot's lies and whoring." Even a churchman of high intellectual standing like More stooped to call Luther "a pimp, an apostate, a rustic, and a friar."

In December 1520 Luther literally set fire to the papal bull. Charles V, frustrated at being placed in the middle of an unwinnable debate, did very much the same to Luther's letters appealing to him as "Caesar." Against the instincts of Charles and the better judgment of Rome, however, both agreed that Luther would be examined again in Germany. This time, rather than being questioned formally by the Holy See, the authorities that would determine Luther's fate were secular figures.

SUMMARY OF ARGUMENTS

A gathering for the governance of the Holy Roman Empire was called a diet. The particular diet that heard Luther's complaints against the church and the church's complaints about Luther met at Worms, in Saxony. It was Luther's home territory, where he had both governmental and popular support.

In effect, though not in form, the Diet of Worms was a trial of Luther. If he proved convincing to those in authority or showed that he had deep popular support, then Luther might be allowed to continue to write and preach. If he insulted the political leaders who managed the proceedings, or while under their protection spoke too boldly against Rome, they might disavow him and turn him over to the good offices of the church.

Luther left two full recollections of his appearance at Worms in April 1521. In those autobiographical accounts he concentrated on the arguments that he put forward as well as the physical danger he faced. He was entering a venue where papal partisans made no apologies for detesting him. During two days of hearings Luther sparred with his critics in the church and those political authorities who saw him (at best) as troublesome. He clearly was under strain, but though he did ask for time to consider some of the church's charges, he did not buckle. He specified that some of his contentions merely were exhortations to good conduct among believers while others were direct criticisms of Rome. Luther said that he would consider recanting some of his views, but if only the church could convince him he was misinformed about Scripture:

> . . . since I am a man and not God, I cannot provide my writings with any other defense than that which my Lord Jesus Christ provided for His teaching. When He had been interrogated concerning His teaching before Annas . . . He said: "If I have spoken evil, bear witness of the evil." If the Lord Himself, who knew that He could not err, did not refuse to listen to witness against His teaching, even from a worthless slave, how much more ought I, scum that I am, capable of naught but error, to seek and to wait for any who may wish to bear witness against my teaching.

At the end of the second day of disputation, the archbishop of Trier made a quite plausible appeal to Luther. How could Luther be certain that he was correct and that the church, which had stood for more than a millennium, was wrong? Why was Luther different from anyone who took issue with the church due to obstinacy or error?

> Your plea to be heard from the Scripture is the one always made by heretics. You do nothing but renew the errors of Wyclif and Hus. How will the Jews, how will the Turks, exult to hear Christians discussing whether they have been wrong all these years! Martin, how can you assume that you are the only one to understand the sense of Scripture? Would you put your judgment above that of so many famous men and claim that you know more than they all? You have no right to call into question the most holy orthodox faith, instituted by Christ the per-

fect lawgiver, proclaimed throughout the world by the apostles, sealed by the red blood of martyrs, confirmed by the sacred councils, defined by the Church in which all our fathers believed until death and gave us as an inheritance, and which now we are forbidden by the pope and the emperor to discuss lest there be no end of debate. I ask you, Martin—answer candidly and without horns—do you or do you not repudiate your books and the errors which they contain?

Luther's answer was justifiably famous:

> Your Imperial Majesty and Your Lordships demand a simple answer. Here it is, plain and unvarnished. Unless I am convicted of error by the testimony of Scripture or (since I put no trust in the unsupported authority of Pope or councils, since it is plain that they have often erred and often contradicted themselves) by manifest reasoning, I stand convicted by the Scriptures to which I have appealed, and my conscience is taken captive by God's word, I cannot and will not recant anything, for to act against our conscience is neither safe for us, nor open to us.
>
> On this I take my stand. I can do no other. God help me.

VERDICT

The formal finding at Worms was against Luther. The emperor Charles was not only a son of Spain, a most Catholic nation; he was politically linked to Rome and would go out of his way to appease the Holy See. The Edict of Worms (published in early May 1521) restated all of the church's objections to Luther's views, particularly those he had voiced in the Ninety-five Theses. Despite the fact that the discourse at the diet often was elevated, the wording of the edict was more practical:

> To put an end to the numberless and endless errors of the said Martin, let us say that it seems that this man, Martin, is not a man but a demon in the appearance of a man, clothed in religious habit to be better able to deceive mankind, and wanting to gather the heresies of several heretics who have already

been condemned, excommunicated, and buried in hell for a long time.

The Edict of Worms also emphasized the fear that political disobedience would follow from a widespread acceptance of such heresy. Luther's books were to be burned, as were the writings of his supporters. Censorship would be mandatory: City authorities and university theologians (and not those infected with the Lutheran heresy) were to approve writings on religion. The Diet of Worms condemned Luther for the crime of high treason against the emperor. The penalty was the loss of his life and his property. As in the case of other traitors and heretics, his possessions were to be sold with half of the proceeds given to the church.

Yet, there was a problem in enforcing the Edict of Worms: Between the time that the diet finished examining Luther and the edict's publication, Luther had disappeared. As he rode away from the diet, Luther's friends and supporters staged a kidnapping, which in fact was a rescue. They spirited him away to Wartburg Castle, the home of Frederick the Wise, elector of Saxony. Their hope was that Luther's political patrons could buy some time, either to allow tensions with Rome to dissipate or to build further political and popular support for Luther.

Luther went into a kind of internal exile. He was protected from those who might wish to try him in Rome and perhaps silence him permanently. Most critical was the support of the elector Frederick, who seemed motivated largely by a sense of Luther's widening popularity. The danger that Luther faced after he had been condemned at Worms seemed to embolden him intellectually. Luther's literary output in the 10 months of his stay at Wartburg Castle was prodigious, including a widely influential translation of the Bible into German. Beyond his theological arguments expressed in prose, his authorship of several hymns, most famously "A Mighty Fortress is our God," alone would have made him a noteworthy religious writer. Luther's critics failed to predict the lasting musical or literary value of his work; for instance, Henry VIII of England called Luther's songs "tavern tunes."

Luther himself argued that he was no saint, and scholars who have studied his life agree that he was a complex person and theorist. His marriage to a former nun in 1525 provided fodder for those who termed him too worldly. More modern theologians located distinctly negative strains in Luther's views, most notably an element of anti-Semitism. Even Luther's admirers could be bitterly disappointed in him. At no time was that more the case than immediately after his triumph over the emperor Charles. Allowed to preach in Wittenberg, he won more and more adherents to his views—so many, in fact, that large numbers of the German peasantry cited him as their inspiration during a rebellion in 1524. He advised them to "render unto Caesar," however, effectively undercutting their position and emboldening the authorities to suppress the revolt with severity.

In a larger sense, though, Luther's appeal to secular authority in 1525 was consistent with his earlier positions. He had pushed for a consideration of his case in Germany and then at the Diet of Worms. He had insisted, in other words, that Rome should not have the right to try him. His forcing of Rome's hand in that manner was a powerful legacy. Luther's trial was the first major instance in which a critic of the church in Rome had thwarted Roman control over such fundamental issues. Luther lost at Worms only in the most technical sense.

SIGNIFICANCE

Acceptance of reformist religious ideas was aided by the political fractures in Luther's homeland and in Europe generally. In 1526 the Diet of the Holy Roman Empire decided that Luther would be left alone if he remained within his region; an edict from the Diet of Speyer limited enforcement of the Edict of Worms to firmly Catholic territories. That containment did not endure. In 1529 a group of secular elites declared themselves in protest against Rome and Roman influence; they were religiously and politically "Protestant." Some of their motivation to break with Rome was religious, but they also were inspired by the wish to avoid paying Rome tributes from their faraway locales. Also, among certain political leaders and in certain nations there was the longstanding argument against Rome's efforts to influence politics. This was especially the case in France, with its tradition of antipapalism that was centuries old, and in England, where Henry VIII's condemnation of Rome had historical, theological, and personal roots.

In the mid-1500s other religious leaders such as John Knox and John Calvin developed interpretations of Christian Scripture. They inspired the building of communities of faith that owed much to Luther and yet broke with even him on key theological points. Faced with the threat of losing parts of its flock to Protestants, the church in Rome reinvented itself. Roman Catholicism saw a revitalization of devotion among many followers. The church used the term *Catholic Reformation,* rather than *Counter-Reformation,* to describe its reform movement in the mid-1500s. The church argued it was not reacting to an external threat such as Lutheranism but rather proceeding along its own path of growth. Groups such as the Society of Jesus, led by Ignatius Loyola, insisted that they were engaging in housecleaning and reinvigoration that would have occurred without Luther.

The diplomatic arrangement known as the Peace of Augsburg in 1555 established the principle that "as a prince worships, so shall his people." It was an acknowledgment that Lutheranism would not be eradicated. Luther's ideas gave rise to the particular Protestant group that bore his name—a major denomination throughout the world and especially in northern Europe and the United States. Those ideas also fueled other critics of the church in Rome, critics who diverged from Luther in some respects but certainly had common roots. Martin Luther did not begin the Protestant Reformation, but he certainly gave it a hard push.

Further Reading

Bainton, Roland. *Here I Stand.* Abington, U.K.: Cokesbury Press, 1950; Erickson, Erik. *Young Man Luther.* New York: Norton, 1958; Furey, Constance. "Invective and Discernment in Martin Luther, D. Erasmus, and Thomas More." *Harvard Theological Review* 98 (2005): 469–488; Luther, Martin. *Opera Latina.* Frankfurt, Germany: Heyder & Zimmer, 1865–73. Marius, Richard. *Martin Luther: The Christian Between God and Death.* Cambridge, Mass.: Belknap Press of Harvard University Press, 1999; Mendelssohn, Felix. Symphony no. 5 in D Minor, op. 107 ("Reformation").

The trial of Thomas More

Date: 1535

KEY ISSUES

If Thomas More could not save himself in an English court, no one else could have expected justice in 1535. Trained as a lawyer, More had served as England's lord chancellor. He was a key adviser to King Henry VIII on legal affairs. Prior to that appointment More had worked for the interests of the monarchy in a number of capacities, including conducting diplomacy and directing prosecutions. Adding weight to his political roles was his status as one of the best-known intellectuals in Europe. More was a participant in critical debates over the power of the papacy, a humanist intellectual admired by Erasmus of Rotterdam and John Colet, and the widely known author of works such as *Utopia* (1516) and the *History of Richard III* (1518). He ranked with the best minds of his generation, although his positions were not always either as consistent or as modern as later admirers would contend.

More's trial has been conveyed in books both scholarly and popular, such as Robert Bolt's stage play *A Man for All Seasons.* The trial is well documented from several perspectives, including those of foreign observers. Europe watched somewhat in shock as Henry VIII dispatched not only More but also Bishop John Fisher and, eventually, the queen Anne Boleyn. There remain several murky questions concerning the testimony that convicted More. Most scholars conclude that More's trial was technically legitimate while being deeply flawed in an ethical sense.

The events that led immediately to More's prosecution, trial, and execution had to do with the king's matrimonial state. The king wished to secure an annulment of his marriage to Catherine of Aragon, his wife of more than 20 years, so that he could marry Anne Boleyn. Henry VIII insisted that he had determined to "put away" Catherine out of a crisis of conscience. He maintained that he had been tortured by the lack of a male heir from his and Catherine's union. He had reflected and prayed, asking for divine guidance as to what could cause such a calamity upon the Tudor line. The Almighty had answered him, Henry said, with the revelation that it was neither he nor Catherine personally that was to blame but rather the fact of their marrying at all.

Catherine was the widow of Henry's brother, Arthur, who was the heir to the throne of Henry VII. Their marriage was the product of a protracted, delicate, and expensive international negotiation between Henry VII and the comonarchs of Spain, Ferdinand and Isabella, culminating in the Treaty of Medina del Campo (1489). The marriage took place in late 1501, but Arthur died in 1502 before ever becoming king. What was Henry VII's court to do with an extra Spanish princess? The simplest solution was to let her marry the other son of Henry VII, Prince Hal (Henry). Hal had not been groomed to be the next king. He had been a studious sort and nursed some aspirations to church administration, yet he understood his duty to step into his brother's position as Prince of Wales.

Neither Catherine nor Henry raised objections to the marriage plan at the time. Catherine probably was used to her role as a tool of diplomacy, and Henry was fond of his former sister-in-law. There was one technical matter to be addressed by the church, however, before the marriage went forward: According to church law, when people married, they became one, so in the church's eyes a person who married a brother- or sister-in-law was committing incest. Other canon lawyers countered that a scripture in Deuteronomy contradicted what had seemed a prohibition on such "incestuous" unions according to Leviticus. Deuteronomy, the later text, admonished men whose brothers had died without heirs to wed their brothers' widows in order to continue the family line.

It was possible, in other words, to argue with the Levitical ban, and for years theologians had posed just such an argument in the abstract. But, in the case of Henry and Catherine's proposed marriage, it was not necessary to ask the Holy See for a ruling on whether Leviticus or Deuteronomy was superior. Catherine declared that it could be a simpler matter entirely, because the marriage to Arthur had not been consummated. In that case it was an easy decision for Rome. Catherine and Arthur never had been married if there had been no physical union, so she and Henry could marry without impediment. Just to make certain that no one raised an eyebrow later, though, the papacy issued a dispensation stating that the marriage between Henry and Catherine was allowable. The ceremony took place in 1509, and the marriage continued until the king's conscience supposedly began to trouble him in the late 1520s. The king argued that it was before he met Anne Boleyn that he had had the revelatory conversation with the Almighty; cynics reversed the order of those events.

Whatever Henry VIII's motives were, once he made up his mind to marry Boleyn, his timing was extraordinarily poor. Other monarchs had cast aside their first wives while availing themselves of the argument that their initial marriages had been prohibited on grounds of consanguinity, or close-blood relationship. The church for hundreds of years had tolerated the practice as long as wealthy individuals (usually men) had bothered to raise at least a pretext for such annulments. Those petitioners to church authorities also had to be willing to pay canon lawyers and sit through a process that could take years in church courts.

Henry VIII's problem with that long-established system for securing an annulment was that he did not want to wait. He had known Anne Boleyn for several years already. She had refused to be his mistress, holding out for marriage. Henry normally would have depended on his chief adviser, Thomas Cardinal Wolsey, to negotiate the intricacies of the annulment with Rome. Wolsey was papal legate as well as Henry VIII's lord chancellor. He was immensely talented and extraordinarily well connected throughout Europe and especially in Rome. He had managed difficult situations for the king before. But Wolsey faced particular problems in this instance because at almost exactly the time that the king of England approached Rome for assistance in "the King's Great Matter," as the euphemism went, the Holy Roman Emperor Charles V controlled most of Italy. Charles did not relish the thought of his aunt, Catherine of Aragon, being declared an adulteress and her daughter, Mary Tudor, a bastard.

Rome stalled, hoping that the situation would resolve itself. Perhaps Henry would grow tired of Anne Boleyn, or she of him, or perhaps she would agree to live with him without marriage or another solution could be worked out. Papal representatives floated the idea, for example, that they would countenance the marriage of an illegitimate son of Henry and Elizabeth Blount to Henry's daughter with Catherine of Aragon. The son, the earl of Richmond, would be the consort of an unquestionably legitimate monarch, Mary Tudor. That these young people were half brother and sister did not seem troubling to the papal lawyers. Henry, though, saw it as an imperfect solution and rejected it out of hand. He dismissed any suggestions short of what was being called, popularly, "the divorce."

The king already had lost patience with Wolsey, but the lord chancellor died in 1529 before the king could have him tried and executed. The monarch turned to other advisers to help in securing what he wanted. No one really was a substitute for Wolsey, but Henry certainly leaned heavily on certain tested administrators and friends to help. He enlisted the support of not only Thomas Cromwell, Wolsey's former assistant, and the theologian Thomas Cranmer but also Thomas More. Above other advisers, those individuals had the connections and talent to help the king both gauge and influence opposition.

HISTORY OF THE CASE

The king requested that the church within England facilitate the annulment. Wary of acting without full cooperation from the Holy See, English church leaders took their cue from Rome and tried to delay a final resolution. Papal representative Lorenzo Cardinal Campeggio journeyed to England to investigate the situation.

As the months dragged into years, Henry determined that he would have to put pressure on both Rome and the English church. He was assisted in that plan by the fact that church lands and money were a great prize. English legislators and the citizenry generally had a history of resisting papal collections, for example, with the Statute of Praemunire (1353). How much more attractive was the possibility of England's magnates gaining permanent control of the valuable land that had

not been out of church hands for a thousand years? If an English person already was upset about venal clergy or had a theological pull toward Lollardy or Lutheranism, then his or her motive was even stronger for consenting to Henry's strong-arming of the church.

Did Henry intend to establish Protestantism in England? Absolutely not. Did some of those who supported his nationalization of the monasteries have such a view? Certainly, although many of the members of Parliament who went along with the king in "the King's Great Matter" simply coveted the property and resources of the church. Those were the rationales behind laws such as the Act of Succession (1534), the Act in Restraint of Appeals (1533), and the Act of Supremacy (1534). The purpose of Henry's introduction of the laws was clear: The king meant to get his way on the divorce, and he would take the country with him if Rome failed to permit it. And yet, there were many who objected passionately to that trajectory, however powerful the momentum (religious, reformist, pecuniary, personal) was in favor of the king. None who stood in the king's way was more articulate than More.

More had agreed to take on the chancellorship after Wolsey's fall from grace, saying to Henry that he wanted to prove himself a loyal servant of the king and to help, specifically, with legal matters. More's critics saw it as an effort on More's part to enforce religious orthodoxy at a time (1529) when Lutheranism was becoming influential in Europe. More wanted to keep Protestantism out of England, and the chancellorship would be a fine position from which to exercise control over the spread of heresy. In 1529 More published one of his most stinging commentaries on religion, the *Dialogue Concerning Heresies,* a rebuttal aimed at both Martin Luther and the Englishman William Tyndale. Some servants of the Crown such as Cranmer distrusted More precisely because of More's reverence for Rome. Increasingly kept out of general discussions among the king's Privy Council, More focused his duties as chancellor on the issue of heresy. He oversaw several prosecutions that resulted in execution during the years 1529 and 1530.

To be near the throne, though, meant being dragged into the King's Great Matter. While More was sure he could avoid that involvement, Henry VIII grew restive. The king required active support and particularly desired a vocal defense of the monarch's position from a man of international reputation. Under pressure to resign More stepped down as chancellor. He risked further trouble by refusing to attend the coronation of Anne Boleyn in 1533. He narrowly escaped entanglement in the prosecution of Elizabeth Barton, the "Holy Maid of Kent," who with several others espousing a pro-Roman position was tried and executed in early 1534. Henry VIII had tried to get Parliament to state that More had directed Barton's words. The lawmakers refused to believe that More would have been so rash and dropped More's name from their condemnation of Barton. The affair clearly demonstrated Henry's ire toward More.

SUMMARY OF ARGUMENTS

On April 17, 1534, More was sent to the Tower of London on a charge of denying the king's authority by refusing to take an oath supporting the Act of Succession. He was held in the Tower for more than a year with only limited outside contact, purposefully kept away from his family. For a while it looked as though such conditions might backfire on the king, for More actually had relished the thought of a monastic life in his younger days. More secretly wore a hair shirt to mortify the flesh and for a while thrived on deprivation. He also welcomed the asceticism of confinement as a release from the pressures of court life. The longer he stayed in the Tower, though, the more frequently he wrestled with the possibility that he could not do anything to save himself. Such reflections are evident in his prison manuscript *The Sadness of Christ*.

The physical conditions of confinement took a toll on More, as did occasional sessions of questioning by his accusers, led by Cromwell. Though the Tower was a notorious site for tortures such as the rack, those who administered inducements to confess found that less obvious methods frequently were preferable. Especially in the case of an eminent prisoner, it might not do to leave marks on his body. Besides, mental deprivation and confusion could produce devastating breakdowns of will.

His captors predicted quite correctly that More would not change his mind in prison and certainly would not buckle at trial. They hoped, however, to catch him in a mistake if they kept querying him under untenable circumstances. Did they trap him into making a rash statement while he was under questioning, or did they simply give up and manufacture incriminating words? The answer may not be discoverable. At any rate the case against More went forward to trial—and concluded—on July 1, 1535.

More's trial occurred in a very public setting. The venue was one reserved for persons of noble status: the hall at Westminster Palace, where More had received his chancellor's chain only a few years earlier. More had the right to be tried by his "peers"—the barons who had forced John I to assent to Magna Carta had ensured that right centuries before. But, having jurors who were "peers" was not the same as having "impartial jurors." This was a panel of jurymen who were in fact quite the opposite of unbiased. In fact, the elevated social rank of this panel worked against More, for these were persons who had already bought in to Henry VIII's actions. Among the panel was Anne Boleyn's father. Though the jury might admire More's intellect, respect his legal skill, and even like him personally, they could not see why he refused to trim his sails to the political winds as they had done. It is vital to note that very few of the jury cared much about More's or Henry's theology. Fifteen judges presided.

More defended himself and very ably. The usual rule was that a defendant was not allowed counsel, nor was the accused entitled to examine the indictment but rather had to listen to it read in Latin and protest errors in it if he could. Most prisoners before the bar found such a situation made argument impossible. How could they present their own cases effectively in such circumstances? To More, of course, these were not great problems. He could banter in Latin with the best minds of his generation, and he knew the law. What he could not overcome was the fundamental prejudice in the proceedings.

The original charge against More was that he had refused to agree to the Act of Succession. At trial, though, the prosecution argued that he had refused to acknowledge the king as head of the church in England—that is, that More was in violation of the Act of Supremacy. And so, in addition to the trial being preordained, it was fallacious. More's best defense was that he had remained silent on both issues (whether Anne Boleyn's children ought to succeed to the throne and whether Henry was the head of the English church rather than the pope). Observers at Westminster noted that the panel appeared moved by More's learned and confident contention that according to legal principle, his silence on those matters should be construed as implying consent. There was legal opposition to that point, however, by Attorney General Sir Christopher Hales, who served as one of the judges.

Originally, More was cited as having engaged in treasonous correspondence with Bishop (later Cardinal) John Fisher, who had been executed just a few days earlier on June 22. More was able to undercut that charge by noting that if such letters ever did exist—and he denied that they did—as they never were produced in court, they could not be cited as evidence at all. More also negated the accusation that he had made public statements calling the Act of Supremacy a two-edged sword because it would cost persons their earthly lives if they refused to swear to it but would bar them from heaven if they assented to it. More demonstrated that he had made such an argument in a hypothetical sense only. His judges and jury seemed to accept his contention that such a brilliant lawyer would have been foolhardy to make an argument against the act as a flat statement. They knew as well as More that he meant his two-edged-sword remark in that way, but they could not convict him if he were speaking only rhetorically.

Besides More's failure to take the oath (whichever one, on succession or supremacy, the prosecution intended), the key evidence against him was a conversation between More and Sir Richard Rich, solicitor general. Rich testified that More had denied the king's authority to lead the English church during an interrogation session in the previous month (June 1535). More reportedly shook his head at Rich's account, supposedly asking under his breath if Rich had gained a lucrative appointment over Wales in exchange for perjury.

Then in full voice More took Rich to task by swearing he never had made such a statement:

If I were a man, my lords, who did not reverence an oath, I need not, as is well known, stand here as an accused person in this place, at this time, or in this case. And if this oath of yours, Master Rich, be true, then I pray that I never see God in the face, which I would not say, were it otherwise, to win the whole world. . . . In good faith, Master Rich, I am sorrier for your perjury than for my own peril.

VERDICT

More's flashes of acumen could not save him. The court easily reached the verdict of guilty. Once the court's decision was announced, More got leave to make a statement. He spoke once again as an advocate who was present in the moment; he could not resist yet a last legal maneuver. But, he also wanted to unburden his conscience by voicing his views of the king's actions, which he long had thought best to squelch.

His first remarks went to the question of his true opinions. More admitted that he had opposed the king's matrimonial designs on account of his (More's) belief in the authority of the Holy See. His statement reminded English politicians that they were small fry compared to the many other leaders who had accepted Rome's governance. In this respect More aimed at the opinion of history.

More also spoke as a skilled lawyer. He parried that the judgment of the court ought to be set aside because the statute in question was contrary to law and thus the indictment had been invalid. For a few minutes those arguments seemed to stump the judges and caused special concern to Lord Chancellor Sir Thomas Audley, who was presiding. But, then Chief Justice John Fitzjames offered an ambiguous retort: If the legislation under which More had been convicted was unlawful, then More's conviction was too. The unspoken question hung in the air: Were any of the judges prepared to deny, right there, the lawfulness of the Act of Supremacy? None dared to take that step, so More had won the point but still lost the case.

As was customary for persons who once had been close to the king (including Anne Boleyn, who suffered a similar fate in May 1536), the king exercised "mercy" by allowing More to be beheaded rather than endure a more gruesome death. More died July 6, 1535, on a small green yard within the walls of the Tower of London. His son-in-law William Roper reported that he appeared composed on the scaffold, even jesting slightly with the executioner. His remains were supposed to be exhibited on London Bridge as a warning, but More's daughter Margaret Roper recovered the head. Although Henry VIII attempted to clamp down on dissemination of More's writings, his works, especially *Utopia,* had enduring popularity. By the time of the reign of Henry VIII's daughter Elizabeth I, More's books circulated widely in England.

SIGNIFICANCE

The trial of Thomas More was one of the most famous legal proceedings in western European history. With the possible exception of the trial of Joan of Arc, it has become the best-known prosecution since the time of Christ. In its own day the trial of More was of great magnitude. More's reputation as an intellectual and a loyal son of Rome guaranteed that his case would garner attention far beyond England. Political observers wondered how far Henry VIII was prepared to go to punish those who stood in his way. More's old friendship with Henry made the trial even more dramatic, hearkening back to the enmity between Thomas Becket and Henry II. It was a showdown in which the outcome was not in doubt, and yet much rode on the unfolding.

If More had implicated others or broken under pressure, the king's victory over his old friend would have been of greater weight, but the trial ended merely as a show of political force. Henry muscled his way through it but lost the moral high ground. History has borne out that opinion. Scholars remind More's admirers that he was no modern defender of civil liberties and that his trial therefore was not a victory for freedom of conscience. Still, More emerged from the courtroom renowned for his obedience to Rome and as an uncommonly well-spoken martyr, at that.

Further Reading

Ackroyd, Peter. *The Life of Thomas More.* London: Chatto & Windus, 1998; Bolt, Robert. *A Man for All Seasons: A Play in Two Acts.* New York: Vintage Books, 1962; Center for Thomas More Studies. "The Trial of Thomas More." Available online. URL: http://www.thomasmorestudies.org/segn/control/initContext?title=His+Trial. Accessed October 4, 2009; Chambers, R. W. *Thomas More.* London: J. Cape, 1938; Guy, J. *Thomas More.* New York: Oxford University Press, 2000; House, Seymour Baker. "More, Sir Thomas (1478–1535)." *Oxford Dictionary of National Biography.* Available online. URL: http://libproxy.eta.edu:2422/view/article/19191. Accessed October 1, 2009; Marius, Richard. *Thomas More.* New York: Knopf, 1984.

The trial of Francisco Vásquez de Coronado

Date: 1544

KEY ISSUES

In 1540 the viceroy of New Spain, Antonio de Mendoza, authorized an expedition to explore the northern portions of Spain's American dominions. The mission of the party was to search for portable wealth that reputedly existed among native peoples. The explorers consisted of Spaniards, indigenous Mexicans, and Africans; their leader was Francisco Vásquez de Coronado. Coronado was a nobleman from Spain. He had immigrated to Mexico, married an heiress, and acted as assistant to Mendoza. He currently was the governor of Nueva Galicia. He was to journey to the area the Spanish had claimed as "Cíbola." Coronado's reconnoitering began at almost exactly the same time as Hernando de Soto's exploration of what became the U.S. Southeast.

The Coronado expedition lasted about two years. The large party traversed an area presently known as northwestern Mexico and the southwestern United States. Coronado and his cotravelers made contact with a diverse native population, including people of the pueblos in present-day New Mexico. They experienced privation due to thin supply lines, reliance on the limited resources of indigenous peoples, and changeable weather on the Great Plains. They fought with several groups and acted violently toward certain individuals, including guides they believed had misled them into fool's errands. Coronado's quest for the "Seven Cities of Cíbola" ended in injury to its leader and deep disappointment to all of its participants. Coronado and his colleagues found no large cities on the order of the principal settlements of the Aztec Empire, no wealthy people, and no gold.

Word of their failure reached authorities in the mother country at a singularly poor time for conquistadores. In 1542 the Dominican friar Bartolomé de Las Casas circulated an exposé among elites in Spain, telling of Spanish relations with the native peoples of the Americas. The imperial court knew of Las Casas's manuscript, *A Brief Account of the Destruction of the Indies,* although the writing was not widely available until 1552. It was a veritable catalog of abuses. Las Casas was a formidable advocate for peaceful religious conversion and humane treatment of the native peoples. He had accompanied Christopher Columbus on his second voyage to the New World and had spent years in Hispaniola, Guatemala, and Mexico. He was dedicated to abolishing the forced labor that Spaniards had imposed on native people under the *encomienda* system.

Although he faced opposition from both his religious superiors and the nobles who operated under such systems of labor, Las Casas gained the ear of several monarchs beginning with Ferdinand II of Aragon. Las Casas was the prime force behind Spain's enactment of the New Laws of 1542, which banned slavery and the *encomiendas.* The friar also had influence in Rome. Las Casas was credited with drafting Pope Paul II's bull of 1537, *Sublimis Deus.* That pronouncement was an endorsement of the humanity of the "Indians" of the Americas, as they were erroneously called. The bull charged those who sought to convert native peoples to Christianity with protecting Indians' lives, freedom, and property. *Sublimis Deus* served as a blueprint for what Las Casas's contemporaries called "peaceful conversion" and modern scholars dubbed "liberation theology." The writings of Las Casas certainly affected the career of Coronado.

History of the Case

Coronado's expedition figured in several judicial proceedings both in Mexico and his homeland of Spain. Coronado himself was the central figure in one of those trials. Coronado faced an official inquiry into who was responsible for atrocities that occurred on his journey. In a larger sense it was not just in his own trial that Coronado was being judged; several related court proceedings featured accusations of cruelty against Coronado as leader of the expedition. Thus, for some months after his return to Mexico in 1542, Coronado's reputation was on the line.

In the wake of the New Laws and the papal bull and after a hearing of Las Casas's passionate arguments, King Charles I of Spain became angered about Spanish treatment of Indians. He ordered the New Spanish provincial court, the *audiencia,* to look into allegations that native peoples had been mistreated during the recent expedition to Cíbola. The royal presumption was that abuse had occurred, and the *audiencia* was charged to find out which persons had inflicted the "great cruelties."

The first phase of the inquiry was for a court in New Spain to gather testimony from witnesses who had been on the expedition, including Coronado himself. In Spanish law the proceeding was called a *pesquisa secreta* (secret inquiry), for while the investigation was announced to the public, each witness could not hear the others' testimony, and the whole affair was behind closed doors. All of the 14 witnesses that the investigating judge heard were of European extraction, although the journey had included more than 1,000 indigenous people and some Africans in addition to the 300 Spanish and Mexican participants. The person in charge of the *pesquisa secreta* was Lorenzo de Tejada, a judge of the *audiencia.* A court reporter took notes at the time, and that record survived in manuscript into the modern era. An additional set of four witnesses testified for Coronado during what were, in effect, rebuttal depositions.

Summary of Arguments

Judge Tejada gathered evidence about Coronado between May and September 1544 from his post in Mexico City. At the *pesquisa secreta* he asked certain recurring questions of Coronado and the other witnesses. He focused on whether the armed resistance of the pueblo dwellers to their "visitors" had been provoked by Spanish actions. Had the Spanish given due notice of hostile intentions before starting military encounters with native peoples? Were Coronado and his followers justified in burning several native settlements? Had the Spanish explorers tortured persons whom they held in captivity? The judge was especially keen to ferret out details of the killings of two native individuals, "Bigotes" and "the Turk," both of whom appeared to have been executed by the expeditionary party in retaliation for their providing false information to the Spanish.

Several of the witnesses testified to events that they had not personally witnessed but about which there had been rumors while they were on the move. The explorers had been split into a number of different parties during the trek—some searching ahead, some staying behind and peopling supply routes, others refusing to go ahead, and a few wishing to stay where they were rather than return to Mexico City when the expedition failed. Under Spanish law such hearsay evidence might be given a certain amount of weight; it certainly was not disallowed as is the case in modern U.S. courts.

Juan Gómez de Paradinas was representative of those who gave evidence as *de oficio* witnesses (those effectively under subpoena to testify). Gómez had joined the expedition as a prosperous tailor. He had personal connections to the Coronado family in Spain. On the trek in the northern lands he and his wife, María Maldonado, usually were in Coronado's detachment. Maldonado had special value to the expedition as a healer, and Gómez was skilled at repairing attire and issuing supplies. They both ended the adventure with no particular grievance against Coronado, although Gómez seemed to have spent most of his funds in the two years he was with the expedition. Although Gómez testified, Maldonado did not; another husband and wife, however, were among the 14 official witnesses.

What the other couple reported were acts of violence against several pueblos, as well as examples of ill treatment of prisoners. Among the cruelties were the Spanish "setting dogs upon" Indians

and burning native people alive while they were tied to stakes. Such seem to have been the causes of death of at least 100 individuals in a single episode, and there were other deaths in smaller incidents. One Indian had his ear and hand cut off. The Spanish sent him back to his people, maimed, as a warning.

Was Coronado personally present during those assaults? From the testimony it did not appear so. The highest-level leader who was directly implicated in such acts was the field commander García López de Cárdenas. The court scribe's notes make it apparent that Judge Tejada was following the royal instructions by leading the witnesses. Tejada was to assume that torture had occurred; his job was to determine who had applied it and whether it was in any way justifiable:

> He was asked what brutality was inflicted on the Indians when the pueblos had been captured and occupied. By whose order was it committed and how many Indians did they burn and set dogs on. [The witness] stated that the company lanced and stabbed a number of people. . . . Francisco Vasquez was not at the place where the burning was done because he was at another Pueblo. However these men were present: don Garcia Lopez de Cardenas and Pablos de Melgosa, captain of the footmen; the councilman Diego Lopez . . .
>
> The burning was done by order of don Garcia Lopez, who was maestro de campo. And the witness believes that it was not done without orders from Francisco Vasquez, who was the general, but he does not know that for certain. He does believe it, however, because Francisco Vasquez was in a pueblo very near the one where the burning was done and the general kept the captains and all the people of the army so obedient and subject to his command that no one would dare disobey and do anything without his order and permission.

Coronado and his *de parte* (in modern parlance "rebuttal") witnesses took issue with the 14 original deponents. While he admitted the commission of acts of violence against native communities, "the general" noted that he had been a stickler for following official instructions on what to say and do when approaching potentially hostile settlements. He was required to read a statement—the *requerimiento*—apprising native people of his intention to make them subjects of the king of Spain. He said that if they surrendered peacefully, they would suffer no harm. Indeed, Coronado recalled his efforts to make those demands plain through signs and interpreters. He portrayed the actions of the Spanish as appropriate responses to enemy attacks. Coronado denied that the acts of torture that others had described ever had taken place.

Tejada sent his findings to both the *audiencia* and to Spain. He got a different response from each place. In Mexico the *audiencia*'s prosecutor acted upon Tejada's recommendation that Coronado and those under his command ought to be charged with six separate offenses; the *audiencia* considered that case beginning in March 1545. In the home country the Council of the Indies entertained the complaint of its own prosecutor (the *fiscal*), a man named Juan de Villalobos. That set of allegations was against the expedition's second in command, García López de Cárdenas; the charges were filed in Spain in January 1546.

VERDICT

In February 1546, the four judges of the *audiencia* in New Spain announced the result of their hearings into the case directly against Coronado. They addressed the accusation that Coronado had personally or officially committed cruelties toward the native peoples of Tierra Nueva (the new lands explored in the expedition). Their decision was in the form of a terse reply to the *fiscal* of the *audiencia*, Cristobal de Benavente, who had lodged charges against Coronado after the report of Judge Tejada had been issued.

The *audiencia* ruled that the charges against Coronado were unproven. They then went further than noting that Coronado was not guilty by urging that no further action be taken against the expedition's leader. Benavente did not appeal the ruling. In 1553 Coronado secured a statement from the king that he as expedition leader was to be commended for his management of the difficult trek and partially compensated for enormous personal losses he had incurred as an investor.

The case against García López de Cárdenas proceeded in Spain while Coronado's unfolded in the New World. The *maestro de campo* had less success in dodging personal responsibility for atrocities such as the burning of villages and the execution of prisoners, and yet in the end, his punishment was mild. He was sentenced to a term of military service. Through legal maneuvers and political connections he got assigned to locations where his friends were in charge. He was fined, but that quickly was reduced to a manageable amount.

Tejada did conduct further inquiries about Coronado, though not concerning the expedition. About four years after the 1545–46 *audiencia* hearings at which Coronado was exonerated, Tejada investigated Coronado's governorship in Nueva Galicia. He found evidence of poor administration—specifically, Coronado had not paid enough attention to the meting out of justice in his territory.

SIGNIFICANCE

Coronado was not the only Spanish colonial governor who was called to answer for his treatment of native people. Around the time of his case two other major figures faced such accusations. Nuño Beltrán de Guzmán and Álvar Núñez Cabeza de Vaca underwent similar judicial inquiries, Guzmán in 1537 with respect to his actions in the Jalisco area and Cabeza de Vaca in 1545 regarding his oversight of Paraguay. Cabeza de Vaca served prison time as a result; Guzmán did not. Some historians conclude that those outcomes should have been reversed. Cabeza de Vaca probably incurred prosecution because he had adopted many of the views of Coronado's critics. It was ironic that Cabeza de Vaca's tender conscience put him on the wrong side of the law.

The reforms proposed by Las Casas did not gain universal approval. Even when he was an elderly man and known in Europe as an expert on "Indian affairs," many elites expressed resentment of his efforts on behalf of native persons. Trouble erupted in spots such as Mexico and Peru over attempts to enforce the more humane regulations that Las Casas helped draft. Revolts led by *encomenderos* (wealthy landowners) forced Las Casas—as they did Cabeza de Vaca—back to Spain.

At the Spanish court in 1550, "the Defender of the Indians" had to defend himself against the taint of treason. Was it disloyalty to the Crown to give native peoples time to renounce their prior allegiances? Should forced conquest be the preferred method of conversion and political control? Arguments similar to what had been at stake in Coronado's trial were hashed out in a series of debates between Las Casas and humanist scholar Juan Gines de Sepúlveda. The so-called Vallodolid Controversy ended in a political draw, but Las Casas's reputation for compassion continued. Historians note similarities between the papal bull of 1537, Spain's New Laws, and modern documents guaranteeing basic human dignity such as the United Nations Declaration of Human Rights.

Further Reading

Elliot, J. H. *Imperial Spain 1469–1716*. London: Penguin Books, 1990; Flint, Richard. *Great Cruelties Have Been Reported: The 1544 Investigation of the Coronado Expedition*. Dallas, Tex.: Southern Methodist University Press, 2002; Udall, Stewart L. *Majestic Journey: Coronado's Inland Empire*. Santa Fe: Museum of New Mexico Press, 1995; Vickery, Paul S. *Bartolome de Las Casas: Great Prophet of the Americas*. Mahwah, N.J.: Paulist Press, 2006.

The trial of Mary, Queen of Scots

Also known as: *The Queen v. Mary Stuart*

Date: 1586

KEY ISSUES

Mary Stuart, the Catholic queen of the Scots, was the leading contender to the throne of England on which Elizabeth I sat after 1558. Scholars note that if either Mary or Elizabeth had been of another gender, their rivalry might have ended very differently—with a marriage that joined the two kingdoms. As it was, friction between the two rulers became a fight to the death.

Mary Stuart was not only queen of Scotland; she had also been queen of France. A native of Scotland, she had gone to her mother's homeland as a five-year-old, destined for the French political match (a brokered engagement to the future Edward VI of England had fallen through). Mary became a young widow in 1560. She returned to Scotland soon after Francis II's death, but her connection with France remained salient. Mary Stuart symbolized the "Auld Alliance" between Catholics in Scotland and France that many English politicians feared.

Queen Mary's presence across the border from England would have given pause to those who distrusted Catholicism and its faithful, even had the situation in Scotland not been tumultuous. But, with the religious and geographical fractures that emerged in Scottish politics in the middle of the 1500s, Mary Stuart's weaknesses as a ruler there became even more apparent. It did not help Mary that John Knox and other Protestant theologians had made great inroads with the population during her few years in France.

She also came in for criticism because of her dramatic personal life. Married in 1566 to her first cousin, Lord Darnley, she and Darnley produced an heir to the Scottish throne, James. The marriage was unhappy; when the queen of Scots became a widow for a second time, rumor had it that Mary was complicit in Darnley's death. She remarried the earl of Bothwell, whom Mary said had kidnapped and raped her in the immediate aftermath of Darnley's demise. A civil war in Scotland was inflamed by Mary's irregular personal life; that civil turmoil sent Mary running for safety from her own subjects in May 1568.

She never returned to Scotland, for the rest of her life staying in English castles under various degrees of confinement. England's leaders offered several pretexts for not allowing Mary freedom of movement. Initially, the English government's stance was that Mary Stuart was under investigation concerning the death of Darnley. A set of commissioners inquired into the events surrounding Darnley's death and Mary's marriage to Bothwell, who himself had secured a hasty divorce. Among the crucial bits of evidence that those investigators found was a series of notes that Mary supposedly wrote to Bothwell—the "casket letters," whose authenticity still is under debate among scholars. William Cecil, Lord Burghley, Elizabeth's right-hand counselor, managed the inquiry. In a tactic that she would use again, Mary Stuart dodged direct questions posed by the English. She insisted that she would participate only if the commissioners would formally recognize her as a queen. The commissioners returned an "open verdict" in early 1569, stating that no charges had been proved against Mary that would make Elizabeth of England think Mary "evil."

In a complicated series of events following that trial, the duke of Norfolk was executed. He had taken part in a pro-Catholic rebellion against Elizabeth that failed in late 1569. Among Norfolk's transgressions was his willingness to offer his own hand in marriage to Mary Stuart, along with his connection to Italian banker David Ridolfi. Ridolfi supposedly acted on behalf of Pope Pius V in attempting to replace Elizabeth with her Scottish counterpart, Mary. Norfolk's treason trial showed that the English government viewed Mary Stuart as an enormous threat. That fear of the queen of Scots no doubt was exacerbated by the hardening papal position on Elizabeth's religious policy. In 1570 the papacy had issued a formal statement excommunicating Elizabeth Tudor; the bull, *Regnans in Excelsis,* sharpened the rhetoric between England and Rome.

HISTORY OF THE CASE

As Mary Stuart's confinement in English castles stretched into years of captivity, it became apparent that neither the leaders of Scotland nor the English knew what to do with the former Scots queen. The head of Scotland's regency government, Mary's brother James, the earl of Moray, viewed Mary as a rival. As Mary's heir, James, grew into young adulthood, James, too, apparently saw his mother's possible return to Scotland as an impediment to his holding the Scottish throne.

The English government made a reasonable argument that Mary Stuart had to be restrained in order to stop rebellion from coalescing around her. Still, her "stay" in England was increasingly arduous, given that the Scots queen was not in a formal sense a prisoner nor was she accused of a crime. She certainly had not been convicted of any offense. The privy councilors allowed Mary's jailors discretion to impose strict conditions. Mary's last guardian, Sir Amyas Paulet, was particularly stern. The queen of Scots was the centerpiece of numerous plots. Secretary of State William Cecil had developed an elaborate intelligence network and soon intercepted most of the correspondence that Mary's proponents smuggled into and out of her residences. Directly in charge of the monitoring of the correspondence was Francis Walsingham, Elizabethan chief of security.

In 1586 the English proceeded with a criminal prosecution against Mary, accusing her of aiding one set of pro-Catholic plotters. The case hinged upon the letters of Anthony Babington, who had proposed to Mary that Elizabeth should be assassinated and Mary released. Scholars remain divided as to whether Babington was so naive as to commit those thoughts to paper on his own accord or whether government agents planted the idea in his mind. The case involved certain related questions. Did Mary conspire to escape? Had she encouraged anti-Catholic conspirators to kill the queen of England? If she did do either of those things, then was she liable for them? That is, was she bound to accept the conditions of her forced residence? Did she owe a duty of loyalty to Elizabeth? Furthermore, just because Babington had written such things to Mary, was she guilty on that basis alone or did there need to be proof of her more active participation in traitorous designs?

The trial took place at Fotheringhay Castle on October 14 and 15, 1586, with the verdict being handed down in Westminster just over a week later. More than 40 dignitaries heard the case. It was not a regular court session in several respects, notably because of the absence of a jury of the defendant's peers. A jury of peers had been mentioned in the Magna Carta: The barons of England had written chapter 39 to guard against bribery of poorer folk by royal officials. Far from providing juries of "equals" for ordinary people, chapter 39 initially offered a considerable advantage to wealthy individuals; only persons of high social rank would judge their fellow elites. In those rare circumstances when noble individuals were on trial, they had the benefit of juries composed of their friends and relatives.

A difficulty arose, though, when a defendant was too high in rank. The deposed Scottish monarch had no social equals in England except Queen Elizabeth herself, and "Good Queen Bess" did not attend the proceedings. A sketch of the trial chamber that was drawn during Mary Stuart's trial makes clear that England's queen was there in spirit; a regal chair was reserved for her but never was occupied. The persons who sat in judgment of Mary Stuart had a clear bias against her. Several were cabinet-level officers (Cecil, for example, and Lord Chancellor Thomas Bromley) who for years had maintained that Mary Stuart posed a danger to England's stability. In the sketch showing the great hall at Fotheringhay at the trial, one hardly notices a small female figure entering the room via a corner door. It was as if the queen of Scots was an afterthought to the artist.

SUMMARY OF ARGUMENTS

Mary Stuart at first refused to accept the jurisdiction of the court on two grounds: She argued that as a Scot she was not subject to English law and that as an anointed queen she could not be charged with any earthly "fault or offence." Such already had been Mary's rejoinder to the jailor, Paulet, when prior to trial he urged her to repent of her sins. She eventually agreed to attend the proceedings at Fotheringhay in order to state publicly that she had never advocated harming Elizabeth I.

The defendant never fully played the role that the trial's managers had envisioned for her. She refused to read from notes, for example, saying that she would not stoop to "play a scrivener." She displayed emotion readily, weeping copiously throughout her remarks. Her tears reminded listeners of the supposed vulnerability of her gender. She wore a white veil, the color of mourning among the French, as a reminder that she was several times widowed. She also evoked a set of religious images at the trial and afterward. She seemed to be insisting that her accusers notice how imprisonment had enfeebled her body, just as Christ had suffered before his death.

Such powerful visual imagery was important to Mary Stuart, for she could not expect to win her case in a legal sense. She conveyed that she was on trial because of her Catholicism. She also appeared anxious to show that she was the rightful queen of Scotland and that her dignity as a monarch was insulted by the trial. In court Mary Stuart refused to accept responsibility for the actions of English citizens who sought to break her out of jail; it was as though such mundane arrangements were beneath her notice. Part of her argument, too, was that as a ruler she never would have countenanced a plot to assassinate another monarch.

Prosecutors argued that Mary Stuart had offended against a statute of recent vintage—the Act of Association, which in 1584 had made it treason to plot against Queen Elizabeth with a view toward supplanting her with another claimant. That legislation, which was strengthened in 1585, had begun as a policy created by Walsingham and the Privy Council. There was little doubt that the law was aimed directly at the rumored conspiracies to unseat Elizabeth and place Mary Stuart on the throne. At her trial the queen of Scots scorned that law under which she was charged, as "most unknown" to her.

VERDICT

At least as interesting as Mary Stuart's trial was the political theater that followed shortly after it. The judges who had heard her case reconvened at the Star Chamber in Westminster at the end of October 1586 and pronounced a verdict of guilty. In their verdict they reverted to the language of English treason law that long preceded the Act of Association. They spoke of Mary Stuart as having "compassed and imagined" the death of the English queen, thus recalling the wording of the great treason statute of Edward III (1351), which usually had sufficed to try traitors. That itself was a telling choice of verbiage, for it hinted that the judges themselves were uncomfortable in evoking the Act of Association.

An intriguing rhetoric accompanied the ensuing public debate about what Mary Stuart's punishment should be. It still remained the prerogative of the monarch, Elizabeth, to sign a death warrant. Would she do so? Or would the queen of England allow Mary Stuart to go abroad—an improbable but permissible resolution? More likely, would the queen delay imposition of a capital sentence, perhaps indefinitely?

Obfuscation was Elizabeth's style, but Parliament, the hawks on her council, and even certain factions within the public called for a swift execution. It was the norm for Elizabeth to be able to manage Parliament, or at least politely explain why she would not do the legislature's bidding. On this issue she could not manage the politicians and the public. Still, it took from late October 1586 until late January 1587 for Elizabeth to authorize the execution to proceed.

Mary, Queen of Scots, long realized that she was going to die for political reasons; she seemed almost relieved that death would come by an ax rather than in the dead of night. Among her last letters were missives to her brother-in-law the king of France and to Elizabeth I. Mary asked the English queen that she be buried in France. She requested of her in-law in France that masses be said for her soul and her devoted servants paid.

Mary Stuart worked even her death scene to great effect, appearing dignified and unafraid. She dressed magnificently in black and then, when baring her neck for the executioner, revealed undergarments that were crimson, the color of bloodshed for her faith. Even the traditional hoisting of the severed head proved a triumph for her; the executioner grasped an autumn-colored wig. Mary's head, with its white hair, rolled away. It was testimony to the stressful nature of her long confinement in England. Both at her trial and execution Mary Stuart had conducted herself according to her social stature and religious zeal; but for her connections with Bothwell and Darnley, Mary, Queen of Scots, might have gained official recognition as a Catholic martyr.

SIGNIFICANCE

It is impossible to separate the trial of Mary of Scotland from the personal rivalry between Elizabeth Tudor and Mary Stuart. At Elizabeth's insistence the two women never met. Still, they were obviously conscious of each other not just politically and religiously but also in an emotional sense. The thrice-married, unquestionably magnetic Scotswoman must have reminded Elizabeth of her famous status as the Virgin Queen. Eliza-

beth, meanwhile, had the enviable position of ruling a country whose citizens largely trusted her.

The imprisonment, trial, and execution of Mary Stuart presented a great challenge for Elizabeth of England. Mary was the nearest peer Elizabeth would have. She was not just a royal family member of the same generation but also cultured and powerful. To approve the execution of another monarch was a most dangerous action; it would focus the ire of several nations upon England and Elizabeth. Making Mary Stuart into a hero was something that Elizabeth I tried desperately to avoid, both because of her innate sympathy for her Scots cousin and because it might create enormous problems for her and England.

Further Reading

Dunne, Jane. *Elizabeth and Mary: Cousins, Rivals, Queens.* New York: Random House, 2004; Fraser, Antonia. *Mary Queen of Scots.* New York: Delacorte Press, 1969; Guy, John. *Queen of Scots: the True Life of Mary Stuart.* Boston: Houghton Mifflin, 2004; Lewis, Jayne Elizabeth. *The Trial of Mary Queen of Scots: A Brief History with Documents.* Boston: Bedford/St. Martin's, 1999.

The Gunpowder Conspiracy trial

Also known as: *The King v. Fawkes, Rookwood, Keyes, Grant, Bates, Thomas Winter, Robert Winter, and Digby*

Date: 1606

KEY ISSUES

England narrowly escaped a severe blow from terrorism in November 1605. A group of well-connected English conspirators had planned to blow up the building where Parliament met, killing all inside. Among the victims were to be most members of the English royal family and the legislature. The plotters had a vague scheme to mobilize pro-Catholic opinion and take over the government, putting the daughter of the present monarch on the throne and marrying her to a Catholic prince.

Just how close a call did King James I and his advisers and legislators have? Whether the Gunpowder Plot came close to fruition is a matter of conjecture among scholars. Some suggest that the government had infiltrated the ranks of the conspirators. Perhaps King James's advisers such as Robert Cecil chose to apprehend the principals at the 11th hour in order to make the plan seem more threatening than it was. Some writers argue that there was no plot. Rather, they said that the whole scheme was manufactured by the regime in order to justify the repressive policies that James I wished to institute upon his succession to the throne after Queen Elizabeth I's death in 1603, but such views are outside the mainstream among historians. Most modern scholars view the conspiracy as a real danger if not to the security of the English state, then at least to the lives of the many persons who would have been within the Parliament chamber.

Who knew what and when in this case are important questions for researchers. The near tragedy and the response to it also illuminate certain larger controversies. In particular, the episode throws into stark relief the division between Protestantism and Catholicism in the early 1600s. Even in nations such as England that had declared a formal preference for one form of Christianity over another, there remained a large religious minority. What was their role in politics? How much leeway would they have to practice their faith? What would be the extent of government involvement in their everyday lives?

Those who aided the Gunpowder plotters did so in part out of frustration that such questions were not being answered to their benefit during the first few years of James I's reign. Unfortunately for the Catholic minority in England, the failure of the plot made their situation far worse both in short- and long-range terms. The trials of the conspirators demonstrated the antipathy of the government toward Catholicism and exacerbated popular resentment of "popery" as well.

HISTORY OF THE CASE

King James VI of Scotland had expected to inherit the throne of England upon the death of his kinswoman Queen Elizabeth I. Much ahead of the queen's death in 1603, several of Elizabeth's advisers entered into correspondence with the Scots monarch. The English councilors hoped to make themselves indispensable to the new ruler; he in turn sought experienced friends at his future court. James, a political survivor, knew how critical it was for him not to alienate any key faction. He spoke out of both sides of his mouth in dealing with his English suitors, especially with regard to the subject of religion. Thus, expectations were high for his kingship in England among both the Protestants who thought Elizabeth reluctant to reform the Anglican Church and the Catholics who sought a relaxation of strictures on the old faith.

Many English Catholics recalled fondly the doctrinal conservatism of the latter part of Henry VIII's reign. They knew that James was the son of Mary Stuart, the Catholic queen of Scotland. While James as king of England would unlikely revert fully to the policies of Mary Tudor, Elizabeth's half sister and Catholic queen of England from 1553 to 1558, perhaps he at least would grant English Catholics more scope for practice of their faith than Elizabeth had done. Both sides who had felt aggrieved under Elizabeth—the radical Protestants and the Catholics—were disappointed when upon taking control in England James fell somewhere in the middle.

Although the new monarch negotiated peace with Spain in 1604, King James made plain that the cessation of hostilities did not mean toleration for English Catholics. It certainly did not encompass equality or a recasting of England as a Catholic nation, which would have been the dream of those faithful to Roman Catholicism. In 1604 the government began enforcing fines against lack of conformity to the established church; not to publicly profess Anglicanism was an offense. That crackdown after an initial hope of leniency from James touched off the Gunpowder Plot.

The idea of the conspirators was to store gunpowder underneath the House of Lords. They would ignite it when Parliament gathered for a session at which the monarch would be in attendance. The plotters procured a house next to Westminster Hall. From beneath that location they could have tunneled toward a spot underneath the legislative chamber. Initially, the conspirators numbered only seven. All were Catholic and most were wealthy. Although most were young they were well versed in political intrigue and combat.

At the center of the plot was Robert Catesby, a well-spoken young man from a prosperous Catholic family in Warwickshire. He had been heavily involved in the rebellion of the earl of Essex against Elizabeth I in 1601 and, as a consequence, had lost his house through forfeiture. Catesby drew in several close associates such as his cousin Thomas Wintour and Thomas Percy, a grandson of the earl of Northumberland. During 1604 they added others who had military experience and were dedicated to the establishment of a Catholic state in England—persons such as Guy Fawkes and John Wright. A few servants and family members came along during late 1604 and early 1605. In the summer of 1605 the plotters sought assistance from other well-placed individuals such as Ambrose Rookwood, Francis Tresham, and Everard Digby. It should be noted that none of those involved in the conspiracy expected or were promised political rewards in a new regime. Theirs was an ideological battle, albeit one that required funds, access to the royal family, and stables full of horses.

The plotters considered the moral implications of an act of terrorism. They proposed to kill not only England's leaders but also a number of "innocents." The victims quite easily could include the queen and several children of King James. Worse for their consciences, the conspirators knew that their own relatives and persons sympathetic to the Catholic cause would die in the expected conflagration. As deeply religious men, those planning the Gunpowder Plot sought counsel from spiritual advisers such as Father Henry Garnet. Garnet, the leading Jesuit in England, did not give a firm answer about whether killing innocent parties was a sin if it were in the service of a great cause. He did express the opinion of the current pope, though, that rebellion was not an acceptable course of action in this case. The plotters then had a dilemma; rebellion was what they proposed to follow the explosion. Their confessors also had a problem, for they now had learned of a murderous plot. Would they keep such knowledge to themselves?

It transpired that the priests would not have to divulge that information because a secular individual did it for them. Francis Tresham was worried about the danger to his brother-in-law Lord Monteagle. Tresham or a member of his family likely composed an anonymous note to Monteagle, vaguely worded yet warning of the danger of attending the opening of Parliament. Upon receiving that letter in late October 1605, Monteagle turned it over to Robert Cecil, the earl of Salisbury and James I's leading adviser. If the government had not yet been aware of the plot, it now was on notice.

Late on the night of November 4, 1605, the king sent his lord chamberlain and then some courtiers to search buildings near the legislature. Both the chamberlain and Sir Thomas Knyvet, on their subsequent forays, encountered a man who first identified himself as a servant of Thomas Percy, the owner of the premises. Upon encountering that man, who called himself "John Johnson," a second time, Knyvet searched the building that Johnson was guarding. He found the gunpowder plus a fuse and a watch on Johnson's person. Knyvet took the man under guard to Cecil. On the way Johnson admitted that his goal had been to explode Parliament. In Cecil's presence he continued to show no contrition. He said that he wished to commit a violence that would have sent the Scots (and of course King James) back to their homeland.

The next four days were not easy for Johnson. Held in the Tower of London, he faced an array of important interrogators including England's attorney general, Edward Coke, and solicitor general, Francis Bacon, as well as Salisbury and Chief Justice John Popham. King James had issued a royal warrant authorizing increasing gradations of torture to make the prisoner talk, and those measures eventually produced the desired result. Johnson spilled the names of most of the conspirators, including his own: Guy (Guido) Fawkes. Both the use of manacles and the knowledge that many of Fawkes's colleagues had been captured helped break his spirit. The signatures of Fawkes on official documents first before and then after torture make plain his suffering.

Meanwhile, the English people believed themselves to have escaped catastrophe. They celebrated deliverance with bonfires. The ambassador from Spain could not but join in. It was the beginning of several traditions: Henceforth, the nation would associate patriotism with November 5, villifying Guy Fawkes and lighting fires in the place of the explosion that never happened at Westminster.

SUMMARY OF ARGUMENTS

The government had the complicated task of not only rounding up conspirators, who had scattered—some to the Continent—but also discovering which persons besides those already implicated might be involved. Of special importance were Jesuit priests such as the well-known Father Garnet. What was the extent of their foreknowledge? As conspirators beyond Fawkes were questioned, they steadfastly refused to implicate Catholic clerics and foreign powers.

Several of the principals had decamped from London upon hearing of Fawkes's apprehension, although not quickly enough to escape abroad. Several, including Catesby, died as local officials tried to apprehend them in country houses. The government posted heads on spikes in the customary spots around London. Those who were taken alive went to the Tower.

For once during James's 22-year reign, Parliament and the king saw eye to eye. The legislature called for the "insurgents" to be punished with more than the usual savagery specified for traitors. James graciously assured the lawmakers that if the plot had succeeded, he would have been pleased to die there among the lords.

The trial of eight conspirators commenced at Westminster on January 27, 1606. The proceedings were in the form of a special commission convened at Westminster Hall. The trials of Guy Fawkes, Ambrose Rookwood, Robert Keyes, John Grant, Thomas Bates, Thomas Winter, Robert Winter, and Sir Everard Digby were all joined. The persons presiding were six earls of the kingdom (Nottingham, Suffolk, Worcester, Devonshire, Northampton, and Salisbury) plus a judge from each of the major royal courts: King's Bench, Common Pleas, and Exchequer. It was not unusual for a person who had been in charge of tracking down the alleged malefactors (in this case, Cecil) or one who had helped interrogate them (here, Popham) then to sit in judgment.

All of the defendants were accused of treason; each had been implicated by someone's confession. Some even had been caught red-handed, notably Fawkes. Yet, a full-scale trial it would be, for all of the accused conspirators except Digby pleaded not guilty. Digby, perhaps emboldened by his high social station, justified his actions after entering his plea. He had joined in the plot in part out of loyalty to Catesby, dedication to the Catholic faith, and anger at King James's lack of concern for the Catholic toleration that he earlier had promised to offer. It was the fullest defense that any of the conspirators would put forward. None had counsel, though several were well educated enough to have spoken for themselves effectively had they chosen to do so.

Through Cecil, the Crown set out the line of argument that the prosecutor, Coke, would pursue. He should focus on the longstanding nature of this treachery—how it reached back into the reign of Queen Elizabeth, was fed by machinations of Rome, and was encouraged by Jesuits abroad and in secret hiding places in England. The hand of King James was prominent in the prosecution's contentions. This monarch was stung by the idea that the plotters had rejected his authority. James kept recalling that he had progressed to London in triumph at his accession, so he wanted it well known at trial that the plotters had borne a grudge against the late queen.

Yet, with the outline of the charges set, the verbiage of the prosecution was all Coke's. Both a well-trained and sharp-tongued lawyer, he mixed Latin quotations from the law books and classical allusions that appealed to his learned and noble audience with plays on words that spoke to a larger crowd. His language was anti-Catholic and could verge on the coarse. The plotters, he said, had sought to invoke "gunpowder law! . . . fit for justices of hell, executed by 'justice' Faux. . . . But as before was spoken of the Jesuits and priests, they all were joined in the ends like Samson's foxes in the tails. . . ."

Coke had to exercise care, for the state was concerned that the trial might inspire anti-Spanish sentiment. As a consequence, the attorney general's rhetoric was aimed at Rome and its agents in England rather than Catholicism generally. Still, Coke personally was so religiously biased that his words veered toward a blanket condemnation of Catholicism as at the root of every plot in recent memory. He reminded the court watchers, for example, that though they could not be directly linked, this case had similar roots to Sir Walter Raleigh's recent trial. What he did not articulate was that he, Coke, had charged Raleigh with making overtures to Spain. Perhaps it was best to go on to less problematic topics. Coke moved along to the matter of the punishment that the Crown sought.

The assembly included a full meeting of the House of Commons. Coke seemed to be speaking toward them when he included a reminder of the punishment for treason. In one of the most famous descriptions ever given of that penalty, the lawyer sketched out what hanging, drawing, and quartering signified:

> After a traitor hath had his just trial, and is convicted and attainted, he shall have his judgment: To be drawn to the place of execution from his prison, as being not worthy any more to tread upon the face of the earth whereof he was made. Also, for that he hath been retrograde to nature, therefore he is drawn backward at horse-tail, and whereas God hath made the head of man the highest and most supreme ornament, he must be drawn with his head declining downward and lying so near the ground as may be, being thought unfit to take benefit of the common air. For which cause also he shall be strangled, being hanged up by the neck between heaven and earth as deemed unworthy of both or either; as likewise, that the eyes of men may behold and their hearts condemn him. Then he is to be cut down alive, and his privy parts cut off and burnt before his face as being unworthily begotten and unfit to leave any generation after him. His bowels and inlay'd parts taken out and burnt, who inwardly had conceived and harbored such horrible treason. After, to have his head cut off, which had imagined the mischief. And lastly, his body to be quartered and the quarters set up in some high and eminent place, to the view and detestation of men, and to become a prey for the fowls of the air.

The application of the traditional punishment when Commons was braying for a penalty that was even more severe allowed King James to say that he was acting mercifully toward the condemned.

VERDICTS

The guilty verdicts were unsurprising. The only drama to be played out with regard to the convicted persons was how they would die. It was a critical question for the crowds of London and also for the authorities. If those who had conspired eschewed their Catholicism in terror of the scaffold, then they would not earn a reprieve but might win less censure in official sermons and accounts of the executions. The government's hopes were not fulfilled. At the executions on January 30, 1606, almost every condemned person faced down the horror awaiting him calmly, taking solace in Latin (Catholic) prayers and brushing off the ministrations of Protestant chaplains.

Those critical of the condemned saw them as "mumbling Popish incantations" just before hanging. More sympathetic observers told stories such as that of the death of Digby. The executioner and the government may have singled him out for especially gruesome treatment because of Digby's refusal to plead guilty at trial. Digby was cut down from the noose while still alive and the dismembering was begun. The executioner displayed Digby's heart and proclaimed that such was the fate of traitors; Digby supposedly cried out "Thou liest!"

There was some unfinished business to conclude. The indictment had opened not with the names of those who had been condemned by the commission, but rather with the names of Jesuits who had yet to be captured: Fathers Henry Garnet, Oswald Tesmond, and John Gerard. Cecil's intelligence had it that with their impeccable connections among the political elite, Tesmond and Gerard almost certainly had already gone abroad. (Gerard had been a close friend of Digby's.) There was an all-out effort to apprehend Garnet. He was found in an expected location: within a secret hiding spot in the household of a known Catholic family and alongside the family chaplain, Father Edward Oldcorne.

Father Garnet was the more important of those recent detainees, for he was well educated, articulate, and widely liked. At his trial beginning on March 28, 1606, at the Guildhall, Coke again had to work under instructions from Cecil and King James about what could and could not be said. Once more he was to lay stress on the disloyalty of Jesuits being of long vintage. He sought to connect the actions of Garnet with the Gunpowder Plot, but also reviewed some of the activities of Jesuits in England during Elizabeth's reign. (The net was wide. The head of the household where Oldcorne and Garnet had hidden and Oldcorne were also tried for treason but at Worcester.)

At Garnet's prosecution Coke took up the matter of other conspirators' denials that the clerics had been involved, plus Garnet's answers under questioning. Garnet had shifted his responses— probably not in response to any torture, but rather because of his use of the Jesuit tactic called "equivocation." It amounted to answering in a technically truthful manner while not baring all to hostile interrogators. Equivocation allowed priests in England to save their consciences by not lying yet also preserve their larger mission of conversion. Coke had only denigration for such techniques:

> God help us! For then shall all conversation, all trading, all trials by juries be useless and mischievous. The law and sanction of nature hath as it were married the heart and the tongue; from them is conceived in adultery, a breed of bastard children, offending against chastity.

Father Garnet tried a defense, but it fell flat. He utterly denied knowing of this plot and decried the Spanish invasion effort of 1588. The judges pressed on about the sanctity of the confessional. They asked whether Garnet would have violated confidentiality if he had known of the conspiracy to blow up Parliament. When the accused man replied that he would not have disclosed that information to authorities, Coke pounced; the common law said that it was an offense of *laesae Majestatis* ("injured Majesty," or high treason) not to come forward with such information. Garnet's jury was out for a quarter of an hour before finding him guilty of just that crime. Garnet died by hanging, but his genial nature spared him the fate of the proud Digby; James apparently gave direct orders that Garnet should be allowed to hang until dead.

SIGNIFICANCE

To the English, Guy Fawkes Day was a commemoration of national deliverance. It became most important at times when either the public or those in power desired to label Catholics as foreigners or enemies. November 5 inspired great fervor, for example, during the Puritans' protests against Charles I and while Catholic emancipation was being considered in the mid-19th century. For the government to have shown at trial that there were connections between Jesuits and armed insurrection was most important. Though English Catholics and their spiritual advisers argued that most of the Catholic faithful were loyal subjects who abhorred bloodshed, the image of wild-eyed bombers who violently served secretive and foreign masters held the collective imagination.

Further Reading

Bowen, Catherine Drinker. *The Lion and the Throne.* Boston: Little, Brown, 1957; Fraser, Antonia. *Faith and Treason.* New York: Doubleday, 1996; Haynes, Alan. *The Gunpowder Plot: Faith in Rebellion.* Stroud, U.K.: A. Sutton, 1994; Nicholls, Mark. *Investigating the Gunpowder Plot.* New York: St. Martin's Press, 1991; Sharpe, J. A. *Remember, Remember: A Cultural History of Guy Fawkes Day.* Cambridge, Mass.: Harvard University Press, 2005; "The Trials of Robert Winter, Thomas Winter, Guy Fawkes, John Grant, Ambrose Rookwood, Robert Keyes, Thomas Bates, and Sir Everard Digby, at Westminster for High-Treason, being Conspirators in the Gunpowder-Plot. 27 Jan. 1605. 3 Jac. l." Available online. URL: http://www.armitstead.com/gunpowder/gunpowder_trial.html. Accessed October 10, 2009.

The trial of Bapaji

Also known as: *Narasoji v. Bapaji*

Date: 1611

KEY ISSUES

The colonial powers that entered India in the early modern era at first were interested in establishing coastal bases from which to secure their sea trade in the East. As those European nations became further ensconced on the subcontinent, they centered attention on influencing politics in the region in order to enhance economic rewards. With the emergence of England and her entrepreneurs as the key Western power in India, the English usually painted Indian society as static and ruled by considerations of caste. Brahmans figured prominently as local influences in Indian society in Anglophone depictions of the region. Although in India there were Muslim (Mughal or Mogul) overlords, many English writers described Mughal rule as only a veneer; to Western eyes it was the Brahmans who were really in charge.

More modern historians see such a portrait of premodern India as simplistic. Such visions were not only grounded in the British imperialists' need to justify their own "reforms," but also based on historical documents such as court records and religious texts that themselves were written to convey stability and a pan-Indian outlook. Besides, the characterization of premodern India as a Muslim state was inaccurate, if only because the vast majority of persons who lived on the subcontinent were Hindus and because the Mughals themselves often were subject to still greater rulers such as Mongol warlords.

Updated accounts of premodern India underline the interactions between various elements in Indian society. Such studies focus on leaders such as the revered Maratha king Shivaji (1630–80). How did Indian rulers appeal to coexistence among religiously diverse subjects? New scholarship also brings the attention of readers to more mundane affairs, such as the ways in which certain monarchs who differed in religion from their people managed to forge bonds of loyalty with their subjects. The connections between governors and the people sometimes occurred through the leaders' astute manipulation of legal processes—or, perhaps it was the subjects who required their leaders to be sensitive in wielding the law.

HISTORY OF THE CASE

Legal historians note that regional leaders in India often used courts to effect "indigenization." It is critical, though, to remember that catering to indigenous people was a two-way process; it ingratiated the rulers with the public but also gave the local folk more say in governance. A case from the sultanate of Bijapur is an excellent example of how Indians and their rulers both employed legal mechanisms for their own ends. Though at first it seems a minor matter, *Narasoji v. Bapaji* (1611) illustrates the operation of justice well. The trial of Bapaji also throws light on the delicate accommodations constantly occurring among communities that easily could have fractured along religious lines.

In the 1500s in the village of Masura there was a shrine to Jalāl al-Dīn Muhammad Balkhī (Rumi), a 13th-century Sufi mystic, poet, and founder of the dancing (or whirling) dervishes. Rumi had been born a Hindu but had converted to Islam. The memorial was a respected location among both Hindus and Muslims. As with such sites in many other places in the world, two religious groups attempted to partition off a physical space for each group of adherents. Trouble erupted when one faction upset the longstanding balance. A group of local Muslim merchants pressured those who oversaw the shrine to channel donations that were left by Hindus to the Muslim side of the facility.

Then came a clash between the village authorities, those in charge of the shrine, and the Muslim businessmen. The local political leader, called the village headman, commanded the administrators of the shrine to restore the old balance of a Muslim-Hindu partition of the facility. For his effort at intervention employees at the shrine killed the headman and one of his sons, apparently at the behest of the Muslim faction. A new mayor who was the brother of the murdered headman took revenge upon three employees at the shrine.

A relative of one of the three murdered employees took a complaint to the deputy governor, 'Abd Allah Husain, who in turn was a representative of Sultan Ibrahīm Adīl Shah II. 'Abd Allah showed considerable sympathy for the petitioner, in part due to a family connection with him. The mayor who had ordered the latest killings refused to put himself under the sultan's justice and was heavily fined as a result. When the mayor finally was located, he was summarily locked up for three years and his office given to the complainant. The new mayor proved extremely unpopular on account of his reputation as a rapacious money-lender. The villagers forced him out of the locality, and the sultan's representative then replaced the absent new headman with his son, Bapaji.

The family of the headman that had been disciplined by the deputy governor had not given up their ambitions to office. At the death of that old headman who had ordered the three murders, his son, a young man named Narasoji, for obvious reasons bypassed the deputy governor and asked for assistance from the sultan. The sultan appointed a type of ombudsman whose suggestion at a resolution—Narasoji's payment of a fine—failed to satisfy the Muslim businessmen who had been involved earlier. The sultan then ordered that a group of arbitrators should make a ruling. They decided that Narasoji, as the descendant of the former headman, should become the new mayor.

Bapaji appealed that decision, asking for a change of venue to a court that would meet far away from local influences. Interestingly, Bapaji's suggestion was that a court in Paithan, consisting of *dharmadhikaris* (Brahman jurists who applied Hindu law), should resolve the case. Such a request intimated that the Muslim-backed faction represented by Bapaji was confident they would get a fair hearing under Hindu law.

SUMMARY OF ARGUMENTS

The parties spoke for themselves before the judges at Paithan. The judges gave them considerable latitude to question each other in front of the court. Bapaji opened his case with a reminder that the venerated Rumi was born a Hindu. He then noted that he, Bapaji, was a descendant of Rumi and that, as such, he also deserved respect as a holy man. Yet, quite the contrary had happened: His relatives had been murdered.

Narasoji broke in, requesting that the judges ask Bapaji "why the shrine attendants killed my grandfather and one of his sons." The judges obliged, requesting that Bapaji answer the query. Bapaji's response came across as flippant. He countered that three of his relatives had died whereas Narasoji had lost only two family members, and besides, the deputy governor had assessed a fine against Narasoji's father that had yet to be fully paid.

Then Bapaji made another mistake. He presumed to know when to invoke an ordeal within a trial. He called for Narasoji to undergo a physical test of his uprightness if he still refused to pay "loans" that Narasoji's father supposedly had owed to Bapaji's father. The court asked Bapaji for documentation that such loans had existed and that Narasoji's father had agreed to pay them. Bapaji responded that Narasoji's father had promised to make the payments while he was in detention under the deputy governor's order. Narasoji remarked that "any such agreement would have been made under duress." The judges were silent, but their lack of comment probably indicated agreement with Narasoji. Bapaji again spoke directly to Narasoji, proposing that an ordeal would establish whether Narasoji owed him anything.

The court had ignored Bapaji's call for an ordeal earlier, but it seemed to have lost patience the second time he brought it up: "We doubt that anybody should be required to perform an ordeal when reliable witnesses and documents are available." It was a fascinating correction. The court was giving the distinct impression that it relied heavily on written—and presumably more rational—forms of evidence as opposed to physical invocations of divine will.

VERDICT

The judges had more bad news for Bapaji. The legal text that they consulted for guidance, the Sanskrit authority the *Mitāksharā*, indicated that the punishment for demanding an ordeal when other credible evidence could be employed was death. The court also observed that to them, Bapaji was a divisive influence within his locality and therefore also deserving of the death penalty. They quickly came to another resolution, however, and on strikingly political grounds. They stated the verdict in a formal document settling the case, the *mahzar*:

> We conclude that you have caused much trouble to Narasoji and his family, and should be executed. But since you are Muslim, and the present government is a Muslim government, you will be pardoned. However we find that you have no valid claim to the position of village headman. And you

have no right to recover money owed by your father's relatives. Nor do you have any right to receive compensation for the murder of your relatives.

The judges showed no hesitation in simply announcing that they did not think it would be acceptable to the present government to execute a Muslim. They decided to take a less drastic course, one that completely exonerated Narasoji.

Moving beyond the application of law to these parties, one can see the case as an example of Indians of varying castes and religions accepting the judgment of a higher court. That court, in turn, operated with an acknowledgment that the sultans were Muslim, but that Hindu law held sway in most aspects of this case, only excepting the death penalty.

SIGNIFICANCE

In the early 21st century controversy emerged over the publication by Oxford University Press of a book by American author James Laine examining the changing historical perceptions of King Shivaji. Laine noted in the book's acknowledgments that he had consulted documents in the Bhandarkar Oriental Research Institute (BORI) at Pune, in the state of Maharashtra. A group called the Sambhaji Brigade, perhaps connected with the right-wing political party Shiv Sena, in January 2004 attacked the archives, inflicting destruction on the facility and contents.

Some scholars deplored the threat to academic discourse and to the preservation of priceless historical documents. Meanwhile, others greatly objected to Laine's work as an insult, perpetrated by a non-Indian, to a revered figure in Indian history. Among the reasons that Shivaji historically inspired such veneration was his emphasis upon persons of different religions getting along. A particular focus of his policies—the preservation of religious sites such as temples, shrines, mosques, and tombs—followed on the heels of local controversies such as had occurred in the aforementioned case of 1611. That disagreement had come to the attention even of the sultan in the early 17th century. Similar controversies very likely occupied the attention of Shivaji as well, about a generation later. Shivaji demonstrated that the parties were to

exercise restraint and mutual respect in resolving their differences.

As a result of court decisions in India clarifying the situation on the Laine book, Laine's study of Shivaji would remain on the market despite attempts to ban it. Even so, booksellers refused to carry the title out of fear of violence. That controversy pointed out enduring misunderstandings over the writing of Indian history that legal historians only recently have begun to address. It remains to be seen, though, how successfully western scholars can allay concerns that they are either ill-informed about or insensitive to deeply held beliefs among Indians about Indian management of religious diversity.

Further Reading

Eaton, Richard Maxwell. *A Social History of the Deccan, 1300–1761: Eight Lives.* Cambridge: Cambridge University Press, 2008; Laine, James. *Shivaji: Hindu King in Islamic India.* New York: Oxford University Press, 2003; Sarkar, Jadunath. *Shivaji and His Times.* London: Longmans Green & Co., 1920; Sherwani, H. K., ed. *History of Medieval Deccan, 1295–1724.* Hyderabad, India: Government of Andhra Pradesh, 1973–74; Smith, Graham, and J. Duncan Derrett. "Hindu Judicial Administration in Pre-British Times and Its Lessons for Today." *Journal of the American Oriental Society* 95 (July–September 1975): 417–423; Stein, Burton. *Vijayanagara.* Cambridge: Cambridge University Press, 1989.

The Overbury poisoning trials

Also known as: *The King v. Frances Howard Carr, Robert Carr, Weston, Turner, Elwes, Monson, and Franklin;* the Great Oyer of Poisoning

Date: 1615

KEY ISSUES

Scandal came very close to the throne of England in the trial that contemporaries called The Great Oyer

[Assize] of Poisoning. Robert Carr, the confidante of King James I of England, was accused of killing his facilitator at court, Sir Thomas Overbury. The victim had gotten in the way of a marriage between Carr and Lady Frances Howard, herself a formidable personality with superb connections in English politics. The controversial trials of Carr, Howard, and several persons accused of carrying out their scheme, were a delicate matter. Whoever oversaw the proceedings would need to step lightly because of the nature of Carr's former relationship with the king. A singularly talented and articulate judge, Edward Coke, presided in most of the trials. England's leading jurist and legal writer at the time, Coke was fully conversant with the law. But, was Coke's personality appropriate to manage a case with such profound political implications? When the trial began, it remained to be seen whether Coke could put aside his growing rancor concerning King James's oversight of justice. In addition, Coke nursed a tendency to envision conspiracies. That strain of paranoia would prove troublesome to many, including the monarch.

HISTORY OF THE CASE

Robert Carr (Kerr) had come to England from Scotland with the court of the new monarch James I in 1603. King James soon gave Carr offices and titles, even granting him ownership of lands forfeited by Sir Walter Raleigh. Beyond his control of access to James as the king's personal secretary, it was clear that Carr had the king's ear. By 1613 Carr was the earl of Somerset and was ready to arrange a glittering marriage for himself. The king approved of Carr's matrimonial ambitions, having somewhat tired of Carr's personal influence on the throne.

Frances Howard's parents, the duke and duchess of Suffolk, had arranged a marriage between her and Robert Devereaux, the earl of Essex, when both of those young people were mere children. It had been a most incompatible pairing. By 1613 Frances Howard wished to continue her intimate relationship with Carr as his wife rather than be married to Essex. Carr was at first ambivalent about whether he would marry Howard. Although she was from an prominent family and very wealthy, as well as famously attractive, several persons spoke to Carr against the union. The most influential of those voices critical of Frances Howard was Thomas Overbury.

Overbury had helped steer Carr's ascent at court. His being English allowed him to mediate some of the jealousy aimed at Carr on account of his Scottish origins. Overbury also was a talented promoter of himself and others, in spite of his own rather difficult personality. Just as Carr granted access to King James, so Overbury controlled access to Carr. The relationship between Carr and Overbury, like that between the king and Carr, was so close as to fuel rumors of sexual intimacy. When Carr conceived the idea to help Howard secure an annulment of her marriage to Essex, Overbury resisted. Overbury incurred Frances Howard's wrath as a result.

Obtaining the dissolution of Howard's marriage to Essex was a problem, for the Church of England frowned on divorce. The marriage would need to be dissolved on grounds such as prior contraction of marriage or bigamy or other specific reasons. Howard chose to pursue the annulment by alleging that Essex was incapable of fathering children. It was obviously an embarrassing charge that would invite scrutiny of the case. The young lovers Howard and Carr found tangible support from a romantic-minded patron—King James himself. He appointed an ecclesiastical commission to inquire about the infertility allegation against Essex. That group ruled in Howard's favor, though on the exceedingly strained grounds that Essex had been impotent with only his wife. Howard secured what was in effect her divorce in September 1613, but the effort cost her, Carr, and James I in political credibility.

Meanwhile, Overbury had gained the king's anger as well as the new couple's. In the spring of 1613 James I decided to send Overbury abroad as an ambassador. It was an appointment designed to get him out of the way, and Overbury almost certainly knew it. Besides, diplomatic posts were expensive to maintain and took one from the center of English politics at London. Overbury took the unusual step of refusing the "honor" from the monarch. James, perhaps with Carr's urging, confined Overbury to the Tower of London. Overbury was accused of the amorphous offense of "contempt of the king."

Overbury tried to gain James's favor or at least get out of confinement. Among his most potent weapons was his old friendship with Carr. Overbury repeatedly wrote to Carr asking for assistance. Carr bargained with Overbury for his freedom, insisting that Overbury cease his opposition to the Howard faction at court. After sending some bitter letters to Carr, Overbury—never in strong health since his imprisonment—died. Carr and Howard married in an expensive ceremony in December. The king and queen of England directed the festivities while gossip circulated about the couple's route to the altar.

Carr's star continued to ascend. Even while anti-Howard factions at court installed George Villiers as a rival for the king's affections, the earl of Somerset gained the position of privy councilor in Scotland and England. In 1615 the earl tried to broker a marriage between Prince Charles and the infanta of Spain; it was a risky maneuver, but Carr felt his position becoming imperiled by his critics and especially Villiers. At midyear Carr tried to secure from King James a pardon for future offenses. After consultation with the lord chancellor, James issued the immunity only for lesser crimes. Scholars have wondered whether Carr had a guilty conscience.

The former favorite was right to be concerned. One of those who sought to undermine Carr at court, the king's current personal secretary, Ralph Winwood, had secured damaging information. The keeper of the Tower of London, Gervase Elwes, told Winwood that he had knowledge of efforts to poison Overbury. According to Elwes, the crime not only involved the person at the Tower directly in charge of Overbury, Richard Weston, but also a friend of Frances Howard, Anne Turner. Also connected was Sir Thomas Monson, a figure at court allied with the Howards. The trail led perilously close to Carr. Winwood prevailed upon King James to initiate a high-level inquiry into the matter. Leading that investigation was Sir Edward Coke, chief justice of the Court of King's Bench. Coke found plenty of damning details.

SUMMARY OF ARGUMENTS

The bringing to justice of those responsible for Overbury's death was made more complicated by the fact that the conspiracy to murder Overbury involved persons of two distinct social categories. According to Coke's investigation, Howard and Carr generated the idea for killing Overbury and managed the affair, while persons of lesser rank carried out their plan. In a legal sense all would be culpable, but the judicial system also was class-biased enough to divide their trials according to caste. Despite Coke's repeated exhortations that justice should be blind to power, the outcome of each case seemed to depend on the wealth and connections of the accused.

As biographers of Coke note, it was the small fry who were tried first. Weston's day in court was typical of the proceedings against the "low-born" in this case. Weston's indictment was read and his trial begun on October 9, 1613, at London's Guildhall. The venue was a municipal one because of the site of Overbury's death, the Tower. First was the summary of several days' worth of inquiries by Coke, then an hour-long coroner's report on Overbury's death, followed by the start of the criminal trial of Weston. Presiding was a panel of seven officials, including Coke and the lord mayor of London; there was a jury of 14.

Coke's initial charge to the jury was sobering, bombastic, and altogether typical of him. The reporter of the case in England's State Trials series says that Coke warned the jurors that "of all felonies, murder is the most horrible; of all murders, poisoning the most detestable; and of all poisonings, the lingering poisoning." Coke went on to remind the court that poisoning was not a typically English crime because it was so cowardly; the offense clearly had the mark of the devil. Coke concluded by reminding the onlookers that this court should "do justice in presenting the truth, notwithstanding the greatness of any that upon their evidence should appear guilty of the same offense." He was exhorting the jurors that they should not be afraid of convicting Weston, though they suspected Carr also might be involved.

Coke faced a major problem with Weston because upon hearing the indictment, the prisoner refused to plead. Coke threatened Weston with pressing to death and starvation, but Weston still stood mute. Coke finally resorted to a sleight of hand; he took testimony from royal attorney Sir Lawrence Hyde concerning a confession that

Weston had signed earlier. It was not strictly speaking a substitute for a plea of guilty or not guilty; still, the device got before the court the information that Coke required—details of Weston's involvement in the plot. Coke then treated the confession as a plea of guilty.

According to that confession cited by Hyde, Weston had helped administer poisonous powders to Overbury in May, July, September, and October 1613. Among the dangerous substances were mercury and arsenic. Other individuals were involved as well, such as an apothecary's assistant and Turner. Monson apparently had made sure that Elwes, the lieutenant of the Tower, gave Weston scope for the villainy. Weston not only had helped commit the murder but also had spread the libel that Overbury died of a venereal disease.

The jury had no trouble in convicting Weston, and Coke sentenced him to hang at Tyburn. Coke, the former zealous prosecutor, had managed a conviction, but he could not leave well enough alone. He seemed determined to politicize the trial to an even greater extent than it already had been corrupted by politics. Coke's charge to the jury included a reminder that poisoning was a "popish trick." To political insiders, such language suggested the wild rumor that the earl of Somerset's ultimate design in murdering Overbury had been to touch off a pro-Spanish rebellion against the king. And so, Coke's imprint already was on the proceedings. He was lead investigator, in effect the voice of the prosecution, and chief judge. It was not an unusual combination of hats for an English judge in that era to wear, but Coke still brought to his role an unusual ferocity.

Turner was heard in court on November 7, 1615. Her trial was at King's Bench and likewise under the direction of Lord Chief Justice Coke. The case against her was in a different location than Weston's because she had conspired to kill Overbury rather than actually administering potions to him in the Tower. It was Turner's tarts, jellies, and pies that were delivered to the victim. Her trial afforded even more sensation than that of Weston. Turner was a longtime friend of Frances Howard. Although different in social station, they had been brought up together. Turner's time in court involved revelations about Howard's earlier efforts to procure "love-philters" from Turner and from Dr. Simon Forman (since deceased).

Apparently, Howard sought potions for several reasons. At first, she sought to increase Carr's romantic interest in her. She also had asked for assistance in rendering the earl of Essex impotent. The advice for the lovelorn tendered by Forman and Turner was irresistibly juicy. Court reporters noted that spectators leaned forward all at once during spicy intervals of testimony, better to catch each word; the scaffolds on which attendees sat literally cracked under the strain of the collective movement. Turner, who like Weston was not represented by counsel, offered only the weak defense that she had been reared in the Howard household and was more Frances Howard's servant than associate. Coke's instructions to Turner's jury were, again, harshly phrased: The defendant was "a whore, a bawd, a sorcerer, a witch, a papist, a felon, and a murderer, the daughter of the devil Forman." After her predictable conviction Turner died on the scaffold, by all accounts humbly.

Next, England's attorney general, Francis Bacon, decided to go after Elwes as a coconspirator, despite the former cooperation by Elwes with Winwood. Apparently, Elwes had not come forward soon enough with his suspicions against Weston. Elwes was a better lawyer for himself than the previous defendants had been. He reminded Chief Justice Coke (again the lead trial judge, back again at the Guildhall) that Coke often had remonstrated juries not to let an innocent man hang; it was better for many guilty persons to be acquitted. Elwes thought his self-reporting of the plot to Winwood would save him from the charge that he ought to have overseen affairs at the Tower more carefully. According to Coke, though, that turning in of others would not serve as an excuse for what had occurred under Elwes's watch. Once again a bit player—albeit a rather articulate one—was convicted and hanged. There was a poignant reprise to Elwes's conviction: the courtier to whom James I gave Elwes's estate returned it to the man's widow.

The apothecary Forman's assistant, James Franklin, fared little better in his King's Bench trial before Coke and Judge Crook on November 27. Franklin confessed his part. He said he had advised

Turner and Howard on the ways that arsenic and the other poisons might work. It took the jurors only 15 minutes to declare Franklin guilty of the capital crime. Once again Coke made a larger point in his summation: ". . . if this had not been found out, neither the court, city, nor any particular family had escaped the malice of this particular cruelty."

At the Guildhall on December 4, Monson's case was heard. This time Lord Coke went too far in hinting of popish plots. As Monson tried to get character witnesses such as Sir Robert Cotton to appear on his behalf at arraignment, Coke struck down these efforts. Coke reminded the court that "more would be discovered by his trial than the mere death of a private individual." The reference was to whispers that Overbury somehow had been involved in the demise of James I's eldest son, Prince Henry, which rumor had as due to poison. Was Coke suggesting that Overbury's death was by royal command and in retribution for the death of the heir to the throne? James stepped in. He ordered Monson sent to the Tower but prorogued the trials of any additional minor conspirators. Monson shortly went free, and Coke was more than ever in the king's bad graces. Henceforth, Coke would only participate, not preside, in the Overbury case.

Though he had refused to speak at his trial, Weston's earlier words to the sheriff of London seemed to haunt Coke and many others in court. Weston had said that he hoped the prosecution would not "make a net to catch little birds, and let the great ones go." The actions of lesser plotters were laid bare. But, would the deeds of the greatest figures also earn stern censure? A key step in a prosecution of this magnitude was to pave the way for it politically. In England at this time it was wise to secure a statement alleging culpability from Parliament—an impeachment—before proceeding to a criminal trial of well-connected folk.

Both Howard and Carr were of noble birth. They could lean on their privilege as guaranteed in the Magna Carta to be tried by a jury of their social equals; that meant their cases would be heard in the House of Lords. Such a right for the social elite usually was thought to confer an advantage on defendants. Their jurors mostly would be relatives and acquaintances of equivalent

rank. But, it also could be that peers had enemies within the upper house. It would have been surprising if the arrogant Carr and the tempestuous Howard had not garnered disapproval or even malice among some peers.

The countess of Somerset faced a formidable array of legal talent when she appeared in Westminster Hall before the House of Lords on May 24, 1616. Her jurors were most of the peers of the realm; six noble absences were unexplained. The steward (chief official) of the court was Thomas Ellesmere, lord chancellor. Joining him were Coke and several judicial colleagues from the Courts of King's Bench, Common Pleas, and the Exchequer. The chief prosecutor was Francis Bacon, England's attorney general. Bacon had assistance from various royal solicitors and attorneys. Among the considerable disadvantages that the defendant would encounter was that several alleged coconspirators already had been tried and executed.

Howard, wielding her fan and shedding tears, tried to save herself by pleading guilty. The responses of the judges were as reassuring as possible under the circumstances. Those who were presiding had to sentence her to death, but they held out much hope that her remorse and grief, so attractively expressed in court, would commend her to the king's mercy. Bacon had prepared a withering argument against the countess should she have decided to try the opposite plea; it probably was fortunate for Howard that Bacon did not deliver it.

Her husband followed at the bar the next day. Carr's appearance in the House of Lords provided considerably more tension, for this defendant argued that he was not guilty. Lord Ellesmere reminded the lords that they ought to remove politics and personal opinion from their considerations; they were no ordinary jurors but yet had the same role. He reminded them especially to be loyal to the monarch but yet free "from all partiality."

Bacon this time got to use his prepared statements. He charged that the earl of Somerset had committed three interrelated offenses, although one, strictly speaking, was a only moral travesty: Carr had killed "by impoisonment," he had done away with the king's prisoner in the Tower, and he had murdered "under the colour of friendship." Bacon echoed Coke's earlier assertion that to administer poison to an enemy was a most un-English offense—indeed, it smacked of Italy (Coke had said Rome). The main line of reasoning from the prosecution was that Overbury knew too much to be allowed to live once he had become hostile to Somerset.

It was a dangerous strain of argument, for Bacon did not want to spell out all of the secrets to which Overbury had access. He merely wished to indicate that Overbury understood "high" matters of state and that Somerset no longer trusted him. Proving such a thing was difficult, however. Convicting Somerset could rest on the testimony of the persons who already had been condemned—excepting the countess of Somerset, who had not implicated her husband. Bacon cited Carr's correspondence to try to show his guilty frame of mind, for example, calling in Overbury's parents and reading Carr's note of condolence to them. What should the jury make of his statements such as "In the mean time, I desire pardon from you and your wife for your lost son, though I esteem my loss the greater"? Was Carr sincere, menacing, remorseful, or rattled? The jury chose to believe the most sinister explanation.

VERDICTS

Thus, both of the principal plotters in the Overbury poisoning trial were found guilty. King James could not bear to see either of them go to the scaffold. In spite of the clear injustice of the chief conspirators' being spared while their minions hanged, the Somersets lived to walk out of the Tower of London in 1621 after a six-year imprisonment. They repaired to a country house with their daughter, Anne, who was born while they were under arrest. Survival was one achievement, but worming one's way back into political power was quite another.

Howard died, probably of a gynecological cancer, in 1632. Some contemporaries uncharitably opined that it was a fitting demise given her reputation as a "temptress." Carr lived on until 1645, but he never recovered his former place at the pinnacle of politics. Not only had he been usurped in the king's affections by a more powerful favorite, Villiers, Carr also lost close connection to the throne when James I died in 1625.

Although the relationship between Villiers and the new king, Charles I, was now one of uncle and advisee, rather than of lovers, he still held the reins of the royal administration.

Somerset never admitted that he directly caused Overbury's death. At most he seemed to regret that he had had Overbury imprisoned. Though most scholars accept that Overbury was murdered, a few posit that he died of overzealous medical treatment. Of course, the stress of Overbury's confinement probably lay behind the man's resort to dangerous purges and emetics. Thus, Somerset still might shoulder moral responsibility for Overbury's death. Did Howard resent Overbury so much that she planned his death? She had at least as much to lose from Overbury's machinations as Carr did, and the corroborating evidence against her was stronger. Legal scholars say that the facts uncovered in Coke's investigations better support Howard's conviction than the earl of Somerset's, but neither is an airtight instance of guilt.

Coke's position with James deteriorated rapidly after the trials. The king removed Coke from office in the same year as the Somersets' convictions, 1616. The rupture was a long time coming. Coke had objected for years to what he saw as the king's overbearing attitude toward judges. To Coke the jurist, the king did not show proper respect for the common law and its courts. The king persisted in viewing judicial officials as royal appointees. He perceived Coke as haughty and disrespectful. In the Great Oyer of Poisoning the king had wanted Coke to confine himself to the case at hand rather than seeking to uncover additional plots. At stake was no less than the royal reputation.

SIGNIFICANCE

Coke had the last word among contemporaries and in history. A member of the legislature after 1621, Coke parlayed his status as the premier scholar of English law into a role as spokesman for parliamentary critics of the monarch's lawgiving. In the Petition of Right of 1628 Coke articulated the principle that the king was not above the law. It was a notion that Coke already had illustrated in the Carr case. A concept that flowed from Coke's views—that popular will limited executive authority—was of profound influence in England in the subsequent years of the 17th century. It remains a cornerstone of the Anglo-American constitutional tradition.

Further Reading

Bellany, Alastair. "Howard, Frances, countess of Somerset (1590–1632)." *Oxford Dictionary of National Biography.* Available online. URL: http:// libproxy.uta.edu:2422/view/article/53028. Accessed November 6, 2009; ———. *The Politics of Court Scandal in Early Modern England: News Culture and the Overbury Affair, 1603–1660.* Cambridge: Cambridge University Press, 2002; Boyer, Alan. *Sir Edward Coke and the Elizabethan Age.* Palo Alto, Calif.: Stanford University Press, 2003; Bowen, Catherine Drinker. *The Lion and the Throne.* Boston: Little, Brown, 1957; Cobbett, Thomas Bayly, et al., eds. *Cobbett's Complete Collection of State Trials,* vol. 2. London: T. C. Hansard, 1806; DeFord, Miriam Allen. *The Overbury Affair.* New York: Avon Book Division, 1960; Lindley, David. *The Trials of Frances Howard: Fact and Fiction at the Court of King James.* New York: Routledge, 1993; Parry, Edward A. *The Overbury Mystery: A Chronicle of Facts and Drama of the Law.* London: T. F. Unwin, 1925; Somerset, Anne. *Unnatural Murder.* London: Weidenfeld & Nicolson, 1997.

The trial of Galileo Galilei

Date: 1633

KEY ISSUES

The Catholic Church in Rome was uncomfortable, to say the least, with the theories of Galileo Galilei. Galileo supported the vision of several philosophers and scientists who recently had been condemned by the church, particularly the Italian Dominican friar Giordano Bruno. Bruno was burned alive in 1600 for teaching that the universe

was infinite; his "plurality of worlds" ran counter to Catholic doctrine that the Almighty had created the Earth and humans and had sent divine redemption for sins in the form of Jesus Christ.

Bruno's and Galileo's work rested on the heliocentric theory of Nicolaus Copernicus, whose ideas were most fully expressed in the 1543 publication *De revolutionibus orbium coelestium (On the Revolutions of the Heavenly Spheres).* While the Roman Catholic Church did not condemn Copernican ideas as heretical during Copernicus's lifetime, Christian religious authorities took a hard look at them a few generations later. It was exactly during the time that Galileo was most active as a researcher and writer that Copernicus's questioning of the Earth as the center of the universe came under church scrutiny.

Part of Rome's nervousness was that Galileo seemed to have much better proof than Copernicus or Bruno: observations of the "heavenly bodies" via telescopes that Galileo began to use in the 1610s. Another reason for the church's repression of Galileo was politics. Galileo was tied to powers in Florence that the current pope wished to see humbled. Adding further dimension to the religious authorities' treatment of Galileo was the fact that he had once been a friend to the man at the apex of the Western Christian world: Pope Urban VIII.

The church's official announcements about Galileo's case in its immediate aftermath—the press bulletins of the day—led scholars to assume for hundreds of years that Galileo had been treated extremely harshly during trial and imprisoned thereafter. But, the history of Galileo's encounter with the Inquisition recently has been rewritten due to the discovery of documents from diplomats and other observers who watched the episode in 1633. Those records confirm that it was Galileo's political connections that probably saved him. Also, Galileo's willingness to trim his sails rather than follow Bruno's course got him a sentence that was bearable.

Modern examinations of Galileo's trial before the grand inquisitors in Rome make clear that Galileo was not as defiant as myth long had it. Nor was the legal confrontation over his work entirely a matter of a clash of ideas. Rather, both friendship and politics played a part.

HISTORY OF THE CASE

Despite the severity of the church's treatment of Bruno, Galileo must have expected better from his encounter with Rome. It was critical in the scientist's thinking about what he could publish concerning Copernicus that Galileo was friends with the man who had been named Pope Urban VIII, Maffeo Barberini. Barberini was well educated and articulate himself, and he was from Florence. From 1610 to 1611, when the ambitious prelate and Galileo both resided in Florence, Barberini had supported Galileo. Barberini made suggestions about how Galileo might phrase his arguments so as not to run afoul of those within the church who were suspicious of Copernicanism.

Upon Barberini's elevation to the Holy See in 1623, he and Galileo engaged in a series of conversations during which Galileo detailed his recent work with telescopes. Galileo proposed that his observations confirmed the validity of Copernican theory. Pope Urban gave his approval for Galileo to explain himself in writing by using a literary device. Galileo would present a view of the solar system and indeed the working of certain processes on Earth, such as the movement of the tides, but only as a hypothesis. In order to secure approval from the church for his book Galileo had to retune his manuscript, playing down the focus on the tides and natural processes. But, in his writing Galileo went further; for example, he purposefully watered down the explanation that the church currently favored concerning the movement of objects in the solar system, a scheme based on the work of Tycho Brahe. Although the Tychonian view was a complex system, ultimately Tycho had argued that planets and the Sun revolved around the Earth.

In 1632 Galileo published his masterwork, the *Dialogue Concerning the Two Chief World Systems*. Pope Urban objected to it for several reasons. First of all, Galileo wrote the *Dialogue* in a way that made the church's position look unscientific, if not ridiculous. The *Dialogue* dubbed Aristotle and Ptolemy the representatives for ancient views of the universe that Galileo rejected; he called the defender of the ancient systems "Simplicio." By contrast, the clear winner of the mock argument in the *Dialogue* was "Salviati," also known as "the Academi-cian"—maybe a representation of Galileo himself. It took no particular knowledge of Latin to recognize the jibes that Galileo intended through those epithets. The very accessibility of Galileo's *Dialogue* made it threatening to those who already were nervous about Galileo's work. This was a book that many educated persons could read; one did not need to be an astronomer nor especially intellectual to grasp it.

The *Dialogue* was dedicated to Galileo's patron in Tuscany, the grand duke Ferdinando II de' Medici. Having the blessing of political authorities in Florence allowed Galileo to get the book published there. He had tried to put the book out in Rome because that would have meant an even wider audience. The leading censor for the church in Rome, however, objected to the book as not theoretical enough as well as contrary to current church policy.

His Florentine protectors accompanied Galileo to answer to Rome. Galileo got a summons from the Inquisition in Rome in late 1632. He tried but failed to move the Inquisition's hearing to Florence. He was in poor health and had to make the trip to Rome in wintertime. He entered the city in mid-February, repairing to the home of his friend Francesco Niccolini, the Tuscan ambassador to Rome.

Galileo later stayed in either private accommodations or at the residences of the Holy Office during his trial. These were unusual arrangements, testifying to the trustworthiness of the defendant and the high placement of his advocates; usually defendants sat in church jails. Galileo had turned down offers of asylum from sympathetic powers such as Venice, believing that he would be protected in Rome. Besides, he had answered questions about his work before.

SUMMARY OF ARGUMENTS

Galileo began talking with inquisitors on April 12, 1633. His first interrogator was the head of the Holy Office, which coordinated all of the other inquisitions within the church and thus was the most prestigious of the inquisitorial venues. The chief commissioner of the Roman Inquisition was the Dominican friar Vincenzo Maculano; Father Carlo Sinceri was the lead assistant to Maculano.

Since the time that Rome began the Inquisition in the 1200s, the Dominicans had been closely associated with the effort to root out heresy.

At the proceedings that continued in May and June, Galileo's 10 judges were all cardinals who sat regularly as part of the Congregation of the Holy Office of the Inquisition. Others, however, were behind the accusations of heresy levied against him: the many conservative friars, especially among the Dominicans, who in recent years had been battling against Copernican theory. Others, such as Father Lorini of Florence, who first formally lodged a complaint with authorities about Galileo's defense of Copernicus in 1615, were not above literally altering Galileo's writings to make them appear more at odds with the church position than they were. In addition, periodically in the trial appeared the words of the pontiff himself, the former Maffeo Barberini.

It is telling that in the formal documents of Galileo's trial there is mention that Galileo had erred in writing of his ideas to "Germans." Barberini partisans at the Vatican were sensitive to the allegation that they were ignoring Catholics in Germany out of undue focus on military affairs in Italy. The papacy was especially wary of Galileo's long correspondence with Johannes Kepler, which had resulted in a productive sharing of ideas.

Galileo did not have counsel, and that put him at some disadvantage in front of such experienced canon lawyers and theologians. The leading exponent of his work within the church, mathematician Father Benedetto Castelli, was one of the few persons that could have explained Galileo's writing to the Inquisition. Galileo's critics made certain that Castelli was not in Rome for Galileo's trial. Still, the accused man made a good start in self-defense at the initial inquiry before a small panel in April, first arguing that he had acted according to religious guidance. He recalled he had been in Rome several times while he was conceiving the *Dialogue*:

Galileo: I was in Rome in the year 1616; then I was here in the second year of His Holiness Urban VIII's pontificate; and lastly I was here three years ago, the occasion being that I wanted to have my book printed. The occasion for my being in Rome in the year 1616 was that, having heard objections to Nicolaus Copernicus's opinion on the earth's motion, the sun's stability, and the arrangement of the heavenly spheres, in order to be sure of holding only holy and Catholic opinions, I came to hear what was proper to hold in regard to this topic.

Inquisitors: Whether he came of his own accord or was summoned, what the reason was why he was summoned, and with which person or persons he discussed the above-mentioned topics.

Galileo: In 1616 I came to Rome of my own accord, without being summoned, for the reason I mentioned. In Rome I discussed this matter with some cardinals who oversaw the Holy Office at that time, especially with Cardinals Bellarmine, Aracoeli, San Eusebio, Bonsi, and d'Ascoli.

Inquisitors: What specifically he discussed with the above-mentioned cardinals.

Galileo: The occasion for discussing with the said cardinals was that they wanted to be informed about Copernicus's doctrine, his book being very difficult to understand for those who are not professional mathematicians and astronomers. In particular they wanted to understand the arrangement of the heavenly spheres according to Copernicus's hypothesis, how he places the sun at the center of the planets' orbits, how around the sun he places next the orbit of Mercury, around the latter that of Venus, then the moon around the earth, and around this Mars, Jupiter, and Saturn; and in regard to motion, he makes the sun stationary at the center and the earth turn on itself and around the sun, that is, on itself with the diurnal motion and around the sun with the annual motion.

Inquisitors: Since, as he says, he came to Rome to be able to have the resolution and the truth regarding the above, what then was decided about this matter.

Galileo: Regarding the controversy which centered on the above-mentioned opinion of the sun's stability and earth's motion, it was decided by the Holy Congregation of the Index that this opinion, taken absolutely, is repugnant to Holy Scripture and is to be admitted only suppositionally, in the way that Copernicus takes it.

Representing himself, Galileo offered several narrow defenses. His argument had to do with the type of instructions that he had gotten from Cardinal Bellarmine. That warning in 1616 had told Galileo it was against church doctrine to hold the view that the Earth moved; likewise one could not be an obedient Catholic and defend others' maintenance of such a Copernican position. Galileo even produced a copy of Bellarmine's letter to that effect. But, the scientist also said that he was acting within the cardinal's warning when he wrote in his *Dialogue Concerning the Two Chief World Systems* that heliocentrism was as yet not established as fact. Bellarmine's position was that he had issued a "special injunction" forbidding any discussion of heliocentrism whatsoever by Galileo. Galileo denied receiving such a blanket prohibition. Indeed, many scholars believe that in 1632 or 1633 his detractors actually planted such a document within the Inquisition's files to make it appear that he had gotten a sharp warning in 1616.

The inquisitors promised Galileo that if he would admit to defending Copernicanism then they would allow him to escape censure with regard to violating the special injunction. It was a kind of plea bargain that, interestingly, was proposed by a member of the larger inquisitorial panel, Francesco Cardinal Barberini, a nephew of Pope Urban. In early May Galileo made good on his part of the agreement. He said in court that he may have given the wrong impression to his readers and had failed to correct his errors when Cardinal Bellarmine pointed them out in excerpts from the *Dialogue*.

But, at some time between the working out of the plea bargain and its ratification by the full panel of the inquisitors, the arrangement fell apart. It is unclear what forces were brought to bear. Perhaps those Dominicans and some influential

Jesuits who worked to influence Pope Urban against Galileo were having an effect. It could have been that the pontiff himself was growing more rigid concerning Galileo's seeming lack of contrition; why was a plea bargain even necessary, Urban may have wondered. Or, foreign affairs may have pressed the pope to make a stronger show against Galileo, simply to demonstrate that he was in charge within his bailiwick.

Some time in mid-June the prosecutors took a decidedly sterner approach to Galileo. The Holy Office said that in their initial examination of Galileo the churchmen could not determine whether he had meant to defend Copernicus's theories after hearing from Bellarmine that he should reject heliocentrism. Galileo had contended that he had bolstered Copernicus without intending to do so.

The Holy Office now was saying that they did not fully accept Galileo's justification for his writings in the *Dialogue*. At this juncture the history of the trial becomes considerably more dramatic, for it was here that the record indicated that "rigorous examination" was to be used against Galileo. That phrase was a euphemism for physical torture. Did the Church order such measures against the old scholar? First, one needs to consider whether the inquisitors legally could have done so, and that answer is yes. Torture was an available procedure among the Roman inquisitors, although it was the Spanish Inquisition that reputedly was most prone to employ it. If a panel of church judges was divided as to whether to accept such an explanation, then they applied torture to determine the accused person's state of mind.

Closer examination of the church announcements after its trial of Galileo had ended leaves much room for doubt, though, as to what type of strong-arming Galileo endured in order to clear things up. In the first place the documents about this Inquisition do not specify whether Galileo was subjected to "real intimidation" (*territio realis*) or only the threat of torture (*territio verbalis*). Other arguments against the imposition of physical intimidation in Galileo's case are that he fit several categories of persons who usually were exempt from physical pressure. For example, he recently had tonsured his hair in the manner of a cleric and thus could argue that he had clerical status; the rules on the torture of clerics were stricter than with regard to laypeople. Galileo was 70 years old and infirm at the time of his summons to Rome; ill health and advanced age also would have exempted him. Finally, one may conclude that Galileo showed no signs of physical coercion, for the forms of torture that the Inquisition employed—usually involving the dislocation of shoulders—were well known and would have been easy to spot.

The likeliest scenario is that Galileo was under psychological stress at his examinations before the inquisitors. He must have been rattled by the turn that the trial was taking. The examiners could have shown him instruments of torture or threatened him with them. While the emotional impact of that duress cannot be underestimated and may have led Galileo to bend to the will of his judges, it was not physical coercion.

At the "rigorous examination" Galileo apparently (in the words of the inquisitors) "answered in a Catholic manner." In other words, June 21, 1633, Galileo was convincing about his motives for writing as he did in the *Dialogue* about Copernicus. He had not meant to go against Bellarmine's orders; when he did so it was out of pride (the record spoke of "vainglory") rather than a wish to hold on to heretical doctrines.

Galileo's signed statement from June 21, 1633, looked like an acceptance of the terms of his accusers, yet the defendant somehow avoided seeming abject. His critics proffered the view that when Galileo had said in the *Dialogue* that "the earth moves and the sun is motionless, he is presumed, as it was stated, that he holds Copernicus' opinion." Galileo's reply was considerably more circumspect than the riposte that he supposedly muttered: "and yet it does move" *("Eppur si muove")*. Rather, Galileo said, "I do not hold this opinion of Copernicus, and I have not held it after being ordered by injunction to abandon it. For the rest, here I am in your hands; do as you please." It was a legalistic response, just as his whole defense had been. The statement verged on the passive-aggressive; still, it was a capitulation.

VERDICT

There were several possible outcomes of Galileo's trial before the inquisitors. He might be found not to have committed the alleged offense. That was a most unlikely outcome in such proceedings. Inquiries at this level rarely went forward without solid proof, especially in a case involving renowned scholars and their wealthy patrons. At the other end of the spectrum the inquisitors could have declared him a heretic, forced him to recant his heresies, and thus put him on notice that any future appearances before them marked a return to heresy. Such a relapse would condemn him to death at the hands of secular authorities, since the church forbade its own courts to shed blood. Seven of Galileo's 10 judges on June 22, 1633, found him to be someone in whom they had a "vehement suspicion of heresy." It was significant that a minority on the ecclesiastical panel voted not to censure him severely. Yet, Galileo certainly was not being cleared, either.

The formal documents indicated Galileo was to be imprisoned at the will of the Holy Office, which usually meant one stayed incarcerated forever. He had to renounce his writings, several of which were put on a list of publications that good Catholics could not read. Along with the uncensored version of Copernicus's *De revolutionibus*, Galileo's *Dialogue* remained on Rome's Index of Prohibited Books until the 19th century. Pope Urban VIII ordered Galileo not to discuss the motion of the Earth and "the stability of the sun" either in conversation or in writing.

Galileo was released to the custody of first the Florentine ambassador and then Florentine church officials. They allowed him to live out his years at a farmhouse. He taught mathematics to private students, including several clerics, but steadily lost his sight and mobility. He died nine years after the trial's conclusion.

SIGNIFICANCE

For centuries most scholars portrayed Galileo's trial simply as a battle over Copernican ideas. Among historians and scientists who wrote about his trial, some defended Galileo openly. They insisted that he represented the forces of truth and progress versus those of mindless acceptance of church authority. Such characterizations are rooted in some of Galileo's own mocking of his detractors. When certain critics of his refused to look through

Galileo's telescopes for fear of being led from their faith, Galileo famously wondered at that benighted attitude. It was as though scholars had imbibed his scorn; how could Galileo's contemporaries not recognize his contributions? Thus, for centuries it was only within scholarship produced by writers sympathetic to the Catholic Church that the Inquisition's treatment of Galileo made sense. Among pro-Catholic historians Galileo was portrayed as knowingly contravening the teachings of the church. According to those scholars, Rome showed mercy in stopping short of a heresy verdict, which was a virtual death sentence.

More modern scholarship has emphasized the political context of Pope Urban's abandonment of Galileo after the publication of the *Dialogue*. Once an admirer of Galileo, by 1633 Urban was more concerned with keeping the Medici in their place than in supporting his former colleague. In allowing the more conservative elements within the church to prosecute Galileo, the pope could shore up support that he needed for political and diplomatic projects. Still, in the treatment of Galileo by the Roman Inquisition one perceives a persistent staying of the hand of judgment. There was the torture that was threatened but not imposed, the heresy verdict that was approached but never reached, and the perpetual imprisonment that was pronounced but not strictly enforced. Such mitigations may have been because contemporaries understood Galileo's intellectual importance, or perhaps they were due to the intervention of an old friend.

Further Reading

Biagioli, Mario. *Galileo, Courtier: The Practice of Science in the Culture of Absolutism.* Chicago: University of Chicago Press, 1993; Brecht, Bertolt. *Galileo.* New York: Grove Press, 1994; Finocchiaro, Maurice A. ed., trans. *The Galileo Affair: A Documentary History.* Berkeley: University of California Press, 1989; Galilei, Galileo. *Dialogue Concerning the Two Chief World Systems,* translated by Stillman Drake. New York: Modern Library, 2001; Halsall, Paul. "The Crime of Galileo: Indictment and Abjuration of 1633." Available online. URL: http://www.fordham.edu/HALSALL/MOD/1630galileo.html. Accessed November 22, 2009;

Numbers, Ronald, ed. *Galileo Goes to Jail and Other Myths about Science and Religion.* Cambridge, Mass.: Harvard University Press, 2009; Rowland, Wade. *Galileo's Mistake.* Toronto, Canada: T. Allen, 2001; Shea, William, and Mariano Artigas. *Galileo in Rome: The Rise and Fall of a Troublesome Genius.* New York: Oxford University Press, 2004; Sobel, Dava. *Galileo's Daughter.* New York: Penguin, 2000.

The trials of Burton, Bastwick, and Prynne

Also known as: *The King v. Burton, Bastwick, and Prynne*

Date: 1637

KEY ISSUES

The editors of England's State Trials series remark that among all of the politically vital cases recorded in that lengthy record, "there were no more willing martyrs than William Prynne, Dr. John Bastwick, and Henry Burton." None of those men actually died for his beliefs at the hand of the courts, but they all underwent gruesome public punishments as penalty for critical words about the leaders of the English state church. Still, the goals of the three defendants came to pass: Those who condemned them lost favor with the public, while the religious ideals that the authors professed became mainstream.

The prosecutors of Burton, Bastwick, and Prynne were no less than the highest administrators of the Church of England. Perhaps the prosecution even had the blessing of the king himself. The accused men argued their cases to great effect despite crude efforts on the part of the court to hobble their defense. The trial of the three thus became an indictment of the specific judicial venue that tried them, the Court of Star Chamber. Still, the defendants did not malign the entire judicial system of their country nor the institution of monarchy.

The case of Burton, Bastwick, and Prynne was connected to reform in England in the defendants' own day. Reaction against their trial factored into the abolition of the Court of Star Chamber in 1640 and the fall from power and execution of Archbishop of Canterbury William Laud. A groundswell of support from thousands of citizens toward these defendants helped bolster the confidence of religious and political radicals during the lead-up to the English Civil War of the 1640s.

Equally intriguing, though perhaps harder to demonstrate, are the links between the trial of these dissidents and longer-range developments in English and Anglo-American history. For example, the ability of Prynne to reconcile religious protest with loyalty to the restored Stuart monarchy may have helped inspire non-Anglican Protestants to wait for religious toleration in the later 1600s.

Finally, there was the matter of the graphic sentences. The spectacle of the grisly punishments endured by Burton, Bastwick, and Prynne was nothing new to English people inured to public executions at such sites as Tyburn. And yet, these cases seemed to mark a turning point in the opinion of the populace. This trial certainly did not cause a repudiation of the scaffold; there is too much evidence of the immense popularity of London "hanging days" in the century following this trial. But for certain offenses, especially those involving "mere" words, after this trial it appeared excessive to impose corporal penalties. Historians of the U.S. Constitution rightly find roots of American prohibitions on "cruel and unusual" punishment in the sufferings of these defendants.

HISTORY OF THE CASE

Burton, Bastwick, and Prynne separately had been irritants to the Anglican establishment for several years prior to their prosecution in the Court of Star Chamber in 1637. The men pursued different courses of argument from one another in the 1620s and early 1630s. Burton homed in on Archbishop Laud's alleged sympathy for Catholicism. Bastwick came to the defense of Presbyterians who were in trouble with the Church of England. Prynne meanwhile focused mainly on moral offenses that he thought the state church was ignoring.

Henry Burton was a minister in the Church of England who served at the royal court. He tutored first King James's son Prince Henry, who died in 1612, and then Prince Charles. His connections, though, neither kept him from dissent nor insulated him from reprimand when he expressed that dissent. Burton thought he detected increasing toleration for Catholic views within the Church of England under his former pupil the young king Charles I. He struck out at the practices adopted by Archbishop Laud, which were termed "Arminianism." Burton's attacks on Laud from 1626 onward earned him censure from the Court of High Commission, like the Star Chamber a prerogative court closely associated with divine-right monarchy.

Burton continued to attract unfavorable notice from such institutions, in 1629 being cited by the Court of High Commission for his book *Babel no Bethel*. Laud's political usefulness to Charles I increased after the assassination of the duke of Buckingham in 1629. Laudian influence progressed further with the king's proroguing of Parliament in the same year. Charles was adopting what became known as his "personal government," relying on trusted administrators to work outside the legislature to effect policy.

Matters came to a dramatic pass for Burton on Guy Fawkes Day, 1636, when he delivered two sermons that the church hierarchy found especially objectionable. He equated the Anglican episcopacy with Roman Catholicism, though once again he adopted the device of saying he was trying to protect the king from the "machinations" of advisers close to the throne. Ordered to appear first before one of the officers of the High Commission and then its full session, Burton refused to take an oath that was demanded of him. The *ex officio* oath was a controversial tool used by prerogative courts. It was a sworn promise that compelled accused persons to tell the truth to court officials before charges were explained to them. Thus, a minister might be required to swear to his innocence and then either find himself committing perjury or refusing to answer questions. Inquisitorial courts such as the Star Chamber and High Commission read unwillingness to speak as an admission of guilt.

After 1634 Dr. John Bastwick did jail time for his work *Flagellum Pontificis*, which was a revision of his 1624 work *Elenchus*. Originally the piece was intended as a series of rejoinders that Protestant travelers in Europe could give when approached by Catholic missionaries, but the implicit criticism of episcopacy also was aimed at the bishops of England. That the tract did not earn Bastwick imprisonment sooner was due to his professional position as a physician and his connections at court. Also, Bastwick initially published in Latin. English courts looked more leniently upon alleged libels that did not reach the masses in the vernacular.

While Bastwick early on was inclined to apologize his way out of legal trouble and had the money to dodge some prosecutions, after being thrown in jail he had a change of heart. During an outbreak of plague in London in the spring of 1636, an unsympathetic jailer left Bastwick behind when Gatehouse Prison was evacuated. During that traumatic stay in a near-empty prison, Bastwick experienced a religious epiphany that made him willing to circulate his writings more widely. He also began to say that he was ready to suffer for his faith. Among the visitors who helped supply him in confinement was a young John Lilburne. Lilburne shepherded Bastwick's prison memoir, called the *Litany of John Bastwick*, into print. It cost Lilburne a whipping and imprisonment himself. Although Lilburne and Bastwick eventually grew estranged, Lilburne developed a taste for resistance to authority under Bastwick's tutelage.

William Prynne at first seemed a pamphleteer concerned only with personal morality. Nevertheless, he got under the skin of members of the royal family for his criticism of the theater, of which the king and queen were great patrons. The publication for which he first was censured was *Histiomastix* (1633). It had a bite that Prynne argued was general in nature rather than aimed at his queen, but to no avail. His invective was stinging enough to draw a stern sentence from Star Chamber in 1633. Besides life imprisonment he was to have his ears cut off and pay a ruinous fine.

The legal persecution only emboldened the radicals. They all endeavored to smuggle writings out of prison and publish them. Bastwick's 1636 account of his trial before the Court of High Commission, titled *Apologeticus*, proved inflammatory

to the ecclesiastics of England. Prynne, perhaps with collaboration from Bastwick and Burton, produced tracts called *News from Ipswich* and *A Divine Tragedy*, both of which the established church found offensive. Burton also disseminated the sermons that he had preached in November 1636, in which he described the Anglican hierarchy as "antichristian mushrooms." That publication was called *An Apologie of an Appeale*; it was a direct attack on the previous legal actions against him.

SUMMARY OF ARGUMENTS

The proceedings at Star Chamber were technical but did not lack verbal drama. The defendants admitted their writings. Indeed, they grasped at the opportunity to discuss and defend the views that had landed them in court. The judges, meanwhile, wished to deny the accused men a platform. Archbishop Laud was a noticeable figure in the prosecution. At several moments he demanded to know why the answers produced by the defendants did not themselves constitute examples of libel. It had been by Laud's order that the case was filed in the first place. Royal officials had the authority to enter cases before the courts on "informations," circumventing grand jury indictments.

The main discussion before the court concerned the provision of counsel and the preparation of the men's formal answer to the charges. Sitting in close confinement, all of the defendants had been denied access to writing implements and attorneys. Faced with a deadline for preparing their rejoinder to the charges, they finally secured access to a lawyer but lacked privacy in which to discuss matters with him. When counsel was able to read the materials that his clients—mostly Prynne—had written up for him to present to the court, the lawyer backtracked. He judged that putting his own imprimatur on the men's justifications would land him in difficulty. He counseled the three accused men that they should amend their answers considerably.

The three defendants opted to take up their case directly with the court. They had good grounds for doing so since Prynne was a member of the bar. The court declined to let him represent himself and his fellow defendants. The court ruled that not filing an acceptable written answer through a court-approved attorney amounted to a confession of the truth of the charges.

The defendants pressed the judges to either let them read their full responses out loud to the Star Chamber or assure that the judges had perused the defendants' published writings. It was a clever argument, amounting to "either let us explain ourselves, or declare that you have read our work, so we can be sure you understand our position." The bench was ever more exasperated at being the objects of the prisoners' sermons:

> Burton: My good lords, your honors, it should seem, so determine to censure us, and take our cause *pro confesso*, although we have labored to give your honors satisfaction in all things. My lords, what you have to say against my book, I confess I did write it, yet did I not anything out of intent of commotion, or sedition. I delivered nothing but what my text led me to. . . .

> Lord Keeper: Mr. Burton, I pray stand not naming texts of scripture now; we do not send for you to preach, but to answer these things that are objected against you. . . . What say you, Mr. Burton, are you guilty or not?

> Burton: My lord, I desire you not only to peruse my book here and there, but every passage of it. . . .

> Lord Keeper: This is a place where you should crave mercy and favor, Mr. Burton, and not stand upon such terms as you do.

> Burton: There wherein I have offended through human frailty, I crave of God and man pardon: and I pray God, that in your Sentence you may so censure us, that you may not sin against the Lord.

VERDICTS

The proceedings ended with the judges commanding the defendants to silence, after which they pronounced verdicts of life imprisonment and mutilation for each accused man. The ears of the three were to be cut off. Upon observing that Prynne had some remnants of ears from his earlier punishment, the judges lamented that he apparently had paid the executioner on the earlier occasion to do an incomplete job. They declared that Prynne was to be branded on both cheeks as a further punishment. They then turned the floor over to Archbishop Laud, who lectured those in court on the impropriety of the writings of the three.

The physical chastisement was carried out on June 30, 1637, at the Palace Yard at Westminster. The sentences that had been handed down could have resulted in death in several ways. Having an ear severed could cause the victim to bleed to death or might create an infection that would dispatch the person within days. Sitting in the pillory was an invitation to taunters (or assassins) to throw objects at an immobilized person. Imprisonment itself was life threatening. As Bastwick had learned at close hand, the jails of 17th-century England were places of contagion and deprivation. Odds were that a prisoner would die of one or the other long before his natural life span ended.

Enduring the ear removal was a great physical challenge. The executioner poked Burton's temporal artery; Burton was fortunate not to have expired from it. Bastwick perhaps had the best excision, having brought his own scalpel. The executioner seemed to Prynne to act with savagery despite oversight by a surgeon near the scaffold. Prynne nearly was poked in the jugular vein, which certainly would have been fatal. As it was, the executioner hacked at his stumps of ears several times before severing them completely. He also seared Prynne's cheek badly during the branding of the letters *SL*, one on each side of the face. (Though the initials were supposed to stand for "Seditious Libel," Prynne later said they meant "the Stigma of Laud.") It cannot have escaped notice from the government that on the scaffold all three men expressed themselves more eloquently than in any of their publications.

Prynne had invited the executioner to do his worst: "I have learned to fear the fire of hell, and not what man can do unto me. Come sear me, sear me, I shall bear in my body the marks of the Lord Jesus." Prynne's comment upon losing the remainder of his ears was "The more I am beat down, the more I am lift up." He smiled and cast his eyes heavenward. Upon approaching the three pillories, Burton already had compared the scene to "Mount Calvary, where [there were] the three crosses. . . ."

As was typical for him, Bastwick saw in the trial and convictions a popish plot. He used the occasion to lament the influence of "Jesuits." He also declared himself ready to make any sacrifice necessary to usher in a new order:

> In a word, I am so far from base fear, or caring for anything that they would do, or cast upon me, that had I as much blood as would swell the Thames, I would shed it every drop in this cause; therefore be not any of you discouraged, be not daunted at their power . . . go on in the strength of your God, and he will never fail you in such a day as this.

Bastwick's wife, Susanna, picked up his ears from the scaffold and kept them. Her devotion to her mate was much admired. She had gone to stay with him at the fetid Gatehouse Prison and, like Elizabeth Lilburne, promoted radical causes energetically.

Almost all of the spectators seemed admiring of the prisoners, shouting out words of encouragement that the sufferers answered warmly. The condemned men got support both large and small—from handkerchiefs that well wishers pressed upon them to staunch the blood loss to flowers strewn in their paths and Bible verses offering cheer. The crowds and the condemned men were persons brought up on John Foxe's tales of Protestant martyrdom in the previous century, and they applied those lessons well.

Significance

All of the prisoners were dispatched to faraway locations for their imprisonments. Even their rides from London turned into a repudiation of Arminianism. Thousands of well-wishers lined the roads that they traveled out of the city. First sentenced to stay at Lostwithiel Castle, Bastwick was relocated to the more remote Isles of Scilly. Prynne and Burton went to the Channel Islands. All of the men suffered quite restrictive confinements. To deprive them of not only their families' presence but also

all books and letters (and in Bastwick's case even a window) was widely perceived as retributive on the part of the government.

The demonstrations of fortitude and religious constancy by Burton, Bastwick, and Prynne were memorable to their contemporaries. Perhaps the most shocking aspect of the prosecutions at Star Chamber was that the court imposed ferocious punishments on well-connected, professional men. Prynne did not hesitate to draw out that point for those in attendance on June 30, 1637:

> You all at this present see there be no degrees of men exempted from suffering: here is a reverent divine for the soul, a physician for the body, and a lawyer for the estate. I had thought they would have let alone their own society, and not meddled with any of them. . . . Gentlemen, look to yourselves; if all the martyrs that suffered in Queen Mary's days are accounted and called schismatical heretics and factious fellows; what shall we look for!

In 1640, when the political tide began to turn against first Laud and then almost all of the judicial institutions connected with Charles I, the three were released by Parliament. The consensus among the House of Commons was that they had been political prisoners. Burton, Bastwick, and Prynne eventually got compensation from Parliament in recognition of their sufferings, though not enough to pay their huge debts from multiple trials and imprisonments. They all continued their criticism of high-church Anglicanism, though in different modes. Burton went back to the pulpit, and Bastwick served in the New Model Army. Prynne became even more closely associated with the radical politics of the 1640s. Frequently iconoclastic and abrasive, he was jailed anew for his criticisms of those in power, including during the Commonwealth. Prynne ended his days as an office holder under Charles II, churning out a series of books on religious subjects.

There was no more avid pupil of Burton, Bastwick, and Prynne than "Freeborn John" Lilburne, the leading radical figure during the Interregnum. In a famous case in 1638, Lilburne contested the Star Chamber's authority to compel him to give witness against himself. The controversy that Lilburne and the three "holy Christian marytrs" fed was a proximate cause of the Star Chamber's abolition. Lilburne's criticism of the *ex officio* oath served as a longer-range inspiration for British North American colonists' insistence that their new constitution include the privilege against self-incrimination.

Further Reading

Gardiner, Samuel R. *Documents Relating to the Proceedings against William Prynne, in 1634 and 1637*. New York: Johnson Reprint Corp., 1965; Gregg, Pauline. *Free-Born John: A Biography of John Lilburne*. London: Phoenix Press, 2000; Lamont, William. *Marginal Prynne*. London: Routledge & Kegan Paul, 1963; Sharp, Andrew. *The English Levellers*. Cambridge: Cambridge University Press, 1998; Trevor-Roper, Hugh. *Archbishop Laud, 1573–1645*. London: Macmillan, 1940.

The trials of Anne Hutchinson

Date: 1637, 1638

KEY ISSUES

Many of earliest residents in Massachusetts Bay Colony were protesters against the religious policies of the English government. It would be a mistake, however, to think of the American Puritans (a name that they often rejected) as believers in religious liberty. Far from it. Many of their leaders had a vision of a theocracy in which freedom to worship differently than in England simply meant the ability to worship in a way prescribed by the elite members of the colony.

Those colonists who disagreed with the authorities on matters of religious principle could find themselves being drummed out of the community or facing death by execution. Anne Hutchinson ran afoul of Boston's civil and reli-

gious managers by expressing her religious views too publicly. Hutchinson was not condemned to death for her views, although she did die in an untimely manner as result of her banishment. Her friend and fellow religious dissenter Mary Dyer was an extreme example of what could occur when one ran afoul of the religious and political establishment in Massachusetts Bay: Dyer was hanged.

Hutchinson's tangle with the colony's legal system was only half of her legal experience, although it is the most famous aspect of her story. She actually appeared in two separate cases: one trial in November 1637 was before the General Court of Massachusetts, and the other in March 1638 was a hearing presided over by ministers in her own church. The result of those trials was her expulsion from the church and the community. She and her family were forced to move away from the comparative safety of the bay area. An examination of Hutchinson's treatment demonstrates not only the sternness with which Massachusetts's governors repressed dissent. It also shows that Hutchinson, unquestionably articulate though she was, was something of a partner in her own martyrdom.

HISTORY OF THE CASES

Hutchinson had learned religious dissent in England, where she was born in 1591. Her father, Francis Marbury, was an Anglican minister with views that got him into trouble with the English government. Queen Elizabeth I prided herself on keeping to a *via media* (middle way) in matters of religion. Elizabeth claimed that the government was not about intruding into consciences and that she was providing a sensible path between Protestantism and Catholicism. Still, persons who veered too far into "popery" on the one hand or radical Protestantism on the other found themselves being prosecuted on a variety of charges. After a trial by the Court of High Commission that included Bishop of London John Aylmer, a cabinet-level adviser to Elizabeth I, Marbury was jailed for two years in Marshalsea Prison in London.

After his release Marbury alternated between being in disgrace and assuring the bishops that he was a good Anglican. Meanwhile, he tutored his several children and found Anne to be an especially gifted pupil with a particular interest in theology. Rehabilitated and entrusted with a parish in London, Marbury and his family came into contact there with others who argued that the English church, though in form Protestant, still was too close to its Catholic roots. Anne Marbury in time married a merchant, William Hutchinson, and began her own large family. Among the critics of the established church in England with whom the Hutchinsons came into contact was a minister named John Cotton. Cotton deemed Anne Hutchinson capable of helping persons to become ready for conversion to Cotton's Puritan views.

Cotton, though a talented theologian, was under pressure from the government to explain his religious tenets. He went into hiding rather than answer a summons from the same court that had dogged Marbury. In 1633 he made the difficult decision to sail for North America. Cotton's admirers, including the Hutchinson family, followed shortly after, arriving in Boston in September 1634. Leaders of the Massachusetts Bay Colony such as John Winthrop had hoped that Cotton would join them; upon Cotton's arrival Winthrop placed Cotton in a prestigious preaching position in Boston. Cotton's views, though, were not without their critics.

Cotton created rumblings when he emphasized the role of grace in salvation. Here, Cotton was describing a believer's self-knowledge of his or her relationship with the Almighty. The more radical among the set of believers that concurred with Cotton were called "Antinomians;" they underlined the "personal experience" of salvation. This was somewhat at odds with the Puritans' idea that God would provide tangible signs that a believer had been chosen for salvation. Anne Hutchinson, a member of Cotton's church in Boston, became a focus for many who disagreed with Cotton's theology or simply were jealous of his influence.

SUMMARY OF ARGUMENTS

Within a few months of her arrival in America, Hutchinson developed a reputation not only in the traditional roles expected of women by the church elders—housekeeper, mother, helper to her husband, and sometime midwife and healer to other women—but also as a teacher of Christian Scripture. Hutchinson held meetings in her house that she said were for other women. Quickly, though, those gatherings saw men in attendance. Most of the attendees appeared to find Hutchinson's knowledge of biblical texts impressive and her personality compelling.

The leaders of the colony took on Cotton by upbraiding Hutchinson on several counts. Those detractors said that Hutchinson had spoken ill of all of the ministers in Massachusetts except Cotton and her brother-in-law John Wheelwright. Hutchinson supposedly had encouraged division and wrong-thinking in the community as a whole and among believers specifically. Her home meetings were further evidence of Hutchinson's rebelliousness against authority, for she had presumed to instruct not only younger women but also men.

An implicit charge against Hutchinson and those with whom she agreed theologically was that they had endangered the safety of the colony with comments about the possibility of salvation for Native Americans. In that regard Hutchinson had common cause with Roger Williams, who was formally expelled from the Massachusetts Bay colony for espousing such views. The founders of Massachusetts had made clear even during their voyage from England that the views of private individuals would not be allowed (in Winthrop's words) to "subsist in the ruin of the public."

The General Court of Massachusetts called Hutchinson to answer for what it termed her transgressions on November 7, 1637. It was usual practice in the early 17th century in the English-speaking American colonies for legislatures also to act as judicial courts. In Massachusetts the situation was striking, for not only did the colony's leaders serve as its legislators and chief judges; they also operated a theocracy. Justice in the colonies was much more based on rules from local English courts over which magistrates presided than on the procedures of royal courts in London.

The fact that immigration to America had been very recent meant that few public officials, even legislators, had legal training. Lawyers were most unusual in colonial courts at this period. In contrast to the practice in many parts of England at the time, courts in the colonies actively discouraged defendants from asking for juries. Thus, those who sat in judgment of Hutchinson were laypeople, and they had a decidedly religious as well as political agenda.

Former governor Winthrop was the chief judge at Hutchinson's civil (that is, secular) trial. The deputy governor and 10 other court officials assisted him and, like some clergymen present, occasionally questioned Hutchinson, but Winthrop was the chief spokesperson for the colony's leadership in this venue. Hutchinson was 46 years old at the trial. The mother of 15 children, she recently had become a grandmother. Her children ranged in age from one-and-a-half to 24. She also was both pregnant and breastfeeding her youngest child.

There was no person serving as a court reporter in the civil trial of Hutchinson, nor was there an official transcript produced, but several listeners with vested interests in both sides took down in some detail the words that were spoken. The record of the proceedings, though not official, conveys a clear picture of Hutchinson's and Winthrop's verbal sparring. Indeed, the court record is the best document available concerning Hutchinson's beliefs and demeanor.

At her civil trial Hutchinson began as defiant and continued on that note. Perhaps her only show of vulnerability was accepting a chair on which to sit. Winthrop's opening statement was that she was "called here as one that hath troubled the commonwealth and the churches," to which he added that she had been warned to desist from her objectionable teachings. Hutchinson retorted that she had not yet heard an actual charge laid against her. Winthrop reminded her that she was supporting a faction, the Antinomians, that had been discredited within the colony. Hutchinson replied that her support of such beliefs was a matter of conscience. Winthrop famously upbraided her: "Your conscience you must keep or it will be kept for you."

And so the exchange went until it became an argument about how the Christian Scriptures applied to the case at hand. Hutchinson insisted that the apostle Paul had recommended that women with a special understanding of Scripture should teach younger women, while Winthrop interpreted the passage more narrowly. Paul, he argued, had

meant that the women should instruct their younger female colleagues in how to serve their husbands. Among the more important pieces of commentary from Hutchinson's judges was a statement from Deputy Governor Thomas Dudley; he had heard Hutchinson express views that worried him while on board the vessel sailing from England in 1634. Hutchinson's shipboard comments were troubling enough that Dudley lobbied to keep Hutchinson from gaining membership in the church at Boston until she could clear up any doubts as to her fitness to be among the congregation. It bears noting that Dudley was serving both as an official of the court and a witness against Hutchinson.

The trial extended to a second day—itself a rare occurrence in the colonies, bespeaking the importance of the issues raised. The momentum shifted for a time toward Hutchinson on that subsequent day, largely because John Cotton decided to make a series of remarks in her favor to the court. Hutchinson, however, had not finished her own declarations. She said that the proceedings were subject to the judgment of the Almighty; that is, her accusers would be assessed harshly. This she said she knew through a divine (she said "immediate") revelation. Hutchinson had barely avoided the taint of Antinomianism earlier; such statements, public and brazen, implicated her again in that heresy. Cotton at that point no longer would defend his friend and supporter.

VERDICTS

The first trial ended with Hutchinson's banishment from the colony. Although a virtual death sentence in wintertime, the punishment was stayed because of Hutchinson's advanced pregnancy. The delay in enforcement in effect gave her the opportunity to sort out the situation with her home congregation. She had time to make peace, if she could, and to convince religious and civic leaders close to her—notably Cotton—that she would be quiet. These things she did not do.

The second trial that Hutchinson faced—an examination in front of her home congregation on March 22, 1638—included only slightly less dramatic exchanges than her tussle with Winthrop. This time she appeared at the church of Boston to answer questions from the Reverend John Wilson and several other ministers. Many of these were men that Hutchinson had criticized as emphasizing a "covenant of works" rather than a reliance on faith and a personal experience of salvation.

It was apparent from the start that Cotton had thrown in his lot with the authorities. He spoke sharply to Hutchinson, warning her that her "forwardness" in mixing the genders in Bible instruction would lead inevitably to adultery. It must have been a painful allegation for both William and Anne Hutchinson, who had been devoted to each other through Anne's legal ordeals. Cotton aimed stern words at Hutchinson's children, urging them to withdraw affection from their mother rather than be led astray. He admonished the women of the congregation and the community that Hutchinson was dangerous, especially to unsophisticated female minds.

To no one's surprise, Hutchinson was excommunicated from the congregation. In a memorable scene Mary Dyer stood up and took Hutchinson's hand, and they exited the church together. Hutchinson's detractors lost no opportunities to malign her and Dyer. When both delivered children with fatal physical disabilities, Winthrop declared it a divine judgment. Cotton had helped to conceal the birth of Hutchinson's child, perhaps because he knew how critics would interpret it. Cotton seemed to feel compassion for Hutchinson and Dyer even while he refused to defend them publicly.

SIGNIFICANCE

Hutchinson had brought out a number of critics, several of whom were respected in the pulpit and in the wider community. Minister Hugh Peters, who later would have a major voice in condemning King Charles I, for a time served as a leading preacher in New England. Peters made it a goal in America to gather resistance to the Antinomians. Yet, even after her two defeats in court and with such skilled opposition, Hutchinson was not without dedicated and influential supporters. One of the secular leaders in Massachusetts with whom she was aligned, Henry Vane, had become governor in 1636. The Hutchinsons joined with William Coddington to move near Roger Williams's settlement in the area that is the modern state of Rhode Island. Anne and William Hutchinson eventually quarreled with Coddington over his leadership, and Anne raised objections to the idea of William Hutchinson serving as a local official in any capacity.

When William Hutchinson died in 1642, Anne and her young children and household members moved into Dutch territory, near present-day New York City. There, native peoples who had been warring with the Dutch settlers massacred all but one of the Hutchinsons in 1643. The lone survivor, one of Anne Hutchinson's daughters, lived as a captive for several years and then moved back into Anglo-American society. Her descendants became leaders in Massachusetts who were prominent at the time of the American Revolution.

Hutchinson's story resonates with many in a more modern era. Among those who have seen her as a hero are persons who advocate for women's rights (she has been called the first American feminist), Baptists (due to her connections with Rhode Island and Roger Williams), civil libertarians (because of her outspokenness at trial), and Quakers (especially with relation to her friendship with Quaker activist Dyer). Even historians who lionize Puritans such as Winthrop find much to admire in Hutchinson. Modern studies of Hutchinson emphasize her connection with not only religious controversy but also the political infighting that went on among the founders at Massachusetts Bay.

Further Reading

Hutchinson, Thomas. *The History of the Colony and Province of Massachusetts Bay.* Cambridge, Mass.: Harvard University Press, 1936; LaPlante, Eve. *American Jezebel.* San Francisco: HarperCollins, 2004; Morgan, Edmund. *The Puritan Dilemma.* New York: HarperCollins, 1958; "Trial at the Court at Newton. 1637." AnneHutchinson. com. Available online. URL: http://www.anne hutchinson.com/anne_hutchinson_trial_001.htm. Accessed December 5, 2009; Winship, Michael. *The Times and Trials of Anne Hutchinson.* Lawrence: University Press of Kansas, 2005.

The trial of Charles I

Date: 1649

KEY ISSUES

Could monarchs commit treason? If subjects could put their rulers on trial, then the powers of queens and kings were not absolute. Furthermore, if kings were traitors, rulers could not be said to have divine authority for their policies. Divine right was a claim that English kings Charles I and his father James I had made, although they did not speak but only acted in absolutist terms in the first half of the 17th century.

The duly consecrated king Charles had claimed to be incapable of making errors that justified his removal. His subjects begged to differ, and in the short term they removed him from power and abolished their monarchy. Never mind that within a generation the English nation reversed itself, hunting down the "regicides" and commemorating Charles I as a martyr. In the longer term much of the nation and the world viewed the trial and execution of Charles I as a legitimate exercise of power by Parliament. To North Americans particularly, England's calling a ruler to account helped refine the notion that government should be "of the people, by the people, for the people."

HISTORY OF THE CASE

The roots of the civil conflict that toppled Charles I from the throne reached back into the reign of his father, James I. Both of the Stuart kings of England had tangled with Parliament on constitutional issues such as the relationship between the judiciary and the Crown, the authority of Parliament versus the monarch to authorize taxation, and the treatment of religious minorities. Charles had headed an army that lost on the battlefield, and from November 1647 onward he was a prisoner.

What his captors would do with him depended partially on their agenda but also on the king's willingness to negotiate a long-term plan for the monarchy's role in English government. By the end of 1648 the king could not reach an accord with the army that had opposed him, an army that effectively was calling the shots in Parliament. It became apparent during December 1648 that the army wished to rid itself of Charles's presence in English political life. A trial for treason would be the vehicle for that removal.

Who sat in judgment of the king? The court consisted of 135 persons. Absences were very common from the proceedings; this was a dangerous and divisive business. Only 70 individuals constituted the court on a regular basis, counting its president, John Bradshawe, and three additional lawyers, John Lisle, William Say, and John Cooke. Bradshawe was not an especially distinguished jurist. Still, he was willing to serve even over his family's objections, and that counted for much among the critics of Charles I. Cooke, who wrote the state's argument against the king, had had a longer and more courageous legal career to date, but he was more of a private advocate than a lawyer experienced in state cases. The other members of the court were Parliamentarians who had survived the winnowing of the legislature by Colonel Thomas Pride, plus assorted members of the army.

At the trial two individuals played key roles not as officials of the court but rather as brokers behind the scenes: Oliver Cromwell and Hugh Peters (Peter). Peters was a minister of considerable influence among dissenting groups. His views were radical enough to have impelled him to go to the New World during the 11 years when Charles I ruled without summoning Parliament—the King's "Personal Rule." There Peters encountered communities that were split by the Antinomian controversy; he proved a leading opponent of Anne Hutchinson. Peters went back to England to work against Archbishop William Laud, the architect of Charles I's religious policy. During the civil war Peters was an influential chaplain in the New Model Army. It was in that capacity that he held much sway with Parliament in the winter of 1648–49. Some scholars credit Peters with using his sermons to exhort the populace of London to go along with severe measures against Charles I. This was key during the trial when the monarch seemed to have scored debating points against his accusers.

Cromwell, the better known to posterity, had been second in command of the New Model Army. The army's commander, General Thomas Fairfax, was only very reluctantly a supporter of trying the king at all. In November 1648 Fairfax tried to broker an arrangement by which Charles would remain a figurehead. Cromwell, in contrast to his nominal superior, had managed the army's disparate factions effectively. When Cromwell made up his mind that the king should be forced to capitulate fully, his view became decisive to those who remained in Parliament. In contrast to Fairfax, who increasingly seemed to want to distance himself from the trial, Cromwell drew nearer to it. It was Cromwell who neatly summarized the prosecution's stance that even if Charles were to remain as king, he could be executed: "I tell you," Cromwell said just before the trial began, "we will cut off his head with the crown on it."

SUMMARY OF ARGUMENTS

At the trial there was one central legal question along with several smaller ones. The charges against Charles revolved around the problem of whether the king could be guilty of treason. According to the most prevalent definition of treason in English law at the time, doubt existed on that point. The Statute of Treasons of 1351 famously defined treason as plotting the death of the king or making war against him, but obviously Charles had not rebelled against himself. In order to bring Charles I within the orbit of that classic understanding of treason, Parliament had to pass another statute tailored to the present circumstances: "It is treason," the legislature mandated in a law of January 1, 1649, "for the king of England to make war against the Parliament and Kingdom of England."

The managers of the trial were moderate toward Charles I in certain procedural matters. He was allowed unusual freedom to speak in court, for example. In England during the 1600s defendants were granted counsel only to plead points of law (which the defendant had to recognize before the court would even assign a lawyer). Otherwise, accused persons were expected simply to answer questions. They were not permitted to take the stand in their own defense. Other comments by defendants were only with the court's forbearance, although it was customary to allow convicted persons to address the court before sentencing.

The court granted additional indulgences that were of even greater weight. For example Bradshawe allowed one royalist witness to stand on his right to refuse to testify on the grounds that his words would be self-incriminatory. Both Cooke and Bradshawe had had a part in the recent case that established such a right to remain silent, a trial involving the radical John Lilburne. At Charles I's trial they had the good grace to allow that precedent to be used against their own cause.

The trial took place in the Great Hall at Westminster, site of other proceedings against famous people. William Wallace got judgment there, as did Thomas More. The spacious room was needed for the crowds that were bound to attend. Since Westminster was not a regular courtroom and there were many bodies packed into the hall, certain formalities did not hold sway. There was more calling out from spectators than usual in judicial venues. At an early point a woman shouted from the gallery that Lord Fairfax should not be numbered among the judges; Lady Fairfax was trying to broadcast her husband's unease with the prosecution of Charles. At other times insults were shouted toward both sides, and a military member of the court spat in the defendant's face.

Two especially memorable moments occurred in Westminster during the proceedings: on January 20 and 22, 1649. Both transpired when the court convened for the day, and both involved the most dangerous arrow that the king had in his quiver: the contention that as the monarch he could not be put on trial.

The first incident was when the government's solicitor general Cooke tried to read the charges against Charles. He was standing near the king. As soon as Cooke began to read, King Charles rapped him on the shoulder with his cane and commanded "Hold!" Cooke tried to continue; again the king, imperiously, struck him with the cane. Cooke took up the charges once more, and Charles dealt another blow, sharp but not injurious. This time the tip of the king's cane fell onto the floor. The king nodded toward the silver tip. Cooke ignored the unspoken order to pick it up and read on. The king, obviously deflated, leaned over and retrieved the missing piece of the cane.

There was a gasp among the spectators, and the trial record noted the gravity of the nonverbal drama. The king had bowed! After the indictment was read, however, Charles I recovered some composure. The president and chief judge of the High Court, Bradshawe, now asked for a plea from the monarch. The king made a memorable rejoinder: "I would know by what power I am called hither."

It was not a rhetorical question; Charles I was challenging the right of the House of Commons, and a denuded one at that, to try him. He expanded his argument:

I do not come here as submitting to the court. . . . I see no House of Lords here, that may constitute a Parliament. . . . Let me see a legal authority warranted by the word of God, the scriptures or warranted by the Constitution, and I will answer.

Charles's failure to enter a plea was a serious problem for those who prosecuted the king. English trials proceeded from the assumption that a defendant would declare him- or herself guilty or not guilty. Those who took an alternative position—who either failed to come to court at all or who attended judicial proceedings and then stood mute—threw a wrench into the works. Absconders traditionally were outlawed; they literally had stood outside the legal process and would no longer be protected by its provisions.

Those who refused to plead were if anything more disruptive. The customary legal response was to force them to talk. Some defendants in Charles I's day endured the physical coercion known as *peine forte et dure* designed to make them plead. Among early Anglo-Normans that phrase meant "being confined to a secure fortress," but it later was translated as "pressing with strong weights"— a terrible legal misunderstanding that was visited upon defendants who chose to remain silent. It would have been extremely impolitic, however, to apply such a measure to the king.

Over a day-long recess following the king's initial appearance, legal experts within and advisory to Parliament conferred in a private session. They met in such conferences during most of the days of the trial. The trial's judges, or "commissioners," decided to offer the defendant three options: pleading guilty, pleading not guilty, or standing without a plea. In that third eventuality the court would declare that the defendant was accepting the charges as if they had been confirmed through a confession. If Charles said nothing, in other words, then he was admitting that the mounting of the prosecution was valid.

No matter how ill grounded their reasoning was in English law—for scholars still debate the legality of the principle that the commissioners called *pro confesso*—it worked beautifully in the end. When Charles appeared in court on Monday, January 22, Prosecutor Cooke and Judge-President Bradshawe had their strategy in place. But again, the king offered an uncharacteristically eloquent retort. The clerk of the court read out the formal charge:

Clerk: Charles Stuart, King of England, you have been accused on behalf of the people of England of high treason and other high crimes. The court has determined that you ought to give positive answer, whether you confess or deny the charges.

King: I will, as soon as I know by what authority you sit.

Bradshawe: If this be all that you will say, then gentlemen, you that brought the prisoner hither, conduct him back.

King: I do desire to give my reasons for not answering: I require you give me time for that.

Bradshawe: Sir, it is not for prisoners to require.

King: Prisoner! Sir, I am no ordinary prisoner.

On January 22 and 23 the judges then proceeded over Charles's objections. In the court's third day of meeting, January 23, Bradshawe ordered the king taken away from court; he ruled that the king had exhausted his opportunity to plead and was to be deemed *pro confesso*. Thus, the monarch lost the chance to justify his recent conduct in detail. Some historians maintain that Charles I remained silent because he realized that his accusers had assembled damning evidence. The prosecution could show that as king, Charles had negotiated with England's enemies even while dangling a rapprochement to his domestic opponents.

What the king did not seem to anticipate, though, was that those in charge of the trial had another way to get evidence of his misconduct before the public. They could present it at a hearing to determine the king's sentence. The prosecutors, led by Cooke, were keen to enumerate examples of the king leading troops in battle against Parliament, approving of war crimes such as the looting of towns, and sending his own handwritten letters to Catholic powers abroad, requesting support against the legislature. The prosecution made this information public in the only portion of the trial at which evidence was heard—the punishment phase on January 24 and 25.

VERDICT

Given the careful planning of the leaders of the rebellion who now were arrayed against the king in court, the court's verdict hardly could have been other than it was. King Charles was guilty and would be put to death. That sentence, though, was not something on which his prosecutors had agreed even in early January. It was the king's conduct during the trial that hardened many parliamentarians' hearts against Charles I. In particular, they were offended at the king's expression to his guards that the only recent death he regretted was that of his adviser Thomas Wentworth, the earl of Strafford, in 1641. It was an ill-considered remark on Charles's part, reflecting badly upon him to two constituencies. To the country at large, the king was indicating callousness about all of the blood spilled during the civil war. Among those who knew politics intimately, the king thus appeared insincere, for it was widely rumored that a word from the king could have saved Strafford from the ax.

The form of the convicted man's execution was a matter of some debate among Charles's accusers. They decided to have him beheaded—to modern observers a fierce punishment, but to the 17th-century English a moderation of the prescribed penalty of hanging, drawing, and quartering. The sentence was carried out on January 30, 1649, on a scaffold outside the magnificent Banqueting House at Whitehall, designed for the king's father by Inigo Jones.

It was a cold day. The king was anxious that those who watched should not think he was shivering from fear, so he donned an extra shirt. On the scaffold he made certain to note that he forgave those who had acted against him, and he professed adherence to the doctrines of the Church of England. Those statements probably had much to do with the king's wish to secure his son's accession to the throne. Two disguised men stood by, one being the actual executioner; those who had condemned the king wished to prevent one person from being identified as the man who had wielded the ax.

SIGNIFICANCE

The 59 men who signed the death warrant of Charles I became known as regicides. With the Restoration in 1660, nine of the legislators of 1649, along with other key figures at the trial (such as Cooke) were prosecuted, convicted, and executed as traitors. The few procedural niceties they had allowed Charles I in 1649 were denied to them. The defenders and heirs of Charles I, in fact, appeared more bloodthirsty than had the king's prosecutors. Charles II demanded and got executions of the regicides by hanging, drawing, and quartering. Those "king-killers" such as Cromwell who had died during the Interregnum were dug up and their bodies mutilated. The total executed undoubtedly would have been higher after 1660 but for the fact that some of the judges of Charles I had fled the country. The monarchists followed them abroad in certain cases; leading regicide lawyer John Lisle, for example, was assassinated at the door of a church in 1664.

As late as 1685 Charles I's son James, newly crowned King James II of England, was pursuing the families of his father's judges. In the wake of the Western Rebellion of that year James II insisted on the execution of Alice Lisle, the elderly widow of John Lisle, upon the flimsiest evidence that she had supported the current rebels. Ironically, that action by James and his royal judges was an important strike against the fourth Stuart monarch and served as a complaint against the king during the Glorious Revolution of 1688.

Further Reading

Hibbert, Christopher. *Charles I: A Life of Religion, War, and Treason.* New York: Palgrave Macmillan, 2007; Hill, Christopher. *God's Englishman: Oliver Cromwell and the English Revolution.* New York: Penguin Books, 1990; Lagomarsino, David, and Charles Wood. *The Trial of Charles I: A Documentary History.* Hanover, N.H.: University Press of New England, 1989; Morgan, Edmund. *Inventing the People.* New York: Norton, 1989; Robertson, Geoffrey. *The Tyrannicide Brief.* New York: Pantheon, 2005; Stuart, Charles. *King Charles, His Speech Made upon the Scaffold at Whitehall-Gate.* London: Peter Cole, 1649. Available online. URL: http://jesus-is-lord.com/kjcharl2.htm. Accessed December 16, 2009; Stuart, Charles. *King Charles I's Speech at His Trial, January, 1649.* Available online. URL: http://www.constitution.org/primary sources/charles.html. Accessed December 16, 2009; "The Trial of Charles I, transcript manuscript in facsimile." Available online. URL: http://www. nationalarchives.gov.uk/museum/item.asp?item_id=22. Accessed December 16, 2009; Wedgwood, C. V. *A Coffin for King Charles.* New York: Macmillan, 1964.

The trial of William Penn

Also known as: *The King v. Penn, Bushel's Case*

Date: 1670

KEY ISSUES

Restoration England provided an unlikely environment for two cases that underscored the power of the jury. The trial of William Penn and a resulting controversy concerning the fate of the jury foreman who wanted to free Penn are cornerstones of modern legal practices in England and the United States. Penn took lessons from his courtroom experience that had ramifications for the British American colonies.

The 1660s and 1670s were a time of some conservatism in England because the nation was tired of infighting and the government was committed to stopping political criticism. The regicides were mostly dead or exiled, and many religious malcontents were quieted or had gone abroad, with one main exception: the Quakers. Why did those in power tolerate Quakerism? Much had to do with the influence of the monarch himself. Charles II's cosmopolitanism extended to religious discussion. While his greatest enemies charged that the king simply was a closet Catholic and that his pleas for religious toleration thus only were a cloak for his wish to bring England back to the fold of Rome, the king apparently did believe in religious diversity to a greater degree than many of his peers. On a personal level Charles liked to discourse about a variety of religions. One of his companions in conversation was Margaret Fell Fox, who with George Fox had founded the Society of Friends.

William Penn at first might seem an odd spokesman for the Quakers. He was born into a well-connected family. His father, Admiral William Penn, was a loyal servant of the Crown. Young William met Charles II and his brother James, duke of York (later James II) while carrying military messages to them on behalf of the senior Penn. The younger Penn had a good education, including two years at Christ Church Oxford. At least two of his fellow undergraduates, Robert Spenser and Lawrence Hyde, later became part of Charles II's cabinet and helped Penn politically. Another key connection for Penn at university was his tutor John Locke; Penn's discussions with a man of such keen intellect sharpened his powers of argumentation. While a student, though, Penn ran into difficulty with his family by aligning himself with the theologian John Owen, who argued for greater freedom in England for religious minorities. Penn was sent to France to complete his university training and cool his reformist ardor.

In France, Penn studied at a Protestant academy and became interested in the principles of nonresistance taught by Moise Amyraut. Amyraut, like Penn, might appear a bit of a contradiction to modern readers because he was both a proponent of free worship and a defender of divine right monarchy. Historians point out, though, that Amyraut was connected to the French court at a time before the revocation of the Edict of Nantes, when it seemed possible for concentrated monarchical power to coexist with religious freedom.

After a stint on family business in Ireland during which he regained some of his father's confidence, Penn returned to London. Like many other young men from wealthy families, he was expected to spend time at one of the Inns of Court, rooming houses specially suited for law students and practitioners. Presumably, simply by lodging at one of the Inns of Court, he absorbed sufficient knowledge of law to one day manage his family's business affairs. Penn appears to have picked up more than a little law—unusual in those of his rank. He also began to speak on behalf of groups of London entrepreneurs (several of whom were Quakers) to Parliament regarding the relaxing of religious exclusions.

Having experienced what may have been a personal religious conversion, Penn began associating more and more with Quakers. He married Gulielma Springett, the daughter of one of his hosts. Penn began to appreciate the straits in which religious dissenters might find themselves if they did not have his illustrious connections. His wife's family had their estates confiscated due to their continued adherence to Quakerism. Penn was a friend and literary collaborator with George Fox. Fox already had established himself as a leading religious figure, but his writing was not as polished as Penn's. Penn brought an infusion of money and social contacts to Quakerism. One of Penn's most important compositions, *No Cross, No Crown* (1669), advanced standards for behavior for Quakers that were to become famous, including the addressing of individuals as "thee" and "thou" and the wearing of plain apparel.

Thus, Penn circulated within several circles simultaneously: among religious dissenters, members of the cabinet, the royal household, and London merchants. He seemed a genuinely likable young man—attractive, athletic, well spoken. Ironically, at the same time that Penn's political and social star was on the rise, he began to express a willingness to sacrifice material comfort for his newfound religious zeal.

HISTORY OF THE CASE

Penn got into trouble with the Church of England due to his criticism of the Trinity in *The Sandy Foundation Shaken* (1668). Penn also ran the risk of alienating Charles II on the question of Catholic toleration, for in that writing Penn said that "popery" was the only major religious belief that should not have legal protection.

In addition to criticism of dissent by the hierarchy of the Church of England and the monarchy, England's legislature condemned nonconformity to the established church. The leading statute on the subject was a prohibition of non-Anglican religious gatherings during the end of Elizabeth I's reign. In that law Parliament barred more than five people from listening to non-Anglican speeches within religious structures. Beginning in 1667 Parliament revisited the regulation of unauthorized religious assemblies (conventicles). When faced with what it perceived to be the threat of Charles II's pro-Catholic stance, in other words, Parliament began cracking down on religious minorities. Quakers typically thwarted conventicle laws by simply stepping outside their meetinghouses and listening from the street.

In London, Quakers were economically influential. There, municipal authorities walked a thin line between allowing such bending of the law against nonconformist meetings and provoking protest by breaking up the gatherings. For many, including Penn, the time was ripe for challenging the situation. Penn got his first chance in 1667 when a roundup ensnared him, but the authorities recognized him as significantly wealthier than his colleagues and offered to let him go. He insisted on being arrested and prosecuted with his friends, spending several months in prison. He made an even more famous stand on August 14, 1670, at Grace Church in London, where there had been Quaker meetings before. Penn and William Mead, a Quaker leader, were tried at the Central Criminal Court in London, the Old Bailey. Penn left a thorough reminiscence of his stint in court, published while his memory still was fresh, just a few months after the trial.

It is important to note that Penn's trial did not represent a united front by the government against

Quakers. The authorities were divided among themselves on how to proceed against nonconformists or indeed whether groups such as Quakers were a threat at all. Penn's defenders included not only Quakers but also many influential Londoners and Penn's royal contacts. In the case of the prosecution of Penn and Mead, at issue was Parliament's Conventicle Act of 1670. The enforcers of that regulation were city officials and judges who wished to curry favor with the legislature. The officials sitting in judgment of Penn included the lord mayor of London, Samuel Starling; five aldermen; and three sheriffs, with Thomas Howel, the recorder of London, acting as the presiding magistrate.

SUMMARY OF ARGUMENTS

Trials at the Old Bailey were designed to impress and perhaps intimidate those in attendance. Judges customarily tried the most serious crimes—murder and treason—early in a judicial session and required other defendants to wait. It might take only a matter of hours or a few days for dozens of those preceding cases to be completed, because English courts worked swiftly. Those waiting to be heard could not fail to be impressed with the severity of sentences handed down in capital cases. Nor could they miss the lesson that the court brooked little impudence. Penn and Mead cooled their heels for a few days until they appeared before the bar.

Penn protested the proceedings from the outset, and soon he was engaged in a contest of wills with the judges. When the indictment was read and Penn and Mead were supposed to plead, Penn raised an objection. He criticized the indictment as vague and said he just now was hearing the charges against him. The indictment said, in part, that Penn and Mead "unlawfully and tumultuously did Assemble and Congregate themselves together, to the Disturbance of the Peace of the said Lord the King. . . ." But where, Penn challenged the court aloud, was it prohibited in law for persons to assemble peaceably on a street? He banked on the fact that no one would testify the gathering had been riotous; the meeting had been calm before and during the arrests. Quakers were famous for not resisting

apprehension, just as Penn's spiritual mentors had taught. In fact, often they refused to petition for release from jail.

The recorder made a series of sharp remarks over Penn's argument that the court had not indicated in the indictment which law he had broken. He also reminded Penn that it was customary for defendants to hear the formal charges against them for the first time in court; that is, the court did not have to show a defendant the indictment ahead of trial. Subsequent legal scholars concluded, though, that Penn was correct on the larger point. The established rule was that the indictment should have been more specific, as Penn stated:

> Penn: I desire you would let me know by what law it is you prosecute me, and upon what law you ground my indictment.
>
> Recorder Howel: Upon the common-law.
>
> Penn: Where is that common-law?
>
> Recorder: You must not think that I am able to run up so many years, and over so many adjudged cases, which we call common-law, to answer your curiosity.
>
> Penn: This answer I am sure is very short of my question, for if it be common, it should not be so hard to produce.

Finally, their case was called for trial, but even as Penn and Mead reentered the courtroom on September 3, they must have understood that some of the presiding officials were biased against them. The bailiff stopped them as they removed their hats, telling them that the judges including the lord mayor had said they should place their hats back on. The defendants complied, only to find themselves lectured by the judges about not showing proper reverence for the court by removing their hats. Penn recalled the moment later in the trial to good effect. It was a needless taunting of the accused from the bench that served the prosecutors ill in the minds of the jurymen.

The bullying from the judges continued, with Penn parrying so ably that eventually his tormenters ordered him placed in a corner of the courtroom that served as a place for holding loudmouthed defendants: the "bale-dock." That spot had walls but no ceiling; Penn could hear and continue to conduct his defense, but he could not see his accusers.

The jury all the while appeared sympathetic to Penn and Mead. There was some indication that the prosecution suspected even before trial that at least one man on the panel, Edward Bushel, harbored views they might not like. John Robinson, an alderman and the lieutenant of the Tower of London, now serving as one of the judges, questioned the seating of Bushel because he thought Bushel was refusing to kiss the Bible when taking the oath as a juror; that is, Bushel was acting as a Quaker might in avoiding swearing an oath. Bushel was impaneled anyway, although Robinson's hunch—or his intelligence— was correct: Bushel was prepared not only to hear Penn out but to go much further on his behalf.

VERDICT

When the judges decided they had heard enough testimony, they specified that they expected the verdict of "guilty" and directed the jury to deliberate. The panel went away and discussed the case for an hour and a half and then sent word that they were divided. Eight on the panel favored conviction, and four were against it. The jury was brought into court. Several of the judges then berated Bushel as the cause of the dissension. The officials sent the jury out again, once more directing them to find against the defendants. When the panel returned a second time, the judges asked the foreman for a verdict. He replied that they had determined that Penn and Mead were "Guilty of Speaking in Grace-church-street." It was a finding of fact rather than a determination of guilt.

The recorder asked whether that was all they had to say. Yes, the foreman replied. Enraged, the judges ordered the panel to consider the case again. The drama played out several more times until the judges declared that the jury would deliberate until the verdict was returned according to their instructions, though it was nighttime: "The Court swore several Persons, to keep the Jury all Night without Meat, Drink, Fire, or any other Accommodation; they had not so much as a Chamber pot, tho' desired." Penn spoke out as the jury were led away to their uncomfortable chamber, admonishing them to protect their liberties as Englishmen by standing up to the judges.

It was not unheard of for an English court to demand that a jury deliberate until they reached a verdict. Other juries certainly had been bullied before by judges to reach particular conclusions. But, this occasion was a very unusual one, for the four jurors who were being coerced did not buckle, even when they experienced what must have been pressure from their eight peers to give in. In fact, the strong-arming from the bench had exactly the opposite effect. The eight who had been in the majority decided to bow to judicial pressure to reach a "positive verdict," but that verdict was in favor of Penn and Mead. When they were hauled out of their cell at Newgate Prison (to which the court finally had sent them to deliberate), they spoke on Penn's and Mead's behalf to the great ire of the lord mayor and his helpers.

The judges finally recorded the "not guilty" verdict, but they were not through with the jury. They fined each member 40 marks and ordered the men jailed until they paid. Penn demanded to be released as having been freed by the jury, but the lord mayor said that he, too, would go to jail until he paid a fine. Penn inquired what the basis of that penalty was; the reply was that Penn and Mead had committed contempt "in the face of the court" by wearing hats.

SIGNIFICANCE

At that point not only Penn and Mead but also the jurors, who had dared to vote in their favor, sat in prison. If the judges were not finished punishing Londoners who sided with Penn, neither were the defenders of Penn idle. Those who thought Penn a hero centered their efforts on freeing Bushel. It took months to do so, but through an application for habeas corpus Bushel and the jurymen who had remained in jail the longest (for some had paid their fines and been released) went free. The chief justice of the Court of Common Pleas, John

Vaughan, along with 11 judicial colleagues, granted Bushel's request for habeas corpus. Cynics observed that the chief justice was beholden to Charles II and, thus, that the decision in Bushel's case was more a mark of Penn's connections than an affirmation of religious liberty. It was a ruling, though, that in time transcended the political climate in which it occurred.

Bushel's case became a memorable acclamation that judges must not intimidate members of a jury. The jury's original finding for Penn was only slightly less famous: Legal scholars soon saw it as a victory for the notion of "jury nullification." To nullify a judge's instructions was to do as Penn's jurors had ventured: to make a determination that might run contrary to the judge's explanation of how to apply the law and thus to give a verdict that undercut judicial authority.

The shorter-term impact of the case upon Penn was that he despaired of gaining religious freedom in England. He set his sights on the New World, using royal connections to obtain the right to found the colony that was named for his father. Among the leading principles of the colony of Pennsylvania were the ideals of trial by an unbiased jury, freedom of written expression, and peaceful coexistence among diverse religious and ethnic groups.

Further Reading

Barbour, H. S. *William Penn on Religion and Ethics: The Emergence of Liberal Quakerism.* Lewiston, N.Y.: Edwin Mellen Press, 1991; *Bushell's Case* 124 ER 1006 (1670). Available online. URL: http://www.constitution.org/trials/bushell/bushell.htm. Accessed December 19, 2009; Geiter, M. K. *William Penn.* New York: Longman, 2000; Halliday, Paul. *Habeas Corpus: From England to Empire.* Cambridge, Mass.: Belknap Press, 2010; Hamilton, Sarah, and Andrew Spicer. *Defining the Holy: Sacred Space in Medieval and Early Modern Europe.* Aldershot, U.K.: Ashgate, 2005; Powell, Jim. "William Penn, America's First Great Champion for Liberty and Peace." Available online. URL: http://www.quaker.org/wmpenn.html. Accessed December 20, 2009; "The Trial of William Penn (1670)." Available online. URL: http://www.1215.org/lawnotes/penntrial.htm. Accessed December 19, 2009.

The Salem witch trials

Date: 1692

KEY ISSUES

The authorities in the Massachusetts Bay Colony who supervised the Salem witchcraft trials were not misguided yokels. Nor were they particularly superstitious or out of touch with current theology concerning witchcraft. Rather, they were part of a much larger trend among Western Christians. Witchcraft hysteria flared up periodically among medieval and early modern communities in Europe before dying down in the 1700s. The Massachusetts outbreak of the 1690s is striking because it occurred late and in North America.

Colonial North Americans turned away from certain legal practices in their mother countries; historians observe that European laws often were adapted to New World situations. The officials in charge of the Salem witchcraft trials, though, were at pains to show how loyal they were to England in the wake of recent political turmoil in New England and Britain. Thus, they applied the English common law rules on witchcraft to the Salem defendants, usually to the detriment of the accused persons.

The Massachusetts judges and magistrates also acted quickly to address witchcraft accusations at Salem because they wished to demonstrate to their superiors in England that they maintained control in the colony. A more normal political environment in New England, in other words, might have meant more deliberation—and less bloodshed—within this emotionally charged case. As it transpired, the northeastern part of Massachusetts was convulsed with the allegations during the year 1692.

HISTORY OF THE CASE

In February 1692 several preteen girls in Salem, a village in the British colony of Massachusetts, began to act oddly. They suffered tics, unconsciousness, and hysterical outbursts. Elizabeth

(Betty) Parris, the daughter of local minister Samuel Parris, and Abigail Williams, his niece, were the most vocal among the handful of girls who were afflicted, along with 12-year-old Ann Putnam. Parris had had a rocky tenure as a minister in Salem. Parris was afraid for the health of his daughter and consulted local physicians. Most of the medical men were baffled, but Dr. William Griggs posited that Betty had been bewitched.

Reverend Parris was of a volatile temperament. The girls could have been afraid to admit that they had been dabbling in charms while in the company of an enslaved woman in the household, Tituba. It may have seemed easier at first to go along with the explanation that they had been affected by supernatural forces than to face the minister. Given his somewhat tenuous reputation in the community, Parris had a motive to shift attention to a great evil—witchcraft—that supposedly threatened Salem. It was probably no accident that Parris had read a book published in 1689 by the influential Boston minister Cotton Mather. Titled *Memorable Providences, Relating to Witchcrafts and Possessions,* the work made a case that witchcraft was widespread. Parris may have thought that he would have powerful men on his side were he to raise the possibility of witches in Salem.

By the end of the month the girls had accused several local women of bewitching them. The individuals that the girls named as their tormenters were varied in social status and reputation. Though several of the suspected witches had reputations as quarrelsome within the locality, others were persons who were well connected in Salem society and were known as both religious and helpful people.

The proceedings against the alleged witches from Salem had four main phases: an investigation conducted by secular authorities but held inside the Salem church between March 1 and 5, 1692; a series of more regular trials held in Boston between June and September; a session to consider a few cases under the Supreme Court of Judicature in January 1693; and several reviews of the trials beginning in 1697. By 1711 the cases had been fully adjudicated and appealed. Controversy about the trials that began at Salem remained, however, and was the basis for historical and literary treatments in the subsequent centuries.

Leaders in Boston got wind of the events in Salem within days and issued orders for John Hathorne and Jonathan Corwin to represent the Massachusetts General Court at an investigation in Salem. A key reason that Corwin and Hathorne were sent to conduct the initial inquiry was that the political scene in the colony was inchoate. New England was in a state of flux as a result of the Glorious Revolution of 1688 and the revocation of Massachusetts's charter in 1684. For the time being, Massachusetts had no formal charter, at least until Governor William Phips instituted a new regime in May 1692. In February the courts in the region were anxious not to proceed too quickly until the colonial charter arrived from England.

Neither Corwin nor Hathorne was a schooled lawyer; each served as a justice of the peace (JP). For such quasi-judicial officials to shepherd a case at an early stage was usual in England. According to English practice at the time, JPs could commit persons for trial. But, the procedure that Hathorne and Corwin followed in considering evidence was not strictly according to common law. It was rather an amalgamation of English legal practice, biblical (chiefly what the Puritans called Old Testament) precepts, and current theories about witchcraft from famous treatises such as the 1486 work *Malleus Maleficarium (The Hammer of Witches).*

From those sources Corwin and Hathorne gleaned several guidelines that they applied to the suspected witches of Salem. They acted on the assumption that involvement in witchcraft was a capital crime because of Christianity's severe injunctions against witches and sorcerers. They understood that witches could be distinguished from others by peculiar marks on their bodies. They took seriously the received wisdom that the devil and those he controlled could change into different shapes, including noncorporeal forms and animals. Hathorne and Corwin accepted that sufferers' dreams might be admissible as proof of bewitchment; this was the use of "spectral evidence." Such principles may appear unjust to modern analysts of the events in Salem. Yet, they were not out of the mainstream in 17th-century Massachusetts, which had been established partially on religious grounds and did tailor English legal practices to the New World courts.

Another guideline governed much of what Corwin and Hathorne allowed into evidence: the notion that if harm befell a person after another individual had wished him or her ill, a court was entitled to assume a connection between the "anger" and the "mischief." That link between ill-will and subsequent injury to person or property does occur in modern United States and English justice, although it no longer has the appellation "mischief following anger."

In the first days of March 1692, information tumbled out from those who said they had been afflicted. At first only three suspects were taken into custody: Sarah Good, Sarah Osborne, and the Parrises' servant Tituba. These were followed shortly by three other detentions: those of Martha Corey, Dorcas Good, and Rebecca Nurse.

Sarah Good was a woman in her late 30s who came from a prosperous family but who had been denied an inheritance. She was destitute at the time of the accusations against her, forced to depend on local charity for food and housing. Apparently, she did not accept assistance with the humility expected of one who had fallen on hard times. At the Salem hearings she expressed no sorrow over the misfortunes of her neighbors. The girls who levied accusations against Good reported her as cursing them and committing acts such as breaking a knife to show her satanic powers. Although a witness came forward to explain that he had lost his broken knife around the accusers and the magistrates scolded the girls for lying, Good's alleged use of magic was still used against her. Even Good's four-year-old daughter, Dorcas, accused Sarah of being a witch; the authorities shortly put Dorcas into prison as well. Good's reply to a minister who urged her to save her soul by confessing hardly endeared her to contemporaries: "I am no more a witch than you are a wizard. If you take my life away, God will give you blood to drink."

Sarah Osborne was very sick at the time that the girls and Sarah Good accused her of witchcraft. She made one damaging admission to Hathorne and Corwin: She said that she had dreamed of "Indians." Such a night vision of native peoples commonly was thought to be a sign of demonic collusion. In spite of Osborne's contention that her ill health made her more likely to have been bewitched than to be a witch, she was sent to jail.

Tituba got into trouble with Reverend Parris for mixing up a potion that she hoped would cure some of Betty's symptoms. Very soon after hearing of Parris's anger that Tituba had made a "witch-cake," the girls began naming Tituba as one of their tormenters. When brought before the magistrates, Tituba "revealed" a web of witchcraft in Salem. It appeared that many citizens were consulting with the forces of evil, attending witches' sabbaths, and casting spells. Rebecca Nurse's presence among the accused witches was a puzzle at the time but also a confirmation of the degree to which hysteria was spreading in the case. Nurse was 71 years old, had a large, close-knit family, and was known as pious and neighborly.

As the accused women answered questions before the magistrates, more names of potential witches came out. One of the newly identified evildoers was George Burroughs, who formerly had served as a minister in Salem. Although generally known as an agreeable and charitable man, Burroughs may have quarreled with the wrong people in Salem over his salary. He had left the village over that dispute in 1683, but now was summoned back to answer charges that he had headed a witches' coven.

The hearings became a spectacle. The girls—and other alleged victims had appeared—showed symptoms of violent distress when an alleged malefactor walked into court. Sometimes the girls' actions mirrored those of the defendants. When an accused person moved her hand, for example, the girls would flail with their hands in a more exaggerated manner as though controlled like a puppet by the defendant. To the arguments of defendants that they had had no contact with the afflicted girls or did not even know them, the accusers replied that they had been oppressed by visions of the accused persons. The April 22 examination of Mary Easty by Hathorne and Corwin was typical. Although there was no official court reporter, several observers took notes in the courtroom, and those records present a good idea of what went on:

Magistrate: How far have you complied with Satan whereby he takes this advantage against you?

Easty: Sir, I never complied but prayed against him all my days, I have no compliance with Satan in this. What would you have me do?

Magistrate: Confess if you be guilty.

Easty: I will say it, if it was my last time, I am clear of this sin.

Magistrate: Of what sin?

Easty: Of witchcraft.

Magistrate (to the accusers): Are you certain this is the woman?

Observer's note: Never a one could speak for fits. By and by Ann Putman said that was the woman, it was like her, & she told me her name.

Easty: It is marvelous to me that you should sometimes think they are bewitched, and sometimes not, when several confess that I never knew.

Observer's note: Her hands [Easty's] were clinched together, and then the hands of Mercy Lewis [were] clinched.

Magistrate [to Easty]: Look now your hands are open, her hands are open. [To the accusers]: Is this the woman?

Observer's note: They made signs but could not speak, but Ann Putman and afterwards Betty Hubbard cried out "Oh, Goody Easty, Goody Easty, you are the woman, you are the woman. Put up her head, for while her head is bowed the necks of these are broken."

Magistrate [to Easty]: What do you say to this?

Easty: Why God will know.

Magistrate: Nay God knows now.

Soon Hathorne and Corwin had to ask for additional hearing officers. In late March and April five other officials, including Lieutenant Governor Thomas Danforth, presided over still further accusations in Salem. Those remanded into custody were housed in Boston and Ipswich as well as at Salem. By the time the new governor arrived in mid-May, more than 100 persons awaited trial.

Governor Phips convened a court soon so that he could empty the jails; prisons in that time were not designed for long-term incarceration. But there were more pressing matters even than the crisis at Salem; he needed to get to the frontier to manage instability there. Besides, he wished to demonstrate firmness to those who had appointed him, back in England, by not letting the local hysteria mount.

The type of court that Phips set up was known in England; it was a special commission to "hear and determine" (oyer and terminer, originally from French) what crimes had occurred in an area. Customarily, the English employed such a device when there had been localized disorder such as rioting. Such a commission of oyer and terminer was separate from the royal courts in London and from the circuit courts that visited communities on a set schedule every few months. It was, in other words, an emergency court established to deal with a unique situation. In England, though, judges from ordinary courts staffed such a commission; indeed, the greater the emergency in England, the more likely it was that a highly trained judge would be appointed to hear a commission of oyer and terminer.

New England was lacking in legally trained persons. Several of the commissioners had little or no legal training; rather, they were political men or had experience as religious leaders. The chief judge of the commission, William Stoughton, had served in Massachusetts government between 1674 and 1686; he came back into power with Phips as the new lieutenant governor. Stoughton had a theological background but no formal legal education (such as attendance at the Inns of Court in London). What Stoughton lacked in legal knowledge he made up for in religious opinion. He was of conservative theological views and was convinced that witchcraft was a real presence in the colony.

Along with Corwin and Hathorne there were six commissioners working under Stoughton.

SUMMARY OF ARGUMENTS

The commission's first trial took place on June 2, 1692. The case of Bridget Bishop seemed straightforward enough. Several witnesses testified that they could connect the defendant to acts of witchcraft. Bishop was unpopular with certain neighbors because she ran a couple of taverns and had been married three times. She also was remarked upon as a woman not sufficiently modest in dress. At trial she refused to say that she was troubled by the physical difficulties of the accusers. Bishop's husband had joined the girls in accusing her—itself a damning factor in that patriarchal society. Bishop was convicted and sentenced to death handily. She was hanged on June 10, but her judges clearly anticipated that other cases might not go so smoothly.

A key procedural question about which the commission was concerned was how to evaluate various types of evidence. In particular, there were problems in applying the "two-witness rule" and considering spectral evidence, issues that were related to each other. English law allowed the testimony of one witness to convict a defendant, even in a death penalty case. The only exception at common law was in treason trials, in which two witnesses were necessary. A confession counted against the total; that is, one could be a witness against oneself. In New England, though, it was customary for two witnesses to be required; this was based on a biblical injunction. To complicate things further, the use of spectral evidence begged the question of whether a vision or a dream was equivalent to traditional eyewitness testimony.

In other words, if the commissioners adopted English practice and allowed spectral evidence the same weight as waking testimony, then an alleged witch could be condemned to death upon the word of one witness that he or she had dreamed the defendant was bewitching the "witness." Although the commissioners, especially Stoughton, leaned strongly toward use of the English principle that one witness was enough, it was time for expert opinion to be consulted with regard to spectral evidence.

Not surprisingly, in this theocracy ministers decided the issue. The reply of a set of divines,

including Cotton Mather of Boston's First Church, was that the situation required "exquisite caution." The problem was that the forces of evil might seek to throw a wrench into the proceedings by taking the shape of innocents. Mather and his respected ministerial colleagues urged that spectral evidence not be the only basis for conviction. Stoughton took the harder line, allowing spectral evidence to convict all on its own. One member of the commission, Nathaniel Saltonstall, resigned in protest at Stoughton's disregard of the pastoral recommendation.

Another session of the court of oyer and terminer on June 30 saw the trials of five women, including Sarah Good and Rebecca Nurse. All were convicted, and all were hanged on July 19. Nurse, as noted, made a particularly sympathetic defendant. Indeed, the jury initially came back with a not guilty verdict. Pressured by Stoughton, though, they reversed themselves.

There was an adjournment for more than a month during the rest of the hot summer. During that time off, though, officials allowed certain suspects to be physically tortured. This was to force confessions. Confessions were satisfying to courts in this era because they were thought the surest form of evidence but also because they could indicate repentance. Often those who confessed got a more lenient sentence. That certainly was the case in the Salem trials. No one who offered and stuck with a confession was executed. It was significant that the two persons who were tortured were men, among the few males accused at Salem.

Modern readers may have the impression that another male defendant, Giles Corey, died under torture. Although Corey did lose his life while maintaining that he would not "put himself upon the country" to be tried, in fact, his death was attributable to the court's pressuring him to submit to its authority. Corey's fate was related to the English practice of confiscating the property of convicted felons. Those who died during judicial proceedings did not suffer the ignominy of forfeiture. Corey went down in history as one of the most defiant of the defendants at Salem. When the inducement of *peine forte et dure* (pressing with large stones) was applied to him, rather than agree to participate in the trial Corey was said to call out for "more weight!"

At an August 5 court session six people were tried and condemned. One of the most fortunate escapes from death was that of Elizabeth Proctor, who was pregnant at the time of her conviction. In the language of English law, Proctor "pleaded her belly"; it was a common temporary reprieve. In this instance the device bought Proctor her life, for by the time the child was born, the hysteria over witchcraft had abated.

The case against George Burroughs turned out to be troubling for those who thought the accusations real; Burroughs was well liked and, after all, had been away from Salem for several years. Especially when Burroughs managed to recite the Lord's Prayer without error while on the gallows, it looked as though officials might exercise mercy. Superstition had it that witches could not speak holy texts without their tongues being tripped by the devil. Some at the execution grounds called for him to be set free, but the authorities strung him up anyway. There were 15 more convictions in August, with eight of those people being executed by the month's end.

When the girls' accusations began to include some of the judges along with Mary Phips, the wife of the governor, the trials ground to a halt. The Boston ministers, including Mather's father, Increase Mather, took to their pulpits and wrote pamphlets to warn that innocent lives were being lost. On October 29 the governor effectively suspended the operation of the special court.

By January of 1693 Massachusetts had set up its regular judicial system and turned the remaining witchcraft cases over to the Supreme Court of Judicature. Judge Stoughton still presided, but according to a declaration from Phips, he could not use spectral evidence alone for a conviction. The only three guilty verdicts in 1693 were for defendants who confessed. Obvious tension existed between Stoughton and Phips. Later that spring the governor issued orders for the most recently convicted persons to be released along with a few defendants convicted in the previous fall but not yet executed. It is hard to escape the conclusion that absent the trials' zealous chief judge, events at Salem would not have gone to such an extreme.

In 1697 the leaders of Salem ordered a day of fasting and prayer. It was an occasion for mourning and acceptance of general responsibility for the events of 1692. By that time many of the accusers had recanted their allegations. Certain others, notably Ann Putnam, did not publicly acknowledge their perjured roles until years later. Although within a generation of the episode some families got compensation, Massachusetts made formal apology to the victims only in 1957.

VERDICTS

Of the more than 141 persons arrested on charges of witchcraft at Salem, 26 heard capital sentences pronounced. There were 19 women and men who actually died by hanging. Contrary to popular myth and in contrast to earlier European practice, no one was burned at the stake at Salem. Corey expired when the court tried to force him to plead, and two people (perhaps several more) died in jail. A few convicted persons such as Proctor escaped the gallows only narrowly. A number of other lives—such as those of children of the executed—were permanently altered.

The specter of a community and its families being ripped apart was horror enough to imprint the episode onto the American psyche. From the efforts of Nathaniel Hawthorne to distance himself from his ancestor Hathorne, to the Hollywood treatments of the Salem witch trials, the proceedings have been condemned as rushed and improperly influenced by religion. Still worse, the trials were often prejudiced against the weakest members of Salem society: the poor, old, and unlikable.

SIGNIFICANCE

Writers have disagreed about the long-term causes and immediate triggers of the Salem witchcraft scare and other such outbreaks. To some, the accusation of so many women reeks of misogyny. But, while the overwhelming preponderance of female defendants in witchcraft cases at Salem and elsewhere suggests distrust of women at an elemental level, the initial accusers also were female. Recent scholars note that the fact that women's and girls' testimony carried weight with the magistrates was a step forward for women's status in court. Also, juries of women got to participate in the proceedings as examiners of the bodies of both accused persons and their victims. Such female "juries" gave women a role within courts that contradicted their limited political and legal status in the larger society.

Researchers have linked witchcraft hysteria to organic causes—molded rye, for example—that periodically affected local populations. Or, the psychological and physiological effects of pre-adolescence may have played a part in the terrors that the accusing girls said they experienced. Perhaps concerns about witchcraft were related to a decline in spirituality among churches. The mystical elements that Europeans had found emotionally satisfying within Catholicism were missing in the more intellectual and abnegating Protestant creeds. Historians focused on community formation note that Salem village and its surrounding locality were in the midst of uncomfortable economic changes in the late 1600s. They posit that the accusations of witchcraft may have been a cover for efforts to wrest property away from certain neighbors.

Or, maybe witchcraft accusations were more grounded in politics than in social tensions, gender bias, or religious belief. It was no coincidence that the outbreak in Salem occurred just as the effects of England's Glorious Revolution of 1688 were filtering into the colonies. The discussion of witchcraft as a manifestation of political anxiety was most widely disseminated in Arthur Miller's play *The Crucible,* which was a parable against McCarthyism. The creation of a minority group who could be purged from Massachusetts society made the mainstream feel more secure against larger external foes such as Native Americans, rival foreign settlers, and even new Anglo governors.

Further Reading

Boyer, Paul, and Stephen Nissenbaum. *Salem Possessed.* Cambridge, Mass.: Harvard University Press, 1974; Demos, John. *The Enemy Within.* New York: Viking, 2008; Karlsen, Carol F. *The Devil in the Shape of a Woman.* New York: W. W. Norton, 1998; Mackay, Christopher, trans. *The Hammer of Witches.* Cambridge: Cambridge University Press, 2009; Norton, Mary Beth. *In the Devil's Snare: The Salem Witchcraft Crisis of 1692.* New York: Vintage, 2003.

The trials of William Kidd

Also known as: *The King v. Kidd, Churchill, Howe, Mullins, Owen, Parrot, Loffe, Jenkins, Lamley, and Barlycorne; The King v. Kidd*

Date: 1701

KEY ISSUES

William Kidd's 1701 trial and execution were well publicized. This was not because Captain Kidd posed a special danger nor because he was unusually successful at his violent craft. Kidd had high-level political connections in England and North America. His spectacular downfall was due to a falling off in influence among his chief investors. Whatever spoils Kidd did not spend immediately—and pirates almost always drank much of their earnings—almost certainly went to his backers or was confiscated by the English government. His demise probably netted no buried treasure, however fervently amateur scholars still wish that to be the case.

The courts of England spoke of Kidd as a brigand and tried him at London's Central Criminal Court facility, though under the rules of the Court of Admiralty. If Captain Kidd's execution could warn ordinary folk against taking up piracy, then so much the better from the standpoint of merchants and the government. The late 1600s and early 1700s were a time of enormous expansion by England and her sailing entrepreneurs. Stopping random attacks by pirates was a priority because doing so made returns on trade more predictable. But Kidd was more a political prisoner than an ordinary criminal. His real offense was having embarrassed the wrong people.

HISTORY OF THE CASE

Kidd was a Scot about whose early life little is known. Like many young men in the British Isles, he found himself at sea—whether by choice or at the hands of a press gang remains uncertain. Also like many of his generation, he sailed throughout the West Indies, sometimes in legitimate naval service under Governor Christopher Codrington but occasionally as a privateer. Under Codrington the crew eventually mutinied because they preferred more lucrative but irregular pursuits. Kidd followed them and the money with which they had absconded and wound up in New York. There, around the year 1690, he set down roots both political and personal.

Among Kidd's close associates were the merchant Robert Livingston and Richard Coote, the earl of Bellomont, who served as the governor of both Massachusetts and New York. The three men soon formed a conspiracy to make riches by employing Kidd's expertise on the sea. They saw immense potential for looting pirate ships that were plying the Indian Ocean in the area between Madagascar, the Indian subcontinent, and the eastern Arabian Peninsula. There sailed not only traders flying non-English flags but also ships of Muslim pilgrims who carried cash to pay for their journeys to holy sites.

Under the guise of apprehending pirates Kidd would act as a pirate himself. He would get investments from his backers in the New World as well as an influential set of Whig politicians in England. His patrons, for example, included the earl of Shrewsbury. Kidd's expectation was freedom from prosecution for his actions. To those who signed on as sailors he offered an unusually high percentage of the booty. The largesse was evidence of Kidd's confidence in this enterprise.

Kidd and his 90 seamen—many experienced pirates, no doubt—sailed from New York on a ship called the *Adventure Galley* in the fall of 1696. By the spring of 1697 matters were going poorly for the expedition. The crew members became frustrated at Kidd's reluctance to approach vessels that they saw as fair game, especially once the ship sailed into known pirate waters near India. But Kidd was waiting for larger prizes. Kidd, for his part, also was frustrated when he had to defer attacking certain pilgrim ships upon finding them accompanied by British naval vessels. During one disagreement over what the crew perceived as his lack of interest in plunder, Kidd assaulted a sailor named William Moore. Moore died the next day of a skull fracture. Kidd expressed no remorse.

The group did capture six ships in all, though only two of those seemed to fall under the terms of Kidd's orders to go after French targets. The *Quedah Merchant* was the most lucrative catch but also the most troublesome for Kidd in the long run. The loss of that ship, owned by Indians, angered the ruler of the Mughal court, the emperor Aurangzeb, who already was incensed at a piratical capture of the Indian ship *Ganj-i-Sawai* in 1695. The pirate John Avery (or Every, or Bridgeman) had led the earlier raid. The English tried and executed several of Avery's men in 1696, but Avery escaped capture.

Aurangzeb was an ally that the English wished to keep happy in order to smooth their business dealings in India. Although the Mughal rulers later were to decline sharply in importance vis-à-vis the British, at the dawn of the 18th century the Mughal was extremely influential in the region. In addition, Aurangzeb felt himself personally affronted by seizures of ships. His daughter was among the passengers aboard the *Ganj-i-Sawai*; that attack reportedly included atrocities against the female passengers. The Great Mughal had many friends in London who put pressure on the government to apprehend Kidd.

Kidd, meanwhile, had trouble on the way back to either England or New York; the planned end point of his expedition was unclear. He claimed that on Madagascar an old rival, Robert Culliford, waylaid him and forced most of Kidd's crew to desert the mission. In June 1698 Kidd either left or surrendered the *Adventure Galley* and resumed sail on the *Quedah Merchant*. Some historians argue that Culliford and Kidd were in cahoots and that Kidd made for the New World with a full complement of spoils. Others maintain that Kidd stashed most of his earnings before departing the Indian Ocean or else left treasure hidden somewhere else along his route, such as the Caribbean.

Before reaching New York, Kidd got wind of the news from London. The Mughal's backers as well as his Whig sponsors had turned against him. Warrants were out for the arrest of Kidd and his crew. Trusting in the support he thought he still enjoyed, and perhaps knowing that he had stored loot as an insurance against a turn in his fortunes, Kidd went to New York. There he buried an amount of treasure that was worth about £2 million in modern currency on Gardiner's Island. He then proceeded to meet with Bellomont in Boston. Kidd gave to his attorney the letters of marque that had granted him permission to attack French ships. That lawyer permitted Bellomont to hold the documents. Bellomont did send the "French letters" to London, but there they became hard to trace.

Bellomont faced pressure from the Crown to turn Kidd over for prosecution. The governor was tainted through association with Kidd. He put Kidd, his crew, and even Kidd's wife into prison, in deplorable conditions. Bellomont searched for and recovered the treasure from Gardiner's Island. After taking depositions from several of those who sailed with Kidd, in the summer of 1700 Bellomont sent the alleged pirates for trial in England.

Kidd and his colleagues were held in London's Newgate Prison for the better part of a year while Parliament and those in the cabinet decided exactly how to proceed. At least seven of Kidd's men died while in custody, most likely of the diseases endemic to hellholes like Newgate. No doubt political bargains were being made in that time. The Whig junta that had been in power and served as major investors in Kidd's scheme were particularly interested in Kidd's legal treatment.

The Whigs had just lost their control over Parliament. The Tories had won a major election and now, under Robert Harley, ran the House of Commons. While Kidd sat in Newgate, his health deteriorating, apparently the Whigs worked out an agreement to sacrifice the pirate leader in exchange for keeping their names out of the case. Kidd was hauled out of confinement at least twice to testify before Parliament and confer with his old backers the earl of Romney and Lord John Somers. On those occasions he must not have said anything either to convince the Whigs to change that political arrangement or to entice Tories to his aid. In April 1701 the Commons formally petitioned King William to commit Kidd for trial.

SUMMARY OF ARGUMENTS

On May 8, 1701, Kidd's murder trial opened on a most unusual note: the reading of an antipiracy proclamation from King William III. The policy

statement had been published first in 1698. It decried the pirates that were harassing East Indian shipping but offered amnesty to those who would surrender to English naval authorities:

> Whereas we being informed, by the frequent complaints of our good subjects trading to the East Indies, of several wicked practices committed on those seas, as well upon our own subjects as those of our allies, have therefore thought fit (for the security of the trade of those countries, by an utter extirpation of the pirates in all parts eastward of the Cape of Good Hope, as well beyond Cape Comorin as on this side of it, unless they shall forthwith surrender themselves, as is herein after directed) to send out a squadron of men of war, under the command of Capt. Thomas Warren. Now we, to the intent that such who have been guilty of any acts of piracy in those seas, may have notice of our most gracious intention, of extending our royal mercy to such of them as shall surrender themselves, and to cause the severest punishment according to law to be inflicted upon those who shall continue obstinate. . . .

The royal letter made an exception in regard to crimes committed in the time for which Kidd was under indictment; those offenses were not pardonable. The king also exempted Kidd and Avery from his consideration of mercy. Although the proclamation of King William had no formal bearing on the court's determination of guilt or innocence, it was an astonishingly prejudicial document to present in a courtroom. (In the 20th-century United States even an accidental mention of the chief executive having formed an opinion on a defendant's guilt was sufficient to bring a mistrial under discussion. Such was exactly the situation, for example, in the Charles Manson trial.)

The Admiralty court had two main wings: It heard prize cases on the one hand and criminal and civil cases on the other. The nonprize cases were said to reside in the Admiralty's Instance Court. Cases there had most of the procedural guarantees for defendants allowed in the common law courts of the day; that is to say, they provided protection for defendants superior to many continental courts but much inferior to the protection afforded defendants in modern Anglo-American trials. The prosecutor at Kidd's grand jury proceedings and criminal trials was civil law expert George Oxenden, who regularly served as a judge in England's High Court of Admiralty. He was called "Dr. Oxenden" in the trial record on account of his doctor of laws degree from Cambridge. Oxenden had several experienced associates.

The reading of the king's proclamation indicated that this case was a matter of state importance. Otherwise, Kidd's appearance at the Old Bailey—albeit under Admiralty jurisdiction—was typical in certain respects. Like most prisoners' trials, Kidd's prosecutions were jumbled in with the cases of others. In this instance, Kidd stood accused of piracy along with his crewmen Nicholas Churchill, James Howe, Darby Mullins, Abeel Owen, Hugh Parrot, Gabriel Loffe, William Jenkins, Robert Lamley, and Richard Barlycorne. Kidd alone was accused of murder in the death of William Moore.

Trials at the Old Bailey were astonishingly quick by more modern standards, with many cases concluded in hours or even minutes. In 1701 it was rare for criminal proceedings to span more than one day. Both of Kidd's hearings as well as the trials of his fellow pirates took less than two days. For the same jury to hear one case after another in rapid succession was routine. Juries might be within earshot. One panel might deliver its verdict while a parallel jury for a defendant in a related (or unrelated) crime still was hearing evidence.

The English promise of swift justice often meant that judges and other court officials such as bailiffs or recorders showed impatience with defendants who insisted on niceties such as defense counsel. Indeed, in Kidd's day counsel was not guaranteed, even in capital cases. The principle still was in force that judges were supposed to look after the interests of defendants. Accused persons who asked for legal representation had to justify that request with an explanation of a point of law—not simply a claim of innocence or a factual question—that was at issue. For instance, one might procure a lawyer if there was an error in the indictment or if the case had been assigned within the wrong jurisdiction. The problem was that it

was very unlikely that a lay defendant such as Kidd could ascertain or articulate such justification for an attorney.

Kidd proceeded as though his trial were not a foregone conclusion. He first objected to the fact that he had to enter a plea without access to counsel and then requested evidence that he thought critical to his defense. Oxenden and the court officials were unsympathetic. They said that Kidd had to plead before the trial could proceed; the six judges led by Sir Edward Ward would decide whether he needed a lawyer or not. Kidd, knowing that the case would roll on quickly once a plea was entered, desperately stalled for time. He hoped that his "French passes" could be located or an attorney could help him explain to the court the centrality of that evidence:

Clerk of Arraignments: W. Kidd, you stand indicted by the name of William Kidd. Art thou guilty or not guilty?

Kidd: I cannot plead to this indictment, till my French passes are delivered to me.

Clerk: Are you guilty or not guilty?

Kidd: My lord, I insist upon my French papers; pray let me have them.

Recorder: That must not be now, till you have put yourself upon your trial.

Kidd: That must justify me.

Recorder: You may plead it then, if the court see cause.

Kidd: My justification depends on them.

Recorder: Mr. Kidd, I must tell you, if you will not plead, you must have judgment against you, as standing mute.

Clerk: What can he have counsel for, before he has pleaded?

Recorder: Mr. Kidd, the court tells you, you shall be heard what you have to say when you have pleaded to your indictment. If you plead to it, if you will, you may assign matter of law, if you have any; but then you must let the court know what you would insist on.

Kidd: I beg your lordship's patience till I can procure my papers. I had a couple of French passes, which I must make use of in order to my justification.

Recorder: That is not matter of law. You have had long notice of your trial, and might have prepared for it. How long have you had notice of your trial?

Kidd: A matter of a fortnight.

Dr. Oxenden: Can you tell the names of any persons that you would make use of in your defence?

Kidd: I sent for them, but I could not have them.

Dr. Oxenden: Where were they then?

Kidd: I brought them to my lord Bellamont in New England.

Recorder: What were their names? You cannot tell without book. Mr. Kidd, the court see no reason to put off your trial, therefore you must plead.

Clerk: W. Kidd, hold up thy hand.

Kidd: I beg your lordships I may have counsel admitted, and that my trial be put off; I am not really prepared for it.

On and on it went, until Oxenden and the clerks wore Kidd down.

Kidd had to argue his own case, though he finally did secure the presence of his lawyers Dr. William Oldys and Mr. Lemmon (whose first name was not in the trial record). It was Kidd who cross-examined witnesses and answered judges' questions. Kidd was mostly an ineffective counsel for his cause, though one must note that he had to contend against frequent interruptions from the judges and the jury panel. Kidd's best defense of himself actually occurred not in the courtroom, but rather just after the trial had begun, in a letter he had sent to an unknown authority—perhaps the trial judge Baron Ward. In that missive Kidd placed responsibility for his actions on Bellomont and the peers who had funded and conceived his mission:

> The more efficiently to work my ruin, he [Bellomont] has sent over all papers that would either do me little service, or, as he thought, would make against me, but has detained the French passes and some other papers which he knew would acquit me, and baffle his design of making me a pirate, and my cargo forfeited.
>
> If the design I was sent upon, be illegal, or of ill consequence to the trade of the Nation, my Owners who knew the Laws, ought to suffer for It, and not I, whom they made the Tool of their Covetousness. Some great men would have me die for Solving their Honour, and others to pacify the Mogul for injuries done by other men, and not my self, and to secure their trade. . . .

Kidd took up the same themes at his trials, but less eloquently. Only in the 20th century did historians uncover the documents that Kidd probably sought; they likely had been misfiled. Thus, scholars conclude that Kidd was incorrect when he accused Bellomont of withholding or hiding evidence. In addition, modern legal historians observe that the documents that allowed Kidd to plunder ships flying a French flag would have helped defend him against only some of the charges of piracy levied against him. Besides, there was the murder charge to be fought; the French letters would have availed him not at all on that accusation.

The killing of Kidd's gunner Moore seems at first glance to have been an effort by prosecutors to persecute Kidd specially. It was long said that captains were wholly in control of their vessels while at sea. But, in fact, according to English law, captains could not murder their crew or passengers. And so, even considering how rough and tumble conditions normally were on English sailing vessels during Kidd's era, captains did not have completely free rein.

It was most unfortunate for Kidd, then, that his prosecutors took the trouble to apply the charge of murder. He had at least a theoretical chance of escaping the five piracy charges against him, for example, through a political bargain before trial. But, there were several eyewitnesses who could testify to his killing of Moore. He and Moore had argued about Kidd's unwillingness to let the crew go after a particularly alluring ship as a prize, and Kidd in a pique had hit a heavy bucket against Moore's head. Kidd's statement that he had not held a grudge against Moore was weak, as was Kidd's effort to connect Moore's criticism with an attempted mutiny that had occurred one month before the bucket was swung.

VERDICTS

Kidd was convicted in rapid succession of both murder and piracy. Kidd's murder jury came back with their guilty verdict and read it in open court while the piracy trial was going on. In a parallel case Robert Culliford, Kidd's likely colluder in Madagascar, surrendered under the terms of the royal proclamation and was tried at the same time as Kidd. His sentence was one year—clear evidence of the monarch's following through with his promise to "repentant" pirates.

At least one of Kidd's men, Robert Churchill, tried to argue that the royal pardon covered him as well; the judges rejected his contention. Kidd and his crew members, in contrast to Culliford, heard a terrible sentence pronounced. They were to be hanged at waterside in London. Their bodies were to be displayed, encased in chains, to the terror and edification of all who passed by.

Kidd tried one last gambit. He wrote to Robert Harley, offering to journey to the Caribbean to turn up the stupendous sum of £100,000 (millions of dollars in modern currency) that he said he had stashed away. He proposed to buy his freedom and promised to forfeit his life if he could not make good on the offer. The authorities declined to negotiate.

At the 11th hour all of Kidd's underlings were reprieved by royal order. Not so the chief and a couple of pirates convicted for crimes separate from Kidd's expeditions. As if to spite his captors and the Newgate chaplain who expected a sorrowful last speech, Kidd proceeded to the gallows drunk and angry. The minister got one last chance to appeal to Kidd, though; the hangman's rope broke as Kidd was pushed off the scaffold. Traditionally the hangman got to fail three times before the prisoner was deemed releasable, so Kidd was hauled back up for another execution attempt; the chaplain implored him to beg forgiveness for his sins. This time Kidd expressed contrition, and the rope held. Kidd's body hung in the gibbet at Wapping for two years.

SIGNIFICANCE

A number of claimants—from the widows of Kidd's crew members who had died at sea to Kidd's widow Sarah in New York and the Indian owners of the *Quedah Merchant*—sought financial satisfaction from the English government. Few saw any proceeds, although Sarah Kidd did obtain some money through self-help rather than government or legal channels. Although Lord Bellomont had died even before Kidd's trial, Kidd probably did not have the satisfaction of knowing that his former partner had predeceased him.

King William of England outlived Kidd by only about a year. His successor, Queen Anne, ordered Kidd's possessions sold at auction. The sum raised went a long way toward the construction of a building at the Royal Naval Hospital at Greenwich that contained a home for retired sailors. The more irregular seamen with whom Kidd consorted, however, most likely did not get to avail themselves of the splendid facility.

Just after Kidd's execution, piracy actually became more of a problem in parts of the Atlantic. In the first decades of the 18th century pirates grew more violent and numerous than they had even in Kidd's heyday. One of the factors that seemed to make seaborne outlaws fiercer was their impression that King William's amnesty had not protected several sailors (such Kidd's crewman Churchill) who had surrendered. Britain and the North American colonies finally brought piracy more under control in the 1730s.

Kidd's story would have been more compelling to Hollywood if Kidd had been a vicious desperado like Edward Teach ("Blackbeard") or a well-spoken dandy like Walter Raleigh. Likewise, Kidd's tale would be more memorable to the larger public if it could be proved that he had left a large fortune unclaimed on some tropical island. Both of those scenarios were the basis of heavily fictionalized treatments of Kidd, most famously in Robert Louis Stevenson's *Treasure Island* and J. M. Barrie's *Peter Pan*. The real Captain Kidd's life was more complex and sad.

Further Reading

Captain William Kidd Web site. "History—Trial Transcript." Available online. URL: http://www.captainkidd.org/TrialTranscript.html. Accessed January 2, 2010; Cordingly, David. *Under the Black Flag*. New York: Random House, 2006; Gascoigne, Bamber. *A Brief History of the Great Moguls*. New York: Carroll & Graf, 2002; Rediker, Marcus. *Villains of All Nations: Atlantic Pirates in the Golden Age*. Boston: Beacon Press, 2004; Ritchie, Robert C. *Captain Kidd and the War Against the Pirates*. Cambridge, Mass.: Harvard University Press, 1986; Zacks, Richard. *The Pirate Hunter*. New York: Hyperion Books, 2003.

The trial of Czarevitch Alexis

Date: 1718

KEY ISSUES

The emperor Peter Romanov, who governed Russia from 1682 to 1725, aimed to unify and modernize the nation. He proposed to bring in Western influences as well as make Russia more of a power within Europe. He insisted on intellectual, economic, political, and military transformation. He was nothing if not ambitious: He planned a greater political and economic role for Russia in the Baltic region and largely succeeded. He proposed a new northern capital as physical testimony to his cultural vision; St. Petersburg showcased his ability to fund such dreams. Even within a line of rulers accustomed to autocracy, this czar had little tolerance for criticism. Physically imposing and accustomed as a child to struggling for position, Peter

styled himself "the Great" and acted the part: imperious, restless, curious, and often cruel. Not only groups but also individuals who got in his way experienced the autocrat's wrath.

HISTORY OF THE CASE

There is no better illustration of this czar's personality than his treatment of the royal heir, Alexis (Alexei Petrovich). His father's grand visions, of course, depended in large part on being able to mold his offspring. But his first male progeny, born to the czar and his first wife, Eudoxia Lopukhina, in 1690, grew into young adulthood as a disappointment to his exceedingly demanding father. This put Peter into a foul temper and placed Alexis in a most vulnerable position.

Several differences of opinion existed between father and son. First of all, the czar had become estranged from Lopukhina when Alexis was a toddler, so there was little sentimental attachment to the child of the estranged mother. For her part, Alexis's mother encouraged animosity toward Peter the Great among those around her. When the czar sent his first spouse to a convent in 1699, he theoretically took a greater interest in the heir's education. What that oversight amounted to, however, was not personal attention from the restless father; rather Peter consigned the boy to tutors. Those instructors promoted study of modern subjects of which his father approved, such as geography and the French language.

Then there was the matter of Alexis's lack of enthusiasm for military affairs. Although when Alexis became a teenager Peter gave him important tasks connected with Russia's war against Sweden, the son's performance was mediocre. The young man proved sickly at times, or at least not as hardy as his robust father. The famously tall and athletic czar took as a personal insult having a child who was not also a fine physical specimen. With more than a little venom he called Alexis "an unworthy son" and a "gangrenous limb."

The czarevitch was uninterested in martial affairs, preferring theology and other intellectual pursuits. That was a problem for him also, for Alexis inclined toward an older approach to religion than was advocated by this czar. Many of the boyars with whom the czarevitch liked to converse were to Peter the Great reactionaries who stood in the way of rational reforms—especially reforms of the church. Even in the matter of Alexis's marriage they exercised undue influence over the young man, according to the father.

The production of a son in 1715 by Alexis and his German wife, Charlotte, failed to quiet Peter the Great's scorn. If anything, the birth of a grandson encouraged the czar to make greater demands of his own progeny, for Peter now perceived that there was another excellent blood alternative (the grandson, who was in fact the future Peter II) to Alexis's holding the throne. Despite the fact that he had an international reputation as a profligate, Peter professed himself indignant over Alexis's preference for the company of a peasant woman to that of Grand Duchess Charlotte. After Charlotte died in childbirth, Alexis appeared even more devoted to his "lowborn" mistress from Finland—yet another reason for criticism by the ruler.

Alexis seemed to take a prudent course in absenting himself from Russia. He decamped for the hospitality of the Habsburg ruler in Vienna, his brother-in-law, Holy Roman Emperor Charles VI. Perhaps his father's anger would subside if he, the crown prince, appeared to renounce his claim with a self-enforced exile.

Peter brooded over the idea that the czarevitch had been at the center of a conspiracy to unseat him. He became determined to obtain answers about the extent and members of the supposed plot. Such a conspicuous escape by Alexis into the protection of another ruler was embarrassing to the Russian leader. Alexis accepted his father's firm requests to return to Russia and explain himself, probably not grasping that Peter intended to unmask disloyalty—real or imagined—at any cost.

SUMMARY OF ARGUMENTS

In late January 1718 Alexis reentered Russia. Through the Russian emissary (Peter Tolstoi) he had extracted from Peter the Great a promise that the father would view the son in future with less distrust. Furthermore, the czar would allow his son to retire to the countryside and marry his beloved Finnish peasant mistress, Afrosinia. Alexis contemplated renouncing his claim to the throne in favor of his half brother (also named Peter), the czar's young son by a second marriage.

Within a few weeks of his arrival in Moscow, the czarevitch realized that his father intended to renege on all of those assurances if Alexis did not disclose his alleged coconspirators. He first attempted to state before a solemn assembly of dignitaries at the Kremlin that he repented of any offenses against the czar, but that confessional session, on February 14, did not satisfy his father. On February 18 Alexis offered up the names of his friends, though there was no plot to disclose. Peter the Great, urged on by both secular and religious councils, became convinced that his son had sought to turn back the clock. He authorized a series of tortures upon Alexis's family members (including the czar's former wife and Alexis's mother, Eudoxia) and political and personal associates.

The Council of Ministers heard the case of the alleged conspiracy, with the crown prince as yet unnamed at the plot's center. That body, which was in effect Peter's cabinet, reassembled as a magistrates' court and began its inquiries in Moscow. In March 1718 the court handed down sentences on several prominent alleged coconspirators. The commissioner of the Admiralty, Alexander Kikin, for example, was accused of being too close to Alexis and his entourage. An officer named Gliebof was charged with having an affair with the czaritsa (former queen) Eudoxia, who was supposed to have been out of the public eye in the convent. Dositheus, a bishop who had expressed some sympathy for Eudoxia, was deprived of his clerical status and then tortured. The two men died after having their bones broken on a wheel and being impaled. Peter the Great personally witnessed several of those actions. Eudoxia was fortunate to escape with her life. After a public self-abnegation, she was returned to a stricter convent.

The council then pointedly moved to St. Petersburg—a tangible sign that its judicial incarnation was in the service of Czar Peter. The investigation was narrowing its focus to the czarevitch. In April 1718 Afrosinia made a bargain for her own safety. She testified of Alexis cherishing "the old people." She reported the heir had said that when he took the throne he intended to deemphasize military affairs, renounce foreign campaigns, and even abandon his father's showpiece St. Petersburg, treating it "simply as any other town." The reformist clergy who supported Czar Peter stated that the czarevitch had "spoken with distaste of the novelties his father had introduced." And so, Alexis was accused of wishing for his father's death and opposing his policies. Afrosinia did ensure her own security; she alone among the key figures close to Alexis did not garner physical torture, prison, or death.

The charges against the grand duke sounded both vague and contradictory throughout the inquiry. Was Alexis lazy and incompetent, or the mastermind of dangerous plot against the czar? Did the czarevitch covet the crown of Russia, or was he perpetually shirking his duty? Among such allegations was Peter's contention that Alexis had trusted foreign allies such as the Habsburg leader Charles to intervene in Russia, unseat his father, and secure his place on the throne. It was widely said among both diplomats and the public, however, that Alexis had turned to foreign assistance only as a last resort when he sought to abdicate the throne; in fact, Peter the Great had summoned his son back to Russia. Recent historical scholarship has uncovered some evidence that Alexis did engage in speculation while abroad about how much foreign support he might expect if he were to mount a challenge to his father's reign. How deep any expectation of success ran in Alexis is open to debate.

There remained Czar Peter's promise not to prosecute his son if Alexis would make a full report of what had transpired. The czar himself drew up a declaration stating that he no longer considered that pact—engineered by diplomat Peter Tolstoi—binding because Alexis had failed to disclose the extent of his treachery. The son's deceitful conduct now had been revealed through the "confessions" of others and the statements of Afrosinia. Peter took the step, however, of asking for an opinion from the church as to how to proceed against his ungrateful son. The theologians temporized, saying that there was scriptural authority both for a father to take vengeance upon a rebellious child and for the parent to offer forgiveness. The prelates were keen to throw jurisdiction in the matter to secular authorities.

VERDICT

In June 1718 a body of 127 men began to consider the evidence that had been presented, determine guilt, and set a sentence. That superior panel, called the High Court of Justice, consisted of the members of the Russian senate—only recently elevated to a dignified status by Peter—as well as the magistrates who had conducted the initial investigation, certain close councillors to the czar, and some military figures. A few days before the body announced its judgment, the government official still in charge of the general investigation—none other than Tolstoi—ordered the czarevitch flogged with a whip called the knout. That weapon had metal barbs interspersed within leather thongs.

Alexis, who already was extremely weak from his imprisonment and never in good health anyway, got 25 lashes. He deteriorated rapidly. The court announced its capital verdict on June 24, but later that same day Alexis was flogged again with 15 strokes. He did not recover from that beating. Alexis was found dead two days later in the new-style political prison that his father had recently ordered constructed inside the Peter and Paul Fortress in St. Petersburg. Several contemporary accounts report on the discovery of Alexis's body. While most concur that the czarevitch succumbed to torture, a few conclude that his death was a secret execution. Peter himself stated that he had heard Alexis had suffered a seizure. The ruler had gone to visit him in jail in his last hours, to offer the son fatherly forgiveness though not political pardon. In the days before the body was laid to rest, Peter the Great pointedly attended boat launchings and celebrated his own birthday.

SIGNIFICANCE

The proceedings against Alexis were the most prominent of the czar's efforts to root out treason during his reign. The trials of the czarevitch and others were a clear warning that no one—however highly placed—would find quarter if he or she were disloyal to Peter. Several hundred individuals were hauled before Russian courts on similar suspicions in the seven years subsequent to the death of the czarevitch. As others had been treated during Alexis's trial, so these new suspects were held incommunicado, tortured, and/or executed using the most brutal methods possible. Among the "grave matters" investigated by the Chancellory for Secret Inquisitorial Affairs—the body that had overseen Alexis's trial—were allegations that certain persons had expressed sorrow at the czarevitch's demise.

The judicial and political pronouncements about Czarevitch Alexis's "conspiracy" constituted a show trial. The main purposes were to ease Peter the Great's mind about the succession and to clear the way for the son of his second marriage. The entire prosecution was designed to demonstrate to foreigners and Russians that this czar was conversant with European sensibilities. Peter seemed to be arguing that if trials in Russia were well publicized, then they were more modern. Such was the reasoning that later Russian leaders—most particularly, Joseph Stalin—put forward in justification for stage-managed trials.

Further Reading

Bushkovitch, Paul. *Peter the Great: The Struggle for Power, 1671–1725.* Cambridge: Cambridge University Press, 2001; *The Economist.* "Show Trial." December 23, 1999. Available online. URL: http://www.economist.com/world/europe/display story.cfm?story_id=346820. Accessed January 17, 2010; Hughes, Lindsey. *Peter the Great.* New Haven, Conn.: Yale University Press, 2002; Massie, Robert. *Peter the Great.* New York: Ballantine Books, 1986; Schuyler, Eugene. *Peter the Great, Emperor of Russia.* New York: Charles Scribner's Sons, 1884.

The trial of the White Lily sect leaders

Date: 1720

KEY ISSUES

How does a court respond to unusual religious practices? When is an unofficial religion a cult in the eyes of authorities? Is such a group so dangerous that it merits prosecution? If the government proceeds against religious figures or groups that are locally popular, could such a trial cause rebellion? These were some of the concerns of leaders in China during the early 1700s in the case of the White Lily sect.

The judge at the trial of the leaders of the group was Lan Luchou (Lu-chow) (1680–1733), who was celebrated as a jurist and administrator. Judge Lan told of the case in his memoirs. It was an account that was by no means an official transcript, nor even a detailed reflection on a trial, as in Edward Coke's *Reports*. Judge Lan's memories of prosecuting the White Lily sect were edited by the jurist's assistant, Kuang Minbin (K'uang Min-pin), in 1729. Based on Lan's and Kuang's writings, one may assume that the trial occurred around 1720.

The prosecution of the White Lily sect advanced Lan's career and enhanced his reputation as a wise leader. Although the trial itself is not well documented, even a short recounting shows Lan's capabilities. Lan was in many respects the ideal imperial judge. He was praised for diligence and selflessness in contrast to judges who misused their considerable power.

The administration of justice in imperial China assumed its modern form during the Ming dynasty (1370–1650) with the development of the Ming Penal Code. The code advanced principles such as respect for authority, deference to elders, loyalty to family, and obedience to the state. The code's stance with regard to religion was relevant to the case. In Judge Lan's day there was no state church in China; Chinese beliefs were too complex to be summed up as a "religion," anyway. Officials tolerated certain religious beliefs and actions that were not officially sanctioned—notably, Buddhism. However, the code and courts in practice discouraged simpler, naturalistic religious beliefs. Many elites adhered to Confucian precepts that emphasized rationality and bureaucratic rule. The code outright forbade sorcery and gatherings that promoted superstition.

Who presided over law courts in the empire? Power, including legal authority, flowed from the emperor through his regional prefects and then through the governors of smaller areas, with the basic unit of local government being the district. Districts were centered in cities, including rural areas for dozens of miles around. District magistrates were the chief judges in the vicinity. Magistrates had a wide range of duties beyond courtroom tasks; they also were tax collectors and record keepers, and they were charged with keeping order.

The term *judge* only partially explains the district magistrate's judicial responsibilities. Each magistrate had the power to apprehend suspected criminals (as U.S. sheriffs did), investigate crimes (like a modern police department), and prosecute (as would a U.S. district attorney). At trial the district magistrate questioned accused persons and victims, family members, experts, and witnesses. He could order certain types of torture, although the judge who seldom resorted to coercion generally was more esteemed. He proclaimed guilt or innocence and might preside over punishments. The Chinese judge was akin to the sheriff of the Old West who, like Wyatt Earp, styled himself simply as "the law."

The district magistrate was busy and powerful. His effectiveness was based on his individual reputation for knowledge, fairness, and diligence, but the judge did not work alone. In addition to the members of the courtroom staff, such as jailers and bailiffs, who were state employees, the judge hired a set of personal assistants. These individuals—and they invariably were male—might be strong-arm men or scholars, or both. A respected magistrate such as Judge Lan could be promoted to regional prefect after he gained the confidence of the central government. In addition to being mentioned in official histories of the empire, some magistrates, such as Judge Dee (Di Renjie, 630–700), were celebrated as the heroes of detective novels.

HISTORY OF THE CASE

When he arrived in an official capacity in the Chaoyang district of the Guangdong Province, probably in the 1710s, Judge Lan realized that he would preside over a citizenry with diverse religious habits. Wealthier families in the area tended to be Taoist (Daoist). Poorer folk (especially women) were devoted to Buddha, while the Qing rulers of the empire favored Confucianism. Such varied beliefs often were compatible with one another; Chinese people for thousands of years had embraced a rich mixture of religious tenets, philosophies, and personal practices.

It would be inaccurate to describe the Chinese central government as requiring a single official religion. Still, in localities there could be a delicate balance among competing worldviews—a balance easily upset by the rise of a powerful religious personality or organization. In particular, if religious groups offered the possibility of a paradise on earth or the spectacle of a messiah figure, they became dangerous in the eyes of the authorities. It was Judge Lan's task to keep watch over such movements so that they did not become too disruptive in Chaoyang.

Judge Lan must have known that his predecessor in office had tried to crush an affiliation called the Hou Tian (Hou-t'ien), or White Aspens, later known as the White Lily sect. The former magistrate had succeeded only in driving the group underground; they returned during Judge Lan's term in office. Their leaders were men named Yen and Chou, as well as a woman who was identified by Judge Lan only as Yen's wife. That woman had a lover named Hu who also exercised a key role. The four leaders claimed that they had spoken directly with divinities (immortals). Hu actually professed to be a divinity, and Yen's wife (Hu's lover) said she was a goddess—"the Lady of the Moon."

SUMMARY OF ARGUMENTS

The White Lilies used a large building as their headquarters, presenting plays that attracted crowds. They performed exorcisms, claimed to control the weather, issued charms to ensure fertility and cure disease, and ran séances. Judge Lan was concerned about the theatrical performances because the Ming Penal Code had strict regulations on theaters and actors. For example, the law forbade actors and actresses from marrying more respectable people. Judge Lan also had heard that Hu, who went by the name "the Immortal of Pencil Peak," had dressed in a feminine manner and danced around the goddess. The fact that some worshippers thought Hu was a woman was to Judge Lan a gross deception. Also worrisome were reports that the White Lilies used strong incense and a form of hypnosis to make their faithful sleepy. The leaders then introduced believers to departed family members and unborn children.

Lan sent constables to shut down the building, but they were unnerved by the threat of being cursed by the White Lilies. Besides, several prominent local families seem to have provided the group with immunity from arrest. Judge Lan decided to visit the group's headquarters himself, banking on his prestige as well as the presence of his aides to keep him safe.

Encountering a warren of rooms as he entered the White Lilies' temple, the judge persisted in searching for ringleaders Hu, Yen, Chou, and the "Lady of the Moon." No doubt with the assistance of his helpers (who traditionally were skilled in martial arts), Lan rounded up the heads of the group. He also located their colorful props, including sleep potions and wigs. The raid went along chaotically but without harm to the investigators. Apparently, once word got out that the district magistrate himself was on the premises, worshippers fairly fell over themselves to turn in the "divinities."

What cannot be gleaned from Judge Lan's account is the perspective of those who were apprehended. Nor does his reader gain much sense of wider public opinion. Judge Lan apparently thought that shutting down the sect was progressive, but one might turn the tables and find in his actions an example of a burdensome imperial government—a national authority that sent its minions to regulate the private beliefs of ordinary people. Even as described by Judge Lan, the activities of the worshippers appear harmless enough to modern minds. Indeed, the sect's "contacts" with deceased relatives and its fortune-telling must have been comforting to people deeply concerned with family and the afterlife. In Lan's memoirs there is a palpable sense of disapproval about the adulterous relationship between Hu and Yen's wife and Hu's cross-dressing; there also is a whiff of misogyny. Perhaps it was the unconventional morality of the cult leaders rather than their religious ideas that really incurred the judge's anger.

VERDICT

Judge Lan gave no formal description of the trial of the leaders and their lieutenants; only hints about the proceedings appear in his memoirs. If the trial was run as was usual in courts in China at the time, then it would have looked much more like an inquiry than a confrontation between accusers and defendants. This particular trial probably was even more a fait accompli than

usual—merely a summary of the case against the accused persons. Certain damning facts already had been uncovered during Judge Lan's investigation and the raid of the White Lily temple. A key bit of information to which Judge Lan alluded in his account of the raid was that he "subjected" Yen's wife to "a searching examination as to the whereabouts of her accomplices." It was the norm for suspects to confess either at trial or beforehand. Physical intimidation (especially at the hands of a magistrate's assistants) might loosen tongues. Judge Lan improved his reputation, however, by not boasting of such methods but rather only suggesting that he had used them.

The judge did note that the case involved depositions, which he must have reviewed in some detail. He passed sentences against the White Lilies after relegating them to three categories: the real leaders, their immediate inferiors, and their followers next in line. In his telling of the tale, the magistrate focused on the aftermath of the trial instead of on courtroom scenes. Lan was most interested in the punishment phase and the effects of the case upon the community.

Having ruled that the masterminds of the cult were Hu and his lover, the "Lady of the Moon," Judge Lan required that they receive 100 blows from a bamboo pole and then be weighed down by a heavy collar called the "cangue" and made to stand at a main gate. Chinese law at the time allowed punishment only for the most serious crime of which a person was convicted. In the cases of Hu and his lover, that crime was adultery, which carried a capital sentence. Although technically Judge Lan did not impose the death penalty, in effect he ensured the same outcome.

Just as judges in European jurisdictions made it likely that certain convicted persons sentenced to the stocks or the pillory would be exposed to well-aimed bricks—defenseless before a hostile crowd—so did Judge Lan make death probable for the White Lily leaders. He turned Hu and his lover over to an angry town; they suffered at the hands of former believers who screeched at them, tore their skin, and finally fractured their skulls. Lan noted aridly that they "passed together into their boasted Paradise."

He sentenced Yen, along with Chou and 10 other leaders of the group, to much lighter fates: to wear the cangue, receive a whipping, or "be punished in some way," as Judge Lan put it. His account offers the distinct impression that he did not know precisely what correction was meted out to those mid-level offenders. Rather, the judge left the exact sentences to another party. Perhaps it was one of his own lieutenants or the public executioner who determined the details.

Judge Lan considered what to do with the other people implicated in the affair—the worshippers in the building at the time of his raid. He offered amnesty to those underlings as long as they promised good behavior. There were two factors that seemed to influence him toward mercy: One of his reasons seems class based to the modern observer, and the other appears more generous. Judge Lan said he hesitated to besmirch the reputations of people from "old and respectable" families by associating them with the case. He burned the depositions because they listed distinguished names. He also argued that the shame of being connected with the affair would be too great a burden to the local people, since the whole area recently had suffered a bad harvest.

Significance

Judge Lan did not go after the small fry involved in the cult. But, besides mercy, what did he offer to the community after these events? He not only eradicated the cult but also replaced it with an institution that he thought wholesome. He ordered a renovation of the White Lily temple, which he changed from a maze of rooms to a more orderly floor plan. He mandated that the place should be ritually purified. Finally, it was turned into a library where scholars, including himself, could read and discuss great literature with an emphasis on Confucian teachings.

Imperial officials told Judge Lan that he would have been completely justified in recommending the execution of more persons who had been involved. Indeed, they said that such a course of action would have spread his renown as a stern judge. Lan's superiors praised the fact that he had concluded the case not in order to punish but to "care for the fair fame of so many people." It did not hurt, as well, that Judge Lan's resolution promoted the type of worldview—Confucian, rational, learned, respectful of authority—that the emperor desired.

Further Reading

Cohen, Myron, and Stephen Teiser. "Living in the Chinese Cosmos: Understanding Religion in Late-Imperial China (1644–1911)." Available online. URL: http://afe.easia.columbia.edu/cosmos/prb/heavenly.htm. Accessed June 8, 2008; Giles, Herbert A. *Historic China and Other Sketches*. London: Thomas de la Rue & Co., 1882; Miller, James. *Chinese Religion in Contemporary Societies*, Santa Barbara, Calif.: ABC-CLIO, 2006; Nimick, Thomas. "The Placement of Local Magistrates in Imperial China." *Late Imperial China* 20 (December 1999): 35–60; Pidhainy, Ihor. "State Ritual in Late Imperial China." *Religion Compass* 3 (2009): 7–17; Van Gulik, Robert, trans. *The Celebrated Cases of Judge Dee*. New York: Dover Publications, 1976.

The trial of John Peter Zenger

Also known as: *The King v. Zenger*

Date: 1735

Key Issues

John Peter Zenger was the target of the prosecution when he was charged with seditious libel, yet, as merely the printer of a newspaper, Zenger was only the bearer of opinion that political authorities did not want to hear. At his trial, then, there were far more dangerous political opponents in the crosshairs of the colonial government. The state wished to silence the critics of New York's governor, William Cosby. To do so, Zenger's accusers underlined the English legal principle of "the greater the truth the greater the libel." Zenger's prosecutors echoed English common law that truth was no defense to an insult. Indeed, if a libel were true, then it made the insult more actionable.

The prosecution had the better case, legally, but fortunately for Zenger, his jury did not much care about the current law.

Although Zenger's lawyers certainly defended him well, their purpose was not so much to free the man as to attack political institutions and persons that they saw as offensive. The objects of the defense team's ire were the present governor of the colony and his political lackeys. If Zenger's defenders needed to revise English common law to win, then so be it.

Zenger's trial resulted in a victory for several portions of the defense agenda. Two principles that the defense championed were of special import. The jury verdict demonstrated that panels might nullify the instructions of even the most politicized judge. Zenger's case also helped establish the notion in the British North American colonies that governments ought not to use ruinous bail amounts to keep their critics in jail. Thus, a case in which the defendant was rather beside the point to both factions turned out to be a building block of the U.S. Constitution's guarantees of reasonable bail and a fair trial.

HISTORY OF THE CASE

Zenger was a German immigrant who arrived in New York in 1710. He struggled to make a living as a printer, first as an associate of prominent New York politician William Bradford and then in a separate business. Zenger's technical experience and access to a press made him an alternative to the better-connected Bradford when opposition arose toward the new governor, Cosby, in 1733. Zenger was a man without much to lose in terms of political connections but much to gain vis-à-vis readership when the detractors of Cosby sought a mouthpiece.

Zenger established a paper, the *New York Weekly Journal,* to serve the needs of political professionals such as Rip Van Dam and James Alexander. Such men had various bones to pick with Cosby. Among Cosby's more controversial actions upon taking office were his demands for a vastly increased salary and his replacement of colonial officials with more slavish operatives. It was not that colonial administrations were immune to political profiteering, but Cosby's actions seemed

to many observers to be unusually corrupt. Cosby's critics called themselves the Popular Party, and they captured the imagination of some ordinary folk.

The *New York Weekly Journal* soon became a hit with the wider public for its broad lampooning of Cosby and his appointees, such as Judge James De Lancey. In one issue, for example, Cosby's critics published a mock interview with a fortuneteller who warned that all governors whose names began with C had proved to be disasters in office. The prognosticator cited several examples including New York's former governor Richard Coote, the earl of Bellomont, who had turned William "Captain" Kidd over to the English but left his own and the colony's affairs in a financial shambles. The newspaper caricatured Cosby as a "monkey of the larger sort" who pretended to be a general; Cosby had an important military assignment prior to his governorship. Certain satires in the paper were not traditional articles at all but rather "editorial advertisements."

The *Weekly Journal* and its main writers, especially James Alexander, also played up news stories in which Cosby's opponents had gained political success. Such a featured episode was the winning of an election by former judge Lewis Morris (whom Cosby had removed from office) despite Cosby's determined opposition. Perhaps even more damaging in the long term for the Cosby faction was the paper's championing of Whig ideology. Through the citation of historical examples of poor performance by rulers, the paper invited its reader to draw parallels with Cosby's present methods.

The governor and those connected to him reacted harshly, turning over copies of the periodical for public burning. Twice during 1734, at regular grand jury sessions, Judge De Lancey requested that jurors enter an indictment against "unknown persons" who had written and published the *Weekly Journal.* Both times the jurors declined.

In November 1734 another of Cosby's placemen, Attorney General Richard Bradley, presented to Judge De Lancey and Judge Frederick Philipse what English courts called an "information." This was an affirmation of the truth of an allegation, backed up by the official's (Bradley's) oath of office rather than a grand jury's oath. The goal was to get the bench to shut down the operation of the paper. This time Cosby named Zenger as the paper's publisher. The use of an information to justify arresting Zenger was unusual though not unprecedented. The specific charge against Zenger was one that courts in England had frequently adjudicated in the 17th century: the hybrid crime of seditious libel.

English criminal law defined libel as the injuring of a person's reputation through writing. Sedition was undermining the government, though it was a step short of treason. Thus, seditious libel was writing about the government or an official in a way that injured his reputation and made it difficult for him to govern. Zenger was accused of publishing writings that had in them "many things tending to raise factions and tumults among the people of this Province, inflaming their minds with contempt of His Majesty's government, and greatly disturbing the peace thereof."

Unfortunately for Cosby, the offense of seditious libel not only was associated with Stuart monarchs such as Charles I. It also was tied closely to the operation of one English judicial court, the Star Chamber. It was at Star Chamber that Puritans such as John Burton, Henry Bastwick, and William Prynne had been prosecuted for seditious libel in the 1630s. The lesson that Cosby ought to have taken from such cases was that strenuous efforts to tamp down written dissent could blow up in a leader's face.

SUMMARY OF ARGUMENTS

Before the trial could get fully under way three procedural tiffs took place. These controversies at the outset influenced public opinion more toward Zenger, for they made the governor look yet more manipulative. First of all, there was the matter of the personnel of the bench in the case. Cosby had made certain that the trial judges were none other than De Lancey and Philipse. Zenger's lawyers, James Alexander and William Smith, protested that these jurists were appointed in an improper manner. They went back to the dismissal of Lewis Morris to demonstrate Cosby's heavy-handed management of the colony. They also contended that De Lancey held several judicial appointments at once—something forbidden among English courts.

Cosby's judges were not pleased with the challenge to their commissions: For their pains, Alexander and Smith got disbarred. Their replacement was John Chambers, of whom Zenger was suspicious because he was affiliated with Cosby. Legal historians say that during the short time he represented Zenger, Chambers was an earnest though uninspiring advocate. The shuffle in attorneys, however, was to prove most advantageous for Zenger. First of all, it won him sympathy. Second, Zenger's backers looked around for another attorney to assist Chambers—really to take over for him—and they found someone of exceptional ability.

Another point to which Zenger's original attorneys objected but which they could not change was the setting of his bail. The amount was exorbitant: £800, which was far beyond the ability of even Zenger's patrons to pay. It kept him in jail throughout the trial, and that was the point: Cosby wanted the paper shut down. Zenger, though, persevered, dictating columns to his wife through the bars of his cell. The public missed only one issue during Zenger's incarceration. Again, the tactic backfired on Cosby and his minions. There was an outcry about the punishing nature of the bail, for in the 18th century prisons not only were incommodious but also were seedbeds of contagion. A long stay often cost prisoners their lives. In all, Zenger sat in jail for eight months.

The impaneling of a jury proved another sticking point. Cosby and De Lancey tried to pack the panel. Chambers had requested and been granted a special, or "struck," jury. Such juries, which were occasionally used in English and colonial courts, were supposed to be made up of unusually well read or specially qualified voters, as when a case was quite technical. But a special jury risked appearing elitist; it was as though the bench did not trust "ordinary" men to give judgment. That was precisely the implication in Zenger's case, but not because of the educational qualifications or wealth of the jurymen.

Zenger's defenders argued that the list from which the struck jury was to be chosen contained only the names of Cosby's friends, appointees, and personal employees. Somewhat backed into a corner by evidence that the proferred list was hopelessly corrupt, De Lancey and Philipse resorted to the regular voter rolls. The 12 jurors who sat in Zenger's case appeared to be a good cross section among voters; that is to say, they were associated with neither faction exclusively.

Zenger's time in court included several dramatic moments. When the case got under way on August 4, 1735, the "Morris faction" had a spectacular gambit in store. They had secured the legal services of one of the best attorneys in the colonies, Andrew Hamilton. Journeying from Philadelphia, Hamilton came into the courtroom as one of the spectators. At one point Hamilton joined in with Chambers's arguments, much to Chambers's relief and the judges' surprise and chagrin. Shortly, Hamilton simply took over the case from Chambers. The alteration in the defense table left De Lancey and Philipse nonplussed, but they could not dismiss Hamilton. In a phrase that came to mean "securing a brilliant and expensive advocate," it was said that the defense had "brought in a Philadelphia lawyer."

Hamilton had a four-pronged argument. He aimed to put Cosby's administration on trial by discussing the truth of the articles Zenger had printed. He then planned to contend that truth could be a defense to a charge of libel—in effect, that English law was not as black and white as the prosecution contended. Next, Hamilton wished to establish that the jury had the right to make a decision about unclear points in the law; that is, if the law on libel were gray, then a jury could sort it out rather than relying solely on a judge's directions. Finally, Hamilton would propose that New World conditions mandated alterations to English legal practice. Thus, Hamilton hoped, a New York jury might alter English libel law so that truth was a defense.

Attorney General Bradley thought that the defense might allege corruption in the Cosby administration, and he came prepared to counter such charges. Early on Bradley and Hamilton engaged in a lively discussion. Bradley hoped to permit a certain amount of debate with Hamilton about whether Zenger had published the paper—only not so much that it would prove politically embarrassing to the governor. Then Bradley expected to turn the case over to the bench; the attorney general would ask for a "special verdict" on whether the publication was a violation of the

law. It would be De Lancey and Philipse who would decide the case, not the jury.

Hamilton forestalled that plan. Hamilton declared that the defense would admit the "fact of publication." As befitted his reputation as a skilled criminal lawyer, Hamilton was correct on procedure; the case now should be in the jury's hands. De Lancey then did the best he could; he tried to shut down Hamilton's oratory and direct the jury on what it should do.

The judge said that the matter now was settled except for the formality of a jury verdict. According to De Lancey, if the defense stated that Zenger had published the alleged materials, then it mattered not whether the writings were true or false. Indeed, the bench opined that if Zenger's paper had published accurate articles, the damage to Cosby and the colony was greater.

Hamilton soldiered on, getting in substantive arguments under the guise of procedural objections. He pointed out to Judge De Lancey that the precedents that the judge was citing to justify the principle of "the greater the truth the greater the libel" were from Star Chamber cases. Surely that court had been abolished as a tyrannical institution in one of the more popular legislative policies of the 1640s? Judge De Lancey was adamant that he knew English law and that that law applied to Zenger. He called for the prosecution and defense to make their final statements to the jury.

Hamilton's summation included much of what he had wanted to say, anyway. Except to the prosecution (and maybe even to them), it was a brilliant effort. Hamilton was defending not so much Zenger personally as he was supporting the right to publish political comment. Hamilton's selection of examples was adroit. He used passages from the book of Isaiah, for example, to contend that an overzealous public authority might object even to sacred words on grounds that they were critical of a corrupt administration:

"The Leaders of the People cause them to err, and they that are led by them are destroyed." But should Mr. Attorney go about to make this a Libel, he would read it thus; "The Leaders of the People [innuendo, the Governor and Council of New York] cause them [innuendo, the People of this Province] to err, and they [the People of this Province meaning] that are led by them [the Governor and the Council meaning] are destroyed [innuendo, are deceived into the Loss of their Liberty] which is the worst kind of Destruction."

Hamilton was arguing on two levels—that the Cosby administration could twist any text into a criticism and that Scripture justified attacks on Cosby.

Hamilton's oratory ranged from abstractions to comments about his own age and infirmity. It was a masterful performance that he designed for the jury; De Lancey already had shut down the case except for jury deliberations. One of the most compelling portions of Hamilton's argument was his appeal to the jury as intelligent citizens. He reminded them that if they freed Zenger they might face judicial ire but would earn the approval of later generations:

> Men who injure and oppress the people under their administration provoke them to cry out and complain; and then make that very complaint the foundation for new oppressions and persecutions. . . . Gentlemen of the jury, it is not the cause of a poor printer, nor of New York alone, which you are now trying. NO! It may in its consequences affect every freeman that lives under a cause of liberty; and I make no doubt but your upright conduct this day will not only entitle you to the love and esteem of your fellow citizens, but every man who prefers freedom to a life of slavery will bless you and honor you, as men who have baffled the attempt of tyranny.

VERDICT

In the face of such eloquence Bradley's reminder to the jurors that they had to convict according to De Lancey's instructions stood little chance of ratification. The jury took only a short time to deliberate. When foreman Thomas Hunt announced that they found Zenger "not guilty," the courtroom rang with "Huzzah's." Judge De Lancey's immediate reaction was not recorded.

SIGNIFICANCE

Just after Zenger's trial judges in England and North America insisted that the case did not establish a clear right to jury nullification. To put it another way, most legal authorities still claimed that the bench was the arbiter of law while juries determined fact. The debate continued all the way to the 1776 revolution. No less than Benjamin Franklin (himself a nonestablishment printer, a parallel in Pennsylvania to Zenger in New York) weighed in on behalf of Hamilton's arguments.

There were direct connections between the Zenger case and the U.S. Constitution's safeguards on freedom of the press and the right to a fair trial. For example, among the political opponents of Governor Cosby had been Lewis Morris. Morris was the member of the colony's Court of Exchequer who resisted Cosby's effort to (in effect) extort money from his predecessor, interim governor Van Dam. Morris's descendant, Gouverneur Morris, helped compose the U.S. Constitution and Bill of Rights. Zenger was on Morris's mind as he considered the wording of the Eighth Amendment. That founding father explicitly cited the Zenger trial as a cornerstone of American resistance to a tyrannical executive.

In the more modern United States judges usually do not remind jurors that they have the right to decide on the law. It falls to individual panelists to suggest nullification to their jury colleagues while in deliberations. Thus, jurors have to help themselves to such a remedy. Still, an important long-term outcome in Zenger's case was not only a victory for freedom of the press but also a vindication of jury independence.

Further Reading

Finkleman, Paul, ed. *A Brief Narrative of the Case and Tryal of John Peter Zenger.* St. James, N.Y.: Brandywine Press, 1997; Jarrow, Gail. *The Printer's Trial: The Case of John Peter Zenger and the Fight for a Free Press.* Honesdale, Pa.: Calkins Creek, 2006; Lehman, Godfrey D. *We the Jury—; the Impact of Jurors on Our Basic Freedoms.* Amherst, N.Y.: Prometheus Books, 1997; Levy, Leonard. *The Emergence of a Free Press.* New York: Oxford University Press, 1985; Putnam, William. *John Peter Zenger and the Fundamental Freedom.* Jefferson, N.C.: McFarland, 1997; "The Trial of John Peter Zenger." Available online. URL: http://www.courts.state.ny.us/history/zenger.htm. Accessed July 3, 2008.

The Boston Massacre trials

Also known as: *The King v. Preston; The King v. Weems, White, Carroll, Warren, Kilroy, McCauley, Hartegan, and Montgomery*

Date: 1770

KEY ISSUES

"Why is it always Boston that breaks the King's peace?" Leaders from quieter British North American colonies put that question to John Adams at the Continental Congress in 1776. The prodding demonstrated a widely held perception of Massachusetts in the late 1760s and early 1770s. It was a characterization common in Great Britain and the thirteen colonies: Boston harbored radicals who were too quick to respond to perceived insults with violence. Since the insults that Bostonians had identified were on the part of British authority, physical dissent meant the real possibility of the home government alleging treason or insurrection. Censure of Boston surely would reverberate elsewhere in North America.

Boston certainly had seen disorder in the years that political fractures widened between the mother country and Britain's New World holdings. Within a couple of years Adams was to become an early advocate of independence; of course, he was a leading figure at Philadelphia in 1776. It was ironic that he should have been tarred with the epithet of rabble-rouser, though, because in 1772 Adams was not known among Bostonians as especially radical.

There had been serious trouble between Bostonians and British troops since large numbers of soldiers had arrived in October 1768. The 4,000

troops were a quite visible addition to the city of about 20,000. Bostonians' objections to the military presence were numerous. First, there were practical concerns, such as the fact that British soldiers supplemented their pay with jobs that locals coveted, yet still could not always pay their bills to area merchants. Lawyers among the colonists voiced a constitutional argument against the quartering of troops in civilian areas that went back at least as far as the reign of England's King Charles I. Parliament famously upbraided the monarch for using soldiers in such a way to dampen dissent, in the Petition of Right of 1628.

The more immediate objection that Bostonians expressed to the newly arrived soldiers was that they were a military answer to the colonials' political dissent—an overreaction, it seemed, on the part of the government in London. The empire was struggling to raise revenue to administer its North American holdings. Ever conscious of the need to balance income from taxes with protests against such levies, the administration of King George III tried several different policies in the 1760s.

The imposition of the Stamp Act in 1764 raised the ire of printers and lawyers, two of the most articulate groups within colonial society. Britain's chancellor of the Exchequer, Charles Townshend, envisioned a replacement for that unpopular legislation; he imposed customs duties on certain imports, including paper and glass. In spite of Townshend's cogent argument that these measures were both necessary and preferable to other possibilities, such as taxes on income, the new measures also proved unpopular. Faced with local opposition to collections, customs officials asked for military backing from the home government. The major port at Boston was a natural site for such a show of force from London. Local hatred of the import duties centered on the Custom House itself.

HISTORY OF THE CASE

At about 9:00 P.M. on March 5, 1770, a lone sentry named Hugh White was guarding Boston's Custom House. Winter stayed late in Boston, and this evening was very cold and snowy. White found himself under siege from a small group of locals. They were festering with resentment over an earlier quarrel about a bill owed by a more senior officer to a local wig maker. White was under the command of that officer, John Goldfinch; White earlier had stood up for his superior as a gentleman who surely would pay his bill.

At first, the ragtag crowd of mostly young men and boys merely pelted White with snowballs. Shortly, though, the sentry faced missiles of hard-packed snow and ice. Someone rang church bells as though a fire had been sighted. It may have been a signal to alert anyone who was interested to come and watch what promised to be fisticuffs. Small riots such as the one involving White at the Custom House were breaking out in several locations. The ranking British officer on duty at the main guard post, Captain Thomas Preston, decided to focus on the most critical situation first.

More Bostonians arrived at the Custom House. So also did a small number of British soldiers in their bright red coats under Preston. Everyone at the scene was shouting, with some city people taunting the soldiers to go ahead and use their weapons. Preston tried to keep discipline among his men. The eight reinforcements did not show patience with the assault. They opened fire on the spectators with their muskets.

There were five fatalities among the crowd, several of whom had been in the original group to tease the sentry: Crispus Attucks, Samuel Gray, James Caldwell, Samuel Maverick, and Patrick Carr. Two of those men lingered before expiring. Six others were injured, some critically; one was a storeowner who was on his premises but in the line of fire. Many observers and Preston himself noted that it was he who made the soldiers stop shooting after their initial volley, for they had reloaded.

The killings were called "a massacre." Among the Bostonians who immediately publicized the event—literally sending out information about it within hours—was the silversmith and political activist Paul Revere. Revere and his radical colleagues referred to the incidents as the "Bloody Massacre" or the "State Street Massacre."

A fine engraver, Revere produced an image of the episode that took considerable liberties with the facts. He depicted the exchange of hostilities as occurring in a well-lit spot, for example, and portrayed Attucks as a white man when in fact Attucks was of mixed race. Revere could have had a major impact on the trial of Captain Preston, for he showed Preston as raising his hand in a signal to fire. Vital to Revere's goal in making the incident an object of anger was his depiction of the British soldiers standing in an orderly line; it looked as though the grenadiers coolly mowed down bystanders.

Scholars note that Revere was engaged in competition with other engravers to get his print out before others did and that he may have copied the drawing of rival Henry Pelham. Still, another drawing by Revere of the scene at the killings indicates that he may have been an eyewitness to the events on March 5. He certainly gave a specific account of where the bodies fell. Accurate or not, Revere's depiction in the engraving was powerful propaganda. It had great influence on the citizens of Boston and, eventually, a much wider public.

Twelve men along with Captain Preston were arrested; four of those individuals were supposed to have fired out of the windows of the Custom House, but they never were tried on that charge. Historians doubt that such shots were fired. But those critical of the soldiers' actions won an early victory when Lieutenant Governor Thomas Hutchinson (a descendant of religious protester Anne Hutchinson) ordered all of the soldiers in Boston to be removed to Castle Island for a time. Within a week a grand jury returned indictments against Preston and eight of his men. Much for their own protection they were incarcerated from that point throughout the trials.

At the request of a Boston merchant who came to him on the morning of March 6, John Adams took the case of both the soldiers and Captain Preston. Adams had experience in defending British troops. Adams's previous such case was on behalf of men who also had killed in what might be argued as self-defense. Within the last year he had represented four seamen charged with murdering a British officer who had tried to press them into naval service. The American public had been very much on Adams's side in that cause because the "impressing" of sailors was most unpopular.

Adams was faithful at keeping a diary even at the busiest times of his life. Now, he noted in his journal that defending the killers of Bostonians would be altogether a different matter from his last famous criminal case. He was nervous that mob violence might turn upon him or that those with whom he was aligned politically might think him a sellout. (His fee turned out to be a modest one.) Still, Adams took very much to heart the words of penologist Cesare Beccaria: To save one person from a wrongful conviction would be "sufficient consolation to me for the contempt of all mankind." He would cite that same quotation from Beccaria during the Boston Massacre trials.

SUMMARY OF ARGUMENTS

Captain Preston's trial occurred first. This was of some importance to the soldiers' situation, for if Preston were acquitted then they would stand a greater chance of conviction. In that event the prosecution could argue that since the soldiers incontestably did fire shots, they must have done so while not under orders from their commander. The jury then could judge the enlisted men to be negligent and perhaps malicious—but certainly they would be called disobedient soldiers. If, on the other hand, Preston were convicted, it might lessen local pressure to convict his men.

The trials of all of the soldiers, Preston included, did not occur until the fall of 1770. The delay was significant because it meant the prosecution went forward not in the immediate aftermath of the killings, when tension was greatest. The spreading out of the trial from the massacre almost certainly was a deliberate effort by Hutchinson to calm the situation.

Preston's trial lasted from October 24 to October 30, 1770. The trial of Captain Preston was not well chronicled by observers, and there was not an official court reporter at Boston's courthouse on Queen Street. Much of what historians know of the proceedings is a distillation of what must have occurred given the arguments in the better-documented trial of the soldiers. The prosecution of Preston, though, was of great importance in the affairs of Massachusetts. The lead prosecutor was Solicitor General Samuel Quincy, assisted by an experienced attorney from Boston named Robert Paine.

The key to Preston's fate was whether he had given an order to the redcoats to fire. Eyewitness testimony was mixed on that point. Though Preston himself was not allowed to testify at trial, he had given a deposition shortly after his arrest in March that supported his innocence. Preston noted that on scene at the Custom House he had been standing in front of the soldiers. If he had told the men to shoot, he would have been their first victim. According to Preston, those who shouted "Fire!" were members of the crowd. Adams surely would have stressed this point to the jury. Preston was acquitted.

The composition of the jury panels at the separate trials of Preston and the soldiers is an element of the case on which legal historians comment. Perhaps motivated by concern that they would have more difficulty defending the men now that Preston had been acquitted, defense counsel apparently honed their strategy on jury selection between Preston's trial and the soldiers'. The soldiers' case—the King v. Weems and others—came up on November 27 and concluded on December 14. At the soldiers' trials Adams and his colleagues made certain to challenge potential jurors who were city dwellers. They hoped that persons from outside the reach of "mob mentality" would be more sympathetic to the soldiers' position.

Adams's presentation of the redcoats' case had several interrelated parts that fit together ingeniously, though at first they did not seem compatible with one another. First, Adams reminded the jury of his duty as an attorney to see "an unfortunate victim of tyranny" (in Beccaria's words) "saved." Indeed, all that spectators in court had to do was to look at counsel for the opposing (prosecution) side, to see how fractured Americans were with regard to politics. For example, Adams's defense associate in the Preston case had been Josiah Quincy, Jr., but Samuel Quincy, Josiah's brother, stood at the bar for the prosecution. And so, Adams's initial point must have gone down well: He represented colonials who believed in justice even above political faction.

Second, Adams proposed that the soldiers had been compelled to fire to preserve their own lives. Self-defense was, in fact, one of the very few justifications for homicide in English law. These men were surrounded by a growing mob and faced real injury, perhaps even death, from objects being hurled at them. Adams focused on the term *mob* itself, mocking the prosecution's efforts to come up with politer designations for the gathering outside the Custom House:

> We have entertained a great variety of phrases to avoid calling this sort of people a mob. Some call them shavers, some call them geniuses. The plain English, gentlemen, [was that it was] most probably a motley rabble of saucy boys, Negroes and mulattoes, Irish teagues and outlandish jacktars. And why should we scruple to call such a people a mob, I can't conceive, unless the name is too respectable for them.

Then Adams embarked upon the cleverest part of his argument: If there was a violent gathering in Boston on March 5, it was because a long-term British policy created it. To quarter troops within a crowded urban environment was to invite disorder: "Soldiers quartered in a populous town will always occasion two mobs where they prevent one. They are wretched conservators of the peace." There was an important factual determination, as well. Had all of the defendants fired? Or, was it only some of them? While Adams did not consciously distinguish between the soldiers, the evidence did point to two of them, Hugh Montgomery and Matthew Kilroy, as having been shooters. The eyewitnesses proved contradictory with regard to the other soldiers' actions, a point that Adams exploited.

The inclusion of testimony from one of the victims who died a few days after the massacre, Patrick Carr, proved to be both dramatic and legally intriguing. English law said that in most cases evidence could not be admitted unless a witness could be put under oath—the so-called rule against hearsay evidence, or second-party testimony. But there was an exception for "dying confessions." If a person gave a statement who knew his time was short to live, it might be employed in court. Thus, Carr's comments to a physician that he forgave the men that shot him because they had been provoked, served as powerful inducement to the soldiers' jury to either excuse or lessen their crime.

VERDICT

Of the eight soldiers accused of the killings, six were acquitted. The length of the jury deliberations—two-and-a-half hours—points to a bargain being easily reached among the panel to spare the younger defendants and punish only Kilroy and Montgomery as tokens. Furthermore, the two convicted men were sentenced on a lesser charge than murder: manslaughter. It was a verdict indicating that the jury thought the men had not planned their reaction but had been goaded into it, although it did connote that the soldiers had fired without orders.

Aside from the time that all of the soldiers already had spent in jail, which was a number of months, they actually walked free. How could it be that Kilroy and Montgomery were released when they were convicted of manslaughter? It was due to a quirk in English law that in the 18th century allowed first offenders to escape hard time. By the era of the Boston Massacre trials, benefit of clergy was an escape clause within a bloody English criminal law.

The device of benefit of clergy had been a matter of contention during the era of Thomas Becket and Henry II. It was originally a way for royal courts to let persons with clerical status (who had been well educated by the church) escape the physical punishments of the king's justice. But, the category of "clergyable offenses" had survived long past the time when only priests could read. To avail oneself of the advantage of not getting physical chastisement (including the death penalty), all that a defendant had to do was ask for benefit of clergy at sentencing. If it were his or her first offense, then the secular court would order the convicted person branded—usually on the thumb. Branding was a mild enough punishment to be considered noncorporal, but it also would allow future adjudicators to see at a glance if they were dealing with a habitual criminal. Thus, while theoretically the sentence that loomed for Kilroy and Montgomery was capital, their being subject to English law bought them their lives.

The soldiers, including Preston, got out of Boston as quickly as they could on boats for England. King George granted Preston a sizable pension. Others who had been pivotal in the episode, notably Hutchinson, could not abide the mounting criticism of the home government and likewise decamped as loyalists for London.

SIGNIFICANCE

It is commonplace to describe the Boston Massacre as one of the sparks that set off the American rebellion of the 1770s. Such a judgment may be more accurate in retrospect than it was at the time; that is, the episode was looked back on as a step toward independence only after the breach had occurred. The killings and trials of 1770 did not kick off a period of confrontation in Boston or elsewhere; the time from late 1770 through 1772 was free of major violence between the British and the colonials. Still, within a few more years those who desired independence, such as Boston merchant John Hancock, later chair of the Continental Congress, had begun memorializing the massacre as a key break by Americans from their British rulers.

Those scholars who characterize Adams primarily as an ambitious and pompous politician paint his role in the Boston Massacre trials as calculating. They maintain that for John Adams to take on the role of lead defense counsel at the Boston Massacre trials required the approval of Samuel Adams, who was the leader of the Boston radicals in 1772. This view either has Samuel Adams thinking that John Adams could not prevail or presenting the Americans as cynical guarantors of a fair trial. A kinder assessment would conclude that John Adams meant what he said in 1772 and at the end of his long and storied life: Providing an effective defense for persons who might otherwise be oppressed by the legal system was a cornerstone of a democratic society. As an old man, John Adams said that he considered his defense of Preston and the British soldiers to be an act of personal bravery, and "one of the best services I ever rendered my country."

Further Reading

Bailyn, Bernard. *The Ordeal of Thomas Hutchinson.* Cambridge, Mass.: Harvard University Press, 1974; Countryman, Edward. *The American Revolution.* New York: Hill & Wang, 1985; McCullough, David. *John Adams.* New York: Simon & Schuster, 2008; Zobel, Hillar B. *The Boston Massacre.* New York: W. W. Norton, 1970.

The James Somerset case

Also known as: Somerset's case; *The King v. Knowles, ex parte Somerset*

Date: 1772

KEY ISSUES

In the late 18th century slavery was a lynchpin of the British economy. Not only did enslavement make possible the production of sugar and other key commodities in the West Indies; it buttressed trade in other areas of the world where Britain had interests, particularly North America. Britain's government and private enterprises were especially dependent on forced labor in the years before the American Revolution.

Within that context, the 1772 decision of one of England's leading commercial judges, William Murray, Lord Mansfield, was quite striking. Mansfield appeared to rule that slavery could not exist in England. Legal scholars during Mansfield's day and ever since have pointed out that Somerset's case actually did not outlaw slavery in England. The decision certainly did not reach out over the empire. But, for opponents of slavery the case proved a major ideological victory. It became commonplace at the time and still is usual among scholars to refer to the great moral force of the Somerset decision.

HISTORY OF THE CASE

James Somerset (Sommersett) was a man of color in the service of Charles Steuart (Stewart). Somerset was born in Africa and sold to slave traders, who took him to Virginia. With Steuart, Somerset lived for a time in Massachusetts. Steuart worked as a customs officer for the British government in North America and the Caribbean. Somerset was typical of enslaved individuals who labored as "house servants" or even personal assistants, such as valets, to wealthy Britons in the colonies. Somerset and Steuart traveled to the home country in 1769. Officials such as Steuart often stayed for long periods in England.

Once in London, Somerset came into contact with abolitionists headquartered in England's capital city. Despite the fact that many of them were members of the Church of England, these individuals constituted a loose organization committed to social action, particularly in regard to race. They called themselves "evangelicals" or "saints" on account of their dedication to moral causes that they saw as grounded in Christian Scripture.

Perhaps emboldened by his discourse with the abolitionists, Somerset ran away from Steuart in 1771. Somerset underwent a baptism at a London church in early fall 1771. Three individuals were his sponsors: Thomas Walkin, Elizabeth Cade, and John Marlow. Though not personally prominent, they almost certainly were abolitionists.

A leader among the abolitionists was Granville Sharp. He had been committed to that cause since 1765, when he helped treat the injuries of an enslaved man named Jonathan Strong who had been hurt by his owner. Sharp assisted Strong in gaining his freedom and embarked on research into the legal status of slaves in Britain. Sharp corresponded with others of like mind, such as Philadelphia's Benjamin Rush and Anthony Benezet.

The Evangelicals drew support from other groups such as Quakers and Methodists. They joined with certain individuals such as the former slave Olaudah Equiano to try to influence policy. It was critical that the Evangelicals worked from within Anglicanism because only professing members of that state church could vote or serve in Parliament at that time, and these abolitionists had a long-range legislative agenda. They also hoped to effect change piecemeal by securing the freedom of individuals who were enslaved. In part they did this by helping slaves escape and then hiding them, and in part they pursued test cases in the courts. They trusted that by building up a series of legal rulings they could demonstrate to Parliament that English justice abhorred slavery.

On November 26, 1771, the slave catchers whom Steuart had hired to find Somerset located him. According to Steuart's instructions, they took him aboard a ship, the *Ann and Mary,* bound for Jamaica. Somerset was to be resold. Clearly Steuart wanted to rid himself of the runaway slave. The captain of the vessel was John Knowles.

Either Somerset's baptismal sponsors or their friends had heard about him being dragged away by the slave catchers. They applied to the Court of King's Bench for Somerset's release under a writ of habeas corpus. That remedy was used in two ways in this situation. First, the applicants wanted to secure Somerset as being under the custody of King's Bench so that Captain Knowles could not sail away. Once that was done, Somerset was allowed to walk free until the court could decide (in effect) on a second application of the writ: whether Knowles was entitled to "detain" Somerset on a voyage to the New World.

The case's form, prepared by Sharp on Somerset's behalf, was noteworthy. The action was neither a suit nor even a criminal prosecution. Rather, Somerset, via Sharp, was asking a judge to compel the sheriff of London to release Somerset from his improper detention on board the ship ready to sail for Jamaica. In Somerset's day the "great writ" of habeas corpus had a long history in England. It was supposed to make citizens secure against arbitrary arrest and detention. To obtain a writ of habeas corpus was to order the persons who wrongfully "held the body" of someone to let him or her go. Granting habeas corpus did not absolve the released person from future criminal charges; it merely bought him or her freedom for the time being.

The use of the writ was something of a cause célèbre in London in the 1760s. Its most famous application was at the hands of John Wilkes, whom King George III had had arrested using a general warrant. Wilkes applied for and got a writ of habeas corpus on the grounds that general warrants were illegal; that precedent obviously helped inspire the U.S. Constitution's Fourth Amendment prohibition of "over-broad warrants." In the case of *The King v. Wilkes* (1764), Wilkes was convicted of libel but won great popular support for his right to publish criticisms of the foreign policy of George III. A leading judge, Lord Mansfield, was pivotal to Wilkes's career; Mansfield presided over Wilkes's libel case.

That Somerset's rescuers chose habeas corpus as a means to their end was partly determined by the facts of Somerset's case. They wanted to get Somerset off the ship as quickly as possible to save Somerset from deportation. But, the abolitionists also were making a stronger point. They contended that James Somerset was not a piece of property but rather a person. He therefore deserved the same right—not to be arbitrarily detained—as other people in Great Britain.

For all of his careful assembly of historical and legal materials on Somerset's behalf, Sharp was not qualified to practice before the royal courts. He had to hire attorneys to actually present Somerset's case. Donations from abolitionists poured in. With those funds, expensive legal help was guaranteed. It turned out, though, that the attorneys for Somerset's cause decided to work without a fee. In particular, Somerset and Sharp were fortunate to get the services of a man only recently admitted to the bar but already a keen legal historian and a dedicated voice against slavery: Francis Hargrave. The Somerset case was his first appearance before a court as a barrister.

SUMMARY OF ARGUMENTS

Steuart did not fight with Hargrave, Sharp, and Somerset personally. Steuart's letters from the time of the Somerset case indicate that the plantation lobby argued on his behalf. Their effort to guarantee that slaves would not be protected if their masters stayed in Britain was, after all, a much larger cause; the slavers' basic tenet was that captured Africans were property. The proslavery position had several precedents on their side. For example, there was the Yorke-Talbot policy of 1729, which came out of a longstanding discussion about how slaves' conversion to Christianity might affect their legal status.

The defenders of enslavement long had justified their holding of human beings in bondage because the Africans were not Christian. Slavery, its apologists said, was good for black Africans' souls. Critics of slavery such as the Quakers responded by wondering if persons of color would be set free if they converted to Christianity. England's two top prosecutors, Attorney General Philip Yorke and Solicitor General Charles Talbot, generated an influential ruling to try to clarify the state of the law:

> We are of the opinion, that a slave, by coming from the West Indies, either with or without his master, to Great Britain or Ireland, doth not become free; and that his master's property or right in him is not thereby determined or varied; and baptism doth not bestow freedom on him, nor make any alteration to his temporal condition in these kingdoms. We are also of opinion, that the master may legally compel him to return to the plantations.

Slaves were property, and their religious conversion did not alter that condition. Yorke later became Lord Chancellor Hardwicke. In 1749 he decided the case of *Pearne v. Lisle,* which equated African slaves with cattle. It would seem that Somerset and Sharp had an uphill battle.

The Evangelicals were not, however, without legal arguments to justify their application for habeas corpus. First of all, there was the old argument about slaves who had become Christians. Since the Yorke-Talbot opinion seemed to have forestalled such a line of reasoning, and since it came from a jurist (Hardwicke) whom Mansfield admired, Sharp did not harp on the point that Somerset recently had been baptized. Sharp instead crafted his argument around the contention that although Somerset had lived in the colonies where slavery had long been allowed, he now was in England. The abolitionists wished for Mansfield to declare that in Britain slavery was illegal. Thus, it was key to argue that slavery had not existed within recent memory—which in the law could be many generations.

Hargrave was known as a halting speaker. Although he was not going to win this case on oratorical talent, he had other gifts. He relished not only reading legal history but also collecting and annotating classic texts, such as writings of Edward Coke. With his superb grounding in medieval and early modern law, Hargrave was admirably positioned to instruct Mansfield on the degrees of force that had accompanied the master-servant relationship in England.

The difficulty that Hargrave faced was that although actual slavery had not existed since around the time of the Norman Conquest, English law had recognized the forced labor known as villeinage, which, though rare, had been present in the 16th century. Hargrave did not try to argue that villeinage never really had existed in England, although some of his legal colleagues and Sharp pushed for such an approach. Instead, he underlined that English common law courts repeatedly had undermined villein status until, in the 1610s, villeinage had faded away; thus, Hargrave played on the pride that Mansfield felt as a member of his profession.

Sharp, Somerset, and Hargrave also had a few judicial rulings as backing, especially the cases of *Shanley v. Harvey* (1763) and *The King v. Stapylton* (1771). The latter decision was especially relevant because it came from the pen of Mansfield. It involved a slaveholder who tried to deport his slave; Mansfield and the jury did not permit him to do so, though Mansfield was careful to say that the case could not be presumed to be a wider judgment on the legality of slavery in Britain. Indeed, Sharp observed that Mansfield changed course several times as he pondered that case. Sharp and the abolitionists did not want Mansfield to renege on any ruling on behalf of Somerset.

But, as he had done with the *Stapylton* case, Mansfield considered Somerset's request for months. The judge appeared most anxious to get the parties to reach a settlement rather than hand down a formal ruling; he pressed Steuart hard to allow Somerset's release. Steuart's backers, though, wanted a clear judicial ruling and expected victory.

Mansfield as an individual believed in abolition. It was well known that he served as the guardian to the daughter of his nephew. The ward was a child on whom he doted, and the girl, Dido Elizabeth Belle Lindsay, was of mixed race. Yet, Mansfield was a superb commercial lawyer, which meant that he almost necessarily had strong sympathy for free trade and British economic superiority. He could not but realize that ruling on Somerset's behalf would be perceived as a slap at merchants, shipbuilders, and plantation owners who depended on slavery for their livelihoods.

VERDICT

Mansfield finally handed down a decision on June 22, 1772. His words were concise in an era when judicial obfuscation was common. Mansfield began his ruling in a businesslike form, but built to a conclusion that was stunning in scope. He started by discussing the Yorke-Talbot precedent and then disregarding it. In essence, the question of Somerset's baptism was irrelevant to the present case.

He next admitted that he understood the ramifications of the case: "We feel the force of the inconveniences and consequences that will follow the decision of this question." And yet, this was a matter of enormous weight—so vital that he would go on to decide it himself without conferring formally with other judges. Mansfield reviewed the facts of the case: Somerset had

> . . . absented himself, and departed from his master's service, and refused to return and serve him during his stay in England; whereupon, by his master's orders, he was put on board the ship by force, and there detained in secure custody, to be carried out of the kingdom and sold.

And then, unexpectedly, the hammer came down. Mansfield termed the conduct of Steuart reprehensible:

> So high an act of dominion must derive its authority, if any such it has, from the law of the kingdom where executed. A foreigner cannot be imprisoned here on the authority of any law existing in his own country: the power of a master over his servant is different in all countries, more or less limited or extensive; the exercise of it therefore must always be regulated by the laws of the place where exercised. The state of slavery is of such a nature, that it is incapable of now being introduced by Courts of Justice upon mere reasoning or inferences from any principles, natural or political; it must take its rise from positive law; the origin of it can in no country or age be traced back to any other source: immemorial usage preserves the memory of positive law long after all traces of the occasion; reason, authority, and time of its introduction are lost; and in a case so odious as the condition of slaves must be taken strictly. . . .

Slavery, Mansfield said, was repulsive. It was not equivalent to villeinage, which in any event no longer existed in England. If slavery were to be allowed in Britain, Parliament would have to authorize it. Mansfield had accepted Sharp's and Hargrave's arguments almost to the letter. Through Mansfield's words the abolitionists had staked out the high ground. While the legislators were not ready to outlaw slavery, they were not about to promote it through "positive law," either.

Although in Great Britain and America the *Somerset* decision did not quickly result in large-scale legal victories for abolition, it served as an inspiration. Particularly in North American colonies such as Massachusetts that already were disposed against slavery, Somerset's case was widely cited as a building block of abolition.

In the 1820s, English judges in at least two major cases expressed the opinion that the *Somerset* decision had ended owners' control over slaves in Britain. Those jurists, however, as always guardians of precedent, criticized Mansfield as having gone against Lord Hardwicke's decisions. Nothing if not perceptive of the potential applications of his ruling, Mansfield himself was at pains to affirm in subsequent cases that the *Somerset* decision was narrow. He maintained that *Somerset* applied only to this instance of a slave being spirited out of the country by his owner to be resold. It was a strained reinterpretation of his own words, given the breadth of Mansfield's stunning language in 1772.

SIGNIFICANCE

The abolitionists publicized the case immediately. It became immortalized as an endorsement of the idea that British soil conferred freedom on anyone who made it to the shores of the mother country—a notion that Mansfield said he did not intend and the decision did not state. William Cowper's long poem *The Task* (1785) echoed the misconception:

Slaves cannot breathe in England,
if their lungs
Receive our air, that moment they are free.
They touch our country, and their shackles
fall.

Slaveholders in the colonies reported, in alarm, that enslaved individuals who got wind of the deci-

sion thought the same thing. Africans in the New World were now desperate to get to Britain so they could gain freedom. If anything, the *Somerset* ruling made conditions for American slaves a bit worse, so anxious were their masters not to allow that possibility.

The hopes of the English abolitionists were elevated. They surely thought that additional judicial rulings would continue to strengthen their cause. But, as partisans such as Equiano soon noted, the antislavery movement was in for bitter disappointment on that score. In 1781 the groups working to end slavery were appalled to hear of an incident on board the slave ship *Zong*. Confronted with an outbreak of disease among his human cargo while sailing for the Caribbean, the captain of that ship (which had English owners) opted to throw 132 Africans overboard. The captain reasoned that he could claim the loss for insurance purposes if the Africans had drowned but not on account of illness. An initial court ruling affirmed the captain's judgment, allowing the ship owners to recover damages for the loss of the "cargo." Sharp hoped that the *Somerset* decision would provide a judicial corrective, especially since appeal lay with Lord Mansfield's court. In his decision in the *Zong* affair, however, Mansfield decided that although the owners could not recover the cost of the slaves, the killings were no more reprehensible than if animals had been tossed into the sea.

Abolitionism continued in Britain long after the Somerset case because Parliament still could not agree to pass a "positive law" concerning slavery. For at least a generation after the *Somerset* decision there was a legislative stalemate. Meanwhile a fervent antislavery parliamentary faction presented compelling testimony of the horrors of the Middle Passage. Thomas Clarkson's models of packed slave ships, shown at Westminster, were vivid reminders of the trade's inhumanity. Persons of unimpeachable character such as William Wilberforce signed on, aided by skilled legislators such as James Stephen. For a time, though, the plantation lobby stolidly blocked them at every turn.

The breakthrough came when slavery began to look less tenable economically and politically, especially after the Haitian revolt ended in 1804. The Slave Trade Act of 1807 was designed to end British commerce in slaves, though it did nothing for those already in bondage. In addition, in Britain persons who recently had been slaves frequently were simply called apprentices and then maltreated much as slaves had been. It took until 1833 for Parliament to declare slaves within the empire free. London's Central Criminal Court, the Old Bailey, saw several prosecutions for the kidnapping of African-born persons such as in the case called *The King v. Pedro de Zulueta* (1843). Clearly, slave shipment still was going on. But, the Royal Navy enforced the legislation that finally had come out of Sharp's endeavors, and British foreign policy condemned African rulers who refused to cease selling to the trade.

A cynical reading of the historical record—from which Somerset promptly disappeared—would be that as an individual, he was not of much consequence to his defenders. When the case was decided in court in his favor, James Somerset undoubtedly joined the abolitionists in exulting. Many persons of color had attended the arguments at King's Bench concerning the writ of habeas corpus. It was probable that Somerset now asked for and got obscurity, even among the community of free black Africans who must have seen him as a hero. In anonymity Somerset must have felt there was safety from the slavers. It would have been out of character, though, for the conscientious abolitionists such as Sharp and Equiano not to take a continuing interest in the man whose cause had so greatly advanced their campaign.

Further Reading

Equiano, Olaudah. *The Interesting Narrative of Olaudah Equiano.* New York: Palgrave Macmillan, 2007; Halliday, Paul D. *Habeas Corpus: From England to Empire.* Cambridge, Mass.: Belknap Press, 2010; *The King v. Knowles, ex parte Somerset.* Lofft 1, 98 E.R. 499, 20 S.T. 1 (1772); "Lord Mansfield's Decision in the Sonnet Case." Available online. URL: http://www.colonialwilliamsburg.com/History/teaching/enewsletter/volume7/feb09/teachstrategy.cfm. Accessed July 17, 2009; Oldham, James. *The Mansfield Manuscripts and the Growth of English Law in the Eighteenth Century.* Chapel Hill: University of North Carolina Press, 1992; Paley, Ruth. "Mansfield, Slavery and the Law in England, 1772–1830." In *Law, Crime* *and English Society, 1660–1830,* edited by Norma Landau, 165–184. Cambridge: Cambridge University Press, 2002; Van Cleve, George. "Forum: Somerset's Case Revisited: Somerset's Case and Its Antecedents in Imperial Perspective." *Law and History Review* (Fall 2006): 601–645; Wiecek, William. *Sources of Antislavery Constitutionalism in America, 1769–1848.* Ithaca, N.Y.: Cornell University Press, 1977; Wise, Steven M. *Though the Heavens May Fall.* Cambridge, Mass.: Da Capo Press, 2005.

The trial of Cho Chae-hang

Date: 1780

KEY ISSUES

Confucian principles guided Korean, as well as Chinese, law well into the modern era. The Ming Penal Code was influential in Korea throughout the Choson (Joseon or Yi) dynasty (1392–1897). In China emperors often made the code an instrument for increasing the power of the imperial government. When Confucian scholars in Korea urged adherence to the code, however, they in effect hemmed in the powers of the Korean throne. Korean bureaucrats and judges who administered the law pointedly did not cite Chinese imperial texts that focused on centralization of power and royal authority. As centuries went by, Korea and China supplemented the code with decisions from cases, pieces of legislation, and pronouncements of policy from government officials.

Efforts by Korean monarchs in the 18th century to systematize that mass of legal precedent proved frustrating to the Crown. The only area of the law over which the monarch had thorough control was in regard to offenses against him: treason, certain other political offenses, and accusations against the governing class. For these there was the State Tribunal *(uigumbu).* A highly organized but not always well-run legal bureaucracy oversaw cases involving private individuals.

The everyday managers of law in Korea were district magistrates. Each magistrate was called a *suryong*. Appointed by the king for 1,800-day terms, the district magistrates were the centers of local political life as well as judicial power. When magistrates heard offenses that carried the penalty of a light beating or less, they had final authority to impose punishment. Magistrates had to submit their judgments to a higher authority, though, if more serious crimes and punishments were involved. Capital cases in the provinces were supposed to be heard directly by one of eight provincial governors; the governors had their decisions reviewed as a matter of course. The analogy to English or U.S. law would be that Korean law provided for automatic appeal in felony decisions, with capital cases receiving particular attention.

The Korean government agency that reviewed cases in which heavy penalties were imposed was the Board of Punishments. The board itself had four main divisions: a section concerned with death penalty cases (the Bureau of Review), another dealing with criminal cases that were not capital (the Bureau of Prohibitions), the Bureau of Legal Research, and a department overseeing all cases involving slaves (the Bureau of Slaves). By the middle of the Choson dynasty, the Board of Punishments employed more than 200 officials; it was one of the largest departments within the government in Seoul.

While certain central government departments such as the Board of War were able to arrest and imprison suspects, offices called the *p'odoch'ong* investigated most cases in the provinces. Their investigators could question suspects and hold them in custody, but they did not have judicial roles. In that sense, Korean criminal justice was similar to Britain's in the 19th century and later. The police did not try alleged criminals but rather looked into suspected crimes. In Korea, as in China, magistrates were not the sole investigators of crimes, but they did carry the authority to make inquiries.

In cases where a death had resulted, magistrates were supposed to order an inquest, which included taking testimony from witnesses and relatives and might involve an examination of the body by forensic experts. Then the magistrate heard a second set of depositions and testimony;

he was looking for inconsistencies or running themes in the accounts. All of the documents of the inquest plus the magistrate's comments went to the Board of Punishments, which sent out a second magistrate to conduct a parallel investigation. Sometimes the first two investigations and reports proved unsatisfactory or irreconcilable, and the board ordered another investigation or more.

Once the board had the magistrate's or governor's set of reports in order, it called for a higher review of the case. The governor reviewed the record of smaller crimes. For capital cases, which already had begun with the governor, it was the board itself that conducted the review within the appropriate division. The final report that the board generated was called a "polished memorial" if the investigation seemed wrapped up succinctly or a "report memorial" if there still were loose ends.

In certain instances the monarch intervened in the process. He might take cognizance of an especially important case by writing a "response memorial" to the Board of Punishments, asking it to take further action. The Board of Punishments typically substantiated its findings by having several parties to a case tortured. At the end of the 18th century the board had to ask for royal authorization to impose a more severe form of torture than that technically allowed by law. In the middle of the 1700s statutes restricted the use of "severe" tortures, but the king could make an exception. This was almost exactly how English law worked in the early 17th century, for instance, during the investigation of the Gunpowder Plot; torture was by royal warrant.

In a case that appeared even more difficult, for example, due to its factual intricacy, the Korean state might impose another layer of oversight: a *simni* review. The *simni* was an adjudication that was solely on paper. It focused on certain elements of an investigation. Was a defendant interrogated correctly? Was an autopsy performed in accordance with proper procedures? Was the correct law applied? Had the case been accurately described in a factual sense? Korean king Chongjo (Jeongjo), who governed from 1777 to 1800, ordered the collation of an important set of *simni* covering his reign. In 1798 the royal secretary Hong In-ho and his brother Ui-ho published that collection, titled the *Simnirok*. It amounted to a casebook for consultation by Korean legal officials. The *Simnirok* describes some of the most vexing criminal cases in late 18th-century Korea.

The highly layered Korean legal process was designed to serve several purposes. It was supposed to increase public confidence in the consistency and fairness of justice. It further aimed to substitute official penalties for private retribution. Enforcement of the Ming Penal Code also propagated certain values, notably respect for authority. The individual cases in the *Simnirok* did not change national policy, nor did any one decision have a large historical impact. As a group, however, they were intended to serve as precedents that were to be *chonsu* (observed with respect). Like the writings of Egypt's chronicler al-Sayrafi, the *simni* are a window into a justice system that was important in one corner of the world for hundreds of years.

HISTORY OF THE CASE

The account of the case against Cho Chae-hang from the *Simnirok* is relatively long, attesting to its difficulty. The charge against the defendant reflected a common scenario: Chae-hang was accused of killing his wife.

Immediately the Ming Penal Code spoke to the situation. Although it was enforced with varying severity over the many centuries of its use in China and Korea, the code was clear in general principle. Women who killed their husbands, even accidentally, almost always were subject to the death penalty. Men who killed their wives might incur death if the killing was intentional. If the wife died accidentally as a result of the husband's action, though, he was not at fault. The code provided no liability for a husband who "merely" beat his wife severely or who drove her to suicide through his abuse. According to the law, if a woman plotted her husband's death, she was to be capitally punished whether or not the plot came to fruition. In the case of a potentially murderous husband, though, he was to suffer only if the plot was carried out.

The trial of Cho Chae-hang at first glance seems to be just such an instance of a double standard. Despite the code's prescription of the death penalty for an intentional killing, in modern parlance Cho Chae-hang "walked." Was the judicial handling of the case all about gender? Male and female roles certainly were at issue. A close examination shows, however, that more may have been at stake.

SUMMARY OF ARGUMENTS

The *Simnirok* tells little of the deceased woman—not even her name appears. Like so many women in the legal accounts, she is identified in connection with men. This victim was the wife of Cho Chae-hang, the daughter of Yun, the niece of Yi Ka-won. The woman died after a quarrel over a "bowl of food." Whether the food was inadequately prepared or scant in amount or in another way offensive to her husband, the record does not indicate. Furthermore, there is no notation that to die over a bowl of food was particularly unusual.

Among both wealthy and poor, of course, spousal abuse could occur. Perhaps the issue of food was a red herring, thrown in by someone who wished to pin blame on the husband for what may have been a natural death. Determining if the woman died violently would be relevant—though perhaps not dispositive—with regard to Cho's fate. The location of the death was listed: Hwanghae Province, Paekchon County.

Another feature of the case was all too prevalent; after the death of Yun's daughter, relatives quickly intervened. According to the Ming Penal Code, obedience and loyalty to one's family were great virtues, yet family connections might create a strain, particularly for married women. Were wives subject first to their husbands and the husband's relatives or to their own kin? Legal rulings over such conflicting loyalties appear throughout the *Simnirok*.

An unusually large number of *simni* hearings (five) followed the initial magistrate's investigation into the death of Cho's wife. Yi Ka-won, the dead woman's uncle, emerges from the record as especially anxious to see Cho convicted. A question for the courts was whether Yi pursued the case so zealously out of real concern for his niece or from another motive, such as greed or malice.

Yi maintained that his niece died at her husband's hands. He began to assert that Cho had committed murder. The *simni* say that the body was not yet cool before Yi insisted on inspecting it himself, looking for bruising that would confirm that his niece had been fatally beaten and kicked. Yi also spread the word that an unknown party was ready to pay for burial expenses if only the burial would be delayed. No one appeared with the money, though, and the burial took place. It was as though Yi wished to convey the impression that the husband wanted the body put away quickly.

Next, Yi enlisted the help of a man named Cho Kyong, who was described in the record as an invalid—whether this indicated old age or physical disability is unclear. To local authorities, Cho Kyong appeared to be an unrelated person and thus more credible than Yi. Forty days after the death, Cho Kyong asked for an investigation. It was a difficult business to determine cause of death in the six months that the initial inquiry lasted, especially given the state of the dead woman's body in that time after burial.

Yi brought a young domestic worker from the household of the dead woman to the magistrate, saying she could testify to Cho Chae-hang's murderous conduct. The investigators determined, however, that the servant was too young to be a valid witness. During a later portion of the investigation Yi made the authorities aware of several other witnesses, but they gave inconsistent accounts of the death. Was the victim killed near a well? Did Cho Chae-hang assault her while she was in the kitchen? The inquiries failed to establish even the location of the death.

Korean law required that once a murder investigation had begun, it must have a forensic component. Yet, the marks on the wife's body that investigators observed post mortem did not necessarily indicate that she was kicked to death at all, never mind by her husband.

VERDICT

The royal report reviewed the initial investigation, the required corroborative investigation, and the subsequent *simni* connected with the case. The case had been adjudicated over a period of three years, and with each inquiry more questions emerged. The king's ruling on the matter, which was final, was sharply critical of how the process had unfolded. Several officials including the provincial governor came in for particular censure. In the royal announcement Governor Cho Sang-jin was relieved of his post. The governor had a personal role to see justice done and had failed at several points to take the matter seriously enough. Even when ordered by royal officials to reinvestigate, the governor had foisted off the matter to a magistrate.

The verdict indicated that forensic experts who had examined the body had been sloppy. Those medical and legal experts reported that marks on the body were not typical of the expected pattern of bruising caused by a foot strike, but they failed to dig further. They also failed to perform certain tests set out in the *Muwollok,* the standard forensic manual, to see if there were other wounds on the body besides the alleged bruises.

Fortunately for both the justice system and Cho Chae-hang, justice had not yet been carried out. If the results of some of the initial investigations had held sway, Cho would have been executed as a murderer. As it was, the investigation eventually determined that Yi Ka-won had accused Cho Chae-hang falsely of murder and had dragged along several others, including Cho Kyong. The specific action of Yi that came in for the greatest condemnation was his circulation of a folk song among local women, pinning blame for the death on Cho Chae-hang. This indicated an effort to pull an entire village in on the ruse. The planting of the song showed willingness to involve "simple" folk, and it demonstrated an extended effort to deceive the legal process.

The verdict noted that technically Yi Ka-won ought to "take the place" of Cho Chae-hang and suffer the punishment to which the falsely accused person had been sentenced. But, the code also provided that if a convicted criminal had not been executed at the time that a plot to frame him was discovered, then the schemer might be reprieved. Fortunately for Yi, this is what the king decreed in the final *simni*. Yi was to be exiled to a "remote place" indefinitely. Cho Kyong, who had taken a bribe to intervene, suffered involuntary servitude. It was up to the magistrates to sentence others who had participated in the effort to deceive. Cho

Chae-hang was to be released, not with an apology but yet with an official explanation.

SIGNIFICANCE

How did Cho's wife die? Suddenly, certainly, but was it due to her husband's brutality? A fatality due to domestic violence would not have been unusual. That was one reason why Yi may have thought himself able to make the charge in the first place: It was imminently believable, at least in the abstract, that a husband might kill his wife over a bowl of food. Whether Yi was correct and he simply overstepped the mark in assembling a case, or was in fact an extortionist and a perjurer is impossible to determine.

The king and his legal advisers wished to emphasize that the case was an example of mistakes compounding mistakes. The interlocking procedures required in the law served as counterweights to one another. When one part of the process malfunctioned, justice was compromised. In this instance, the authorities concluded that they had rooted out a conspiracy.

Whether or not that was true, Korean legal officials had conveyed a lesson about the necessity of following legal forms carefully. Without such attention to detail, the king concurred, an innocent man might have been executed. When the process of delivering justice worked, the monarch said, all was well: "For the truly guilty one to be caught and the innocent to be enabled to get off is a brilliant exemplification of the heavenly principle." In the case of Cho Chae-hang, although the death in his house remained a mystery, at least justice appeared to be done.

Further Reading

Haboush, JaHyun Kim, trans. *The Memoirs of Lady Hyegyong*. Berkeley: University of California Press, 1996; MacCormack, Geoffrey. *The Spirit of Traditional Chinese Law*. Athens: University of Georgia Press, 1996; Pratt, Keith. *Everlasting Flower: A History of Korea*. London: Reaktion Books, 2006; Shaw, William. *Legal Norms in a Confucian State*. Berkeley, Calif.: Institute of East Asian Studies, 1981; ———. *Social and Intellectual Aspects of Law in Yi Dynasty Korea, 1392–1910*. Berkeley: University of California Press, 1979.

The trial of Joaquim José da Silva Xavier

Also known as: The trial of Tiradentes

Date: 1790

KEY ISSUES

The gold mines of Brazil supported the Portuguese Empire, but in the 18th century the valuable ore began to peter out. The mother country still wanted the revenue from once profitable areas such as Minas Gerais and pressed for taxes to be paid. The citizens of the region objected to such exactions on several occasions, exploding into open revolt against the government in Portugal. In 1720 a protester named Felipe dos Santos organized resistance to the stern controls over gold that the rulers in Lisbon had instituted. In spite of his being a man of some local influence, the authorities responded to dos Santos ruthlessly. His protests were swept aside, and dos Santos was tried and executed. His mutilated body was exhibited as a gruesome reminder of the fate of traitors.

At the center of tax protests in the latter part of the 1700s was a group of rebels known as the Inconfidência Mineira (Minas Conspiracy). The movement's leader was a man from a middling background, orphaned at age 11 and reared by a guardian who had him well educated. Joaquim José da Silva Xavier was a native of Minas Gerais. He served in the military, becoming a minor officer but advancing no further because of a lack of social connections. He held a variety of side jobs, including the occasional practice of dentistry, at which he was skilled. He also was a bit of a small businessman. He tried his hand at mining in his home region and had a plan for a waterworks in Rio de Janeiro but felt his economic goals stymied by lack of political pull.

Through militia service Silva Xavier was able to travel widely within Brazil. He made journeys from his hometown of São José del Rey to Rio along the route on which gold was shipped for export. He saw firsthand the impoverished conditions of persons along the Estrada Real, that main shipping artery. In Rio in 1788 he came into contact with visitors and wealthier locals who had traveled to Europe and North America, imbibing the ideas of Jean-Jacques Rousseau, Thomas Jefferson, John Locke, and Voltaire. Among those who shared his admiration for republicanism was José Álvares Maciel, the son of the colonial administrator of Vila Rica (modern Ouro Prêto). Silva Xavier became convinced that for Portugal to require the same levels of colonial tribute as in the past was economically oppressive as well as politically tyrannical.

Although adherents of independence and republicanism included entrepreneurs such as Inácio José de Alvarenga Peixoto, writers such as Cláudio Manuel da Costa, clergy such as Luis Vieira da Silva, and bureaucrats such as Tomás Antônio Gonzaga, it was the lower-born Silva Xavier who kept urging on a conspiracy to bring about such change in Brazil. Perhaps the greatest influence for Silva Xavier was the newly formed United States. He carried around copies of the documents that the founders of the United States had just composed—inspirations for a new Brazilian nation—in both French and English editions. Silva Xavier could read neither language, but it seemed important to him that the effort to expel the Portuguese should have the support of intellectuals and common people.

HISTORY OF THE CASE

The vision of the revolutionaries was idealistic and their scheme inchoate. They plotted an uprising to coincide with a renewed royal effort at tax collection. The new agent in Brazil acting in the name of Portugal's queen María was Luís Antônio Furtado de Mendonça. The conspirators decided that they would assemble on a *derrama* (tax collection day) in February 1789, in Vila Rica, and declare Brazil a republic. Their aim was for ordinary people to join the movement rapidly and decisively.

They hoped to establish a capital in the city of São João del Rei, as well as a university dedicated to the championing of liberty and equality. Several of the participants aspired to bring to Brazil the industrial progress that they had seen or heard about from trips to England. In social goals, though, the group was badly divided. There were those among the revolutionaries who thought Silva Xavier too moderate. Despite his own lack of social standing, he headed a faction that argued slavery should not be abolished for all persons in Brazil but only for individuals who had been born there.

The group had a mole; upon learning of the planned rebellion, Mendonça canceled the collection and moved to arrest members of Inconfidência Mineira. Silva Xavier escaped to Rio and met up with his supposed comrade Joaquim Silvério dos Reis, who betrayed him to authorities. Silvério dos Reis had made a bargain with the government to infiltrate the movement in exchange for remission of his own taxes. In May 1789 Silva Xavier was apprehended by military officials and held for questioning along with a number of his comrades.

SUMMARY OF ARGUMENTS

The roundup netted 84 alleged traitors who were interrogated in Rio. The judicial proceedings against the principals consisted of an investigatory portion and a sentencing phase, held before two separate courts. The colonial government first conducted an official inquest, called a *devassa,* into the detainees' parts in the conspiracy. It was a complex story. The plans had been poorly laid out, and there were many different motives for participating in the scheme: intellectual, religious, political, economic, and even personal. Those threads took some time for the authorities to unravel.

On January 18, 1790, Silva Xavier made a full confession of his part in the conspiracy to the investigating court. Initially he offered only a general account of the plot, saying that he had spoken with a lot of people about his wish for rebellion. As the *devassa* continued to focus on him in seven subsequent interrogation sessions, though, Silva Xavier began to take on more of the responsibility for what had occurred. He said that personal disappointment at his lack of military advancement inspired him to consider rebellion. He confessed that he had made up reports that foreign assistance was forthcoming. He had hoped that the citizens of Rio would flock to a revolt that began in Minas. In other words, Silva Xavier admitted he had created the rumors that the rebellion would win support from outsiders to interest local people in joining.

At the inquest Silva Xavier found himself lampooned as a jack of all trades. In particular, his vocation as a dentist was a matter for ridicule; the government pointedly called him "Tiradentes," or "tooth puller," trying to underline his lack of professional status. In Silva Xavier's era, attending to dental needs was not considered a profession but was likened more to surgery—a line of work that could be gory. Although their intention was derision, *Tiradentes* became a popular way of referring to Silva Xavier; it reminded his admirers of the rebel's humble origins.

The inquest turned up further evidence of the role played by Silva Xavier. The government claimed that his part was crucial and emphasized that he had manufactured the idea of support from abroad. Its contention was that he was a personally disaffected man who, using deceit, had urged others to join him. Modern scholars who have examined the trial record, however, take issue with that line of reasoning. They locate much more widespread support for the revolt than the prosecution would admit at the time. Historians identify adhesion to the ideals of the rebels from a variety of interests and among a cross section of Brazilians.

As formal sentence was considered by another court, the *alçada*, the lawyer who represented Silva Xavier had a difficult task. The defense attorney struggled to make Silva Xavier somehow worthy of the court's mercy, even while the defendant wanted to shift all blame onto himself. The attorney's method for appealing for gentle treatment was to paint Silva Xavier as having a longstanding reputation as mentally unstable. The defense's line of argument was that Silva Xavier was well known as being unreliable and given to grandiose talk. Even though he had spoken openly of rebellion, the defense contended, Brazilians knew better than to take him seriously.

VERDICT

Of the original defendants in the Minas Conspiracy, 24 were found guilty; 10, including Silva Xavier, were given the death sentence. One of the ringleaders, Cláudio da Costa, committed suicide between the time of his apprehension and the end of the trial. Silva Xavier, who seemed more and more at peace as the trial proceeded, made a memorable statement to the court pleading that others should not be executed because he had led them astray: "I am the cause of death of these men. I wish I had ten more lives and would give them for all of them. If God would hear me, I alone shall die and not they."

He got his wish. Silva Xavier was the only convicted person whose sentence was not commuted by order of the queen of Portugal. The other major participants were to be exiled to Africa. Subsequently, four of the exiles were pardoned and allowed to return to Brazil; three of those individuals were clerics. Silvério dos Reis, who had betrayed the plot, was rewarded with a handsome pension and residence; he found his reputation among the common people, though, to be that of a Judas.

The chronology of the distribution of clemency was telling. On October 15, 1790, not long after she could have received reports of Silva Xavier's admissions of his main role in the rebellion, Queen María wrote to the *alçada* specifying that only the leader or chief leaders were to die. The judges of the *alçada* did not deliver their sentence until April 18, 1792. At that time, they first ordered that all 10 of the ringleaders were to suffer a capital sentence, but two days later they announced the queen's decision to spare the lives of all except Tiradentes. The viceroy admitted that he had imposed delays in sentencing in order to make a public show of the queen's piety and mercy. Such actions give credence to the idea that the trial of the conspirators was engineered to shift blame onto Tiradentes, who gladly accepted that responsibility. Both Lisbon and its South American governors did not desire the rebellion to become a broader-based protest against Portuguese rule.

The sentence given to Silva Xavier was carried out on April 21, 1792. Wearing a simple white garment and speaking graciously to a priest, Silva Xavier was hanged. He then underwent "three or four more deaths": His dead body was quartered, his blood used to write a document justifying the execution, and portions of his corpse displayed in locations around Brazil. In addition, his house was destroyed, his small estate confiscated by the government, and his children anathematized.

SIGNIFICANCE

Subsequent events bore out the vision of Silva Xavier and his fellow revolutionaries. The royal government of Portugal itself was displaced within a generation of the Minas Conspiracy. It fell not due to rebellion but military occupation. The rulers of Portugal journeyed to Brazil in 1808 to escape Napoleon's invasion of the Iberian Peninsula. In 1822 Brazil separated from the mother country. Independence, however, was under the auspices of the same royal family that had overseen the crushing of the rebels of 1789; it took until 1889 for Brazil to declare itself a republic.

With Brazil's rejection of a monarchical form of government came official embrace of hero status for Silva Xavier. The accused man's behavior in court and on the scaffold came in for special praise: When Tiradentes saw that it would be impossible to emerge alive from the trial, he sought to save his fellow plotters and to die courageously. His selflessness became celebrated, and his vision for an independent republic acknowledged.

His hometown was renamed Tiradentes. The square in Rio de Janeiro where he was hanged is now known as Praça Tiradentes. The state of Minas Gerais adopted the flag and slogan created by the conspirators as its official symbol and motto: *"Libertas Quae Sera Tamen"* (Freedom, even if it comes late). The date of Silva Xavier's execution became a national holiday. Each year on April 21 people in his homeland celebrate Tiradentes as one of the originators of not only Brazilian freedom but also Latin American independence.

Further Reading

Fausto, Boris. *A Concise History of Brazil.* Cambridge: Cambridge University Press, 1999; Garcia, Rodolfo. *Autos da Devassa da Inconfidência Mineira.* Rio de Janeiro, Brazil: Biblioteca Nacional, 1936–38; Levine, Robert M. *The History of Brazil.* Westport, Conn.: Greenwood Publishing, 1999; Marchant, Alexander. "Tiradentes in the Conspiracy of Minas." *Hispanic American Historical Review* 21 (May 1941): 239–257; Maxwell, Kenneth R. *Conflicts and Conspiracies: Brazil and Portugal, 1750–1808.* Cambridge: Cambridge University Press, 1973.

The *Bounty* court-martial trial

Also known as: The court-martial of Burkett, Byrn, Coleman, Ellison, Heywood, McIntosh, Millward, Morrison, Muspratt, and Norman

Date: 1792

KEY ISSUES

It is no wonder that the last voyage of HMS *Bounty* has served as the basis for several Hollywood films. The ship saw plenty of drama in her sailing from 1797 through 1789. The maritime adventure began in England and ended in the South Pacific, with a reprise in the mother country. The cast of characters was not only memorable but also typical of British vessels in that era. The ship held career naval personnel, an ambitious captain, at least one "gentleman," two civilians, and a crew of able sailors. The purpose of the trip, too, was a standard trope: the *Bounty*'s mission to far-flung lands was to enhance the imperial economy.

Things went terribly awry for the captain and those who respected his authority. But, in a remarkable twist, the man who had been the leader on board when the *Bounty* left London lived to tell the tale of a mutiny. British justice assigned blame for what had happened on the trip. A naval court-martial settled the famous case but not all of the mysteries surrounding the events connected with the *Bounty* in the Tropics.

HISTORY OF THE CASE

The voyage of the *Bounty* in 1787 was the brainchild of Sir Joseph Banks, the head of England's royal botanical gardens (later Kew Gardens). Banks had a scheme to bring breadfruit to Jamaica from Tahiti. Banks had sailed with James Cook in 1769 and seen the fruit in Tahiti then. Through the

Royal Society, Banks promoted breadfruit as a cheap source of nutrition for slaves in the Caribbean. He got the support of the British navy, which appointed Lieutenant William Bligh as officer in charge of the *Bounty*. A merchant ship had been commandeered and refitted (at no special expense) for the purpose of the voyage to the South Seas. Bligh had commanded a ship on Cook's third expedition and so was fairly experienced, but no other officers of rank went along on the *Bounty*.

Due to the somewhat specialized nature of this voyage, the seamen who were hired on to the *Bounty* tended to be more experienced and skilled than was usual for mere trade ventures. The only two persons who really had no naval skills were a botanist, David Nelson, and a visually impaired man named Michael Byrne who was the ship's musician. There was a divide among the crew of the *Bounty*, though, that was typical on British ships of sail. This division was between "gentlemen" and "commoners." Persons from wealthy backgrounds might join voyages out of motives including scientific interest, wanderlust, friendship, or a desire to enhance career options in politics or the military. Such gentlemen's presence on board might inspire tension, accustomed as persons of comparative privilege were to deference and comfort on land.

The trip began on December 23, 1787, out of Spithead, England. It was not an easy voyage, first simply on account of the dangerous sail around South America at Cape Horn. Despairing of making that treacherous passage, the crew of the *Bounty* finally headed in the opposite direction. They sailed around the southern tip of Africa and then eastward, near Australia, New Zealand, finally reaching Tahiti on October 26, 1788. Such long voyages over open water could see privation, but apparently Bligh was more than usually stingy with rations. He had a volatile temper and managed to alienate even the master's mate, the well-born Fletcher Christian. Christian and Bligh had already twice sailed together, and Christian seemed a man of fairly amiable disposition, but even he found Bligh mercurial. Apparently, Bligh was not so much physically as verbally abusive. His invective must have been exceptionally demeaning and incessant for the seasoned sailors to be affected by it.

Fractures among the men continued in spite of, or perhaps because of, a several-month respite on Tahiti while the crew gathered and cultivated breadfruit for their return voyage. Bligh feared that the Englishmen had "gone native," tattooing themselves and associating with Polynesian women. He worried that the mission was faltering because the men would rather stay in the South Seas.

Those fears were shown to have some basis when three men, William Muspratt, Charles Churchill, and John Millward, actually deserted. Bligh showed uncharacteristic mercy by having them punished with a whipping rather than hanging; it was a decision he would regret. If Bligh had executed the men summarily, he probably would have found the law on his side. At the court-martial of U.S. ship commander Alexander Slidell Mackenzie in 1845, for example, Mackenzie was acquitted of murder when he used hanging to suppress a mutiny on the high seas.

Resentments festered among the men as they embarked on the return voyage with the precious breadfruit plants in early April 1789. By the end of the month there was an open breach. Christian and several of the most skilled navigators waylaid Bligh in his cabin. Without any bloodshed the mutineers determined to take over the ship and set adrift Bligh and anyone else who wished to join him. The ship's crew of 42 was divided almost evenly between those favoring Christian and those remaining loyal to the commander.

The choice facing the neutral crewmen was stark. On the one hand, venturing out at sea in a lifeboat was far more perilous even than in a regular vessel. Somewhat to the chagrin of the mutineers, several of the crew took to the lifeboat with the unpopular Bligh, although a few men assigned to his company begged not to be.

And yet, according to the regulations for conduct of persons on ships, not staying with Bligh also could prove lethal. According to Britain's Articles of War, amended by Parliament in 1749 and 1779, anyone who did not assist a ship's commander against mutineers was presumed to be a mutineer himself. Those rules were well known among seamen; thus, if the *Bounty* mutineers were apprehended, they probably would die by hanging. The *Bounty*'s rebels counted on being able to disappear among the tropical islands that they found so attractive.

Though Christian and his partisans had no stomach for a summary execution of Bligh, they must have assumed that the master would not survive in his small craft long enough to reach land or be rescued. Much to their surprise, he did both. Bligh later wrote a self-congratulatory account of his piloting of the 23-foot launch and its 18-man crew across open water. While fighting against natives who prevented them from landing and getting more supplies, the "loyalists" and Bligh prevailed against incredible odds. Bligh used only rudimentary tools to navigate. He and all but one of his men survived until they reached Timor in the Dutch East Indies 47 days after the mutiny, having logged over 3,500 miles. Bligh may have been unlikable, but his leadership on that journey was among the great feats of seamanship.

Of course, the deposed commander reported everything that had transpired to his superiors in London. The Royal Navy went searching for the mutineers. Many of them were located on Tahiti in the spring of 1791. Captain Edward Edwards apprehended all 14 of the Englishmen that he found among the Tahitians. There was another faction among the men from the *Bounty,* though, that had settled on Pitcairn Island. Those gone from Tahiti, and thus not put in irons on board Edwards's ship, the *Pandora,* included Fletcher Christian.

In the Torres Strait between Australia and New Guinea, the *Pandora* ran into disaster. At the last minute one of her crew let most of the *Bounty* crewmen out of their confinement in cages on deck; still, only 10 of the original captives survived the wreck. Also lost were several dozen men from the *Pandora.* Struggling again in lifeboats, the survivors of the accident reached land and were shipped off again to England.

SUMMARY OF ARGUMENTS

In September 1792 the court-martial of the *Bounty* crew was held on board the HMS *Duke,* which was anchored in Portsmouth harbor. Presiding over the forum was Admiral (later Viscount) Samuel Hood, a distinguished naval man. His 12 assistant judges were all naval captains. The court met in the largest cabin on the vessel, obviously restricting the number of persons who could attend from the public.

One individual who took a close interest in the case was Edward Christian, already a distinguished legal scholar and soon to be Downing Professor of Law at Cambridge. Edward Christian gave advice to at least some of the accused men before and while they stood trial, although discreetly. It would not have done the defendants much good to be closely associated with the brother of the mutiny's ringleader.

The prosecution technically was in the hands of the judge advocate general of Britain, Moses Greetham. In practice, though, and certainly in contrast to more modern procedures, the roles of Greetham and Hood were reversed. Greetham was the person present who knew most about procedural matters, while Hood advised the prisoners when they needed prodding about how to conduct their defenses. Greetham, who was what one might call a career Admiralty law expert, actually swore in the judges.

Among the 10 men brought to trial were four individuals who were only reluctant members of the mutineers' company. Bligh, rancorous as he was, admitted that all four of those crewmen really were not culpable in his eyes. The navy's regulations were strict, however, and those men— Michael Byrne, Joseph Coleman, Thomas McIntosh, and Charles Norman—faced trial alongside the six more active mutineers in custody.

The prosecution had a good witness in ship's master John Fryer. Fryer's recollections of the mutiny were particularly damaging to crewmen John Millward, Thomas Ellison, Thomas Burkett, and James Morrison because that testimony placed the four men in positions at the center of the action against Bligh—for instance, guarding him and threatening nonmutineers with weapons. Morrison managed to make some headway against the allegations in two respects: He caught a couple of witnesses against him in contradictory statements, and he cited good evidence that he had tried to join Bligh in the launch but could not do so due to the mutineers' insistence that he stay on the *Bounty.*

William Muspratt also suffered from the testimony of prosecution witnesses. Although

Muspratt supposedly held a weapon in his hands at the time of the mutiny, he told the court that he could call witnesses to gainsay that. The judges would not allow it because the witnesses he wished to summon were two of his codefendants. While he contended with the judges on that point, Muspratt was fortunate to have the advice of attorney Stephen Barney. The few *Bounty* defendants who relied on legal counsel were careful to keep their consultations low key. Even in capital cases, the Admiralty lagged behind the common law courts in allowing legal counsel for defendants.

The testimony against Peter Heywood was similar to that concerning Muspratt. He had his hand on a cutlass at the time that Bligh was being placed on board the launch. Surely, the prosecution argued, that gesture was to show his support for the mutineers who at that moment were in charge. Heywood, though, countered that he was young and just had been awakened when Bligh was being put off the ship. He said that he did not realize the gravity of the situation, and one witness did indicate that he thought Heywood simply was paralyzed with indecision.

It was a subtle point, but there was one other element that the prosecution seemed to be taking into account when making its case against the mutineers. Some had come aboard the *Pandora* voluntarily, while Edwards had to round up others over a course of days. Those groups were listed separately in a document similar to an indictment: a preamble to the case called a "circumstantial letter." Heywood and Coleman, and two of the men who perished en route to England were specially noted as boarding the *Pandora* of their own volition.

VERDICT

The judges handed down their verdict on September 18. The trial had lasted six days. The Admiralty had held the trial to help prevent future mutinies. Although it was a military proceeding, the principle at work was the same as in the rest of English justice. Not many criminals were caught in the 18th century. Those who were apprehended were held up as notorious examples. Absent effective enforcement, judicial authorities employed terror for the few persons who were snared. In this instance six men heard the death sentence pronounced.

The four least blameworthy defendants in the view of the court-martial were the men that even Bligh looked upon favorably: Byrne, Coleman, McIntosh, and Norman. They all were acquitted of being mutineers. It was especially helpful to those crewmen that in their statements to the court before deliberations they could read a letter of support from Bligh. Perhaps the most sympathetic figure was the near-blind Irishman, Byrne. Clearly the mutineers had kept him aboard out of charity, for he would have been at great peril in the open launch.

Heywood and Morrison got an "earnest" recommendation to mercy from the court, fairly guaranteeing their pardon by King George. That result came through, but only three days before the executions of their mates. Heywood undoubtedly was helped because of excellent connections within the navy and his fairly high social station. Bligh's father in law had procured Heywood a place on board the *Bounty*. Morrison appeared to have swayed the judges with his explanation of being compelled to remain onboard with the mutineers. The mutineers did want certain men to stay with them, despite their lukewarm support for the rebellion, because of their abilities as seamen. While the men had been on Tahiti gathering breadfruit, Christian apparently chose to associate with the most able sailors.

The president of the court, Lord Hood, advised Heywood to continue his naval career. It no doubt also was of use to Heywood that he was young, only 15 at the time of the mutiny. The court's opinion that he had a useful life to lead proved correct. Heywood went on to establish a very competent service record, prospering in several commands during the Napoleonic conflict. Heywood also contributed to the military as a hydrographer for South America and the South Pacific. His experience on Tahiti allowed him to give advice to the London Missionary Society on the native language in that faraway region. In other words, Heywood's association with the mutiny did not bar him from success in a variety of endeavors. Still, one must conclude that class bias helped save him at trial.

Millward, Ellison, and Burkett died by hanging on the ship *Brunswick,* on October 29, 1792. Muspratt, whose case at that time was still unresolved, was badly affected by the executions. For Muspratt the court delayed the carrying out of sentence because of the legal objection he had raised. Could he be denied witnesses who were codefendants, when the decision to try all of the men together was an arguable point? Others who might have helped Muspratt were either dead or at great distance; for example, Bligh was not in attendance because he had embarked on another voyage. Muspratt's case for a pardon was not as strong in terms of the facts of the mutiny that were demonstrated in court, but he had a good point that he had not been allowed to make a full case. The royal pardon eventually extended to him as well, but his mental state was fragile ever after.

The rigidity of navy rules extended to the actions of captains, too. Bligh and Edwards were subject to court-martial for "losing" their ships. Their prosecutions were mere formalities, though, and came after those of the crewmen. Both commanders eventually were acquitted and went on to higher commands.

SIGNIFICANCE

The sea and human nature took a toll on some of the mutineers. Four men in custody had drowned in the wreck of the *Pandora* in 1791. A group of mutineers led by Fletcher Christian settled on Pitcairn Island in 1790. Divers in 1957 definitively identified the sunken remains of the *Bounty* near Pitcairn. It was almost certainly burned by Christian so that his fellow settlers could not leave. That lonely outcropping was not well mapped by Europeans at the time of the mutiny. When the British finally began to locate it accurately, in 1808, visitors noted that the former mutineer John Adams managed the island's small mixed-culture community. Many scholars believe that Christian and the other surviving mutineers died as a result of feuding in the interim, although there remained tantalizing reports of Christian being sighted in England after the turn of the century. The modern residents of Pitcairn Island and nearby Norfolk Island trace their ancestry to both Polynesians and the English mutineers.

Again at the behest of Banks, Bligh made another expedition to secure breadfruit to nourish the Caribbean slaves. This time he and the prized plants made it to the West Indies as well as the Atlantic island of St. Helena, where in both spots the breadfruit was unloaded and planted. In Britain, Bligh and Banks were lauded for their efforts, but slaves in the Caribbean found the plant not to their taste as a staple.

Bligh continued in naval commands, although his reputation suffered for a time as a result of the publicity of the *Bounty* mutineers' trial and subsequent publications about the case. He endured two more mutinies in 1797 and 1804, these times as Captain Bligh. Banks continued to champion Bligh, helping him gain appointment as governor of New South Wales in 1805. That stay in the South Seas was unsuccessful, too. In 1808 Bligh faced an uprising among British troops in Australia. In 1810 he was replaced by Lachlan Macquerie as governor. Despite that political setback he remained in line for promotion. In recognition of long service and perhaps still in tribute to his epic navigation in the *Bounty*'s lifeboat, Bligh gained the rank of rear admiral and then vice admiral. He died in 1817.

Among the leading actors to portray the principals in the *Bounty* affair have been Charles Laughton, Trevor Howard, and Anthony Hopkins (as Bligh), Errol Flynn, Clark Gable, Marlon Brando, and Mel Gibson (as Fletcher Christian). Clearly, the tale resonates with modern audiences, but the real mutiny on the *Bounty* is more than just the basis for dramatic treatment. It also has a striking historicity.

The episode occurred during the great age of sail, during Great Britain's most grasping reach for empire. The economic goals of the *Bounty*'s mission were vast, as was the risk of most imperial enterprise. Bligh had much authority over the crew, but the rebellion of April 1789 made clear that custom put some limits on that suzerainty. It remained for legal forces to assign blame and inflict punishment when voyages went off course. The resolution of the trouble on the *Bounty* was typical of other episodes of mutiny. The verdict of the forum at Portsmouth contained a show of severity but yet also a demonstration of leniency and legal precision.

Further Reading

Alexander, Caroline. *The* Bounty. New York: Penguin, 2003; Barrow, John. *The Eventful History of the Mutiny and Piratical Seizure of H.M.S. Bounty: Its Cause and Consequences.* Boston: D. R. Godine, 1831; Bligh, William. *A Voyage to the South Sea.* London: George Nicol, 1792; Christian, Glynn. *Fragile Paradise: The Discovery of Fletcher Christian,* Bounty *Mutineer.* Boston: Little, Brown, 1982; Dening, Greg. *Mr. Bligh's Bad Language: Passion, Power and Theatre on the* Bounty. Cambridge: Cambridge University Press, 1992; Kennedy, G. *Captain Bligh: The Man and His Mutinies.* London: Duckworth, 1989.

The trials of Louis XVI and Marie Antoinette

Date: 1792–1793

KEY ISSUES

One of the most important events in France during the late 18th century was the Tennis Court Oath of June 20, 1789. On that day the Third Estate, the commoners among the French national legislature, declared that they represented the will of the people of France. It was up to their class of citizens, they said, to frame a constitution for the nation. They acted in opposition to alternative notions about who should hold the balance of political power in the nation. The Third Estate took issue with the theory that the great nobles—the Second Estate—of France should rule. The rebels also contested that the nobility ought to control affairs in connection with the First Estate, the clergy. Finally, they debated the longstanding claim of French kings that the monarchy embodied the state.

The actions of June 20 were a threat to not only royal prerogative but also the traditional structure of the Estates-General. The events of that day altered the course of both immediate and long-running political change in France. No longer did it appear that the nobility were directing resistance

to royal power, as was traditionally the case in the nation and had been true in the past few months.

Three days later, in his official declaration responding to the actions of the lowest estate, King Louis XVI attempted to sound interested in a new method of doing political business. He reminded those assembled that he had taken the initiative to call the legislature into session after its one-and-a-half-century hiatus:

> It would seem that you have only to complete my work; and the nation awaits, with impatience, the moment when, by the harmony of the beneficent views of its sovereign with the enlightened zeal of its representatives, it can enjoy the well-being that such harmony will produce.

Louis XVI went on to detail specific reforms that he would support, among them tax restructuring, abolition of privileges that denied liberty to individuals—such as the *corvée*, which required laborers to build roads, and the royal use of indeterminate jail time—a reexamination of censorship, and a streamlining of law codes. To the king's critics it all seemed a sop.

Their distrust increased as the monarch reinforced the military presence around court and got rid of at least one well-known adviser, Jacques Necker, who represented moderate reform within the monarch's inner circle. On July 14, Parisians expressed their discontent with the pace of transformation by storming the Bastille. It did not take long for provincial French people to cast out administrators of high social class and replace them with individuals from the Third Estate.

In a convergence of events quite favorable to those newly powerful elements, French peasants voiced grave distrust in both the monarchy and the nobility who had soaked them since time immemorial. The "Great Fear" in the countryside allowed the Third Estate to present itself as the guardian of order.

For some months in 1789 the monarch was under siege at Versailles. Eventually, the royal family was forcibly removed to the Tuileries Palace in Paris. In June 1791 King Louis and Queen Marie Antoinette tried to escape France, heading in disguise toward Belgium. They were detected at

Varennes and brought back to Paris. Louis's unpopular management of foreign affairs then sunk him completely in the mind of the public. He had gotten involved in a war with Austria (his wife's homeland), and that conflict had gone poorly for the French. After several days of rioting and radical speechmaking within the Paris Commune, the French legislature acted boldly. The National Constituent Assembly suspended the king from office and jailed him and his household.

Since their effort to leave the country, the royal family had lost considerable support among the radical elements in Paris. The press turned vicious toward both monarch and monarchy. But the most savage invective seemed reserved for Queen Marie Antoinette. In journals such as *Le Père Duchesne,* journalists like Jacques-René Hébert vilified the consort of Louis XVI, painting her as immoral and a spendthrift. She was in many ways an easy target, having come to France young, being of somewhat too gentle nature to earn her stripes among sophisticated courtiers, and being of course identified with Austria, now the enemy. It also was a simple matter to paint Louis as under her influence. Such damning of the monarch as a man was a long-tested method of criticizing the king. One could condemn his policies via the assertion that his wife or advisers had led him astray, without risking a charge of treason.

HISTORY OF THE CASE

France still had a constitutional monarchy in the fall of 1791, although many French people had lost confidence that Louis XVI was working honestly with the legislature. After September 1791 that body was termed the Legislative Assembly. With a new constitution the French nation rejected orders of nobility—clearly also a strike at hereditary monarchy. The legislators were divided among themselves about whether a monarchy was desirable, with the faction known as the Jacobins favoring abolition of kingship in France and the Girondists (Brissotins) leaning toward establishing a constitutional monarchy along the lines of the British model.

Meanwhile, outside the halls of power raged even more radical forces, in particular, the sans-culottes, made up of ordinary citizens so-called because they rejected the formal knee breeches of their supposed social superiors. The sansculottes rioted ever more frequently during late 1791 and into 1792, making it apparent that the legislature was not completely in charge of the direction of politics. The Paris Commune, heavily influenced as it was by the sansculottes, played a pivotal role during that time. On August 10, 1792, a mob of sansculottes stormed the Tuileries Palace, where the royal family was under house arrest. Louis's captors eventually demanded to try the king on a charge of treason. Within a few weeks France had been declared a republic, the legislature reconfigured as the National Convention, and the fate of Louis XVI put up for political debate in the legislature.

There were revolutionaries who did not want to try the king and queen at all. Maximilien Robespierre and fellow Jacobins argued that to offer Louis XVI and Marie Antoinette any type of trial would be to question the legitimacy of the rebellion that dethroned them. In this instance, however, moderate voices prevailed: The ruler was to be charged and made subject to a public proceeding as to his guilt. Louis's odds of demonstrating innocence, of course, were close to zero.

Very much as with Charles I of England, Louis's judge and jury were the members of the legislature that had decided to try him in the first place. Another parallel with Charles I's trial was that in Louis's case the 721-member legislature recently had been purged of almost anyone who might have advocated for the monarch. Those two trials of monarchs, though, diverge in certain ways. Most important, Charles I was an ongoing presence at his trial. He attended it regularly and reacted to it (though often without words) at many turns. Scholars note that in contrast, Louis XVI, as an individual, seemed to be forgotten at many points in the proceedings against him. The French king appeared on only two days of the trial: December 12 and 26. The arguments discussed in court were much larger than he. The place at which the trial of Louis took place also was different from England's great space at Westminster Hall. The Manège was a converted riding academy from Louis XV's reign, a thoroughly uncomfortable meeting spot. It was a location that seemed to split factions in a physical sense. Early in Louis's trial those rifts showed themselves in ideological terms.

SUMMARY OF ARGUMENTS

On December 12, 1792, the Assembly's president, Bertrand Barère, read charges against Louis to the defendant. The accused was supposed to respond briefly to each charge, in turn, as if pleading guilty or not guilty to each point. It was an extended reading of a something like an indictment. But the accusation also was an exchange between accuser and accused. Throughout the interchange neither side changed its stance much, with Barère speaking more of Louis's political philosophy than of specific crimes and Louis insisting that he had the authority to do what he did:

> Barère: Louis, the French people accuse you of having committed a multitude of crimes in order to establish your tyranny by destroying its liberty. You suspended the meetings of the Estates-General, dictated laws to the nation at the royal séance, and posted armed guards: What do you have to say?

> Louis: There did not exist any laws concerning such things.

> Barère: You ordered troops to march on Paris and in the days before the fall of the Bastille you spoke as a tyrant.

> Louis: I was then the master of whether or not the troops marched; but I have never had the intention of shedding blood.

When Barère ceased the accusations, he asked Louis if he had anything to say. Louis asked for a lawyer and to see documents that would substantiate the charges. Early in the fall the National Convention had appointed a commission of 24 to investigate the king's actions. Girondist in sympathy, it was headed by a bookish though not especially scholarly or lawyerly man named Charles Éléonor Dufriche de Valazé. Upon collecting that documentation concerning the king, Valazé's attitude toward the monarch hardened somewhat. By

the time Louis asked to see proof of the charges, Valazé was so angry that he literally refused to look Louis in the face. He handed sheaves of papers to the monarch over his shoulder. Louis's response upon seeing the papers was to remind the legislature that just because documents contained the royal seal did not mean he had signed them or approved them personally.

Louis was dismissed for the day, and his accusers dissolved into argument. Jean-Paul Marat and the members of the most radical faction in the National Convention, nicknamed "the Mountain" due to their lofty physical position within the chamber, contended that the king's responses were slippery. Marat argued that the previous exchange only demonstrated that the king would be evasive at a trial; better to dispense with the formalities. Appointing a lawyer for Louis was a waste of the revolutionaries' time. The Girondists, on the other hand, maintained that usual legal procedures ought to hold sway. The moderates prevailed once again.

The king requested a first and second choice for his counsel, both experienced lawyers. The first nominee declined on grounds of ill health, but the second, 66-year-old François Denis Tronchet, accepted the brief. It was an extraordinarily risky assignment. Tronchet took the precaution of sending back his consent but identifying himself as republican. Among several other attorneys who volunteered to attend to the king's legal brief was Guillaume-Chrétien de Lamoignon de Malesherbes, an even more senior person, who treated his royal client with great deference. When members of the court objected to Malesherbes's antirevolutionary respectfulness toward Louis and asked him what could have made the lawyer employ genteel words, Malesherbes famously replied "Contempt for life." It was an apt observation, for while Tronchet managed to outlive the Terror, Malesherbes was to become a victim of the guillotine in April 1794.

Faced with a mass of documents to read through, the lawyers for Louis requested more time to prepare their defense. They also petitioned for a third attorney. They got the added manpower, the fine orator Raymond Desèze, but lost on the request for a postponement. Even after more legal counsel was provided, the political factions bickered with one another over the terms of

Louis's access to his lawyers. Should the attorneys have pen and paper? How thoroughly should they be searched before gaining admission to Louis's quarters? The situation was complicated by the fact that the members of the National Convention were Louis's judges but the Paris communards were his captors. Even discussion of such questions brought howls of outrage from Robespierre and his colleagues in the Paris Commune: "Measures should be taken so that we do not have to hear, each time someone prejudges the destiny of the accused, these insults of cannibals."

The defense got to state its case on December 26. It fell to Desèze to make the legal speech on behalf of his client, a formal summation called the *plaidoyer*. He had the unenviable task of justifying Louis's actions, particularly in the period since 1791, without antagonizing or insulting the convention. His argument was bold, though not as sweeping as he first had proposed to Louis. To the assembled legislators, Desèze maintained that, as Louis earlier had argued, the king legitimately issued decrees after 1789. He developed the theme that Louis had made many concessions to popular wishes: "The people wanted the abolition of servitude. He began by abolishing it on his own lands. The people asked for reforms in the criminal law . . . he carried out those reforms."

On account of the overflowing crowd the Manège was sweltering even in the winter. Desèze himself was exhausted and had to change shirts halfway through his three-hour peroration. Despite the members' physical discomfort and the length of counsel's speech, they appeared riveted by Desèze's words. To win the respect of virulent enemies of the regime, such as Marat, the *plaidoyer* must have been powerful. Making any arguments on behalf of Louis certainly represented an extraordinary act of personal courage on the part of the lawyers for the defense.

VERDICTS

While it appeared easy for the National Convention to decide that Louis XVI was guilty, it had much greater difficulty declaring his punishment. On January 15, 1793, the day of its decision for the death penalty, the policymakers were badly split as to whether execution or exile would be the better course. Only a narrow majority of 361 members preferred a swift execution. A large number, 288, voted against the death penalty, and the rest hedged their bets, arguing for delay in the application of punishment. More moderate members argued for a reprieve, but their colleagues voted down a remission in the sentence. Again, that decision was by only a slight majority.

About one week later (January 21, 1793) the former king was executed via the guillotine at the Place de la Révolution. According to most witnesses, he was calm. He made a statement absolving his captors of his death but also saying he had committed no crime. Before he could conclude the remarks, a military commander on the scene ordered a drumbeat to drown out the speech. Although the crowd generally sounded hostile to the condemned man, after his death several people tried to retrieve Louis XVI's blood.

It remained to be decided what should be done with the former queen. The revolutionaries now termed her "the Widow Capet," in reference to the family name of Louis's branch of the French royal house. The case against Marie Antoinette was even more difficult to make than that concerning her husband. She held no public office and was assigned no official role according to any of the recent constitutions of France. Still, a common public sentiment was that she had exercised control over Louis. If he was guilty of capital crimes, then she was complicit in those offenses.

As with Louis's case, there was the matter of exactly how to try her. The legislature's Committee of Public Safety took less care in framing a justification for a proceeding against Marie Antoinette. Even at the moment of Louis's death, the revolution was moving into a still more radical phase. Not only were legal niceties falling by the boards, but those members of the National Convention who expressed reservations (largely the Girondists) were losing control of the political process.

Those who supported the royalist cause, or who argued that to try Marie-Antoinette was without precedent, floated plans. Thomas Paine suggested she could be exiled to the United States. Perhaps there could be a prisoner exchange with a foreign power. Maybe her nephew, the young emperor Joseph II, would make a plea for her life. From the time of Louis's death through the summer of 1793, the three main factions (Jacobins, Girondists, sansculottes) considered the situation. Meanwhile, the Widow Capet's physical deterioration was noticeable and her mental state poor. She was despondent over the taking away of her son Louis-Charles, whom she and the royalists considered the dauphin. She could hear the eight-year-old boy being beaten. The jailers of the former royal family had declared that the boy would be reeducated to love the revolution.

On August 13 Marie Antoinette was transferred from the Temple, a kind of exclusive jail for prisoners of high rank, to the Conciergerie, a much more dismal facility alongside the Palais de Justice. It cannot have seemed a good omen to the prisoner and her family. Indeed, those who sought to either please or further inflame the most radical elements in France—especially the Paris Commune—specifically decided at about the time of the transfer to the Conciergerie that Marie Antoinette's head was required as a sacrifice. It was Hébert who led the fray.

Hébert, who had sharpened his skills as a journalistic critic of Marie Antoinette, now began to gather evidence against the former queen. A shocking piece of that evidence was a series of depositions from Louis-Charles that his mother, sister, and aunt had sexually abused him while they were jailed in the Temple.

On October 12, 1793, Marie Antoinette faced a secret interrogation led by the president of the Revolutionary Tribunal and attended by public prosecutor Antoine Fouquier-Tinville. Her accusers made clear the line of their future charges—that she had unduly influenced Louis XVI, especially in regard to trying to leave the country in 1791. Some scholars perceive the effort to paint Marie Antoinette as a harpy was emblematic of a larger shift among Jacobins toward marginalizing the position of women as revolutionaries. A key goal in framing such accusations against the former queen, in other words, was to warn women against trying to assume public roles.

Like her husband, Marie Antoinette asked for and got capable counsel. Just as with the former monarch, though, her lawyers had an extraordinarily short window in which to digest the mass of alleged documentation about their client's offenses.

In the case of the Widow Capet they had merely hours instead of the days allotted to Louis's legal defenders. The trial began on October 14 at the Palais de Justice. The most serious of the political charges against the former queen were that she had composed the speech that Louis XVI had given on June 23, 1789, at the royal séance that had proved so unsatisfactory and that she had inspired Louis to flee toward Austria in the summer of 1791. Of course, the queen was called a spendthrift. It was a criticism that she acknowledged had merit. Still, some of the particulars alleged against her, even concerning her carelessness with money, simply were untrue. For example, the prosecution cited her building of the Petit Trianon (a chateau) as a personal retreat, when in fact it was constructed under the previous monarch.

Other information that witnesses at the trial gave hardly constituted evidence at all. It was mostly reports and rumors, testimony that collapsed when questioned by Marie Antoinette's counsel. One of the guardsmen who brought the royal couple back from Varennes, for example, reported that the queen had looked at him in a critical manner; he took this as if she meant to seek revenge upon him.

And then Hébert moved in for the kill. He described items from the prisons where Marie Antoinette had stayed that showed she had been engaged in Catholic worship. He noted that young Louis-Charles had reported efforts by the former royals to maintain contact with supporters while imprisoned. And then he brought out the allegations of sexual impropriety.

Many who were present recalled that the prisoner sat absolutely still, stunned by Hébert's gambit. Finally, goaded by a female member of the crowd to answer the allegations, Marie Antoinette cried out, "If I have not replied, it is because Nature herself refuses to respond to such a charge laid against a mother. I appeal to all mothers who may be present." Clearly, she had touched some of the spectators, if only the females and if only for a moment. The prosecution made haste to follow up on that favorable performance by the accused with more details of her alleged meddling in politics. The jury, made up of ordinary people and Jacobins, decided Marie Antoinette's guilt quickly. She was to die, and soon.

The journey of Marie Antoinette to the guillotine was, if possible, marked by even more scorn from a huge crowd than had been the case with Louis's death. On October 16, 1793, on her way to the scaffold, Jacques-Louis David sketched the former queen. The republican artist may have wished to portray her in as unregal a pose as possible, but there is no reason to doubt the accuracy of his drawing. She sat in the humble cart bolt upright, hands tied behind her, looking older than her 37 years. The exhibitionist Madame Toussaud took wax impressions of the heads of both Louis and Marie Antoinette shortly after their deaths. Before many months had elapsed, those relics were on display alongside models of the heads of the king's and queen's judges and prosecutors, including that of Hébert.

SIGNIFICANCE

The queen's trial and execution were almost without historical precedent in western European history, and yet Marie Antoinette's violent end probably did not affect history much in a direct sense. The protracted, brutal confinement of Louis-Charles, followed by a sudden announcement of his death in 1795, gave rise to persistent rumors that he eventually was spirited away by supporters. Modern scholars give no credence to the revolutionaries' assertions of sexual abuse by his female relatives; they contend that the boy was coerced to make false accusations.

In contrast to the fate of Marie Antoinette, the condemnation of Louis XVI had long-range political consequences. Just as had Charles I, Louis quickly became a martyr for monarchists and, indeed, many who saw fault with the revolution. Although he had been a mediocre ruler in many respects, fellow monarchs in Europe were inclined to defend Louis's memory. His death, in other words, was yet another reason to detest the French revolutionaries.

From the late 18th century onward scholars have argued that exile would have done just as well for Louis and Marie Antoinette. Their deaths seemed to move the revolution along an even bloodier road. Compassion toward the deposed monarch and his spouse might have conciliated foreign opinion and laid the groundwork for a more moderate path within France.

Further Reading

Feher, Ferenc. *The French Revolution and the Birth of Modernity*. Berkeley: University of California Press, 1990; Fraser, Antonia. *Marie Antoinette—the Journey*. New York: Anchor, 2002; Jordan, David P. *The King's Trial: Louis XVI vs. the French Revolution*. Berkeley: University of California Press, 2004; Marie Antoinette. *The Genuine Trial of Marie Antoinette, Late Queen of France*. London: J. S. Jordan, 1793; Schama, Simon. *Citizens*. New York: Penguin, 2004; Tackett, Timothy. *When the King Took Flight*. Cambridge, Mass.: Harvard University Press, 2003; Walzer, Michael. *Regicide and Revolution: Speeches at the Trial of Louis XVI*. New York: Columbia University Press, 1993.

The trial of Wolfe Tone

Also known as: The court-martial of Wolfe Tone, *The King v. Tone*

Date: 1798

KEY ISSUES

The Irish were deeply divided among themselves in the 1790s, but many of them shared a distrust of England and a wish to achieve greater separation between the two. At the same moment, however, the English government had plans to adhere Ireland to Britain even more closely in a constitutional and political sense. To some articulate and influential Irish people, the French Revolution offered an alternative to English political forms and English authority.

No one in Ireland represented disparate factions more capably than Theobald Wolfe Tone. Tone gained the respect of both the United Irishmen, who were Protestants critical of English control in Ireland, and Catholics, many of whom were agitating for independence. Tone, like them, at the fall of the Bastille turned his attention to France as a savior. It was not only French political philosophy that appealed to radical Irish people such as Tone but also French military assistance to effect an anti-English revolution in Ireland.

HISTORY OF THE CASE

Educated at Trinity College Dublin and the Inns of Court in London, Wolfe Tone began attracting attention for his political activism in the early 1790s. With the help of his friend William Russell, Tone published a series of pamphlets aimed at the Protestant elite in Ulster. He hoped to sway them toward toleration for Irish Catholics, who at the time did not enjoy full civil and political rights. The Ulster Presbyterians, as they often were known, already were chafing at English domination in Ireland. It was a testimony to Tone's success as an advocate for both positions—Catholic emancipation and Irish independence—that in 1791 and 1792 he was invited to join high-level groups in Belfast agitating for both causes. Tone's manifesto, *An Argument on Behalf of the Catholics of Ireland* (1791), was widely read, being eclipsed in popularity only by *The Rights of Man* by Thomas Paine. And yet, change in Ireland, particularly Catholic Emancipation, did not proceed as quickly as its proponents such as Tone hoped. During 1793 and 1794 Tone turned to legal practice.

The revolution in France had grown ever more radical since the executions of Louis XVI and Marie Antoinette. Fear of the importation of French radicalism led to crackdowns against political liberals in the British Isles. Tone sympathized with a member of the United Irishmen named Archibald Rowan and wrote materials that, like Rowan's publications, the pro-English authorities in Dublin considered disloyal. It hurt Tone's case with the government that his opinions as to what might happen if France invaded Ireland were found in the possession of a French agent. Since he ran the risk of being prosecuted for either sedition or treason, Tone made an agreement with those in power that he would leave the country voluntarily.

Although Tone had the opportunity to go to France, he chose to decamp for the United States in the summer of 1795. His departure brought home to his Irish colleagues who had hoped for reform or even independence that the government was in no mood to compromise. Even while living in Philadelphia, Tone's thoughts were cast toward the French. He made several useful diplomatic contacts including future U.S. president James Monroe who then was serving as American ambassador to France. Leaving his wife and children in the United States, Tone went back to Europe less than a year after he had arrived in North America. He traveled to France as an agent on behalf of Irish reform.

He convinced several key leaders in France, such as diplomat Lazare Carnot and General Lazare Hoche, that French interests would be well served through association with the United Irishmen. Tone asked to be named an adjutant general in the French army. He was motivated partly by ambition but as well by the fear that if he were captured, without a high rank he would be treated dishonorably as a prisoner of war. It turned out that his concern was well founded.

In December 1796 the French attempted an invasion of Ireland, with Tone and Hoche in commanding positions. The weather proved disastrous for the effort, with some ships being forced to return to France en route and others having to turn around even after landing at Bantry Bay. Tone retreated to Germany and the Netherlands, disappointed at not being able to intervene to assist his colleagues in Ireland who were being arrested, jailed, and, in some cases, executed. The effort to crush resistance in Ireland was spearheaded by Lord Lieutenant of Ireland Charles Cornwallis, who had been defeated in North America but had found more success closer to home. Tone for a time lost support for another invasion effort within France in 1797 when Hoche died of natural causes and Napoleon Bonaparte replaced Carnot and other republicans.

It was not that Tone lacked the confidence of that ascendant leader. Before embarking on a second invasion Tone spoke with Bonaparte. In response to Tone's worry that he did not have sufficient military experience, Napoleon had responded, "But you are brave . . . that is enough." With Napoleon concentrating on a campaign in Egypt in 1798, Tone's renewed effort was not nearly as well provisioned as it had been at Bantry Bay. Again the weather was uncooperative, and this time the British were better apprised of the progress of the ships. The British captured Tone's ship, the *Hoche,* and took it ashore in Ireland on October 31, 1798. Those who were present at the landing noted that Tone was dressed as a French officer.

SUMMARY OF ARGUMENTS

Tone was treated as a military figure in one important respect: His trial was in a military court. But in other ways his officer's rank did not aid him. As Tone noted in letters of protest to government and military officials, he was shackled, as prisoners of war should not have been. Even more detrimental to Tone's situation was that he was charged as a British subject who had committed treason, rather than being identified simply as a captured enemy soldier.

The court-martial took place over one day, Saturday, November 10, 1798, convening in the Riding School of the Dublin Barracks. The venue was swamped with spectators, many of them members of the Protestant Ascendancy and therefore hostile to the prisoner. Tone insisted on reading a statement of justification to the court over the objections of his judges. Although he resented being termed a traitor, he accepted the idea that his actions had been illegal under English law. He did not, in other words, question the jurisdiction of the court. He asked to be executed by firing squad, quickly. As usual, Tone's prose was flowing yet to the point:

> What I have done has been purely from principle and the fullest conviction of its rectitude. I wish not for mercy—I hope I am not an object of pity. I anticipate the consequence of my capture, and am prepared for the event. The favourite object of my life has been the independence of my country, and to that object I have made every sacrifice.

Tone was aware that his military failure might mean he would be judged harshly in future:

> Success is all in this life; and, favoured of her, virtue becomes vicious in the ephemeral estimation of those who attach every merit to posterity—In the glorious race of patriotism, I have pursued the path chalked out by Washington in America and Kosciuszko in Poland. Like the latter, I have failed to emancipate my country; and, unlike both, I have forfeited my life.

The government faced down Tone's claim that he was first and foremost a French officer, contending that he was a British subject and owed allegiance to the Crown. It had plenty of evidence, of course, that Tone had conspired to lead an invasion by a foreign power that would ignite a revolution in Ireland.

VERDICT

The verdict of guilty was no surprise, but Tone waited to hear what form the capital punishment would take. Some time on Sunday evening, the day after his trial, he heard that he was to be publicly hanged the next day.

Tone's father and his fellow radicals quickly cast about for legal means to avoid the gallows. The elder Tone hired the capable and politically sympathetic lawyer John Philpot Curran to appear before the Court of King's Bench to argue that the court-martial was an incorrect forum for Tone's trial. Curran's contention was that the proceedings should have been in the form of a criminal trial in a royal court because Tone was not a British soldier. Lord Chief Justice Kilwarden concurred; he immediately issued a writ of habeas corpus, sending the sheriff to the barracks where Tone was imprisoned to secure his release so that a trial could be held before civil authorities.

The sheriff rushed back into court. He reported that the commander of the barracks had refused him entry. But, there was worse news yet: Tone had cut his own throat, apparently just that morning (Monday, November 12), and physicians reported that he probably would not survive the injury. Although in great pain from the throat wound, with characteristic wit Tone remarked upon the fact that he had not succeeded in the suicide: "I find, then, that I am but a bad anatomist."

Tone's attitude about his probable fate was relevant during his trial. Some biographers note that Tone consistently argued against suicide. Others see him as condoning it for captives under certain circumstances. Additional scholars have said that Tone's closeness to his wife and family precluded his taking drastic action to end his own life. Another point of view, though, emphasizes his public statements that contain marked fatalism.

The doctors patched up the prisoner. British authorities said their medical care was with a view toward executing Tone despite his injuries. The preparation of the civil court's writ meant, however, that the execution was temporarily postponed. Lord Kilwarden and the Court of King's Bench persisted in their contention that civil authority superseded military authority. Despite Curran's best efforts, a civilian surgeon was not allowed to examine the condemned man, nor was Tone moved out of the barracks. The military surgeon, a French royalist named Benjamin Lentaigne, treated Tone but failed to stop him from bleeding to death. Other surgeons argued that the wound must have been inadequately dressed, because although Tone's windpipe was severed his carotid artery was not punctured. It was, in other words, an injury that he could have survived had enough pressure been applied to staunch the blood loss.

Tone died at age 35 on November 19, 1798, and was buried in a family plot in Dublin. Many of Tone's colleagues were either hanged or exiled as a result of their support for the French invasions, with a number of persons being transported to Australia.

SIGNIFICANCE

The Irish rebellion, although contained for the moment, continued. Elements who had allied with Tone were especially angered by the imposition of union between the English and Irish Parliaments in 1800. In severe rioting in Dublin in 1803, Irish protesters lynched Lord Justice Kilwarden (who had spared Tone's life) as an example of the British authority that they so detested. Those who continued to fight for Irish autonomy and independence regarded Wolfe Tone as a hero. He was an inspiration to the Young Ireland Movement in the 1840s as well as more radical figures in the 20th century.

Controversy over Tone's fate endured, with some scholars contending that his death was the result of an assassination attempt rather than self-destruction. Certain historians point out that even

if Tone had had a trial outside a military venue, he probably would have forfeited his life via execution, as did so many of his fellow rebels. And yet, Lord Kilwarden's reprieve of Tone might have succeeded in allowing a prisoner exchange had Tone not died in the interim, for Tone was a high-profile prisoner in whom no less than Bonaparte had reposed confidence.

Further Reading

Curran, W. H. *Memoirs of the Legal, Literary, and Political Life of the Right Honourable John Philpot Curran.* Cambridge, U.K.: Chadwyck-Healey, 2000; Elliott, Marianne. *Wolfe Tone: Prophet of Irish Independence.* New Haven, Conn.: Yale University Press, 1989; O'Donnell, Patrick Denis, and T. Gorey. "Wolfe Tone: Suicide or Assassination." *Irish Journal of Medical Science* 57 (1997): 57–59; Thomas, Donald, ed. *State Trials, Treason and Libel.* London: Routledge & Kegan Paul, 1972; Tone, Theobald Wolfe. *An Argument on Behalf of the Catholics of Ireland.* Belfast: Society of United Irishmen of Belfast, 1791.

The trial of Thomas Picton

Also known as: *The King v. Picton*

Date: 1806

KEY ISSUES

How far did British legal principles hold sway in the empire? Bringing the blessings of British law to faraway corners of the earth sounded noble in principle, but applying that goal could prove slippery. The time period in which a new British possession was in transition from a previous system of law to British governance was especially fraught with complexity. The late 18th and early 19th centuries were an era when Great Britain was extraordinarily self-assured about the superiority of its institutions, most especially legal institutions. The spreading of the British Empire in that same era afforded ample opportunities to bring British justice to other societies. But, that imperial and legal expansionism was not always a smooth process; it could inspire self-doubt.

HISTORY OF THE CASE

Thomas Picton, a native of Wales, had a distinguished military record in Europe and the West Indies. His work life spanned the period from 1777 at the Battle of Gibraltar to his death in battle in 1815. A political and legal scandal interrupted that career and made for one of the most famous trials in 19th-century England. The great controversy of Picton's life involved his military governorship of Trinidad between 1797 and 1802.

Britain wrested control of Trinidad from Spain during the Napoleonic conflicts. Picton had been aide-de-camp to Sir Ralph Abercromby, British commander in chief in the West Indies. Abercromby rewarded him with the post of interim governor of Trinidad. Picton immediately set about with two agendas: notifying London that Trinidad would be a fitting base of operations for a native-led anti-Spanish revolt in South America and setting up the island as a model of order. He was most keen to establish respect for British authority among the many enslaved persons on Trinidad. Those thousands of individuals with darker skins vastly outnumbered the newly arrived Anglos and the Spanish who remained.

Under what type of law, though, should Picton provide stern discipline? He already was well known in military circles as a stickler for the rules, but as Trinidad's leader he was acting in more than a military capacity. He was being asked to administer a British government, although British law had not been formally implemented, by a parliamentary enactment, a treaty, or the writing of a new constitution for the island. Indeed, Abercromby appeared to have given him a brief to employ Spanish legal forms.

Picton made examples of several local people who were charged with crimes, most notably during the first year of his leadership. He was anxious to head off slave rebellions as well as to establish that he would brook no misbehavior among the 500 or so troops on the island. And, it was no acci-

dent that hangings occurred at a place visible to the entrance to the Port of Spain; anyone arriving on a ship was sure to take note of the harsh justice that prevailed. The jail on the island, already known as incommodious, acquired an even worse reputation under Picton, in part owing to overcrowding.

Picton was well liked by the slaveholding plantation owners, some of whom were refugees from French Caribbean islands. They appreciated his domineering methods and focus on political conservatism and had no objection to his use of Spanish law. As part of a political bargain in the home country in 1802, though, Picton's position on the island changed. London sent two men, Commodore Samuel Hood and William Fullarton, to administer Trinidad with Picton as a three-man commission. It was a consolation prize to Fullarton, who had wanted a more prestigious appointment than that of first among equals on a tropical island. To Picton, the arrangement was an insult. At the least, he expected from London an acknowledgment of his success in promoting British interests and maintaining order.

Although Hood appeared impressed with Picton, Fullarton and Picton quickly discerned reasons to dislike each other. Picton perceived Fullarton's political ambitions, and Fullarton found much to abhor in his tour of the island jail. It was not long before Fullarton provoked a crisis among the commissioners. He began investigating the administration of justice during Picton's tenure. In a huff Picton tendered his resignation and headed for London. Fullarton had become determined to make Trinidad more hospitable to antislavery campaigns. He seemed motivated by the hope that his accusations about Picton would raise his own profile, but he also was impelled by a moral aversion to Picton's leanings toward the slaveholders. Fullarton pursued the former military governor, literally and figuratively. He incited opinion against Picton through letters to London and then followed Picton there to lead the campaign for a prosecution.

Picton's two trials in England (first in 1806 and then in 1808) involved the recapping of two other proceedings, a criminal case of 1801 in which Picton had participated, on the basis of which Picton was accused of torture, and an 1805 inquiry in Trinidad into Picton's official conduct.

During the 1805 investigation Picton and Fullarton already had left the island.

In the 1805 inquiry and the 1806 trial and appeal, Picton's detractors concentrated on eight episodes in which persons had died after summary treatment by Picton's orders. During seven of those instances the alleged criminal had died due to severe treatment. But one purported malefactor had survived, and she would provide the testimony against Picton that Fullarton was convinced would demonstrate Picton's overreach.

The alleged criminal's name was Luisa Calderón. She was a young woman of mixed race. She was 13 or 14 years old when she was charged with theft in 1801. Her accuser was Pedro Ruíz, a man in whose home she was a domestic worker. Ruíz very well may have sexually abused Calderón. Certain court documents describe her as Ruíz's mistress. Calderón had been briefly involved in a (more) consensual relationship with another man named Carlos González. Ruíz alleged that together Calderón and González had plotted to rob him. Calderón refused to confirm any such plan to the officials who arrested her.

The local court official hearing the case was an alcalde, the parallel to a magistrate in English law. That judge, Hilaire Begorrat, applied for a routine permit to question Calderón under duress; in other words, he asked for authorization to torture her. Picton signed the order, just as he had initialed several others. Picton also personally told Calderón that the hangman would see to her fate if she did not cooperate.

The alcalde had Calderón "picketed" to make her talk. Picketing was a form of torture in which the jailer hoisted the prisoner by a rope attached to one arm. He then let the victim hang in the air with a big toe just barely touching a picket or sharp board. The procedure at best was extremely uncomfortable and could dislocate the shoulder. Most prisoners quickly admitted whatever the authorities asked of them in order to be released from the painful suspension.

Under that treatment Calderón lasted about an hour before confessing to a sexual connection with González. The officials who presided at the interrogation kept close watch on the time, for they had the impression that they could not continue to apply torture for more than an hour.

Another turn at the picket convinced Calderón to say that she had seen González take money from Ruíz's house and had not alerted anyone about the robbery. A third interrogation under torture failed to force Calderón to admit that she knew where González had hidden the money or that she had helped him break in. In 1802 González was convicted of the robbery, ordered to pay back a considerable sum to Ruíz, and banished from Trinidad. Calderón was released with no further charges. She had been held in jail, shackled, for eight months. Fullarton brought Calderón to London as the key witness against Picton.

SUMMARY OF ARGUMENTS

Picton was arrested soon after he arrived in England in 1803 by order of the Privy Council. He had been delayed by a military action in the Caribbean on his journey away from Trinidad. Thanks to a wealthy relative, Picton made bail. That sum had been set at £40,000. Picton's biographers note that such a large recognizance practically announced that the court thought him guilty.

The first case to be heard against Picton, however, was not in England. It was rather in the form of an investigation by the British leaders who remained in Trinidad. Key to that commission's findings was the testimony of several alcaldes who had served under Picton and had heard the case involving Calderón, Ruíz, and González. Those men, Begorrat and Francisco de Farfán, each insisted that they considered Picton to have been a reasonable administrator. Far from indicating any resentment of Picton among the Spanish administrators that he had superseded, Farfán praised Picton as "a man of considerable talents, doing honor to his own country." The inquiry in Trinidad absolved Picton of cruelty and sent word that many on the island wished Picton's reinstatement as governor.

The second examination of Picton, that at his trial before the Court of King's Bench on February 24, 1806, was a far greater threat to his freedom. Edward Law, Lord Ellenborough, the chief justice of the Court of King's Bench, presided. There was a special jury, meaning, in this case, that the jurors were better educated and wealthier than average, but not indicating any particular expertise on the part of the panel members.

Picton stood accused of allowing torture, which the prosecutor admonished had not been used in England since at least the time of Charles I. In Britain it was an important principle that custom could make or unmake laws. The judges in the late 1620s had refused to authorize torture for legal ends even though it had been employed at earlier times for political purposes. (Admittedly, the distinction between politicians' sanctioning of torture and the courts' authorization of it was lost upon torture victims.) That refusal to allow torture in England had continued, so torture was no longer legal in England in 1806.

The prosecution faced an interesting dilemma, for they had to note that Trinidad in 1797 stood poised between British and Spanish law. The island was under British rule, but there were no forms of British law that yet had been imposed. The prosecution correctly predicted that Picton's lawyers would argue that he was justified in applying torture according to Spanish law.

Fullarton and the others arrayed against Picton had an answer for that, too, as stated by lead prosecutor William Garrow:

> . . . if it were written in characters which no man could misunderstand, and which he who runs may read, that the laws of Spain as applicable to Trinidad permitted, in any given circumstances, the infliction of torture, this would afford no justification to a British Governor. . . . It was his duty in the first moment of his government to have impressed on the minds of the people of this new colony a conviction of the perfect security they would acquire, of the abundant advantages they would derive, from the mild, benign, and equitable spirit of British jurisprudence.

Garrow was at the start of his career in the Picton trials. Against Picton he proved a capable adversary, though perhaps his heart already lay in the defense work that later made his fortune. Among legal historians Garrow is thought to have originated the phrase "innocent until proven guilty," but that was not a phrase he employed in this case.

Garrow relied on Calderón herself to demonstrate the cruelty of Picton's actions. She still could show rope burns on her wrist. She also could recall Picton's direct threats that if she did not testify before the alcalde she might be executed. Garrow did stretch the truth in one crucial respect: He underestimated Calderón's age at the time of the offense, describing her as 10 or 11 when she probably was three years older.

Several other devices that Garrow employed were quite effective. He made a pun on picketing, which he said henceforth ought to be called "Pictoning." The prosecutor circulated in court a drawing of woman being tortured on the picket. Judge Ellenborough warned that the drawing might be inflammatory, but Garrow pressed on and got permission to show it to the jury. He also produced a volume of Spanish law that he said was in force at the time of the torture. Garrow further substantiated his case by bringing to the stand a Spanish lawyer named Pedro Vargas. Vargas affirmed that the compilation cited by Garrow, the *Recopilación*, did not contain any reference to picketing. Garrow's argument was that Picton had acted contrary to not only British but also Spanish law. Picton, he contended, had adapted a military punishment for civilian purposes.

The argument from leading defense counsel Robert Dallas was as muted as Garrow's presentation was sharp. Dallas opened with a long comparison between the episode involving Calderón and a recent case in which a British magistrate on the island of St. Vincent had ordered an enslaved man to lose a hand, the harsh penalty being imposed not for his original crime but for resisting arrest. Dallas said he was contrasting Picton's actions against a person who was suspected of committing a felony with another British criminal judge's cruelty toward an innocent slave. It was an argument designed to play well among antislavery crowds, but it fell flat in this instance; Dallas had managed to describe two tyrannical acts by British leaders in the West Indies.

Dallas had not had time to digest the *Recopilación*, so he more or less accepted Vargas's interpretation of it. Counsel for the defense asked the jury to consider only that Picton might have sincerely believed that Spanish law did sanction torture like picketing. Dallas proposed that Picton's authorization of the torture was "a mere error of judgment, for which no criminal responsibility attaches."

VERDICT

After an intricate debate concerning whether the law of Old Spain applied in Trinidad in 1797, whether the island conformed to a newer form of Spanish colonial law, and then whether torture was a part of either of those legal codes, Lord Ellenborough charged the jury with its task. The panel was to decide "whether torture could be applied at the discretion of the judge and, if so, whether the application of torture to witnesses formed part of the law of Trinidad at the time of the cession of that island." The jury replied that they were not convinced that a law was in force that allowed torture in Trinidad when Picton became governor. He had acted *ultra vires* (outside the law) and, thus, was guilty.

Dallas immediately asked for a new trial based on technical points he had raised. That opportunity to clear Picton's name became available in 1808. It was a proceeding that, while not called a retrial, was one. Between the 1806 trial and the 1808 hearing, Picton's fellow commissioner Hood had helped Picton's cause through his own notable war record and persistent advocacy for Picton. Hood also had a good showing at a by-election in Westminster. Most helpful for Picton was Fullarton's death in February 1808. Fullarton's family and friends carried on the case without him, but with less passion. This time the defense attorney Dallas showed thorough familiarity with Spanish law. He made the case in the 1808 trial that Spanish law did allow torture. At Picton's urging Dallas had investigated Vargas thoroughly; upon retrial the defense could disparage Vargas's credentials.

The jury in the second English trial temporized. Governor Picton, they said, had applied the relevant law yet should have refrained from relying on Spanish rules allowing torture because he represented Britain. In other words, the panel decided that the right decision lay somewhere between Garrow's argument that morally a British official should hold to a higher standard than other leaders and Dallas's contention that Picton had been technically correct in authorizing the picket.

SIGNIFICANCE

The case against Picton had broken Fullarton's health. It affected his quarry far less. Picton got offers to pay the costs of the legal action from several sources, including through donations from Trinidad. He declined such testimonials and went back to active military service. His discipline continued to be a matter of comment, but also his bravery. He insisted on wearing a high hat into battle, thus marking him out among military enemies. Picton's leading of a charge at a critical moment during the Battle of Waterloo killed him. That sacrifice established him as a national hero. The disgrace of Picton's torture convictions was largely forgotten.

Further Reading

Fry, Michael. "Fullarton, William, of Fullarton (1754–1808)." *Oxford Dictionary of National Biography.* Available online. URL: http://libproxy.uta.edu:2422/view/article/10226.Accessed February 1, 2010; Havard, Robert. *Wellington's Welsh General: A Life of Sir Thomas Picton.* London: Aurum Press, 1996; MacCarthy, Captain. *Recollections of the Storming of the Castle of Badajos: By the Third Division, Under the Command of Lieut. Gen. Sir Thomas Picton GCB, on the 6th of April, 1812.* Charleston, S.C.: The History Press, 2001; Naipaul, V. S. *The Loss of El Dorado.* New York: Alfred A. Knopf, 1973; Thomas, Donald, ed. *State Trials,* vol. 2: *The Public Conscience.* London: Routledge & Kegan Paul, 1972.

The trial of Queen Caroline

Also known as: The Bill of Pains and Penalties against Queen Caroline

Date: 1820

KEY ISSUES

The British monarchy was not a well-loved institution in the 1810s. A large part of the problem was the two men who laid claim to royal authority in that time: the old king, George III, and his son George, Prince of Wales. Since taking the throne in

1760 George III had been something of an enigma to the public. He was unusually conservative, even moralistic, in personal matters. Some considered him unsuccessful in imperial affairs; that is to say, he had no hold on the public imagination, as did monarchs who readily acquired foreign territory and mistresses. And there was the matter of George III's mental state. The king's grasp on reality could be precarious. Particularly after about 1800 this created an opportunity for the future George IV to set up an alternative court.

The primary purpose of that anticourt was pleasure. The prospective king George had extremely expensive tastes. The Prince of Wales had a keen appreciation for cultural matters and particularly architecture, but he also liked the company of attractive companions and enjoyed gambling and other social pursuits. The younger George was no cipher, yet the political participation of the heir to the throne was constrained by custom. If the powers of the British monarch in this era were already hemmed in by Parliament, then those of the king or queen in waiting were even more restricted. The prospective ruler was to play no partisan role, indeed, little part at all in the affairs of state. He had little to do besides spend money.

In addition to the holders of the throne, there were other forces conspiring against monarchism. For decades, movements had been afoot that promoted independence from royal governance—notably those in France and the United States, of course, but also nascent efforts in Greece, for instance, and South America. Despite the fact that many governments in western Europe tried to institute a conservative bent after the Napoleonic Wars, radicalism, or at least liberalism, kept popping out and, with it, critiques of hereditary kingship.

In England the disaffection with monarchs and monarchy was palpable. It spread beyond intellectuals and artists, affecting the newly educated middle class, as well as the poorer folk. After Waterloo there was widespread talk of fundamental reform in Britain. Reformers envisioned change that would realign institutions to better reflect the growing prosperity of urban workers and the new, non-noble owners of land. There was no better illustration of the political instability in England

after the Napoleonic Wars' end than the controversy surrounding the Peterloo Massacre.

Peterloo was the derisive name for the shooting of civilians who had gathered in a large field near Manchester to stage a mock election for a "representative" to Parliament. The goal was to draw attention to the need for electoral reform. In 1819 even large cities such as Manchester and Birmingham could not send members to Parliament because of a patchwork of voting regulations dating back to the medieval era. The local authorities panicked at the sight of such a "monster meeting," a crowd of tens of thousands. Troops that had been there supposedly to control the crowds overreacted to being surrounded by a sea of people; they charged the unarmed demonstrators, resulting in the deaths of 15 and injury of hundreds.

The British government's response was not shame but rather repression. Parliament passed the Six Acts; the legislation curtailed the right to assembly, limited publication of controversial materials, cut access to bail, and limited the possession of firearms. No less a talent than Percy Bysshe Shelley took the opportunity to lambaste the state of the nation in "England in 1819":

> An old, mad, blind, despised, and dying
>   king,—
> Princes, the dregs of their dull race, who
>   flow
> Through public scorn,—mud from a
>   muddy spring,—
> Rulers who neither see, nor feel, nor know,
> But leech-like to their fainting country
>   cling,
> Till they drop, blind in blood, without a
>   blow,—
> A people starved and stabbed in the
>   untilled field. . . .

HISTORY OF THE CASE

For several years one of the few bright spots for the British government and certainly the royal family had been the wife of the Prince of Wales. Princess Caroline and the heir to the throne had married in 1794. It was an arranged match, of course; the two had not met before their engagement. They were first cousins. In many respects they were an odd couple even by the standards of royal unions. A native of the German principality of Brunswick, Caroline was vivacious without being refined. She lacked the discretion necessary to get along with a bon vivant like the younger George. He, meanwhile, had no intention of reining in his wandering eye nor of trying to understand Caroline's background or personality. George had been romantically involved with a woman, Maria Fitzherbert, with whom he was rumored to have contracted an unauthorized marriage. The situation was potentially explosive for the Prince of Wales because Fitzherbert was Catholic, and it was forbidden by statute for the heir to the throne to marry into that faith.

George and Caroline had a daughter, the progeny of the few months they lived as man and wife. At first they managed to show some civility to each other, but that veneer wore thin as Prince George continued to use the daughter to try to assure the compliance of Caroline with his rules of behavior. The heir seemed to resent Caroline's development of her own orbit of friends at another alternative royal residence, her home at Blackheath. Only the intervention of King George III permitted Caroline access to her daughter.

Prince George listened avidly to rumors about Caroline's conduct. He engineered a secret but much-whispered-about investigation into her conduct in 1806. That inquiry quashed stories that Caroline had produced a child out of wedlock. It also hinted that the future queen should be made welcome at court. It was a warning shot at Caroline, though, that her flirtatious behavior, especially involving talented and well-known men, was unbecoming to a woman of her social standing.

The Princess of Wales suffered from the fact that her estranged husband was made regent in 1810, owing to the mental incapacity of his father. At that juncture the Prince of Wales could and did restrict her contact with their daughter, Princess Charlotte. Caroline decamped for the Continent. She traveled widely, almost obsessively, inspiring increasingly vivid reports of her behavior. George was especially angered by word that Caroline was spending time with a man named Bartolomeo Bergami, an Italian of obscure origins. It was one thing for Caroline to be linked with an English admiral or a cabinet minister—which she had

been—but it was of a different order for her to consort with a foreigner of much lower social rank.

With the death of Princess Charlotte in 1817, the gloves really came off. Prince George began earnest discussions with legal experts about how to divorce Caroline. A process was available through ecclesiastical courts in England, but it was time consuming. More frustrating for the future king was the fact that he almost certainly would have to disclose his repeated acts of adultery if he wished to allege the same about Caroline.

The Prince of Wales gathered more information beginning in 1818. He relied now not on lower-level spies but appointed three Englishmen (two of them lawyers) to travel to Italy and assemble damaging details about his wife's movements. The so-called Milan Commission returned to England. Prince George bided his time until he could act not as the prince in waiting but as king.

George began to consider asking for a private act of Parliament to cover the situation. It was not without precedent for the legislature to grant a divorce. (Such a course of action was undertaken only on behalf of extremely powerful petitioners.) Of still greater concern was the fact that although they were to be heard first in the House of Lords—which George might expect to be more sympathetic to him than the House of Commons—the proceedings would be quite public.

Still, the risk might be worth taking for George because of one enormous procedural advantage. In a bill for divorce Caroline would be forced to justify herself. She answered those who argued for the bill on the grounds of her misconduct, rather than standing formally charged with a crime. It was to be in effect a trial of Caroline, yet without the procedural guarantees that would have helped her in court. In particular, she would be denied the right to confront her accuser, for in such a proceeding there was no identified plaintiff. Caroline and her lawyers also would not be allowed to know ahead of time who was being called as witness against her.

SUMMARY OF ARGUMENTS

In early 1820 the mood of the populace, certainly in London, was overwhelmingly on the side of

Caroline. By now the object of the proposed political action called herself queen, although George IV and she had not yet been crowned. George III had died in January. Aside from the unpopularity of the new king, Caroline had the benefit of Whig politicians who pushed her case in the press. Persons such as radical London leader Matthew Wood urged her to fight George's offer of a settlement that would have kept her on the Continent in fine style. Such an arrangement would have forced Caroline to renounce her title as queen consort and would have granted her husband a divorce.

Caroline was fortunate to have the services of Henry Brougham, a talented and ambitious Scots lawyer. Brougham was called Caroline's attorney general (chief lawyer) and another skilled advocate, Thomas Denman, her solicitor general. Brougham had been advising her as Princess of Wales, as well as negotiating with the government for a solution that would ease the prince's embarrassment while providing for Caroline's upkeep.

Brougham did his best to put a positive face upon the scurrilous information that the king sent over from the Milan Commission to the House of Lords. Brougham really began his arguments before Parliament when the government coyly suggested that the legislature should decide what to do with that information from the three commissioners who had been appointed, after all, by George. Brougham, a member of the House of Commons, went on the offensive. It was a perversion of justice, he argued, for the Church of England to have removed Caroline's name from prayers for the royal family contained within the liturgy. Did the king wish to go around ordinary processes? Was George serious about wishing for advice from Parliament? Why would members of the legislature consider discussing this matter in the absence of witnesses from the Continent?

Brougham could not prevent the matter from being put forward for formal debate, however. A "secret" committee of the lords, which was secret in name only, soon had digested the Milan Commission's findings. On July 4 those 15 lords recommended that the legislature give the matter open discussion. The committee reported that the queen's conduct seemed of "the most licentious character." Robert Jenkinson, Lord Liverpool, responded that they soon would have a bill to

consider. The controversy involved political considerations of some complexity. For example, former foreign secretary George Canning withdrew from public life for a time due to the persistent rumors that he had been intimately involved with Caroline while she stayed at Blackheath. He could not lead opposition to the king within the House of Commons, given such a compromising position.

Once Parliament formally began to consider the case, on August 17, 1820, Brougham did not have to resort to such legalistic lines of argument any more. He ridiculed George (though never naming him) for hiding behind the smokescreen of the Bill of Pains and Penalties rather than confronting his wife in open court. The astute lawyer also attacked several witnesses as unreliable. He said that the evidence against Caroline amounted to mere rumor and emphasized her well-known devotion to children, including her deceased daughter. Brougham did not have to underline the fact that many of those who spoke during the proceedings against the queen were foreigners or persons of lower social standing. Their lordships could draw that conclusion for themselves merely upon hearing the witnesses.

The initial scenes inside the "court"—really the meeting chamber of the House of Lords—were a matter of some comment in the press. The first order of the day was for the house to ascertain which of the lords would attend and which would be excused. Customarily, many of the peers were absent due to advanced age, illness, or simple disinterest in public business, but this was going to be an intriguing discussion, so attendance was high. One of the peers who did not attend was George Gordon, Lord Byron, although Caroline had wished he would because he leaned toward her side. Brougham, though, was relieved, for Byron nursed an old grudge against the Scot and had threatened to duel with him. Another dramatic moment occurred when the duke of Hamilton demanded to know on whose behalf England's attorney general, Robert Gifford, was appearing. The point was to force Gifford to admit that he worked directly for George IV, but Gifford refused to say that aloud.

All ears waited for Brougham to speak. Those who knew him well realized that recently he had come to have grave doubts about the queen's moral position. This was the result of his conversations with Caroline but also his reading of the materials that George and the Milan Commission had assembled. He was going to have to defend Caroline, in other words, without a passionate belief in her innocence. He chose to do so on legal grounds, but Brougham's contentions went beyond narrow argument. His first point was that this was legislation not for the public benefit but rather for a private purpose. This was a bill, in addition, that made the queen's conduct illegal after the fact. As such, the law compared unfavorably even with some rare precedents, such as the lords' hearing of the cases against two of Henry VIII's wives. The queen's second-ranked lawyer, Denman, followed up with remarks that also were lauded as argument, though perhaps not as much admired for phrasing.

Brougham warmed to his task as the proceedings continued for the next several weeks. Though he did not believe in his "client's" integrity anymore, he summoned great rhetorical skill in presenting her case to best advantage. The speech he made in conclusion of Queen Caroline's case lasted two days. Brougham's performance broadened his political appeal beyond those groups such as London merchants and antislavery activists that already admired him. Reportedly one peer, Thomas Lord Erskine, departed the House of Lords in tears at the conclusion of Brougham's summation. Henceforth, Brougham was a figure of national prominence. He would go on to become Britain's lord chancellor and a key liberal reformer in education and law.

In the fall of 1820 both mainstream writers such as William Cobbett and authors for cheaper newspapers such as William Benbow had a field day over what they called "the Divorce Trial." Some of the publications were witty, as with the oft-repeated quip, allegedly from Caroline, that "she had committed adultery but once, and that was with Mrs. Fitzherbert's husband." The press offered numerous caricatures of the main characters in the drama, concentrating their satire on George IV. In the publications of reformer William Hone, one of George Cruikshank's cartoons depicted the new king as a bloated dissipate. Supporters of the king tried to purchase as many of the most insulting periodicals as they could; it cost them thousands of pounds.

VERDICT

The case never reached a formal conclusion. The government, through its leader, Lord Liverpool, did not ask for a subsequent reading in the House of Commons, so the bill died. The Bill of Pains and Penalties had passed through the House of Lords with only a nine-vote margin in early November 1820. Liverpool had warned George that it very well might fail in the lower house. The supporters of both parties also seem to have decided that if there were a firm resolution in Parliament, it would spur further controversy and possibly even violence among the public.

Initially, the queen was acclaimed as vindicated. She attended a triumphant service at St. Paul's Cathedral later in the month to the enthusiastic shouts of large crowds. Among her many supporters were women, who saw her as a symbol of females trapped in loveless marriages. The nation still had no easy form of divorce. The case had pointed out how indissoluble even abusive unions could be. Those close to the monarch called the proceedings "tantamount to a defeat." King George even spoke of abdicating.

The government again held out an offer of £50,000 for the queen to depart the country. Caroline continued to press to be crowned as consort to George. He and the Privy Council fought her, saying that to be crowned with the king was a privilege that she had not earned. George IV succeeded in locking her out of the coronation ceremony at Westminster Abbey on July 20, 1821.

The coronation of the new monarch appeared to turn public opinion toward George and away from Caroline. She was ill and depressed from the revelations about her conduct that she had to sit through. George IV, of course, had endured no such formal recitation of his indiscretions. The general opinion was that Caroline would do the nation more good with her absence than by staying. The anonymous poem went around London:

Most Gracious Queen, we thee implore
To go away and sin no more;
But, if that effort be too great,
To go away, at any rate.

Sir Walter Scott, who was trying to ingratiate himself with the new king, called Caroline the "Bedlam Bitch of a Queen." Caroline, still uncrowned, died within weeks of the coronation of George IV. She was laid to rest in Brunswick. A plaque on her coffin read "Caroline, the injured Queen of England." George IV lived for 10 more years, increasingly taking solace in brandy and opiates. His passing was remarkably little mourned. Newspapers commented in memoriam upon his "unbounded prodigality" as well as his "indifference to the feelings of others."

SIGNIFICANCE

The trial of Queen Caroline served as a juicy bit of political theater. It was extremely unusual for a British monarch to go so public in his repudiation of a spouse. Perhaps, as Brougham had said, the only precedents were what Henry VIII did to Anne Boleyn and Catherine Howard. Even those women, though, had the benefit of criminal trials among the lords rather than the subterfuge of a condemnatory bill. That the animosity between George and Caroline went so far and lasted so long had to do with many factors, not least of which was George's protracted wait for his father to die. Until he was monarch in his own right, rather than regent, even the egotistical Prince of Wales hesitated to push his luck. The partisans of Caroline, on the other hand, may have waited a bit too long after Peterloo to make their case, for while they unquestionably tapped into popular resentment about the regent's deplorable morals, they did let the public's enthusiasm for protest lose momentum.

Further Reading

Bennett, Anthony. "Broadsides on the Trial of Queen Caroline: A Glimpse at Popular Song in 1820." *Journal of the Royal Musical Association* 107 (1980): 71–85; *Caroline. The Important and Eventful Trial of Queen Caroline, Consort of George IV. For 'adulterous intercourse,' with Bartolomo Bergami.* London: George Smeeton, 1820. Available online. URL: http://vc.lib.harvard.edu/vc/deliver/~scarlet/004380129. Accessed March 5, 2010; Folkson, Sheree (dir.), *A Royal Scandal.* British Broadcasting Corporation, 1996; Fulford, R. *The Trial of Queen Caroline.* London: Batsford, 1967; Robin, Jane. *The Trial of Queen Caroline.* New York: Free Press, 2006; Smith, E. A. *A Queen on Trial: The Affair of Queen Caroline.* Phoenix Mill, U.K.: A. Sutton, 1993.

The trial of William Burke and Helen McDougal

Also known as: *The King v. Burke and McDougal;* Burke and Hare case; body snatchers case; trial of the resurrectionists

Date: 1828

KEY ISSUES

In the early 19th century Edinburgh boasted one of the finest medical schools in Europe. Its success, however, was provisioned in part by a dark secret: the illegal purchase of cadavers for dissection by medical students and physicians. The law within the British Isles already provided for the bodies of condemned criminals to be offered for medical study. In fact, the courts touted such a use of dead bodies as one of the terrors of the scaffold. If hanging were not frightening enough to deter offenses, then perhaps the knowledge that one's body would be cut apart would serve the purpose of crime prevention.

The procurement of bodies for dissection, though, was unpredictable. Relatives and friends of condemned criminals frequently objected to the post-mortem examinations. Hangings at Tyburn, for example, had been interrupted by rescues of corpses, and there had been protests, even riots, "against the surgeons" at several times during the past century.

The problem was even more serious than a set of objections to turning over felons' corpses. The surgeons had also created a market that led to the plundering of cemeteries. The bodies that grave robbers supplied as often as not were the remains of persons whose loved ones were not present; that is, consent was not granted to such a transaction. Few people, however, reckoned that persons might go beyond digging up graves to make money from the Edinburgh and London doctors. William Burke and William Hare, two of the most notorious criminals in British history, did not simply desecrate graves and steal bodies; they created corpses. Their own destitution and the poverty of people like them set up a situation where their personal greed and cruelty could hold sway.

HISTORY OF THE CASE

Burke left a wife and children behind when he went to Edinburgh as a laborer in 1826. The larger cities of Britain in the early 19th century were awash with individuals who might have few close friends or kin in the vicinity. In Edinburgh, for example, thousands of Irish people had migrated to serve as laborers on the new canal between Edinburgh and Glasgow. A few decades later, of course, the Irish also toiled as "railway navigators." Migrant laborers had to put up with substandard lodging. They reasoned they could make do in terrible housing for the brief time that they would be earning decent enough wages at this temporary work.

Among his fellow workers and Irish folk in Scotland, Burke met a woman named Helen McDougal. Upon her acquaintance with Burke, she abandoned her own kin and went with him to Edinburgh, where they rented rooms in a house claimed by William Hare in the West Port neighborhood of the city, in a squalid courtyard called Tanner's Close. Hare was also Irish. He had gained control of the lodging house by wooing the wife of the ill owner of the place. When the man died, Hare moved in as the new landlord. The widow of the former owner was called "Lucky" or (as William Hare's common law wife) "Mrs. Hare."

In 1827 the two men and their female partners conceived a plan to make money from the natural death of another lodger. That man, named Douglas, had owed Hare a sum of money; upon Douglas's demise, Hare and Burke decided they would substitute a heavy bag in Douglas's coffin while offering the body to Dr. Robert Knox, an anatomy instructor at the University of Edinburgh. Knox paid them £7, a hefty sum that more than repaid the debt Douglas had owed. The rest of the money Burke, Hare, McDougal, and Mrs. Hare spent on a drinking binge.

Scholars are divided as to the impetus for the subsequent actions of the four. Did Dr. Knox hold out the temptation of further rewards if they could provide "fresher" bodies? Or, were the body snatchers simply inspired on their own? In the spring of 1828 another lodger at Tanner's Close became very ill. Burke and Hare hastened his death with a pillow over his face. They delivered the body to Dr. Knox at Surgeon's Square in return for a payment of £10. It was a short step from there to waylaying an elderly woman named Abigail Simpson who had just collected her pension, plying her with liquor, and getting her to stay the night. For Simpson's body Dr. Knox paid Burke and Hare what was becoming the customary fee.

In late April 1828 two known prostitutes accepted an invitation from Burke to come home with him and drink. One of the young women eventually left for a nearby pub; her companion, the beautiful Mary Paterson, was never again seen alive. Paterson's corpse turned up, of course, on Dr. Knox's dissecting table, where her good looks attracted comment and recognition from medical students. Something similar occurred when Burke, Hare, and the women killed a young man named James Wilson. Wilson had been well known in the neighborhood as mentally challenged. The medical students identified "Daft Jamie's" body.

On October 31, 1828, Burke met an older Irish woman in a tavern and invited her to his lodging house to stay. There he introduced the new "guest," Mary Docherty, to some lodgers named Anne and James Gray. After a night of drinking, about which neighbors commented on account of its rowdiness, Docherty went missing. McDougal, Burke's companion, stated that she had turned Docherty out of the lodging house due to Docherty's drunken advances toward Burke. Somewhat suspicious of that explanation, Mrs. Gray looked around the house, finally discovering Docherty's body on a bed. She confronted McDougal, who offered to buy Ann Gray's silence. The Grays went to the police. When investigators arrived at the house, though, Docherty's body had disappeared.

The authorities questioned Burke and McDougal, who both said that Docherty had left the residence at seven o'clock on the day in question. But, the two had not gotten their stories completely straight: William Burke said it was 7:00 A.M., while McDougal asserted Docherty had departed at 7:00 P.M. An anonymous tip (by a medical student or a local resident?) led the police to call at Dr. Knox's medical office, where they found the body of Mary Docherty. People in the area whose family members were missing began to associate their disappearances with Burke and Hare. In fact, a new verb entered the lexicon of Britons: *burking*, the killing of a person in order to provide his or her body to an unquestioning anatomist.

The police searched the lodging house and found items that belonged to Mary Paterson and James Wilson. There still was difficulty in showing, however, that those persons had been murdered. No one officially had identified their remains at dissection, though the strong suspicion was that the two victims were those missing persons. While James Gray had identified Docherty's body, the autopsy on her was inconclusive as to a cause of death. The public prosecutor told the police that better evidence of the Burke-Hare connection to the dead people was required.

The Scottish official charged with ascertaining whether enough solid evidence existed to go forward with a trial was called the lord advocate. This particular officeholder (the Scottish parallel to an English public prosecutor or a U.S. attorney general), Sir William Rae, determined that even the interviews with the four suspects had failed to yield a good case. He recommended that prosecutors try to arrange plea bargains with some of the suspects. McDougal refused the arrangement. This was workable, to authorities anyway, since they already considered Burke to be the criminal mastermind. They concentrated on extracting information from William Hare, assuring Hare that he would not be prosecuted if he gave up evidence about Burke. Lucky Hare, meanwhile, was spared prosecution because a husband was not required to give evidence against his wife. William Hare supplied names of victims and details of witnesses. The case now could go forward. Interestingly, then, although the public usually spoke of "the case of Burke and Hare," the formal charges actually were against "Mr. and Mrs. Burke" (William Burke and Helen McDougal).

SUMMARY OF ARGUMENTS

The trial took place beginning on December 24, 1828, at the courthouse in Edinburgh's Parliament Close. A four-judge panel supervised the proceedings, led by Lord Justice Clerk David Boyle. Scotland had an advanced system for the provision of counsel at no charge when needed. Clearly, the defendants qualified. Burke and McDougal got the services of two superb advocates, Henry Cockburn and James Moncrieff.

The initial problem before the court was a defense objection to the indictment as overly broad. The charge had included allegations about three separate murders, widely separated in time. Judge Boyle determined that he would proceed first only in the case of the death of Mary Docherty. For prosecutors this was not a terrible blow, for her death was the most recent. Though the cause of her death was not fully established, Docherty's identity was. Also, the prosecution appreciated the fact that the judge had chosen to focus on the one of the three murders alleged in which McDougal's leading role was most clear.

Still, that initial decision by Judge Boyle came in for considerable criticism both during and after the trial. Certain members of the public maintained that the defendants ought to be held accountable for all three murders—those of not only Docherty but also Wilson and Paterson. There also was considerably strong feeling against William Hare, who carried through on his part of the plea bargain but also seemed smug in court; he knew he would not hang. Finally, the entire trial more or less ignored the role of Dr. Knox.

The testimony of Hare seemed specially framed not to implicate the anatomist. Cockburn tried repeatedly to get information before the court concerning Knox's role, but Judge Boyle would not allow it. Hare's major theme in testimony was that the murders were never his idea and that it was Burke who invariably pocketed the money. The court would not permit Cockburn to establish even that Hare had visited a surgeon with a body.

Lucky Hare took the stand with a baby in her arms. It was a device that Cockburn saw through as an effort to gain sympathy for her tale even though Mrs. Hare was not under indictment. The baby also provided an excuse for Lucky Hare not to answer questions; when an inconvenient query arose, she would act as though the baby needed tending.

In its summation the defense laid stress upon the heavy drinking that had gone on in the household on the days surrounding Docherty's death. The implication was that neither of the Hares had the wherewithal to remember what had occurred; everyone on the premises, including the deceased woman, was extremely impaired. Burke's lawyer also emphasized that the neighborhood and indeed the entire city were wracked by rumors about the Burkes and the Hares; such an atmosphere of prejudice precluded a fair trial. The final point of the defense was the matter of corpus delicti. The need for corpus delicti, or hard evidence of a crime being committed at all, such as a corpse, was a principle usually applied when there was no body. But, in this instance the defense was saying that the body of Docherty could not be connected with a criminal act.

Cockburn was not averse to a last-minute alteration of strategy based on his reading of how the trial had gone. His final effort as defense counsel was to ask the jury to separate the cases of Burke and McDougal. He requested that even if the panel determined Burke to be guilty, they ought to consider that McDougal was "under the influence" of her husband. Scottish law was different from English legal regulations in certain respects, but none were better known the availability of a "third verdict." Besides "guilty" or "not guilty" a jury might say that the case was "not proven." Lawyers and judges contended that this meant that the prosecution had not established such a person's guilt. Cockburn suggested that this jury return a verdict for McDougal of "not proven." In the popular mind such a decision was said to mean that a defendant was either more sympathetic than his or her codefendant(s), or else simply less involved in the crime in question.

Verdict

The jury took less than an hour on Christmas morning 1828 to announce verdicts of "guilty" for Burke and "not proven" for McDougal. The court had been in session around the clock, but the principle of justice occurring swiftly was preserved. The one bit of mercy that Justice Boyle displayed toward Burke was that his body would not have to hang in chains. The jurist did offer a particularly apt refinement on the death penalty. After the convicted man was executed, his body was to be "given over" for dissection. Then Burke's skeleton was to be preserved as a warning against similar crimes.

In the days just before his execution on January 28, 1829, Burke gave confessions about 16 murders that he and Hare had committed. He detailed how the murders were carried out to escape detection. Burke lured victims to the lodging house, all four persons helped get them deeply intoxicated, and then Burke held the victim's mouth closed while Hare sat on his or her chest. The condemned man declined to implicate the women. Though the women almost certainly had participated in assuring "marks" that they were safe at the house, they likely had not seen anyone killed. Probably only Lucky Hare still could have been tried. Burke's hanging saw a crowd that raucously cheered his death.

Knox was been a young member of the Royal College of Surgeons of Edinburgh at the time of the trials. He was a specialist in anatomy rather than much of a practicing physician. It would have been unusual for Knox not to accumulate a working list of irregular suppliers of bodies via grave robbing, people termed in that day *resurrectionists*. Knox did delegate certain tasks to those with whom he worked at his office, including his brother and a doorkeeper. Still, those in his own time and ever since have pointed out that a specialist in anatomy ought to have been suspicious when he kept receiving very recently deceased persons from one source. (The tally of Burke and Hare's victims seen by Knox usually is set at 17.) Knox continued in his position in Edinburgh for several years after the scandals broke, later moving to a cancer hospital in London. He was pilloried in the press, especially via numerous puns on his name, such as "obnoxious" to his profession. One of Knox's assistants, William Fergusson, went on to become an eminent physician. Fergusson gave great credit to Knox's tutelage, even during what he called the "eventful period" of the Burke and Hare scandal.

The three surviving murderers, Lucky Hare, Helen McDougal, and William Hare, all felt the effects of the trial keenly. Mrs. Hare left for Ireland without William Hare. People were reported as recognizing and hounding her. McDougal had to go to Australia to escape most of the ignominy. William Hare got the worst of the reprisals. An angry crowd in Carlisle, northwestern England, drove him into a lime pit. The incident left him blind.

SIGNIFICANCE

It has been said that Burke and Hare are the best-known duo in Scottish history. They certainly were notorious in their day throughout Britain. Legal officials and literary figures such as Walter Scott and Robert Louis Stevenson either attended or followed the trial closely. Stevenson's tale "The Body Snatcher" was a riff upon the medical students and anatomists who were connected with such enterprises.

Well before this case arose, the British Parliament had been considering legislation to change the existing regulations on the provision of bodies for anatomists. The previous relevant law had been the Murder Act of 1752 that had allowed dissections on the bodies of executed murderers. The demands of the anatomists for more bodies were increasing, though, with a greater emphasis on dissection in medical curricula. Also, with greater availability of both prisons as punishment and transportation and a growing sense of revulsion at capital sentences, fewer persons were being convicted of murder.

The Burke and Hare case showed that holes existed in the system of provision of bodies. Although a few pioneering spirits such as Jeremy Bentham advocated the donation of corpses for scientific study, such views were not at all mainstream. Indeed, many persons and groups who believed in the resurrection of the dead on the Day of Judgment argued that dissection was sacrilegious.

In the aftermath of the trial of these offenders Parliament drew up a measure that shifted provision of cadavers onto the poor. Even after the enormous publicity attendant on Burke's trial, religious objections remained. An effort in 1829 to enlarge the old law, for example, was blocked by the archbishop of Canterbury. Parliament settled on a measure that allowed relatives to opt out of the donation of bodies to science. The new measure also set up a system that centralized the acceptance of bodies at medical schools in the hands of one or two licensed anatomists. The Anatomy Act of 1832

stated that the bodies of persons who died in workhouses would be forfeited to the anatomists unless family members came to claim the remains within 48 hours. Another element of the 1832 law was its abolition of the penalty of hanging in chains.

Further Reading

Bailey, B. *Burke and Hare: The Year of the Ghouls.* Edinburgh and London: Mainstream Publishing, 2002; Barzun, Jacques. *Burke and Hare: The Resurrection Men—A Collection of Contemporary Documents Including Broadsides, Occasional Verses, Illustrations, Polemics, and a Complete Transcript of the Testimony at the Trial.* Metuchen, N.J.: Scarecrow Press, 1974; Bates, A. W. *The Anatomy of Robert Knox: Murder, Mad Science, and Medical Regulation.* Eastbourne, U.K.: Sussex Academic Press, 2010; Behlmer, George. "Grave Doubts: Victorian Medicine, Moral Panic, and the Signs of Death." *Journal of British Studies* 42 (April 2003): 206–235; Gordon, R. Michael. *The Infamous Burke and Hare: Serial Killers and Resurrectionists of Nineteenth Century Edinburgh.* Jefferson, N.C.: McFarland Publishers, 2009; Marshall, Tim. *Murdering to Dissect.* Manchester, U.K.: Manchester University Press, 1995; Richardson, Ruth. *Death, Dissection, and the Destitute.* Chicago: University of Chicago Press, 2000; Roughead, William. *Notable British Trials: Burke and Hare.* London: William Hodge & Co., 1948.

The trial of the *Amistad* mutineers

Also known as: *United States v. Cinque et al.; The United States, Appellants v. the Libellants and Claimants of the Schooner* Amistad

Date: 1839–1840

KEY ISSUES

By 1839 many nations had banned slavery within their borders and as a part of their trade, and yet slavery persisted. In the Caribbean region particularly, the buying and selling of black Africans continued, supplying planters who demanded cheap labor. Much of that trade was in contravention of explicit legal bans on commerce in slaves. The antislavery policies of Old World nations such as Spain were widely ignored and poorly enforced by certain colonial governments such as that of Cuba.

An abolitionist movement grew more vocal in the United States in the early 19th century, in part due to the influence of antislavery forces from Great Britain. Britain had taken the forefront in outlawing slavery first within the homeland and then through its ships. Other powers such as the United States followed suit by way of international treaties. In the United States there was considerable moral pressure for a national policy of abolition.

Still, the United States was a union of many states, the southernmost of which saw slavery as necessary to their economies. North American slavery was not about to be abolished simply due to the nation's treaty obligations. In the 1830s the U.S. federal government under President Martin Van Buren was at pains not only to keep southern planters happy but also to get along with nearby foreign neighbors that had a more lax attitude toward slavery.

HISTORY OF THE CASE

During the age of sail, mutiny was an eventuality that loomed large for the commanders of vessels of all types. Shipboard rebellion was a special threat when travel distances were great, for dissatisfaction could build up for months among a crew. But, other circumstances besides a shortage of rations on a long voyage might inspire those on board to take over a ship. Such was the situation among, not the crew, but rather certain other persons sailing off the coast of Cuba in June 1839. This episode was not a traditional case of mutiny, for the identity of the mutineers was fundamentally different from that of crew members or even passengers.

The *Amistad* was a Spanish ship plying the waters near Cuba with a cargo of enslaved persons. The "human cargo" had recently been apprehended in Africa, brought to Havana, and purchased by slave owners José Ruíz and Pedro Montez. On the voyage from Africa, the slave ship that had carried these captives to Havana had dodged British vessels that were patrolling in search of such ships, which operated in contravention of an 1817 international treaty that outlawed slave trading.

Ruíz and Montez were transporting the 49 adult Africans and four children to another spot in Cuba, Puerto Príncipe, via the port of Guanaja, when trouble broke out aboard. The enslaved persons were already traumatized by their capture, journey across the Atlantic, and sale. They spoke almost no words of the language of their tormentors but managed to make signs to the crew, asking what was to become of them. When a cook made a gesture across his throat to the prisoners and joked that they would be killed and eaten, their anxiety turned to panic. Fearing for their lives, the slaves organized an overthrowing of the authorities on board.

On July 1, led by a man from the Congo named Joseph Cinque (Cinquez), the mutineers subdued their oppressors. They killed the captain of the *Amistad*, Ramón Ferrer, and the cook named Celestino who had taunted them, as well as two other crew members. They kept Ruíz and Montez alive because the Spaniards had navigational skills. The goal of the rebels was repatriation to Africa. Ruíz and Montez thwarted the plan, however, by steering the *Amistad* westward at times when the Africans were asleep. The Cubans missed their mark as well, though; the ship ended off the coast of the northern United States.

On August 26 crewmen on a U.S. revenue cutter called the *Washington* sighted the *Amistad*. Lieutenant Richard Meade on the *Washington* thought that the *Amistad* was full of smugglers or pirates, especially because he saw blacks and white together on that unknown vessel. The *Washington*'s commander, Thomas Gedney, ordered the *Amistad* boarded to find out what the *Amistad* was doing in the coastal waters near Long Island.

The ship and its occupants all were taken to Connecticut. Gedney's main goal was to claim salvage rights on the ship, which he could argue he had "rescued" from destruction by the Africans. Since the Africans could be claimed as property in Connecticut but not New York, and since they formed a valuable portion of the "cargo," it was a conscious choice by Lieutenant Gedney to land in Connecticut instead of New York.

When the Africans as well as Ruíz and Montez were ashore, the authorities at New London, Connecticut, notified the federal government of the incident. President Van Buren was interested in keeping peace with Spain and Cuba as well as pacifying slaveholders at home. He encouraged the U.S. attorney for Connecticut, William Holabird, to mount a prosecution of the mutineers for piracy and murder. Abolitionists such as Lewis Tappan of New York were geographically well placed to hear quickly of the *Amistad*'s arrival in the United States and the potential prosecution of Joseph Cinque and his peers. In September Tappan had formed the "*Amistad* Committee" to publicize the plight of the Africans and to defend them in court.

SUMMARY OF ARGUMENTS

The "trials" of Cinque and 38 other Africans (aside from the children and several other Africans on the *Amistad* who had died en route) turned out to be more complicated than a criminal prosecution for murder and piracy. The government initiated such a course but was rebuffed. The federal government then stood behind the efforts of Ruíz and Montez to secure a civil judgment. The point was to get a judicial determination of the status of the Africans. The arrival of the *Amistad* in U.S. waters posed several murky questions of law, morality, and diplomacy.

An initial hearing before Judge Andrew Judson was concerned with the circumstances under which the *Washington* crew boarded the *Amistad* and kept the Africans from running away. Holabird emphasized the account of the mutiny that he had gotten from Ruíz at the time of the discovery by the crew of the *Washington*. The attorney referred to the captured Africans as the property of Ruíz and Montez; Judge Judson agreed, committing the Africans to trial at a U.S. circuit court in New Haven for murder and piracy. U.S. circuit court judges were like the English assize court jurists who went out from a central location several times a year to "clear the jails." In this instance, the judge who was slated to preside over the criminal trial was Justice Smith Thompson, who also sat on the U.S. Supreme Court.

Defense counsel Roger Baldwin (a descendant of founding father Roger Sherman and himself later a U.S. senator and governor of Connecticut) played a key role in argument before Judge Thompson. The defenders of the Africans and those representing Ruíz and Montez immediately broached major topics. Holabird emphasized the authority of the U.S. president to manage foreign affairs. He proposed that the Africans should be released into the custody of President Van Buren. The abolitionists, through Baldwin, fought that idea strongly, for they suspected that Van Buren intended to give them back to Cuba. They also knew that if the administration were to hand the mutineers to the Cubans, they very likely would be punished with death or, at best, continued enslavement.

Judge Thompson decided not to commit the Africans for trial on criminal charges. His justification for lifting the criminal charges was that the offenses of murder and piracy (if they had occurred as crimes), certainly had happened out of U.S. jurisdiction. The rebellion, in modern terms, occurred in international waters. Furthermore, the mutiny did not involve any U.S. citizens; clearly, U.S. criminal law was not involved. The decision was a major victory for the abolitionists, and certainly for Cinque and the Africans, but it did not settle the question of what would become of the mutineers. If they were considered property, they still could be sold into slavery as part of the salvage operation. Strictly speaking, then, the Africans no longer were defendants, but in fact, they were on trial, for if their side lost the civil case, their freedom and perhaps their lives would be forfeit.

President Van Buren gave orders that the moment the Africans were declared to be Ruíz's and Montez's possessions, they were to be hustled aboard a waiting ship and taken to Havana. The government's documents give clear evidence that federal authorities planned to undertake that action so quickly that an appeal against the judgment for the Cubans would be useless in practice. It was an extraordinary demonstration of the administration's commitment to undercut the judicial process and to placate Spain and Cuba.

The civil case began on November 19, 1839, and lasted until January 13, 1840. Abolitionists in the United States saw the case as extremely important and had set about securing superb representation for the accused men. At the head of the defense table was Baldwin, joined by Joshua Leavitt and Seth Staples. Holabird again spoke for the prosecution.

The lawyers for Cinque and the Africans based their defense on several elements. The foundation of their argument was the contention that the black men were not in fact slaves in a legal sense. Spain had outlawed slavery via its signing of the international treaty of 1817, therefore the original capture in Africa was a criminal act and the sale to Ruíz and Montez in Cuba was invalid. It was, of course, an argument that was a slap at both Cuba and Spain for not enforcing the abolitionist treaty obligations of Spain.

The prosecution backed the slaveholders' claims that the black men had Spanish names and therefore were from Cuba; thus, they were not recently imported captives. The defense presented witnesses such as Dr. Richard Madden, who had examined Africans in Cuba and seen the conditions under which detainees were held there. Such testimony demonstrated that those who said the persons of color were longtime inhabitants were, simply, lying. The black individuals spoke African languages, answered to African names, followed African traditions, and in short had to be very recent arrivals to Cuba. The linguistic evidence from the defense was creative; they had scoured urban areas looking for experts in Mende, the native language of Cinque and his men. With good translators on their side, the defense had communicated fully with the captives.

Another key component of the defense argument was that any person had the right to keep from being killed. The Africans had thought that they were going to be murdered by their captors, so they rebelled in self-defense. The murders on board the *Amistad* were incidental to the mutiny, which was justified. The defense laid stress on factors that exacerbated the fear of the Africans on the *Amistad,* especially the trauma of the recent Middle Passage. Their not knowing the language of the captors also was key, for it meant that the captives could not grasp the grim humor of those who taunted them.

The defense had still larger points to make. Staples, for example, framed his argument that the

Africans had a claim to "the inherent property of liberty" on the writings of John Locke. Staples referred to inherent or natural rights as superior to the human-made laws that still allowed slavery to exist in the United States. He also held up a challenge to lawmakers: bring their current positive law into line with the Lockean principles so grandly stated in the Declaration of Independence.

Judge Judson's decision was a shock to the powers in Washington. The Africans were set free and were supposed to be returned to Africa. The determination of the circuit court was a vindication of the Africans' right to rebel and to kill their captors, but only under the particular circumstances of this case. It was not a wholesale affirmation of the evils of slavery, which would have been the ideal outcome for abolitionists. Ruíz and Montez got their ship, but it was not enough for the Cubans or the administration. Again with the approval of the U.S. government, the prosecution appealed the civil decision to the U.S. Supreme Court.

VERDICT

Along with a political motivation, there was a tactical reason to take the case further. In terms of diplomacy the federal authorities wished to signal to Spain that the United States valued Spain as an ally. The U.S. government expected a sympathetic hearing from the Supreme Court, owing to the presence of a majority of justices on the Court who were either slaveholders themselves or from pro-slavery states.

The major addition to the defense when it appeared before the high court within the U.S. Capitol was not an argument but rather an individual. Tappan had convinced former U.S. president John Quincy Adams to defend the Africans. It was a personal as well as a political watershed. Adams had kept himself somewhat distant from abolitionism prior to that point, but his conscience no longer would let him appear neutral. His arguments to the Court encompassed the autobiographical (including reflections on his father's career and his own appearances before the Supreme Court as a young man), the moral, and the partisan. He remarked with particular acidity on Van Buren's actions in the case; they boded ill for the civil liberties of American citizens, he said. He also had harsh words for the prosecution's effort to read into the treaty banning slavery certain exceptions. Adams reminded the Court that he knew the treaty well, having been U.S. secretary of state when it was negotiated.

Baldwin confined himself to a less expansive plea similar to what had worked in New Haven, although he did criticize the government's stance as being contrary to its treaty obligations:

> If the government of the United States could appear in any case as the representative of foreigners claiming property in the Court of Admiralty, it has no right to appear in their behalf to aid them in the recovery of fugitive slaves, even when domiciled in the country from which they escaped: much less the recent victims of the African slave trade, who have sought an asylum in one of the free states of the Union. . . .
>
> The American people have never imposed it as a duty on the government of the United States, to become actors in an attempt to reduce to slavery, men found in a state of freedom, by giving extra-territorial force to a foreign slave law. Such a duty would not only be repugnant to the feelings of a large portion of the citizens of the United States, but it would be wholly inconsistent with the fundamental principles of our government, and the purposes for which it was established, as well as with its policy in prohibiting the slave trade and giving freedom to its victims.

The Supreme Court decision in *U.S. v the Libellants and Claimants of the Schooner* Amistad, like the Connecticut ruling that it examined on appeal, was restrained. Justice Joseph Story composed the majority opinion. Legal historians describe Story's writing in this instance as balm for troubled waters on the high court and in general in U.S. society. Story was personally opposed to slavery, but he must have thought it best to soften that opposition for the purposes of reaching an agreement with his proslavery judicial colleagues. (The waters were stirred up again, however, in another Supreme Court decision in 1857, this time enunciated by Chief Justice Roger Taney for the *Dred Scott v. Sandford* case.)

In their decision, the Supreme Court justices did affirm the earlier judgment freeing the African mutineers, but they also underlined that this was an unusual scenario that was unlikely to be replicated. These black African men had the right to kill their captors. The decision certainly did not mean that slavery was banned in the United States, among several reasons because the mutiny had occurred outside U.S. waters.

SIGNIFICANCE

As in the Somerset case, the acquittal of the *Amistad* mutineers was more of a symbolic than a legal victory. The ruling of the Supreme Court in 1840 in *U.S. v. Cinque* was narrowly worded, just as Lord Mansfield had taken care to phrase his holding to apply closely to the case at hand in 1772. In a response similar to that of the British abolitionists of the 1770s, New World antislavery forces took immediate moral inspiration from the courts' decisions in 1839 and 1840.

Cinque and his colleagues got their individual freedom from the famous decision. It took several months to raise the funds to ship them back to Sierra Leone, but Tappan and the abolitionists managed it. The Americans presumed that Cinque and the returning Africans would be educated within the colony of free black Africans, largely run by missionaries. Early reports on that effort were not encouraging.

The Africans then slipped back into obscurity, just as James Somerset had disappeared from public view. It was not that the subjects of each case were mere tools of the abolitionists. There is much to indicate genuine friendship between the blacks and their white legal supporters both in the early 1840s and the 1770s. Rather Cinque and his fellow Africans, like Somerset, probably preferred the anonymity that might protect them from reprisals.

Perhaps because they grasped the temporizing nature of the Supreme Court's *Amistad* decision, the abolitionists soon realized that they might not defeat slavery in the courts. Rather, like the British abolitionists, they were going to need to put their trust in "positive law." But, would Congress or another elected authority have the courage to abolish slavery as Parliament had done? For another generation after the *Amistad* case, the answer was no.

Further Reading

Cable, Mary. *Black Odyssey: The Case of the Slave Ship* Amistad. New York: Penguin Books, 1977; Friedman, Lawrence. *Gregarious Saints: Self and Community in American Abolitionism, 1830–1870.* Cambridge: Cambridge University Press, 1982; Jones, Howard. *Mutiny on the* Amistad. New York: Oxford University Press, 1987; Osagie, Iyunolu Folayan. *The* Amistad *Revolt: Memory, Slavery, and the Politics of Identity in the United States and Sierra Leone.* Athens: University of Georgia Press, 2003; Rediker, Marcus. *The Slave Ship: A Human History.* New York: Penguin, 2008. Spielburg, Steven (dir.), *Amistad.* Dreamworks Productions, 1997; *The United States, Appellants, v. the Libellants and Claimants of the Schooner* Amistad, *Her Tackle, Apparel, and Furniture, Together with Her Cargo, and the Africans Mentioned and Described in the Several Libels and Claims, Appellees.* 40 U.S. 518 (1841). Available online. URL: http://www.archives.gov/education/lessons/amistad/supreme-court-opinion.html. Accessed September 25, 2009; Young, Kevin. *Ardency: A Chronicle of the* Amistad *Rebels.* New York: Knopf, 2011.

The trial of Marie Lafarge

Also known as: The Lafarge Affair

Date: 1840

KEY ISSUES

Poison detectives were the most famous expert witnesses in French courts in the mid-19th century. Those who studied the effects of toxic substances in the human body offered science as a solution to the "hidden" crime of poisoning. Along with academics such as chemists and medical specialists such as anatomists, the public was fascinated with the new technologies for assessing the amount of poison in a corpse. Poison detection represented the advancement of knowledge in the service of solving murders, just as to late 20th-century court watchers DNA evidence promised a higher degree of certainty in difficult cases.

Poisoning was an interesting crime not only because it was hard to detect but also because of who seemed to be committing it. Some argued that murder by poisoning was characteristically "female." The administration of poison could be accomplished through control of domestic items such as food and drink. It often worked subtly and slowly—ideal for the supposedly patient and calculating female temperament. Even when poison acted quickly, it easily could be passed off as an illness, for women often nursed the sick at home.

HISTORY OF THE CASE

Marie Fortunée Cappell was from a "respectable" background. Like many women of her day, she was considerably constrained by her gender. Having lost both of her parents, Marie found that her marriage prospects were in the hands of an uncle. In 1838 Cappell's guardian located a prospective mate who was the master of an iron forge. Marie soon discovered that the man had misrepresented himself as wealthy when in fact his home and finances were in poor condition. She married him anyway, but the young bride balked at sexual intimacy until Charles Lafarge cleaned up the premises and his prospects. At one point in those personal negotiations, Marie Lafarge also threatened to take arsenic to put an end to her misery. Charles Lafarge began to make improvements, but not before family and domestic workers were alerted to the tension between the young couple.

In January 1840 Charles Lefarge began having intestinal distress and severe nausea while away in Paris. He said that he thought that a cake Marie had sent to him had spoiled. Upon his return Marie nursed him with foods such as truffles, venison, and eggnog that were supposed to bring him strength. A member of the household, Anna Brun, observed Marie stirring a white powder from a malachite box of hers into Charles's liquid refreshments. Marie identified it as "orange blossom sugar" and said it always helped her. Two physicians, Dr. Bardon and Dr. Massenet, thought that Charles Lafarge had cholera, a disease that raged in urban areas in that era.

Brun told Lafarge family members of her suspicions about Marie, and on January 13 the Lafarges confronted Marie. She told of buying rat poison; the creatures were scurrying around the decrepit house and disturbing Charles's sleep. But, within a matter of hours, someone noticed a white powder at the bottom of a glass of sugared water that Marie had given to the ill man. By that time a third physician, Dr. René Lespinasse, had been called in. He suspected poisoning.

When Charles Lafarge died later on the day of January 13, the family summoned assistance from a justice of the peace in their town of Brive. That legal official, Monsieur Moran, took away several food and liquid items from the scene that were left over from being given to Charles by Marie. He examined the house and found that the substance that the gardener identified as rat poison had been placed on the premises; the rats had ignored the bait. Moran requested that the physicians who had seen Lafarge perform tests on his body for the presence of arsenic.

One particular test, developed by Englishman James Marsh, had been used only since 1836, so Lespinasse and his colleagues were not trained in its use. Instead, the doctors used older methods of testing. They reported to Moran that they had found large amounts of arsenic in Charles Lafarge's tissues. At about the same time other tests showed that the ostensible arsenic left out for the rats was a harmless paste made from flour. Moran committed Marie Lafarge for trial on the theory that she purchased arsenic but used it on her husband instead of the rodents. The accusation gained further credence when Dr. Lespinasse gained access to Marie's malachite box through one of her friends; it held arsenic.

SUMMARY OF ARGUMENTS

While Madame Lafarge awaited trial for murder she became the subject of public comment on another score. Before her marriage she had stayed at the home of Vicomtesse de Léautaud, who was the mother of a friend from school. Some jewels had gone missing during the visit. The *sûreté* (local police) thought Marie responsible, but the hostess' husband had refused to pursue the matter further because it seemed impolite to suspect the attractive

friend of their daughter. Now the wealthy family reconsidered and asked the police to search the Lafarge household. Sure enough, the missing valuables were found at the old converted monastery in Le Glandier, the run-down building that had been Marie and Charles's home.

Marie had a complex and, to some observers, credible explanation: She said she had agreed to fence the jewels for her friend, who was involved with a disreputable lover and needed to buy him off. Lafarge straightaway was tried for theft, however. She earned a two-year sentence even before facing the more serious charge of causing the death of her husband.

Due to the high profile of the *vicomtesse*, Marie Lafarge now was getting a great deal of attention from the French press. It was a time in which sensational journalism was burgeoning, reaching an ever more literate public in western Europe and North America. In the United States, "yellow journalists" such as James Gordon Bennett at the *New York Herald* were discovering that stories involving attractive young women—whether as suspects, crime victims, or wronged spouses—sold newspapers. In France, prints of the delicate-looking Marie Lafarge became a hot commodity.

The court at Tulle that heard Marie Lafarge's trial for murder was packed with spectators. That the case attracted attention from all levels of society was obvious in the attire of the "audience"; many seemed to be dressed as though for the opera. The proceedings opened on September 3, 1840. Then, as in more modern cases, observers watched the deportment of the defendant closely. Surely a guilty woman would betray her sinister nature in some way. Early reports of Marie Lafarge in the courtroom, though, were sympathetic. She appeared to need smelling salts, and she dressed modestly in widow's garb.

The accused had a team of appointed lawyers. The lead *avocat*, Charles Lachaud, was a young man who was joined by Masters Théodore Bac, Paillet, and Desmont. Paillet had as one of his clients the best-known toxicologist in France, Mathieu Orfila. Armed with a statement from Orfila that cast aspersions on the competence of Charles Lafarge's physicians to perform the Marsh test, Paillet asked the court to run the test again with Orfila in charge.

The judges agreed to retest for arsenic in Lafarge's body but said that calling in Orfila was unnecessary. The judges summoned three local men, an apothecary and his son, named Dubois, and Monsieur Dupuytren, a chemist from Limoges. The experts reported that they had detected no arsenic in the body of the deceased. The trial became a series of questions and counter-questions on the methods that these most recent experts had used to administer the Marsh test versus those employed by the Lafarge family physicians.

The prosecution asked for the food items that the local magistrate Moran had taken from the household to be evaluated for arsenic. The poison turned up and in far more than trace amounts. The eggnog was especially toxic. Finally, the judges agreed to a motion from the prosecution to bring in Orfila himself.

It was a fascinating turn of events, for Orfila's participation originally had been requested by the defense. But now, prosecutors were convinced that Orfila's expertise would show that Charles Lafarge's body contained arsenic—only diffused throughout tissues beyond the sites that the family doctors had examined just after his death. Prosecutors also posited that the chemists from Tulle and Limoges did not know how to detect arsenic in small amounts. Furthermore, they had confidence that Orfila could tell the difference between arsenic in a body that had been the result of poisoning and arsenic that had leeched into a corpse from surrounding soil. Finally, they knew that Orfila could explain his methods in court.

Orfila proved their judgment correct. He was a master of presenting evidence. He answered concerns about his personal bias (presumably toward the defense) by asking the most recent set of chemists to stand by and watch him perform the Marsh test. He even used the materials that they had employed earlier. To the embarrassment of those experts Orfila reached a different result: There was arsenic in Charles Lafarge's body that indicated poisoning. In combination with the presence of arsenic in the recently tested food samples, the court could draw but one conclusion.

Verdict

The defense, shocked, tried to summon a person who might refute Orfila's report, François-Vincent Raspail. An important and early proponent of cell theory, Raspail already clashed with Orfila on several occasions in court concerning the way to conduct the Marsh test. There was a general professional jealousy between the two men, as well. Marie Lafarge sent Raspail a note pleading for his help; it reinforced her image as a wronged woman:

> In my trouble I call both your science and your head to my aid. The experiments of chemists had given me back much of the reputation torn from me in the last eight months. But now M. Orfila has come and I have fallen back into the abyss. I now put my hope in you, Monsieur. Lend the aid of your science to this poor maligned innocent. Now that everyone is abandoning me, come and save me.

Raspail took up the opportunity to confront Orfila again. When he got to court, though, the verdict already had been pronounced. Marie Lafarge was guilty. The president of the assize court sentenced her to life in prison with hard labor, which soon was commuted to life without hard labor. She gained compassionate release in 1852 due to her tuberculosis. Marie Lefarge died within a few months of getting out of prison.

Significance

Along with the Dreyfus Affair of the 1890s, Lafarge's case was one of the most polarizing trials in 19th-century France. Those who were officially a part of it referred to the trial often in later life, usually with some regret. Raspail did not miss an opportunity to impugn Orfila's pronouncement of a definitive toxicological result. Lachaud went on to other cases, where he found greater success as a defense lawyer.

The partisans of the defendant such as novelist George Sand insisted that Marie Lafarge was a loving wife who had been wrongly accused by Charles Lafarge's coarse family. Lafarge's memoirs make for a less literary but more poignant self-defense along the same lines. Even those who watched the trial and did not take sides took notes. Writers such as Gustave Flaubert in *Madame Bovary* included arsenic poisonings prominently within their plots.

Medical and pharmaceutical personnel saw the controversy over the Lafarge evidence as an opportunity to enhance their professional standing and to eliminate irregular practitioners. Perhaps it was better to prevent such occurrences than to resort to poison detectives once harm had occurred. In England, where citizens followed the Lafarge case avidly, Parliament considered limiting the purchase of arsenic to males and then solely in drug stores. The Arsenic Act of 1851 placed only one control on arsenic sales; it required purchasers to sign a register. That legislation was testimony to the insecurity that the public felt after episodes such as the Lafarge trial. Expert testimony might sway a jury, but it was no guarantee of longer-term certainty about a case.

Further Reading

Burney, Ian. *Poison, Detection, and the Victorian Imagination.* Manchester, U.K.: Manchester University Press, 2007; Chenal, Pierre (dir.), *L'Affaire Lafarge.* Trianon Films, 1938; Cullen, William R. *Is Arsenic an Aphrodesiac? The Sociochemistry of an Element.* Cambridge, U.K.: Royal Society of Chemistry, 2008; Downing, Lisa. "Murder in the Feminine: Marie Lafarge and the Sexualization of the Nineteenth-Century Criminal Woman." *Journal of the History of Sexuality* 18 (January 2009): 121–137; Hartman, Mary S. *Victorian Murderesses: A True History of Thirteen Respectable French and English Women Accused of Unspeakable Crimes.* New York: Schocken Books, 1977.

The trial of Daniel M'Naghten

Also known as: *The Queen v. M'Naghten*

Date: 1843

KEY ISSUES

English terminology for persons with mental illness changed greatly in the 18th and 19th centuries. In the early 1700s individuals with mental problems might be called "lunatics," and their condition, ascribed to the phases of the Moon. Within a century such men and women were accorded more dignity among medical specialists. In court as well, in the 1800s accused persons had a much better chance of being allowed to "plead insanity," that is, to argue that they had a disease of the mind that exempted them from the full rigors of the law. By the middle of the 1800s defendants with mental conditions no longer were said to be "mad." Nor were they warehoused in appalling lockups such as the old Bethlehem Hospital in London. Rather, upon being found "not guilty by reason of insanity" they were said to be ill and were treated, not in "madhouses," but "asylums." The mentally ill could stay in places where they might find refuge and recovery instead of being exhibited as curiosities for tourists.

Courts did declare defendants incompetent to stand trial prior to the mid-18th century in England, and a few accused persons even were judged "not guilty by reason of insanity" in trials. Such findings were fairly rare, though, and tended to apply to only certain types of individuals; that is, one generally had to fit a certain stereotype to be insane according to the law in England. He or she had to exhibit obvious symptoms on a lifelong basis and had to be in the terminology of the time *furious,* or in more modern parlance *maniacal* or *frantic.* One's mental disability had to be quite serious and sustained. The lawyers called one famous test of insanity "the wild beast test"; if a defendant had no more reason than a rabid animal, then he or she could qualify in court as insane. Insanity according to the law was permanent and obviously incapacitating. It caused an individual to be incapable of ever distinguishing right from wrong.

There were a few exceptions to such a narrow legal view of insanity prior to about 1800, such as persons who through illness (a high fever) or injury (a skull fracture) suddenly began to act insane. Outside the courts, physicians and others such as those acting from religious principles argued for more humane treatment of the mentally ill and a relaxation of the legal standards. But legal exemptions to the strict application of England's insanity law were rare.

With change in medical prognoses for the mentally ill in the late 18th century, transitions to different types of care facilities, and an improvement in the reputation of medical persons who specialized in diseases of the mind, the legal picture changed. In the early 1800s physicians who used to be called "mad-doctors" embarked on a campaign to change lawmakers' and the public's perception of their profession. They founded groups such as the Association of Medical Officers of Asylums and Hospitals for the Insane in England and the Association of Medical Superintendents of American Institutions for the Insane, which became effective lobbying organizations. They also strove to make names for themselves in a judicial setting in Great Britain and the United States, volunteering to serve as expert witnesses.

Judicial authorities in early 19th-century Britain were receptive to new ideas about mental illness. It was a time when legal reform was in fashion. From abolition of the more gruesome forms of capital punishment to the banning of slavery and the reorganization of certain courts, progressive voices seemed to prevail. In particular, British courts accepted arguments from the new profession of psychiatry that persons could suffer from insanity without being wholly given over to it; insanity could be temporary or "partial." Medical experts on mental illness had new opportunities to observe their patients within facilities that emphasized familial settings and the absence of physical restraints. These physicians had seen improvements among patients over time, and they had observed gradations of disease among the mentally ill.

An early case indicating willingness to entertain such relaxation in the judicial rules on insanity involved a British soldier from the Napoleonic Wars. James Hadfield had tried to assassinate George III. Hadfield's lawyer defended his client by noting Hadfield had sustained a head wound from combat for which he was released from military duty. That honorable discharge was a powerful indication of the severity of the injury, for not many soldiers were formally permitted to leave the battlefield during the fight against France. At the time of his trial Hadfield could speak rationally on occasion, but his actions clearly had begun to be erratic after his injury. The judge instructed the jurors to find Hadfield not guilty by reason of insanity because Hadfield's criminal conduct, though of recent vintage, obviously was of physical origin.

Judges' willingness to hear medical arguments, however, only went so far. By the 1840s some jurists argued that medical experts were on thin ice with their notion of "partial insanity." The public had another objection to findings of not guilty by reason of insanity. When defendants who succeeded in pleading insanity were sent to psychiatric facilities rather than prison, there was a contrast between their treatment and the incarceration that other accused persons suffered in jails. Never mind that, as modern historical scholars have pointed out, mental institutions were not luxurious but merely less objectionable than they had been. Never mind, also, that jails were improving somewhat due to the reforming efforts of the same groups such as the Quakers who had insisted on changes in mental institutions. The perception remained that criminals sent to asylums had an easier go of it than those consigned to jails.

HISTORY OF THE CASE

On January 20, 1843, in London, Daniel M'Naghten shot a man who he thought was Prime Minister Robert Peel. The victim, who in fact was Peel's secretary, died on April 25. Peel was unhurt. M'Naghten was accused of murdering the secretary, Edward Drummond, in the assassination attempt. M'Naghten singled out Peel for his anger because he believed that he was being persecuted by the police. Peel was the founder of a modern police force in London. M'Naghten, a Scottish woodworker, recently had perceived the British government, in general, and the new police force, in particular, as singling him out for persecution. His ideas showed a bit of paranoia, perhaps, but M'Naghten had delusions not wholly untenable in an age when the government informer was a standard tool for gaining information about sedition and the London "bobby" was still an innovation.

SUMMARY OF ARGUMENTS

M'Naghten faced the prosecution beginning on Friday, March 3, 1843, at London's Central Criminal Court, the Old Bailey. The case clearly was of the highest level of importance to the government and the public. Prince Consort Albert appeared among spectators, and the prosecution was headed by Solicitor General Sir William Webb Follett. Three judges sat on the bench: Justices Edward Williams and John Coleridge, and, presiding, the Lord Chief Justice of the Court of Common Pleas, Sir Nicholas Tindal.

The prosecution turned the attention of the court to well-known definitions of insanity as enunciated most famously by Sir Matthew Hale in the late 1600s. Those definitions emphasized the capacity of the defendant to know right from wrong and implied that accused persons who responded normally to matters of everyday existence could not be legally insane. Prosecutors then extracted testimony from several witnesses about M'Naghten's ability to recall details such as railway timetables and the names of ships. The defense countered with witnesses from Glasgow—both M'Naghten's fellow mechanics and civic and police authorities—who testified to the prisoner's previous industriousness and efforts at self-education and then increasingly erratic behavior during 1842.

The court heard testimony from major figures among the English medical community who for years had been recognized as experts in mental illness, such as Dr. Edward Monroe and Harley Street physician Sir Alexander Morrison. Both had interviewed M'Naghten for several hours at the behest of the defense. A few other witnesses, such as the physician to the main asylum in Glasgow, questioned M'Naghten less extensively but still had examined him in person. The judges also allowed the admission of testimony—written and oral—from psychiatrists who had not laid eyes on M'Naghten but only read about him or spoken to those who had seen him. A least one witness who argued for M'Naghten's insanity, Dr. Forbes Winslow, admitted that he simply had reached that conclusion while listening to the proceedings at trial.

A major contention among the medical experts who argued for M'Naghten's acquittal was that a person might slip in and out of sanity. He or she might be able to distinguish right from wrong at one point in life, lose that ability, and then recoup it. Their focus was on the moment when the alleged criminal act occurred. This was in contrast to an earlier view that the inability to tell right from wrong must have been permanent or, alternatively, must have been caused by an identifiable physical injury or illness. The medical testimony centered on the defendant's inability to control himself, yet admitted that "a man might go on for years quietly."

The court report on M'Naghten's case highlights that medical testimony. The judges appeared especially impressed by the work of writers on insanity who argued for a modernization of British insanity law. It was the well-known contention of American physician Isaac Ray, for example, that an offender might be "partially" insane. M'Naghten's lawyer, Alexander Cockburn, emphasized just that to the court.

VERDICT

Chief Justice Tindal's instructions to the jury, though quite abbreviated in the case report, seemed to point toward a verdict of not guilty by reason of insanity. The jury complied; M'Naghten went not to the gallows but to Bethlem Hospital and eventually to Broadmoor Asylum, where he died of natural causes in 1865. Parliament and the queen wanted to hear why such an offender was not termed guilty. The influential testimony of psychiatrists in particular had stirred up controversy. Even before Drummond had expired, members of Parliament had discussed the state of insanity law. Immediately upon hearing the verdict, that discussion became a demand: The most august members of Britain's judiciary would please explain how such a verdict could occur. The judicially qualified members of the House of Lords conferred to draw up answers to the questions put by the legislature and, by extension, their constituents.

Parliament was asking the "law lords" to backtrack on recent judicial rulings that had allowed medical experts greater sway in insanity cases; a few defendants had escaped the noose by successfully using devices such as partial insanity. The lords issued a multipart statement on where the law presently stood. In effect, they wrote a retraction of some of their own recent rulings on insanity and a repudiation of much of what had gone on at M'Naghten's trial. Their statement henceforth was called the "M'Naghten Rules," but ironically so, because if they had been enunciated before Daniel M'Naghten's indictment, he would have hanged.

The M'Naghten Rules specified that a defendant should be classified as legally insane if she or he did not know what he or she was doing or did not recognize the wrong quality of the act. This point represented no change in the law, for if a person was "deprived of reason" completely, he or she might have fitted under the wild beast test, and if he or she did not realize that what he or she was doing was wrong, the defendant would have been judged insane under the right-wrong test. The innovative portion of the M'Naghten Rules lay in their insistence that to qualify as insane a defendant was required to have "a disease of the mind" during the time that the alleged act was committed. In one respect, the rules supported the role that medical experts had been playing: Who better than physicians to determine what constituted a disease of the mind? Yet, in another way the M'Naghten Rules were a way of putting medical experts on notice; the disease of the mind needed to be widely agreed upon among the medical community for courts to recognize that it existed.

The rules, then, renounced the verdict in the M'Naghten case. Although leaving some room for interpretation by judges, juries, and medical witnesses, the M'Naghten Rules became widely adopted in principle in Britain, the United States, and other jurisdictions influenced by English law. By the late 19th century most U.S. state courts used a variation of the M'Naghten Rules as their basis for insanity law. The chief exception was New Hampshire, which adopted a rather different emphasis based on the writings of its native son Isaac Ray. In New Hampshire, courts left the question of insanity to jurors rather than medical experts or even judges. Furthermore, the New Hampshire Rule presumed that jurors would make their decisions about a defendant's sanity based on commonplace examples of the defendant's behavior rather than extensive medical testimony.

SIGNIFICANCE

The M'Naghten Rules proved popular with the public and many English and U.S. judges for well over a century. In the 20th century medical experts, especially psychiatrists, increasingly

argued that the standards were out of date, but those calls for change usually did not prevail. The electorate was angry when "the insanity dodge" seemed to keep a well-known offender out of jail. Accused assassins who availed themselves of the insanity defense came in for particular public ire, such as in the cases of President James Garfield's assassin, Charles Guiteau, and President Ronald Reagan's attempted assassin, John Hinckley, Jr. The vast majority of defendants did not attempt the insanity defense, even in capital cases. Despite the fact that most defendants who pleaded insanity were unsuccessful, it was the few well-known cases where they were that influenced public opinion and drove changes in the law.

Further Reading

Daniel M'Naghten's Case. All ER Rep 229 [1843–60]. Available online. URL: http://libproxy.uta.edu:2156/hottopics/inacademic/?. Accessed August 1, 2009; Diamond, B. L. "Isaac Ray and the Trial of Daniel M'Naghten." *American Journal of Psychiatry* 112 (February 1956): 651–656; Moran, Richard. *Knowing Right from Wrong: The Insanity Defense of Daniel McNaughtan.* New York: Free Press, 1981; West. D. J., and A. Walk, eds. *Daniel McNaughton: His Trial and the Aftermath,* Ashford, U.K.: Headley Bros., 1977.

The trial of Bahadur Shah Zafar II

Also known as: *The Queen v. Bahadur Shah*

Date: 1858

KEY ISSUES

Indians rose up against foreign rule several times during British occupation, but no rebellion was more threatening to the imperialists than the revolt of 1857. The roots of that episode, which the British called the Sepoy Mutiny, are well known among scholars. The deep-seated causes were political and economic. Britain had established a presence on the subcontinent in the 1700s in order to support the nation's foreign trade. The British East India Company operated in India at first only at the sufferance of local and regional Indian leaders. As the company's profits grew, so did its ability to play one local ruler off against another. By the middle of the 1800s there was no Indian authority that could challenge the British for suzerainty in a practical sense, although Indians still offered de jure allegiance to several once-powerful rulers.

The uprising flared in 1857 specifically over another set of long-term issues. There was grave misunderstanding between Europeans and Indians over matters of religion and custom. In certain campaigns of the 1850s British military leaders managed to insult the religious beliefs of both Hindu and Muslim soldiers who served the British Empire. Famously, the British required Indian soldiers to grease their bullets in beef and pork fat, an offense to both the Hindu and Muslim faithful. Whether that really was the impetus for revolt on the part of every mutineer, the rumor of such British insensitivity rang true among Indians. And this much was clear about the mutiny: A shared resentment of the British united even the most religiously divided elements among the indigenous population.

The insurrection saw atrocities on all sides. Local leaders at Cawnpore, for example, sanctioned the slaughter of noncombatants to whom they had initially granted shelter. In retaliation, British troops forced those killers to lick the blood-soaked walls of the house where dozens of Anglo women and children had died and tied Indian soldiers to the fronts of live cannons. After months of violence the British quelled the mutiny in a military sense, but the rulers of the empire still had a point to make: In the political sphere they were no longer mere traders, asking for permission via the East India Company to control India. They now aimed to govern outright. The plan was for India to become part of the British Empire. All that really stood in the way of that ambition was the existence of the old forms of Indian government and the few high-profile Indian leaders who had not been killed during the Sepoy Mutiny. Chief among those remaining figureheads was the Muslim ruler in Delhi, Bahadur Shah Zafar II, often simply called by his title, the Mughal.

HISTORY OF THE CASE

Bahadur Shah was an unusual Mughal in several respects. First of all, he was elderly—in his early 80s—which led some among the British to question whether he really exercised much power at all or, rather, delegated responsibilities to powerful nobles and family members. Unquestionably, there was dissension from the Mughal's views at the Red Fort in Delhi, his headquarters. While ordinarily this would simply be a matter of palace politics, such a split within the court of the Mughal was decisive amid the chaos in Delhi during the 1857 rebellion. Among those within the royal household who favored the rebels and supported reprisals against Europeans were Bahadur Shah's favorite wife, Zinat Mahal; his personal assistant, Basant Ali Khan; and one of his sons, Prince Mirza Mughal. Arrayed against those influential individuals were the Mughal's physician, Hakim Ahsanullah Khan, and an in-law, Mirza Ilahi Baksh. During the Sepoy Mutiny the Mughal's inability to force his own moderate views on those close to him meant that those who disagreed with him prevailed. When the British finally subdued the Mughal court in September 1857, after Delhi had been in rebel hands nearly half a year, it must have been obvious to the victors that the Mughal was a prisoner in his own court.

Secondly, the Mughal was unusual in personality. He was not inclined to politics as much as to poetry and religion. The ruler was known by a combination of his family name and his nom de plume (Zafar). Before Bahadur Shah took the throne he dressed simply in the manner of a cleric or teacher. He was respected for his piety and religious scholarship. He was a devout Sufi, an adherent to a branch of Islam that places emphasis on the most spiritual or inner explorations of faith. Zafar took on pupils and was called a dervish in recognition of his focus on poverty and self-denial. Such persons in medieval western Europe often had served as mendicant (begging) friars, like those whom John Wycliffe supported. They, like Zafar, were considered holy persons who humbled themselves in order to seek spiritual truth.

Another unexpected characteristic of the Mughal was his deep commitment to soothing religious tension. Despite a lifelong study of his own faith, Bahadur Shah showed great respect for Hindu beliefs and ceremonies. He made a point of having his court celebrate Hindu festivals such as Diwali, Dusshera, and Holi. He noted with approval that prominent Hindu holy men honored the memory of deceased Sufi leaders. Within his poetry he noted the common features of Hinduism and Islam. At several points in his reign Zafar interceded with extreme Muslim ideologues. He stated he did so to protect his Hindu subjects.

Bahadur Shah may have been a ruler in name only, yet he was a widely revered person and a symbol of unity among Indians. Thus, the British accorded the Mughal the dignity of surrender terms that guaranteed his own life and the lives of certain family members. At the same time the victors in the Sepoy Mutiny engineered a public trial to strip away the Mughal's remaining prestige. The revolt had appeared to coalesce in Delhi under the authority of the Mughal, and at his home it would meet a legal end.

SUMMARY OF ARGUMENTS

The British admitted within diplomatic correspondence and even in the newspapers that framing a charge of sedition against Bahadur Shah was tricky, for he was a ruler himself. Indeed, the British even had trouble deciding how to refer to the Mughal during the proceedings; they finally came up with the phrase "the titular majesty of Delhi." This uncertainty about what to call Bahadur Shah reflected a larger ambiguity. Though some native rulers were dispersed and others bought off or discredited, a few natural-born rulers in India such as the Peshwa never had formally ceded their authority to the British Crown. The British were working toward such an arrangement at exactly the time that the mutiny occurred. Thus, in the strictest sense the outbreak of violence was not a mutiny, for *mutiny* implied allegiance to a military authority. Nor was the revolt a set of treasonous acts, for that would have meant that Indians owed deference to an imperial government in London.

The court came up with a phrase that sounded as though (but did not outright say that) the Mughal was bound to show loyalty to the monarch of Great Britain: The Mughal was charged with allowing his commander in chief, Muhammad Bakht Khan, to rebel against the British. The first count of the indictment called Bahadur Shah "a pensioner of the British government." The description was technically correct, for the British did pay the Mughal a small sum each year and allow him to keep troops. Still, it gave the wrong legal impression—that Bahadur Shah had officially ceded his political authority to the British. Other counts alleged that the Mughal had allowed the royal princes to participate in the rebellion, had wrongfully styled himself "the sovereign of India," and on May 16, 1857, had allowed the massacre of 49 civilians who had taken shelter in the palace five days earlier.

It fell to Major F. W. Harriott, deputy judge advocate general, to articulate the prosecution of the Mughal. His contentions, as well as the court's makeup and its general hearing of the case, were fully in line with neither English military nor English civilian justice. In form the court looked like a court-martial. Its personnel all were military. The president of the court was Lieutenant-Colonel M. Dawes; four military officers, called "commissioners," assisted him. There was no jury, only the group of hearing officers that resembled a judicial panel. That the court was called a "commission" implied its role was to determine facts, but the inquiry's sole purposes were to decide whether Bahadur Shah had committed the offenses in the indictment and what to do with him. Thus, it functioned as a court rather than a fact-finding body.

The prosecution spent some time trying to establish that the Mughal had held at least nominal authority in Delhi at the time of the rebellion. They asked members of his household such as royal physician Hakim Ahsanullah Khan to verify Bahadur Shah's signature on a number of documents from 1857. What those accusing the Mughal did not emphasize was the content of several of those official letters and proclamations: The documents made it apparent that during the hostilities Bahadur Shah was calling for calm and restraint.

Very few Indian witnesses were called. The court made plain that they, the judges, considered native persons untrustworthy, although the prosecution did summon a few Indians to testify against Bahadur Shah. Interestingly, in at least one instance the commissioners' xenophobia trumped their wish to discredit the Mughal. Former secretary Mukand Lal began to testify against the ruler, but the court upbraided him for his haughty demeanor. When he spoke again, Lal retracted his earlier assertion that Bahadur Shah had ordered prisoners in the palace killed.

Other testimony corroborated the ruler's reluctance to support the mutineers. During one episode while the violence raged, Indian troops stormed into the royal residence, firing their weapons. They announced that they had massacred civilians at Meerut owing to the Indian soldiers' objections about the animal fat used to lubricate bullet cartridges. What they got was not commendation from the Mughal but instead a lecture on deportment and ethics: "I did not call for you; you have acted very wickedly."

Witnesses also reported that the ruler desperately tried to intervene to save the lives of Europeans who had been captured by rebels, such as the British commander of the guard at the royal palace, and Judge Fraser, the district magistrate. Bahadur Shah's efforts were for naught, however, especially after an announcement by Basant Ali Khan from within an official audience courtyard at the palace that the king's personal guard should go round up the Europeans.

The ruler had counsel, Ghulam Abbas, during the proceedings, but that man also was called as a witness for the prosecution. Abbas had been in the company of the Mughal during the rebellion. He testified in some detail about Bahadur Shah's reactions to the news of escalating violence in Delhi and elsewhere. The Mughal himself obviously was weak and ill during the trial. He walked into the courtroom (an audience chamber of his own palace) with assistance, attended by his surviving son. A well-known photograph of Bahadur Shah just after the trial shows him reclining on cushions and looking like a frail elderly man.

In his summation Harriott admitted that it was impossible to reconstruct the ruler's actions and words during the worst of the violence in Delhi in May. Even so, Harriott contended that the Mughal was responsible for atrocities such as the killing of refugees at the palace: "If I have not succeeded in tracing to the King himself a foreknowledge of the leading events that were to take place on Monday, the 11th of May [the date that

Europeans had asked for the Mughal's protection in the palace], I trust it has been made obvious that the secret was in the possession of some influential inmates of the palace." In other words, the prosecution argued that the ruler was not the legitimate leader in Delhi, plus he was not in control of his own household. And yet, Harriott maintained that Bahadur Shah ultimately was responsible for the safety of British people within and outside his residence.

VERDICT

The commissioners did not expand on their reasons for convicting the Mughal on all the counts with which he was charged. They simply stated that he was guilty. They did honor the agreement by Major William Hodson who had negotiated Bahadur Shah's surrender, to spare the ruler's life and that of his wife and one son. Hodson personally had executed two other sons, Mirza Mughal and Mirza Khizr Sultan, and a grandson, Mirza Abu Bakr, of the Mughal. The British officer himself was killed shortly afterward.

The court stated that ordinarily it would consider the death penalty appropriate. Under the circumstances, though, the Mughal and the remainder of his family were sent away permanently to Rangoon (Burma), where they lived in custody until the former ruler's death in 1862. Through the poetry that he wrote while in exile Zafar mourned that he would not be buried in his homeland.

SIGNIFICANCE

Bahadur Shah Zafar did not initiate the uprising of 1857 against the British. Nor did he approve of it, apparently. He was of quite limited political authority in the 20th year of his reign over what was left of the Mughal Empire. The esteem in which he was held by a variety of religious groups, however, made him a focal point for the Indian rebels. The British centered their resentment about the mutiny on Bahadur Shah. To them, Bahadur Shah was a Muslim who united diverse populations in resisting British occupation. In modern India and Pakistan Bahadur Shah has been honored as an early hero in the resistance to British rule.

Further Reading

Chakravarty, Gautam. *The Indian Mutiny and the British Imagination.* Cambridge: Cambridge University Press, 2005; Dalrymple, William. *The Last Mughal.* New York: Knopf, 2007; Eraly, Abraham. *The Mughal Throne: The Saga of India's Great Emperors.* London: Weidenfeld & Nicolson, 2003; Hussein, Syed Madhi. *Bahadur Shah Zafar and the War of 1857.* Delhi, India: Aakar Books, 2006; Nayar, Pramod K. *The Trial of Bahadur Shah Zafar.* Hyderabad, India: Orient Longman, 2007; Noorani, A. G. *Indian Political Trials, 1775–1947.* New York: Oxford University Press, 2006.

The trial of John Brown

Also known as: *Virginia v. Brown*

Date: 1859

KEY ISSUES

The battle over slavery in the United States in the 1850s sometimes was fought in unexpected places. Of course, there was discord in the halls of Congress and near the Mason-Dixon line and in countless locations throughout the South. Violence also permeated the American West, particularly the territory of Kansas and the state of Missouri, even though there were not many slaves in total in those lands.

According to the terms of the Kansas-Nebraska Act of 1854, it would be the choice of Kansas residents whether to enter the Union as a free or a slave state. Missouri slaveholders did not fancy being hemmed in by free states on three sides; Missouri already had borders with the free states of Illinois and Iowa. Contrary to the expectations of some who voted for the compromise that allowed "squatter sovereignty" on the issue of slavery in prospective states such as Kansas, Kansas actually began to attract slave owners in that time period. Kansas had sections near the Missouri border, in

particular, with agricultural potential that could be supported by slavery.

To those U.S. citizens who were slavery activists—either for it or against it—Kansas quickly loomed as a spot for a showdown. If slavery were to become well established there, then the territory likely would become a slave state. If slavery were rejected, then Missouri's slaveholders were in a much worse position; moreover, an antislavery decision among Kansans would establish momentum against additional new slave states on the western frontier.

Into this delicate and dangerous situation, in October 1855, came a most unusual individual. John Brown was an abolitionist determined to sway Kansas toward the side of antislavery. In his mind the conflict in Kansas was a divine cause. He was prepared to use any methods necessary to secure victory. In certain respects Brown was an unlikely leader. He was a poor man, the son of a tanner, and he was getting on in years by the standards of the era. When he arrived in Kansas, he was 55 and looked even older.

Throughout his life Brown had used his meager funds to support antislavery campaigns. He impressed no less than Frederick Douglass, who first met with Brown in 1847, as being "in sympathy a black man, and as deeply interested in our cause, as though his own soul had been pierced with the iron of slavery." Brown, in other words, was not a white man motivated by noblesse oblige or even strictly religious zeal—although Brown did have plenty of that. Rather, Brown expressed a genuine emotional connection with people of color and was willing to die on their behalf.

Brown spearheaded abolitionist agitation in Kansas for about a year, leading several murderous raids and outright battles (such as at Osawatomie) against the proslavers. For example, at Pottawatomie Creek in May 1856, Brown and several of his sons dragged seven of their opponents out of their homes and killed five of them using swords. That raid apparently was in reaction to the famous incident a few days earlier in the U.S. Capitol, when Representative Preston Brooks of South Carolina severely beat Senator Charles Sumner of Massachusetts. Sumner, a leading abolitionist, was highly regarded by antislavery forces. He had been delivering a speech on the escalating violence in Kansas at the moment that Brooks charged toward him with a cane. In the years that it took for Sumner to recover from the attack, he received a stream of admirers, John Brown among them. Sumner, even as deeply committed to the cause as he was, reportedly was taken aback by the intensity of Brown's devotion to abolition.

Kansas proved to be indeed troublesome in regard to not only the violence that occurred there but also how that violence played into the political process. Election outcomes seemed to be greatly affected by voters' fears. Was a proslavery territorial constitution that had been drafted in 1857 valid? Although U.S. president James Buchanan gave an opinion declaring that document suitable as the basis for statehood, the legal situation officially remained in limbo.

Meanwhile, Brown's actions in "Bleeding Kansas" had earned him a reputation for action among abolitionists, which he parlayed into further influence. He decided to travel east, canvassing for funds. Among his financial supporters were the members of "the secret six," eminent abolitionists such as Samuel Gridley Howe who had grown impatient with constitutional and political solutions. Brown's hope appeared to be not so much an armed insurrection but that he could enjoin massive numbers of slaves to join with him. If many enslaved persons left their owners, Brown's theory was that the Southern economy would collapse through want of labor. Though there were holes in Brown's plan, he did have a personal history of effecting freedom for slaves and links with members of the Underground Railroad. Still, scholars debate whether those who bankrolled Brown knew of the details of his plot.

HISTORY OF THE CASE

In July 1859, a man identifying himself as a cattle farmer named Isaac Smith used $35 in gold coins to rent a farmhouse in Maryland on the Potomac River just across from Virginia. (In more modern times the area was at the three-state intersection of Virginia, West Virginia, and Maryland.) "Farmer Smith," who, of course, was Brown, trained 21 men for several months. His aim was to lead a raid on the nearby federal arsenal at Harpers Ferry; he had been planning the attack since at least 1858.

Brown hoped to give arms to slaves who would flock to join the insurrection. He envisioned setting up a free state consisting of persons of color.

For all his groundwork the raid itself was poorly executed. Brown left three men to guard the farmhouse as a base of operations. The rest went with him on the night of October 16, 1859, to the village surrounding the arsenal. His party captured the arsenal, but word got out to nearby towns via a train that had gone through Harpers Ferry (under fire) during the initial strike. Local people besieged the raiders. Brown's attackers got reinforcements in a detachment of marines led by Colonel Robert E. Lee and Lieutenant J. E. B. Stuart. On October 18, the marines overwhelmed Brown and his remaining colleagues, who had suffered heavy casualties already. Two of Brown's sons were among the 10 dead raiders. Those who defended the arsenal against Brown lost four citizens and one military man.

The choice of a site for the prosecution of Brown and four of his surviving coconspirators was loaded with difficulty, for where Brown was tried was sure to have great influence on the outcome of the case. Also at issue was the nature of the charges against them, which helped determine where trial was held. If Brown and the others were charged with trying to seize the federal weapons facility, they each would have to be tried in federal court, the most likely location of which would be Washington, D.C. There, a judicial proceeding would be delayed because of its complexity and the difficulty of transporting the badly injured Brown to the nation's capital. Once Brown and the others arrived in Washington they would have had much better access to legal talent and direct abolitionist support.

Although the cases of each of the other men were different from Brown's in certain legal respects, Virginia authorities were most concerned about what they did with Brown, and where and when. Brown's trial was to them by far the most important proceeding. It would set the tone for the trials of the other men. Also, it was Brown who Virginia expected would attract the most fervent defense efforts and the widest press coverage.

Virginia was keen to try Brown near the scene of the raid for several reasons. Local whites were likely to view Brown as an interloper. Needless to say, there were no African Americans in Virginia jury pools. Virginia officials also wanted to make the point that Brown had offended against Virginia sensibilities and Virginia law. They insisted that the raid at Harpers Ferry was an effort to start a slave revolt. They wished to make clear that inciting such a rebellion among slaves would be punished severely. In addition, Virginia authorities were in great haste to conclude a trial. They rightly feared that any delay would allow Brown's supporters to marshal arguments—both legal and moral—on his behalf.

The gravity of the legal dilemma provoked by Brown's actions was apparent in the decision by three major political figures to interview Brown personally after his capture. Visiting him at Harpers Ferry were the governor of Virginia, Henry Wise, Congressman Clement Vallandigham of Ohio, and Senator James Mason of Virginia. Despite being from a Northern state, Vallandigham was known to be sympathetic to Southern principles. Indeed, during the Civil War he fled Ohio to Canada, himself the target of prosecution for sedition.

Wise's role in the prosecution cannot be overstated. With most other captives the visit of the dignitaries would have amounted to an interrogation session, but in the case of Brown the officials had their hands full. Governor Wise emerged from the meeting fully determined to prosecute Brown, perhaps because Wise also saw in Brown immense vitality: "They are mistaken who take him to be a madman. He is the best bundle of nerves I ever saw—cut and thrust and bleeding in bonds. He is man of clear head, of courage, of simple ingeniousness. He is cool, collected, and indomitable."

SUMMARY OF ARGUMENTS

The state of Virginia prevailed over every effort to relocate the trial or prosecute Brown on federal charges. Trial for Brown and separate proceedings against several of his coraiders were scheduled for Charles Town, Virginia, the nearest settlement with a courtroom. The other defendants were John Cook, John Copeland, Edwin Coppock, and Shields Green. One of the very few escapees among the raiders was Brown's son Owen. "Old Man" Brown had been punctured in the ribs with a saber

or bayonet. His captors allowed him to lie on a cot in court.

Of the three counts lodged against Brown, two were particularly controversial in his own time and afterward. He was charged with committing treason against the state of Virginia, conspiring with persons of color, and first-degree murder. Only the murder charge was free from the taint of legal bias. Brown and his men clearly had shot a railroad porter (ironically, a black man) as well as a marine and three other local people at Harpers Ferry.

During the trial several of Brown's supporters urged him to plead insanity. Such a plea had only a long shot at being accepted in the court at Charles Town but perhaps could have been the basis for launching an appeal to a higher court. A comparative lack of expertise and commitment among Brown's lawyers made them either unlikely or unwilling to try that gambit. Brown himself was absolutely against the insanity plea.

The prosecution relied on evidence that demonstrated Brown had planned the raid for many months. Found on the farm in Maryland where he had trained were documents from a "constitutional convention" some time before in Canada, where Brown helped draft a blueprint for a new state made up of freed slaves. It was that material that bolstered the state's case for conspiracy to incite slave rebellion as well as treason.

The state had an exceptionally good witness against Brown in regard to the engagement at Harpers Ferry—a person whose testimony might even play well beyond the South. Brown had kidnapped none other than Lewis Washington, the great-nephew of George Washington. Washington was held with the raiders as a hostage while they and Brown's men were surrounded, holed up in the arsenal.

The defense lawyers who initially were appointed by the court, all Southerners, did not put their hearts into saving Brown, although they were polite and observant of legal forms. They persisted in apologizing to the court and the jury for doing their duty as counsel to the accused. Brown did not confide in them and said so, although he said that he respected them. Although Massachusetts attorney George Hoyt joined the defense after the trial had been under way several days, he got in on the proceedings too late to reroute the defense strategy. Hoyt had difficulty in catching up on what had gone on at trial already, for the court would not permit a delay in order for him to confer with Brown. By the end of the trial yet another attorney had come to aid Brown: Hiram Griswold of Ohio. But Griswold mostly figured in the closing statement for the defense. That summation was an effective raising of certain points that the defense had not emphasized during the bulk of the trial.

After Brown's trial was all but over, yet while the remaining four defendants waited to be heard in court, enough legal talent had arrived from outside the South to make a considerable difference in the other accused men's chances. But, for Brown such legal assistance was too late. He argued personally to Judge Richard Parker that he should have a postponement to allow late-coming attorneys to familiarize themselves with the case materials, or a longer delay to bring in further lawyers. Parker refused.

Brown's attorneys made several arguments that sounded procedural in nature, but that did have a bearing on the fairness of the trial. For example, the defense asked for a separation of the counts of the indictment, rather than the jury being asked to find the defendant guilty on all charges or none. Brown's lawyers also contended that the actions of local citizens had amplified the violence at the arsenal at a point even before the marines arrived. Those local persons had ignored a flag of truce raised by the raiders and shot at Brown and his men.

The argument mentioned at trial by the defense that carries the most weight among modern legal scholars was that Brown had been acting against a federal facility, and thus, the case should have been heard in federal court. The prosecution's reply was that Brown's victims had fallen not within the arsenal but rather on the soil of Virginia.

A related defense contention was that Brown was not living in Virginia (rather the farmhouse was in Maryland) and therefore did not owe any allegiance to the commonwealth. The prosecution dispensed with that argument on two narrow grounds—that Brown had "resided" in Virginia during the raid and that Virginia soldiers were among his targets. Interestingly, one of the other raiders, blessed as he was with superb legal counsel, was able to get the court to rule that he was not a resident of Virginia; that defendant actually had lived in Virginia for a number of months prior to the raid, whereas Brown's "residence" amounted to hours.

Throughout the trial Brown was a memorable presence. Rarely would he respond to something that was said, for example, becoming angry at the account by a prosecution witness of how raider William Thompson was captured, then shot. That reaction was one of the only occasions when Brown objected to the trial as unfair. Brown also became upset about his counsels' attempt, early on, to have Brown declared unfit for trial on mental grounds based on a claim of hereditary insanity. At that juncture he dismissed two of the court-appointed lawyers. For most of the trial, though, Brown lay on the stretcher, seemingly calm. At certain moments, presumably for greater effect, he would draw a blanket over his face.

VERDICT

In the month between Brown's conviction and the carrying out of his sentence, those trying to save him from the gallows campaigned hard within the press, in legal circles, and to politicians. Among the reasons that supporters voiced for clemency for Brown was how he had conducted himself at trial. In contrast to Brown's reputation for ferocity, he appeared poised and even gracious toward his accusers. In his statement to the court after learning the verdict, Brown accepted the judgment with equanimity:

> Now, if it is deemed necessary that I should forfeit my life for the furtherance of the ends of justice, and mingle my blood further with the blood of my children and with the blood of millions in this slave country whose rights are disregarded by wicked, cruel, and unjust enactments, I submit; so let it be done.

In the interval between judgment and punishment, citizens across the United States and elsewhere were deeply invested in John Brown's fate. French author Victor Hugo, for example, wrote to try to obtain a pardon for Brown. Back in the

United States, Henry David Thoreau composed a poem in honor of Brown, and Ralph Waldo Emerson spoke admiringly of the convicted man, as did John Greenleaf Whittier and William Lloyd Garrison. Several persons tried to intercede with the governor of Virginia on grounds of Brown's mental incapacity, but all of those efforts went nowhere. Brown himself appeared resigned to his fate and discouraged those who sought to rescue him by force.

Brown died at the scaffold on December 2, 1859, by all accounts stoically. His wife, Mary Ann, was allowed to visit him in prison and to accompany the body to its resting place at a family burial ground in New York. Even some of the guards who witnessed the hanging remarked on Brown's extraordinary calm in meeting his fate.

The men who had been captured and tried just after Brown as coconspirators all had their own trials, several of which were marked by sophisticated legal arguments. In the weeks between the outset of Brown's trial and the hearing of the others' cases, even the more obscure defendants got legal assistance of better quality than Brown had had. Some of Brown's Southern lawyers seemed to warm to the task of representing the other men, who they claimed were "misled" by Brown into joining the raid. But, the most effective representation was from outsiders.

Among the clever legal strategies that those newly arrived lawyers attempted to save raiders Green and Copeland was the contention that since those men were persons of color they could not be citizens under Virginia law. This also was according to the recent *Dred Scott* decision by the U.S. Supreme Court. Thus, the defense maintained that Copeland and Green could not be charged with treason against the state of Virginia. Judge Parker granted that point in regard to Green, but not to Copeland, who was of mixed race. It mattered little to the jury; the men were convicted of murder and incitement of slave rebellion—both capital offenses, anyway.

A talented attorney from Indiana, Daniel Voorhees (later a U.S. senator and renowned orator), struggled valiantly both in court and through petitions to Governor Wise to save John Cook. Cook was related by marriage to the governor of Indiana and thus had unusually good access to

assistance. Cook's best chance, as Brown's had been, lay with getting the trial removed to federal court. Wise seriously considered that possibility as an opportunity to broaden the discourse on slavery. For reasons that remain somewhat unclear, though, Wise ultimately left the case in Charles Town. He also refused to grant Cook clemency in spite of Cook's confession. The four coraiders were hanged on December 16, 1859. Two other of Brown's colleagues who were apprehended later followed them in early 1860.

SIGNIFICANCE

Among more ordinary citizens Brown rapidly became larger than life. Many Southerners wished him good riddance. They applauded the trial as an effort by Virginia authorities to avoid mob violence against the raiders. Southern jurists congratulated themselves on the civility that they thought had marked the trials. The few demonstrations of overt hostility to Brown in court were decried as indecorous. Among most Southerners Brown was a terrorist. Although many moderates thought Brown intemperate, misguided, and perhaps unhinged, they also admitted that he had shown admirable character while under threat of hanging. In the North, generally, Brown was celebrated as a person who had perhaps his finest hour while in the courtroom. All his life seemed to be leading up to the statement he made after the verdict was pronounced:

> Had I interfered in the manner which I admit, and which I admit has been fairly proved (for I admire the truthfulness and candor of the greater portion of the witnesses who have testified in this case), had I so interfered in behalf of the rich, the powerful, the intelligent, the so-called great, or in behalf of any of their friends, either father, mother, brother, sister, wife, or children, or any of that class, and suffered and sacrificed what I have in this interference, it would have been all right; and every man in this court would have deemed it an act worthy of reward rather than punishment.
>
> This court acknowledges, as I suppose, the validity of the law of God. I see a book kissed here which I suppose to be the Bible,

or at least the New Testament. That teaches me that all things whatsoever I would that men should do to me, I should do even so to them. It teaches me, further, to "remember them that are in bonds, as bound with them." I endeavored to act up to that instruction. I say, I am yet too young to understand that God is any respecter of persons. I believe that to have interfered as I have done as I have always freely admitted I have done in behalf of His despised poor, was not wrong, but right.

One abolitionist hymn especially resonated with antislavery activist Julia Ward Howe. She penned "Battle Hymn of the Republic" to the tune she heard Union soldiers singing in Washington, D.C.:

> John Brown's body lies a mould'ring in the
>   grave
> John Brown's body lies a mould'ring in the
>   grave
> John Brown's body lies a mould'ring in the
>   grave
> His soul goes marching on.

Whether the John Brown named in that marching song was "Old Osawatomie Brown" or simply a Northern soldier of the same name is an academic question. Many U.S. residents in the 1860s considered the John Brown who was hanged at Harpers Ferry to be a spark to the Civil War. On his way to execution Brown handed a note to one of his supporters. It was a last, prescient warning: "I John Brown am now quite certain that the crimes of this guilty land will never be purged away, but with Blood."

Some contemporaries thought him a madman, others a martyr, but Old Man Brown certainly captured their attention. Brown's trial drove consideration of larger questions. Was the South committed to the rule of law? Did abolitionists have the stomach for the types of guerrilla actions that Brown undertook? Was slave rebellion possible, or, on the other hand, desirable? The most fundamental query of all, of course, was whether slavery was an issue over which the nation was prepared to go to war.

Further Reading

Banks, Russell. *Cloudsplitter.* New York: Harper-Flamingo, 1998; Earle, Jonathan Halperin. *John Brown's Raid on Harpers Ferry: A Brief History with Documents.* New York: Bedford/St. Martin's, 2008; Furnas, Joseph C. *The Road to Harpers Ferry.* New York: W. Sloane Associates, 1959; McGinty, Brian. *John Brown's Trial.* Cambridge, Mass.: Harvard University Press, 2009; Oates, Steven. *To Purge This Land with Blood: A Biography of John Brown.* New York: Harper & Row, 1970; Peterson, Merrill. *John Brown: The Legend Revisited.* Charlottesville: University of Virginia Press, 2004; Rehnquist, William H. *All the Laws but One.* New York: Vintage Books, 1998.

The trials of the Lincoln conspirators

Also known as: *The United States v. Powell, Atzerodt, Herold, O'Laughlin, Spangler, Arnold, Mary Surratt, and Mudd*

Date: 1865

KEY ISSUES

The assassination of President Abraham Lincoln was one of the most traumatic events in United States history. Coming at the end of a catastrophic civil war and masterminded by a Southern sympathizer, the murder of Lincoln threatened to rip apart the president's plans to "bind up the nation's wounds." There were many personal tragedies within the story of the assassination as well as collective sorrow. The First Family was left with a fragile matriarch to have charge of the Lincolns' sons. The chief assassin came from a brilliant family of actors and had been a most promising performer himself.

In the immediate shock of the assassination government officials may have overreacted by charging too many people with helping the conspiracy to kill the president. The trial of the conspirators, therefore, cast a wide shadow over the lives of certain individuals who may not have been involved in the plot at all. There was a lingering perception, too, that the trials were unfair because they were not held in civilian courts. But the most enduring legacy of the Lincoln assassins' trials was the sense that the great villain in the episode had escaped: John Wilkes Booth had cheated the American people of the satisfaction of learning his motives and then exacting revenge.

HISTORY OF THE CASE

On April 14, 1865, the war intelligence was encouraging. General Robert E. Lee had surrendered at Appomattox on April 9, and Confederate forces were expected to lay down their arms shortly in North Carolina. President Lincoln met with his cabinet that morning and talked with General Ulysses S. Grant about an engagement to attend the theater that evening. Grant declined, although Lincoln told him and several others that a laugh would do him good. A police guard was stationed outside the door of the private box where Lincoln and his wife, Mary Todd Lincoln, sat with another couple. Aside from the guard, there was no other armed protection for the president.

While the play *Our American Cousin* was in progress, the guard left his post to get a drink across the street. At 10:13 P.M. the door to the presidential box—closed but not locked—opened. A man stepped in and aimed a derringer at the president's head. He fired one shot, hitting his mark. The other male occupant of the stage box struggled with the shooter and was stabbed. The assassin jumped over the rail of the box onto the stage floor, falling partially into the audience. The 12-foot drop broke his foot, but he managed to shout: *"Sic semper tyrannis"* ("So it is always with tyrants"). The saying was the state motto of Virginia. He jumped onto a waiting horse and rode away. Members of the theater staff instantly recognized the shooter as John Wilkes Booth, a 26-year-old actor and Southern sympathizer, who had been at the theater as recently as that morning.

A physician in the audience at Ford's Theatre attended to Lincoln immediately, seeing that the gravely wounded man was moved to a house across the street. The doctor helped Lincoln's heart beat again but realized that the victim had suffered a critical brain injury. Within an hour the District of Columbia police had entered the crime into their log. Several cabinet officials gathered at the residence where Lincoln lay. One observer noted the contrast between Lincoln's gaunt frame and his powerful arms. Within a few more hours at least six doctors were in attendance. All concurred that Lincoln had only hours to live.

The news got worse. Secretary of State William Seward also had been attacked. Seward was in his own house recuperating from a carriage accident, with two sons present, when a man named Lewis Powell (also known as Lewis Paine, or Payne) talked his way into the residence. He slashed Seward's throat and badly injured one of Seward's sons. At first, Seward seemed fatally wounded, but timely medical intervention saved him from bleeding to death. Lincoln, however, died just after 7:00 A.M. on the morning after the shooting.

A search for the two attackers proceeded under the direction of Secretary of War Edwin Stanton. It soon became apparent that the assaults had been coordinated and that other individuals were involved. George Atzerodt and Michael O'Laughlin, for example, were also principals in the assassination scheme. Atzerodt's mission had been to kill Vice President Andrew Johnson and O'Laughlin was to dispatch Secretary of War Stanton, but neither plotter completed his task.

Early on the morning of April 15, Booth and a companion, David Herold, showed up at the home of a physician in Maryland, Samuel Mudd, asking for help with Booth's injury. Mudd was asleep when Booth arrived; he tended to the foot and made Booth rest on a couch. By the end of the day the conspirators had decamped for Virginia, where they hoped they would be safer. In a few more days they crossed the Rappahannock River with the help of Confederate soldiers.

Powell was arrested on April 17, along with other alleged coconspirators O'Laughlin, Edman Spangler, Samuel Arnold, and Mary Surratt. Mrs. Surratt was the owner of the boarding house where meetings among the men had occurred. While he was on the run, Booth got welcome information: Much of the nation was in mourning for Lincoln.

Early on the morning of April 26, Union troops tracked Booth and Herold to a barn where they were hiding. Herold gave himself up, but Booth held out. He was mortally wounded when the pursuers set the barn on fire and then shot him. He died within a few hours. The government confiscated Booth's diary and talked with many persons who knew him. Authorities were anxious to discover Booth's motives, movements, and coconspirators.

SUMMARY OF ARGUMENTS

The government would make its case against Powell, Atzerodt, Herold, O'Laughlin, Spangler, Arnold, Surratt, and Dr. Mudd. Once the surviving main plotters were in custody, the U.S. government under President Andrew Johnson had an interesting dilemma: how to try them. Certain government officials of high rank, including Secretary of the Navy and former U.S. attorney general Edward Bates contended that the civilian courts ought to handle the matter. A further argument against a military trial was that it later would be seen as a contravention of ordinary (civilian) justice and that its findings, thus, might seem suspect.

In theory, the nation still was at war; portions of the rebel army had not formally surrendered and, indeed, would not do so until early summer 1865. Secretary of War Stanton, a hard-liner with regard to the treatment of the Southern rebels, argued in emergency cabinet meetings for a trial before a military commission. Attorney General James Speed, later a Radical Republican, also made a fervent case for a military trial in a memorandum to the new president. Though his argument amounted to the contention that a state of war still existed, Speed addressed concerns that a military court would be retributive in nature and that military justice in this case would be contrary to the U.S. Constitution's guarantees of a fair trial:

> The laws and usages of war contemplate that soldiers have a high sense of personal honor. The true soldier is proud to feel and know that his enemy possesses personal honor, and will conform and be obedient to the laws of war. In a spirit of justice, and with a wise appreciation of such feelings, the laws of war protect the character and honor of an open enemy. When by the fortunes of war one enemy is thrown into the hands and power of another, and is charged with dishonorable conduct and a breach of the laws of war, he must be tried according to the usages of war. Justice and fairness say that an open enemy to whom dishonorable conduct is imputed, has a right to demand a trial. If such a demand can be rightfully made, surely it can not be rightfully refused. It is to be hoped that the military authorities of this country will never refuse such a demand, because there is no act of Congress that authorizes it. In time of war the law and usage of war authorize it, and they are a part of the law of the land.

> That portion of the Constitution which declares that "no person shall be deprived of his life, liberty or property without due process of law," has such direct reference to, and connection with, trials for crime or criminal prosecutions, that comment upon it would seem to be unnecessary. Trials for offenses against the laws of war are not embraced or intended to be embraced in those provisions. If this is not so, then every man that kills another in battle is a murderer, for he deprived a "person of life without that due process of law" contemplated by this provision; every man that holds another as a prisoner of war is liable for false imprisonment, as he does so without that same due process.

Speed and others highly placed in the federal government had practical reasons for desiring a military court. Such a proceeding would get under way more quickly. Military trials also tended to be more rapid once they began due to the lack of certain procedural guarantees that characterized civilian justice. Those pressing for a military trial won out. President Johnson authorized a trial by military commission on May 1, 1865. The judge advocate general of the army, Joseph Holt, was to be lead prosecutor. Holt, like most of the government officials associated with the case, had a record of opposition to black slavery.

Eleven men served as judges for the commission. The court sometimes was called the Hunter Commission, recognizing its ranking member, Major General David Hunter of the U.S. Volunteers. The court consisted of eight generals, a colonel, a lieutenant colonel, and two specially appointed judge advocates (one not an officer), chosen by Holt. Thus, in the personnel of the commission one sees immediately a contrast with civilian justice in the 19th-century United States: The prosecutor had a hand in selecting two judges who would hear his case.

All eight of the main plotters were accused of conspiracy to commit murder and treason. The government considered charging several others who had heard discussions at the Surratt house but instead allowed certain of those witnesses to turn state's evidence, especially regarding Mrs. Surratt's role. Mudd and Surratt were charged with harboring, concealing, and aiding conspirators, which legally made them part of the conspiracy itself. Prosecutors related that Surratt had given instructions for one of her boarders to be ready with certain items such as binoculars should someone call for them after April 14. The charges against Mudd included the report that after treating Booth's leg on April 20, Mudd had run an errand, heard of the shooting of Lincoln, and then returned home and told Booth to leave. The allegation, in other words, was that at the least Mudd had suspected Booth was the assassin and had not detained him.

An example of the haste with which military proceedings took place was the formal convening of the commission on May 9, followed by a deadline of May 12 for the prisoners to secure counsel. Fortunately for the accused, they all got access to well-qualified legal representatives. Several lawyers—Thomas Ewing, Jr., William E. Doster, and Frederick Stone—defended more than one accused person. Ewing and Surratt's lawyer, Reverdy Johnson, both had long experience at the bar and in politics, and Ewing was related by marriage to Union general William Sherman. But Johnson left the everyday management of the Surratt case to two younger legal associates, Frederick Aiken and John Clampitt. Inexperience hampered their ability to defend Mrs. Surratt. Still, the attorneys who worked for the accused conspirators seemed to have taken their tasks due to belief in the principle that every defendant—no matter how unpopular—deserved representation.

The commission heard testimony for six weeks. The War Department took special care to obtain a full stenographic record of the proceedings. The prosecution's main focus was not so much on these conspirators but on uncovering further plots to overthrow the U.S. government and wreak havoc among the Northern civilian population through acts of terror. It was a case that had political implications; at times, it seemed it was the Confederacy and its president, Jefferson Davis, on trial. The gravity of the case was reflected in the harsh conditions of incarceration for the prisoners. They were held in shackles, their heads covered with canvas bags.

Despite the fact that the cases against most of the defendants looked unassailable, two individuals among the accused did give the prosecution pause. There was real question as to how involved Surratt and Mudd were in the conspiracy to kill the president and, indeed, whether they knew of that particular plot at all. Some of the most damning evidence against Surratt came from John Lloyd, a former policeman who had bought out Mrs. Surratt's interest in the family inn after Mr. Surratt died in 1862, and Louis Weichmann, a boarder at the Surratt rooming house.

There was prominent mention at trial of the fact that Surratt and her family were Catholic. Some scholars argue that far from her religiosity being evidence of good character, affiliation with Roman Catholicism made Mary Surratt a kind of outsider in U.S. society. She could be painted as a person likely to associate with foreign powers and dark conspiracies. Defense attorney Aiken made a thinly disguised argument that the government's pursuit of Surratt was so dogged because the prosecution could not locate the real conspirator in the Surratt household, Mary Surratt's son John. John Surratt indeed was a Confederate sympathizer and fled abroad rather than face trial. While his mother fought for her life in court, John Surratt was in hiding in Catholic religious institutions.

Mudd was linked to the conspirators because Weichmann said that it was Mudd who had introduced John Surratt to John Wilkes Booth. Surratt apparently had agreed to participate in a conspiracy to kidnap President Lincoln. The plan was to exchange Lincoln for Southern prisoners and certain political concessions. Such a notion was what Booth had originally envisioned. His resentment of Lincoln escalated, however, when Booth heard

Lincoln give a speech in early April at which the president promised to work for voting rights for persons of color. Enraged, Booth turned to murder. Were the others fully aware of the change of course, though? In particular, was Mudd at all involved in the plot prior to his tending of Booth's leg after the assassination? Did he recognize Booth then, or was Weichmann's story a fabrication? Scholars are divided as to Mudd's complicity, if any. Some historians critical of Weichmann's role in the trial argue that Stanton may have suborned perjury by Weichmann.

Ewing's summation in defense of Mudd emphasized that the prosecution's case against his client contained two other holes:

> Now, as to Dr. Mudd, there is no particle of evidence tending to show that he was ever leagued with traitors in their treason; that he had ever, by himself, or by adhering to, and in connection with, others, levied war against the United States. It is contended that he joined in compassing the death of the President ("the King's death"). Foster [an English legal historian and authority on treason], speaking of the treason of compassing the king's death, says: "From what has been said it followeth, that in every indictment for this species of treason, and indeed for levying war and adhering to the king's enemies, an overt act must be alleged and proved."
>
> The only overt act laid in these charges against Mudd is the act of assassination, at which it is claimed he was constructively present and participating. His presence, and participation, or procurement, must be proved by two witnesses, if the charge be treason; and such presence, participation, or procurement, be the overt act.

VERDICT

The verdict came down on June 30, 1865: All of the eight accused persons were guilty, with four—Surratt, Atzerodt, Herold, and Powell—slated for the ultimate punishment. The commission's small concession to Mrs. Surratt was that its findings did not connect her with all of the conspirators—only Booth, Herold, and Powell. There was some talk that President Johnson would reprieve Mrs. Sur-

ratt; five of the commissioners had recommended mercy for her on account of her gender and age (above 40). Johnson, though, claimed never to have received that official commendation to moderate Mrs. Surratt's sentence.

All of those who had gotten capital sentences, including Mrs. Surratt, died by hanging at the District of Columbia's penitentiary on July 7. So superstitious were the soldiers about being associated with the grim enterprise that it was difficult to locate men to open the drop apparatus and to dig the graves.

The four people who had known of the plot but had not taken key roles were given sentences of either six years' imprisonment with hard labor (Spangler) or life with hard labor (Edman, O'Laughlin, and Mudd). Eventually, those four were imprisoned in Florida in a location known for its miserable weather and frequent epidemics. O'Laughlin died of yellow fever in 1867. President Johnson released the other three in 1869, although their reputations were severely affected by the conviction.

Mudd fought hard to secure a full pardon. It was a battle taken up by his descendants that continued well into the next century. John Surratt was extradited to the United States from Egypt in 1866–67. He appeared before a Maryland state court, charged with conspiracy to kidnap but not murder. John Surratt's jury failed to reach a verdict, and he was not retried because the statute of limitations had expired in his nonmurder case. In 1870 Surratt made a public speech in which he explained that he had supported Booth's plans for kidnapping Lincoln but was utterly unaware of the change in direction among the plotters to an assassination.

SIGNIFICANCE

The magnitude of the tragedy of Lincoln's death hardly can be overestimated. His passing affected the course of the nation's recovery from the Civil War by infusing that process with even more bitterness and sorrow than it ordinarily would have contained. Those government leaders who in late April 1865 argued that the trial of Lincoln's killers ought to take place in a regular court correctly predicted that a military proceeding would be subject to criticism as irregular in process, no matter how just the outcome.

With the benefit of hindsight historians now generally perceive that most of the convicted conspirators had been heavily involved in Booth's plan to kill the president. Serious scholars doubt that the Confederate government engaged in an effort to kill Lincoln or to inflict terror on the Northern population through spreading smallpox or poisoning water supplies, theories that the prosecutors had broached at trial. Reservations have existed among scholars, though, about the roles of Mrs. Surratt and Dr. Mudd.

There remained, though, a question of lasting legal importance after the conspirators' trials: When were ordinary courtrooms preferable to military proceedings? John Surratt faced a regular court hearing in 1868 because in the decision of *Ex parte Milligan* (1866) the U.S. Supreme Court ruled that military tribunals were inappropriate venues for the trials of ordinary citizens while the regular courts were functioning. Had the *Milligan* decision been in force in 1865, there would have been serious legal objection to the trial of the Lincoln conspirators before a military commission. The availability of justice through regular courts is an aspect of the United States's constitutional system of which the nation has been most proud throughout its history. What better time would there have been to demonstrate the effectiveness of American justice than when the country was suffering from the loss of its greatest president?

Further Reading

Chamlee, Roy Z., Jr. *Lincoln's Assassins.* Jefferson, N.C.: McFarland & Co., 2009; Donald, David Herbert. *We Are Lincoln Men: Abraham Lincoln and His Friends.* New York: Simon & Schuster, 2004; Good, Timothy S. *We Saw Lincoln Shot: One Hundred Eyewitness Accounts.* Jackson: University Press of Mississippi, 1996; Kauffman, Michael W. *American Brutus: John Wilkes Booth and the Lincoln Conspiracies.* New York: Random House, 2005; Larson, Kate Clifford. *The Assassin's Accomplice: Mary Surratt and the Plot to Kill Abraham Lincoln.* New York: Basic Books, 2008; Surratt House Museum. "Proceedings of the Conspiracy Trial." Available online. URL: http:// www.surratt.org/su_docs.html. Accessed March 10, 2010; Swanson, James L. *Manhunt: The Twelve-Day Chase for Lincoln's Killer.* New York: HarperCollins, 2007.

The trial of Chief Langalibalele

Also known as: *The Queen v. Langalibalele*

Date: 1874

KEY ISSUES

In historians' accounts of clashes between white Europeans and native inhabitants in South Africa, the Zulu Wars of the 19th century have played a prominent role. The situation faced by the neighbors of the Zulu, however, is less often discussed. The amaHlubi were a group that had moved south from within an area near the present-day Democratic Republic of the Congo. They were a flourishing people for hundreds of years until the Zulu, under their famous leader Shaka, displaced them in the early 19th century. That period of Zulu activity kicked off a time of internal warfare among Africans known as the Difiqane. The discord, in turn, made it possible for some white powers—notably the British—to exploit African disunity.

It was by no means a given that the British would move to consolidate their authority in a repressive manner among black Africans in the middle of the century. There were several examples of moderate policy toward native peoples among British leaders in South Africa. Beginning in the 1840s, for example, the British secretary of state for native affairs in Natal, Theophilus Shepstone, had managed to resettle Bantu people who were on the run from the Zulu. Rather than instituting a British-style government among the Bantu, Shepstone kept native groups and lands under the control of their own chiefs. It was a kind of home rule policy, with Shepstone showing considerable respect for native laws and traditions. The Bantu, in turn, regarded him favorably as Somtseu, "the Mighty Warrior."

Shepstone's plans to resettle those displaced by the Zulu ran into difficulty with the amaHlubi, under their leader Langalibalele, whose name means "the sun is shining." The chief held out for more favorable terms before agreeing to be moved. But eventually the amaHlubi were relocated in the northwest portion of Natal, near Basutoland, where they served as a buffer between white settlers and marauding Bushmen. In that area the amaHlubi seemed prosperous enough. They also appeared content under the leadership of the well-established Langalibalele, who was 30 years old at the time of the "tribal relocation." Shepstone, meanwhile, thought himself the architect of a successful policy. White settlers felt reasonably safe, Africans were empowered in local governance, and the British Empire was assured that it was in control. The situation remained fairly stable for the next 20 years.

HISTORY OF THE CASE

The discovery of diamonds in the southern part of Africa threw off that balance. The movement of black persons to and from mines in areas adjacent to the Natal region proved unsettling for whites. Further complicating the picture was the fact that some mine owners handed out firearms in lieu of wages, although in Natal, guns had to be registered. Anglo settlers were uneasy about gun running and free spending among African mine workers. A crisis arose involving the amaHlubi because British authorities, most particularly Shepstone himself, insisted that Chief Langalibalele was failing to maintain order among the native people. The resident magistrate in Escourt, John Macfarlane, charged that Langalibalele was not sufficiently overseeing the activities of young men among the amaHlubi who had been carrying unauthorized guns.

Langalibalele replied that he could not personally account for every gun within the vicinity, an area of about 130 square miles. The lieutenant governor of Natal, Sir Benjamin Pine, ordered Langalibalele to appear to explain himself in Piet-ermaritzburg. Among other tensions that had arisen between Pine, Macfarlane, Shepstone, and, on the other side, Langalibalele, were questions about Langalibalele's payment of taxes and his practice of polygamy. Rather than answering the summons, first Langalibalele delayed and made excuses. Of special importance were his actions and words in answering representatives sent to him by Macfarlane, especially a man named Mahoiza. Finally, Chief Langalabilele went on the run, crossing into Basutoland.

Almost immediately, white settlers and the provincial authorities panicked. They had visions of a massive native rebellion. Their fears were fueled by rumors that Langalibalele had been negotiating for months with leaders in Basutoland and had been stockpiling weapons. The government of Natal pursued Langalibalele, saying by leaving his post as leader, he had betrayed the trust of the government. Among the force sent against the amaHlubi leader, there were about 80 whites; the rest of the 1,500-man array was black African. There was a bloody encounter at Bushman's Pass during the pursuit, but that was not directly Langalibalele's doing. The government forces had seized cattle to assuage hunger during their march without offering compensation to the native people, as was customary.

With the flight of Langalibalele and the spilling of British blood at Bushman's Pass, the government of Natal now felt itself completely justified in removing the chief from his position and "dispersing" the amaHlubi. The dispersal in fact was a series of reprisals against persons who refused to exit their homes quickly, who hid from British and pro-British troops, who attempted to run to neighboring lands, or who belonged to groups, such as the amaPutini, who had allied with the amaHlubi. Perhaps 200 persons died in the action. More than 300 individuals were marched to the capital as prisoners, and others simply were made homeless. Although official reports acknowledged only one killing of an unarmed prisoner, there were rumors of many acts of great violence by whites against blacks in the aftermath of Langalibalele's decision to flee.

The amaHlubi leader and more than 80 of his closest associates surrendered peacefully on

December 13, 1873. Significantly, this took place at the homestead of Molapo, a Basuto who had allied himself with the government of Natal. Some of those who turned themselves in were released immediately. A handful of the leaders, including Chief Langalibalele and five of his sons, were immediately bound over for trial.

SUMMARY OF ARGUMENTS

The court in Langalibalele's case consisted of the lieutenant governor of Natal, Pine; the secretary for native affairs, Shepstone; three white magistrates, three native chiefs, and four native men who held offices within the European-led government. Every person on the bench or assisting with the trial had either an official or personal interest in convicting Langalibalele. For example, several members of the Cape Colony's Executive Council who were present in an ill-defined but official capacity were related to men who had been casualties at Bushman's Pass. Lieutenant Governor Pine, who had helped direct Langalibalele's pursuit, presided. The persons of native ancestry on the court were either directly in the employ of the government or heavily indebted to the British politically. The lead prosecutor was John Shepstone, younger brother to Theophilus Shepstone.

The trial took place in a tent outside Government House in Pietermaritzburg. The public was allowed to attend and seemed fascinated to do so; the onlookers included many women. Throughout the proceedings Chief Langalibalele was under armed guard. The court convened on January 16, 1874, and went on for a week. Each afternoon when the court adjourned, the judges and prosecution met to go over the proceedings and develop a strategy for the next day.

The first important decision of the court was the determination of which type of law would govern the case. Would Langalibalele be tried under the rubric of British rules governing trials or using African customary law? Pine declared that the proceeding would be (in the language of the time) a "Kafir court," meaning it would rely on Natal's common law. In modern parlance in the region, to call a person "kafir" has been highly objectionable—indeed, a legally actionable insult.

During the 19th century, however, the word simply was a reference to native legal practices.

There were several difficulties in overseeing a trial using native law, the most important of which, in this case, was that the native law of Natal had not been committed to paper. It also was crucial that Pine was far from being an expert in native law. Even to communicate effectively with Langalibalele (who in court always was referred to as "the prisoner" instead of using the more neutral English term *defendant*), Pine and the court relied on Shepstone rather than an African interpreter.

During the trial Pine assumed the guise of the overlord of the amaHlubi. He began by charging Chief Langalibalele with treason against Britain. According to the indictment, the chief had deserted his post as representative of the queen to the amaHlubi, decamped with his cattle, conspired to gather arms with other rebels, and insulted the messengers sent to bring him to justice. In response to the court's requirement that he enter a plea, Langalibalele tried to discuss his own actions, that is, to provide justification or extenuation. Somewhat impatiently Pine told him that it was appropriate at that time only to enter a plea. He also dismissed Langalibalele's request to call witnesses who had fled, opining that such persons were disreputable and thus would not be taken seriously by the court, anyway.

The next set of remarks issued from the native persons who were serving on the judicial panel. They came forward to condemn Langalibalele. Each declared that the chief was most fortunate to have a trial at all, for according to a strict application of native justice, he would have forfeited his life for rebelling against a lord.

The leading witnesses against Langalibalele were several *indunas,* native officials who personally had spoken on behalf of the government to Langalibalele urging him to answer Macfarlane's charges concerning gun possession. The individual named Mahoiza gave a vivid account of degradation at the hands of the amaHlubi chief. He testified that Langalibalele's associates had required him to strip naked to appear before their leader, a clear affront to the dignity of Mahoiza's position representing Natal authorities and, ultimately, the British Crown. The trouble with that spectacular evidence was that before the trial ended it had been discredited. In fact, Mahoiza had been searched for weapons but otherwise treated respectfully when he took the government message to Chief Langalibalele.

Langalibalele appeared weak and dejected before and during the trial, but he had sufficient verve to send messages to persons who he hoped might assist in his defense. He was especially interested in obtaining legal advice and, if possible, a lawyer to speak for him in court. The court seemed to consider two written offers from potential counsel but rejected both. Langalibalele was not allowed to speak with a lawyer, nor could he consult with anyone friendly to him, inside or outside court. This was in direct contravention of native law, which allowed every person on trial the right to dispute the facts alleged and provided for each adult male charged with crimes to serve as a witness if he wished.

VERDICT

It was no surprise that Langalibalele was sentenced to a life in exile, although exile was a punishment unknown in native law. No one among British officials in Natal thought it politic to execute him, for that would make the chief a martyr and might incite more violence. But, to which place should Langalibalele be sent? According to a British law from the 1860s, it was illegal to exile a prisoner to another British colony. Having been warned by the colonial secretary in London of the extralegality of imposing exile, South African authorities such as Pine, who had managed the trial, moved to cover their tracks politically.

The Cape Colony legislature supported the outcome of the trial. That parliament quickly passed an act specifically aimed at Langalibalele's situation, called the Natal Criminals Act, that ordered the convicted man held at Robben Island. It was a forbidding spot several miles off the coast. The Anglican bishop of Natal, Dr. John Colenso, helped secure Langalibalele's release from the penal institution about a year later.

Colenso's part in the story of Langalibalele cannot be overstated. The bishop had earned the trust of Zulu and other black African people through some years of service as a Christian mis-

sionary. Modern scholars regard Colenso as a forerunner of liberation theology. Organizations that he and his daughters assisted were progenitors of the African National Congress. Much like modern Anglican dignitaries such as Archbishop Desmond Tutu, Colenso was an intercessor between black and white. He was, as well, a prolific writer whose accounts of military clashes provide invaluable details (such as troop numbers) about engagements between blacks and whites. Once the situation had gotten out of hand before Langalibalele's surrender, Colenso had attempted to reason with Shepstone. He was dismayed to find Shepstone's attitude had hardened toward the native peoples in general. He next tried to secure legal representation for Langalibalele at trial, without success. Colenso then decided to intercede with London to bring pressure on Shepstone and Pine and to ameliorate the situation of Langalibalele while he was jailed.

Colenso took an active role in the case during trial and afterward, journeying to England to campaign for redress with officials at the British cabinet level. He had an impact, notably with Secretary of State Henry Herbert, Lord Carnarvon. Carnarvon pressured Natal to moderate the punitive legislation and thus Langalibalele's incarceration. Although Colenso led the effort to appeal the sentence of exile, several of the same persons who had sat in judgment originally made up the appeals court, a violation of principles of English law. With the legislature's retraction of the Natal Criminals Act, Langalibalele's sentence in effect was commuted to house arrest. He was taken to Uitvlugt farm near Pinelands in Cape Town but found detention there unhappy, especially due to the fact that one of his favorite wives either could not or would not join him. Chief Langalibalele died in 1889, a few years after Colenso. One of Colenso's daughters reported on the reverence with which the amaHlubi laid Langalibalele to rest.

In the eyes of the British government compensation was due to certain persons who had been displaced in the roundups at the time of Langalibalele's arrest. In general, however, those who had lost homes and lands were not made whole. The careers of Pine and Macfarlane suffered palpably from their association with Langalibalele's trial.

Although Shepstone extricated himself in London by casting blame on his underlings, his career advancement stalled.

The amaHlubi remained broken up as a people. The British had considerably more trouble with the Zulu. The war that erupted with them in 1878 cost thousands of British lives despite greater British troop strength. The white men prevailed, though, and the Zulu land was torn apart just as had been the kingdom of the amaHlubi. There continued to be trouble among native rivals for the former Zulu territories. To keep order the British decided to make the Zulu territory a formal colony in 1887.

SIGNIFICANCE

Immediately after the trial a number of criticisms of its conduct emerged, particularly among the press in Britain but also, in more constrained tones, within Natal itself. The most lamented aspect of the trial was the denial of legal counsel to Langalabilele. Without a lawyer, the argument went, he neither fully understood the proceedings nor challenged irregularities. Denial of legal advice was contrary to Natal's statutory law in any legal proceeding—African or English. In other words, according to positive law in Natal, the right to counsel superseded any common law tradition that withheld legal expertise to a prisoner. Most critics also decried the fact that the court employed an odd mixture (the term *hybrid* appeared several times in descriptions of the trial) of native law and English law. It seemed, in other words, as though the authorities were cherry-picking legal forms and rules that suited their goal—conviction—rather than following any established format for the conduct of the trial.

In a ceremony during October 2004 the British government officially addressed the treatment of Langalibalele. Speaking to the modern chief of the amaHlubi, Muziwenkosi Langalibalele II, and a number of the amaHlubi, British high commissioner to South Africa Ann Grant did not go so far as to issue a formal apology for the trial and imprisonment of Chief Langalibalele. Her words, though, were an effort at reconciliation. Commissioner Grant symbolically handed back authority to the amaHlubi monarchs. Muziwenkosi Langalibalele II noted that the amaHlubi had never accepted that they were a part of KwaZulu-Natal. He said that it was their wish for the amaHlubi's present leaders to attain the same status as elites among the Zulu—to be accorded the high level of respect that Langalibalele had had before his trial.

Further Reading

Deacon, Harriet, ed. *The Island: A History of Robben Island, 1488–1990.* Bellville, South Africa: Mayibuye Books, 1996; Guy, Jeff. *The Heretic: A Study of the Life of John William Colenso, 1814–1883,* Johannesburg, South Africa: Ravan Press, 1983; Herd, Norman. *Bent Pine (The Trial of Chief Langalibalele).* Johannesburg, South Africa: Ravan Press, 1976; Kunene, Mazisi. *Emperor Shaka the Great: A Zulu Epic.* London: Heinemann Educational Books, 1979.

The trial of Vera Zasulich

Date: 1878

KEY ISSUES

Russia began widespread reform of its criminal justice system in the middle of the 19th century under Czar Alexander II. Russians had access to jury trials beginning in 1864, according to the laws known as the Judicial Statutes. In theory, the law provided for justice that was modeled along English lines, with guarantees of speedy trials and equitable treatment for all participants. In a terrible irony, though, among the most brutal trials of the reformist era were the proceedings against several persons involved in the assassination of Czar Alexander in 1881. In addition, the assassination of the czar kicked off a time of repression against political dissenters that spurred on more radical schemes for change in Russia. But what inspired the radical reaction against a reformist czar? It was another trial, a judicial proceeding against a young woman named Vera Zasulich in 1878, that spurred on the better-remembered events of 1881.

Alexander II embraced a program of reform that encompassed political as well as legal change. Coming to the throne in 1855, he swiftly embarked on transformations that in Russia were called "westernization." The most famous of his actions was the abolition of serfdom in 1861. Alexander's favorite nickname was "the Czar-Liberator." The freeing of the serfs was a massive change that bred domestic discontent. Wealthy nobles objected to the loss of free labor on their estates. Newly emancipated persons still felt tied to now-angry landlords and grumbled that the pace of change was too slow. Payouts from national funds to the former controllers of the serfs left the czar's treasury in precarious straits, and the ex-serfs complained about plans to pay back authorities for their new lands.

The czar insisted on personally directing social, political, and legal transformation. He brooked little criticism with his authority and methods. In particular, he bristled at agitation from leftist organizations, perceiving that such groups envisioned the abolition of the monarchy. Radicals, in turn, engaged in violent schemes to destabilize the state and to kill the czar. During 1879 and 1880 four serious attempts were made on Czar Alexander's life in Russia; another had occurred in France a few years prior. The czar survived each of the conspiracies, but in the last of these efforts there were 11 fatalities and many injuries at the Winter Palace. The assassins contrived to blow up a dining room where the czar was supposed to be eating with his guests and family. They succeeded in setting off the explosion, but the ruler had delayed the meal and thus was spared.

Alexander's responses to the assassination efforts varied. At times, he cracked down on dissent, for example, in the late 1870s authorizing military authorities to engage in severe censorship. Among the many tactics that the czar's minions employed was the physical maltreatment of prisoners. Among the most disliked officials on behalf of the czarist state was the governor of St. Petersburg, General Fydor Trepov.

HISTORY OF THE CASE

Trepov was a longtime servant of the Russian monarchy. He had held an important military position in putting down the November Uprising in Poland under the previous czar. Trepov continued to be of service to Alexander II in crushing Polish rebellion in 1863. In Poland and through his management of the police in St. Petersburg, Trepov developed a reputation for gratuitous violence. He was especially severe toward persons accused of political radicalism. He exhibited signs of paranoia and was, besides, rumored to be a sycophant. Despite some evidence that Alexander II himself did not much like Trepov, the ruler continued to allow Trepov free rein within the capital. It was no surprise that radical groups singled out Trepov as a target for assassination.

The task fell to a bright and articulate young woman named Vera Zasulich. Zasulich was the daughter of a family described as impoverished nobles. She joined a group led by Sergei Nechaev and later associated with Mikhail Bakunin. The radicals with whom she met frequently were on the run from authorities. Although Zasulich held a job as a typesetter for a revolutionary publication, she found other work difficult on account of her record with the police and having served prison time.

For 13 months during 1869 and 1871 Zasulich was confined in isolation at a prison called the Castle and then at the Peter and Paul Fortress. "The Russian Bastille" long had been home to Russia's most important political prisoners. There, for example, the czarevitch Alexis was tortured to death upon his father's orders. As a part of Alexander II's reforms, though, the place had been made less grim. The comparative freedom of the latter part of Zasulich's incarceration seemed to enrage her further. She resented the seemingly capricious treatment she got in contrast to other prisoners. She fed her anger with the uncensored reading materials that fortress administrators allowed her.

The leftist protesters chose a moment to dispatch their enemies that they thought would punctuate a larger radical agenda to greatest effect. They waited until the trial of a large group of student protesters ("the 193") had concluded and then delivered their own "verdicts" against officials whom they thought especially brutal: Trepov and the prosecutor of the 193, Vladislav Zhelekhovskii. The radicals were moved to choose Trepov as a target because of Trepov's beating of a political prisoner, Arkhip Bogolubov, in 1877.

The plan had mixed results. The woman who was to shoot Zhelekhovskii was unsuccessful. On January 24, 1878, Zasulich gained entry to a public session at which petitioners presented requests in person to Trepov. She was able to shoot Trepov with a revolver at close range. She shouted "Revenge!" at the moment of the crime. She appeared not to care whether she herself perished in the attempt. The target of Zasulich's action, however, did not die from his injuries, and Zasulich was held for trial.

The government had good evidence that Zasulich was part of a leftist-anarchist conspiracy. State Prosecutor Count Konstantin Palen decided, however, to try the case as though Zasulich were a single individual who was disaffected and perhaps unbalanced. Palen's reasoning was complex. The government was disheartened at the results of the trials of radicals that had just concluded: those of the 193 and the 50. Despite the fact that the Russian Senate conducted the trials, the court acquitted about half of the defendants. Further, the defendants had seized every opportunity in court to articulate their agendas. Even moderate reformers groused that the proceedings were not in front of juries. Conservative voices, meanwhile, objected that the radicals had gained a public forum in which to propound their ideas.

The regime also still wished to underline its commitment to jury trials. Alexander II hoped to demonstrate that its reforms of the justice system were working. Palen and the czar calculated that the Russian state did not have to rely on a semi-secret trial before a Senate tribunal in order to secure a verdict against Zasulich. The goal was to make these proceedings narrow in scope. Zasulich's time in court was supposed to be simply the trial of an attempted murderer.

Zasulich sat in prison lamenting that she again might be detained indefinitely and would never get another chance at martyrdom. She had little idea how poorly the state was faring in its effort to line up the case against her. The first major difficulty that Palen faced was finding a lawyer who was willing to speak for the prosecution in court. Several talented prospects declined to participate, perhaps themselves unnerved by the radicals'

recent success. Palen sounded out the prospective trial judge, Anatolii Koni. Koni gave advice but would not promise that he would side in every instance with the government. Quoting a justice who upbraided Louis XIV upon a similar request, Koni said, "Sire, the court renders decisions, but not services."

SUMMARY OF ARGUMENTS

Zasulich was fortunate to secure the services of an eloquent attorney, P. A. Alexandrov. The defense strategy was to emphasize to the jury the emotional impact of the beating of Bogolubov upon a supposedly impressionable Zasulich. It was a clever approach because it could play upon the comparative youth and gentility of the defendant. In his opening statement at trial, on January 24, 1878, Alexandrov recalled Zasulich's prison time earlier in the decade:

> . . . during those years of nascent sympathies, Zasulich forever created and strengthened in her soul one sympathy—a selfless love for everyone who, like herself, was forced to drag out the miserable existence of a political suspect. The political offender, whoever he might be, became a dear friend to her, the companion of her youth, her comrade in upbringing. The prison was her alma mater, which strengthened this friendship, this association.

If Alexandrov wanted to make the case that the beating had motivated Zasulich, then he needed to move the argument away from the fact that the defendant only had read about Trepov's actions in the newspapers. Alexandrov wished to personalize Zasulich's motivation, to make the treatment of Bogolubov vivid for the jurors. Getting the court to agree to hear from witnesses who had seen Trepov attack Bogolubov was key to that line of argument.

First, Alexandrov asked the court to summon persons who had been incarcerated with Bogolubov to testify at Zasulich's trial. That request was refused. But, using a provision in the newly revised Russian Criminal Code, Alexandrov requested that such witnesses should be summoned at the expense of the defense. According to the reformed law, this had to be permitted; it was an innovation aimed at giving accused persons more of a chance to conduct their defenses.

And so, Alexandrov presented evidence of Trepov's controversial action toward Bogolubov. He focused on Bogolubov's standing as an intellectual to reach out to the better-educated observers of the present prosecution. The defense thus put Trepov on trial. Alexandrov also argued that Zasulich did not have personal animosity toward Trepov; she did feel sympathy, though, for Bogolubov. It was a difficult task that Alexandrov took on, to paint the defendant as both a political novice and also a person fired by the need to demonstrate a larger point. He managed to pull it off:

She was and she remains the selfless slave of her idea, in the name of which she raised the bloody hand. She came in order to submit to you all the burden of her grieved soul, to release before you the mournful story of her life, to relate honestly and truly all that she had endured, thought, and felt, what had moved her to commit a crime, and what she expected from her action.

VERDICT

The jury took only a short time to do its duty according to the reformed law. The panel had to compose a list of questions that it had addressed during deliberations, and then, once decided, read that list and the verdict to the court. The judge's role under the reforms of 1864 was more as a supervisor than a director of the proceedings. The scene at the reading of the results was most dramatic. The foreman began with the queries they had considered and then said "not guilty." He barely could get the words out, so overcome was he with emotion.

There was an immense uproar in the hall. Almost everyone reacted with joy. Many shouted out a diminutive—an approving nickname—for the defendant: "Verochka! Verochka!" The roar of approval came from not only the lesser attendees in the faraway seats but also dignitaries near the bench.

The trial of Zasulich had been a sensation in St. Petersburg. Wealthy residents had snapped up tickets to sit inside. Poorer folk awaited word from the courtroom while standing in the cold. The proceedings inspired publicity nationwide as well as across the Continent. Zasulich was a physically attractive person from a "good" family. She made a sympathetic rebel, both to reformist Russians and literati elsewhere.

Ivan Turgenev, for example, probably used Zasulich as the model for a key character in his poem "Threshold." According to Turgenev, a group of revolutionaries grilled an attractive young woman on the seriousness of her intentions. As she was accepted into their ranks, one radical shouted out that she was a fool, and another dubbed her a saint.

A play that was one of Oscar Wilde's earliest works, *Vera, or the Nihilists*, was obscure and inferior in comparison to the playwright's later dramatic output. It certainly was a muddling of the historical record involving Zasulich. Still, the drama made clear that Zasulich's trial was a kind of referendum on the czar himself. Wilde had the monarch ponder whether the Russian ruler was respected because of his reforms: "Am I a tyrant? I'm not. I love the people. I'm their father." Henry James's novel *The Princess Casamassima* fictionalized Zasulich but underlined her intellectual talent and the "nobility" of her birth. James also portrayed accurately the connection that Russian radicals had with London; it was a place where ideas germinated when their homeland proved too repressive for long residence.

Zasulich saw that the acquittal had made conservative forces within St. Petersburg angry. She fled the country literally overnight, taking refuge in Switzerland and then elsewhere in Europe. The "Angel of Vengeance," as her admirers called her, returned to Russia only on the morning of the great revolutions of the 20th century.

SIGNIFICANCE

Before 1878 Czar Alexander vacillated on how to address political protest. Sometimes he responded to criticism of his policies with the curtailing of civil liberties. Such was the situation that gave rise to the case of Zasulich. Alexander had allowed General Trepov a certain leeway to rough up opponents of the regime. Occasionally, though, the czar determined that measured reform might win over his moderate domestic critics while undermining the revolutionaries. In 1864 Alexander II had announced the creation of district councils called *zemstvo*. In 1879 Alexander decided that these local assemblies needed to be tied in with a national governing body. The question was how to do so without threatening the old noble families who were powerful both at court and within their regions. During early 1881 Interior Minister Loris Melikof sketched out a new constitution that both royal adviser and czar hoped would address the varied calls for reform.

In February 1881 a group called Narodnaya Volya (people's will) was the latest cell of leftists who plotted to kill the czar. The group aimed to toss bombs at him while he rode in St. Petersburg. Alexander had taken the precaution of traveling in a closed coach. Thus, when a bomb exploded among his guards as he was riding by coach on March 1, 1881, the monarch initially was unhurt. Against the advice of his guards, Alexander climbed outside to tend to two wounded persons and became an easy target for a second assassin. This bomb exploded practically in the face of its intended target, while mortally wounding the assassin.

As biographers of both Zasulich and Czar Alexander note, the Zasulich trial did away with much hope among both radical and moderate reformers that legal niceties would promote civilized political discourse. For one thing, the trial had a negative effect on the careers of several legal figures connected with it. Palen ensured that those potential prosecutors whom Palen had approached and who refused to participate were dismissed from their government jobs. Judge Koni resisted pressure from Palen to resign his judicial position. Koni used the legal reforms of 1864 to secure his post, but he did have to stop hearing criminal cases in future.

There were specific changes in trial procedures as a reaction to the Zasulich verdict. In May 1878 the government sponsored legislation limiting recourse to juries in cases where defendants were accused of violence toward officials—a clear slap at the verdict that had just been pronounced. According to a new law of August 1878, many such cases were to be heard in courts-martial. It was a provision that would have favored unpopu-

lar officials like Trepov because of their military connections.

If the Zasulich trial left any commitment to legal reform within the government, then the killing of Alexander II washed away the remnants of that commitment. In contrast to the trial of Zasulich, the six surviving assassins of Alexander II did not benefit from the judicial reforms that the czar had implemented. In particular, they were subject to the death penalty, which, though it had been abolished years before, was reinstituted in this instance for "czaricide."

Among the vast changes accompanying Bolshevik victory in 1917 was the abolition of jury trials. With the end of the Soviet state came a reexamination of the need for juries once again in Russian courtrooms. According to legislation that the Supreme Soviet of the Russian Federation enacted in 1993 and confirmed in a new constitution the same year, Russian citizens would have a choice of methods of trial. They might opt for trial along Soviet-era lines, with a panel of one professional judge plus two laypersons (called "lay assessors") who sat on the bench with the judge. Those coming before the court might request a panel of three professional judges. Or, hearkening back to the 19th-century system, they could elect to have a judge plus 12 jurors; in such a system the jurors were the final arbiters of law. The court named jurors at random from among local residents.

At the end of the 20th century, just as at Zasulich's trial, parties to cases had access to lawyers. Jurors headed cases in a manner similar to that in Western (especially English and U.S.) courts, with consideration of evidence, presentations by prosecution and defense, and opportunity for the defendant to speak. Jurors determined guilt or innocence and could make recommendations as to sentencing. As in the English system, appeals to a supreme court were to be on points of law rather than constitutionality. Jury trials did not prove immediately popular again in Russia, but in the 21st century, as in the 19th, they slowly gained in usage until a perceptible minority of defendants requested them. Zasulich's trial was in many ways a high-water mark for jury trials in Russia, but in a centuries-long view it was not typical of Russian justice.

The Zasulich trial freed the defendant to continue her political activities from abroad, including collaboration with Friedrich Engels and Karl Marx and association with V. I. Lenin and Leon Trotsky. Zasulich personally proved a hero among radicals, although she was not without critics due to her eventual break with Bolshevism. Several of Zasulich's fellow radicals emerged from the reformed Russian courtrooms of the 1870s emboldened to more drastic action. At least two exonerated persons from the trial of the 193, for example, helped plan the killing of Alexander II. The trial of the "Angel of Vengeance," while in its own time an example of liberal reform, fostered autocracy in the Russian courtroom.

Further Reading

Avrich, Paul. *Anarchist Portraits*. Princeton, N.J.: Princeton University Press, 1988; Bergman, Jay. *Vera Zasulich: A Biography*. Stanford, Calif.: Stanford University Press, 1983; Dostoevsky, Fyodor. *Notes from the Underground*. New York: Penguin, 1991; Kucherov, Samuel. *Courts, Lawyers, and Trials Under the Last Three Tsars*. New York: Praeger, 1953; Radzinsky, Edvard. *Alexander II: The Last Great Tsar*. New York: Free Press, 2005; Siljak, Ana. *Angel of Vengeance*. New York: St. Martin's Press, 2008; Zasulich, Vera. *Vospominaniia*. Cambridge, Mass.: Harvard University Library, 1980.

The trial of Ned Kelly

Also known as: *The Crown v. Kelly*

Date: 1880

KEY ISSUES

The Kelly gang stole horses and robbed coaches. Its members, though youthful, knew the territory well and could hide out in underpopulated regions of Australia. Within a few years of the gang's formation in the middle of the 1870s, the ruffians expanded their scope from crimes against individuals to larger prey, such as banks. There were occasions when it appeared that whole towns were under the thumb of the lawbreakers. Many communities were afraid of the gang's precipitous arrival. Law enforcement was aware of their activities, but the rustlers seemed able to either evade apprehension or escape captivity. Perhaps there was sympathy among the local citizenry for the perpetrators. Were the members of the gang simply high-spirited youth, or were they redistributors of wealth? Did they display an expansionist spirit, or were they merely brigands?

The activities of Australia's Kelly gang blurred the lines between the good and the bad guys, just as groups like Jesse James's gang confounded U.S. society in the same era. The Kelly gang's time in the spotlight was brief and ended badly for all of the members. Still, the Kellys were long remembered, even glorified, as exponents of a wilder time in their nation's history. Justice prevailed over their mayhem, but that victory was not necessarily celebrated. With the demise of the Kelly gang some of the romance of the frontier was gone. At least, that is what persons who did not encounter them at close range concluded.

HISTORY OF THE CASE

The Kellys and their associates were mostly small-time, young criminals. They came out of an Australian tradition of "bushranging." Originally that term referred to convicts from the British Isles who had been transported to Australia but managed to escape from custody after arrival. They then moved around sparsely settled areas, sometimes disappearing into the vegetation. As convict transportation was coming to an end around 1840, the term *bushranger* evolved to mean a person who lived on the fly and made a living by extralegal means. The bushranger was the Australian equivalent of the English highway robber or the American Wild West outlaw.

In the late 1850s and 1860s Australian society already was divided in opinion about the bushranger. Some country folk thought him heroic, a kind of latter-day Robin Hood who stole from rich farmers, railways, and banks. The reading public gobbled up stories of bushrangers such as "Brave" Ben Hall, who directed more than 600 robberies but never killed any victims of those thefts.

Bushrangers such as the Clarke brothers and Captain Thunderbolt (Frederick Ward), along with the occasional female partner in crime such as Ward's companion Yellilong, were as well known for their skill at riding and rustling horses as for their brazen holdups of mail coaches. At their hands robbery acquired a certain cachet among particular segments of the population. Hall reputedly said that one "may as well have the game as the blame." It did not hurt their reputations, of course, when bushrangers shared their proceeds with local folk who sheltered them, provided supplies, and misled search parties.

The police considered such persons to be nuisances and worse. Political authorities voiced plenty of criticism for local lawmen's inability to capture those who hid in the bush. Beginning in 1865 the governments of New South Wales and Victoria pushed through their legislatures acts that identified certain bushrangers as especially dangerous. Those individuals were listed in Supreme Court warrants attached to the acts. The named persons could be shot on sight and their bodies claimed for a reward rather than the fugitives being brought in alive for a trial. Anyone who aided a specified felon in escaping or even harbored him was an accessory to a criminal act. These laws were a resuscitation of medieval English outlawry.

Another departure from modern legal practice was the twist that this outlawry was created not by judicial order but rather through statutes that amounted to "private legislation." Laws such as Victoria's Felons' Apprehension Act of 1878 were aimed at individuals rather than a class of criminals. Although England in earlier times had seen its share of legislation that addressed particular episodes of lawlessness, for a measure to be so directly targeted was not the norm in the modern era.

Another striking characteristic of the acts in New South Wales and Victoria was their reversal of the presumption of innocence—a cornerstone of English law. The lawmakers dispensed with such concerns due to their fear that the bushrangers were out of control in the countryside. As one proponent of the legislation of 1878 put it,

The Bill is framed for the purpose of enabling the ends of justice to be carried into effect against a gang of ruffians that have committed grave and serious outrages during the last few days . . . sometimes occasions arise—and the outrages lately committed form one—in which we may fairly assume from the facts revealed that the accused is guilty and we may come to that conclusion even before conviction. . . . Now this Bill is to enable every well-disposed subject of Her Majesty, whether a police officer or civilian, to take and apprehend these men—to take them alive or dead.

The members of the Victorian Legislative Assembly took exactly three days to pass the legislation; Governor Ferguson Bowen approved the measure, formally making it a law on November 1, 1878. As the speaker indicated, the rush was in response to the activities of one gang that was helping itself to loot, seemingly with impunity, in areas of Victoria.

From the viewpoint of the police and the government, the Kelly family was made up of prototypical criminals. John "Red" Kelly had come to Australia as a man convicted of pig stealing in his native Ireland. Others among the transported Irish had been charged with political protest rather than mere property offenses. Still, ordinary crime was a well-known reason for being sent to the faraway colony. Red Kelly's wife was Ellen Quinn.

Life in Australia was not easy for small farmers, and Red Kelly was known to steal a horse or two on the side. Red died in jail, and Ellen found herself in a worsening economic state. She moved to a settlement called Eleven Mile Creek and lived in a poor dwelling there. The Kelly homestead was analogous to the sod huts on the American Great Plains, with livestock sometimes sheltering indoors. Her young teenage son Edward ("Ned") had a penchant for the theft of animals. He got training in that occupation under a bushranger named Harry Power, himself a transportee who had escaped from jail in Australia. Ned Kelly was a proficient fighter both in the ring and out. Another sibling, Dan Kelly, was suspected of horse stealing.

A newly promoted 21-year-old constable at the police station at Greta made it a personal mission to take on the Kellys. Against advice of several of his peers, Constable Alexander Fitzpatrick set out in April 1878 to arrest Dan Kelly. When he arrived at the Kelly hut, though, Fitzpatrick ran into difficulty, starting with the Kelly women. In the version of events coming from the Kelly family, Fitzpatrick made a sexual advance toward Ned and Dan Kelly's sister Margaret ("Maggie"). According to Fitzpatrick, several family members assaulted him with items including a shovel. The constable eventually took a bullet in the wrist from Ellen Kelly, a wound that would prove minor. Fitzpatrick said that he bargained for his life with the promise that he would not divulge the incident. He got away and promptly broke that pledge.

As Fitzpatrick eventually told the story, Ned Kelly had done the actual shooting, though witnesses would swear that Ned had been hundreds of miles distant at the time. The lawman implicated Ellen in the attempted murder, though, and got her sentenced to a three-year term in jail. The sentencing official was Judge Redmond Barry. Ellen Kelly had a baby that came into confinement with her. Ned Kelly nursed a grudge against Constable Fitzpatrick, who eventually lost his position due to his excessive drinking.

Ned and Dan Kelly retreated to a spot in the Wombat Ranges where they thought they could not be tracked. The government brought in aboriginal people to try to locate the fugitives. Ned resented both the law that singled him out for harsh treatment, as well as the use of what he called "black trackers." It was as though employing native peoples appeared unsporting to the gang.

The gang sneaked up on a police party that had been dispatched to find them at Stringybark Creek in October 1878 and killed three officers. They robbed a bank at Euora and the Faithful Creek station in December of the same year, calling down the wrath of the New South Wales governors. The Kelly gang became known for other, smaller gestures of contempt for conventionality. For example, they wore the ties of their hats under their noses rather than chins, as if constantly to thumb their noses at those in power. Also of consequence were certain symbolic acts such as the Kellys burning townspeople's mortgages during one bank robbery.

This was the juncture at which the legislature of Victoria passed its Felons' Apprehension Act with an expiration date of June 26, 1880, hoping it would spur those who were on the fence about their loyalties to help round up the perpetrators. In February 1879 the Kelly gang paralyzed law enforcement and robbed a bank at Jerilderie, netting a very large sum.

Ned Kelly handed over to a bank officer a written justification of his actions and continued to threaten more. The manifesto came to be called the Jerilderie Letter. Kelly's writing is one of the most unusual documents connected with any alleged brigand's life—a long, passionate condemnation of not only the treatment of him by police, but also the living conditions for Irish immigrants in Australia. His contempt for the lawmen was exacerbated by a resentment of English authority:

I have seen as many as eleven, big & ugly enough to lift Mount Macedon out of a crab hole more like the species of a baboon or Guerilla than a man. actually come into a court house and swear they could not arrest one eight stone larrakin and them armed with battens and neddies without some civilians assistance and some of them going to the hospital from the affects of hits from the fists of the larrakin and the Magistrate would send the poor little Larrakin into a dungeon for being a better man than such a parcel of armed curs. What would England do if America declared war and hoisted a green flag as its all Irishmen that has got command of her armies forts and batteries even her very life guards and beef tasters are Irish would they not slew around and fight her with their own arms for the sake of the colour they dare not wear for years, and to reinstate it and rise old Erins isle once more, from the pressure and tyrannism of the English yoke, which has kept it in poverty and starvation, and caused them to wear the enemys coats.

The governments of Victoria and New South Wales offered a total £12,000 in rewards for the capture of the men—enough incentive to cause some Kelly partisans to switch allegiance. But, the government crackdown also may have caused the fugitives to consider moving on, perhaps to California. The Kelly gang ultimately responded to the government action with reprisals against their former friends, such as Aaron Sherritt. Apparently the Kellys carefully timed their revenge on Sherritt to coincide with the expiry of the 1878 legislation. Historians speculate that the police had used Sherritt as much to smoke out the whereabouts of the gang as to get specific information about them. Still, to the Australian public at the time, the police appeared unable to stop the Kellys even when constables literally were in the house with Sherritt before the gang arrived.

On June 28, 1880, the Kellys holed up in a hotel at Glenrowan, Victoria. They took 70 people hostage. The gang's plan was to derail a train loaded with police that had been sent to confront them. The malefactors had torn up the tracks nearby, but a hostage who got out of the hotel managed to alert the train before it wrecked. The police attacked despite the danger to townsfolk. In the chaos the hotel caught fire, and all the gang members except Ned Kelly were either burned to death or fatally shot. Ned hid in some undergrowth. At dawn on the morning of June 29 he emerged behind police lines, wearing a crude suit of armor and firing at his pursuers. Multiple police rounds merely grazed his metal cladding, until a policeman had the presence of mind to shoot at Kelly's unprotected legs.

SUMMARY OF ARGUMENTS

After being committed for trial at Beechworth, the injured Kelly stood trial at Melbourne on October 18, 1880. He was charged with the killing of Constable Lonigan (Lonergan) in the ambush at Stringybark Creek. Ned Kelly's survival and trial amid the deaths of his friends presaged the capture of bank robber Frank James (older brother of Jesse) in Missouri three years later, although Frank James's trial had a better outcome for the defendant. A barrister named Mr. Smyth presented the government's case, backed up by the Victoria crown solicitor (chief lawyer) Henry Field Gurner. Presiding at Kelly's capital trial was none other than Redmond Barry, chief judge of Australia's Supreme Court.

Those who stood with Kelly were alert to the fact that politics entered into the case; some among the public had regarded the government's passage of the Felons' Apprehension Act as heavy handed, while, of course, the state defended its actions as necessary to maintain order. David Gaunson, a Legislative Assembly member, acted as Kelly's solicitor. An inexperienced barrister, Henry Bindon, was the government-appointed advocate within the courtroom. Gaunson denied that he had a political motive in representing Kelly. He was helpful to Bindon in the role of "instructing solicitor," really the senior lawyer in the case. Gaunson in turn got assistance from his brother William Gaunson. Kelly's sister Maggie Skillion struggled to pay the solicitors.

Some of Bindon's early arguments at trial were procedural. He laid stress upon the poverty of Kelly's family, which needed time to raise more funds for the defense. The newspapers meanwhile reported that the police were searching through Kelly hideouts, expecting to locate loot. In court Bindon emphasized that Kelly had acted honorably toward hostages. He reminded the jury that only the dead policemen or Ned Kelly could say with certainty what had occurred at Stringybark, but was it not possible that Lonigan had died from "friendly fire"? Furthermore, the rules of evidence at the time prevented Kelly from testifying in his own defense:

> The prisoner's mouth is shut; but if he could be sworn, then he would give a totally different version of the transaction. . . . There is no ground for saying the police fell in with a gang of assassins. The whole career of the prisoner shows that he is not an assassin, a cold-blooded murderer, or a thief. On the contrary he has shown himself to have the greatest possible respect for human life. I ask: will the jury convict a man on the evidence of a single witness and that a prejudiced witness? If you have the smallest doubt, gentlemen, I trust you will give a verdict in this case different from that which the Crown expects.

The defense tried to counter a stream of witnesses who told of the gang's bank robberies.

Prosecutors also called to the stand persons who said they had heard Kelly brag about taking items from the dead policemen's bodies. The most vivid evidence against Kelly came from Constable McIntyre, who had escaped the carnage at Stringy-bark Creek. In McIntyre's version of that episode Kelly came across as an accomplished killer who took special pleasure in shooting Lonigan. Bindon may have made one critical error at trial: failing to get the Jerilderie Letter introduced into evidence. Legal historians and Kelly biographers speculate that that document—which was not released to the public until the middle of the 20th century—would have created sympathy for Kelly among the jury panel.

Judge Barry's instructions to the jury made clear where he thought blame lay for the shooting of Lonigan:

> The jury must realise that the confessions made by the prisoner at various times were not made under compulsion, but when the prisoner was at liberty; and if he had made them in a spirit of vainglory or to screen his companions, then he had to accept full responsibility.
>
> The prisoner's mouth was not closed. He could not give sworn evidence, but he could have made a statement, which, if consistent with his conduct for the past eighteen months, would have been entitled to consideration. But the prisoner had not done so.
>
> Whether the prisoner shot Lonigan or not is an immaterial point. The prisoner was engaged in an illegal act. He pointed a gun at McIntyre's breast. That circumstance is enough to establish his guilt. . . . The jury will, however, have to regard the evidence as a whole and say accordingly whether murder has been committed. It cannot be manslaughter. Your verdict must be either guilty of murder or an acquittal.

It took the jurors approximately 20 minutes to convict Kelly. But, the man who had to keep silent in his own defense finally got his chance to comment publicly on the proceedings when the clerk requested if he had anything to say to the court before sentencing. Kelly summarized his view of the trial (and what he thought had occasioned it):

For my own part I do not care one straw about my life, nor for the result of the trial; and I know very well from the stories I have been told, of how I am spoken of—that the public at large execrate my name. The newspapers cannot speak of me with that patient tolerance generally extended to men awaiting trial, and who are assumed, according to the boast of British justice, to be innocent until they are proved to be guilty. But I don't mind, for I am the last that curries public favour or dreads the public frown. Let the hand of the law strike me down if it will; but I ask that my story be heard and considered—not that I wish to avert any decree the law may deem necessary to vindicate justice, or win a word of pity from anyone. If my lips teach the public that men are made mad by bad treatment, and if the police are taught that they may exasperate to madness men they persecute and ill-treat, my life will not be entirely thrown away. People who live in large towns have no idea of the tyrannical conduct of the police in country places far removed from the court.

VERDICT

In the English tradition of death penalty cases, Judge Barry placed a black handkerchief on his head before pronouncing the formal judgment of the court that Kelly was to be hanged. Kelly responded much to the effect of "I will meet you on the other side." Kelly's supporters eventually could not resist noting that Judge Barry died within a fortnight of the execution.

It was no surprise when Judge Barry sentenced Kelly to death, and yet sympathy for the outlaw remained. Thousands of people turned out at a public meeting on November 5, 1880, to protest the capital sentence and appeal for mercy from the governor. Although a petition requesting clemency boasted more than 30,000 signatures, the official response on November 8 was negative. The punishment was carried out at Melbourne Jail on November 11, 1880. Kelly's last words reportedly were "Such is life."

Between 1881 and 1883 a royal commission in Victoria inquired into the operation of police forces. The major reasons for that investigation were the allegations in the Kelly case that the police were corrupt and that they enforced the law selectively, singling out poor Irish settlers for the harshest treatment. The commission did not excuse the Kelly gang's activities, nor did it undermine Ned Kelly's conviction. Many among the public, however, perceived the inquiry as bolstering claims that the lawmen had not enforced justice fairly—a core complaint of the Kelly family.

Eventually several people got shares of the reward money for killing or capturing the Kellys, although discussion raged about how much the police were due. Public opinion leaned toward a high monetary reward for the schoolteacher Thomas Curnow, who had made his way out of captivity in the hotel at Glenrowan and flagged down the police train. The government resisted paying any reward to the aboriginal trackers who had assisted with the search for the Kellys.

SIGNIFICANCE

Ned Kelly and his colleagues remained controversial figures in Australian history. The presentation of the Kelly gang as modern Robin Hoods began in their own generation with a touring stage play run by Dan and Ned's sister Kate. Ned Kelly was the subject of several motion pictures, including *The Story of the Kelly Gang* from 1906, which may have been the first full-length dramatic film in the world. That cinematic treatment included the actual armor that Ned had worn at the gang's last stand at Glenrowan. Although the film conveyed disapproval of Kelly's "life of crime," audiences tended to cheer Ned Kelly on. A number of talented historians, novelists, musicians, and visual artists have made the Kelly gang the centerpiece of their work.

Ned Kelly's protective steel suit became perhaps the most iconic artifact in Australian history, though it represented different things to those who saw it. To some, the homemade armor conveyed the image that Kelly was a chivalrous character who protected impoverished rural folk from the depredations of the wealthy. Others perceived Kelly as an exemplar of a frontier mentality, a person from a hardy generation who helped settle land that was new to Europeans. Certain persons imbibed Kelly's resentment of England for forcing the Irish into first poverty and then immigration;

to them the armor was a defense against corrupt police and other leaders whom Kelly saw as allied with England. To those who supported the opinions of the police and legislators that the Kelly gang were desperadoes who had to be stopped quickly, the crude armor was sinister, a symbol of criminality that met an early end.

Further Reading

Baron, Angela N. *Blood in the Dust: Inside the Minds of Ned Kelly and Joe Byrne.* Greensborough, Australia: Network Creative Services, 2004; Brown, Max. *Australian Son: The Story of Ned Kelly.* Melbourne, Australia: Georgian House, 1948; Carey, Peter. *True History of the Kelly Gang.* New York: Random House, 2000; Douthie, Judith. *I Was at the Kelly Gang Round-Up.* Greensborough, Australia: Network Creative Services, 2007; "The Nolan Gallery's Foundation Collection." Available online. URL: http://www.pictureaustralia.org/nolan/. Accessed March 4, 2010; Jones, Ian. *Ned Kelly: A Short Life.* London: Little Brown, 1995; Moloney, John. *I Am Ned Kelly.* New York: Penguin Books, 1980.

The trial of Charles Guiteau

Also known as: *The United States v. Guiteau*

Date: 1881–1882

KEY ISSUES

The assassination of a country's leader often has been cause for national self-examination, with the main function of the assassin's trial being such. But what if neither assassins nor citizens get that day in court? Whether from overreaction on the part of guards at the scene or a suicide wish on the part of the killers, assassins often have not survived to stand trial. Thus, the courtroom drama of those who have been apprehended and charged is usually magnified.

After the death of President Abraham Lincoln, of course, U.S. citizens never had the benefit of the assassin's trial to work through their grief. Though the Lincoln conspirators were convicted and several hanged, Lincoln's assassin, John Wilkes Booth escaped that formal condemnation, having been mortally wounded in a shootout with Union troops as they hunted him down in 1865. Then, in 1881, there was an outpouring of sorrow at the death of President James Garfield—a politician with no particular hold on the public imagination and a new officeholder at that. In fact, the grief and the outrage heaped upon Garfield's killer had much to do with unresolved national rage from 15 years prior.

HISTORY OF THE CASE

Charles Julius Guiteau seemed odd to those who knew him. Guiteau appeared quirky, opinionated, a bit of a huckster. But, did being unusual mean that he was dangerous? Born in 1841, fairly well educated and from a middle-class background, he nonetheless had difficulty finding his place either among peers or in a job. For a short time when he was about 20 years old, Guiteau lived in the Oneida Community, at first admiring the utopian community's founder John Humphrey Noyes. In time, though, Guiteau became disenchanted with the place and the role model.

He lived for a time with the assistance of his sister Frances and her husband, attorney George Scoville. Guiteau studied law, married, and wrote for a variety of publications. He had no particular success at any of those ventures. When his wife left him, alleging physical abuse, Guiteau's actions grew more erratic. Frances Scoville consulted physicians about his physical threats to her. Guiteau distanced himself from his family and began preaching in revivals. During the 1880 presidential campaign Guiteau—always a news hound— showed great interest in the complex political contest. He particularly focused on maneuvering between Republican factions. He became fixated on James G. Blaine, who played a key role in the election of James Garfield as president.

Blaine, who was rewarded by being named secretary of state under Garfield, received dozens of letters from Guiteau. Those communications variously offered advice (both religious and political) and begged for preferment. Eventually Guiteau's tone changed, and he began sending criticism to Blaine and other authorities. Guiteau now concentrated his threats on President Garfield. On July 2, 1881, Blaine, Garfield, and other presidential advisers were at a train station in Washington, D.C., when they were met by Guiteau (whom they did not recognize). Without a word Guiteau shot toward Garfield, hitting the president in two locations on his body. It was the bullet in Garfield's back that was to prove the more dangerous, although at first the president did not appear to be mortally injured.

The fact that Garfield initially survived the assassination attempt for a few weeks helped Guiteau. When Guiteau was arrested, word quickly spread through newspapers of his undistinguished careers and difficult personality. Though he never had spent time in an institution for the mentally ill, his eccentricity made it possible that he could plead insanity. But, as Garfield's prognosis grew worse, so did Guiteau's chances of engendering sympathy because of his mental state. Garfield died on September 19; Guiteau went on trial on November 14.

SUMMARY OF ARGUMENTS

Medical opinions figured into Guiteau's case in two ways—one obvious and the other oblique. The less apparent medical factor at Guiteau's trial was a point raised by Guiteau himself: The president's physicians had dickered among themselves about how to treat him and made his condition worse through clumsy attempts to locate the bullet in his back. Alexander Graham Bell even participated in a search for the bullet that had come to rest near Garfield's spine. Although most of Guiteau's arguments in court were harebrained, medical historians looking back on the record credit Guiteau with at least one reasonable contention, that it was the aggressive treatment by Garfield's doctors (and their probing with unwashed fingers) that had finally dispatched Garfield. The president might have lived if physicians had left the bullet alone.

Guiteau's trial went on for several months, with the verdict delivered on January 25, 1882.

The major factor in its unusually long duration was medical testimony. As in the prosecution of Daniel M'Naghten for attempting to assassinate British prime minister Robert Peel, the trial of Guiteau was a clash between experts on mental illness.

Some of those who weighed in about Guiteau's mental condition took the view that the accused ought to be termed *insane*. Such experts tended to see mental illness as a disease that was both physical and inheritable; most persons who held to such views at Guiteau's trial were psychiatrists or anatomists. An opposing group of experts argued strongly against that characterization, sometimes from their training as physicians but also due to experience as superintendents of prison and psychiatric facilities. These specialists frequently characterized insanity as a rare phenomenon that created a lifelong disability, though they did admit certain circumstances (such as head injuries) that could induce insanity. The experts who doubted Guiteau's insanity characterized him as a cagey and immoral individual. It was in that context that Guiteau's connection with Oneida came back to haunt him.

Representing the organic view of insanity at Guiteau's trial was physician Edward Spitzka, head of the New York Neurological Society. Among those who testified powerfully that Guiteau was more a sinner than a diseased person was John Gray, the editor of the *American Journal of Insanity* and the superintendent of the Utica Insane Asylum. It was the first great contest in a U.S. trial between expert witnesses. If Spitzka and his views had prevailed at Guiteau's trial, Guiteau would have been recognized as insane and would have been put into an institution for the mentally ill, much as happened to M'Naghten. Gray and those who agreed with him, however, said that Guiteau was, in the parlance of the day, "foxing" (outwitting) them and deserved to hang. According to Gray, the M'Naghten Rules ought to apply because Guiteau suffered from his own "depravity" rather than mental disease.

There were complexities at the trial in addition to the medical arguments. Chief among the legal difficulties of running the trial was Guiteau's vocal and erratic presence. Trained as a lawyer—albeit a barely competent one—he insisted on participating loudly in his own defense. Rather than counting himself lucky to have the counsel of his long-suffering brother-in-law, George Scoville, Guiteau went about proving the maxim that "he who defends himself has a fool for a client." Not only did Guiteau periodically disagree with Scoville's decision to use an insanity defense, insisting that he (Guiteau) had received instructions from the Almighty to commit the assassination; he frequently interrupted Scoville and Judge Walter Cox, insisted on handing prejudicial statements to the press, and insulted potential jury members.

Commenting on Scoville's contention to the jury that Guiteau could appear normal but that he also had a "want of mental capacity," Guiteau interjected, "I had brains enough, but I had the theology on the mind and this is the reason I did not go on in the law business. There is no money in theology." Guiteau sparred with the district attorney, telling him: "I have just as good a right to talk as you have. You are altogether too talky this morning. You are worse than a boar with the diarrhea. You had better go home." Finally, the judge threatened to have Guiteau gagged if he did not control himself. It proved difficult to retain counsel for Guiteau given his behavior. Judge Cox took the tack that to avoid a mistrial and to allow the jury to assess Guiteau's mental state themselves, he had to give Guiteau a certain amount of leeway in court.

Public sentiment ran very high against Guiteau. Increased security was necessary when Guiteau was in jail, and even then Guiteau narrowly missed being shot and killed by one drunken critic. Guiteau insisted that he had many visitors who applauded him and gave him money (though not as much as had been sent to Mrs. Garfield, he regretted), but that claim seemed delusional to anyone who read the papers. Thomas Nast's bitter cartoon, published in *Harper's Weekly* in December 1881, summed up most laypeople's view of Guiteau. Nast drew Guiteau as a smirking jester, in terrible contrast to Garfield's coffin. The defendant was a shyster who mocked the judicial process and had threatened to wreck the political system as well.

VERDICT

When the jury returned its verdict of guilty, Guiteau reacted strongly (the transcript said "excitedly") as he so often had done during the proceedings. On February 3, 1882, when Judge Cox pronounced the traditional sentence that Guiteau would be "hanged by the neck until you are dead. And may the Lord have mercy on your soul," Guiteau could not help responding, "And may God have mercy on your soul, I had rather stand where I am than where the jury does or where your Honor does. . . . I am not afraid to die . . . I know where I stand on this business. I am here as God's man and don't you forget it. God Almighty will curse every man who has had anything to do with this act."

Attempts by Guiteau's counsel and certain medical figures to obtain a Supreme Court review of the case or a pardon from President Chester Arthur were unsuccessful. Guiteau continued to suffer from delusional behavior long after hope of a remission of sentence had passed, and he sang a bizarre song on the scaffold. Guiteau's sentence was carried out at the District of Columbia jail on June 30, 1882. His execution, ironically, both seemed to expiate his guilt among critics and bear out those who had argued he was insane. Anatomical examination of his body upon autopsy showed evidence of his having contracted syphilis some years prior. That finding, of course, bolstered the view of those convinced of Guiteau's insanity and that his mental state had an organic cause. His detractors, though, concluded that syphilis was contracted through Guiteau's moral failing—probably while at the Oneida Community.

SIGNIFICANCE

The assassin Guiteau's trial had a perceptible effect on U.S. law and public opinion. Many members of the public began to associate the insanity defense with seedy and manipulative defendants, an association that has persisted. Jurisdictions beyond those that already had applied the M'Naghten Rules began to look more favorably upon the rules' strict standards for determining insanity. From Guiteau's trial onward it would be a great challenge to convince juries that an accused person was legally insane.

Further Reading

Ackerman, Kenneth D. *Dark Horse: The Surprise Election and Political Murder of President James A.*

Garfield. New York: Carroll & Graf, 2003; Cawthon, Elisabeth. "Public Opinion, Expert Testimony, and 'the Insanity Dodge.'" In *Historic U.S. Court Cases, 1690–1990,* edited by John W. Johnson, New York: Garland Press, 1992; Clark, James C. *Garfield: The President's Last Days and the Trial and Execution of His Assassin.* Jefferson, N.C.: McFarland & Co., 1993; Georgetown University Library. "Charles Guiteau Collection." Available online. URL: http://www.library.georgetown.edu/dept/speccoll/cl133.htm. Accessed September 23, 2007; Rosenberg, Charles. *The Trial of the Assassin Guiteau.* Chicago: University of Chicago Press, 1968; *United States v. Guiteau,* 1 Mackey 498 (D.C. Cir. 1882). Available online. URL: http://libproxy.uta.edu:2156/hottopics/inacademic/?. Accessed September 20, 2007.

The trials of Alfred Packer

Also known as: *Colorado v. Packer*

Date: 1883, 1886

KEY ISSUES

Seafarers, frontier people, and explorers shared a dirty secret: cannibalism. Whether one was marooned on a deserted island, adrift in a lifeboat, holed up in a makeshift windbreak during winter, or simply lost, after a few weeks of privation the mind turned to survival. Staying alive might necessitate the consuming of companions. Many who had to eat human flesh did not live to tell the tale. That was the fate of most of the Donner party, for example, in the American Sierra Nevada in the 1840s, and surely must have happened among sailors. Most who did survive preferred not to discuss the matter, whether from guilt or fear of moral condemnation or prosecution.

The law in several nations was unclear about whether cannibalism ever was justifiable, perhaps because there was a variety of dire circumstances in which the eating of human flesh might occur.

And so, for example, legal authorities in England generally accepted that cannibalism usually was defensible (perhaps not even prosecutable) if it meant that an individual in mortal fear of starvation had eaten the body of a person who had died of natural causes. On the other hand, if a desperate and starving individual killed a companion for the purpose of eating him or her, then English law deemed the killer a murderer. What, though, of some middle cases? For example, what if the person who died had somehow volunteered to be eaten, say through the drawing of lots to determine the sacrifice? What if there had been a physical struggle concerning the issue, and one person had killed another in self-defense and then consumed him?

Gray areas in the law were not simply theoretical disputes. Several cases of cannibalism did come before courts in various nations during the great age of sail and New World exploration. Even the 19th century saw shipping routes opening rapidly. Owing to advances in navigation and vessel design, sailors and passengers could travel the oceans with deceptive ease. But, when they were left alone on the ocean or even on barren land, travelers were unable to summon help for weeks or longer. During that time their situation could deteriorate rapidly. The exploration of far-flung areas of the globe such as Antarctica engendered both heroic sacrifices and agonizing moral dilemmas such as the possibility of cannibalism. In slightly less exotic but no less dangerous locales, including the American West, cannibalism could be the result of factors as mundane as not traveling with enough pack animals or underestimating the distance between supply posts.

Such were the rather ordinary circumstances that made Alfred Packer notorious and brought him within the purview of the U.S. judicial system. Packer's treatment under the law was complicated by several lapses of time. There were key gaps between the alleged crime and its discovery and then between his identification as a suspect and Packer's detentions and convictions. Packer's case also was muddled due to the fact that between the time of his supposed offense and Packer's first trial, Colorado had changed from a territory to a state. Packer's convictions drew fire in his own time and have garnered criticism since because of

the difficulty of gathering conclusive evidence from the crime scene.

HISTORY OF THE CASE

Alfred Packer had an undistinguished career as a prospector, trapper, and guide in the western territories of North America. He hailed from a prosperous family in Pennsylvania. He had left home as a young man. He joined the Union army during the Civil War on two occasions, both times being honorably discharged due to epilepsy. Packer was not known for being lucky; when he got a tattoo while in service, for example, the artist misspelled his name *Alferd*. But, he also seemed to take poor fortune with good humor.

In 1873 he joined a group of 21 gold prospectors who were headed from Utah into southwestern Colorado territory; Packer was hired because he supposedly knew the mountains in the region well. His party left Provo, Utah, in November 1873 and quickly ran short on provisions. The men were forced to make do with horse feed and the occasional badger. Fortunately they were discovered by a band of Ute Indians, whose leader was called Chief Ouray by U.S. authorities. Although the Ute were initially suspicious of the interlopers, upon assurance that the men were prospectors and not settlers, they welcomed the whites to their camp.

Upon hearing of their planned route through the Uncompahgre wilderness, Ouray warned the prospectors not to try to go farther in the dead of winter. He offered to let them stay in comparative shelter until the weather moderated. On February 6, 1874, a group of five men, led by prospector O. D. Loutsenhizer, insisted on trying to reach their next stop: Los Pinos Indian Agency, near modern Gunnison. They finally trekked the 85 or so miles to Los Pinos but barely escaped dying of starvation after becoming lost.

Another portion of the original party also decided to set out, leaving over Ouray's objections on February 9. This group consisted of Packer, Israel Swan, Frank Miller, George Noon, Shannon Wilson Bell, and James Humphrey. Among the men who stayed with Ouray and the Ute was a man named Preston Nutter, who later would become important in assessing Packer's account of events.

Eventually, all of the 21 men who had begun the journey in Utah would be accounted for, except for the five companions of Packer.

Among the group of six, only Packer survived the trek to Los Pinos. He walked into the Indian agency on April 6, carrying a coffee pot with live coals and telling an ever-shifting but initially plausible story of what had occurred in the mountains. At first Packer related that his fellow travelers had left to try to find help when he became ill. They never returned, he said, and he made his way alone out of the wilderness.

What raised suspicions about Packer were two items that he carried—money (he was reputed to be always short of it) and certain weapons. Those items had been known to belong to others in his party. What also made Packer's position less tenable was the appearance of other persons who had been in the original party of 21 and who insisted that their colleagues would not have left Packer to fend for himself while ill. When Native Americans coming out of the wilderness brought back human flesh that obviously had been prepared for eating (one newspaper called it "human jerky"), local opinion turned further against Packer.

Packer traveled to another settlement nearby, at Saguache. There the Indian agent, Charles Adams, asked Packer to make a formal statement on May 8, 1874. That account by Packer sometimes was called his first confession, for it implicated him in the death of Bell and was an admission of cannibalism.

According to that version of events, the party had run into trouble quickly. Within 10 days of leaving the Ute, Swan had died, and his body was eaten; Humphrey died naturally a few days later and was eaten. It is not clear, but one assumes from Packer's telling that the party traveled some in this time. Packer left the camp—he did not say for how long—and returned to find Miller had died accidentally; his body also was consumed. Bell then shot Noon and tried to hit Packer with the rifle he was carrying, but Packer fought off the attack and shot Bell. According to Packer, after the death of Bell it took him 14 days to reach Los Pinos.

Adams ordered a search of the area to uncover the bodies. Packer went along as a guide, but he either could not or would not locate the corpses.

He found himself in the custody of the sheriff in Saguache. In August 1874 Packer heard news that could not have been welcome to him: The five bodies had been found. It is debatable who discovered the remains, but in early August the most important bit of information to date concerning the men's deaths surfaced: a series of sketches by artist John Randolph of a campsite with the men's corpses scattered about it. The scenes were published in *Harper's Weekly* in October 1874. Although Randolph may have taken small liberties with his depiction, it was apparent through his visual record as well as the word of others who had seen the site by then, that none of the victims had expired naturally. Nor were their bodies scattered along any route; rather, they seemed to have been killed close to one another and at about the same time. At the least, Packer's confession was inaccurate.

SUMMARY OF ARGUMENTS

Before Packer could be tried for murder, however, he had to be located. Somehow he had secreted a penknife and escaped from the jail at Saguache. He was on the run for the next eight and a half years. Eventually he was identified as living near Cheyenne, Wyoming, having been discovered by a member of the original party who heard Packer's distinctive voice and alerted authorities. Charles Adams again took a statement from Packer, this time in Denver on March 16, 1883.

Packer's second confession to Adams was much more detailed than the first. It also differed in certain vital respects. In the second account Packer says that he was away from his five colleagues most of one day, trying to scout out their location. He admitted that he did not know "that side" of the mountains. He returned to the campsite to find Bell (who Packer said had "acted crazy in the morning") roasting a piece of Miller's leg. The other three men's bodies were lying nearby; they appeared to have been killed with a hatchet. Bell came at Packer with a hatchet, and Packer shot him. Packer noted that he had subsisted on the meat from the men for "the better part of the 60 days" that he had been lost.

Packer stood trial in 1883 in Lake City, near Gunnison, which was the largest town close to the scene of the deaths. He was charged only with the murder of Israel Swan. Perhaps the prosecution's selection of Swan as the key victim had to do with Swan's age (60) making him the most sympathetic figure among the prospectors. If age alone were taken into account, Swan presumably would have been the least likely to be able to defend himself.

Some of the most compelling testimony at Packer's trial for the killing of Swan came from witnesses who had come upon the bodies of the victims. Preston Nutter, for example, testified that Swan's body showed evidence of head trauma (a cut) through a blanket that covered the skull. If the jury believed that Packer had killed Swan, therefore, they had to assume that he had struck a blow with a hatchet while Swan and several others slept. Other witnesses related that the only body that did not seem to have hatchet wounds was Humphrey's; his skull was crushed. Miller had been decapitated. All of the bodies were found within a single campsite, though animals had disturbed the remains since the killings.

Another element of the trial that received notice in the press was Packer's insistence upon making a rambling statement in justification. Although Packer had not pleaded insanity, he might have done so under the circumstances, had his counsel advised it. Still, it was a particularly bad moment in U.S. history even to suggest that temporary derangement had motivated Packer, whether that was his formal plea or not. A Denver newspaper noted that Packer's efforts in court to paint himself as unhinged by fear and starvation came off as similar to the self-serving courtroom antics of Charles Guiteau, who just had been tried and convicted of the assassination of President James Garfield.

VERDICTS

It took the jury a few polls, but in the end they did convict. Judge Melville Gerry delivered a florid, mournful statement in sentencing Packer, saying in part:

> It becomes my duty as the Judge of this Court to enforce the verdict of the jury rendered in your case . . . it is a solemn, painful duty to perform. I would to God this cup might pass from me! You have had a fair

and impartial trial. You have been faithfully and earnestly defended by able counsel. . . .

> In 1874 you in company with five companions passed through this beautiful mountain valley where stands the town of Lake City. At this time the hand of man had not marred the beauties of nature. . . . No eye saw the bloody deed performed. No ear save your own caught the groans of your dying victims. You then and there robbed the living of life. . . . To other sickening details of your crime I will not refer. Silence is kindness. . . .

> For nine long years you have been a wanderer upon the face of the earth, bowed and broken in spirit; no home; no loves; no ties to bind you to earth. I hope and pray that in the spirit land to which you are so fast and surely drifting, you will find that peace and rest for your weary spirit which this world cannot give. . . .

The popular account of Judge Gerry's admonition was considerably more colorful, however, with the judge reputedly ordering Packer to

> "Stand up, y'voracious man-eating son of a bitch. Stand up." Then, pointing his finger at him, so raging mad he was, he says, "There was seven democrats in Hinsdale County, and you've ate five of them, God damn you. I sentence you to be hanged by the neck until you is dead, dead, dead, as a warning against reducing the democrat population of the state. Packer, you republican cannibal, I would sentence you to hell but the statutes forbid it."

Packer did not hang. He was convicted of murder under territorial law, but legislation in 1881 had brought an aspect of that older law (the need for a jury to be convinced of the element of premeditation in murder cases) under scrutiny. Packer's lawyers contended on appeal that Packer should be freed because his trial had been invalid.

The Colorado Supreme Court agreed; Packer's conviction, with those of several others who had been sentenced under territorial law for unrelated crimes, was reversed. But even as Packer remained the ultimate survivor, he also remained out of luck.

He had never been charged with the deaths of the other four men, nor had he been accused of manslaughter. The district attorney's office decided to pursue manslaughter verdicts against Packer for all five deaths. The most conservative course of all would have been to omit Swan's death from consideration, but there is no indication that this was considered as a strategy. Conviction on all counts would mean that Packer would avoid the death penalty but serve life in prison.

His second trial in 1886 proceeded exactly as the prosecutors hoped. Packer certainly was a pathetic figure yet an unsympathetic defendant. His insistence on speaking in court again was ill advised. His remarks were inconsistent, rambling, and perceived as not remorseful enough. He was convicted handily and sentenced to eight years on each of the five counts charged. Sent to the state penitentiary immediately upon conviction, he served time without making any trouble.

While incarcerated, Packer was the focus of a number of efforts to moderate his sentence. Investigative journalists obviously found his story lurid. In response to their interest Packer actually composed a third "confession" in 1897. In tone and in detail this account was different from Packer's earlier versions of events. There was more emphasis than before, for example, on Packer's contention that both he and Bell suffered from mental breakdowns—Bell before he killed the other four and Packer after killing Bell.

A change in state leadership allowed the outgoing governor to bow to pressure for a pardon. Packer went free in 1901 and lived quietly. He eventually became a sort of tourist attraction for travelers who wished to glimpse an authentic "mountain man" from the days before Colorado statehood. Parents apparently felt little concern about letting their children visit Packer, who gave them candy and regaled them with stories about old days on the frontier. He died of natural causes in 1907.

SIGNIFICANCE

Cannibalism was rare, though it was a phenomenon that was underreported. It was an opportunity not to be missed, however, when it did become the basis for a trial. The eating of one's fellow humans made for such fundamental moral dilemmas—and such good copy—that contemporaries could not look away.

Packer's handling by Colorado authorities was uncomplicated compared to the management of defendants from another famous cannibalism trial in his day, *Regina v. Dudley and Stephens* (1884). The charging of two English sailors with murder after their lifeboat went adrift and they killed and ate a cabin boy involved rarefied legal arguments. *Regina v. Dudley and Stephens* still is debated in law school classes involving moral quandaries.

Packer's situation in the Colorado wilderness underlines for modern scholars the harshness of the frontier. The courts' response to his crime underscores how sophisticated the U.S. legal system could be, even in such a wild west. Packer had able legal representation, articulate judges, and thoughtful jurors; he benefited from a quick appeals process and public pressure for a moderation of his fate.

In the hundred years after his death Packer became an object of fun. Trail mixes and cooking contests were named after him. More seriously, researchers inquired into the deaths of Packer's companions in an effort to determine through forensic examination whether Packer's versions of events were plausible. Their efforts were inconclusive in answering the question of whether Packer was both a cannibal and a murderer.

Further Reading

"The Alfred Packer Collection at the Colorado State Archives." Available online. URL: http://www.colorado.gov/dpa/doit/archives/packer.html. Accessed September 15, 2007; Curtis, Bill, ed. "The Ballad of Alferd Packer." Available online. URL: http://web.cecs.pdx.edu/~trent/ochs/lyrics/ballad-alferd-packer.html. Accessed September 16, 2007; Hodges, Joseph G. "The Legal Experiences of Mr. Alfred Packer." *Dicta* 19 (June 1942): 149–154; Jessen, K. *Eccentric Colorado: A Legacy of the Bizarre and Unusual.* Boulder, Colo.: Pruett Publishing, 1985; Scientific Sleuthing. *Alfred G. Packer Exhumation Project, Lake City, Colorado, July 17, 1989.* Washington, D.C.: George Washington University, 1989; Simpson, A. W. Brian. *Cannibalism and the Common Law.* Chicago: University of Chicago Press, 1984.

The Haymarket trials

Also known as: *Illinois v. Schnaubelt, Schwab, Neebe, Fischer, Engel, Fielden, Parsons, Spies, and Lingg, et al.*

Date: 1886

KEY ISSUES

There were many reasons for the residents of Chicago to be on edge during the year 1886. The city was growing rapidly, spurred by booming investments and a surge in immigration. With that physical and demographic expansion came opportunity but also challenges. In particular, there was the issue of how the many persons new to the area would get along with established residents and one another. There also were issues surrounding employment. Would new arrivals underbid the wage requests of established residents in search of jobs? Were recent immigrants willing to work longer hours, at more dangerous tasks, than workers who "knew the system"? Workers recently arrived from abroad brought with them not just different languages but also different ideologies. How would divergent views on employment, religion, family structures, and politics affect neighborhoods and workplaces?

There was news from other nations that seemed to bode ill for the smooth incorporation of nonnative folk into a dynamic environment. Innovative theories on the economy and politics were all the rage in Europe, and those discussions were not only theoretical. European working people were supporting strikes, for example, and some groups who were resorting to violence said that they acted with the poor in mind. The actions of even women might be murderous in pursuit of anarchism, as the case of Vera Zasulich in 1879 had shown, and yet Zasulich had received sympathy from many liberals in Europe. The anarchist assassination of Russia's Czar Nicholas II in 1881 seemed an ominous sign that political extremism was on the rise in the Old World. What if persons

of German and Slavic heritage brought such ideas and actions to Chicago?

For some in the United States it was easy to conflate agitation for an eight-hour day, for example, with the organization of unions. Also one might associate labor organizations with syndicalism or anarchism. Anger had surfaced as a result of the downturn of the 1870s, especially with the Panic of 1873 and a series of railroad strikes in 1877. Working people were not of a single mind, as was claimed by persons who feared that radicalism was spreading through new immigrants to the American Middle West. Some labor groups opposed strikes altogether. Certain radical cliques disdained employee groups that concentrated on wage and hour improvement as merely "bread and butter" unions. In other words, there was no unanimity among workers or immigrants and no master ideology that drove protests.

Still, the rhetoric was heated. Among the chief voices concerning Chicago's economic situation in the 1880s were middle-class individuals who ran political institutions and law enforcement. These people often assumed that labor groups had a destabilizing and politically extreme influence and that labor was allied with violent upheaval. Many working-class people, conversely, proclaimed an effort to oppress employees in every management decision. They romanticized the acts of labor's "martyrs" and overlooked self-aggrandizement by labor leaders.

HISTORY OF THE CASE

Several of the people who got into trouble with the forces of authority in Chicago in the 1880s did fit the profile of foreign agitators. The city's lively underground press served a diverse nonnative population. Writers for alternative publications expressed much radical sentiment. Recent arrival August Spies, for example, was the editor of the *Arbeiter Zeitung,* a periodical that circulated among German-speaking immigrants in the Chicago area. His associate editor was Michael Schwab.

On the other hand, some of the most prominent radicals were not of late European vintage. It was true that Albert Parsons was from well outside Chicago and began as an advocate of socialism, but he had migrated from Texas rather than central Europe. Parsons wrote for mainly English speakers in his paper *The Alarm*. Both Spies and Parson were nationally active, for example, in 1881 helping to produce a call to action for working people called the "Pittsburgh Manifesto." But, both men eventually strayed from a theoretical adherence to socialism, believing that no one political ideology was a panacea.

It would take a shock to the capitalist system to effect a meaningful transformation of how workers were treated. The goal was not just a better workplace experience but also more justice from the courts and the police. These individuals believed the immediate mechanism for creating a new order was speech, both written and oral. Spies, Parsons, and anarchist associates such as small business owner Oscar Neebe and teamster Samuel Fielden were inveterate public speakers and composers of editorials.

In time, several persons who had heard about anarchism from such publications and their editors broke off with their former colleagues, accusing men like Parsons and Spies of being too slow to effect change. People such as Louis Lingg, a 22-year-old immigrant from Germany in 1884; George Engel, a small businessman; and Spies's coworker, compositor Adolph Fischer, hoped to bring immediacy to anarchism through the use of a specific medium: dynamite. Lingg, for example, was familiar with a manual for how to assemble bombs, a book called *Revolutionary War Science* by Johann Most. The notion was to grab public attention and inflict casualties, especially among the hated police. In this, the ultra-radicals played into the hands of those who said that all immigrants were in league with European assassins.

The Chicago area saw several confrontations between striking workers, employers' representatives such as the private Pinkerton security agents, and the police, in the years between 1884 and 1886. Those episodes resulted in several deaths and injuries, chiefly among working people. On occasion, the police struck out at not only picketers but also persons who simply happened to be in the vicinity of labor agitation. Spies, Parsons, and their fellow "talking anarchists" kept calling for a show of support for anarchism. They meant to demonstrate to the authorities how many people stood with them in sympathy. On May 1, 1886,

the more moderate anarchists seemed to have prevailed. Nationally, they had organized an eight-hour walkout from work. Such an action was to symbolize that direct action rather than either union negotiation or violence would improve conditions of work.

Flush with what Spies thought was that success, he went to address a meeting of lumber workers on May 3. It happened that a confrontation among union strikers, nonunion "scabs," and police was going on nearby at the McCormick Reaper Factory. Spies saw the police overreact to the situation, killing two workers and injuring several others. He returned to his newspaper and composed an angry editorial about the McCormick strike. Some of the other anarchists met and planned a public meeting at Haymarket Square to protest the recent police actions. The more radical Fischer inserted language into the announcement of that May 4 gathering, telling spectators to arm themselves. Spies objected to that wording and got the handbills reprinted, although a few remained in circulation; Spies did agree to speak at the rally.

The protest meeting did not attract as many people as the organizers had hoped. The sky was gray and threatened rain. Spies arrived late and sent word to summon others who were not there—including Parsons and Fielden—to follow him in addressing the crowd. The police were present, mostly in plainclothes. Law enforcement had been on alert after reading the handbills announcing the meeting. They had heard rumors that this meeting was merely a distraction and that the real trouble would be at the McCormick Works.

Chicago mayor Carter Harrison made certain that attendees saw him at the Haymarket. Harrison did not wish to associate himself with the organizers, yet he thought his presence might ingratiate him with working-class voters during a reelection campaign. Harrison said to a colleague that he thought the situation was thoroughly under control. He later spoke of Spies's talk as unremarkable.

Although the meeting had begun with a few thousand in attendance, by around 10:00 P.M. there were only a hundred or so listeners as Fielden wrapped up his speech. The police decided at that point to break up the assembly. Inspector John

Bonfield, who was the local supervisor of the police, ordered Captain William Ward to approach the wagon on which Fielden was standing and demand that the meeting cease. Fielden asked if he might finish his remarks, but Ward insisted that the proceedings stop at once.

Ward was stepping off the makeshift platform when from behind him a bomb came through the air. It exploded among the policemen, killing a lawman named Mathias Degan. It was not apparent who had hurled the bomb nor exactly whence it came. Gunfire then erupted. Many (if not all) of the shots were from the police. Within the next few days at least seven policemen died of their injuries; perhaps 60 persons suffered gunshot wounds.

The response by law enforcement and city authorities was sweeping. Many mainstream newspapers as well as the city's business leaders such as Marshall Field encouraged police to round up radicals. Public opinion seemed sharply condemnatory of the radicals. Working-class folk kept to their homes in fear that they might be connected with anarchism. The authorities questioned dozens of radicals, including most of the people who had met after the McCormick incident to set up the Haymarket gathering. A few of the anarchists quickly offered to turn state's evidence.

Only two individuals that the police considered prime suspects escaped custody: Parsons made it to the home of friends in Wisconsin, and a man named Rudolph Schnaubelt, the brother-in-law of Schwab, absconded to points unknown. Parsons eventually returned to Chicago voluntarily to face justice. Lingg reportedly fought with the officers who searched his rooms.

SUMMARY OF ARGUMENTS

On May 27, 1886, a grand jury approved a multiple-part indictment of nine anarchists—Schnaubelt, Schwab, Neebe, Fischer, Engel, Fielden, Parsons, Spies, and Lingg—as well as Lingg's landlord and the leader of the Haymarket planning meeting. They were charged with the murder of policeman Degan, whose death was the only fatality certainly caused by the bomb blast instead of bullets. The indictment listed additional alleged offenses, including rioting, but the defendants were tried first on the murder charge, and so the other cases were never heard. The indictment noted the missing Schnaubelt specifically as the bomb thrower.

It took three weeks to impanel a jury from among the 1,000 persons who were subject to voir dire. Most potential jurors stated that they would find it difficult to be completely unbiased. Judge Joseph Gary allowed such individuals to sit anyway. It was the judge's role to screen jurors who admitted that they already thought the defendants were guilty, but Judge Gary refused to do so, making it imperative that the defense should dismiss such persons from the jury pool. The defense had only a certain number of challenges that it could make on a preemptory basis. Thus, toward the end of the process of empanelment, Judge Gary's leaning toward the prosecution left the defense without the ability to remove jurors who were overtly biased. The 12 jurors finally selected were small shopkeepers and businessmen, almost all of them born in the United States.

The case proceeded in Cook County Criminal Court between late June and early August 1886. The site of the trial was the new Cook County court building. The state made its case through Illinois prosecutor Julius Grinnell. Grinnell began his specific arguments by trying to demonstrate that Schnaubelt had thrown a bomb that Spies had lighted. It was fairly easy for the defense to attack that scenario, because the only person willing to testify to such a set of events was a man who was not known for his good character. Thus, Grinnell had to change direction somewhat. He contended that the anarchists had hoped for a violent confrontation and had planned for a showdown for months. They had laid groundwork such that a melee was inevitable. Grinnell also attempted to demonstrate that the police, far from overreacting to a small protest meeting, had through a disciplined response at Haymarket kept the city from a far worse anarchist event. In Grinnell's presentation the police were martyrs for a much larger cause:

> Law is on trial. Anarchy is on trial. These men have been selected, picked out by the Grand Jury, and indicted because they were leaders. There are no more guilty than the thousands who follow them. Gentlemen of

the jury; convict these men, make examples of them, hang them and you save our institutions, our society.

The defendants had had difficulty even putting together a team of lawyers. At first, a Chicago labor group had volunteered the services of its organization's counsel, but it seemed wise also to enlist the help of persons who knew the criminal law well. The addition of William Black and William Foster as defense counsel bolstered the chances of the accused men. Black, in particular, was an attorney with extensive experience and a former Union army officer.

The defense had many weak spots to attack in the state's case. Black focused, for example, on expert testimony indicating that the bullets that killed and injured several officers had to have come from police guns. He noted that several anarchists had been hit by gunfire. The defense also brought in a witness who spoke of the police chief, Bonfield, as itching for a fight on the day of the Haymarket gathering. And, although the defense admitted that the throwing of the dynamite bomb almost certainly was an anarchist act, legally if the state could not identify the bomb thrower, then a conspiracy case revolving around the bombing was weaker.

Black and Foster maintained that there clearly was disagreement among the anarchists about their goals. Some were more enamored of violent action than others. The defense had to be careful in making such a contention, for it practically invited the jury to distinguish among the accused men. Black had been in favor of Parsons's gesture of sympathy with his fellow radicals—the decision to turn himself in. He had hoped it would sway the jury in Parsons's favor and indeed color all of the defendants as honorable persons who trusted that they would get justice.

Therein lies a mystery for scholars who study the Haymarket trials. Did the defense lawyers suggest to the defendants that they might be able to save some among them from a murder conviction if the attorneys could paint certain anarchists as more moderate? That type of arrangement was pursued in other capital cases such as during the Scottsboro trials of the 1930s. In effect, the defense lawyers might have gained lesser sentences for some defendants by casting less sympathetic defendants to the wolves, but this was not something that Black and Foster attempted for the alleged Haymarket offenders. Rather, the defense in Chicago simply said that the anarchists as a group had deplored the loss of life at Haymarket, without noting that some among the men (such as Lingg) probably had voiced little regret. Legal historians do note that the defense initially worked hard to get the trials of the defendants separated, but Judge Gary would not allow it.

Judge Gary's charge to the jury was decidedly anti-anarchist, as indeed had been the jurist's running of the trial. He laid emphasis on the general activities of the anarchists in the months preceding the Haymarket incident. The charge from the bench to the jury implied that the anarchists were guilty because of their general beliefs rather than specific actions.

VERDICT

On August 19, 1886, the jury took a few hours to reach a decision. The guilty verdict was announced the next day. Judge Gary sentenced all but Neebe to death. The executions by hanging were scheduled for December 3. In another court session in October, Gary provided the condemned men the formal opportunity to speak in regard to the carrying out of the sentences. Usually such a chance for convicted persons to make statements occurred immediately after sentencing, but in this case there had been so many defense objections to Gary's handling of the trial that Gary had to postpone the formality of the defendants' statements until he could rule on the numerous points of law that defense counsel raised. Among the most serious objections to the conduct of the trial was that the bailiff who had summoned jurors had boasted he was going to make certain that anyone who answered the call was opposed to radicalism. As expected, Gary did not censure his own conduct at trial. He did, however, allow the statements by the convicted men to proceed.

The anarchists got their forum on October 7. As might be expected, seasoned speakers such as Spies and Parsons held forth for hours. Spies, for example, refused to concede that the prosecution had a corner on good values:

It is true we have called upon the people to arm themselves. It is true that we have told them time and again that the great day of change was coming. It was not our desire to have bloodshed. We are not beasts. We would not be socialists if [we] were beasts. It is because of our sensitiveness that we have gone into this movement for the emancipation of the oppressed and suffering. It is true we have called upon the people to arm and prepare for the stormy times before us.

This seems to be the ground upon which the verdict is to be sustained.

"But when a long train of abuses and usurpations pursuing invariably the same object evinces a design to reduce the people under absolute despotism, it is their right, it is their duty, to throw off such government and provide new guards for their future safety."

This is a quotation from the Declaration of Independence. Have we broken any laws by showing to the people how these abuses, that have occurred for the last twenty years, are invariably pursuing one object, viz: to establish an oligarchy in this country as strong and powerful and monstrous as never before has existed in any country? I can well understand why that man Grinnell did not urge upon the grand jury to charge us with treason. . . . You cannot try and convict a man for treason who has upheld the constitution against those who try to trample it under their feet.

Lingg's statement in contrast was striking because he made no attempt to couch his contempt for the nation, democracy, Chicago officials, or judicial proceedings:

You have charged me with despising "law and order." What does your "law and order" amount to? Its representatives are the police, and they have thieves in their ranks. Here sits Captain Schaack. He has himself admitted to me that my hat and books have been stolen from him in his office—stolen by policemen. These are your defenders of property rights! . .

While I . . . believe in force for the sake of winning for myself and fellow workmen a livelihood such as men ought to have,

Grinnell, on the other hand, through his police and other rogues, has suborned perjury in order to murder seven men, of whom I am one.

It is hardly incumbent upon me to review the relations which I occupy to my companions in misfortune. I can say truly and openly that I am not as intimate with my fellow prisoners as I am with Captain Schaack.

The universal misery, the ravages of the capitalistic hyena have brought us together in our agitation, not as persons, but as workers in the same cause. Such is the "conspiracy" of which you have convicted me.

I protest against the conviction, against the decision of the court. I do not recognize your law, jumbled together as it is by the nobodies of bygone centuries, and I do not recognize the decision of the court.

The defense made serious legal objections to what had transpired in the courtroom at Chicago, despite Judge Gary's satisfaction with how he had administered the trial. Attorney Black was confident that the Illinois Supreme Court would hear an appeal. The higher court did postpone the executions of the seven men while they listened to defense arguments. On appeal in March 1887 the defense focused on the amorphous nature of conspiracy charges. Black, for example, reiterated his stance that since no one had been proved to have thrown the bomb (which had been the cause of Degan's death), the condemned men could not be conspirators to murder.

Most journalists and writers as well as many union leaders remained either neutral or on the side of those who wished to see the anarchists hanged. Some prominent individuals, though, joined in pleas for a remission of sentence on the moral ground that Judge Gary had been obviously biased. The Illinois Supreme Court rejected the legal contentions of the defense, setting a date for execution of the seven men on November 11, 1887. On jurisdictional grounds the U.S. Supreme Court refused to take up the case.

Those who defended the convicted men, including persons supporting the Haymarket Defense Fund Committee, argued to the governor of Illinois, Richard Oglesby, for clemency. In that action the defenders of the anarchists again faced disunity among the radicals. Some, such as Lingg, rejected appealing to the hated authorities at all. Parsons contended that to do so was an admission of guilt. Parsons's wife, Lucy, herself a political activist, played a prominent role among those writing about the case from a perspective sympathetic to the defendants. She continued in that cause for many years, being politically active until her death at age 90.

Only Spies and Schwab formally petitioned on their own behalf for the governor to give them a lesser sentence. One day before the executions were to take place, Lingg killed himself by exploding dynamite in his mouth. The governor decided to let the sentence stand for Parsons, Fischer, Engel, and Spies, although he did commute the sentences of Fielden and Schwab. The men were executed on schedule, all expressing defiance of those who had convicted them.

The defenders of the three men still in jail (Neebe, Fielden, and Schwab) continued their efforts to lessen their multiyear sentences. The position that the trial was unfair, of course, was not necessarily the same as the argument that the convicted men were not guilty. Perhaps the greatest sympathy for the Haymarket defendants emerged not in their adopted land but rather other nations, particularly Europe. There they were remembered as spokespeople for the working class and victims of American justice. Certain American reformers did say that they were either inspired or angered by portions of the Haymarket story. Eugene V. Debs, for example, composed an account of the case in 1898, and the young lawyer Clarence Darrow took part in defense and clemency efforts.

Under a new governor, in 1893 the critics of the Haymarket trials got even more than they had hoped: a statement from Governor John Peter Altgeld that the proceedings had been so tainted with misconduct and bias that the men deserved to be pardoned and released. It was a bold move on Altgeld's part, which almost certainly cost him reelection in 1896.

SIGNIFICANCE

Altgeld did not suffer the only loss in the Haymarket affair. Groups of laboring persons also were affected by the tendency among the press and prosecutors to paint all workers' organizations as anarchistic and violent. The advocates of the eight-hour day noticed a drop-off in public support after the Haymarket trial. That diminution of support occurred even though employee groups said that they envisioned only moderate reforms of workplace conditions and wages.

Socialists in the United States likewise thought that the forces of law were putting them on notice. To be radical was to be disloyal, many newspapers said. The police seemed to concur. If one were an outspoken socialist, the editorial writers implied, then he or she was likely to have a cache of dynamite in the basement.

The police in Chicago expressed pride about their role in suppressing violent agitation such as at Haymarket. Law enforcers in the city took to heart prosecutor Grinnell's characterization of them as shielding the public from the anarchists' bombs and bullets. Despite a tradition of alternative political thought within the Second City, there lingered after Haymarket the belief that order would prevail against radicalism. The police were on the front lines of that effort, but just behind them were mainstream media publishers and their editorialists along with business owners and politicians. It was a sense that would come out again in force as late as the Democratic Party's convention in 1968, when the police acted once again to discourage the speeches of radicals in public meetings.

Further Reading

Avrich, Paul. *The Haymarket Tragedy.* Princeton, N.J.: Princeton University Press, 1984; Busch, Francis X. "The Haymarket Riot and the Trial of the Anarchists." *Journal of the Illinois State Historical Society* 48 (Autumn 1955): 247–270; Chicago Historical Society. "The Dramas of Haymarket." Available online. URL: http://www.chicagohistory.org/dramas/overview/main.htm. Accessed May 3, 2010; Duberman, Martin. *Haymarket: A Novel.* New York: Seven Stories Press, 2003; Green, James R. *Death in the Haymarket.* New York: Anchor Books, 2007; Smith, Carl. *Urban Disorder and the Shape of Belief.* Chicago: University of Chicago Press, 1995.

The trial of Lizzie Borden

Also known as: *Massachusetts v. Lizbeth Borden*

Date: 1893

KEY ISSUES

"Lizzie Borden took an axe and gave her mother forty whacks.
When she saw what she had done, she gave her father forty-one."

The ditty about a double murder in late 19th-century Fall River, Massachusetts, makes it clear that the perpetrator was the daughter of the victims. And so the case passed into popular memory. The result of Lizzie Borden's criminal trial, however, was utterly at odds with the singsong recollection.

The case was well known at the time. Such brutality seemed in sharp contrast to the reputation of the defendant. Lizzie Borden belonged to an upper-middle-class family. Her life prior to the day of the murders appeared, if anything, rather dull. There was a disconnection between the refined public face of the defendant and an explosive anger that had inflicted terrible injuries on the Borden parents. Therein lay an intriguing set of questions for the public and the jury: Was a woman physically capable of committing such a crime? Would a female's supposedly higher sense of morality prevent her from perpetrating an act of such ferocity? If Lizzie Borden was the killer, then what were her motives for patricide? How could she have hidden the tangible evidence of her actions so quickly? Was she acting alone or in concert with a paid assassin? To watch a Sunday school teacher on trial in such circumstances was mesmerizing to Borden's contemparies.

HISTORY OF THE CASE

The two victims died at the hands of an assailant who came armed with an ax or hatchet. The elder Bordens seemed to have been caught unawares; they had no defensive wounds, although the rooms where they died were spattered with blood. Each victim had been struck a dozen times (not 40 or 41), with almost all the blows falling on the face. The grisly nature of the deaths was captured in some of the earliest crime scene photographs in U.S. history.

An immediate search of the premises failed to turn up the supposed weapon, though several tools of the type that had been used were on the grounds. One hatchet had its head cleanly broken off, the shaft buried in ashes. The condition of the bodies indicated to contemporary investigators that Mrs. Borden had died about an hour before her husband. Establishing the times of the victims' deaths relative to each other was important not only for the purpose of reconstructing the time line of the crimes but also in settling the Borden estate. If Mrs. Borden died first, then her husband inherited her resources; that wealth in turn was passed along to his children. If Mr. Borden died first, then Mrs. Abby Borden's sister got the considerable Borden inheritance.

Mr. and Mrs. Borden had been at home on a very hot day, August 4, 1892. Andrew Borden had attended to business earlier in the morning and returned to take a nap. Abby Borden, stepmother to the two Borden children, was completing household chores in a bedroom. Lizzie was in or near the Borden residence at the time of the attacks.

Also at the house was Bridget Sullivan, the Bordens' domestic worker. Bridget had been washing windows inside and outside the house, visible to neighbors. It was odd that Bridget did not hear Mrs. Borden being killed, for Abigail Borden weighed about 200 pounds and must have struck the floor with some force. Another person was staying at the house besides Lizzie, her father and stepmother, and Bridget Sullivan: For a night only, also resident was Lizzie's maternal uncle, John Morse. Both Morse and Lizzie's sister, Emma Borden, were outside of the house at the time of the crime, with Emma visiting in a nearby town.

Lizzie Borden said that she discovered her father's body. She called for help from neighbors, who in turn summoned official assistance. The neighbors and Bridget went through the house to look for Mrs. Borden, although Lizzie said that she recalled Abby Borden had gone out after answering a note to attend to a sick friend. The police arrived quickly, getting to the scene minutes after the crime was reported and just after Mrs. Borden's body was found. Several medical doctors also showed up in short order. The Borden family physician, Dr. Seabury Bowen, lived in the neighborhood; he viewed the bodies as they lay in the crime scenes and prepared them for autopsy.

Early in the effort to find the killer police interviewed Lizzie. Upon the initial search of the house she seemed faint, and Dr. Bowen prescribed her a sedative. Perhaps as a result of trauma or the effects of that medicine, she then appeared unusually calm. Certain statements that Lizzie made in recounting events sparked the attention of the police and the district attorney. For example, Lizzie had varying explanations for exactly what she had been doing at the time of the murders. In one version she was in the upper level of the barn out back, eating a pear, while at another time she said she was searching for supplies for a fishing trip.

At a coroner's inquest Lizzie's story was even more inchoate. Two other witnesses came forward with stories that cast suspicion on her. A drugstore clerk recalled that the day before the murders Lizzie had tried to purchase prussic acid, saying she needed it to remove insects from a sealskin cape. The clerk replied that she needed a prescription for the poison, and she left. Alice Russell, a neighbor and friend of both Emma and Lizzie, recounted that a few days after the murders she had found Lizzie stuffing a dress into a stove. When Russell warned Lizzie that such an action might be incriminating under the circumstances, Lizzie replied that it was an old dress stained with paint and continued the burning. That information, taken together with reports from Dr. Bowen and others that Mr. and Mrs. Borden and Bridget had suffered from a stomach complaint the night before the murders, appeared suspicious. Lizzie was charged with murder as a result of the coroner's inquiry.

SUMMARY OF ARGUMENTS

Lizzie Borden retained expensive and influential lawyers. The defense consisted of the attorney that the Bordens regularly consulted, Andrew Jennings, as well as a younger criminal law expert from Boston, Melvin Adams. The third person at the defense table was George Robinson, a former gov-

ernor of Massachusetts who had returned to private legal practice. It was not without importance that as governor, Robinson had appointed to the bench one of the three men who presided over the trial, the Honorable Justin Dewey.

Hosea Knowlton, the district attorney in Fall River, headed the prosecution team. His able assistant was county district attorney William Moody. Knowlton went on to become attorney general of Massachusetts, while Moody had an even more distinguished career; he eventually served in the cabinet of Theodore Roosevelt and as a member of the U.S. Supreme Court. With such experienced counsel involved on both sides, it was no surprise that the trial was protracted by 19th-century U.S. standards. It ran for two weeks, concluding on June 20, 1893.

The case against Lizzie Borden was circumstantial. There was no confession. No eyewitnesses placed her with her parents at the moment of the crime. The murder weapon had not been found. No physical evidence (such as bloody garments or wounds on her own body) established her guilt. In such cases where circumstances rather than connected objects or irrefutable witnesses pointed to a perpetrator, it was critical for the prosecution to link to the defendant the three classic elements of motive, means, and opportunity.

In this trial motive should have been easy to demonstrate. The state maintained that the reason for Lizzie to have committed the murders was greed, supplemented by family discord. Several times the prosecution was able to remind jurors that Lizzie Borden pointedly rejected Abby Borden as a mother figure. Just minutes after Abby Borden's body had been discovered, Lizzie corrected those who referred to the victim as her mother; the murdered woman, she said, was her stepmother. In response, the defense relied on Emma Borden's testimony that Lizzie was not concerned about the inheritance, nor was she angry with her father and stepmother.

Also related to the question of motive were Lizzie's actions in the day preceding the deaths. The prosecution tried to introduce testimony from Russell that sounded as though Lizzie was setting up the murders. One day before the crimes Lizzie had confided to Russell that she was fearful that some (unnamed) person was trying to harm her father. The defense countered that line of thought with witnesses who saw an unidentified man in the area at the time of the crimes. The state also wanted to remind jurors at trial about the drugstore visit Lizzie had made concerning prussic acid. In rulings critical to the trial's outcome the judges determined that such evidence concerning Lizzie's supposed efforts to poison her parents would not be admitted.

It appeared at the start of the trial that the question of opportunity was an area where the state could make inroads. Lizzie was one of only a handful of people who were known to have had access to the Borden home during the morning in question. The house was a confusing jumble of rooms, many of which were kept locked from inside due to the family's fears about burglaries and Andrew Borden's general irascibility. The state tried to demonstrate that for a stranger to have made his or her way into the rooms where the victims were, killed them, and then escaped undetected in daylight, strained credulity. But, in a remarkable coincidence there was a seemingly unrelated ax murder in a nearby community between the time of the Borden deaths and Lizzie's trial. The man who was convicted of the other murder was out of the country when the Bordens died in August 1892, yet the defense for Lizzie Borden maintained that another total stranger could have crept in and killed the Bordens in a similar random act of violence.

And what of the question of means? The prosecution did not have ready answers to the query about how the crimes were committed. They relied on a more general argument—that despite women's reputations as being weaker than men, women were cunning and capable of destructive emotional outbursts. In answering that contention, the defense was greatly aided by the fact that searchers inside the Borden home had failed to locate either the murder weapon (or at least the blade portion that had touched the Bordens' bodies) or the bloody clothes that the killer must have worn. Lizzie's attorneys hammered away at the fact that there was not "a spot of blood connected with her." How, they asked, could she have committed the carnage and not been stained?

The defense went even further. Knowlton and Moody based much of their appeal to the jury on Lizzie Borden's character. She was a well-brought-up woman and looked it throughout the trial. She made only one statement in court, a deferential answer that she was innocent and would rely on her lawyers to defend her. Moody maintained that Lizzie had a cordial relationship with her father in spite of his penny-pinching reputation. Even as he died, Andrew Borden was wearing a single ornament, a ring that Lizzie had given him many years before. Attorney Robinson also played on the idea that there was a typical appearance of guilt about murderers and that Lizzie Borden fell far outside that stereotype. "Gentlemen," he inquired of the jury, gesturing toward the primly dressed, poised defendant, "Does she look it?"

Judge Dewey voiced instructions to the jury in terms that were quite favorable to the defense. He spoke negatively of circumstantial evidence as though a case could not rest wholly upon it. He told the jury to disregard several initial statements that Lizzie had made to the police because at the time of those answers she was not formally charged with the crime and may have been in shock. He urged the jury to "rise above passion" in making its decision, reminding the jurors that they did not have to convict Lizzie, even if they desperately wished to see the murders solved.

VERDICT

The jury needed just over an hour to decide that Lizzie Borden was not guilty. Legal scholars who have analyzed the case contend that key to the jury's decision were the judicial instructions favorable to the defendant. In retrospect, Moody comes in for praise among researchers interested in the case for his astute questioning of witnesses. Yet, it also appears that to contemporaries, the presence of Robinson was important. By his very willingness to represent Lizzie, that well-known politician served almost as a character witness on her behalf. His influence on the judges may have been decisive as well.

SIGNIFICANCE

The murders of Andrew and Abigail Borden remain unsolved in a legal sense. Of course, after a certain point in time anyone who could have been the killer had died, and a resolution of the crime became academic. Debates then emerged among historians, scholars of crime, and those interested in psychology and gender relations. Why and how had Lizzie Borden committed the killings? If she was not the murderer, then who was?

The most usual explanation for the crimes among writers who wish to "solve" the murders is the argument put forward by the prosecution at trial: Lizzie and Emma Borden resented living in the restricted financial circumstances imposed by their frugal father. Perhaps they were impatient for an inheritance; they certainly did not want to share the estate with a stepmother. Lizzie's and Emma's uncle John testified at trial that Andrew Borden had told him that he was considering changing his will (the original of which had been lost) to greatly reduce the amount given to his daughters. The bulk of the estate was to be distributed to Abby.

Two of the most convincing proponents of theories castigating Lizzie were from the era in question: Edwin Porter, a Fall River newspaper reporter who had followed the trial as it transpired, and Edmund Pearson, an early 20th-century crime writer. Porter's writing is particularly interesting. He published a book reviewing the evidence in the case in the same year as the trial, but almost every copy was bought up before it could be distributed among the public. The rumor was widespread that Lizzie and Emma Borden had attempted to purchase all of the volumes.

One of the provocative theories concerning the murders was that they were perpetrated by Lizzie and supported by Emma as a result of simmering resentment at the daughters having been sexually abused by Andrew Borden. Authors have portrayed Lizzie as suffering from medical conditions including premenstrual syndrome and epilepsy. Some writers have framed theories around the alleged guilt of the maid, Bridget, while still further explanations involve a disgruntled commercial tenant of Andrew Borden or even his illegitimate son. A few works insist that the killings were the work of a complete stranger.

Although many researchers conclude that the bulk of evidence points to Lizzie Borden's guilt, her life after the trial appeared low key. She never married, though biographers note her close friendship with an actress that caused a rift between Lizzie and Emma. She traveled less than one would have expected given her range of cultural interests and

resources. Her one large purchase after the trial was a new house. Much in contrast to the 21st-century expectation of tell-all autobiographies, the acquitted woman never wrote a memoir or gave an interview. When she died in 1927, Lizzie Borden left a considerable portion of her estate to animal welfare organizations. If Lizzie Borden did hack her parents to death with an ax, then that terrible act allowed her to live in apparent peace and prosperity for some years afterward.

Further Reading

Aiuto, Russell. "Lizzie Borden." Available online. URL: http://www.trutv.com/library/crime/notorious_murders/famous/borden/index_1.html. Accessed January 7, 2008; Brown, Arnold R. *Lizzie Borden: The Legend, the Truth, the Final Chapter.* New York: Dell, 1992; Engstrom, Elizabeth. *Lizzie Borden.* New York: Tor Books, 1991; Fall River Historical Society Museum. Available online. URL: www.lizzieborden.org. Accessed January 9, 2008; Lincoln, Victoria. *A Private Disgrace: Lizzie Borden by Daylight.* New York: Putnam, 1967; Pearson, Edmund. *The Trial of Lizzie Borden.* Garden City, N.J.: Doubleday, 1937; Porter, Edwin H. *The Fall River Tragedy.* Fall River, Mass.: J. D. Munroe, 1893; Spiering, Frank. *Lizzie.* New York: Random House, 1984; Sullivan, Robert. *Goodbye Lizzie Borden.* Brattleboro, Vt.: S. Greene Press, 1974.

The Dreyfus case

Also known as: The court-martial of Alfred Dreyfus; Dreyfus affair; trial of Zola

Date: 1894–1899

KEY ISSUES

In the last quarter of the 19th century France was torn among several factions. Among the contenders for the nation's soul were those who yearned for a return to premodern, conservative, largely Catholic values and those who saw current France as the direct heir to the enlightened revolution of the 1790s. Architectural historians maintain that the two great structures built in Paris in the 1870s and 1880s, the Basilica of Sacré-Coeur and the Eiffel Tower, epitomize tension between the sacred and the secular in French national consciousness. Such divisions also existed within institutions such as the French military.

The case of Alfred Dreyfus was more complex than it seemed on the surface: the treason prosecution of a French army officer. In fact, the Dreyfus affair was not much so much about military concerns but rather social and religious fractures within France, although France was indeed wary of a militaristic Germany. Concerns over German expansionism affected many other nations. Great Britain, for instance, passed a series of Official Secrets Acts beginning in the 1880s. The legislation threatened harsh penalties for journalists, media distributors, and even whistle-blowers who printed information that the government considered confidential.

German spies were bogeymen in the late 19th century to many across Europe. Careless, greedy, or disloyal diplomats who fed German imperial ambitions were no less dangerous to their home countries than German secret agents. This was expressed culturally as well as politically and legally: Arthur Conan Doyle's tale "The Adventure of the Bruce-Partington-Plans," for example, revolved around the theft of military secrets by a government official. The story is set in 1895, while the Dreyfus affair raged.

Dreyfus's case involved several courts-martial (two of Dreyfus) as well as prosecution of the novelist Émile Zola. Zola had defended Dreyfus memorably in print. The legal proceedings were a test of the place of military courts within France and a gauge of the relationship between civilian and military institutions. Dreyfus was accused of passing along military secrets, but among his colleagues within the army, his greatest crimes were his hailing from a border region and being Jewish. To civilians who latched onto the case because of a chauvinistic agenda, the young army officer made an excellent target because he was not French enough.

History of the Case

The Statistical Section (counter-intelligence section) of the French intelligence service was charged with keeping a lookout for suspicious activities at the German embassy in Paris. An office cleaner collected the Germans' trash and periodically turned it over to French intelligence for analysis. In 1894 a handwritten short document, pieces of paper torn in half but otherwise undamaged, passed through the hands of French intelligence officer Major Hubert-Joseph Henry. Henry was working directly under Colonel Jean Conrad Sandherr, the head of the intelligence office. The papers pointed to sensitive information being sent from the French to the Germans. Specifically, it appeared that information about French artillery weapons, formations, and movements was being transferred to the German attaché in Paris. The newly discovered document was a cover letter (bordereau).

Investigators made a set of assumptions about the traitorous information that proved to be critical in their search for the perpetrator. First of all, lead investigator Major Armand du Paty de Clam deduced that the details in the bordereau came from within the General Staff of the War Office, a comparatively well-educated group of men. He knew that the person who wrote the bordereau spoke German, which again narrowed the list of suspects. Du Paty also suspected that the writer of the cover letter was an artillery officer who was being trained for intelligence work and that the bordereau was composed no later than mid-August 1894. Among the matters that du Paty failed to consider was why Henry had held such a document for a week or more before informing his superiors of its existence.

Those who sought to find the writer of the bordereau compared handwriting samples from personnel who seemed to fit the profile they had assembled. In early October they came up with a suspect: Alfred Dreyfus. Dreyfus had a fine mind and a good service record. Only the judgment of one of his examiners that "Jews were not in demand on the General Staff" kept him from finishing first in his class at the École Supérieure de Guerre in 1892.

Colonel Sandherr pressed his allegations. When the secretary of war, General Auguste Mercier, heard that Dreyfus was the major suspect, he constituted a committee of fellow cabinet-level officials to investigate the matter. He asked them to work quickly so as not to be accused of a cover-up. The committee first asked for a judgment as to whether the script on the bordereau was the same as in a dossier (Dreyfus's dossier, it turned out). A writing expert from the Bank of France reported that the writers might have been different persons. The committee, however, summarized the conclusions of the expert, Alfred Gobert, as "neutral" and called for another handwriting analysis. A police officer named Alphonse Bertillon who already knew the details of the matter performed a second analysis; he declared that Dreyfus was the writer of the bordereau.

When the investigators determined to bring Dreyfus in for questioning on October 15, 1894, they had a plan to gather more evidence of his guilt, induce him to confess, and perhaps even to encourage him to commit suicide on the spot. The idea was to summon Dreyfus to a meeting with General Mercier. While waiting for the superior's arrival, du Paty was to ask Dreyfus to take dictation of a letter. The wording of the letter was similar to that of the bordereau. Dreyfus wrote the missive without pause. His superiors, seeing their plan to expose Dreyfus falter, stopped the experiment and arrested him for treason.

SUMMARY OF ARGUMENTS

Dreyfus appeared completely taken aback and protested his innocence. He asked which documents had been the basis of the charge of treason. As he was driven to the Cherche-Midi, a military prison, he continued to ask Major Henry what he had done. He gave permission for his home and belongings to be searched. Nothing incriminating turned up. Even the expenditures of the household seemed ordinary. If the Germans were paying Dreyfus, then he was hiding the money well.

Du Paty interrogated Dreyfus in his cell, demanding that Dreyfus complete handwriting samples. None matched the script on the bordereau. No foreign notepaper was found anywhere near Dreyfus. Du Paty told the keeper of the prison, Major Ferdinand Forzinetti, not to divulge anything to Dreyfus about the case, nor was Forzi-

netti to tell his own superior that Dreyfus was incarcerated. The superintendent reported to du Paty that Dreyfus was so distraught as to be in physical and mental peril. Dreyfus became more focused on October 29, when du Paty finally revealed the document in question to the prisoner. Dreyfus denied having written it.

The police handwriting expert Bertillon continued to insist that Dreyfus was the writer of the treasonous letter. He explained divergences from Dreyfus's normal writing that were apparent in the bordereau as deliberate efforts to disguise his hand. General Mercier ordered another set of handwriting experts to make a report; two fingered Dreyfus as the bordereau's writer on the same grounds as Bertillon, and one strongly disagreed.

General Mercier still was considering what to do with that conflicting information when he found out that conservative newspapers had printed reports of Dreyfus's arrest on a charge of treason. Major Henry had leaked the information. The minister of war now decided that he had to make the case known to civil authorities in Paris or else be accused of collusion. Interestingly, the military attachés of both Italy and Germany spoke with each other when the accusations hit the press, asking if the other had benefited from secret information from Dreyfus. They discovered that neither had had any contact with Dreyfus. That information effectively exonerating Dreyfus was intercepted by French intelligence on November 2.

The press outcry against Dreyfus was harsh. He had sold secrets of paramount importance to the national defense, the papers said, and had cost French spies their lives. Newspaper editorials wondered why Mercier had sat on the information for two weeks or more. Why was Mercier protecting "the Jew"? Mercier, in turn, acted as though his own political survival was at stake. He superintended the preparation of a dossier from the War Office on Dreyfus, eventually turning over a sealed copy to the judges that heard charges of treason. Not only did Dreyfus's attorneys lack pretrial access to the information in the file, they did not even know of its existence until they got to court.

The formal decision on whether to prosecute Dreyfus was left up to Major Bexon d'Ormescheville, who was the leading judge-advocate of the first court-martial of the department of the Seine. He took reports from Dreyfus's colleagues that amounted to innuendo about the officer's personality, but no clear picture emerged of a traitor or even a free spender. Indeed, Dreyfus had considerable family resources that made him unlikely to succumb to the temptation of a financial motive. His reputation was one of hyper-patriotism, especially hailing as he did from a region that the Germans had occupied within living memory. Still, d'Ormescheville pressed further. Mercier and others, including Henry, urged a prosecution.

The Dreyfus family lawyer, Edgar Demange, was reluctant to take on the case. He told Dreyfus's wealthy brothers and his wife that he would agree to the brief only if he was completely satisfied of Dreyfus's innocence. Upon his own investigation he did take the case. He pushed hard for a public inquiry, assuring the prosecution that he would not divulge state secrets in order to clear his client. The War Office refused; Mercier claimed that the safety of France demanded a secret proceeding.

The court-martial that took place at the prison of Cherche-Midi on December 19, 1894, began with formal arguments from Demange to open up the case to public scrutiny. Again the court rebuffed him. Major Jean-Pierre Brisset, the chief lawyer (commissary) for the state, insisted anew that a secret trial was imperative. Colonel Émilien Maurel-Pries, the president of the court, acceded to requests from the prosecution that a very limited number of people should be present at trial.

The state's evidence was not impressive. The report of the scene in which Dreyfus was forced to take dictation from du Paty seemed inconclusive at best for Dreyfus's accusers. The handwriting analyses did not bear close scrutiny, either. But there was one decisive moment: Major Henry testified that a foreign informer had warned him months before of a mole within the War Office. He said that the unnamed person had implicated Dreyfus.

Demange based his defense mostly from the bordereau itself, contending that its contents and wording spoke against Dreyfus's authorship. Its grammar was poor, for example, in contrast to Dreyfus's well-schooled prose. The cover letter's references to technical aspects of artillery were amateurish, whereas Dreyfus knew the artillery

well. Would not a spy wish to convince his handlers of the value of the information he was divulging?

However convincing Demange's contentions were, based on the evidence there were two areas in which the defense faced an uphill battle. First, there was the presence of the defendant himself. Dreyfus seemed stiff, proud, and uncommunicative. He did not plead for his career with the judges. Even more damaging was the delivery of the secret dossier to the court. Historians cannot know precisely its contents, although one interested party later reconstructed portions of that file. But the judges were convinced by it.

VERDICT

The seven-judge panel pronounced Dreyfus guilty and sentenced him to a military prison for the remainder of his life. He was to lose his rank in a public ceremony of "degradation" before being sent to Devil's Island, in French Guinea. On January 5, 1895, the day of Dreyfus's public humiliation on the Champ de Mars, many French people acted as though Dreyfus was a great villain. He bore the stripping off of his military insignia and the breaking of his sword with enormous fortitude. He faced a huge crowd that bayed for his life and called out religious slurs. Dreyfus continued to insist to military officials such as du Paty that he was completely innocent of any wrongdoing— even in the face of du Paty's offer of a lighter sentence if Dreyfus would confess. The support of Dreyfus's wife and family as well as certain other individuals, such as the jailer Forzinetti, was critical in keeping up his spirits.

Certain other individuals, meanwhile, started to take up Dreyfus's cause, even at the risk of their careers. A striking example was General Paul Darras, the man who read the order of degradation at the Champ du Mars. As soon as he pronounced the sentence to the crowd, Darras loudly proclaimed: "You are degrading an innocent man!" There was another defender who would prove invaluable to Dreyfus, although he was at first an unlikely friend. Major George Picquart of the intelligence service had been the official observer from that office at the secret court-martial. The more he saw in the military court proceeding, the more suspicious he became that something was amiss.

A new French president sent Dreyfus into foreign exile. Dreyfus was placed in confinement on a tropical island, where he lived with little mobility in filthy conditions. Mrs. Dreyfus's efforts to join him were refused. Dreyfus's family kept up a stream of comment to the press about the deplorable circumstances of his imprisonment and his deteriorating health. Dreyfus's brothers also insisted that inquiry should continue in a search for the real author of the bordereau.

With the change in presidential administration came a new leadership in the intelligence service: Picquart now was at its head. Coincidentally, Henry was not overseeing the reading of the trash from the Germans as closely during March 1896 as in the past because of personal business. On one particular day Picquart delegated the job to another officer named Captain Jules Lauth. After a few hours of gluing together slips of paper, Lauth reported back to Picquart with real concern. He had pieced together a small card *(petit bleu)* used to communicate through a pneumatic tube. The *petit bleu* contained a note from Colonel Max von Schwartzkoppen of the German emissary to French intelligence officer Major Charles Esterhazy. The note seemed very much like communications that had convicted Dreyfus.

Lauth and Picquart at first wondered if there was another spy in their midst. Picquart kept this new finding under very close guard while he investigated whether the original charges against Dreyfus might have been a terrible mistake. The more that Picquart delved into Esterhazy's background, recent conduct, and skills, the more worried the intelligence chief became. Esterhazy had worked closely with German intelligence at a post in Tunis, was fluent in the German language, and at times was badly in debt. His knowledge of artillery matters was scattershot—the type of random intelligence reflected in the bordereau.

Esterhazy somehow got wind of the suspicions and tried taking the offensive in discussing the matter with superiors. Picquart, meanwhile, grew more convinced of Esterhazy's involvement in the earlier treason. Picquart heard from a double agent in Berlin that the Germans were puzzled by the whole Dreyfus affair, as they never had had any

dealing with Dreyfus and had tried to spread word to that effect in the French press at the time of Dreyfus's initial detention. When Picquart made his superiors General Raoul Le Mouton de Boisdeffre and General Jean-Baptiste Billot aware of his fears, they told Picquart to keep quiet. The higher-ups did not want to preside over another Dreyfus scandal. The word came down that Esterhazy should be let go in a subtle manner.

Picquart compared handwriting samples from Esterhazy to the script in the bordereau; it was identical. He took Esterhazy's writing from office files (with identifying marks removed) to his superiors du Paty and Bertillon. They pronounced the samples to be from either Alfred's brother Matthew Dreyfus or the bordereau itself. Picquart explained that this writing had been produced more recently. The superior officers then speculated that "the Jews" had been training people to write in a script like Dreyfus's hand. Picquart, undeterred, then located the secret dossier within Henry's safe. He perused it and found nothing there to incriminate Dreyfus. It looked to Picquart as though Dreyfus had been wrongly convicted. He also theorized that several highly placed individuals either had known about the injustice and looked the other way or had colluded in the process.

After Picquart made his official report to his superiors, he was told that they thought there must have been two spies. The Esterhazy matter, in other words, was separate from the Dreyfus case. What were the motives of the two generals in opposing Picquart? General de Boisdeffre seemed impelled by religious bias; he was influenced by his Jesuit spiritual adviser to suspect disloyalty among Jews. General Billot simply did not want to stir up trouble. Picquart also faced opposition from men below him in rank, including Lauth and particularly Henry, who it turned out was a close associate of Esterhazy. Other superiors advocated keeping the matter secret. It later came out that a general, Arthur Gonse, had tried to dissuade Picquart from digging any deeper. In one conversation Gonse asked Picquart why he cared if "this Jew remains at Devil's Island or not." Picquart's response reportedly flabbergasted the general: "But he is innocent."

When Dreyfus's family managed to make public a photographic reproduction of the bordereau in *Le Matin* on November 10, 1896, independent handwriting experts began to weigh in. Word about Esterhazy's possible involvement was leaking out, and his script could be compared with that in the bordereau. Those who wished to neutralize Picquart, however, were at the same moment having him transferred to a faraway position (at Tunis) where he would not be closely involved in the investigation.

Picquart was so worried that he would be forcibly silenced that he left word of his findings in a codicil to his will. He took leave and returned to Paris, where he consulted a lawyer. He also prepared to confront none other than Henry, who now was in Picquart's old post as head of the intelligence service. Picquart was convinced that Henry was occupied with covering up his own role in Dreyfus's unjust conviction, literally through the manufacture of documents. Picquart and others who sought to clear Dreyfus guessed that the Staff Office was beginning to warn Esterhazy. Schwartz-koppen, meanwhile, retired to Berlin; he realized that "his man," Esterhazy, had been found out. Though Esterhazy was being protected, Schwartz-koppen no longer saw him as a viable intelligence source and wished to be free of the scandal that might erupt if Dreyfus were cleared.

The conservative press vilified those who defended Dreyfus in all this, charging that Picquart and other Dreyfusards were attempting to "substitute Esterhazy for the Jew" at Devil's Island. Faced with that apparent support and angered by arguments by Dreyfus's brother Matthew that handwriting experts now had conclusively matched the bordereau script with his own, Esterhazy demanded a court-martial for himself. In December 1897 General Billot restated within the Chamber of Deputies that he was absolutely convinced of Dreyfus's guilt.

Esterhazy's court-martial on January 10 and 11, 1898, was a triumph for him and a brush-off of the Dreyfus family. Though they had lawyers ready to represent them, the pro-Dreyfus faction was not given an official role in the inquiry. Besides trying to clear Alfred Dreyfus's name, the Dreyfusards also argued that any "revision" of the case ought to be in a public forum. There, too,

they lost. The military court was not enamored of making Picquart's evidence readily available.

Esterhazy's defense was that the *petit bleu* was a forgery. The real focus seemed to be, in fact, on neither Esterhazy nor Dreyfus but rather the troublemaker Picquart. Picquart was confined for a 60-day period for his whistle-blowing. The court advised him to expect further investigations into his actions. The most critical remark that the judges made about Esterhazy in their statement of acquittal was that with his dissolute habits Esterhazy was not an ideal role model for young soldiers.

The affair got more contentious as additional voices entered the discussion. The acquittal of Esterhazy touched off protest among the "revisionists," those who wished to revisit the case and clear Dreyfus of any wrongdoing. Most sharp among those cries for justice came from the novelist Émile Zola. Zola was not the only person with academic or literary credentials to take up the case, but he was arguably the most talented. He declared Dreyfus innocent, condemned the military officials who had colluded in his persecution, and castigated the civil authorities who had acceded to demands that the intelligence service should police its own. His declaration of these injustices, "J'accuse," appeared on January 13. It was an intemperate but compelling call for further action on behalf of Dreyfus.

The War Office immediately filed charges of defamation against Zola. The jury of the Seine heard that case in February 1898. The president (chief judge) of the court, Albert Delegorgue, seemed anxious to allow no evidence that would be helpful to Dreyfus or Zola but permitted much to be introduced that pointed to Esterhazy's honorable intentions. Zola had extremely capable counsel in Albert Clemenceau and Fernand Labori. They did get Picquart to testify, and he held up well even under close questioning. A dramatic moment occurred when Henry, on the stand, accused Picquart of lying; Esterhazy did practically the same. After the trial of Zola concluded, Picquart challenged Henry to a duel as a result of the affront. Picquart refused, though, to give Esterhazy the satisfaction of treating him as a "gentleman" with such a test of honor. Picquart said "that man belongs to the justice of the nation."

Zola's trial had been going fairly well for the defense until February 17, when General Georges-Gabriel de Pellieux, a legal expert with the Staff Office, dropped a "thunderbolt" into the proceedings. He had seen a communication from one foreign attaché to another (presumably the German to the Italian) that Dreyfus was their contact in Paris. General Gonse affirmed de Pellieux's testimony. Zola's counsel objected strenuously. Why, Labori asked, did the generals not produce the document? Picquart suspected that Henry had forged the communication. He said as much under cross-examination. The government declared that such sensitive evidence should not be subject to inspection in open court because foreign powers might be offended. General de Boisdeffre made a statement supporting the testimony of Pellieux, and the court left it at that. The jury found Zola guilty, sentencing him to a year's imprisonment and levying a large fine. The publisher of the libel also was fined and jailed. On a technicality an appeals court annulled the sentences. The stated reason for the nullification was that the court-martial should have pursued the libel case because its judgment was what Zola had impugned.

Though certain civil officials warned against it, the court-martial laid a second case against Zola. Rather than appear at the Court of Assizes of Seine and Oise at Versailles, Zola fled to England. This court reimposed the previous punishment; it was the maximum penalty allowed for defamation that had no extenuating circumstances.

The French national legislature was fractured by the case. Dreyfusards accused the defenders of the army of being anti-Semites, while anti-revisionists painted the pro-Dreyfus deputies as intellectuals or radicals. But, just when things looked bleakest for those who defended Alfred Dreyfus—still sweltering on Devil's Island—the case began to go his way. Within the War Office in late summer 1898, quite by accident documents came to light that showed that Major Henry in fact had forged certain materials damaging to Dreyfus. When he was confronted with that evidence, Henry broke down and admitted he had committed the offense in order to protect Esterhazy. Henry was put into custody at the same prison where Picquart had been confined. On August 31, 1898, Henry committed suicide. The cover-up was unraveling and becoming public at the same time. Esterhazy promptly fled for London. General de Boisdeffre resigned.

The legal system prepared to hear a revision of the Dreyfus case as of September 27, 1898. There were two major schools of thought on what form a reconsideration of the case should take. The attorney general, Manau, argued that the proceedings should be a complete voiding of Dreyfus's sentence—a repudiation of the court-martial of 1894. Others maintained that there should be merely an inquiry on the whole situation. An investigation would issue a report and acquaint the public with the facts as they now were known, and that would suffice.

The decision was to combine the approaches. In mid-November the case went to the Criminal Chamber of the Court of Cassation. The civilian court would take under advisement Mrs. Dreyfus's petitions to reconsider her husband's case in light of new evidence but would proceed with an inquiry rather than a formal trial. At that moment the court informed Alfred Dreyfus of what was to transpire. Until then Dreyfus had been allowed mail, but it was heavily censored to contain only family news and no information about his case.

Picquart and his lawyers had to engage in complex political and legal maneuvers in order to prevent a court-martial of him from going forward prior to the revision of Dreyfus's case. They managed it, though. Picquart's fate was put in the hands of civil justice.

As the proceeding on Dreyfus went forward, much information favorable to Dreyfus made it into the newspapers. The graphologists now were unanimous in declaring the bordereau to be not in Dreyfus's hand but rather in Esterhazy's. One of those experts was among those who had testified against Dreyfus in 1894. It carried much weight with this court, too, that the type of paper on which the bordereau was written had been found elsewhere in Esterhazy's correspondence. No one had turned up any paper of the sort among Dreyfus's possessions.

From his self-imposed exile Esterhazy released a statement that he had written the bordereau but that he had done so under instructions from above. On May 29 the president of the Court of

Cassation read a statement expressing regret that Esterhazy could not be retried, for he surely had composed the document that began the whole affair. The court nonetheless could do something to help bring about justice. It could and did recommend that Dreyfus should be reheard in another court-martial. It would be a long-overdue opportunity for Dreyfus to clear his name.

Dreyfus's second court-martial still would be under the auspices of the military, which had thought its reputation impugned in the affair. The rules of evidence for that venue meant that Dreyfus was being retried on much the same evidence as had been offered in 1894. Dreyfus's case also was damaged when his lawyer, Labori, was shot while the court-martial was on going.

The new trial began on August 7, 1899, in Rennes. Except for the chief judge, all of the men who would decide the case were artillery officers. Dreyfus was in poor mental and physical health. Though he attempted to appear robust by stuffing his clothes, he was almost in shock. He remained composed in what must have been a supreme effort at self-control. To his judges Dreyfus offered a formal statement expressing confidence in this court's ability to assess his actions fairly:

> I am absolutely sure, I affirm before my country and before my army, that I am innocent. It is with the sole aim of saving the honor of my name, and of the name that my children bear, that for five years I have undergone the most frightful tortures. I am convinced that I shall attain this aim today, thanks to your honesty and to your sense of justice.

Much to his surprise and that of the nation as a whole, the court-martial convicted him again. It was as though the wounded pride of the army would not admit error. General Mercier thus was cleared of his involvement in the cover-up. The court-martial, however, declared an extraordinary postscript to its verdict—that there had been extenuating circumstances to Dreyfus's treason. The court recommended he should be detained for 10 years. They further let it slip out that they had asked the War Office to treat Dreyfus gently. On September 19, 1899, France's president, Émile

Loubet, declared him pardoned. This also reversed Dreyfus's military degradation, although it did not make the career soldier eligible for further military service. In 1906 the verdict of the court-martial at Rennes was vacated so that Dreyfus could again serve in the army.

SIGNIFICANCE

After his reinstatement to army rank Dreyfus served another year before an initial retirement. World War I brought him back to active duty. He saw battle at Verdun but survived, living almost to the next international conflict. Picquart resigned his commission in protest of his treatment by the French military. Zola came back to France but was denied many of the honors that his literary talent otherwise would have earned for him. He died of carbon monoxide poisoning owing to a closed chimney in 1902. Rumor had it that his death was no accident but rather the result of his outspoken advocacy of causes such as Dreyfus's.

At the end of his many trials Dreyfus would have been more at home near to Eiffel's engineering marvel than within the great Catholic edifice of Sacré-Coeur. But, when the Dreyfus case reached a legal resolution, Dreyfus still did not seem comfortable in belonging to either side of the controversy. Rather, he insisted that the furor had been about an error among his superiors. Until his death in 1935, Dreyfus maintained only that he had been wrongly accused. He did not accept the role of a martyr nor even the mantle of a defender of justice.

Further Reading

Bredin, Jean-Denis. *The Affair: The Case of Alfred Dreyfus.* New York: George Braziller, 1986; Brown, Frederick. *For the Soul of France: Culture Wars in the Age of Dreyfus.* New York: Knopf, 2010; ———. *Zola: A Life.* New York: Farrar, Straus & Giroux, 1995; Fischman, Lawrence. *The French Artillery Officer.* Dallas, Tex.: Gram's Group, 2009; Forth, Christopher. *The Dreyfus Affair and the Crisis of French Manhood.* Baltimore, Md.: Johns Hopkins University Press, 2006; Harris, Ruth. *Dreyfus: Politics, Emotion, and the Scandal of the Century.* New York: Metropolitan

Books, 2010; Johnson, Martin P. *The Dreyfus Affair*. New York: St. Martin's Press, 1999.

The trials of Oscar Wilde

Also known as: *Wilde v. Douglas; The Crown v. Wilde*

Date: 1895

KEY ISSUES

Late 19th-century Britain supposedly was a place marked by conformity to traditional sexual values. Yet, in a variety of subcultures English people ran counter to the Victorian stereotype. Some individuals bridged the gap between those worlds: the expected and conservative versus the alternative and subversive. Writer Oscar Wilde did just that for several years of his well-known life. In three separate trials, however, his leading role within the homosexual community became public. The trials of Wilde—one of which he initiated as a lawsuit, the other two of which were prosecutions of him for sexual offenses—were tests of conventional norms regarding sexuality.

The Wilde trials sent a chill through the homosexual underground, literally causing some persons to flee England for locations (particularly Paris) more conducive to their personal, social, literary, and artistic activities. In a legal sense the cases involving Wilde were a gauge of authorities' willingness to prosecute using the Criminal Law Amendment Act of 1885, which some of its critics called "the blackmailer's charter." Legislation regarding consensual homosexual activity in late Victorian Britain was nowhere near as severe as the statute of 1533 that Henry VIII passed to suppress supposed sexual immorality within monasteries. That famous "buggery law" had made certain sexual acts between men punishable capitally. And yet, the Victorian law still provided for a term of hard labor upon conviction. For Wilde, the combination of his trials and prison time in effect were a death sentence. His reputation among polite society was shattered, and his health and spirits were destroyed by incarceration.

HISTORY OF THE CASE

Wilde enjoyed a considerable reputation among a wide public as a writer, an art critic, and even what one might call a celebrity from the late 1870s into the early 1890s in London. He was a notable promoter of the aesthetic movement in the arts, along with persons such as his sometime rival James McNeill Whistler. By the early 1890s Wilde had several plays running in the fashionable West End. Wilde was at the epicenter of not just English theater but also the literary world.

He had toured Europe and the United States in the 1880s, lecturing on subjects ranging from the silver works of Benito Cellini to home decoration. Wilde's formal speeches were tolerably received, but he made a greater impression in other respects. He was described as a brilliant conversationalist, equally at home with the Prince of Wales as with the miners of the American West. Like the woman whom he frequently called his muse, actress Lillie Langtry, he marketed himself skillfully. Those around him perceived his commercial value. The photographer Napoleon Sarony, who took a famous series of photographs of Wilde during a New York stop, successfully pressed for a clarification of United States law so that he, the photographer, could control the iconic images that he and Wilde had produced.

In the United States, Wilde was known simply as "Oscar" in places as diverse as Cambridge, Massachusetts, and Leadville, Colorado. His affectations—knee breeches (better to show off a man's calf muscles), a green carnation in the lapel (rumored to designate him as a "molly"), long hair atop his noticeably large head—were unconventional. His critics lampooned Wilde, the most famous send-up appearing in William Schwenk Gilbert and Arthur Seymour Sullivan's light opera *Patience*. Wilde seemed to celebrate caricatures, though, as recognition of his distinctive persona.

Wilde did observe some conventionalities. He came from an upper-middle-class Irish family; his father, William Wilde, was knighted for achievements as an ophthalmologist in Dublin. As Oscar

Wilde entered young adulthood, his mother, Jane Elgee Wilde, still was active as "Speranza," a poet and advocate for Irish nationalism. Wilde attended Trinity College, Dublin, and Magdalen College, Oxford. At university he carefully cultivated an image of indolence while showing promise as a scholar of the classics. He graduated with a "double first" degree, finally bringing to the surface his academic prowess.

He moved to London to try his hand at writing, beginning with editing magazines. His literary career went much better after the American tour had established his celebrity. He got married, and he and his wife, Constance, had two boys upon whom they doted; several of Wilde's better-known stories were composed for the children. Constance Wilde, quiet and bright, seemed willing to try out his theories on aesthetic dress and was generally tolerant of his free spending and traveling. Theirs appeared to be a companionate, though perhaps not passionate, marriage.

Wilde was a successful playwright and author and a recognizable figure around town. He also had a secret life, spending a great deal of time with young men from Oxford and Cambridge who idolized him. They, in turn, introduced Wilde to the London homosexual underworld, socializing not only with well-known artists and writers but also professional male prostitutes. With characteristic wit Wilde referred to these shadier associations as "feasting with panthers." Wilde had many friends and a few lovers among the diverse group of persons he met in the "molly subculture," but no relationship was as important to him as his connection with a young nobleman named Alfred Douglas.

Douglas, who also had attended Magdalen College, Oxford, became close friends with Wilde in June 1891, when he was 21 and Wilde was 36. At the time of their acquaintance Wilde was enjoying successful reviews from *The Picture of Dorian Gray* despite some difficulty in getting that work published. Douglas, whom his friends called "Bosie," came from a quarrelsome family. His father, John Sholto, the marquis of Queensberry, was a man who enjoyed the outdoors and sports such as bicycling and shooting.

Queensberry was an enthusiastic promoter of pugilism; it was for him that the Queensberry rules of boxing were named. There were rumors that

Queensberry's oldest son had committed suicide as a result of being discovered as homosexual; Queensberry, partly as a result, had a keen aversion to men who did not act "manly." He therefore was incensed at the developing relationship between Wilde and his youngest son, Alfred, and was determined to break it apart. He engineered face-to-face meetings involving Wilde and his son, discussions that ended with insults flying. Queensberry sent "toughs" (the more modern term would be *enforcers*) to Wilde's house to warn him to stay away from Lord Alfred. He arranged for protesters to appear at Wilde's plays. None of it worked, and Lord Alfred appeared to glory in his father's increasing distress. By late 1894 Wilde had three very successful plays either in composition or running in London's West End: *The Importance of Being Earnest, Lady Windemere's Fan,* and *A Woman of No Importance.* He was balancing marked professional success with an increasingly turbulent private life.

The full truth about that delicate balance finally came out in the courtroom. Always the master of epigrams, Wilde composed a saying that neatly summarized what happened at his trials: "The truth is never pure and rarely simple."

Queensberry's anger escalated, and he attempted to pull Wilde into a public fight. Wilde thought it time to confront his chief critic. Both Queensberry and Wilde, in 1894, had talked with lawyers about how to employ the legal system to achieve their desired results. Wilde was confident about his ability to get Queensberry to desist in his persecution of him and Bosie Douglas through legal action. Queensberry, armed with the reports of private detectives who had tailed Wilde, honed his offensive strategy. His lawyers advised him that the act of sodomy was the most serious offense with which Wilde could be charged. Yet, sodomy would be difficult to prove. While keeping the charge of sodomy in reserve as a weapon, Queensberry crafted a more manageable accusation.

In late February 1895 Queensberry left his calling card with the porter at the Albemarle Club, to which Wilde belonged. On the card Queensberry had scrawled "to Oscar Wilde, posing somdomite." The key word, though misspelled, was one that would be actionable in a libel suit. Queensberry had thrown an insult at Wilde to which he hoped

Wilde would react. It was a clever bit of wording, reflecting Queensberry's legal consultations: He was accusing Wilde of looking like a sodomite, rather than being one. Wilde did file suit against Queensberry for libel. It would be up to Queensberry to "justify" his writing, that is, to offer evidence that would support his words being truthful. Queensberry also would have to show that the insulting phrase was written for a defensible purpose under the law; this was called "justifying" the libel.

It was pivotal that attorney George Lewis, whom Queensberry originally had engaged to represent him in court, withdrew from that role after initially arguing on Queensberry's behalf at the arraignment. Lewis considered himself a friend of Wilde and would not appear against him. His withdrawal, however, left room for Queensberry to engage a brilliant barrister named Edward Carson, who had been in school with Wilde and apparently did not like Wilde. Wilde, accompanied by Bosie Douglas, had conversations with solicitor C. O. Humphreys in which he assured Humphreys that there was no truth to Queensberry's accusations. Humphreys, in turn, told Wilde and Douglas that the case was winnable. Wilde later wrote that he felt contempt for Humphreys for not being more discerning.

Before trial Queensberry's legal team had to release the details of his plea of justification. The plea provided damaging and detailed information about Wilde's contacts with various young men who were known as prostitutes, blackmailers, or both. Queensberry's lawyers intended to supplement that data gathered by his detectives with letters that Wilde had sent to Alfred Douglas. The correspondence appeared to describe a romantic relationship between the two men.

SUMMARY OF ARGUMENTS

Wilde's suit against Queensberry was heard beginning on April 3, 1895, at London's Central Criminal Court, the Old Bailey. Edward Clarke, Wilde's barrister, argued that Queensberry had besmirched Wilde's reputation. Queensberry's barrister, Carson, replied that the truth of the libel could be proved and that it was published for the benefit of the public. The trial largely was a contest of verbal skills on the part of Wilde and Carson, who, as Wilde had predicted, would perform "his task with the added bitterness of an old friend."

Wilde was at his most effective in the witness box when he defended the content of his literary works as well as private letters. Wilde's own lawyer, Clarke, admitted that Wilde had bought back letters from a blackmailer, Alfred Taylor. Wilde memorably described the effort at blackmail:

> I felt that this was the man who wanted money from me. I said, "I suppose you have come about my beautiful letter to Lord Alfred Douglas. If you had not been so foolish as to send a copy to Mr. Beerbohm Tree, I would gladly have paid you a very large sum of money for the letter, as I consider it to be a work of art."
>
> He said, "A very curious construction can be put on that letter."
>
> I said in reply, "Art is rarely intelligible to the criminal classes."

And, he parried ably with Carson, who questioned the morality of *Dorian Gray:*

> Carson: The affection and love of the artist of Dorian Gray might lead an ordinary individual to believe that it might have a certain tendency?
>
> Wilde: I have no knowledge of the views of ordinary individuals.
>
> Carson: Have you ever adored a young man madly?
>
> Wilde: No, not madly. I prefer love—that is a higher form.
>
> Carson: Never mind about that. Let us keep down to the level we are at now.
>
> Wilde: I have never given adoration to anybody except myself.

But, the details of Wilde's meetings with the young male prostitutes began to emerge through Carson's dry, methodical questioning, and Wilde's wit finally wore thin:

Carson: Did you ever kiss him?

Wilde: Oh dear, no. He was a peculiarly plain boy. . . .

Carson: Was that the reason why you did not kiss him?

Wilde: Oh, Mr. Carson, you are pertinently insolent.

Clarke stopped the proceedings before a number of young men could be put on the stand to speak in person about the acts alleged. Wilde's side, in other words, withdrew the libel action against Queensberry before any more damaging information came out about Wilde. Justice Henn Collins directed the jury to reach a "Not guilty" verdict; he further allowed the defense to state that the offensive words had been published "for the public benefit." To cheers from onlookers the court adjourned. Shortly afterward, Justice Collins sent Carson a note congratulating Carson on his superb oratory and "having escaped the filth."

VERDICTS

Wilde already had considered advice to decamp for the Continent. His supporters as well as his lawyers foresaw that Queensberry would not be content until Wilde was in jail. They expected that they could delay another trial until Wilde was safely out of reach of English law. In one of the mysterious aspects of his case—one much debated among Wilde's and Douglas's friends and subsequent biographers—Wilde refused all such offers to escape. Did he expect that he could outtalk his tormentors? Was he paralyzed with conflicting emotions? Did he nurse the sense (perhaps fed by his mother) that it was dishonorable to run from a fight?

Against mounting evidence that Queensberry did intend to spearhead a prosecution and that the case against him would be devastating, Wilde stayed to face trial. The case stretched into two trials, one after another. The prosecution was mounted by the government via a public prosecutor but also fed by Queensberry's animus. In those latter two of Wilde's three trials, Wilde faced charges of both sodomy and multiple acts of indecency. Prime Minister Archibald Primrose, Lord Rosebery, had per-

sonal motives for wishing the government to appear strict toward Wilde and his ilk. While he was foreign secretary a few years prior, Rosebery was rumored to be a lover of Queensberry's eldest son.

It did not take long for the prosecution to gear up. The second trial in which Wilde participated—now as a defendant—began on April 26, 1895. Clarke again represented Wilde, refusing to accept a fee. He no doubt seemed moved to help Wilde because of the bankruptcy proceedings against Wilde that had gone on days before. The calling in of Wilde's debts, urged on by Queensberry, ended with the forced sale of Wilde's valuable manuscripts and artifacts. Sir Frank Lockwood, Britain's solicitor-general, led the prosecution. He was assisted by Charles Gill and C. O. Humphreys's son Travers. Justice Arthur Charles presided. Wilde, who had been denied bail, appeared pale and thinner after only a few days behind bars.

Again, much of the memorable rhetoric of the trial revolved around Wilde's letters to Alfred Douglas:

Gill: Is it not clear that the love described relates to natural love and unnatural love?

Wilde: "The Love that dare not speak its name in this century" is such a great affection of an elder for a younger man as there was between David and Jonathan, such as Plato made the very basis of his philosophy, and such as you might find in the sonnets of Shakespeare. . . . There is nothing unnatural about it. It repeatedly exists between an older and a younger man, when the elder man has intellect and the younger man has all the joy, hope, and glamour of life before him. That it should be so, the world does not understand. The world mocks at it and sometimes puts one in the pillory for it.

Wilde had the disadvantage of his case being joined with a supposed coconspirator, Alfred Taylor. Taylor, in whose quarters several of the alleged assignations took place, had refused to participate in a plea bargain in exchange for his testimony against Wilde. Despite that handicap to Wilde, both the jury and the judge in the case found the evidence against Wilde in the second trial to be unconvincing. The jury refused to convict Wilde and Taylor. Admittedly, it was not a huge vote of confidence; rumor even among Wilde's friends had one or at most two jurors voting for acquittal. Justice Charles, however, had directed the jury to clear Wilde. He characterized the defendant Wilde as "one of our most renowned and accomplished men of letters of today." Justice Charles discounted the testimony of witnesses that he termed blackmailers and rejected the negative prosecutorial interpretation of Wilde's literary work.

The prosecution did not rest, however, largely because of Queensberry's pursuit of the case and Lockwood's fear that the government would be seen as too sympathetic to Wilde. Wilde went free on May 1, 1895, but was rearrested within a matter of hours. Lockwood, with his greater trial experience than Gill, took a more active role in the second prosecution of Wilde (his third trial), which focused on Wilde alone. Taylor already had been convicted. This trial repeated much of the evidence from persons who had tried to blackmail Wilde but without the brilliant sparring that previously marked Wilde's and Carson's interchanges. Wilde, perceptibly haggard, seemed resigned to a conviction.

There still were interesting points for discussion among the lawyers. Clarke asked the jury to consider Wilde's early literary productivity as well as his potential for future writings. He fretted that a person of Wilde's genius could be convicted upon the word of criminals. Replying in his summation, Lockwood made short work of the argument that anyone should place an innocent meaning upon Wilde's letters to Douglas. He also asked a question that many of Wilde's supporters would not: Why was Bosie himself not called to give evidence? At various times during the proceedings prosecutors referred to Wilde as having written pieces that were in fact composed by Douglas, or having committed acts that seemed more in line with Douglas's prior behavior. Douglas had headed for the Continent rather than be called to the stand, or worse.

Justice Alfred Wills's directions to the jury made plain his disgust at the content of the trial; his statement upon passing sentence was an even plainer condemnation of Wilde: ". . . People who do these things must be dead to all sense of shame, and one cannot hope to produce any effect upon them. It is the worst case I have ever tried. . . ." Wills sent

Wilde to hard labor in prison for two years, the maximum sentence allowed under the law for a conviction of indecency. Due to some legal wrangling the sodomy charge had been dropped; in this case, as in most other such prosecutions, it was practically impossible to substantiate.

SIGNIFICANCE

Wilde's trials had personal, literary, legal, and social implications. As a person, Wilde was irreparably harmed by his time in court. He languished in prison for two years, during which time his career was severely damaged. He sustained a serious injury in a fall in prison, which probably led to his death (in a small hotel in Paris) in 1900. The fate of his immediate family was regrettable and preventable. Ordered by the court to pay the costs associated with his prosecution of Queensberry, Constance Wilde had to sell all their household possessions at great loss and put her children into the trust of relatives. Constance Wilde never divorced her husband, though she renamed the children for their guardians. She died after a botched back surgery just about the time Oscar Wilde was released from prison. Given the relatively large resources of Queensberry's family, the bankruptcy proceedings against the Wildes were punitive.

Wilde's output as an artist ceased for a time and never did regain its former sparkle, although in prison he produced two memorable works. He composed a bitter autobiographical letter to Alfred Douglas, titled *De Profundis,* and a rumination called *The Ballad of Reading Gaol,* which was a criticism of prison conditions. Although *The Ballad* was widely known to be Wilde's, it was published without his name attached. *De Profundis* was circulated only in part for about half a century, finally appearing in a complete edition long after the deaths of both Wilde and Douglas.

For decades after Wilde's conviction Europeans referred to Great Britain as a bastion of conservative laws concerning sexual behavior. In 1918, at another trial involving artistic expression, *Rex v. Billings,* prosecutors argued that Wilde's influence had corrupted the youth of the nation and made them unfit to compete militarily against the Germans.

Commemorations of the 100th anniversary of Wilde's trials included the designation of a spot for

Wilde in Poet's Corner of Westminster Abbey. That honor was a tribute to Wilde's potential and his fame, if not his talent. Wilde defies the efforts of scholars to pigeonhole him: His positions are not consistent enough to make him a hero of literary freedom, Irish national consciousness, aestheticism, or gay rights. Wilde's long-term historical reputation ultimately may rest upon the resilience of his writings; their quality still is under discussion among literary scholars. He remains, though, a dazzling wit and a self-promoter of the first order, at once engaging and self-destructive.

Further Reading

Blanchard, Mary Warner. *Oscar Wilde's America.* New Haven, Conn.: Yale University Press, 1998; Edwards, Owen Dudley. "Wilde, Oscar Fingal O'Flahertie Wills (1854–1900)." In *Oxford Dictionary of National Biography.* Available online. URL: http://libproxy.uta.edu:2422/view/article/29400. Accessed November 4, 2007; Ellmann, Richard. *Oscar Wilde.* New York: Random House, 1987; Fischer, Trevor. *Oscar and Bosie.* Thrupp, U.K.: Sutton Publishing, 2002; Holland, Merlin. *The Wilde Album.* New York: Henry Holt, 1997; Hyde, H. Montgomery. *The Trials of Oscar Wilde.* London: William Hodge, 1948; "Reading Wilde, Querying Spaces: An Exhibition Commemorating the 100th Anniversary of the Trials of Oscar Wilde." Available online. URL: http://www.nyu.edu/library/bobst/research/fales/exhibits/wilde/00main.htm. Accessed April 15, 2007.

The trial of Harry Thaw

Also known as: *New York v. Thaw*

Date: 1907

KEY ISSUES

The Harry Thaw case of 1907–08 did not break new legal ground. The justification that the defense proffered, though temporarily successful, was far too transparent to convince jurists to alter the law. Rather, this was a trial that compelled attention because of the outsize personalities of its major players. There were three main figures in the case: the alleged murderer who was a playboy millionaire of uncertain mental stability; the victim, who was the leading architect of his day in the United States; and the object of both men's affections, who was a most attractive young woman. When one considers that all of those individuals were galvanic personalities, each quite prominent in his or her environment, there was every reason for the trial to become extremely well known. The crime that gave rise to the trial took place in New York City, which was a center for newspaper reporting. It would have been remarkable for the case not to attract wide comment.

HISTORY OF THE CASE

The facts of the case were common enough: the crime at issue was a shooting. On June 25, 1906, the perpetrator had shot his target three times in the head at close range in front of numerous witnesses. The victim was a man who had been involved with the wife of the man who pulled the trigger, though that affair happened before the murderous man and his wife were married. It seemed that the husband could not let go of his jealousy of the man who had preceded him in his young bride's affections—so far, a usual enough scenario. What elevated the episode to national prominence was, in particular, the identity of the victim. The dead man was Stanford White, a regular in the glittering social scene of New York City and a creator of buildings all over the country. A principal in the architectural firm of McKim, Mead, and White, he had constructed buildings for the robber barons as well as the public. He was the designer, in fact, of the very structure in which he died: Madison Square Garden. White, who was in his mid-40s, also was a lothario with a penchant for young showgirls.

The shooter was Harry Thaw, a wastrel son of a family in Pittsburgh who gained a fortune in the coke business, an offshoot of steel production. There had been disharmony between Thaw's parents about how much rein he should be given. His mother indulged the profligate son, while the father attempted to put him on an allowance. So mercurial was his personality that Thaw often had to spend money to buy friends; that was especially his modus operandi with women. Particularly alarming was Thaw's propensity for sadism. Like White, Thaw admired young singers and dancers on the New York stage. There is some indication that Thaw at one time considered White a bit of a role model. White was vigorous, appeared wealthy, and the ladies flocked to him. Those aspiring actresses and the occasional actor who fell in with Thaw, though, might find themselves not only seduced but also beaten.

The third point in the love triangle was Evelyn Nesbit, a 15-year-old when she arrived in New York in 1900 and gained the attention of both men. Nesbit was from an obscure (if not impoverished) background. Like Thaw, Nesbit and her ambitious mother came to the big city from Pittsburgh. She sought modeling prospects and got attention quickly from artists and photographers searching for a new muse. Nesbit had a lithe, fresh beauty. She came across stunningly in photographs, in a variety of guises from sultry to naive. Nesbit's greatest opportunity as a model was when the artist Charles Dana Gibson employed her to pose for one of his Gibson Girl drawings, which had become famous as a prototype of fashionable young womanhood. She soon broke onto the stage with small parts, thus gaining the attention of both Thaw and White who were avid theater attendees. White asked his friends in the theater to grant more opportunities to Nesbit. Her new benefactor had done the same for many other young actresses.

Though White paid no attention to Thaw, Thaw was obsessed with Nesbit in part because she soon became linked with White. Those who knew White assumed that Nesbit and White were lovers. After Nesbit had to be hospitalized with appendicitis, Thaw stayed by her side to nurse the young woman. White, meanwhile, had other mistresses, as well as his regular family. In time his attention to Nesbit diminished.

Thaw bombarded Nesbit with requests to know about her involvement with White—this at a time when the men were no longer rivals for Nesbit's attention. Intimidated by Thaw's physical threats and perhaps hoping that Thaw would desist from asking about White if she disclosed her involvement with the much older man, Nesbit provided details. She recalled that White had wooed her after seeing her in a musical. He set both her and her mother up in a good apartment. She told of being left in "the care" of White while her mother was out of town; White had put a drug in her champagne and had raped her.

Nesbit told Thaw of White's actions while they were on a trip to Europe. Thaw became so unhinged that he beat Nesbit. She fled to the United States and asked for assistance from White. White sent lawyers to take Nesbit's deposition about Thaw's abuse. In her recollection in the deposition Nesbit said that Thaw had pressured her to accuse an (unnamed) man of statutory rape:

> Thaw had begged me time and time again to swear to written documents which he had prepared, involving this married man and charging him with drugging me when I was 15 years of age. This was not so; and I so told him. But because I refused to sign these papers said Thaw not alone threatened me with bodily injury, but inflicted on me the great bodily injury I have herein described.

Thaw retaliated by hiring detectives to tail White. He also assembled information about White's treatment of other young actresses besides Evelyn Nesbit.

Thaw pursued Nesbit; he was alternatively charming and unstable. Surprisingly, he finally got her to marry him. Although she was alarmed by Thaw's episodes of violent jealousy, she must have been drawn to the security that his family's money offered. After the wedding, in April 1905, they took up residence in Pittsburgh. The couple made occasional trips to New York. It was on one of those occasions that Thaw "encountered" White at Madison Square Garden. It surprised almost no one who knew "Mad Harry," least of all Evelyn Nesbit Thaw, that Harry Thaw should have killed Stanford White. It appeared that Thaw had stalked White for months, if not years.

SUMMARY OF ARGUMENTS

Thaw spent his time awaiting trial in comfort, eating meals from the fashionable restaurant

Delmonico's. He doubtless also was fortified by assurance from his mother that she would exhaust the family's considerable financial resources in his defense. Along with several other highly competent attorneys the Thaws hired a lawyer from California, Delphin Delmas, renowned for his skill in criminal defense work. But, despite the depth of experience on the defense side, getting a jury to excuse Thaw's murder of White would be no easy task.

The circumstances of the killing made it difficult to justify. District Attorney William Jerome reminded the jury that White had been shot in cold blood:

> Justifiable means self-defence, and when a man sits with his head in his hand, quietly looking at a play, his arm thrown over another chair that has been pushed away from the table, and is shot down by an enemy with a revolver, held so close that his very features are so disfigured that his brother-in-law does not recognize him, even the wildest stretch of the imagination will hardly picture that to a jury east of the Mississippi River it is a case of self-defence.

The classic rationalization for a husband killing his wife's lover would have applied to this case if Thaw had acted after finding his wife and White in flagrante delicto. But Thaw had known of his wife's prior involvement with White before his marriage, by which time the connection between White and Nesbit was over. Thus, it was not a case of infidelity at all, nor could the crime have been said to occur in the heat of passion.

The only other reasonable legal possibility for the defense would be to claim that Thaw had been insane at the time of the crime. There were two major pitfalls, however, to such an approach. First of all, the insanity defense was unpopular with juries, particularly so after the notorious case of Charles Guiteau, the assassin of President James Garfield. The man who killed President William McKinley, Leon Czolgosz, found to his regret that both judges and jury members were most unsympathetic to an insanity plea in the killing of a high-profile individual. Secondly, if Thaw's lawyers were to broach an insanity defense, there were

really only two ways of presenting such an argument. Either Thaw had been insane all of his life—in which case his mental difficulty would have been hereditary but also obviously disabling—or he had been temporarily (or "partially") insane at the time of the crime.

Mental health professionals in Thaw's time might see gradations of mental illness; they argued for peaks and valleys in an individual's mental disability. But courts and jurors tended to think in starker terms. A person either was born insane or went insane from an organic cause such as a brain injury. If a person showed temporary mental distress, it almost always was because the individual lacked self-control, for example, when the person had indulged in drink or drugs. Nesbit had said in her deposition in 1903 after running from Thaw in Europe that Thaw appeared to be (in the language of the time) a "morphine fiend." It would be unwise to call attention to Thaw's mental state if he might be accused of exacerbating any instability through drug use.

Thaw's defense lawyers and his doting mother had to be cautious about leaning hard on an insanity defense, among other reasons because Thaw himself initially was averse to such a plea. In fact, Thaw had dismissed his original chief attorney, William Delafield, for trying to broker an arrangement involving an insanity plea. Besides, if the defense built too strong a courtroom record of Thaw's mental instability and secured a verdict of not guilty by reason of insanity, then Thaw would end up in a mental institution. Such places were hardly conducive to the lifestyle of the scion of "the Pittsburgh Thaws." Also, when might Thaw expect to be released from an asylum for the mentally ill if the court committed him for treatment?

And so the high-priced lawyers took a gamble. They struck out in uncharted legal territory, formulating an argument that was a hybrid of the defense of the enraged husband who had happened upon his wife and her lover and the defense of partial insanity. Defense attorney Delmas coined the term *dementia Americana* to describe Thaw's state of mind when he shot White at the theater. Any red-blooded American male would have been driven partially insane, Delmas maintained, by the mental image of an older man raping an innocent girl. It was an outrage upon the family's honor, which the dutiful husband had a right to avenge.

The defense took the precaution of submitting affidavits that showed Thaw to have been extremely concerned about White's proclivities in the weeks leading up to the murder; that is, the defense attorneys tried to demonstrate that Thaw was "laboring under a delusion" for some time before he shot White. Such a contention would help to explain away some of the obvious calculation that accompanied his murderous act. It was a clever strategy, for that line of reasoning allowed the defense to maintain that, although deluded, Thaw had been concerned about White's "ravishing" of underage girls. Thus, for example, the defense summoned the recollection of none other than Anthony Comstock. Comstock remembered Thaw calling upon him to report on White's seduction of girls. That evidence was designed also to vilify White by bringing in evidence that the moralist Comstock disapproved of him and took Thaw seriously.

The use of the novel defense in large part depended on the ability of Thaw to play the concerned husband. It also depended on the skill of Evelyn Nesbit Thaw at filling the role of the wronged young woman. For "dementia Americana" to work in court Evelyn Nesbit Thaw had to garner sympathy for herself at present but also for the young person she had been when she first arrived in New York. The defense further needed the jury to believe that Thaw had found Nesbit's tale of abuse by White to be credible. The *New York Times* reporter who reported on the trial clearly thought that Thaw had succeeded in conveying his mental agony:

> It was manifest as she [Evelyn Thaw] spoke that the prisoner [Harry Thaw] was again going through the torture of that night. Prepared by his counsel for a day of mental agony, he had seemed when he came into court to have his heart steeled against the pain of an old wound begin reopened. But when his wife, with her soft, black hair dressed so that the coiffure rested between her shoulders, with a linen collar, simple black tie, and blue jacket that a child might

have worn accentuating the girlishness of her form, began to tell of her meeting with White, Thaw shuddered, drew his brown overcoat closer about his shoulders and began to sink in his chair.

Recognizing the effect of such drama in court, prosecutor Jerome urged the jury not to succumb to the inflammatory appeals of the California lawyer Delmas. He reminded the panel of the calculated manner in which Thaw had pursued White:

> Locate your enemy. Locate a man who had blackballed you at clubs, locate the man who had wronged the woman that you had married, locate the man who had spread your scandals broadcast through the town, locate him carefully for half an hour or more, and then go over and shoot him in a way that "it seems it was done very quietly," and then come with your dementia Americana to a jury, east of the Mississippi River, and ask them to see in it anything but a premeditated and deliberate design to take the life of the man you hate. Was there not absolute premeditation? Was there not absolute motive?

Jerome was saying that a sophisticated New York jury would not accept the legal shenanigans that Delmas was trying to foist off on them. While making that argument, Jerome came close to saying that Nesbit was responsible for the whole scandal:

> A vulgar, ordinary, low, sordid murder. The married man getting away with the girl from the unmarried one, and the unmarried one taking her back and living with her, and finally marrying her; and fearful that the married man would get her back again—the man whom he hated, the man who had kept him out of clubs, the man who had circulated, as it is said here, scandals about him, the man who said that he could get the girl back and would, the man who had described him as a dope fiend, whom he had every reason to hate; and the girl lying between them like a tiger egging them on. With

Thaw she is wronged by White; with White she is lashed by Thaw. Why, the same old elements that existed since the foundation of the world, and because she has a childish garb and a childish face, is she coming here to tell a tissue of lies like this, to work on you, gentlemen, to acquit a cold-blooded, cowardly murderer, on the ground of dementia Americana.

VERDICT

Given the state of the law on insanity, the power of the prosecution's verbiage, and the fact that Thaw had killed White in front of hundreds of witnesses, anything short of a capital sentence for Thaw would have been a victory. But Thaw got something better: a mistrial. The jury could not agree whether he fit any definition of insanity, but enough of the panel (five men) had bought the idea of "dementia Americana" to deadlock the deliberations. On April 11, 1907, Thaw's first brush with the legal system ended on that inconclusive note.

The prosecution refiled charges. Between the first and second trials of Thaw, there was a shuffling within the Thaw legal camp, mainly on account of the lawyers' lack of confidence that the novel defense would work again. The notion of "dementia Americana" had shock value once, but the prosecution now had gained time to attack its legal validity. In addition, Thaw's appeal wore thin with the public and the jury after a certain amount of exposure to him. The new defense table thought it prudent to fall back upon a more traditional defense plea. This time they would contend that Thaw had been unstable in the long term and that there was a family history of serious mental illness. The new trial began in January 1908.

Prosecutor Jerome answered the argument that Thaw was insane with a reminder to the jury of which people had not testified to Thaw's supposedly lifelong mental fragility: his attorneys, bankers, poker-playing friends, the police who arrested him. Jerome told the court that it was only journalists (sensationalizers, presumably) and Thaw's employees who gave evidence of his insanity. The implication was quite clear: The "servants" had been bought off.

Faced once more with the beautiful, mournful Evelyn Nesbit Thaw—whom they wanted to believe—the jury gave the argument of hereditary insanity the benefit of the doubt. On February 1, 1908, the jury in Thaw's second trial pronounced a verdict of "not guilty by reason of insanity." Thaw would be confined to the Matteawan Hospital for the Criminally Insane in Fishkill, New York, for an infinite period. Most commentators saw the verdict as a legal subterfuge that was morally justifiable because of the trial's revelations about White's lechery and general high living. In sparing Thaw from execution, the jurors had come to Evelyn Nesbit Thaw's rescue. The unlikable Thaw was almost beside the point.

But, what would become of Thaw? His mother would not rest until Thaw was truly free. She spent many more tens of thousands of dollars—a fortune in that day—to get him released from strict confinement. Thaw did obtain enough latitude to break free during one outing from Matteawan. He made it to Canada but eventually was returned, later residing in an institution in Pennsylvania.

Finally the psychiatrists deemed Thaw no longer a threat. Since he had been found "not guilty," if he were sane then Thaw did not have to be incarcerated further. Rumor had it that the elder Mrs. Thaw's contributions to the institution where Harry Thaw was held had helped the doctors see their way clear to release him. Thaw's behavior, however, continued to be problematic. He spent money wildly and got into at least one more serious scrape with the law—a near-fatal assault—that cost his family still more money. He died in 1947, by all accounts in poor mental health.

Nesbit tried a stage career, including vaudeville. In 1915 she claimed that a child she bore was Thaw's, the result of one of Thaw's relaxed confinements at Matteawan. Thaw divorced her straightaway, and the Thaw family fought a long battle to disestablish Thaw's paternity of the child. Nesbit's fame originally had been based on her dewy good looks. When her youth faded, so did her professional prospects. Her autobiography emphasizes that she thought White had made only one major mistake (rape) in his treatment of her. Nesbit contended that it was she who insisted that she and White had no future together. Nesbit died in 1967 after pursuing a quiet life in middle age as a visual artist.

When White was killed, the elaborate picture of material success that he had assembled crumbled. He was deeply indebted because of his extravagant lifestyle. Had White lived, however, there remained the possibility that his immense talent could have dug him out of financial distress. As an architect, White was more than an apologist for the Gilded Age plutocrats for whom he designed mansions. His demise at the apex of his career deprived the world of a flawed human being but also an unquestionably gifted artist.

SIGNIFICANCE

The early 20th-century public gleaned morals from the Thaw-White-Nesbit case but perhaps not the same lessons that more modern observers would take away from the episode. To persons at the turn of that century, for example, the Thaw trial cast light on the perils of being a starlet. The case provided an exposure of the casting couch that would surprise few people 100 years later. The public in 1907 also listened, fascinated and appalled, to stories of behavior of the captains of industry at their New York bacchanalia. White had been in the midst of such behavior. The trials of Thaw did not quite conclude with the finding that the victim deserved to die, but they came very close. If White's life was a perfect example of the brilliant excesses of the era, then the reprieve of Thaw signified that Americans had grown weary of such decadence.

Further Reading

Fleischer, Richard (dir.), *The Girl in the Red Velvet Swing*. Twentieth Century Fox, 1955; Gillman, Susan. "'Dementia Americana': Mark Twain, 'Wapping Alice,' and the Harry K. Thaw Trial." *Critical Inquiry* 14 (Winter 1988): 296–314; Nesbit, Evelyn. *Prodigal Days*. New York: Julian Messner, 1934; Thaw, Harry. *The Traitor*. Philadelphia: Dorrance & Co., 1925; Uruburu, Paula. *American Eve: Evelyn Nesbit, Stanford White, the Birth of the "It" Girl, and the Crime of the Century*. New York: Riverhead Books, 2008.

The trials of Sinnisiak and Uluksuk

Also known as: *The Crown v. Sinnisiak and Uluksuk*

Date: 1917

KEY ISSUES

Europeans first explored the region known as the Coppermine, in present-day Northwest Territories, Canada, in 1771. The British were looking for the source of copper that Inuit peoples were trading in more southerly areas. It took more than a century for broader interest in the area to develop. In the early 1900s several distinct groups began to penetrate the northern frontier by land, journeying around Great Bear Lake and dragging themselves painstakingly along the Bear and Coppermine Rivers. Great Bear Lake had portions north of the Arctic Circle, and nearby waterways frequently remained frozen well into July. The land drained by the Coppermine River all the way to Coronation Gulf was sparsely populated with Inuit. Far to the south were other native populations of the American plains, such as the Chippeweyan, Blackfeet, and Cree.

One set of non-native individuals who lived in the area in the early 20th century were trappers. The British government funded expeditions to the Coppermine, and a number of explorers were working on behalf of the Hudson's Bay Company. Other residents in the region represented the Canadian government, which established police posts at spots such as Fort McFerson and Herschel Island. Private individuals such as George and Lionel Douglas gained familiarity with the region through their prospecting for copper. Ethnographers such as Vilhjalmur Stefannson found the vicinity a fertile ground for examining indigenous people who had had little or no contact with outsiders. Then there were clerics, usually either Roman Catholic or Anglican missionaries, who saw it as their duty to bring Christianity to both the people they called Indians and the "Stone Age" folk, the Inuit.

HISTORY OF THE CASE

It took months for the clerical colleagues of Fathers Jean-Baptiste Rouvière and Guillaume Le Roux to become alarmed at not hearing from them. Word traveled very slowly in the northern lands where the priests had begun a mission among the Copper Inuit people. Rouvière had gone north out of Fort Norman in the summer of 1911. Le Roux joined him in the summer of 1912. Both were younger men (30 and 28, respectively), and priests from the Oblates of Mary the Immaculate. They had the blessings of their bishop to convert the Inuit. They and their order were in a bit of a hurry because they had gotten word that Anglican missionaries recently had made inroads among the Inuit in the region.

Despite the immense distances involved, the missionaries were expected to report back on their efforts, and Rouvière in particular was a good correspondent. He relayed messages that made clear the physical challenges of the work. Simply building a dwelling place proved exceedingly trying, for example, although eventually they adapted an existing hut on the bank of the Dease River. Rouvière and Le Roux also were confounded by the shyness of the Inuit, most of whom had seen few if any white faces and whose limited experiences made them wary of whites' intentions. Although occasionally the priests got advice from non-native trappers and explorers, they generally labored alone to try to win the trust of the native people.

Perhaps most difficult of all their tasks was the learning of the Inuit language. Although bright and multilingual men, Rouvière and Le Roux struggled to be understood and to grasp what the indigenous folk said to them. In translating, the missionaries had an added complexity. They strove to convey concepts to the Inuit that they insisted the Inuit should accept as key to conversion: the necessity of monogamous marriage, for example, and the sinfulness of theft. Such notions appeared foreign to Inuit culture. In turn, there seemed to be Inuit values that they could not express to the missionaries.

In 1914 several ominous reports filtered into the Diocese of Mackenzie and to its bishop, Gabriel Breynat. An ethnologist brought back news that in the hut of an Inuit family he had seen artifacts that related to the Catholic faith, as well as a Hollis double-barrel gun. In a separate incident an explorer named D'Arcy Arden had heard from a group of Indians that they had seen a demolished hut near the Dease River. Bishop Breynat called in the authorities.

The Royal North West Mounted Police (RNWMP) devoted considerable resources to a search for Fathers Rouvière and Le Roux. The police sent out two full-time investigators to the north, one inquiring openly and the other undercover. Those policemen, Inspector Denny La Nauze and Corporal Wyndham Valentine Bruce, had to engage the services of several other individuals including independent ethnologists, guides, and translators in order to untangle the disappearances.

The investigators gathered details connected with the missing men and recovered several items that had belonged to them. In the spring of 1916 at an Inuit camp certain Inuit came forward to speak with the investigators. First among them was an elder named Koeha. Koeha described an incident in which another Inuit, Kormik, had appropriated a gun belonging to the fathers, a weapon that Kormik believed Father Rouvière had promised to give him.

After hearing of that episode, which had occurred in 1914, the police believed they had solved the case. The worst, of course, had happened: Father Rouvière and Father Le Roux were dead. The gist of the tale was that several Inuit had killed the priests on account of the quarrel over the gun. The whole story behind the deaths was actually more complex and would come out in public at trial. It took about a year to obtain evidence to build a case, but evidence finally did include confessions from the supposed killers. Another year elapsed before the police could bring two of the admitted perpetrators within the scope of Canadian justice. A considerable amount of that intervening time was spent simply traveling back south to a location where courts actually met: Edmonton.

SUMMARY OF ARGUMENTS

The two accused killers were named Uluksuk and Sinnisiak and were the first Inuit to face justice in a white man's court. The Canadian government was fully cognizant of the importance of the situation. The case involved certain legal vexations, not least of which was the novelty of trying defendants who literally had no knowledge of the white man's law. The language barrier was imposing. At trial it proved necessary to lean heavily on two of the few translators who were available, the native men named Ilavinik and Patsy Klingenberg. Adding more difficulty to the case was the fact that during the proceedings Ilavinik's work became suspect as biased. Klingenberg became the translator of choice.

More than its concern about establishing the legal precedent that the Inuit ought to be held accountable for killing whites, the government had a political point to make. All native people in Canada were to be subject to Canadian political authority. The north was now the provenance of the nation as a whole rather than of indigenous people. The legal and political lessons were intertwined. If white explorers, entrepreneurs, government officials, and settlers were to venture in future to the north to consolidate their vision of a Canadian nation, then they expected a guarantee of personal safety. If the Inuit were not put on notice that it was wrong to kill whites, then all whites who ventured into the northern regions were at risk.

As if to indicate the importance of the lessons that the government wished to impart, the trials began under the direction of the chief justice of Alberta, Judge Horace Harvey. The crown prosecutor was Charles McCaul and the defendants' lawyer was James Wallbridge. All were respected legal figures. Judge Harvey made it a point to say that he had required the officials of the court to secure the service of esteemed citizens as the six required jurors. The case, he indicated, would be examined closely, and he wanted to guarantee the integrity of the process. One of the jurors, Alfred Fugl, was a district manager for the Hudson's Bay Company and had lived for years in the north. The court convened on August 14, 1917.

Local citizens flocked to court, and the case attracted national attention in the press. Some attendees came from the United States. No small part of the allure of the case was the opportunity to observe the two defendants in court. Uluksuk and Sinnisiak, for their part, appeared mostly unmoved by white man's justice. On several occasions they fell asleep in court. Often the accused men seemed not to understand much of what was said, even with the laborious translations.

A significant announcement by the prosecution was an early point of interest in the case. The Crown proposed to charge Uluksuk and Sinnisiak separately. It would proceed first with the trial of Sinnisiak for murdering Father Rouvière. McCaul had two reasons for that separation of the defendants at the commencement of the case: Father Rouvière had been unarmed when he was killed, and Sinnisiak appeared to have been the instigator of the decision to commit the crime. The division of the defendants and the taking up of a case only concerning Father Rouvière were to prove quite important late on.

The Crown made several arguments at the outset. None was more vital to the defendants than a point that the government stated quite clearly: If Uluksuk and Sinnisiak were convicted, they would not die. The state would request conviction, and, yes, the penalty for murder was death, but the prosecution was ready to petition that that sentence not be imposed. McCaul was in contact with the ministers of Indian affairs and justice. They gave him instructions on how to try the case. Scholars contend that McCaul was telegraphing the goal of the trial. Its purpose was not to see Sinnisiak and Uluksuk hanged but rather to impose and announce British justice on the northern frontier.

McCaul enlarged upon that theme. The prosecution was not about this particular set of defendants or victims. It was focused on the conveying of vital lessons to northerners like the Copper Inuit:

> The Indians of the Plains . . . have been educated in the ideas of justice. They have been educated to know that justice does not merely mean retribution, and that the justice which is administered in Court is not a justice of vengeance. . . .
>
> These remote savages, really cannibals, the Eskimo of the Arctic regions have got to be taught to recognize the authority of the British Crown, and that the authority of the Crown and of the Dominion of Canada, of

which these countries are a part, extends to the furthermost limits of the frozen North. It is necessary that they should understand that they are under the Law . . . that they must regulate their lives and dealings with their fellow men, of whatever race, white men or Indians, according to, at least, the main outstanding principles of that law, which is part of the law of civilization.

During the trial of Sinnisiak the prosecution underlined certain points in the story of the priests' deaths. For example, McCaul emphasized that in the north almost everyone who could, carried a gun. Although the Inuit were not all in possession of firearms, they coveted them. Even priests needed guns, for the primary food source in the Coppermine region was caribou. Thus, the argument about the priests' gun was a disagreement over a tool essential for survival—certainly for the two white men who said they were about to leave the Inuit camp and go out on their own for a time.

Attorney Wallbridge also pursued certain consistent lines of argument during the case. He emphasized that the jury should consider the killings of the priests acts of self-defense. He recapped or leaned on witnesses' accounts of events leading to the priests' deaths. Wallbridge reminded the court of the confessions of Uluksuk and Sinnisiak, which tallied remarkably well with one another and remained consistent over subsequent retellings.

In the confessions of the defendants the episode had begun when the Inuit named Kormik had taken one of the priests' guns. The father had gotten it back only after he threatened the native folk with another firearm. The Inuit were angry about the priests' wielding of guns and their seemingly going back on their word to make a gift of the gun to Kormik. Still, due to the intercession of Kormik's mother and the elder man Koeha, they let the priests go away unharmed from the Inuit camp.

Uluksuk and Sinnisiak then happened upon the white men several days later. Wallbridge contended that that meeting was by chance. The prosecution maintained it was deliberate tracking of Rouvière and Le Roux. The defense explained that the missionaries at that point were desperate for assistance to travel to a location where they could build shelter and find food. Here, Wallbridge had the advantage of a piece of evidence that supported this line of thought: a portion of Father Rouvière's diary that the police had recovered from the death scene. The last entry in that journal was one apparently written by Rouvière around the time of the trouble over the gun: "We are at the mouth of the Coppermine. Some families have already left. Disillusioned with the Eskimoes. We are threatened with starvation; also we don't know what to do."

Wallbridge sketched out for the jury what his client said had occurred upon Uluksuk and Sinnisiak's meeting with the priests. Rouvière and Le Roux demanded that the two Inuit men pull their heavily laden sled. For a couple of days the Inuit complied, but they grew more and more fearful as the whites seemed increasingly hostile. The priest that they called Ilogoak (Le Roux) appeared more threatening. When Uluksuk and Sinnisiak got the chance, they unhitched themselves from the load and attacked the priest who was carrying the gun, Le Roux. Both of the defendants agreed it was Sinnisiak's idea. When Rouvière tried to run away, Sinnisiak followed and shot him, completing the killing with an ax and a knife.

Wallbridge had an explanation for the most shocking aspect of the crimes: the fact that the killers had cut open the priests' bodies and eaten part of the men's livers. The defense argued that this was not an act of savagery or even cannibalism per se but an effort by the Inuit to guarantee that the spirits of the priests would not haunt their killers.

Judge Harvey's instructions to the Edmonton jury on August 17, 1917, favored the prosecution in no uncertain terms. He told the panel that in present law, this case did not permit the application of an argument of self-defense. He complimented McCaul for his unwillingness to appeal to prejudice but to present the case as one that would impart a lesson about the superiority of British justice. He reminded the jury of the government's promise to spare the lives of Uluksuk and Sinnisiak, even if both were convicted of murder and he as a judge had to impose the death penalty.

VERDICT

Very much to the surprise of all in court, not least of Judge Harvey, the jury returned a verdict of "not guilty" against Sinnisiak. At that juncture the decision of the prosecution to seek separate trials looked exceedingly wise. Now Uluksuk could be charged with the murder of Father Le Roux, as could Sinnisiak; the Crown entered just such a case only days after the verdict was announced favoring Sinnisiak. Trusting in Judge Harvey's dismay at the verdict, on August 20 McCaul applied to Judge Horton for a change of venue. McCaul contended, and Horton apparently concurred, that the Edmonton jury had been affected by pro-Inuit propaganda. There also were whispers that juror Fugl was anti-Catholic.

Judge Harvey presided over the next proceeding, which began in Calgary on August 22, 1917. It was a controversial ruling from the bench, since he had expressed himself strongly in favor of the prosecution at the other trial's end. In Calgary, Harvey announced, the jury would be sequestered. In many other respects the case was the same. The arguments of counsel were less protracted than at Edmonton, but they concentrated on the same themes.

McCaul insisted on the letter of the law with regard to the definition of murder. He painted Kormik as a thief and Ulukshuk and Sinnisiak as anxious to ingratiate themselves with their Inuit peers by "recovering" the priests' cache of weapons, supplies, and trinkets. He hammered home the fact that the priests were utterly dependent on their rifles and that they were acting sternly toward their former Inuit friends because they were desperately hungry. In the prosecution's scenario the Inuit had turned the fathers Rouvière and Le Roux out of their settlement with little hope of the white men finding either shelter or food.

Wallbridge persisted in portraying the Inuit as trusting, amiable people, straight out of the Stone Age. Sinnisiak and Uluksuk had turned to violence only when facing what they thought was an imminent threat to their own lives. He reminded the jury that a reprieve was not absolutely guaranteed.

Judge Harvey repeated his earlier instructions to the jury. Once again his words leaned heavily toward conviction and practically promised a non-capital outcome. This time the jury decided that Ulukshuk and Sinnisiak were guilty—though this time, technically, of the murder of Father Le Roux. Judge Harvey and the government were true to

their word. From the bench came the mandatory death sentence, and from Ottawa within days, the expected reprieve. The convicted men spent two years in minimum-security confinement at Fort Resolution, after which they returned to their own people. Although Ulukshuk and Sinnisiak did assist in constructing a rough police barracks for the Coppermine region, they mostly traded on their notoriety. Ulukshuk expired after a fight in 1924, and Sinnisiak died under less dramatic circumstances around the year 1930.

SIGNIFICANCE

Despite the determination of Canadian authorities to frame the prosecution as a warning to the Inuit, the native people of the north continued to kill whites. Indeed, some observers argued that the lesson of the 1917 Inuit trials was that whites could be dispatched, if only the defense could establish enough sympathy for defendants in the eyes of the jurors. The RNWMP remarked on a spate of violent crimes by Inuit in the mid-1920s. In 1924 the first Inuit executed after a trial was hanged for murder for killing a constable and a trader at Tree River; the perpetrator already had been under confinement concerning a third murder.

The period in which the trials of Ulukshuk and Sinnisiak took place was one of first contact between colonial authorities and the premodern people of the Coppermine region. Scholars observe that the Inuit did not convert easily to white ways despite the best efforts of Christian missionaries, traders, police, and officials of the criminal justice system.

Further Reading

Eber, Dorothy. *Images of Justice.* Montreal, Canada: McGill-Queen's University Press, 1997; Hippler, Arthur E., and Stephen Conn. *Northern Eskimo Law Ways and Their Relationship to Contemporary Problems of "Bush Justice."* Fairbanks: University of Alaska, 1973; Jenkins, McKay. *Bloody Falls of the Coppermine: Madness, Murder, and the Collision of Cultures in the Arctic, 1913.* New York: Random House, 2005; Keedy, Edwin M. "A Remarkable Murder Trial: *Rex v. Sinnisiak.*" *University of Pennsylvania Law Review* 100 (1951): 48–67; Morse, Bradford.

Aboriginal Peoples and the Law. Ottawa, Canada: Carleton University Press, 1985; Moyles, R. G. *British Law and Arctic Men.* Burnaby, Canada: Simon Fraser University Publications, 2004.

The trials of Roscoe Arbuckle

Also known as: *California v. Arbuckle*

Date: 1921, 1922

KEY ISSUES

During the early years of the 20th century, film-making emerged as a prominent enterprise in southern California. Although some films were created for educational and political purposes, their vast audience was interested primarily in entertainment. "Moving pictures" made fortunes not just for producers and distributors but also for their most popular stars. With the enormous visibility of actors on screen came a satellite industry devoted to watching the private lives of screen figures.

Even in the formative era of Hollywood film-makers were concerned with image control for their players. Thus, it served the film industry when the press christened Canadian native Mary Pickford as "America's sweetheart"; her reputation for demure behavior was as endearing on celluloid as in real life. And press portrayal of Rudolph Valentino as a real-world lothario supported his casting as a heartbreaker on the silent screen.

Silent film comic Roscoe Arbuckle found that publicity could unmake a career. Arbuckle fell from public favor and the good graces of Hollywood because his image in the headlines was sharply at odds with his film persona. Arbuckle also epitomized the excesses of other film stars—indeed, Hollywood in general—among an American public that lionized screen heroes and yet was not entirely comfortable with their increasing role in U.S. culture.

Once Arbuckle was hauled into court in the lurid case that ruined his career, Hollywood found itself under an unwelcome spotlight. It had gained the attention of individuals who called for oversight of the film industry so as to prevent Hollywood from corrupting the nation's morals. For decades after Arbuckle's trials in 1921 and 1922, filmmakers themselves sanitized their output in lieu of submitting to regulators. That self-censorship extended even to the early days of television.

HISTORY OF THE CASE

Considering that his time in court was connected with censorship of the big screen, it is ironic that Arbuckle's film roles were not at all scandalous. Indeed, as an actor, Arbuckle was as wholesome as the two persons with whom he often was compared as a comic: Buster Keaton and Charles Chaplin. A 1921 depiction in *Vanity Fair* shows a group of film celebrities "leaving work." Just next to Arbuckle in the crowd were Gloria Swanson, Pickford, and Chaplin. In this depiction Arbuckle is instantly recognizable because of his size as well as his bowler hat.

Having started his career on stage in vaudeville, Arbuckle at first was ashamed of acting in films. He warmed to film, though, joining Keystone Studios in 1913. He quickly became one of the studio's most popular actors along with his frequent costar Mabel Normand. "Fatty and Mabel" were an early mixed-gender comedy team. Arbuckle was an endearing screen presence. He was an everyman who triumphed in the face of adversity. His girth made him seem approachable rather than a dandy. He was amazingly agile; fellow performers said he was a gifted ballroom dancer.

Arbuckle moved to Comique Studios in New York in 1917, gaining creative authority over his films and continuing to mentor younger talents such as Keaton. Arbuckle's popularity often was said to be second only to Chaplin's. The "fat man's" fame only increased in 1919 when Chaplin stopped acting for a few years. Arbuckle returned to the West Coast in 1919 to star at Paramount. The work was lucrative, but he had a hectic schedule and little control over his films. He went to San Francisco to escape the grind on September 5,

1921. He checked into a luxury hotel, hosting a party in several rooms. Many of the people who attended knew Arbuckle only casually, but they all were Hollywood types—producers, agents, cameramen, aspiring performers, and their managers.

During the party Arbuckle found a young woman named Virginia Rappe in distress in his bathroom. He helped her to her feet and then onto a bed. Arbuckle gave Rappe some ice to rub on her abdomen. He assumed she was intoxicated, for although Prohibition was in effect, alcohol was flowing freely at the gathering. Rappe's companion, Maude Delmont, though very intoxicated, insisted on supervising Rappe's care. Convinced that Rappe was not seriously ill and that others were looking after her, Arbuckle left the event on schedule with friends, eventually returning to the Los Angeles area.

Rappe died four days later in a hospital of peritonitis and a ruptured bladder. Immediately, her companion, Delmont, began speaking to the press with a horrifying story. Delmont contended that Arbuckle had pursued Rappe while at the studio. She stated that in San Francisco he had invited the actress to the party and made sexual advances that Rappe repulsed. Delmont intimated that Arbuckle had sexually assaulted Rappe using either his body or foreign objects such as a champagne bottle and a chunk of ice; her story changed with subsequent retellings. According to Delmont, the violence of the assault combined with Arbuckle's weight had caused enough pressure to do damage to Rappe's abdominal organs, leading to Rappe's death.

The police knew Delmont as an extortionist. On several occasions she had introduced young women to stars or wealthy men and then helped the alleged victims claim that they had been assaulted. Rappe was known to become loud and remove her clothes when she drank heavily. Delmont's story would not have convinced the authorities to pursue the case but for two other powerful influences: the public prosecutor and the newspapers.

The ambitious district attorney in the area, Matthew Brady, saw prosecuting Arbuckle as an opportunity to enhance his career. Several news outlets, particularly William Randolph Hearst's *San Francisco Herald-Examiner,* perceived that the situation was prime fodder for increasing sales. Hearst had another motive for whipping up public opinion: He was famously resentful of the fact that southern California had been chosen as the site for the film industry. This case would allow Hearst to claim that he and the denizens of northern California were guardians of morality in contrast to Hollywood.

Much to his surprise, Arbuckle was arrested in connection with Rappe's demise. The district attorney aimed to charge him with murder because the law said that to cause a death while committing another grave offense, such as a rape, raised the level of the crime. (Brady did not file a separate rape charge.) The judge at the police court where Arbuckle was arraigned refused to give credence to the murder allegation and instead committed Arbuckle to trial for manslaughter. It was the first of many indications that the prosecution was deeply flawed.

Still, the state went ahead with the case against Arbuckle, armed with claims that in the hours before her death Rappe accused Arbuckle of injuring her. Only one other witness besides Delmont came forward to contend that Arbuckle had committed an assault—a woman at the party named Zey Prevon, who allegedly had heard Rappe on her deathbed say that Arbuckle had "hurt" her. Alleged evidence against Arbuckle emerged in the press. The headlines were sensationalist even in staid papers such as the *New York Times.* Among the groups that called for a boycott of Arbuckle films were women's organizations. In the majority of press accounts Rappe appeared to be a babe in the woods and Arbuckle a monster.

SUMMARY OF ARGUMENTS

Beyond the ambitions of Brady and the desire of Hearst to sell newspapers, Arbuckle faced another distinct disadvantage in the case: his weight. When he was in good standing with the press and the public, his size was associated with good humor; once he was accused of assault, the fact that he was large made him a threat. The newspapers alleged that his sheer bulk had contributed to Rappe's death and that he had a history of using his weight to force himself on other women. His coworkers in the film industry responded that though he had a taste for alcohol, cars, and fine clothes, Arbuckle was shy with women.

What most newspapers did not note was that it was Rappe who had a reputation for promiscuity. Medical testimony indicated that Rappe may have undergone several abortions, with one procedure occurring shortly before her death. She also suffered from gonorrhea and frequent pelvic infections; doctors had warned her that drinking inflamed her condition.

Those medical findings were discussed in court in November 1921, when Arbuckle appeared in what was to be the first of three trials of the case. Although the hotel doctor who had been first on the scene to examine Rappe argued on the stand that an "external force" had ruptured Rappe's bladder, Arbuckle's defense attorney discredited that testimony. The defense also demolished claims that Arbuckle's bloody fingerprints had been found on a hotel door. The defense further presented information about Arbuckle's behavior at the party and afterward that contradicted the prosecution's picture of Arbuckle as brutish toward Rappe and uncaring after she became ill.

Belying the legal wisdom that defendants only could lose by giving testimony, Arbuckle made a good impression on the stand. He spoke calmly and extensively, and his account had no contradictions. District Attorney Brady made the decision not to allow Delmont to appear at the trial; her absence hurt the prosecution's case. Despite screaming headlines critical of Arbuckle, the trial had gone well for the defendant inside the courtroom, and yet the jury did not exonerate him.

The jury could not reach a unanimous verdict, though they ended their deliberations at an 11–1 vote in favor of acquittal. Helen Hubbard, the lone panel member who insisted on conviction, declared that she had gone into the trial convinced of Arbuckle's guilt. She was married to an attorney who had professional contacts with District Attorney Brady. If the district attorney had been willing, he might have dropped the case after the mistrial, but such a move did not suit Brady's plans to run for governor.

It was at this juncture that several Hollywood studio executives decided to impose voluntary restraints on their industry in order to demonstrate to the public that they were working to uphold a high moral tone. A consortium of producers hired Postmaster General Will Hays to serve as an arbiter of film standards, and he performed the job zealously. Hays gave his name to a set of guidelines that Hollywood imposed on itself until the motion picture rating system was adopted in 1968. Immediately, Hays pushed the studios to insert morals clauses into individual actors' contracts. The Hays Code also had the effect of fending off government-imposed censorship, although it did not prevent religious groups, notably the Catholic Church, from having a major impact on films' content.

At a second trial that began in January 1922, lead defense attorney Gavin McNab emphasized forensic evidence that showed Rappe had been seriously ill before the party. He contended that Rappe did not die from an assault. In fact, McNab argued that such an attack never took place. The defense also continued to shake the validity of the supposed fingerprint evidence. Most significant was the defense's line of argument that Brady had threatened potential witnesses into testifying negatively about Arbuckle. Such revelations completely undercut the testimony of Prevon, who had been key to securing an indictment against Arbuckle in the first place.

But the defense made critical errors. Most important was assuming Arbuckle's testimony had been so conclusive in the first trial that he need not appear again on the stand in a second proceeding. Confronted with Arbuckle's nonappearance, the second jury inferred that he either did not take the new trial seriously or that he was unable to tell a straight story. It may have hurt Arbuckle's standing with the jury, as well, that McNab also was serving as counsel in a case that tarnished the reputation of none other than Pickford, who was seeking a "Nevada divorce" so that she could marry Douglas Fairbanks. As at the first trial, the jury engaged in lengthy deliberations about the Arbuckle case, and again they announced that they were deadlocked. This time, however, the vote initially was 9–3 for conviction. Indeed, if it had not been for one particularly stubborn pro-Arbuckle juror who announced to his peers on the panel that he would not switch his position, Arbuckle probably would have been convicted.

At a third trial in March 1922, the defense put its experience to good use. McNab called Arbuckle back onto the stand, where for the second time Arbuckle gave a believable account of himself at the San Francisco party. The defense scored points when they pointed out that Delmont was giving paid lectures about the trial but was not speaking in court, where she would have been cross-examined. McNab also included more evidence about Rappe's heavy drinking and her shady association with Delmont.

The jury had no hesitation about Arbuckle's credibility. On April 12, 1922, they found in his favor after approximately one minute of deliberation. In an action with few precedents in criminal trials the jurors composed a statement that Arbuckle had been railroaded:

> Acquittal is not enough for Roscoe Arbuckle. We feel that a great injustice has been done him. We feel also that it was only our plain duty to give him this exoneration, under the evidence, for there was not the slightest proof adduced to connect him with the commission of a crime. He was manly throughout the case and told a straightforward story which we all believe. The happening at the hotel was an unfortunate affair for which Roscoe Arbuckle, so the evidence shows, was in no way responsible. We wish him success and hope that the American people will take the judgment of fourteen men and women that Roscoe Arbuckle is entirely innocent and free from all blame.

VERDICT

Although Arbuckle was acquitted resoundingly, his troubles were not finished. Within a week the new president of the Motion Picture Producers and Distributors of America, Hays, sent word that Arbuckle was to be banned from performing in films. The heads of Paramount Studios had pushed for Hays's decision. The prohibition extended to the showing of films that were already made. The blacklisting in effect lasted until 1925, when Arbuckle began to direct again using his father's name, William Goodrich. Several actors who worked with Arbuckle reported that he had lost his typical good spirits.

Ten years after the trials the head of Warner Brothers Studio decided to cast Arbuckle in a series of comedic films. Those "shorts," such as *In the Dough* and *Tomalio,* proved a hit with audiences, who apparently had forgiven or forgotten Arbuckle's legal set-to. On June 28, 1933, Arbuckle was officially again in the good graces of Hollywood. On that day he signed a contract for a longer film. He never enjoyed the comeback, however; a few hours later he died in his sleep of a heart attack. Arbuckle's friends stated that they believed the stress of the trials finally had killed him.

SIGNIFICANCE

Those who worked alongside Arbuckle had great respect for his talent and were almost universally convinced of his innocence in the Rappe case. They did not testify on Arbuckle's behalf because their handlers warned that to defend Arbuckle in public would destroy their careers. A few brave souls—notably Keaton—spoke openly of their trust in Arbuckle and their wish that he would return to the screen. And there were subtle tributes. In his iconic, recurring role as the Little Tramp, Chaplin wore a small bowler hat. The rumor around Hollywood was that in 1913 Chaplin had borrowed it from Keystone Pictures' rising star, Roscoe Arbuckle.

Further Reading

Brownlow, Kevin. *Hollywood: The Pioneers.* New York: Knopf, 1980; Long, Bruce. "Roscoe 'Fatty' Arbuckle." *Taylorology.* Available online. URL: http://www.public.asu.edu/~ialong/Taylor28.txt. Accessed January 20, 2010; "Mable and Fatty Viewing the World's Fair at San Francisco, Cal." *Early Motion Pictures.* Available online. URL: http://www.sfmuseum.org/loc/fatty.html. Accessed January 21, 2010; Oderman, Stuart. *Roscoe "Fatty" Arbuckle: A Biography of the Silent Film Comedian, 1887–1933.* Jefferson, N.C.: McFarland & Co., 2005; Stahl, Jerry. *I, Fatty: A Novel.* New York: Bloomsbury, 2004; Young, Robert, Jr. *Roscoe "Fatty" Arbuckle: A BioBibliography.* Westport, Conn.: Greenwood Press, 1994.

The Sacco-Vanzetti trials

Also known as: *Massachusetts v. Sacco and Vanzetti;* the Sacco-Vanzetti case

Date: 1921

KEY ISSUES

For many people in the United States in the early 20th century, the term *radical* conjured up the image of foreign revolutionaries. Some thought of radicalism as a creed of violence. They associated leftist thought with terrorism, specifically bomb throwing. Radicalism was connected in certain minds with the struggles of working people; to be a radical meant to be a union member and an advocate of strikes. Those who adhered to radical agendas saw themselves as striving for better living and working conditions and more rapid change in society, but they might differ widely from radical peers about preferred methods.

Events in Russia in 1917 gave new urgency to debates on the place of political alternatives on the left, as did World War I. European upheavals spurred immigration to the Americas in the late 1910s, and the sheer number of fresh arrivals exacerbated nervousness about the presence of possible radicals. Persons already resident in the New World worried about job displacement, political unrest, and even criminality among their new neighbors. The newcomers were concerned about economic opportunities, and they sometimes found cultural adaptation difficult.

The case of Nicola Sacco and Bartolomeo Vanzetti underlined such apprehensions on the part of political and legal authorities, U.S. residents, and newly arrived persons. The prosecution of the two immigrants was connected to perceptions of their politics and origins. Their trial was linked to the Red Scare in several respects. But was the case all about the radicalism of Sacco and Vanzetti?

HISTORY OF THE CASE

Sacco and Vanzetti had come to the United States from Italy in 1908 but left the country during World War I to avoid military service. Upon their return Sacco (a married man with a family) worked in a shoe factory and Vanzetti (who was unattached) sold fish on the streets. Both lived in what were then outlying areas of Boston. The men apparently did not know each other until 1917.

They met because they both were sympathetic to anarchism. Like some of their fellow immigrants in the Boston area, Sacco and Vanzetti rejected the idea of political authority and supported efforts by anarchist leaders such as Luigi Galleani to disrupt governmental operations. Many Galleanists projected ire toward officials who deported individuals on account of their political beliefs. After Galleani was sent back to Italy in June 1919, some of his followers arranged to bomb the home of the attorney general of the United States, A. Mitchell Palmer. Palmer was unhurt, but the bomber died. Several other prominent citizens had been targeted in that plot.

On April 15, 1920, police were called to the scene of an armed robbery at a shoe factory in Braintree, Massachusetts. They found the paymaster, Frederick Parmenter, and a guard, Alessandro Berardelli, with fatal gunshot wounds. Parmenter was able to speak just enough to indicate he did not know the gunman who had shot him. Witnesses described a blue Buick that was a getaway vehicle, with at least three men besides the gunmen inside. More than $15,000 in cash was stolen. The Braintree robbery was similar to a failed heist in Bridgewater, Massachusetts, several months earlier. In Bridgewater, however, the weapon had been different—a shotgun rather than a pistol—and no one had died.

Anarchists had to know that government agents were watching them. They also suspected that authorities might be roughing up anarchists and other alleged "reds" while in custody. Such manhandling might have been to obtain information concerning bomb-throwing plots. It also may have involved the police suspicion that anarchists were connected with the robberies in Braintree and Bridgewater.

A general step-up in governmental spying against leftists made the anarchists of southern Massachusetts jumpy. Some of them attempted to leave the area. The chief of police in Bridgewater, Michael Stewart, thought that an anarchist named

Ferruccio Coacci might have been involved in the robberies. Coacci had worked at both of the factories that had been targeted. On April 16, 1920, Stewart went to interview Coacci, who had missed a date to be deported. Coacci appeared suddenly anxious to comply with the deportation order, and detectives actually escorted him to a point of embarkation. Stewart then tailed one of Coacci's friends, Mike Boda (Mario Buda), to see if Boda would lead them to any evidence. Within a couple of days a car matching the description of that used in the Braintree robbery-murders was found near a house in which Coacci and Boda had stayed.

Of particular concern to anarchists in the area was the death in custody of one of their number, Andrew Salsedo. On May 3, Salsedo fell from a window while Department of Justice officials were questioning him in New York City. Radicals and the authorities alike suspected Salsedo died while withholding information about the Braintree and Bridgewater crimes. The government and local police theorized that the robberies were engineered to fund the Galleanists' bomb construction projects.

The nervousness of the radicals increased still further. Chief Stewart waited for Boda to pick up a car that was under repair, thinking that Boda planned to use that vehicle to move incriminating written materials, or worse. (Some historians agree with the contemporary theory among police that when anarchists spoke of "radical literature" it was a code phrase for "explosives.") On May 5, the owner of the garage where Boda's auto was located alerted police when Boda and three other men called for the car. Upon the arrival of the police the four suspects tried to flee, two by motorcycle and two on a streetcar. The two on the motorcycle escaped. The men on the streetcar were Sacco and Vanzetti. At that point they were unknown to police. Chief Stewart had simply put the word out along the streetcar line to look for two foreigners.

The apprehension of Sacco and Vanzetti was a pivotal moment, for later their behavior and comments when approached by police would be analyzed in some detail. Of special importance was the discovery on their persons of weapons (some armed), ammunition, and a draft of an announcement about an anarchist speech written by Vanzetti. At the scene where police confronted them, the men gave what police said were elusive and contradictory answers about why they were carrying weapons for which they had no permits and where they were going.

After a warning that they would not have to answer his questions but that he would use any replies against them, Chief Stewart asked Sacco and Vanzetti about their political associations. They denied knowing Coacci and Boda, refused to admit being anarchists, and claimed never to have been in Bridgewater before the current day. The police detained them on a concealed weapons charge but did not immediately ask them about either armed robbery.

Frederick Katzmann, the district attorney for Plymouth and Norfolk Counties, interviewed the suspects as well as a number of witnesses to both the Braintree and Bridgewater robberies. Katzmann and the police operated under the assumption that the two crimes were connected. The modus operandi was similar in each and the targets both were shoe factories on payday. The authorities constructed a rationale for the linked crimes; they were to obtain cash to fund radical activities, specifically bomb making. Although the working theory was that five men—Sacco, Vanzetti, Boda, and Coacci, plus another man, Ricardo Orciani—had been at both Bridgewater and Braintree, only Sacco and Vanzetti were not on the run.

Katzmann then ran into difficulty because Sacco had a good alibi for the Bridgewater crime. Although his case against Vanzetti for the nonfatal Bridgewater robbery was relatively weak, he decided to go ahead with that prosecution. It would serve as a bellwether for the more serious case against the two men in the Braintree murders. Vanzetti's trial took just over a week, concluding on July 1, 1920. Vanzetti was convicted on this, his first offense. He received a sentence of 12–15 years.

SUMMARY OF ARGUMENTS

The judge who had heard the case against Vanzetti for the Bridgewater crime was Webster Thayer, a decidedly antiradical individual. In a case in 1920 Thayer had reprimanded a jury for acquitting an anarchist against his pointed instructions to convict. The jurors at that trial stood their ground, however, and refused to change their verdict or apologize for it.

Thayer apparently lobbied hard to hear the subsequent case that Katzmann put forward: the prosecution of both Vanzetti and Sacco for the Braintree robbery-murders. Thayer's deportment during trial, not just in the courtroom but also in off-the-bench comments, became one of the most controversial elements of the case. The trial opened on May 31, 1921, in state court in Dedham, Massachusetts.

The defendants had competent counsel, although at times they quarreled with those lawyers. The chief defense attorney, Fred Moore, came to the case from California. Leftist groups funded the defense. Moore was a dogged fighter for his clients though some even among the defense team accused him of coaching witnesses inappropriately. Moore clearly irritated Judge Thayer, who sub rosa referred to him as a "long-hair" (an intellectual out of touch with mainstream society). Moore was known for making numerous motions for the defense at trial. His record for getting motions approved under Judge Thayer was notably poor.

Although lawyers for the defense, the defendants, and their supporters accused Thayer of barely disguised bias against them, the jury in the "Braintree trial" (also called the "Dedham trial") consistently praised the judge's management of the courtroom. They insisted that his guidance of the panel had been temperate. The jury of 12 men was impaneled from two calls among more than 600 potential jurors. The jury was attentive to the complex recitation of evidence.

The documents and testimony in the case filled several volumes. Among the more lengthy portions of the record were eyewitness accounts of the Braintree crime, testimony from witnesses who gave information about the movements of Sacco and Vanzetti on April 15, 1920, and forensic evidence. Certain forensic material, specifically information about the bullets that killed Berardelli and Parmenter, proved decisive among jurors and vexing to subsequent scholars of the case. In the courtroom the jury panel leaned heavily on the state's argument that the bullets found in the bodies of the deceased men had come from firearms recovered from Sacco and Vanzetti. The state contended

that Sacco had been apprehended while carrying Berardelli's gun.

The state needed to establish that Sacco and Vanzetti were at the scene of the Braintree killings. Both said that they were not present, and the defense produced witnesses who swore to their being in other locations on April 15. The ballistics evidence was key to placement of the two accused men at the fatal location. The prosecution maintained that Sacco and Vanzetti could not prove they were elsewhere. Such an argument discounted the testimony of several persons of Italian origin. Some, for example, said they had seen Sacco in a restaurant in Boston on April 15 after he had visited a passport office earlier.

Katzmann also put emphasis on the actions and words of Sacco and Vanzetti at the time of their apprehension on May 5, 1920. He posited that their fleeing the garage where Boda's car was located, as well as their confused answers to police, demonstrated a "consciousness of guilt" about the Braintree crime. The defense responded that Sacco and Vanzetti spoke untruthfully to the police out of the fear of being labeled anarchists rather than due to guilt.

The defense rested much of its hope in creating doubt in the jurors' minds that the two accused men were at Braintree at all. Moore and his legal colleagues spent time debunking prosecution assertions about the items that connected Sacco and Vanzetti to the scene. It was not just the ballistics that were at issue. A cap supposedly belonging to Sacco, for instance, had been found near the victims. In a courtroom episode that eerily prefigured a pivotal moment at O. J. Simpson's 1995 murder trial, prosecutors required that Sacco try on the cap to demonstrate it would fit him. Sacco acted as though the cap were too large. The prosecution produced witnesses who indicated they had glimpsed Vanzetti holding a shotgun as the getaway vehicle sped away; among Vanzetti's possessions upon apprehension were shotgun casings.

In the Dedham courtroom there was little talk of the defendants' radicalism. The defense did not want to bring up Sacco and Vanzetti's politics, of course, but the prosecution also trod lightly on that topic so as not to be accused of feeding public fears about anarchism. Even when Vanzetti explained his effort to help pick up Boda's car as related to spiriting away radical publications, the prosecution refused to capitalize upon that opportunity to open up a discussion about the men's politics.

Despite the persistent talk of Judge Thayer's prejudice against the defense, his charge to the jury was measured. Thayer cautioned the jurors not to let their biases interfere with a fair assessment of Sacco and Vanzetti:

> Guilt or innocence, gentlemen, of crime, do not depend upon the place of one's birth; the proportion of his wealth, his station in life, social or political, or his views on public questions prevent an honest judgment and impartial administration and enforcement of the law, for when the time comes that these conditions exist to an extent that men, because of these conditions, cannot be indicted, tried, acquitted according to the laws of the commonwealth in a court of justice, the doors to our court house should then be closed and we should announce to the world the impotency of our courts and the utter failure of constitutional or organized government.

VERDICTS

On July 14, 1921, the jury deliberated for several hours before finding both men guilty of armed robbery and murder. The killings were considered first-degree murder because they occurred in the course of another potentially capital crime.

The guilty verdict and Judge Thayer's death sentence set off immense controversy. The defense launched appeals, not only in a legal sense but also in the mass media and through radical channels. Even mainstream publications tended to be critical of the convictions; among such pieces was an article by Felix Frankfurter in the *Atlantic Monthly*. Those who supported Sacco and Vanzetti decided that attorney Moore was a greater liability than help. William Thompson of Massachusetts replaced Moore.

As the case was appealed, pressure mounted for a political intervention. Would Massachusetts governor Alvan Fuller issue a reprieve? Fuller sought the advice of an expert panel, directed by Harvard president Abbott Lowell. The committee reviewed the extensive trial record as well as hearing from additional witnesses. It concluded that some of Judge Thayer's remarks outside of court had been not the best examples of a balanced judicial temperament but also asserted that the trial as a whole had been fair.

That report supported Governor Fuller's decision to let the sentence stand. The Massachusetts Supreme Court denied an appeal. Upon hearing the decision of the Massachusetts Supreme Court, Sacco and Vanzetti chose to speak about their core beliefs. They continued to profess innocence of the crimes, but they freely admitted to political disaffection. Sacco addressed the court in class-conscious terms:

> I never knew, never heard, even read in history anything so cruel as this Court. After seven years prosecuting they still consider us guilty. And these gentle people here are arrayed with us in this court today.
>
> I know the sentence will be between two classes, the oppressed class and the rich class, and there will be always collision between one and the other. We fraternize the people with the books, with the literature. You persecute the people, tyrannize them and kill them. We try the education of people always. You try to put a path between us and some other nationality that hates each other. That is why I am here today on this bench, for having been of the oppressed class. Well, you are the oppressor.

Vanzetti's statement was more personal and perhaps more convincing of his innocence, but he also set forth deeply held political beliefs:

> What I say is that I am innocent, not only of the Braintree crime, but also of the Bridgewater crime. That I am not only innocent of these two crimes, but in all my life I have never stolen and I have never killed and I have never spilled blood. That is what I want to say. And it is not all. Not only am I innocent of these two crimes, not only in all my life I have never stolen, never killed, never spilled blood, but I have struggled all my life, since I began to reason, to eliminate crime from the earth.

Everybody that knows these two arms knows very well that I did not need to go into the streets and kill a man or try to take money. I can live by my two hands and live well. But besides that, I can live even without work with my hands for other people. I have had plenty of chance to live independently and to live what the world conceives to be a higher life than to gain our bread with the sweat of our brow.

My father in Italy is in a good condition. I could have come back in Italy and he would have welcomed me every time with open arms. Even if I come back there with not a cent in my pocket, my father could have give me a position, not to work but to make business, or to oversee upon the land that he owns.

. . . Now, I should say that I am not only innocent of all these things, not only have I never committed a real crime in my life—though some sins but not crimes—not only have I struggled all my life to eliminate crimes, the crimes that the official law and the moral law condemns, but also the crime that the moral law and the official law sanction and sanctify,—the exploitation and the oppression of the man by the man, and if there is a reason why I am here as a guilty man, if there is a reason why you in a few minutes can doom me, it is this reason and none else.

The U.S. Supreme Court determined not to accept the case on appeal. The furor continued, not just rhetorically but also on the streets. Demonstrations abroad in support of the convicted men occasionally turned into anti-American outbursts. Literati were deeply engaged in the discussion. John Dos Passos and Edna St. Vincent Millay, for example, penned critiques of the case.

Those who argued that anarchists were prima facie criminals seemed to be proved correct in several incidents directly related to the trial. Boda set off a bomb in New York City after his colleagues were indicted but before trial. That demonstration of anarchist frustration killed 33 people and injured scores more. It would be the deadliest deliberate detonation in U.S. history until the Oklahoma City bombing of 1995. Boda escaped

the country. At least one key witness told authorities that he would not testify at the Braintree trial due to fear of retaliation by anarchists. While the defendants were on death row, the home of the brother of the garage owner who had called police about Boda's car was the site of a bomb detonation. Presumably the radicals had mistaken one brother for the other.

President Lowell of Harvard University came in for sharp criticism and direct threats for his committee's report on the case. In 1932, which was well after the execution of Sacco and Vanzetti but within the time that the case still was recalled vividly, Judge Thayer's house was bombed. Thayer was unhurt, although his wife and a domestic worker were injured. The jurist was badly shaken by the reprisal. He lived under guard at another location until his death about a year later.

SIGNIFICANCE

The Sacco and Vanzetti case was extremely contentious while the defendants were alive, and it continued to create division after their deaths in the electric chair on August 23, 1927. Both amateur and professional investigators have reexamined the two crimes that were at issue, with special focus on the Braintree robbery-murders. The most prevalent line of thought about the case has been that both of the men were innocent of committing the crime, though they may have had some hand in planning one or both robberies. They were convicted, this argument goes, because of class and ethnic prejudice and with the cooperation of the judiciary (especially Judge Thayer) and law enforcement. A somewhat narrower view of the trials is that the man that police suspected as the ringleader, Coacci, had absconded. To law enforcement, Sacco and Vanzetti were likely stand-ins.

According to this view, police, prosecutors, and forensic experts either withheld exculpatory information or manufactured false evidence against Sacco and Vanzetti. Although several details support that contention, there are bits that point the other way. The prosecution, for instance, did not introduce into evidence hairs found on the cap from the crime scene. While those hairs supposedly matched Sacco's, Katzmann apparently rejected the option that the case should be decided "by a hair."

Certain scholars present an alternative scenario for the robberies: They were carried out by a local crime group known as the Morelli gang, one of whose number made a jailhouse confession that absolved Sacco and Vanzetti prior to their execution. At the least, critics of the trials say, Sacco and Vanzetti's case should have been reopened on the grounds of that confession and other new evidence of which authorities were aware prior to the executions.

Those who take issue with such an interpretation of the trials as unfair pursue several arguments. Some contend that Sacco and Vanzetti may not have been triggermen but that they did conceive of the crimes or at least ride along in the Buick. Other significant theories are that Sacco was a killer but Vanzetti was innocent—either completely or to a certain degree—of the murders. These discussants have not convinced many of the defenders of Sacco and Vanzetti of their complicity in the crimes at Bridgewater and Braintree, but such arguments have altered the perception that the accused men were political innocents.

Legal historians find a number of aspects of the case worthy of discussion. The role of Moore comes in for examination not just because of his outsize reputation for radicalism but also due to certain strategies he adopted in handling the case. For example, there is some indication that Moore foresaw it as easier to defend Vanzetti than Sacco and that he considered arguing for Vanzetti's innocence in stronger terms than Sacco's. Perhaps the jury would acquit one and convict the other. He discussed such a strategy with Vanzetti, who vetoed the idea. Sacco, Vanzetti said, had a family; Moore should try to save him.

The case of Sacco and Vanzetti revolved around an everyday crime, and yet, the defendants' days in court made for two spectacularly well-known trials—especially the prosecution of both men at Dedham, which garnered interest all over the world. Though less well known in the later 20th century than among the generation that witnessed the case, the story of Sacco and Vanzetti continues to inspire popular interest as well as debates among specialized scholars. The enduring reputation of the judicial proceedings is that they were biased against Sacco and Vanzetti. Although the men may have been criminals, the question remains whether the taint of official misconduct in this case should have trumped the defendants' guilt.

Further Reading

Avrich, Paul. *Sacco and Vanzetti: The Anarchist Background.* Princeton, N.J.: Princeton University Press, 1991; *Nicola Sacco and Bartholomeo Vanzetti v. Commonwealth of Massachusetts* 25 U.S. 574 (1927). Available online. URL: http://libproxy.uta.edu:2156/hottopics/inacademic/?. Accessed May 15, 2010; Davis, John. *Sacco and Vanzetti.* Melbourne, Australia: Ocean Press, 2004; Ehrmann, Herbert. *The Case That Will Not Die: Commonwealth vs. Sacco and Vanzetti.* Boston: Little, Brown, 1969; Kadane, Joseph B., and David A. Schum. *A Probabilistic Analysis of the Sacco and Vanzetti Evidence.* New York: Wiley, 1996; Miller, Peter (dir.), *Sacco and Vanzetti.* First Run Features, 2007; Russell, Francis. *Sacco and Vanzetti: The Case Resolved.* New York: Harper & Row, 1986; Watson, Bruce. *Sacco and Vanzetti: The Men, the Murders, and the Judgment of Mankind.* New York: Viking, 2007; Young, William, and Kaiser, David. *Postmortem: New Evidence in the Case of Sacco and Vanzetti.* Amherst: University of Massachusetts Press, 1986.

The trial of Mohandas Gandhi

Also known as: *The King v. Gandhi;* the Great Trial

Date: 1922

KEY ISSUES

In this rare instance the maxim "he who defends himself has a fool for a lawyer" does not apply. During the case of *The King v. Mohandas Gandhi* the defendant presented his position memorably. Although Gandhi lost in court, he won praise for his honesty and eloquence as a self-advocate. But, the episode was more than an enhancement for Gandhi's growing personal stature. The trial of Gandhi proved an instance of good judgment by the British Crown as it tried to retain control over India. The Mahatma represented a growing movement for Indian self-government that the British ultimately recognized as viable only decades after the conclusion of this case. But, in the courtroom, at least for a time, the representatives of the British Crown seemed to understand the unique appeal of Gandhi among Indians. In contrast to earlier and later prosecutions in India the case against Gandhi went forward and was concluded in an atmosphere of mutual respect.

HISTORY OF THE CASE

Mohandas Karamchand Gandhi came from a wealthy background in India. He completed university studies in England and trained to be a lawyer at London's Inns of Court. He practiced law in India for a few years and then moved to South Africa with its large Indian population. During his years there Gandhi was moved by the restrictions on all people of color. He served the British as an ambulance corpsman during two military confrontations in Africa but at the same time was refining his belief in self-determination for Indian people both in South Africa and in India.

Gandhi's philosophy of satyagraha was both spiritually based and pragmatic. It involved telling the truth and seeking truth, refusing to make others suffer, allowing oneself to be hurt if necessary, and providing an opportunity for an opponent to emerge gracefully from conflict. It was a set of ideals that could cross religious boundaries. Persons in many of the world's belief systems could appreciate such tenets. Gandhi liked the term *civil resistance* as a shorthand English expression for satyagraha, for it conveyed that nonviolent methods gave strength to those who employed them. When Gandhi advocated the use of civil resistance in the service of Indian self-determination, he did not propose inactivity. Rather, he expected that nonviolent methods would prove powerful weapons against imperial rule.

The British had been in India for hundreds of years, and Indians had become accustomed to British goods and culture. Part of Gandhi's goal was to help Indians see that they could govern and sustain themselves. Given poverty and religious divisions within the subcontinent, though, such a campaign

to infuse Indians with self-confidence faced large obstacles. A key barrier to Indians' uniting against the British was the great divide between Muslim and Hindu people. After World War I many Indian Muslims and Hindus were angry at the ruling nation—Muslims due to British policy toward Turkey and Hindus in connection with British rule in India.

Muslim Indians centered much of their political action in the years after 1919 on the Khilafat movement, which supported the caliph of the Ottoman Empire. The Ali brothers Maulana Muhammad Ali Jouhar and Maulana Shaukat Ali were especially influential with Muslim Indians. From within the Indian National Congress, Gandhi at times worked alongside the Alis and the Khilafat to oppose the British. It was only a temporary alliance, however, based much more on shared dislike of British foreign policy than common domestic goals.

Gandhi and those who admired him had evolved in their aims and their methods. Gandhi, in 1921, had not yet come to the advocacy of complete independence but rather was still a "home ruler" in the language of the day. Like certain factions among the Irish, Gandhi at the time was recommending that Indians should govern themselves in daily matters, perhaps with the British Crown as a figurehead. Also, except for his links with those who opposed British policy toward Turkey, Gandhi's focus in the postwar era was as much inward as in regard to foreign affairs. It was during this time that Gandhi concentrated on promoting Indian textiles, especially through hand-spinning, and on improving the lot of lower-caste Indians.

In two particular incidents in 1921, political protests linked with Gandhi's words got out of hand. In Bombay in November 1921 many objected to the visit of the Prince of Wales (the future Edward VIII), and Gandhi had urged Indians not to celebrate that state visit. Large numbers of people rioted, resulting in deaths and loss of property. At Chauri Chaura, near Agra, in February of 1922, after police shot three persons during a protest about liquor sales, a mob followed 22 policemen to their station and burned the building. Gandhi condemned such violence, even taking it upon himself to fast as an act of repentance for any part he had played in atrocities. Still, the British blamed him as a leader among Indians, for inspiring them to rebel.

In an issue of his magazine *Young India,* on September 29, 1922, Gandhi published three articles that the British government found particularly objectionable. In those articles he answered questions from critics who could not grasp why nonviolent protesters would risk apprehension:

> We seek arrest because the so-called freedom is slavery. We are challenging the might of this Government because we consider its activity to be wholly evil. We want to overthrow the Government. We want to compel its submission to the people's will. We desire to show that the Government exists to serve the people, not the people the Government.

Gandhi had special scorn for the principles and practice of imperialism:

> No empire intoxicated with the red wine of power and plunder of weaker races has yet lived long in this world, and this "British Empire" which is based upon organised exploitation of physically weaker races of the earth, and upon a continuous exhibition of brute force, cannot live, if there is a just God ruling the universe.

Beyond those more abstract arguments, Gandhi warned that he envisioned asking Indians who were serving the British as soldiers to lay down that allegiance and turn toward their native land. This was an invitation made more complex by Gandhi's desire for assistance from Muslim partisans of independence:

> I shall not hesitate (when the time is ripe), at the peril of being shot, to ask the Indian sepoy individually to leave his service and become a weaver. For, has not the sepoy been used to hold India under subjection, has he not been used to murder innocent people at Jalianwala Bagh, has he not been used to drive away innocent men, women, and children during that dreadful night at Chandpur, has he not been used to subjugate the proud Arab of Mesopotamia, has he not

been utilised to crush the Egyptian? How can any Indian having a spark of humanity in him, and any Mussalman having any pride in his religion, feel otherwise than as the Ali Brothers have done? The sepoy has been used more often as a hired assassin than as a soldier defending the liberty or the honour of the weak and the helpless.

On the basis of those words Gandhi was charged with sedition.

SUMMARY OF ARGUMENTS

Gandhi's trial was a brief one, held at Ahmedabad on March 18, 1922. The judge was C. N. Broomfield of the District and Sessions Court. Thomas Strangfield, the advocate-general of Bombay, prosecuted. A trial in recent Indian history loomed as a precedent: the second prosecution, in 1909, of Lokmanya Bal Gangadhar Tilak (*Lokmanya* was an honorary form of address meaning "the Beloved") for sedition.

Tilak had written an article in his own publication, the *Kisari,* defending two Bengali bombers who had killed several women while attempting to assassinate British official Douglas Kingsford. Tilak thought that the action ought to inspire Indians toward self-rule, which he called *swaraj.* The British accused Tilak of sedition. In an acrimonious proceeding he was convicted and sentenced to six years' imprisonment. The connection with Gandhi was close. Gandhi associated with Tilak through the Congress Party. Also, despite Gandhi's advocacy of nonviolence, he and Tilak had assisted the British government in finding Indian recruits for World War I. At Tilak's death Gandhi paid public tribute to Tilak as a founder of "the maker of modern India."

Tilak had defended himself ably at his trials. He proposed that in presenting to his readers the motivations of the bombers, he was more a journalist than an agitator. Judge Davar, however, disagreed. In a strong charge to Tilak's jury, he told the panel that Tilak had erred in holding up Irish rebels against British authority as examples to Indians. Such words showed Tilak's intentions to be dishonorable. There were Indians on the jury as well as British-born subjects. The vote to convict Tilak was along national lines. Davar's reprimand to Tilak was harsh. He said that The Lokmanya's words had been "seething with sedition" and had praised the use of deadly weapons. The defendant, though, seemed to accept the criticism with good grace.

Like Gandhi, Tilak espoused the belief that progress toward self-governance for India might require personal sacrifice on his part. At the end of his trial Tilak proclaimed: "In spite of the verdict of the Jury, I maintain that I am innocent. There are higher powers that rule the destiny of men and nations and it may be the will of providence that the cause which I represent may prosper more by my suffering than by my remaining free." Lokmanya Tilak's exile to Burma and fine were moderated to mere imprisonment as a result of civil unrest involving hundreds of thousands of participants. Clearly, the convicted man had many admirers.

Thus, at Gandhi's trial the prosecution was well aware of the interest that would prevail in the case of Gandhi, especially since Tilak had died just two years prior and now Gandhi was the unquestioned head of the movement for Indian self-rule. The British government appeared to be determined not to overreact in Gandhi's case as some (even among its own ranks) had accused the authorities of doing in 1908–09 with Tilak. Still, Gandhi's profile was so high that those in power apparently could not refrain from censuring him in a judicial setting.

The "Great Trial," as it came to be called, was almost over before it really got under way. As the prosecutor began to list the charges against Gandhi, the defendant broke in, forestalling both further details and a jury trial. Gandhi pled guilty. But, for the government this case was as much about stating its reasons for opposing self-determination as about convicting this individual in the dock. Sir Thomas Strangman continued to explain why the authorities linked Gandhi's words with the bloodshed that had erupted of late.

The prosecutor implicitly brought to mind an old principle in British law: the more that an inciter spoke to the lower classes, the more dangerous he was. Gandhi was well informed and articulate. He was the product of an elite British university (University College London), yet he addressed the ordinary folk of India. He reached across classes and religious divides—a peculiarly un-British notion and a potentially effective one. Strangman recommended a "severe" sentence that would be a stern comment on how writings could incite violence.

VERDICT

It remained for Judge Broomfield to determine a sentence. He invited Gandhi to present a statement to the court, knowing that this would be the defendant's opportunity to state his case more fully. Gandhi obliged, in one of the most unusual responses ever voiced by an accused person. Gandhi spoke to the court first without notes, simply in addressing the accusations of Advocate-General Strangman. He then added a longer, more formal prepared speech, but it was the Mahatma's spur-of-the-moment reply that went down as practically unprecedented—a verbal and legal example of satyagraha:

> I would like to state that I entirely endorse the learned Advocate-General's remarks in connection with my humble self. I think that he was entirely fair to me in all the statements that he has made, because it is very true . . . that to preach disaffection towards the existing system of Government has become almost a passion with me. The Advocate-General is also entirely right when he said that my preaching of this disaffection did not commence with my connection with "Young India" but much earlier. . . . It commenced much earlier than the period stated by the Advocate-General.
>
> I wish to endorse all the blame that the Advocate-General has thrown on my shoulders in connection with the Bombay occurrences, Madras occurrences, and the Chauri Chaura occurrences. Thinking over these things deeply . . . I have come to the conclusion that it is impossible for me to dissociate myself from the diabolical crimes of Chauri Chaura or the mad outrages of Bombay. The Advocate-General is quite right when he says that as a man of responsibility, a man having received a fair share of education and experience of this world, I should know the consequences of my acts. I knew them. I knew that I was playing with fire. I ran the risk; and if I am set free, I would still

do the same. I wanted to avoid violence. Non-violence is the first article of my faith. It is the last article of my faith. But I had to make my choice.

I had either to submit to a system which I considered has done an irreparable harm to my country, or incur the risk of the mad fury of my people bursting forth when they understood the truth from my lips. I know that my people have sometimes gone mad. I am deeply sorry for it; and I am, therefore, here to submit not to a light penalty but to the highest penalty. The only course open to you, Mr. Judge, is, as I am just going to say in my statement, either to resign your post or inflict on me the severest penalty.

Judge Broomfield's pronunciation of sentence on Gandhi could only be characterized as gracious:

Mr. Gandhi, you have made my task easy in one way by pleading guilty to the charge. Nevertheless, what remains, namely the determination of a just sentence, is perhaps as difficult a proposition as a Judge in this country could have to face. The law is no respecter of persons. Nevertheless, it would be impossible to ignore the fact that you are in a different category from any person I have ever tried or am likely ever to try. It would be impossible to ignore the fact that in the eyes of millions of your countrymen you are a great patriot and a great leader; even all those who differ from you in politics look up to you as a man of high ideals and of noble and even saintly life. I have to deal with you in one character only. It is not my duty, and I do not presume to judge or criticise you in any other character. It is my duty to judge you as a man subject to the law, who has by his own admission broken the law, and committed what to an ordinary man must appear to be a grave offence against such law. I do not forget that you have consistently preached against violence, or that you have on many occasions, as I am willing to believe, done much to prevent violence.

But having regard to the nature of your political teaching and the nature of many of those to whom it was addressed, how you can have continued to believe that violence and anarchy would not be the inevitable consequence, it passes my capacity to understand. There are probably few people in India who do not sincerely regret that you should have made it impossible for any Government to leave you at liberty. But it is so, I am trying to balance what is due to you against what appears to me to be necessary in the interest of the public; and I propose, in passing sentence, to follow the precedent of the case, in many respects similar to this case, that was decided some twelve years ago, the case of Mr. Bal Gangadhar Tilak, under the same section. The sentence that was passed upon him as it finally stood, was a sentence of simple imprisonment for six years. You will not consider it unreasonable, I think, that you should be classed with Mr. Tilak; and that is the sentence two years' simple imprisonment on each count of the charge, six years in all, which I feel it my duty to pass upon you. If the course of events in India should make it possible for Government to reduce the period and release you, nobody would be better pleased than I.

The ending of the trial was a high point in Anglo-Indian jurisprudence. Although Gandhi's supporters shed tears, so did prosecutor Strangman. Gandhi appeared quite cheerful. The parties shook hands, and the courtroom emptied with respectful calm.

SIGNIFICANCE

Gandhi's reputation only grew within India and elsewhere as a result of the Great Trial. Among a number of important advocates for Indian independence at the end of World War II, Gandhi was the person with enough internal and international prestige to broker not just separation from Britain but also the subsequent partition of the subcontinent. His participation in that separation of parts of India from each other on the basis of religion, however, earned him the enmity of persons from within India who arranged his assassination in 1948.

The influence of Gandhi's advocacy of nonviolent resistance on other campaigns for human rights and independence cannot be overstated. Satyagraha informed the tactics of civil rights reformers in the United States such as Dr. Martin Luther King, Jr., and antiwar protests worldwide. The efforts of persons such as Mother Teresa to eradicate discrimination based on caste also can be traced to the ecumenical outreach of the Mahatma.

Scholars of imperialism frequently argue that the British forgot nothing and learned nothing in India. The trial of Gandhi appears an exception. In that episode, at least once the case reached the stage of argumentation, those in court appeared keenly aware of not only the unusual character of Gandhi but also his historical significance.

Further Reading

Attenborough, Richard (dir.), *Gandhi*. Columbia Pictures, 1982; Chada, Yogesh. *Gandhi: A Life*. New York: Wiley, 1999; Gandhi, Mohandas K. *Gandhi, an Autobiography*. Boston: Beacon Press, 1993; Strangman, Thomas. *Indian Courts and Characters*. London: W. Heinemann, 1931; Watson, Francis. *The Trial of Mr. Gandhi*. London: Macmillan, 1969; Wolpert, Stanley. *Gandhi's Passion: The Life and Legacy of Mahatma Gandhi*. Oxford: Oxford University Press, 2002.

The trials of Nathan Leopold and Richard Loeb

Also known as: *Illinois v. Leopold and Loeb*; the Thrill Killers' trial

Date: 1924

KEY ISSUES

The case of Nathan Leopold and Richard Loeb was a curious mixture of horrific criminality, scientific argument, public interest, and lawyerly skill. The 1924 trial was of two young men who coolly abducted and murdered a young boy, apparently to experience the sensation of killing. Such a proceeding could not fail to grab headlines. The accused teenaged millionaires were defended by the ablest criminal trial lawyer of the day, Clarence Darrow. That Darrow often had championed the cause of powerless individuals made his choice to represent these despised, privileged, and well-educated defendants all the more striking.

HISTORY OF THE CASE

Leopold and Loeb (aged 19 and 18, respectively) were involved in a homosexual relationship. Both were college graduates recognized for their brilliant minds. Both already were enrolled in postgraduate programs at the University of Chicago, near where they grew up. Loeb was the more forceful of the two, but they shared the notion of committing "the perfect crime," an undetectable murder. The purpose was dual. In the short term the perpetrators wanted to see what it felt like to kill. Through their holding out of the promise of a ransom and then the denial of a resolution to the case, they also hoped to demonstrate to themselves that they were brighter than the police.

They put their plan into effect on May 21, 1924. The choice of victim was somewhat random, though they did pick from among boys at an exclusive preparatory school. It would not have seemed unlikely for such a victim to be held for ransom. Loeb and Leopold were able to lure into their rented car a boy they knew, a 14-year-old cousin of Loeb's named Bobby Franks.

At first the scheme seemed to work smoothly for the criminals. They offered Franks a ride home from school and then bashed his head in. They rode around until they thought it safe to dispose of the body in a location that they had selected, a culvert. Loeb and Leopold had envisioned that the action of water in a drain would decompose the body quickly. They cleaned up the car, burned some of Franks's clothes, buried other of his personal items such as a belt buckle, and proceeded to mail off their demands for a ransom. The point was not the money. Loeb and Leopold regularly received ample distributions from their indulgent families.

The plan began to unravel within 24 hours. First of all, Franks's body was found. With it was a pair of glasses easy to connect with Leopold. The police also located a typewriter that the killers had tried to dump; it also was traceable to Leopold. The more that the police and newspapers inquired into the movements of Leopold and Loeb on the day of Franks's disappearance, the shakier the two teenagers' stories became.

The police also proved abler than the plotters had expected at pitting them against each other. In a series of interviews with police the two offered confessions. The public prosecutor Robert Crowe was certain that the capital charge he proposed to file would result in a conviction. Surely a jury would not fail to chastise severely the two rich "thrill killers."

SUMMARY OF ARGUMENTS

Darrow often had defended persons with unpopular political views or minority status. The public and his peers credited Darrow with having saved dozens of alleged criminals from execution. He was a well-known trial attorney in the United States in 1924, although his choices of clients often raised eyebrows. In the 1910s Darrow's defense of Industrial Workers of the World leader Bill Haywood and the McNamara brothers of Los Angeles—all accused of murder—cost his reputation for integrity considerably.

Many of Darrow's cases did not pay the bills; however, this one promised to be lucrative and was not without ideological appeal for the progressive attorney. He had fought against the death penalty repeatedly, and Darrow could not resist another chance to do so, especially under these seemingly insurmountable odds. Faced with public skepticism about his taking a supposed "million dollar fee" from the deep pockets of the Leopold and Loeb families, Darrow suggested that the Chicago Bar Association should mediate the question of his payment.

The prosecution assumed that the mental state of the killers would be at issue in the trial. Indeed, much of the prosecution lawyers' preparation did not center on the facts of the crime or even its investigation but rather the state of knowledge about killers' motivations. In particular, the state expected that this trial would consider the question of insanity.

Obviously, these killers did not lack mental capacity: One, Leopold, had a Phi Beta Kappa key, and the other was the youngest person ever to graduate from his university (Michigan). Could an individual be rational, even a genius, and yet so emotionally damaged that he could not conform to the dictates of the law? It was a complex query, made more tangled by the mutually dependent and sexual relationship between the defendants.

There was another factor that Darrow hoped to exploit but the prosecution expected to explain away: the ages of the accused. They were in a gray area chronologically. Although Loeb and Leopold held college degrees, they were minors according to Illinois law. Darrow's research into other death penalty cases involving young people in Chicago indicated that not one individual of these men's ages or below had ever been executed as long as he or she had admitted culpability. The prosecution, meanwhile, would maintain that the defendants' intelligence and advanced educational attainments mitigated against their being insane by current legal standards.

For several reasons, then, Darrow took an enormous gamble. When the case came up for trial on July 23, 1924, in Cook County's Circuit Court, Darrow announced that his clients would plead guilty. Darrow's reasoning was based on his understanding of precedent, which he hoped to convey to Judge John Caverly. Darrow had a negative motivation, as well; he wished to keep this case out of the hands of a jury. He might boast an astonishing record of extricating defendants from the death penalty, chiefly by appealing to the common decency of the ordinary American juror. But, Darrow recognized that these clients would appear to be extremely objectionable human beings to the "twelve good men and true" who would be impaneled. His best opportunity to save Leopold's and Loeb's lives lay in reason and law.

No longer a trial, the month-long hearings in the Chicago courtroom, then, concerned what punishment Judge Caverly would impose. Would the judge direct that Leopold and Loeb should be put to death, or was there some ground for moderating their sentences? Psychiatric experts had labored for months after the arrests, compiling lengthy reports on the upbringings and current mental states of the two accused persons. Both the defense and the prosecution had their share of experts, several of whom now took the stand before the judge.

The prosecution's contentions were simple: These were spoiled, wealthy young men. They had no consciences. First-class educations only filled the young men's heads with philosophy, such as that of Friedrich Nietzsche, that Leopold and Loeb applied selectively to themselves. Loeb envisioned himself as an exemplar of a super-race, and Leopold worshipped him. They were bored with their usual pursuits, which included homosexuality, and so they developed a new "game" involving murder. They had not outsmarted the authorities; their only regret was being caught. They were dangerous criminals who deserved to die because of their amorality. They were a continuing threat to public safety.

Darrow for the defense had the more intricate task. He made the most of the opportunity. The mental health experts that he summoned described a lifelong sense of unreality and lack of connection to their surroundings, in both Leopold and Loeb. It was a point that could have been dangerous to the defense, but Darrow had to acknowledge it. To Leopold and Loeb, Franks meant nothing, and yet they ran a great risk in killing the younger boy. As Darrow stated,

> [Leopold and Loeb were] boys of distinguished and honorable families, families of wealth and position, with all the world before them. And they gave it all up for nothing, for nothing! They took a little companion of one of them, on a crowded street, and killed him, for nothing, and sacrificed everything that could be of value in human life upon the crazy scheme of a couple of immature lads.
>
> Now, your Honor, you have been a boy; I have been a boy. And we have known other boys. The best way to understand somebody else is to put yourself in his place.
>
> Is it within the realm of your imagination that a boy who was right, with all the prospects of life before him, who could choose what he wanted, without the slightest reason in the world would lure a young companion to his death, and take his place in the shadow of the gallows?
>
> . . . How insane they are I care not, whether medically or legally. They did not reason; they could not reason; they committed the most foolish, most unprovoked, most purposeless, most causeless act that

any two boys ever committed, and they put themselves where the rope is dangling above their heads. . . .

> Why did they kill little Bobby Franks?
>
> Not for money, not for spite; not for hate. They killed him as they might kill a spider or a fly, for the experience. They killed him because they were made that way.

In that brief stretch of argument Darrow turned attention away from the victim of a brutal crime to its perpetrators. In his explanation Leopold and Loeb also were "boys" who could not help themselves. Not only were the accused individuals poorly brought up (especially by Leopold's allegedly abusive governess). The defendants' emotional ties to each other only complicated the already-troubled state of their minds.

Darrow further concentrated on the larger meaning of the case. How it would look to the world if the state of Illinois executed Leopold and Loeb? This was the main plank of Darrow's argument. He was asking Judge Caverly to disregard the intense media pressure for hanging, which no doubt also reflected popular preference for a capital sentence. Darrow proposed that this was an opportunity for the judge to move forward to a new era in sentencing, informed by scientific opinion rather than mob justice or ignorance:

> I suppose civilization will survive if your Honor hangs them. But it will be a terrible blow that you shall deal. Your Honor will be turning back over the long, long road we have traveled. You will be turning back from the protection of youth and infancy. Your Honor would be turning back from the treatment of children. Your Honor would be turning back to the barbarous days which Brother Marshall seems to love, when they burned people thirteen years of age.
>
> And for what? Because the people are talking about it. Nothing else. It would not mean, your Honor, that your reason was convinced. It would mean in this land of ours, where talk is cheap, where newspapers are plenty, where the most immature expresses his opinion, and the more immature the stronger, that a court couldn't help

feeling the great pressure of the public opinion which they say exists in this case.

Though he usually excelled in speaking to juries when he had the opportunity to provide a summation, in this instance Darrow needed to direct all the force of his oratory toward Judge Caverly. For 12 hours on August 24 he held forth in a plea to spare the young men's lives. It was an extraordinary speech, exceptional even within the career of a world-class advocate:

> I am pleading for life, understanding, charity, kindness, and the infinite mercy that considers all. I am pleading that we overcome cruelty with kindness and hatred with love. I know the future is on my side. Your Honor stands between the past and the future. You may hang these boys; you may hang them by the neck until they are dead. But in doing it you will turn your face toward the past. In doing it you are making it harder for every other boy who in ignorance and darkness must grope his way through the mazes which only childhood knows. In doing it you will make it harder for unborn children. You may save them and make it easier for every child that some time may stand where these boys stand. You will make it easier for every human being with an aspiration and a vision and a hope and a fate. I am pleading for the future; I am pleading for a time when hatred and cruelty will not control the hearts of men. When we can learn by reason and judgment and understanding and faith that all life is worth saving, and that mercy is the highest attribute of man.

Among the few dry eyes in the courtroom when Darrow concluded his remarks were those of Leopold and Loeb.

Verdict

Judge Caverly announced his verdict several days after the two sides had presented their final statements. He awarded an extremely long sentence to both Leopold and Loeb: life for the murder of Bobby Franks plus 99 years for the separate offense of the boy's kidnapping. The goal was for the convicts to die in jail. Perhaps in the interim, science could learn about criminality by studying them. The judge leaned heavily on the argument that history was already on his side. He noted that he could find only two instances in which minors had been given the death penalty in Illinois. Judge Caverly also reminded his critics—of whom there were sure to be many—that to these coddled young men the prospect of life behind bars was perhaps worse than execution.

Both of the convicts began serving time at Illinois's Joliet state prison. Loeb died in prison at the hand of another inmate in 1938. Leopold got a reduction in sentence in 1958, and then was paroled, partially on his promise that he would leave the country. He settled in Puerto Rico, where he continued his lifelong hobby of birding, learned languages (27 in all), and eventually married. He died in 1971. Leopold's autobiography, published upon his release from confinement, made evident his emotional dependency on Loeb. It also demonstrated that as he got to know Darrow during the trial and afterward, Leopold developed a profound respect for his defender:

> He [Darrow] hated superficiality; he refused to conform for conformity's sake. One result was that he often espoused unpopular causes. It may be said of him that he was one of the best-hated as well as one of the best-loved men of his day. Clarence Darrow came to visit me a few months before his death. Physically, he had grown feeble; the mark of death was on his face. But age and illness had not dimmed that piercing inner light. His wisdom, his kindliness, his understanding love of his fellow man shone out from under the wrappings of his flesh as brilliantly on this last day I saw him as it had on the first.

Significance

For Darrow, Judge Caverly's decision was a triumph. That Leopold's and Loeb's lives were spared was recognition of a celebrated lawyer's powers of persuasion. Darrow succeeded in his short-term task, but his arguments earned enormous negative comment. In this case he had taken the rich boys' side, channeling the arguments of psychiatrists.

Lost to many observers were Darrow's appeals to focus the case on humanitarian concerns, specifically a repudiation of the death penalty. What stuck in the public's mind was that he had accepted a large fee to argue for two wealthy young men who had killed in a singularly cold-blooded manner.

Further Reading

Baatz, Simon. *For the Thrill of It: Leopold, Loeb, and the Murder That Shocked Chicago.* New York: HarperCollins, 2008; Higdon, Hal. *The Crime of the Century: The Leopold and Loeb Case.* New York: Putnam, 1975; Jensen, Richard. *Clarence Darrow: The Creation of an American Myth.* New York: Greenwood Press, 1992; Leopold, Nathan. *Life Plus 99 Years.* Garden City, N.Y.: Doubleday, 1958; Rich, John (dir.), *IBM Presents Clarence Darrow.* NBC television special production, aired September 4, 1974; Stone, Irving. *Clarence Darrow for the Defense.* Garden City, N.Y.: Doubleday, 1941.

The trial of John Scopes

Also known as: *Tennessee v. Scopes,* the Scopes Trial, the Scopes Monkey Trial

Date: 1925

KEY ISSUES

The most famous trial in United States history seemed to begin in a junior high school classroom. The controversy that brought John Scopes into a courtroom in Dayton, Tennessee, during the summer of 1925 concerned, in theory, Scopes's duties as a public school teacher. Formally at issue was whether Scopes could teach current scientific opinions about the biological origins of humans. Specifically the question was whether the law in Tennessee permitted teachers to discuss the theories of Charles Darwin concerning human evolution. To those alarmed at Scopes's effort to bring

his university training in Darwinian biology to bear on his young students, evolutionary theory was not only unproven; it was sacrilegious. In the minds of Darwin's critics Scopes was teaching that humans were descended from lower orders of animals. This gainsaid a literal interpretation of Christian Scriptures that God had created people in the image of the divine.

Darwin himself had inspired bitter responses, although many persons who considered themselves religious did not find Darwinian ideas incompatible with their beliefs. A famous discussion of Darwin in connection with Christianity had taken place shortly after the publication of Darwin's *On the Origin of Species* (1859). At the reading of a scientific paper at Oxford University in 1860, two well-known partisans of the pro-Darwin and anti-Darwin positions, Thomas Huxley and Bishop Samuel Wilberforce, exchanged sharp insults with each other. Darwin's *The Descent of Man* (1871) proved even more of a lightning rod for religious objections than *On the Origin of Species* had. The subsequent work specifically mentioned humans whereas Darwin's original book on evolution had a much narrower argument. Still, the Wilberforce-Huxley exchange (sometimes called the Oxford Debate) was the most public airing of concerns about Darwin's applicability to religious belief prior to the set-to in Tennessee in 1925.

Scopes was heard in a local court on charges of violating a Tennessee statute forbidding non-"creationist" instruction. But the case originated less in one teacher's conscience than in the fact that local citizens saw an opportunity to make their town famous. They invited scrutiny of the case among national media, which in the 1920s included radio as well as newspapers and other periodicals. Outsiders proved a source of revenue to the town, but they brought unfavorable comment in addition to their purchasing power. To certain acid-tongued observers, Dayton and its "trial of the century" cast into high relief reluctance toward progress. It was a focus, these critics argued, that was grounded in Christian fundamentalism.

HISTORY OF THE CASE

The Butler Act was a statute passed by the Tennessee legislature in March 1925. Its author, John

Butler, was frank in admitting that he was inspired to write the law after hearing a Baptist sermon. That message declared that students who learned public school biology would lose their Christian religious faith as a result. The governor who signed the measure observed that he expected state officials not to enforce its provisions forbidding public educational institutions from teaching Darwin's theories on human evolution. The law was written in a manner that made it more a general policy statement than a detailed prescription for classroom instruction (or lack thereof).

Professors at Tennessee's institutions of higher learning ignored it, as did many teachers at elementary and secondary schools. The American Civil Liberties Union (ACLU), however, was actively searching for statutes on evolution to contest, on the theory that eventually such measures would be more strictly enforced. In spring 1925 the ACLU placed an advertisement in the *Chattanooga Daily Times* asking for high school teachers to volunteer to help test the constitutionality of the Butler Act.

Mining engineer and transplanted New Yorker John Rappalyea, who was living in Dayton, saw in the ACLU request a happy confluence of principle and economic opportunity. Rappalyea, who attended a local Methodist church, nevertheless remained a bit of an outsider in Dayton. Rappalyea was put off by certain fundamentalist credos that he had heard in the town. In particular, at the funeral of a boy killed in an accident a local minister told the victim's mother that her son would go to hell because he had not been baptized. Rappalyea vowed to show up the fundamentalists. After reading the notice from the ACLU, Rappalyea explained to local teacher Scopes that here was a chance to put Dayton on the map by centering the town amid an important debate. Scopes was not deeply invested in Darwinism as a cause. In fact, he was not even a full-time biology instructor. Rather, Scopes was trained in the teaching of physics, but he finally agreed to help test the law. With the full cooperation of local authorities Scopes began reading to students from a textbook that mentioned evolution. He promptly was arrested and charged with violating the Butler Act. Scopes faced punishment as a misdemeanor offender of a fine between $100 and $500.

SUMMARY OF ARGUMENTS

On the first day of trial, July 10, 1925, the Rhea County Courthouse in Dayton was packed with people from the outlying countryside as well as farther afield. The town had a carnival atmosphere. There were hawkers selling religious tracts and the writings of some of the famous individuals who had been drawn into the case, especially as legal talent. Foremost among those outsiders who would participate in the trial of Scopes were two men: William Jennings Bryan and Clarence Darrow. Although legal historians note that Darrow and Bryan were not necessarily the main strategists for their sides in the case, they had the highest profiles at the time that the trial occurred. They were known both as national figures and within the locality. Thus, observers perceived the trial as a showdown between two aging leaders in their fields of law and politics.

Bryan had been the Democratic nominee for the U.S. presidency in 1892, 1896, and 1908. He was an old-fashioned, bombastic orator. He could hold forth for hours while still holding listeners' rapt attention. His "Cross of Gold" speech at the 1896 Democratic nominating convention was considered one of the great orations in U.S. history. A genuine populist in many respects, his nickname was "the Great Commoner." As a veteran of the Chautauqua circuit, he was familiar with small-town America.

Bryan could be of an independent mind. As secretary of state under President Woodrow Wilson, he resigned rather than back what he perceived as Wilson's bellicosity. Bryan closely identified with evangelical Christianity. He agreed to represent the state in the Scopes case out of a wish to defend a literalist religious position in the controversy. In mid-May 1925 a Christian fundamentalist group secured Bryan's position at the defense table.

Darrow was fresh from his legal victory in the Leopold and Loeb criminal trial of the previous year. To some, he was a kind of legal magician, able to convince juries and judges to see his way even if to the broader public his message remained illusory. His willingness to defend persons who were of minority status was celebrated as representing one of the best impulses in the legal profession. Still,

Darrow's unwillingness to be connected with organized religion made him notorious in some circles, especially the rural South.

There was a team of lawyers representing Scopes. While Darrow was its most recognizable figure, the everyday management of the case rested with New York attorney Arthur Garfield Hays. Hays helped frame the defense's legal strategy. His plan was to bring to Dayton several experts on evolution who would try to convince the court that Darwinian theory was accepted among scientists and thus ought to be allowed in Tennessee schools. He arranged for such persons to travel to Dayton and oversaw their billeting in makeshift accommodations. It was difficult to find boarding space, so packed was the town with visitors, including the press.

The prosecuting attorneys, aside from Bryan, were native sons. Though nowhere on a par with Darrow or Bryan in speaking skills, they nonetheless had the ability to play to local sympathies—key to securing a favorable outcome in any jury trial. The assistant attorney general for the state of Tennessee, Ben McKenzie, did not hesitate to exploit the usual charge from southerners that those who came from out of town were there to make trouble:

As for the Northern lawyers, who had come down to teach the "ignorant yokels" what to believe, they had better go back to their homes, the seat of thugs, thieves, and Haymarket rioters, and educate their criminals rather than to try and proselyte here in the South, where people believe in the Christian religion, and know that Genesis tells the full and complete story of creation.

Those remarks, of course, were a particular jibe at Darrow, who had gained an early reputation in Chicago cases such as the Haymarket trial. The chief lawyer for the prosecution was A. Thomas Stewart, McKenzie's immediate superior in the Tennessee attorney general's office. Stewart took a straightforward approach to the case. The legislature had the right to regulate teaching in Tennessee public schools, and Scopes had knowingly violated the law. Those who objected to the Butler Act should go through legislative processes to get it removed from the statute books. Stewart's main line of argument was that the case was not about religion or science at all but rather public education.

It was that direction that the state pursued and that ultimately prevailed. But Judge John Raulston appeared unwilling to control the momentum of the trial, that is, to shut down its potential as a drama with the stunning cast of outsiders. Raulston played into the hands of those who thought of local officials as old fashioned when he answered Darrow's objection to Bryan being labeled with the honorific "Colonel Bryan" in court. The judge decided that, in fairness, all of the lawyers (especially Darrow) henceforth would be addressed as "Colonel." Raulston also earned the censure of those who thought him biased toward the prosecution when he insisted on beginning and ending each day's session with a benediction.

Both Raulston and locals wanted to hear more from Bryan (whom many idolized) and Darrow (of whom many had heard). Raulston therefore permitted the proceedings to go on in much greater detail than would have been expected, given his concurrence at an early stage with the prosecution's key contentions that 1) the case revolved around whether Scopes broke the law, and 2) no amount of expert testimony would change that fact.

After the prosecution and defense delivered their opening statements, the defense tried to get its experts on the stand. In line with Stewart's strategy the prosecution strenuously objected to such testimony as beside the point. Judge Raulston allowed testimony for the time being so that he could make a ruling. He decided within a day that the proposed witnesses—those whom the defense proposed would explain Darwinism as good science—should be excluded. The defense read in the testimony, however, so it could be looked at upon review by a higher court. Such a move was in line with the defense's long-range plan. The case was to be the basis for an appeal, perhaps to the U.S. Supreme Court, about whether the Butler Act contravened the U.S. Constitution's First Amendment.

At that moment in the trial Judge Raulston chose to move the proceedings outside into the July heat. He took the unusual step, he said, because the crush of people in the old building might make the structure unsafe. In an age when microphones were crude, however, Raulston's decision probably had more to do with letting a wider audience hear the trial first hand. For those not in the immediate vicinity, there were radio transmissions and telegraphed newspaper reports about the sensational case.

The trial then took on an even more surreal atmosphere, with thousands of spectators cheering and booing at various moments. All present fanned themselves constantly. It got still more dramatic, however, when Judge Raulston asked the defense to wrap up its case. Darrow, frustrated at not being allowed to present the expert testimony, hit upon a way to put his skills at cross-examination into play. He asked that Raulston allow Bryan to serve as an expert witness on the book of Genesis. Darrow argued that this was so that the defense might explore the biblical account of creation that the Butler Act supposedly protected.

Against the wishes of his colleagues on the prosecution Bryan jumped at the chance to showcase his own skills in public speaking. What followed was an extraordinary contest between the two leading lawyers. It was exactly the head-to-head contest that many had been seeking at the trial, but that Judge Raulston's exclusion of the expert scientific evidence earlier had seemed to preclude. Bryan began confidently by asserting the literal truth of passages of Christian Scripture, even in regard to accounts of miracles:

Darrow: You claim that everything in the Bible should be literally interpreted?

Bryan: I believe everything in the Bible should be accepted as it is given there: some of the Bible is given illustratively. For instance: "Ye are the salt of the earth." I would not insist that man was actually salt, or that he had flesh of salt, but it is used in the sense of salt as saving God's people.

Darrow: But when you read that Jonah swallowed the whale—or that the whale swallowed Jonah—excuse me please—how do you literally interpret that?

Bryan: When I read that a big fish swallowed Jonah—it does not say whale. . . .

That is my recollection of it. A big fish, and I believe it, and I believe in a God who can make a whale and can make a man and make both what He pleases.

Darrow: Now, you say, the big fish swallowed Jonah, and he there remained how long—three days—and then he spewed him upon the land. You believe that the big fish was made to swallow Jonah?

Bryan: I am not prepared to say that; the Bible merely says it was done.

Darrow: You don't know whether it was the ordinary run of fish, or made for that purpose?

Bryan: You may guess; you evolutionists guess. . . .

Darrow: You are not prepared to say whether that fish was made especially to swallow a man or not?

Bryan: The Bible doesn't say, so I am not prepared to say.

Darrow: But do you believe He made them—that He made such a fish and that it was big enough to swallow Jonah?

Bryan: Yes, sir. Let me add: One miracle is just as easy to believe as another.

Darrow: Just as hard?

Bryan: It is hard to believe for you, but easy for me. A miracle is a thing performed beyond what man can perform. When you get within the realm of miracles; and it is just as easy to believe the miracle of Jonah as any other miracle in the Bible.

Darrow: Perfectly easy to believe that Jonah swallowed the whale?

Bryan: If the Bible said so; the Bible doesn't make as extreme statements as evolutionists do. . . .

So far, Bryan was holding his own, but Darrow's relentless reasoning wore down Bryan's ready responses. Under a barrage of questions about biblical episodes Bryan became flustered and argumentative. His self-assurance melted, and Judge Raulston had to step in to save him from further humiliation:

Darrow: Would you say that the earth was only 4,000 years old?

Bryan: Oh, no; I think it is much older than that.

Darrow: How much?

Bryan: I couldn't say.

Darrow: Do you say whether the Bible itself says it is older than that?

Bryan: I don't think it is older or not.

Darrow: Do you think the earth was made in six days?

Bryan: Not six days of twenty-four hours.

Darrow: Doesn't it say so?

Bryan: No, sir. . . .

Judge Raulston: Are you about through, Mr. Darrow?

Darrow: I want to ask a few more questions about the creation.

Judge Raulston: I know. We are going to adjourn when Mr. Bryan comes off the stand for the day. Be very brief, Mr. Darrow. Of course, I believe I will make myself clearer. Of course, it is incompetent testimony before the jury. The only reason I am allowing this to go in at all is that they may have it in the appellate court as showing what the affidavit would be.

Bryan: The reason I am answering is not for the benefit of the superior court. It is to keep these gentlemen from saying I was afraid to meet them and let them question me, and I want the Christian world to know that any atheist, agnostic, unbeliever, can question me anytime as to my belief in God, and I will answer him.

Darrow: I want to take an exception to this conduct of this witness. He may be very popular down here in the hills. . . .

Bryan: Your honor, they have not asked a question legally and the only reason they have asked any question is for the purpose, as the question about Jonah was asked, for a chance to give this agnostic an opportunity to criticize a believer in the world of God; and I answered the question in order to shut his mouth so that he cannot go out and tell his atheistic friends that I would not answer his questions. That is the only reason, no more reason in the world.

Another riveting presence at Dayton was a person who had no official connection with either defense or prosecution. In fact, though, writer H. L. Mencken already was playing a part in the controversy over the Butler Act in Tennessee. As the editor of the *American Mercury* and a reporter for the *Baltimore Sun,* Mencken was aware of the prosecution and attuned to national interest in the case. He knew Darrow and urged him to become involved. At first Mencken's strong sense of libertarianism caused him to urge that outsiders should leave the citizens of the state to their own devices. Before the trial began, he had pondered: "What could be of greater utility to the son of a Tennessee mountaineer than an education making him a good Tennessean, content with his father, at peace with his neighbors, dutiful to the local religion, and docile under the local mores?"

But Mencken became more vitriolic as he observed the trial in person. On July 14, for example, the third day of trial, Mencken raged that Darrow's fluid arguments seemed to fall unappreciated and that Bryan was feted among the Tennessee folk as a hero:

The net effect of Clarence Darrow's great speech yesterday seems to be precisely the same as if he had bawled it up a rainspout in the interior of Afghanistan. That is, locally, upon the process against the infidel Scopes, upon the so-called minds of these fundamentalists of upland Tennessee. You have but a dim notice of it who have only read it. It was not designed for reading, but for hearing. The clangtint of it was as important as the logic. It rose like a wind and ended like a flourish of bugles. The very judge on the bench, toward the end of it, began to look uneasy. But the morons in the audience, when it was over, simply hissed it.

During the whole time of its delivery the old mountebank, Bryan, sat tight-lipped and unmoved. There is, of course, no reason why it should have shaken him. He has these hillbillies locked up in his pen and he knows it. His brand is on them. He is at home among them. Since his earliest days, indeed, his chief strength has been among the folk of remote hills and forlorn and lonely farms. Now with his political aspirations all gone to pot, he turns to them for religious consolations. They understand his peculiar imbecilities. His nonsense is their ideal of sense. When he deluges them with his theologic bilge they rejoice like pilgrims disporting in the river Jordan.

Mencken's judgments made for astonishing newspaper coverage—some of the most pointed commentary ever penned with regard to any trial. His words did not endear him to the local folk. Before the trial was over, he returned to Baltimore, unapologetic but out from under the risk of being tarred and feathered. Perhaps it was fortunate for Bryan that Mencken did not personally witness the humiliating cross-examination to which Darrow subjected Bryan on the seventh day of the trial.

VERDICT

Despite its enormous acrimony while in progress, the trial of John Scopes ended on a curiously harmonious note. To no one's surprise, the defendant was found guilty. Judge Raulston affixed the fine at the minimum amount of $100. Each side made gracious remarks about the service of the jury and the hospitality of the townsfolk, and yet both Bryan and Darrow seemed to aim more at the

judgment of history. Bryan's closing remarks had little power in them, yet they sounded heartfelt:

> There can be no settlement of a great cause without discussion, and people will not discuss a cause until their attention is drawn to it, and the value of this trial is not in any incident of the trial, it is not because of anybody who is attached to it, either in an official way or as counsel on either side. Human beings are mighty small, your honor. We are apt to magnify the personal element and we sometimes become inflated with our importance, but the world little cares for man as an individual. He is born, he works, he dies, but causes go on forever, and we who participated in this case may congratulate ourselves that we have attached ourselves to a mighty issue.

Darrow continued on his longtime theme that court cases—whatever their immediate outcomes—could help in the rejection of reactionary ideas:

> I fancy that the place where the Magna Carta was wrested from the barons in England was a very small place, probably not as big as Dayton. But events come along as they come along. I think this case will be remembered because it is the first case of this sort since we stopped trying people in America for witchcraft because here we have done our best to turn back the tide that has sought to force itself upon this—upon this modern world, of testing every fact in science by a religious dictum.

The case ended at the appellate level on a surprisingly muted note. In 1927 the Tennessee Supreme Court ruled that Judge Raulston had erred in setting the fine when the jury had failed to specify one. State law said that juries had to set fines above $50. It was, in other words, a technical voiding of the outcome in Dayton. Tennessee officials, who had argued to the state supreme court that the point at trial was moot now because Scopes had left Tennessee and its schools, were content not to pursue another prosecution.

Scopes's lawyers expressed frustration that the state appellate court had not seemed to take seriously their learned arguments on the separation of church and state and about Scopes's right to free speech. They suspected—and legal historians have echoed the point since—that the Tennessee appellate decision was less to help Scopes escape his fine than to prevent an appeal to the U.S. Supreme Court at a time when the defense team still was prepared for that fight.

SIGNIFICANCE

Persons and groups far beyond the Dayton Chamber of Commerce saw a chance to advance their aims through Scopes's case. The case thus grew to be much more than a local episode. It was watched nationally at the time, and it has been periodically revisited ever since. Among the reasons that historians still discuss the trial in some detail is the fact that they sense the public has been influenced by nonscholarly portrayals of the events in Dayton.

In particular, the 1955 stage play *Inherit the Wind,* which was made into several films, has colored general perceptions of the episode. That treatment makes it appear that the quest to overturn Tennessee law largely was based on Scopes's exercise of conscience or academic freedom. With strong celluloid performances by actors such as Spencer Tracy (as Darrow) and Frederic March (as Bryan), the dramatization also plays up the tension between those two characters at the expense of the key roles played by certain other participants—notably talented lawyers on the defense side.

The Scopes Trial still serves to highlight attitudes toward religion and the classroom, science and faith, small-town values and cosmopolitanism, and other important elements in U.S. life. It remains a divisive moment in U.S. history. For those who celebrate Darrow's skepticism about organized religion and see science as a progressive force that should lead academic inquiry, the case is an affirmation. Although Scopes did not prevail formally at Dayton when he challenged the Butler Act, the trial showed that his cause was the wave of the future.

The episode drew in an impressive cast of advocates, especially on the side of the defense. Persons such as Hays were among the most committed civil libertarians of their generation. Indeed, Hays was a founder of the ACLU and a participant in several other major legal contests of the early 20th century including the Sacco and Vanzetti case and the Scottsboro trials. Hays even served on the defense team of Georgi Dimitrov at the Reichstag fire trial in the next decade. Dudley Field Malone, who ironically had worked in the State Department under Bryan, likewise took time off from a highly profitable private law practice in New York to lend aid to Scopes's side. Although Darrow's role is the most remembered from the Scopes case by those who were not present, it was Malone's defense of the right of Scopes to speak the truth within a classroom that struck perhaps the loudest chord with observers at Dayton:

> There is never a duel with the truth. The truth always wins and we are not afraid of it. The truth is no coward. The truth does not need the law. The truth does not need the force of government. The truth does not need Mr. Bryan. The truth is imperishable, eternal and immortal and needs no human agency to support it. We are ready to tell the truth as we understand it and we do not fear all the truth that they can present as facts. We are ready. We are ready. We feel we stand with progress. We feel we stand with science. We feel we stand with intelligence. We feel we stand with fundamental freedom in America. We are not afraid. Where is the fear? We meet it, where is the fear? We defy it, we ask your honor to admit the evidence as a matter of correct law, as a matter of sound procedure and as a matter of justice to the defense in this case.

Those who were present noted that the applause following Malone's remarks was sustained and genuine and that it included persons of all persuasions. Beyond those who attended the trial, the defense got valuable advice from seminal individuals such as future Supreme Court justice Felix Frankfurter.

The Tennessee legislature repealed the Butler Act in 1967. Among those who applaud challenges to Darwinism and evolution, the case serves to demonstrate that "creationism" had articulate defenders. Furthermore, Scopes was convicted: The law stood as a protection to impressionable children and would be an inspiration against further attempts to bring "unproven" science into schools. Though legally an unimportant case, the Scopes Trial is a key reference point for leading decisions such as *Edwards v. Aguillard* (1987), in which state laws concerning the teaching of evolution versus creationism again were considered.

Bryan died in his sleep of a stroke only five days after the conclusion of the Scopes Trial. Some of Rappalyea's local detractors had no hesitation about telling him that he had killed their hero by pressing for a test of the Butler Act. But for all of the criticism that they took from Mencken and others about being benighted, the opponents of evolutionary theory still had the final word on the Scopes case. In many minds the trial is known not by Scopes's name, nor by the year and location of its hearing, but by a derisive nickname. It was an appellation bestowed by those who boiled down Darwinism to the concept that people were descended from apes: the Monkey Trial.

Further Reading

Caudill, Edward. *The Scopes Trial: A Photographic History.* Knoxville: University of Tennessee Press, 2000; Chapman, Matthew. *Trials of the Monkey: An Accidental Memoir.* New York: Picador USA, 2002; Conkin, Paul. *When All the Gods Trembled: Darwinism, Scopes, and American Intellectuals.* Lanham, Md.: Rowman & Littlefield, 2001; *John Thomas Scopes v. The State,* 154 Tenn. 105 (1927); Kramer, Stanley (dir.), *Inherit the Wind.* United Artists, 1960; Larsen, Edward. *Summer for the Gods: The Scopes Trial and America's Continuing Debate over Science and Religion.* Cambridge, Mass.: Basic Books, 1997; Lienesch, Michael. *In the Beginning: Fundamentalism, the Scopes Trial, and the Making of the Antievolution Movement.* Chapel Hill: University of North Carolina Press, 2009; McRae, Donald. *The Old Devil: Clarence Darrow, the World's Greatest Trial Lawyer.* London: Pocket Books, 2010; Mencken, H. L., and Art Winslow. *A Religious Orgy in Tennessee: A Reporter's Account of the Scopes Monkey Trial.* Hoboken, N.J.: Melville House, 2006.

The Scottsboro Boys' trials

Also known as: *Alabama v. Wright, Wright, Weems, Montgomery, Roberson, Williams, Patterson, Powell, and Norris*

Date: 1931

KEY ISSUES

It is rare for a famous trial to make great law. Well-known trials often are sensational in their own times, such as during the 1990s when the O. J. Simpson case galvanized public attention. Only a few courtroom episodes lead to key historical change, especially when those proceedings create martyrs from defendants. Particularly unusual is it for a case to be widely publicized in its day while also creating a long-term imprint on the law. The trials of nine young African-American men that began at Scottsboro, Alabama, in 1931 made news in the United States and abroad for years during the 1930s. The case also left a constitutional legacy in two separate U.S. Supreme Court judgments.

Immediately upon hearing the name of the Scottsboro case, one is confronted with the issue of race. For a person with white skin to term a male of color a *boy* in the early 20th-century United States was to hurl an insult. The put-down had a racist tinge that similar expressions in other locations (terming a French peasant *Jacques,* for example) did not approach. And it was not only the defendants who were labeled for great effect in the case. Even at the level of the Supreme Court arguments the alleged victims were called "girls" although one of the young women was 19 and the other 21 years old and married.

Thus, the youth of the accused persons and the alleged victims was at issue. Were the defendants men whom southern whites called boys out of denigration, or were they teenagers who at law ought to be considered as minors? The Scottsboro defendants' most prominent disability was their ethnicity, but they also labored under the considerable disadvantages of youth and inexperience. At times even the advocates of the "Scottsboro Boys" pointed to the defendants' ages (ranging from 12 to 20) to underline their difficulty in obtaining a fair trial. The accused young men were in a gray area of law, being neither unquestionably children nor fully grown. And were the alleged victims to be called adult women because they held jobs, lived away from their parents, and had been married? Or did their comparative youth and the violence of the purported crime make them girls, who thus implicitly deserved the special protection of the court?

HISTORY OF THE CASE

The Scottsboro case began in an ordinary enough fashion. On March 25, 1931, several groups of young people were riding a freight train in northern Alabama. In the early 1930s in the United States the economy was depressed, and even seasoned workers had trouble finding employment. Those with more limited skills or with fewer family attachments, such as younger people, sometimes "went on the tramp." They walked from one town to another in search of work, hopping onto freight trains and traveling without buying a passenger ticket to cover longer distances.

In areas served by trains around the nation a kind of rough equality emerged among the "down and out" persons who were riding the rails. Men and women of different ethnic and economic backgrounds and skin colors coexisted and indeed formed bonds through shared misery. The particular train in question in northern Alabama in early 1931, though, ran through a portion of the nation that was not so cosmopolitan with regard to issues of class, gender, and especially race. The biases that simmered in northeastern Alabama combined disastrously with the personalities of two persons who were to claim that they were victims in the case. A couple of young women, Victoria Price and Ruby Bates, had failed at finding jobs in textile mills in Chattanooga, Tennessee. Price and Bates were riding from Chattanooga through northern Alabama on the train bound for Memphis.

There were at least three distinct groups of illegal riders on this particular freight train that was carrying cars of coal: several young men who were white, a group of nine young African-American men, and two young white women. Words and fisticuffs erupted among the whites and blacks while the train was moving. At one point when the train slowed down, some of the white youths were forced off or elected to jump from the train to avoid further trouble. Once they landed, they and local people spread the word to stations farther along the line that black hoboes aboard the train had attacked the white boys. At the small town of Paint Rock a group of whites gathered, determined to haul the African Americans from the train and avenge the perceived insult of black-on-white violence.

The crowd got more than it expected. In addition to the nine young men of color, there emerged from the train two white females, dressed in overalls. These young women, Bates and Price, asserted they had been raped by the young black men. The black males and white females were conveyed to the Jackson County seat, Scottsboro. While Bates and Price were taken for a medical examination, the mood among whites in the town quickly grew uglier.

The sheriff and the mayor of Scottsboro pleaded for calm among the whites who had gathered outside the county jail. That armed crowd demanded that the accused persons be subject to rough justice. Finally, the sheriff made an urgent call to the governor of Alabama, who ordered National Guardsmen dispatched to secure the jail. Local opinion was that the only reason that a lynching did not proceed was that the alleged victims were strangers in town.

The young men who were accused of rape were teenagers, with the exception of 20-year-old Charlie Weems. Some of the boys were from Georgia and knew one another; two, Andrew (Andy) and Leroy (Roy) Wright, were brothers; others had come from Chattanooga. The physical state of the defendants was relevant to their ability to commit a violent sexual assault. Among the observations that even the hostile "posse" who had apprehended the young men at Paint Rock made was that several of the alleged perpetrators were either childlike or physically infirm. Olen Montgomery, for example, was largely blind; Willie Roberson had a physical disability (later determined to be syphilis) that required him to walk with a cane; Eugene Williams and Roy Wright each had barely reached their teens and looked even younger. The other individuals—Haywood Patterson, Ozie Powell, Clarence Norris, as well as Andy Wright—appeared healthy despite having spent time recently riding the rails.

Besides its persistent difficulty in keeping the defendants safe, the court in Jackson County had trouble with the issue of legal representation for the multiple defendants. Another legal quandary was whether the try the accused persons together or separately. Since the defendants were accused of rape, which was a capital crime, Judge Alfred Hawkins tried to ensure that the accused had counsel. He named each of the seven men who practiced law in the county as attorneys for the defense. All but one, a semi-retired man named Milo Moody, temporarily demurred. In Chattanooga, African-American friends of some of the accused hired lawyer Stephen Roddy to join in the defense. Neither Moody nor Roddy was highly experienced in criminal matters, certainly not capital crimes, and Roddy had a drinking problem.

SUMMARY OF ARGUMENTS

As their cases were heard and appealed, the Scottsboro Boys sat in jail. Due to the fact that certain of the defendants' cases were being retried at the time that other defendants were in limbo, the chronology of the episode is complex. The Scottsboro trials amounted to an interlocking series of judicial proceedings lasting from 1931 through 1937. In theory each defendant had a separate trial, but in practice, especially in the early hearings, the trials proceeded with the same judge and jury one right after another. At certain moments those in court could hear cheers break out when a verdict had been reached against one defendant, while arguments proceeded against one of his peers in an adjoining courtroom. The first trials of the Scottsboro defendants were each concluded in about one day.

There were three main prosecutions (or sets of criminal trials) that covered the nine Scottsboro defendants. The initial prosecution of all of the defendants at Scottsboro under Judge Hawkins beginning April 6, 1931, was called the "Scottsboro trial." Two subsequent trials at Decatur, Alabama, under Judge James E. Horton beginning March 27, 1933, and succeeded under Judge William Callahan beginning November 20, 1933,

were called the "Decatur trials." A separate trial for Patterson began in January 1936. That was followed in mid-summer 1937 by new trials of defendants Andy Wright, Norris, Weems, and Powell. Thus, before the criminal charges were completely disposed of, six full years had elapsed. Although the strategies of the defense and the prosecution shifted some during that period, several arguments on each side remained important throughout.

The defense contended that the rapes had not taken place. According to the defenders of the Scottsboro Boys, there had been a fight between white and black youths on the train. The whites who were ejected from the railcars sought revenge once they told their story to sympathetic local folk. Price and Bates, meanwhile, had concocted their story to avoid being charged with vagrancy, accused of engaging in interstate prostitution, or upbraided by the townspeople of Paint Rock for riding in a railroad car with black males.

The prosecution rested its argument on the simple assertion—a time-honored maxim in southern society—that sexual contact between white females and men of color was so disgraceful that a white woman would never fabricate such a tale. In other words, any reports of black-on-white rape were prima facie true; a trial was not even needed, many argued. A sub rosa theme in the entire case was that for many southerners, having a trial at all under the circumstances was an act of generosity. The alleged perpetrators were not being lynched; they should be grateful that the rule of law was being upheld. Indeed, many Alabamans expressed exactly that sentiment.

As the succession of trials unfolded, certain issues emerged as especially contentious. The matter of provision of counsel was pivotal. From the first appearance of the defense lawyers in the Scottsboro, Jackson County, courtroom, Roddy's competence and willingness to serve as defense counsel were under discussion. Judge Hawkins sounded ready to allow Roddy to act as sole attorney on behalf of the defendants despite Roddy's apparent unease in that role and lack of experience. Moody's agreement to serve with Roddy gave Judge Hawkins the opportunity to absolve every other member of the Jackson County bar from assisting the defense. Roddy had only hours to prepare his defense and at times seemed impaired in court.

On appeal the defense contended that inexperienced and ineffective counsel had represented the Scottsboro defendants and that Judge Hawkins had failed to protect the young men's right to counsel under the Sixth Amendment of the U.S. Constitution. Such, eventually, was the conclusion of the U.S. Supreme Court in the case of *Powell v. Alabama* (1932):

> In the light of the facts outlined in the forepart of this opinion—the ignorance and illiteracy of the defendants, their youth, the circumstances of public hostility, the imprisonment and the close surveillance of the defendants by the military forces, the fact that their friends and families were all in other states and communication with them necessarily difficult, and above all that they stood in deadly peril of their lives—we think the failure of the trial court to give them reasonable time and opportunity to secure counsel was a clear denial of due process.

Luckily, the defendants' legal representation did not remain subpar. The Scottsboro Boys' plight attracted the attention of extremely skilled lawyers, notably defense attorney Samuel Leibowitz of New York. Leibowitz led the defense team beginning in 1933 and did not accept a fee for his work. Ironically, Leibowitz's presence was a mixed blessing to the defense. While he was unquestionably skillful as a cross-examiner, indeed as an advocate in general, Alabama jurors clearly regarded him as an outsider. He also rankled local observers and newspaper writers. His sharp questioning of the female accusers on the stand earned him the scorn of southerners, who considered him impolite—if not ungentlemanly—toward those white women. As a northerner and a Jew, Leibowitz was alien and therefore stirred hostility among both judges and jurors. In the state's summary to the jury in April 1933, assistant prosecutor Wade Wright delivered an anti-Semitic diatribe that embarrassed even the lead prosecutor, Alabama attorney general Thomas Knight: "Alabama justice," shouted Wright as Knight flushed and looked at the floor, "cannot be bought and sold by Jew money from New York." Leibowitz's motion for a mistrial was denied.

Also damaging to his reputation among southerners was Leibowitz's connection with the International Labor Defense (ILD), a leftist organization that enthusiastically assisted the Scottsboro defendants. The ILD, which had ties to international communist groups, admitted that assistance to the defendants at Scottsboro would further its own political agenda. The ILD not only sent legal counsel to the Scottsboro defendants; it also organized rallies in support of the Scottsboro Boys, lending the case an even higher profile. Leibowitz eventually broke with the ILD over their tactics during the case. He was most perturbed with their effort to bribe Price into changing her testimony. While never himself a Communist, Leibowitz's effectiveness was compromised by association with such radicals.

Another important aspect of the trials was the presentation of medical evidence concerning the alleged rapes. Just after their arrival in Scottsboro and about an hour after the supposed attack, Bates and Price underwent examinations by two local physicians who collected samples of fluids from their bodies and looked for indications of emotional and physical trauma. Doctors R. R. Bridges and Marvin Lynch both testified that there was conclusive evidence that the women had engaged in sexual intercourse within the previous days before examination, but they also swore that the sperm they recovered was nonmotile. The doctors' testimony supported the defense theory that Price and Bates both had had consensual sexual relations some hours prior to boarding the train—a scenario later supported by a male defense witness who had participated in that activity before the women left Chattanooga. Both physicians carefully used only medical terminology, and they answered questions from the defense in a narrow manner.

Throughout the trials the state's attorneys objected strenuously to the admission of evidence about Price's and Bates's sexual history, including their actions in the 24 hours immediately prior to the alleged assault. Prosecutors managed to exclude most testimony about Price's marital situation (she was twice divorced). Particularly under Judge Callahan, the state managed to exclude arguments that both women had engaged in prostitution, including interracial sexual relations, while in Chattanooga. Among the few points that the defense was able to score was that the women lied about their movements around Chattanooga just before boarding the train. The defense contended that the women had stayed out late and had sexual intercourse with other homeless persons, while Price and Bates insisted that they had lodged at a particular boardinghouse. The prosecution also fought to keep the doctors from reporting their conclusions about the accusers' demeanor, which had been fairly calm in spite of their supposed victimization in a brutal gang rape shortly prior to examination.

Jurors never learned that the physicians had concluded, privately, that the women never had been assaulted at all. It was a critical observation, discussed in conference (that is, not in front of the jury) between Dr. Lynch and Judge Horton at the first Decatur trial. Although Horton allowed the trial to continue because he was certain that defendant Norris would be acquitted given the devastating blows to the accuser's credibility that he was seeing in court, the jury convicted Norris anyway. Judge Horton then granted a defense motion for a new trial. He next withdrew from hearing the case, ceding judicial authority to Judge Callahan. Due to those actions implicitly critical of the accusers, Horton gave up any hope of obtaining future public office, including the bench, in Alabama.

VERDICTS

The defense eventually determined that it stood the best chance of winning release for some of the accused if the youngest and most infirm defendants could be separated out. In other words, the defense thought it necessary to save as many of the defendants as it could. Otherwise, it looked as though juries would levy death penalties against every defendant. The Scottsboro jury in 1931, for example, defied Judge Hawkins's instructions and the state's request that Roy Wright (12 years of age at the time of the incident) should be sentenced to life imprisonment. That jury held out 11 to 1 for the death penalty, necessitating a mistrial for Roy Wright but also alarming the defense with the prospect that an argument solely based on the young age of defendants would not move jurors to mercy.

The situation was further complicated by the fact that initially a few of the defendants alleged that their peers had committed the crimes but that they were innocent. Although the defendants later argued that such statements had been made under duress, the damage was great. It was Liebowitz who finally brokered an arrangement to spare a few of his clients. In 1936 the four defendants who were most sympathetic to the public outside of Alabama were not recharged after the U.S. Supreme Court once again called the trials into question.

In the cases of *Norris v. Alabama* and *Patterson v. Alabama* (1935) the court had thrown out the convictions of several of the defendants (Montgomery, Roy Wright, Williams, and Roberson) based on evidence that the voter rolls in Jackson County were manipulated in order to exclude blacks from jury participation. Thus, in an arrangement between the state and those four defendants, those four persons went free. The 1936 conviction of Patterson (given a 75-year term), stood; Norris, who had been assigned the death penalty, saw his sentence commuted to a life term by the governor. Andy Wright and Weems were convicted of rape with long prison terms. The rape charges against Powell were dropped, though he had to serve a sentence for assaulting a deputy during an escape attempt. Given the ultra-violent prejudice that had existed prior to the trials, it was a stunning victory for the defense to have achieved anything but death sentences.

The settlement of the case in such a manner, however, was inequitable. The accusers initially had testified that they were assaulted by all of the defendants. Price kept to that story throughout the trials. But, in a dramatic twist during the proceedings Bates at one point retracted her accusation, saying that Price had coached her. Jurors discounted that recantation; they believed the prosecution's argument that the ILD had tainted Bates, literally buying her support in exchange for new clothes and publicity. The convictions of four of the defendants as rapists stood. Although all four eventually were paroled or pardoned, they suffered the injustice of doing jail time for crimes on which their former codefendants were not recharged.

SIGNIFICANCE

The lives of all of the men of the Scottsboro trials, even those released without retrial in 1937, were profoundly influenced by their involvement in the case. Those who served long prison sentences fared the worst. Patterson managed to escape from prison in 1950 and evade detection for some months. Alabama's governor refused to extradite him, but he shortly was convicted in an unrelated case and died in prison in 1952. Although he was paroled in 1943, Weems suffered serious health problems as a result of his incarceration. Norris went north after his release from prison, but he and Andy Wright lived under the shadow of having violated parole by leaving the state of Alabama.

Bates faced scorn in her native South for having aided the ILD. Price lived in obscurity as a textile worker until 1976, when she took umbrage at a television documentary on the case. That program focused on Judge Horton's dismissal of the charges when he heard evidence from Dr. Lynch of the accusers' calm demeanor just after the alleged attack. Price's suit for defamation was dismissed. She died a few years later, never again commenting publicly on the episode.

The Scottsboro case remained in the minds of many southerners an example of the role of "outside agitators" in fuelling racial tensions. Some southern politicians and jurists saw the avoidance of summary justice as evidence that the region had outgrown the lynch mob; the courts had proceeded in an orderly fashion. The specter of trumped-up rape accusations lingered as a hindrance to truly injured women. A scenario of false accusation based on race was the heart of the bestselling novel and film *To Kill a Mockingbird*. To observers critical of the proceedings, the Scottsboro Boys' case seemed to epitomize southern justice—racist and self-satisfied, with an inaccurate outcome.

Further Reading

Acker, James. *Scottsboro and Its Legacy: The Cases That Challenged American Legal and Social Justice*. Westport, Conn.: Praeger, 2008; Carter, Dan. *Scottsboro, a Tragedy of the American South*. Baton Rouge: Louisiana State University Press, 1969; Miller, James. *Remembering Scottsboro: The Legacy of the Infamous Trial*. Princeton, N.J.: Princeton University Press, 2009; *Norris v. Alabama* 294 U.S. 587 (1935); *Powell et al. v. Alabama, Patterson v. Same, and Weems et al. v. Same* 286 U.S. 540 (1932). Available online. URL: http://libproxy.uta.edu:2156/hottopics/inacademic/?. Accessed July 12, 2009.

The Reichstag fire trial

Date: 1933

KEY ISSUES

The most striking aspect of the Reichstag fire trial is that any defendant managed to walk away from it. The National Socialist (Nazi) Party expected to turn the burning of the German parliament building, the Reichstag, into political capital. To publicize the fire's supposed threat to Germany, Adolf Hitler and his followers insisted on full-scale judicial proceedings against five individuals who allegedly set the blaze. The courtroom drama went on from late September to late December 1933. The entire episode allowed the party to consolidate its hold on the legislative process, in turn cementing the Nazis' leverage in policy making.

HISTORY OF THE CASE

In late 1932 several parties were campaigning for leadership in the German legislature and political primacy in the nation. The groups with the most momentum were the German Communists and the National Socialists, with the Nazis holding a plurality of seats in the Reichstag. In late January 1933 German president Paul von Hindenberg named Hitler as chancellor. The appointment made Hitler in practice the head of state. Scheduled elections of representatives to the Reichstag on March 5 would decide whether Hitler had an electoral mandate strong enough to push through sweeping pro-Nazi policies.

On the night of February 27, 1933, a policeman outside the Reichstag noticed a fire in the building. Through windows he also glimpsed a person inside who was running and apparently setting set small blazes. Although fire trucks arrived quickly, the conflagration progressed so rapidly that much of the structure was destroyed. A later inspection revealed at least 20 separate fires, carefully set. All appeared to have been lit at about the same time, pointing to either an extremely agile arsonist or a set of perpetrators. Though the shell of the 70-year-old building remained, the structure was a total loss.

While trying to determine where fires were burning within the large building, firefighters searched it and discovered a distressed young man hiding in an anteroom. He was identified as a Dutch laborer named Marinus Van der Lubbe. The accused arsonist was 24 years old; he had come to Germany a few months before. His own government pensioned Van der Lubbe after he suffered a work injury that impaired his vision considerably. Although he had attended Communist meetings in Berlin and had expressed sympathy for communism, Van der Lubbe's precise political ideology was difficult to establish at the time just after the fire. He appeared disoriented and perhaps of limited mental capacity. While first in custody Van der Lubbe confessed to setting the fire and insisted that he had acted alone.

Before the fire was wholly quelled at around midnight, Nazi leaders, including the influential Hermann Göring (Hitler's close associate and the president of the Reichstag), came to the scene, stating that the fire had to be the work of Communists. Hitler quickly remarked that the fire was a gift from heaven; one assumes from such a remark that Hitler expected to blame the event on the Communists.

Even investigators without overt links to the Nazis worked on the assumption that the Reichstag could not have suffered such devastating damage through the work of only one arsonist. Investigators also posited that Van der Lubbe could not have planned and carried out the operation on his own owing to what appeared to be physical and mental infirmities. The authorities followed up on reports that a leading Communist member of the Reichstag, Ernst Torgler, had been in the building about one hour before the fire's discovery. Torgler volunteered for questioning and was arrested. Several witnesses reported seeing Van der Lubbe chatting with three persons of yet-unknown identities on the day of the fire. When those men were located, identified, and detained, it came out that they were Bulgarian Communists. One of them, Georgi Dimitrov, was highly placed within international Communist groups.

On the day after the fire President von Hindenberg approved a measure popularly known as the Reichstag Fire Decree. Its wording had come directly from a council headed by Göring. The decree had six sections, all of which undermined civil rights: besides limitations on press, assembly, and speech, telephone and mail communications were subject to interception and private property to search and confiscation at the hands of the Reich government. The deliberate burning of a public building was made punishable by death. Nazi publications followed up the events of February 27 and 28 with lurid anti-Bolshevik propaganda.

SUMMARY OF ARGUMENTS

Who had set the fire and why? Prosecutors sought to establish that Van der Lubbe lit the blaze and had acted with others. They maintained that the young man worked in concert with a Communist conspiracy based in Germany and abroad. The plotters' goal supposedly was to inaugurate a period of chaos, destroying the electoral process and ending in a Communist takeover of Germany that would garner foreign support.

The fire had a galvanizing effect upon public opinion. As they went to the polls, many Germans appeared shaken by Nazi propaganda that a Communist insurgency was imminent. Still, the federal elections of 1933 did not go as well as Hitler had hoped. He aimed to command most of the seats in the Reichstag, but in the election on March 5 got only 49 percent. That forced the National Socialists into coalitions with both the German National People's Party and the Center Party. The Nazis needed such support to assemble a two-thirds majority of the legislature in order to pass the Enabling Act on March 23, which bestowed on Hitler near-dictatorial powers. From the Nazi perspective the most effective aspect of the Reichstag fire was that it incapacitated the Communists from serving in Germany's parliament in the spring of 1933; after the fire most German Communists were either under arrest, expelled from the Reichstag, or laying low.

Did the fire result from the actions of one person, Van der Lubbe, at an especially propitious moment for the Nazis? Or had Van der Lubbe served as the triggerman for a plot by the Communists? As their ranks were decimated in Germany, Communists in the rest of western Europe put together a third alternative: Van der Lubbe actually was in the service of the Nazis. That explanation for the Reichstag fire was very widely circulated in the summer of 1933 in a leftist publication called *The Brown Book*.

According to the Communists, a Nazi-led anti-Communist conspiracy had culminated in Van der Lubbe being given access to the Reichstag through a passageway to the parliament building from the home of none other than Göring. The Dutchman was, in other words, a tool of the Nazis—whether a willing and active participant or somewhat mentally impaired, it did not matter for the purposes of the anti-Nazi theory. Even though the press in Germany was now increasingly under the will of the Nazis, those who prosecuted the case were sensitive to foreign opinion. *The Brown Book*'s explanation for the fire became a presence within the courtroom; leading Nazis called it "the sixth defendant."

Groups who were intrigued but not necessarily convinced by the theory early on held an alternative to the legal proceedings that were under way in Germany. That "third trial" concluded that the evidence did not support the theory of a Communist plot. The inquiry, managed as it was mostly by the Left, did implicate Van der Lubbe; it was ambivalent as to whether the accused Dutch arsonist had received direction from the Nazis.

The first German inquiry into the fire commenced in March 1933 and wrapped up at the end of August. Judge Paul Vogt, at the time a Nazi Party member, was in charge. The inquiry's purpose was similar to that of a U.S. grand jury: to hear evidence relevant to whether a crime had been committed and recommend any likely suspects for trial. During the months of the formal investigation all of the defendants were shackled in prison although they were allowed to correspond with outsiders.

On September 21, Van der Lubbe, Torgler, Dimitrov, and the two other Bulgarians, Blagoi Popov and Vassili Tanev, all were charged with treason before members of Germany's imperial supreme court, the Reichsgericht. They were said to have violated the Reichstag Fire Law of February 28. The trial clearly was as much concerned with politics as crime—a characterization that was admitted by both the Nazis and their critics. Given that highly charged focus, some historical scholars have found it surprising that all of the defendants had competent counsel.

Dr. Philipp Seufert represented Van der Lubbe in an evenhanded fashion. Seufert's role, though, was diminished on account of the defendant's consistent position that he wished to confess and that he was the lone arsonist. It was not insignificant that in an unrelated case several years before, Van der Lubbe had offered a similar confession. This had been in regard to an incident at a workplace where he had been organizing a trade union. In that episode he also argued that other suspects should be exonerated.

Van der Lubbe frequently appeared not to understand the proceedings, perhaps due to difficulty with the German language. He also seemed lethargic; several observers assumed he had been drugged or beaten. Some Western observers were scandalized that he should have been allowed to stand trial at all, so uncertain seemed his grasp of basic aspects of the trial. Photographs of Van der Lubbe as a young laborer in his homeland and those taken at trial (no more than 10 years later) offer a shocking contrast.

The German Communist leader Torgler had benefit of representation by a leading attorney who also was a Nazi. Torgler's lawyer, Alfons Sack, made certain that Torgler's arguments were considered as separate from the Bulgarians'. Sack must have presumed the others to be at a disadvantage because of their foreign status. The Bulgarians employed a team of experienced effective counsel including Dr. Paul Teichert. In a potentially risky move, however, Dimitrov effectively assumed responsibility for conducting the Bulgarians' case. Such active participation was possible due to the German courts' tradition of allowing defendants to respond directly to questions from the bench, opposing lawyers, and even other witnesses. The freedom to address points under consideration and then elaborate on them with further questions was in contrast to the English system of setting separate periods for the presentation of the defense and prosecution cases.

Dimitrov seemed fearless in conducting his own defense. He was sarcastic to the court's president–chief judge, Dr. Wilhelm Buenger. A number of times at trial Buenger silenced him, but Dimitrov appeared unconcerned. Dimitrov baited witnesses including hostile and powerful figures such as Joseph Goebbels and Göring. His exchanges with Göring roused Göring to anger, a dangerous proposition at any time:

> Dimitrov: Mr. Goering is making National Socialist propaganda here! (After that he turns to Goering). This Communist outlook on life prevails in the Soviet Union, the largest and best country in the world, and here, in Germany, it has millions of followers among the best sons of the German people. Is this known . . .
>
> Goering *(yelling loudly):* I shall tell you what is known to the German people. The German people know that here you are behaving insolently, that you have come here to set fire to the Reichstag. But I am not here to allow you to question me like a judge and to reprimand me! In my eyes you are a scoundrel who should be hanged.
>
> President: Dimitrov, I have already told you not to make Communist propaganda here. That is why you should not be surprised if the witness is so agitated! I most strictly forbid this propaganda! You can only ask questions referring to the trial.
>
> Dimitrov: I am highly pleased with the reply of the Prime Minister.
>
> President: Whether you are pleased or not is quite immaterial. Now I deprive you of the right to speak.
>
> Dimitrov: I wish to put one more question pertaining to the trial.

> President *(still more abruptly):* Now I deprive you of the right to speak.
>
> Goering *(yelling):* Go out, scoundrel!
>
> President *(to the policemen):* Take him out!
>
> Dimitrov *(whom the policemen have already seized):* You are probably afraid of my questions, Mr. Prime Minister?
>
> Goering *(shouting after Dimitrov):* Be careful, look out, I shall teach you how to behave, only come out of the courtroom! Scoundrel!

In the end Dimitrov made it clear, even to the judiciary who may have wished to convict him if only to keep themselves out of trouble, that he and his fellow foreigners had not been implicated in the arson. Defended as he was by able counsel who kept the courtroom discussion of his client on a very narrow path, Torgler was almost as safe.

Van der Lubbe, however, had confessed. Regardless of whether that confession had been coerced, it was fatal to the Dutchman that he had been on the scene. He had been caught with incriminating evidence and was identified as a person who was running through the Reichstag while the fires were flaring.

VERDICT

Van der Lubbe was convicted and sentenced to death. He was beheaded by guillotine on January 10, 1934, in Leipzig. The guillotine was not a deliberate refinement in this case to underline Van der Lubbe's notoriety; the device remained in widespread use throughout Germany and France. His alleged accomplices were acquitted. The presiding judges tried to protect themselves against Nazi anger at such a "soft" verdict by composing a statement that condemned the Communists as "the party of treason." "The crime," they stated, "can only be the work of left-wing elements."

Dimitrov, Tanev, and Popov were allowed to leave Germany in exchange for a group of German airmen who were being held in the Soviet Union. Dimitrov assumed Soviet citizenship and went on to become the leader of Communist Bulgaria.

Eventually, he fell out with Stalin and died suddenly in 1949, his demise hastened perhaps as a result of that quarrel.

After the Reichstag fire trial the Nazis closely controlled Torgler's movements. During World War II Torgler wrote anti-Communist propaganda for both Goebbels and Reinhard Heydrich; he later maintained that his cooperation was coerced due to pressure on his family. Although Torgler attempted to regain a position within the German Communist Party, former colleagues distrusted him. That rift had begun when Torgler turned himself in for questioning on the morning after the Reichstag fire.

SIGNIFICANCE

Even with Nazi strategists such as Heinrich Himmler and Göring arrayed against the defendants, all but one of the persons formally accused of causing the Reichstag fire survived their judicial ordeal. Largely this was due to Dimitrov's legal skill. Furthermore, the Nazis' insistence on publicizing the trial widely may have backfired; the case was closely watched in Germany and abroad. The Reichstag fire trial, though hardly a bright moment in German jurisprudence, offered the possibility that the Nazis did not yet have total control over public affairs. At this juncture in 1933 the courts remained reasonably independent. Hitler reportedly was furious at the outcome. He already had moved to ensure that "people's courts," which would be more responsive to his political pressure, would hear subsequent cases of alleged treason.

The central factual question at the trial—who set the blaze—remained unresolved long after the trial's conclusion. At the Nuremberg War Crimes Trials in 1946, prosecutors again brought up the 1933 case. The Allies cited General Franz Halder's remembrance that Göring had joked (in Hitler's presence) of setting the fire himself. Göring gave a detailed reply dismissing Halder's recollection as preposterous. Göring's responses at Nuremberg mostly indicated Göring's contempt for that current legal proceeding. Still, his comments at Nuremberg do betray that at the Reichstag fire trial Göring and the Nazis were obsessed with countering allegations from *The Brown Book:*

That accusation that I had set fire to the Reichstag came from a certain foreign press. That could not bother me because it was not consistent with the facts. I had no reason or motive for setting fire to the Reichstag. From the artistic point of view I did not at all regret that the assembly chamber was burned; I hoped to build a better one. But I did regret very much that I was forced to find a new meeting place for the Reichstag and, not being able to find one, I had to give up my Kroll Opera House, that is, the second State Opera House, for that purpose. The opera seemed to me much more important than the Reichstag.

Long after the war ended, historians and forensic specialists weighed in on the proceedings at the Reichstag fire trial. They engaged in scholarly debates about the two main conspiracy theories that had been proposed in 1933 (that the fire was a result of either Nazi or Communist plots). They also considered the proposition that Van der Lubbe had acted alone but reached no consensus about any of those possibilities. Among the many questions that remained was that of Van der Lubbe's mental capacity before the fire and at trial. Those who argued for a Communist-led plot called Van der Lubbe either an ideologue or a dupe. Persons who contended that the Nazis arranged the burning proposed that Van der Lubbe either was of limited faculties or simply was himself inspired to commit arson, thus playing into Nazi aspirations.

The opening of archives in the former Soviet Union in the 1990s allowed researchers to ponder the situation anew when they located records that the Soviets had purportedly seized from Germany. Some of those documents indicated a high-level plot to torch the Reichstag and pin blame on the Left. That type of conspiracy almost certainly would have had the connivance of Goebbels and his peers, though Hitler's prior knowledge of the plan remained murky. Other writers dismissed such materials as Soviet forgeries.

In Berlin in the late 20th and early 21st centuries a historical and commemorative site called Topology of Terror drew attention to the conditions in which political prisoners during the prewar and wartime era were detained. Several cells in the "House Prison" in the cellar of the Gestapo headquarters at Prinz-Albrecht-Strasse 8 stood as a reminder of the brutalities endured by the important prisoners of the regime. As the National Socialists consolidated their grasp after 1933, even those persons who had the opportunity to defend themselves in court rather than being dispatched out of hand were subject to horrific measures while in custody. In that sense Van der Lubbe was quite representative of many thousands of other political prisoners, for while he may not have been detained at the House Prison, there is much to suggest he was horribly maltreated before and during trial.

Coming to terms with the events of the 1930s and 1940s continued to be a struggle for Germany into the 21st century, including with regard to this case. The conviction of Van der Lubbe was the focus of several appeals by his brother; those efforts were to clear Van der Lubbe's name and perhaps establish a compensation scheme for his heirs. In a set of decisions from 1980 through 1983 German courts first moderated the sentence against Van der Lubbe, then overturned the guilty verdict, then reversed that decision. Among the arguments for Van der Lubbe's pardon was his supposedly fragile mental state; according to the law of many nations at the time of the trial he ought to have been declared *non compos mentis,* or unfit to participate in his own defense.

In 1998 Germany passed a major law "rehabilitating" many Nazi-era convicts. That measure allowed persons prosecuted under the Nazis (or the families of defendants) to ask for an overturning of the verdicts against them. The grounds for rehabilitation were that the whole system of justice in Germany from 1933 onward was so politicized that any conviction had to be suspect. German officials considered Van der Lubbe's situation in 2008. Although Van der Lubbe's family won for him the reversal of his conviction, Germany did not issue a finding that the case against him was incorrect—only that the whole judicial process was flawed.

Further Reading

Avalon Project. "Nuremberg Trial Proceedings, Vol. 9, Eighty-fourth Day, Monday, 18 March 1946." Available online. URL: http://avalon.law. yale.edu/imt/03-18-46.asp. Accessed March 17, 2009; Bahar, Alexander, and Wilfried Kugel. *Der Reichstagbrand—Wie Geschichte gemacht wird.* Berlin, Germany: Quintessenz Verlag, 2001; Dimitrov, Georgi. *The Reichstag Fire Trial: The Second Brown Book of the Hitler Terror.* 1934; Kuijpers, P. *The Reichstag Fire in West German Historiography.* Rotterdam, Netherlands: Erasmus University, 2009; Mueller, Ingo. *Hitler's Justice: The Courts of the Third Reich.* Cambridge, Mass.: Harvard University Press, 1992; Robinbach, Anson. "Staging Antifascism: The Brown Book of the Reichstag Fire and Hitler Terror." *New German Critique* 103 (Winter 2008): 97–126; Tigar, Michael, and John Mage. "The Reichstag Fire Trial, 1933–2008." *Monthly Review* (March 2009). Available online. URL: http://www.monthlyreview.org/090309tigar-mage.php. Accessed March 25, 2009; Tobias, Fritz. *The Reichstag Fire: Legend and Truth.* London: Secker & Warburg, 1963; U.S. Holocaust Memorial Museum. "The Reichstag Fire—Historical Film Footage." Available online. URL: http://www.ushmm.org/wlc/en/gallery_fi.php?ModuleId=10007657. Accessed March 18, 2009.

The trial of Bruno Richard Hauptmann

Also known as: *New Jersey v. Hauptmann;* the Lindbergh kidnapping trial

Date: 1935

KEY ISSUES

Trials that involve famous people have been irresistible for court watchers, especially with the advent of the broadcast media. The Lindbergh baby case of 1935 presented such a spectacle. What would have been a heartrending situation if it had involved ordinary parents now transfixed the entire nation with grief and anger. The local police and other law-enforcement authorities such as the national Bureau of Investigation were desperate to locate a perpetrator. But were they so anxious to provide a solution that they framed an innocent man? The trial of the accused person in the case presents several dilemmas even beyond whether the man who was convicted of the crime was guilty. The Lindbergh baby case also involves questions of the value of circumstantial evidence, the presence of the press in the courtroom and private persons' lives, and the development of forensic investigative techniques.

HISTORY OF THE CASE

Charles Lindbergh was more than a celebrity in the United States during the late 1920s; he was a hero. In May 1927 Lindbergh was the first person to fly solo across the Atlantic Ocean. His achievement spawned national celebrations, won him individual recognitions, and earned him almost unprecedented attention from ordinary folk as well as the national media. After Lindbergh married a bright and attractive woman, Anne Morrow, in 1929, the couple found the crush of attention difficult. They tried to find a more calm life in a small town in New Jersey.

Their effort to shake fame, however, came to a terrible end: On March 1, 1932, their young son, Charles Jr., disappeared from the family home. The Lindberghs notified nearby authorities immediately upon discovering the boy missing at around 10:00 P.M. Local police called in the state police, and the national Bureau of Investigation (later the FBI) offered assistance. The news horrified the nation. Lindbergh the father was identified with the American eagle; the Lindbergh baby was nicknamed "the Eaglet."

After receiving more than a dozen notes asking for ransom, the Lindberghs, through an intermediary named John Condon, paid a $50,000 ransom. The serial numbers of the bills and gold certificates that they used were recorded. Negotiations about the ransom were complicated and went on throughout March. After paying the money the Lindberghs were told they could find their child on a boat offshore. Charles Lindbergh went on an aerial search but spied neither the boat nor his son. The boy's body was found within a few miles of the Lindbergh home about two

months later. The child was determined to have been dead for about two months—in other words, since shortly after he disappeared. A blow to the skull had caused the death.

The case went unsolved for two years. At President Franklin Roosevelt's direction the Bureau of Investigation took over the case. Federal, state, and local authorities interviewed hundreds of persons who had offered tips. They ended up prosecuting a few con artists who had seized upon the case as an opportunity to swindle the public with what they said was information about the kidnapping. So desperate were ordinary citizens to help solve the mystery that they occasionally put up their own money to assist in the effort and of course lost those funds to the swindlers. Celebrities—and more notorious individuals such as incarcerated gangster Al Capone—offered to post reward money.

Investigators thought it critical to keep watch for the gold certificates and numbered bills that formed the ransom. Law enforcers issued a series of bulletins to banks and retail merchants who might receive those tokens connected with the crime. In May 1933 the Federal Reserve Bank in New York detected about $3,000 of the ransom among gold certificates that had been deposited there. The depositor could not be located despite an intensive search.

Investigators also went about profiling the person who had met with the intermediary Condon and had taken away the ransom money. The authorities used a sketch artist and formed a whole personality portrait of the individual, a man who called himself "John." They determined they were searching for a man who spoke English as a second language (as evidenced by his accent and writing) and was from Scandinavia or northern Europe (through a physical description). Those trying to solve the case also paid close attention to the ladder that had allowed the kidnapper access to the baby's second-floor room and had been left at the kidnapping scene. The Bureau of Investigation called in wood expert Arthur Koelher of the U.S. Department of Agriculture to analyze how and where the ladder had been hand-built and what types of skills might have been needed to do so.

In August and September 1934 several of the missing gold certificates began showing up in circulation in the New York City area, particularly in Harlem and Yorkville. Investigators mapped out where they had been used, tracked each bill through several hands, and began to focus on one common user. That link was a man who seemed to match the description of "John," according to Condon's identification of the man who took the ransom money.

A German immigrant named Bruno Richard Hauptmann used some of the bills from the ransom payment to purchase motor fuel. The gas station attendant, knowing of the search for gold certificates, became suspicious when the man had paid using one; he had written down Hauptmann's license plate number and called the police. Hauptmann not only was a close match to the drawings that authorities had generated of "John"; he fit their profile in other key ways. Hauptmann had been convicted and served time for robbery before immigrating. He had been in the United States for 11 years after leaving his homeland and had worked as a carpenter. Hauptmann had not followed that trade lately. He had begun trading in stocks shortly after the kidnapping.

After his arrest several items tying him to the kidnapping were found. More of the ransom money was stashed in his garage. A tool kit of Hauptmann's was missing a chisel that was recovered on the Lindberghs' property. The ladder from the kidnapping scene matched wood that was found in Hauptmann's attic. Among Hauptmann's papers was a sketch of the two-story ladder. The phone number of the man who had effected the transfer of the ransom money was scribbled in a closet at Hauptmann's home. The script on the ransom notes matched Hauptmann's, according to handwriting experts. Hauptmann and his car had been seen near the Lindbergh home the day before the kidnapping. It was a very strong circumstantial case.

SUMMARY OF ARGUMENTS

Hauptmann was indicted in New York for extortion in late September 1934. In New Jersey he faced trial for murder. New York allowed him to stand trial on the more serious charges first. His day in court began on January 3, 1935, in the Hunterdon County Court of Oyer and Terminer in Flemington, New Jersey.

Hauptmann's defense was that he did not know the origin of the money. He said that he was keeping the cash for a friend who had died, Isidore Fisch. Hauptmann's defense lawyer, Edward Reilly, came up with few credible witnesses to Hauptmann's character. Reilly probably erred in putting out a public request for persons who could aid in Hauptmann's defense. The call seemed to draw individuals who were unstable, and Reilly admitted as much in the courtroom. Confronted with a great deal of expert testimony and the eyewitness reports of Condon and Lindbergh, Reilly was forced to lean on the idea that the prosecution's case was a frame-up. He hinted in cross-examination that the New York police had beaten Hauptmann and that they had coached Hauptmann to spell certain words incorrectly to match words from the ransom notes. The defense's elaborate conspiracy theory involving Lindbergh household workers, Condon, Fisch, and perhaps police connivance, however, was hard to prove.

The prosecution relied on a number of links between Hauptmann, the ransom, and the crime scene. It also stressed that Condon had positively identified Hauptmann as "John," despite some hesitation on Condon's part at a police lineup. Long before Hauptmann had been a suspect, Condon helped generate a sketch that bore a striking resemblance to Hauptmann. In addition, Lindbergh had gone along on one of Condon's rendezvous with "John." Lindbergh had been close enough to their conversation that he identified in court Hauptmann's voice as being that of "John." Such eyewitness evidence from Lindbergh carried great weight with the jury.

The county attorney general David Wilentz spelled out the way the state thought the crime had occurred: Hauptmann had planned the crime for some time in advance, but the plot went awry when the ladder broke as he descended it holding the Lindbergh child. The toddler died as a result of the fall, but Hauptmann pressed on to demand the ransom. That scenario would fit a description of Condon's recollection of a conversation he had had with "John" while transferring the ransom money. "John" had hinted that the baby might already be dead, a fact that only a kidnapper himself could know. It was a reconstruction of the crime that made Hauptmann seem not only guilty but also particularly cruel.

The evidence concerning the ladder turned out to be vital to the jury. Witness Koelher's careful investigation of the wood and nails used to construct the ladder, the tools in Hauptmann's possession, and very similar wood found in Hauptmann's house seemed to seal the opinion of the panel of 12 jurors that Hauptmann had planned the crime methodically. Either police had been extraordinarily astute in choosing a person to set up, or Hauptmann had the skills and criminal background needed to bring such a crime plan to fruition.

The defense ended its time in court with its contention that the crime was an inside job. After remarking that the Lindberghs' scrappy terrier did not bark to alert the family of an intruder, Reilly intoned, "I say the circumstances point absolutely along a straight line of guilt toward that butler and the servants who were disloyal to the Colonel." It was a line of argument not without some backing, but it also was not something Reilly had proved. The jury must have perceived that Reilly was trying to distract them from the evidence of Hauptmann's involvement.

Wilentz's summation included a lengthy review of the forensic evidence, but it also was an interesting comment on his own view of the case. He abhorred prosecuting, he said (though most observers thought him adept at it), and would be glad to go back to a quiet life at home. In addition to his point-by-point citation of the many elements that linked Hauptmann to the crime, he provided a character appraisal of the baby's killer. It was not an assessment devoid of prejudice, but neither was the prosecution's comment on Hauptmann as inflammatory as it might have been:

> Now what type of man would kill the child of Colonel Lindbergh and Anne Morrow?
>
> He wouldn't be an American. No American gangster and no American racketeer ever sank to the level of killing babies. Ah, no! Oh, no, it had to be a fellow that had ice water in his veins, not blood.
>
> That is the first thing. It had to be a fellow who thought he was bigger than Lindy, that when the news of the crime came out he could look at the headlines screaming across the page. It had to be a fellow that was an egomaniac, who thought he was omnipotent. It had to be a secretive fellow. It had to be a fellow that wouldn't tell his wife about his money, who would conceal the truth from her. It had to be a fellow that wouldn't trust a bookkeeper, the kind of fellow that could undergo hardship, that could stow away on a boat and travel three thousand miles to sneak into this country in a coal bin, without food, without water, and when he was apprehended in court he would say he would go back again and try it over again. That's the type of man. Try it over the second time and then the third time. It would have to be the type of man that wouldn't think anything of forsaking his own country, that would leave everything behind and flee to another land. It would have to be the type of man that would forsake his own mother, sixty-five years of age, and run away. And let me tell you, men and women, the State of New Jersey, the State of New York and the Federal authorities, have found that animal, an animal lower than the lowest form in the animal kingdom, public enemy Number 1 of this world, Bruno Richard Hauptmann; we have found him and he is here for your judgment.

VERDICT

Hauptmann's guilty verdict came on February 13, 1935. His defense lodged appeals with the New Jersey Supreme Court and the U.S. Supreme Court; both of those authorities denied the motions for a reversal of judgment. Despite a 30-day reprieve from the governor of New Jersey, who had interviewed the convicted man and doubted Hauptmann's guilt, the New Jersey Pardon Board finally rebuffed Hauptmann's effort to gain clemency. Hauptmann rejected several pleas to confess, even some offers involving payments to his family. Hauptmann died on April 3, 1936 in New Jersey's electric chair, still insisting on his innocence.

The case for Hauptmann's innocence was carried forward by a number of scholars, conspiracy theorists, and, chiefly, Hauptmann's widow, Anna. Those who criticized the verdict noted investigators' anxiety to wrap up the investigation, prejudice against the German-born Hauptmann (who had been a German soldier in World War I), and pressure to convict quickly. Some of the more conspiracy-minded writers on the case came up with alternative versions of who had committed the crime: a domestic worker in the Lindbergh home named Violet Sharpe, who had committed suicide during the investigation, or other household workers, or Lindbergh neighbors, or Condon, or Hauptmann's friend Fisch.

SIGNIFICANCE

Some later investigators of the Lindbergh baby's kidnapping and murder who insisted that defense attorney Reilly was correct were motivated as much by their own suspicions about police and FBI misconduct as by the evidence in the case. Others who kept the case alive sympathized with Anna Hauptmann. The convicted man's widow lived to an advanced age, always insisting on her husband's lack of culpability.

Lindbergh lost some of his popularity in the 1930s and 1940s when he expressed admiration for Nazi Germany, opposed U.S. entry into the World War II, and made anti-Semitic remarks. Anne Lindbergh, herself an accomplished flier, also became a well-known writer. During their long lives neither of them expressed doubt in the validity of Hauptmann's conviction.

Further Reading

British Pathé. "Lindbergh Baby Case: Video Newsreel Film." Available online. URL: http://www. britishpathe.com/record.php?id=5790. Accessed April 6, 2009; Fisher, Jim. *The Ghosts of Hopewell: Setting the Record Straight in the Lindbergh Case.* Carbondale: Southern Illinois University Press, 2006; Kennedy, Ludovic. *Crime of the Century: The Lindbergh Kidnapping and the Framing of Richard Hauptmann.* New York: Penguin, 1996; Lindbergh, Anne Morrow. *Hour of Gold, Hour of Lead: Diaries and Letters of Anne Morrow Lindbergh, 1929–1932.* Boston: Mariner Books, 1993; New Jersey Division of Archives and Record Management. "Lindbergh Kidnapping Evidence Photographs." Available online. URL: http://www.state.

nj.us/state/darm/links/guides/slcsp001.html. Accessed April 6, 2009.

The trial of Nikolai Bukharin

Also known as: Trial of the Twenty-one

Date: 1938

KEY ISSUES

Nikolai Bukharin was a leading member of the Bolshevik Party during its formative years. A well-educated man, he had earned his credentials as a radical during protests against the czarist government. He was forced to flee Russia in 1911 because of his dissent. Bukharin served as an intellectual and diplomatic counterpart to Joseph Stalin and an assistant to V. I. Lenin while all three plotted the revolutions of 1917. Some ideological divisions erupted between the three men, particularly concerning Bolshevik overtures to Germany when Russia withdrew from World War I. Those differences healed, though, particularly in view of Bukharin's talent for political writing. His gifts as a theoretician made him a valued exponent within and outside the Soviet state. It was a mark of Lenin's confidence that Bukharin held several key posts: editor of the leading newspaper for the masses, *Pravda;* member of the Central Committee of the Politburo; and partial author of the Program of the Communist Party. At one time Bukharin also was the head of the Communist International (Comintern).

Once World War I ended, Bukharin took on the task of directing the Soviet economy. He was the director of the New Economic Policy (NEP). The plan was for the national government to control heavy industry and transportation, while farms and light industries would operate according to market (capitalist) principles. Organizations of trade workers and farmers gradually would fall under state control. The NEP was recognition that the Soviets could not immediately initiate a truly communist society.

Even as Bukharin assumed the dominant position in Soviet economic policy, he faced a formidable political challenge to inherit the mantle of the ailing Lenin, who died in 1924. Lenin may have thought of Bukharin as a worthy successor; after 1920 Lenin hinted that other likely candidates for supreme leadership, especially Stalin, had serious flaws. From about 1925 until 1928 the two revolutionaries who held the most power in the Soviet Union were the intellectual and economic expert, Bukharin, and the master of bureaucracy, Stalin.

In 1928 there was a falling out between those two leaders. Stalin reversed many of his previous arguments advocating a measured pace of economic change through the NEP. He committed himself and the nation to forced collectivization in the countryside, destruction of wealthy farmers, and a rapid concentration of resources in heavy industry. Stalin made certain that anyone who had a record of opposing such plans was removed from positions of highest influence. Bukharin had written extensively on the subject in recent years, so he lost his highest official roles. But, deeply devoted to communism as he was, Bukharin rejected the idea of appealing directly to the masses to challenge Stalin. He thought it vital that the party should present a united front, especially abroad.

HISTORY OF THE CASE

Stalin's series of five-year plans displaced, imprisoned, starved, or killed outright many thousands of Soviet citizens. Bukharin, along with other officials whom Stalin needed but no longer fully trusted, began circulating criticisms. Bukharin's main contention was that the trajectory of the Soviet economy was no longer in line with Lenin's ideas. From his position as editor of the forum for discussion within the party, the newspaper *Izvestiya*, Bukharin made comparisons between Adolf Hitler's and Stalin's methods.

Stalin was especially angered by a pamphlet composed by a party leader with great influence in Moscow, Martemyan Ryutin. Ryutin called for an end to the brutality in the countryside, calling for the government to make "peace with the peasants." He offered a rapprochement among factions within the party, notably the leftists under

Leon Trotsky. Several persons who had close ties to Bukharin, a group calling themselves "the Red Professors" because of their academic and Bolshevik credentials, helped disseminate the publication.

Stalin ordered the secret police, the People's Commissariat for Internal Affairs (NKVD), to round up persons who held copies of Ryutin's writing. Sergei Kirov, a leading figure in the party's Central Committee, argued that those who had composed and possessed the offending printed matter should be exiled rather than executed. Stalin seemed to go along with such a moderate solution, even offering Kirov a position in Leningrad (St. Petersburg). In that capacity as a special envoy for Stalin, on December 1, 1934, Kirov wound up dead.

Stalin blamed the murder on old revolutionaries who remained alive, notably Grigory Zinoviev and Lev Kamenev. Under torture, they professed "complicity" in the assassination of Kirov. They were handed long prison terms. But, Stalin's supposed efforts to get to the bottom of the assassination of Kirov were in fact a sweep of political circles to eradicate Stalin's remaining opponents. In this effort, later termed his Great Purge, Stalin was particularly keen to neutralize persons with long histories in the party and links to Lenin.

As the hunt for malcontents continued, even persons like Zinoviev and Kamenev who already had been examined and sentenced were hauled back before courts specially designed for a new inquiry. This new prosecutorial effort began in earnest in the summer of 1936, with the restructuring of the State Prosecutor's Office under Andrei Vyshinsky. On behalf of Stalin, Vyshinsky prosecuted three major sets of trials in the next few years: Kamanev, Zinoviev, and their close colleagues in 1936 (Trial of the Sixteen); another group of alleged conspirators including Yuri Pyatek, Karl Radek, and Grigory Sokolnikov, in early 1937 (Trial of the Seventeen); and Bukharin, along with colleagues such as Alexei Rykov and Genrikh Yagoda (Trial of the Twenty-one) from March 2 to 13, 1938. Along with the prosecutions of certain military officials in those years, the trials of 1936–38 eventually were called the Moscow show trials.

SUMMARY OF ARGUMENTS

The charges against the 16 key Bolsheviks in mid-1936 included not simply being "morally complicit" in Kirov's death but also forming a terrorist organization (the Trotskyite Zinovievite Terrorist Center) aimed at destroying the Soviet state. The defendants were accused of allying with capitalist powers and certain foreign leaders. The trials were held before the Military Collegium of the Supreme Court of the Union of Soviet Socialist Republics, the Soviet Union's highest court.

One of the striking features of the three sets of trials was the active role of the USSR's chief prosecutor. In effect, he was the nation's attorney general. Vyshinsky cut a professional figure in court, but his rhetoric became shrill on many occasions. Vyshinsky's argument for the death penalty for "the Sixteen," for example, attacked the contention that the accused persons were heroes of 1905 and 1917 and thus deserved special consideration:

> The comparison with the period of Narodnaya Volya terrorism is shameless. Filled with respect for the memory of those who in the times of the Narodnaya Volya sincerely and honestly, although employing, it is true, their own special, but always irreproachable methods, fought against the tsarist autocracy for liberty—I emphatically reject this sacrilegious parallel. I repeat, this parallel is out of place here. Before us are criminals, dangerous, hardened, cruel and ruthless towards our people, towards our ideals, towards the leaders of our struggle, the leaders of the land of Soviets, the leaders of the toilers of the whole world!
>
> I demand that dogs gone mad should be shot—every one of them!

As the trials continued, the allegations became wider and included more supposed conspirators. Vital to the carrying on of the Moscow show trials were the efforts of the NKVD, headed by Nikolai Ezhov. Indeed, at the time of the proceedings, well-connected Russians usually referred to them as "*Ezhovshchina*" rather than as Stalin's show. Many historians conclude that Stalin perfected a strategy about how to rid himself of rivals via judi-

cial actions from about 1934 onward. Ezhov provided the evidence, and Vyshinsky the verbiage in court.

The importance of the trials of such high-level figures was twofold: These were rivals of Stalin who were old fellow revolutionaries, and as high-profile figures they could not simply be dispatched in the night. His perceived enemies of lesser status, whose fates might not be tracked on the international stage, Stalin was quite content to dispose of with less formality. It was critical, Stalin thought, to appear to give well-known persons fair trials if he, Stalin, were to maintain respect within the international community. Stalin largely did not succeed in engendering that respect.

Defenders of Leon Trotsky (who was in exile in Mexico) initiated an inquiry into the Moscow trials; Stalin had been going to special pains to impugn Trotsky's reputation. That investigation, the Dewey Commission, found the Moscow trials to be a sham:

> . . . The conduct of the Moscow Trials was such as to convince any unprejudiced person that no attempt was made to ascertain the truth.
>
> . . . While confessions are necessarily entitled to the most serious consideration, the confessions themselves contain such inherent improbabilities as to convince the Commission that they do not represent the truth, irrespective of any means used to obtain them.
>
> . . . We therefore find the Moscow Trials to be frame-ups.

Although the Dewey inquiry clearly had its own political bias, diplomats in most Western nations, including the United States, concurred early on that the Moscow trials were only for show.

Poor individuals in the Soviet countryside died by the millions in the mid- to late 1930s. Perhaps 5 million people were arrested during 1937–38, of whom nearly a million got death sentences and the majority of the others brutal internal exile. The Red Army saw a purge in the same years, with 98 of the 108 members of the Supreme Military Council being executed, along with dozens of commanders, divisional commissars, admirals, and field marshals. The Communist Party's Central Committee was not immune to the bloodbath; all but 41 of the 139 persons elected to its membership in 1934 were dead by the end of 1938.

In the proceedings at Moscow against the old revolutionaries, Stalin wanted confessions. Almost every defendant complied. The accused persons were imprisoned for months, beaten or otherwise tortured, and were pressured to cooperate with news of family and friends who were in danger. The rare individual who came to court determined to let the record show that he pleaded not guilty invariably changed his mind after a night of "persuasion" by the authorities. Conclusive evidence could not be established for such tactics at the time, but historians uncovered overwhelming evidence for such strong-arming with the opening up of Soviet archives during perestroika and afterward.

Bukharin's was a particularly interesting case because there is some indication that he more willingly confessed to his "crimes" than did his peers. Perhaps, in other words, Bukharin required less or even no torture to admit his complicity in internecine rivalry. He stated in his confession that he had opposed Stalin through his writings and that that had the potential to weaken his country.

Several writers, including Arthur Koestler (whose *Darkness at Noon* was heavily influenced by Bukharin's trial), commented on the unusual, complex language in which Bukharin wrapped his "admission" of guilt. The confessions were shifting and general; never did Bukharin admit particular actions that were treasonous. Bukharin must have known that he was doomed, but he accepted his fate in the name of the continuing success of the Soviet state and communism:

> May this trial be the last severe lesson, and may the great might of the U.S.S.R. become clear to all. It is in the consciousness of this that I await the verdict. What matters is not the personal feelings of a repentant enemy, but the flourishing progress of the U.S.S.R. and its international importance.

It is possible that Bukharin bargained with the authorities to allow such a general confession in exchange for promises that his family would be unmolested and that he would be allowed to write in prison. Bukharin's wife eventually was sent to a prison camp, although she did emerge alive from it.

In addition to the conviction of Bukharin, the prosecution and conviction of his codefendant Yagoda was especially ominous for anyone who hoped to oppose Stalin. Yagoda's presence among the defendants indicated that the purges were turning upon themselves. He had been the head of the NKVD and now, in 1938, was accused of participating in the effort to destabilize the nation. Stalin obviously hoped to get rid of not just his rivals but also accomplices.

VERDICT

The great majority of the defendants in the Moscow show trials were sentenced to death by firing squad. Despite international efforts on behalf of several defendants and Bukharin's own personal appeals to Stalin, Bukharin was executed just hours after the conclusion of his trial. He died on March 15, 1938. With very few exceptions, those who did not get death sentences at trial died in labor camps or were executed by the Soviet secret police upon Stalin's orders during World War II.

SIGNIFICANCE

Just after the Moscow show trials some leftists in the United States and Europe maintained that the proceedings were valid expressions about real threats to the Soviet state. Thus, they contended, the verdicts against Bukharin and others were justified. But, several other prominent Soviet sympathizers found the episodes repellant and from that point renounced Stalin and communism, even while the USSR was among the Allies during World War II. Nikita Khrushchev's "Secret Speech" of 1956 cast shadows upon Stalin's actions preceding the trials. Stalin's prominent successor, in other words, painted Stalin as a tyrant and the trials as a farce. Between 1968 and 1988 the Soviet government repudiated the verdicts against most of the defendants. An official form of that reconsideration was "rehabilitation," which amounted to posthumous acquittal in the case of Bukharin.

Scholars who have reexamined the Moscow show trials after the fall of the Soviet Union note that there is some evidence of an organized conspiracy to unseat Stalin, perhaps with foreign assistance, among the old revolutionaries. Bukharin's part in such a plan has not been fully ascertained. His words at trial and his writing while in prison remain enigmatic. The most likely scenario for Kirov's death is that Stalin engineered the assassination as an excuse to implement his purges. The best explanation for Bukharin's fate continues to be that he was an articulate and popular individual with links to Lenin and, thus, a threat to Stalin.

Further Reading

"August 22, 1936 (morning session): Speech for the Prosecution." Available online. URL: http://art-bin.com/art/omosc22m.html. Accessed October 14, 2008; Bukharin, Nikolai. *The Prison Manuscripts: Socialism and Its Culture*. Translated by George Shriver. New York: Seagull Books, 2006; Cohen, Stephen F., and Robert C. Tucker. *The Great Purge Trial*. New York: Grosset & Dunlap Publishers, 1965; Conquest, Robert. *The Great Terror: A Reassessment*. Oxford: Oxford University Press, 1990; "Footage from Infamous Moscow Show Trial." Available online. URL: http://www.youtube.com/watch?v=nFB9G1HINXI. Accessed October 14, 2008; Katkov, George. *The Trial of Bukharin*. London: B. T. Bratsford, 1969; Medvedev, Roy A. *Nikolai Bukharin: The Last Years*. New York: W. W. Norton & Co., 1980; Thurston, Robert. *Life and Terror in Stalin's Russia, 1934–1941*. New Haven, Conn.: Yale University Press, 1996.

The trial of Aleck Bourne

Also known as: *The King v. Bourne;* the case of Miss M

Date: 1938

KEY ISSUES

In both Great Britain and the United States well into the modern era, the law on abortion dated from the middle of the 19th century. The United States did not have a national statute outlawing abortions but instead employed state-by-state regulations. Those proscriptions on abortion ranged from prohibitions that were nearly absolute, allowing exceptions only in the event that the life of the mother was at stake, to slightly more permissive. Some states, for example, permitted a range of exceptions allowing abortions to be performed in the event that a pregnancy had occurred as the result of rape or incest. The English law was more uniform because the policy was national in scope. The key law was a statute from 1861 called the Offenses Against the Person Act. Section 58 of that legislation allowed the possibility of a lifetime prison term for anyone who procured a miscarriage through the use of instruments.

The anti-abortion laws that were instituted in the mid-1800s were promulgated at the behest of a medical profession—almost exclusively male—that was becoming more professional. Allopathic medicine was competing for business and respect with homeopathy and other less "mainstream" forms of medical treatment. Allopathic physicians specializing in women's health particularly sought to distinguish themselves from "irregular" practitioners such as midwives. Physicians educated at universities and increasingly affiliated with hospitals made the argument to both legislatures and state licensing boards that only they could provide state-of-the-art care. They warned against the wielding of medical tools in untrained hands. In no field of medicine were their alerts more urgent, they contended, than in regard to obstetrics.

HISTORY OF THE CASE

The fact that doctors had set the legislative agenda with regard to abortion, however, still did not make some physicians completely comfortable as the 20th century wore on. To be sure, abortion was marked off as the bailiwick of allopathic practitioners. It was a procedure to be undertaken in hospitals. And yet, there were gray areas in practice. When the English act of 1861 prohibited "unlawfully procuring an abortion" through the use of instruments, what did the word *unlawfully* mean? Was it simply a reference to a back-alley procedure by anyone, or did it refer specifically to unlicensed abortionists? British doctors assumed that if they indicated within medical records that a woman's life was in danger or even seriously imperiled by a pregnancy, they could perform abortions. But, that was merely an inference. The law spoke not at all to cases, for example, where the mother's mental health was in danger due to a pregnancy—where, say, the pregnant woman threatened to commit suicide if her doctor would not perform an abortion or in which her husband promised to kill her if she did not abort.

In the 1920s and 1930s, certain physicians found themselves in the legally awkward position of defending themselves against charges of infanticide. Activist forensic pathologists such as Dr. Bernard Spilsbury spurred on such cases. A law of 1929, the Infant Life Preservation Act, encouraged prosecutions of doctors who either killed newborns or let infants die during delivery, including delivery in the course of an early induced labor. Spilsbury, the leading forensic pathologist of his day, was personally opposed to abortions and sought out opportunities to testify against doctors he thought were performing too many obstetrical procedures in which unborn children died.

Doctors' organizations including the British Medical Association (BMA) decided that they must seek a clarification of the law. They hoped not simply to inure themselves against prosecution; they also wished to make the statement to the public that if trained physicians had greater latitude to perform abortions, then irregular practitioners would have less allure and the public safety would benefit. That argument hearkened to the contentions of U.S. allopathic physicians who had lobbied in state legislatures for the laws that currently were in force. Such laws, said the doctors' groups, were a guarantee that abortions would be rare because doctors rather than abortionists would perform them. The procedures also would be safer because they would be regulated.

Through members of the BMA such as the young Dr. Aleck Bourne, who had happened to be one of Spilsbury's more promising students, British medical groups kept on the lookout for an appropriate case through which to test the law of abortion in the courts. They found a fact situation in 1938 that they thought lent itself to discussion in a judicial venue.

The pregnant person in question was a 14-year-old girl who had been raped by strangers. The child, who later was referred to in court documents as "Miss M," had been lured into the barracks of the Royal Horse Guards in London. Soldiers had told the victim that they would show her a "horse with a green tail." Several of the perpetrators were arrested and prosecuted for the crime. Although the penalty imposed was for sexual assault rather than the more serious offense of rape, Miss M clearly fell within a category of women who engendered great sympathy when they had unplanned pregnancies.

On the other hand, those who sought to use Miss M's tragedy to delineate the law on abortion had several obstacles to overcome. There was the possibility that very conservative elements might argue that no abortion could be justified, even in the case of rape. Some U.S. jurisdictions, for example, specifically did not allow abortions in cases of rape but only to save the life of the mother. If Bourne were prosecuted, he might face such contentions. An even more likely rejoinder to Bourne and the BMA was an argument that Miss M was not at any peril from continuing the pregnancy to full term. The prosecution might posit that Parliament's law of 1861 did not intend to exempt persons who were emotionally traumatized by a pregnancy, only those physically imperiled by it.

Bourne had his own concerns about the case. Before agreeing to perform the abortion on the rape victim, he wanted to satisfy himself that she was not, in his words, "of the prostitute type." He had several reasons for visiting Miss M and interviewing her with such a question in mind. In a medical vein Bourne wanted to be certain that Miss M was not affected by any venereal disease or infection that an abortion might spread. He also was trying to ascertain if Miss M were of "normal" mental capacity. Part of his argument at trial was going to involve the psychological effects of a pregnancy due to rape. He hoped that Miss M was not of limited mental faculties, for that would impinge upon her ability to appreciate (and presumably be depressed by) her situation.

Politically, he wanted to confirm that the young woman was a suitable representative for the BMA campaign for law reform. If she were later found to have had consensual sexual relations with others, it would undercut her image as a virgin who had been raped and thus her effectiveness as a sympathetic example. Bourne also said that he wanted to know in his own mind that Miss M was telling the truth about the assault. He assumed he could tell if she genuinely had been victimized by her reactions to his physical appraisal. Miss M passed all of Bourne's tests. He noted that she cried when he examined her.

Bourne commented that Miss M's parents seemed "so respectable" that they did not know the name of any local irregular abortionists, hence they had come seeking help from the medical establishment. The parents tried to get help at St. Thomas's Hospital, but the first physician they approached was unsympathetic. He commented that the rapists were from polite society and that Miss M "might be carrying a future Prime Minister." He also ventured the opinion that "girls always led men on."

At St. Mary's Hospital, Bourne carried out the abortion with the full permission of Miss M's parents. He did so while not keeping the procedure secret from other staff. He was inviting prosecution, and he got it. Within a few days the director of public prosecutions filed charges against Dr. Bourne under the 1861 act. Bourne, the BMA, and other medical groups could now ask the English courts to define more clearly the scope of doctors' abilities to perform abortions.

SUMMARY OF ARGUMENTS

Bourne's case was heard at the modern incarnation of the Old Bailey (London's Central Criminal Court) during July 1938. There was a jury of 12, including two women. The importance of the case may be surmised from the fact that England's attorney general, Sir Donald Somerville, was the leader of the prosecution.

Bourne contended that the object of the Offenses Against the Person Act of 1861 was to stop the dangerous practices of unlicensed abortionists. The defense proposed that the purpose of the legislation was not to interfere with the professional judgment of licensed physicians, particularly those prominent in their fields such as Dr. Bourne. Those in Bourne's camp maintained that a physician had to be able to act "in good faith to preserve the health" of his patient. But such an argument was making the role of physician discretion a bit broader than perhaps had earlier been contended. While it was commonplace to interpret the 1861 act as protective of patients' lives, their health had not been much discussed as an issue.

It was an even more difficult matter to argue that Miss M's life was endangered by the pregnancy, though Bourne certainly had a case to make that her mental health might be at stake. The question of the physical and emotional effects of pregnancy upon persons of Miss M's age was one that the medical community had debated recently. In 1936 the BMA had issued a report endorsing the view that pregnancy in young teenagers was to be avoided due to serious physical and psychological consequences. Bourne had been a member of the committee that generated the report. He later commented that he thought himself well supported by the medical community in bringing a test case. He assumed the "official" medical position already had been clearly stated in favor of revision of the Victorian law and that the courts would respect medical opinion in the matter.

Bourne's leading attorney, Roland Oliver, however, did not emphasize the fact that Miss M was well under the legal age of consent. Instead, his strategy was to throw the interpretation of the legislation in question—the acts of 1861 and 1929—into the judge's hands. This was something of a risk to Bourne, for Judge Malcolm Macnaghten might have directed the jury that the law had been getting progressively more protective of the unborn. Instead, Macnaghten reasoned that the 1861 act referred to "unlawfully procuring of miscarriage." He therefore surmised that there was room for physicians to act "lawfully" in performing abortions. The 1929 law the jurist interpreted as filling in a loophole with regard to when in pregnancy abortions might be performed. The 1929 act, therefore, did not speak much to the present situation; rather, Bourne's actions needed to be considered in relation to the Victorian law.

Justice Macnaghten's direction to the jury favored the defense, for it implied that the 1861 law had allowed room for lawful performance of abortions. Who was fitter to perform that procedure than a respected leader in his profession at a hospital in the current circumstance? It would have been difficult for the prosecution to undermine Bourne's position, and indeed, they did not.

Verdict

The jury's decision in *The King v. Bourne* (1938) reflected the direction of Judge Macnaghten, which in turn mirrored the defense arguments. The court said that Bourne's action had been within the scope of the 1861 act. The court went out of its way to note Bourne's seriousness in undertaking the case.

Britain's leading medical journal, *The Lancet*, wrote shortly after the *Bourne* decision that the trial had a worthwhile result: "Compulsory pregnancy for the victims of criminal assaults . . . is an idea abhorrent to civilised Society." Bourne later obtained leadership roles in medical societies. He continued a well-respected writing and teaching career as a gynecologist. Some recent scholars, though, argue that Bourne was denied a position within the most prestigious medical fraternity, the Royal College of Obstetricians and Gynecologists, because of his championing of a relaxation in the law.

Even after 1938 lesser-known health-care providers did well to consult with at least one other medical colleague before performing abortions; that helped insulate them from charges of profiting from abortions. Validation of the decision to perform an abortion by one's licensed medical colleagues was a good idea even when physicians were regular rather than nontraditional practitioners. Meanwhile, the trade in irregular abortions in Britain continued.

Significance

Between the decision in Bourne's trial and 1967, British doctors who performed abortions in hospitals usually were left alone. Occasionally prosecutors went after physicians who seemingly "made their livings" by performing abortions. Often the mode of determining who fell into that category was simply how much an abortionist charged for his or her services. (To ask too small a fee was to invite prosecution, for then one seemed to be trying to accumulate cases.) If one were unlicensed as a physician or operated outside regular medical

facilities, then one also ran a grave risk of arrest. The *Bourne* decision often was spoken of as heralding the "medicalization" of abortion in Great Britain.

The 1967 legislation that decriminalized abortions in Britain really was a legislative follow-up to *Bourne*. That newer law, however, did indicate to many medical practitioners that there was another element that would be key in legal abortions: the concurrence of mental health professionals in decisions about whether abortions were medically necessary. Bourne had used his prominence within the medical community to good effect at the trial in 1938, but he was not altogether pleased at the 1967 law. He did not believe in what was being called "abortion on demand." He supported abortion only in cases where pregnancy would cause serious medical (he said mental or physical) harm to the mother. Bourne in later life joined groups that called for legal protections for the unborn.

The parallel to the Bourne case in the United States was the twin set of decisions called *Roe v. Wade* and *Doe v. Bolton* (1971). While *Roe* and *Doe* did involve several of the same issues as the Bourne case, reaction to abortion's medicalization in the United States was very much more contentious than in Britain. Although in both *Bourne* and *Roe/Doe* the cases had been pushed by large medical groups, in the U.S. cases no single prestigious doctor was putting his career on the line. Also, the defendants in *Roe/Doe* were less the objects of sympathy among the public than Miss M had been. One was a young woman who claimed rape but never pressed charges, while the other woman who sought an abortion was a married person who felt pressured by her husband to limit their family size. It made a large difference, too, that *Roe* and *Doe* came along later in time. In the 1970s in the United States the medical profession was viewed with less deference than it had been in Britain in the 1930s.

While the 19th-century laws on abortion were substantially revised in Britain due to the Bourne case, such change occurred in the United States only with *Roe* and *Doe*. When Parliament saw fit to draft legislation on abortion, it leaned on the *Bourne* decision, a considerably well-established precedent. Some legal historians contend that the reason that the U.S. Congress never has drawn up a policy similar to Britain's Act of 1967 is the comparative weakness of the major American cases on abortion. That was in marked contrast to Britain, a country in which the leading abortion case included both a pitiable victim and a respected abortionist.

Further Reading

Bourne, Aleck. *A Doctor's Creed*. London: Gollancz, 1962; Brookes, Barbara, and Paul Roth. "*Rex v. Bourne* and the Medicalization of Abortion." In *Legal Medicine in History*, edited by Michael Clark and Catherine Crawford, 314–343. Cambridge: Cambridge University Press, 1994; Cawthon, Elisabeth. *Medicine on Trial*. Santa Barbara, Calif.: ABC-CLIO, 2004; De Costa, Caroline M. "The King versus Aleck Bourne." *Medical Journal of Australia* 191 (2009): 230–231; Keown, John. *Abortion, Doctors, and the Law*. Cambridge: Cambridge University Press, 1988.

The trial of Weerasamy and Velaithen

Also known as: *The Crown v. Ramasamy Weerasamy, Iyan Perumal Velaithen, Iyan Perumel Iyan Perumel, Ramasamy Rengasamy, Kalimuttu Sinne Muniandy, and Marimuttu Velaithen;* the Pope murder case

Date: 1941

KEY ISSUES

The Pope murder case took place during the twilight of British colonial control of the island then called Ceylon. Modern Sri Lanka was born in 1948, an independence closely tied to India's break with the British Empire. Britain had controlled Ceylon—though with some serious native resistance in 1818 and 1848—since the time of the Napoleonic Wars. With British governance was introduced the English legal system, with its focus on jury trials and adversarial justice.

Although that manner of resolving disputes had the potential to sit awkwardly in Ceylon throughout the almost two centuries of British rule, in fact, the people of Sri Lanka took to many British legal customs. The islanders, though at times deeply divided according to caste and ethnicity, employed certain elements in the meting out of justice that the British considered old fashioned but not necessarily invalid. For example, testimony might be supported by ordeals such as a witness plunging his hand into hot oil, or those called to the stand might take oaths while touching their foreheads three times. Scholars of the island's culture note that native people placed great store by the accurate and repetitive performance of rituals. A minor mistake by a sorcerer amid a complex rite could render the entire ceremony void. Such practices obviously called to mind earlier English legal customs, and thus, Anglo jurists often folded indigenous beliefs into courtroom procedure in Ceylon.

Indeed, the residents of British Ceylon had a reputation of being quite litigious. Colonial lawyers noted that the average individual in Ceylon followed court cases avidly in the newspapers and relished attending trials. Moreover, the ordinary person was likely to be involved in a civil case at least once during his or her life, irrespective of caste. The number of cases litigated there was noticeably high, even in comparison to nearby India.

The imperial legal administrators were less comfortable, though, with the Ceylonese attitude toward veracity in court. To British minds, the native people had an expansive definition of the truth. For instance, Sri Lankans might have no compunction about lying in court concerning a person accused of cattle theft—a crime often transpiring at night and difficult to prove—if the defendant was rumored to be a serial transgressor. Therefore, British officials were constantly discussing the issue of truthfulness among the native folk who came to court, especially in complex cases or trials involving more than one defendant.

Besides their law, another feature that the British introduced to Ceylon was plantations. Such places were sites for the growing of profitable crops such as tea, coffee, and rubber. British landlords concentrated on those enterprises to the detriment of an older focus on rice, which was the staple food in Ceylon. As less rice was grown, more had to be imported. The cash crops preferred by the imperial overlords drove the economy, and plantation owners became very powerful. In the meantime, rice was far less available and more expensive, and hunger grew in Ceylon. The British reliance on the tea crop was exaggerated when disease wiped out much coffee production on the island in 1875. Even prior to that shift British plantation owners had offered incentives to certain residents of southern India, the Tamils, to immigrate to Ceylon as plantation laborers working with both coffee and tea crops.

Tea production was even more labor intensive than coffee growing, and Tamil migration therefore continued through the late 19th century. The employment conditions for Tamil people on tea plantations were similar to circumstances faced by indentured persons elsewhere in the British Empire. The potential employer paid for one's passage, and then the worker was heavily indebted for his transport. In theory, the laborer could work off the debt and send money to his family back home, perhaps eventually returning to India himself. In practice, the plantation owners often imposed high costs for housing and food, placing the employees in a kind of semi-permanent bondage. The quarters of many plantation workers were sub par. Tea pickers usually lived in places called line rooms, which some likened to chicken coops for humans.

By the 20th century Tamils said that they felt estranged from other non-Anglos in Ceylon such as the higher-caste Sinhalese, who were concentrated in areas to the south and in western coastal towns. By the 1930s the Tamil laborers on tea estates had begun to agitate for workers' rights, with some affiliating with communist or leftist organizations such as the Sama Samajists and many expressing interest in trade unions. The estate workers' movements fed into organizations agitating for greater political and social rights based on Tamil ethnicity. Such groups, including such militant offshoots as the Tamil Tigers, became influential in the late 20th century in Sri Lanka.

HISTORY OF THE CASE

The Stellenberg estate was a tea plantation located near the small settlement of Pussellawa in the high-

lands of Ceylon, roughly in the center of the southern half of the island. Its environment, the mountainous Central Region, was prime growing land for tea. The area was dotted with similar large agricultural holdings, all managed by British landlords and their large staffs. Attached to most of the farms were processing facilities, called factories. The town of Gampola was the nearest community of any size near to the estate. Not far away was the "up-country capital" of Kandy, a center for the Kandyan kingdom that had flourished in the 16th through 18th centuries, before Dutch occupation.

In 1940 and early 1941 there had been labor unrest at the estate, as had occurred in several plantations in the region. An officer of the Estate Workers' Union headquartered at Kandy, a man named Meiappen, had been working at Stellenberg until January 1941, when he was dismissed. The person who did the firing was C. A. G. Pope, the superintendent (overseer) of the estate. Pope reportedly was angry about Meiappen's role as a labor organizer as well as his championing of the case of another worker, Ramasamy Weerasamy, whom Pope had let go in late 1940. Meiappen persisted in trying to get Weerasamy and himself reinstated, making certain that several letters from the Estate Workers' Union about the matter went to Pope. That correspondence became more and more demanding during the late winter and spring of 1941. The dispute culminated in a letter sent on April 26, 1941, that included a demand for a resolution in the workers' favor.

Meiappen himself had complicated reasons for standing up to Pope. First of all, he was friends with Weerasamy. Secondly, he appeared to believe that this was a chance to make the point that management ought not to bully the union. Finally, Meiappen and the union were engaged in something of a local power struggle with a nearby gang leader, Thatan Kangany, for the allegiance of workers. A demonstration of muscle against Pope would solidify the union's position as a defender of the employees so that they would not return to Kangany's gang.

Pope was infuriated with Meiappen, particularly after the superintendent received the threatening letter in late April. He knew that Meiappen not only was behind the demand letters from the union but also had refused to vacate his company lodgings at the estate. Pope swore out a formal complaint against Meiappen for criminal trespass. The police went looking for Meiappen, searching his room and inquiring after him among his coworkers and fellow union members. At some point after the launching of that search on May 7, 1941, Meiappen and several estate workers met at the union headquarters. Meiappen surrendered to the police the next day and was bailed out on the morning of May 9.

On the evening of May 9 Pope drove his car to another plantation to have dinner with its superintendent. Pope had gotten the invitation very recently and only on the 9th had told members of his staff where he was going. He left the other spot, the Le Vallon estate, at 11:00 P.M. As he approached the Stellenberg estate, he passed the tea-processing facility. The night watchman there called ahead to Pope's residence, as was his custom, to alert staff there to have Pope's garage open. Pope did not arrive as expected; the garage employee at the house called the factory security guard back. The guard went to find out what had happened. He found Pope lying on the road, unconscious and bleeding from several severe wounds to the head. Logs lying across the road had blocked the path of the auto. Those initially on the scene surmised that Pope was attacked when he got out of his vehicle to remove the obstacles.

Near the car were several objects out of place in that setting: a wooden club that was broken into several parts, an iron pipe, two bloodstained handkerchiefs, and a piece of broken cord of the type used to hang pictures. Pope died in about three hours without ever regaining consciousness. The police suspected that Meiappen was involved and quickly began inquiring after him. They also wanted to know who among Mieappen's associates might have known of Pope's dinner invitation.

The investigators identified a man named Iyan Perumel Iyan Perumel, who had been working inside Pope's residence on May 9 and had asked other domestic workers about Pope's plans. Later in the day Iyan Perumel was seen talking with a man named Iyan Perumal Velaithen, along with Weerasamy. The police began looking for these three laborers and Mieappen, as well as a man

called Ramasamy Rengasamy. Several people had told the police that one of the handkerchiefs at the murder scene was Rengasamy's. The second handkerchief was even more important, for attached to it was a key. When the police used the key to try to open doors on the Stellenberg estate, the only one it fit was the door to Weerasamy's line room.

Then police kept watch on the office of the Estate Workers' Union, thinking that some of the persons they had identified as suspects might go there for help. On May 11 authorities located an individual who they suspected was Weerasamy; he had shaved his head in a fashion unusual for Tamil workers and gave an improbable name. The police interrogated the man, who admitted that he was Weerasamy. Weerasamy gave a statement to police confessing to having helped his coworker Velaithen waylay and then bludgeon Pope. The investigators redoubled their efforts to locate Velaithen, sending out wanted notices.

On May 15, an employee named Santiago at Frotoft estate observed a person who looked to be of Tamil origin loitering on the premises. Especially after seeing what appeared to be bloodstains on the man's clothes, Santiago suspected that the man was Velaithen. He questioned the stranger, aided by another estate employee, Magarajah, who spoke Tamil. Magarajah inquired of the intruder who his confederates were—referring to the crime against Pope about which there had been word in the Tamil language newspapers. The visitor, who seemed desperate for food, quickly related six names. Magarajah jotted them down on an envelope that he happened to be carrying. He and Santiago turned over both the envelope and the stranger—who in fact was Velaithen—to the police. The police promptly arrested several people on the list.

The state alleged that a group of persons—prisoner no. 1, Ramasamy Weerasamy; prisoner no. 2, Iyan Perumal Velaithen; prisoner no. 3, Iyan Perumel Iyan Perumel; prisoner no. 4, Ramasamy Rengasamy; prisoner no. 5, Kalimuttu Sinne Muniandy, and prisoner no. 6, Marimuttu Velaithen—had conspired to murder Pope. According to the prosecution, the motive was simply revenge for Pope's firing of Meiappen and refusal to reinstate him and Weerasamy. Reading between the lines, however, it is not difficult to perceive a deeper theme: the perception that Pope represented a class of persons—plantation owners and their European overseers—who were exploitative to the Tamil tea workers.

The law in Ceylon allowed a case to be brought before a magistrate to determine if defendants should be committed for trial; that is, there was no necessity for a grand jury indictment. The magistrate's inquiry thus followed pretrial inquiries but preceded the criminal trial itself. In this case as with many others in Ceylon, the magistrate's inquiry allowed the lawyers for both sides to rehearse the arguments they would employ at trial.

There was a large and very active bar in Ceylon. This case was typical in that the prosecution lawyer was of European origin while the defense lawyers were primarily of Asian descent. The chief attorney for the Crown, O. L. de Kretser, Jr., was of mixed Dutch-British heritage, nicely reflecting Ceylon's history as first a Dutch and then British colony. A team of four attorneys represented all of the prisoners except Rengasamy, who retained two lawyers of his own.

Although the magistrate in Gampola, Ivor de Saram, committed the case for trial, he had to sort out which of the numerous statements made by potential defendants could be admitted into evidence. The law in Ceylon was somewhat more protective of defendants' rights in regard to confessions than even English law at the time. Thus, Weerasamy's confession to the police was not legitimate in court because he already was under suspicion and de Sarum was not convinced that Weerasamy had been thoroughly apprised of his rights. The magistrate, however, did allow the prosecution to present Velaithen's statements to Santiago and Magarajah. The issue there was not the incriminating nature of the statements nor even the point during the investigation in which the statements were made but rather the identity of the questioner. The Crown argued that Santiago was not "a person in authority" according to the law but rather simply a private citizen who had detained Velaithen and turned him in.

The Fourth Western Circuit of the Main Assize Court of Ceylon met at the island's largest city, Colombo. It heard the case against Weerasamy, Velaithen, and their four colleagues. The trial went on between December 1 and 19, 1941. Kandy had a circuit court, but the defendants were awarded a change of venue to try to guard against prejudice owing to the publicity that Pope's murder had engendered already.

SUMMARY OF ARGUMENTS

The defense made its case based on arguments of law and fact. In a legal sense the defense concentrated on the confession of Velaithen as well as the statements made by other defendants to magistrates upon their apprehension. The lawyers for prisoners 3–6 contended that the police had beaten or otherwise coerced their clients. Those defendants retracted their earlier statements of complicity in the killing of Pope. The Crown viewed such a line of argument as typical of native persons' slipperiness in court. It tried to establish that there was a pact among the defendants for Weerasamy and Velaithen to take the blame for the crime and then for the defense lawyers to allege police misconduct and the legality of the two principals' statements.

The lawyers for the accused men contested the admissibility of Velaithen's remarks to Santiago, maintaining that Santiago had the role of a person with authority over individuals such as Velaithen. Thus, Velaithen deferred to Santiago and gave him information that he would not have given a person more equivalent in social station. The prosecution responded that Velaithen was desperate for food because he had been on the run for a week after fleeing the scene of a brutal assault. In that condition—a situation of his own making—the fugitive had offered information that proved helpful to the formal authorities.

The defense also argued that one of the bloodstained handkerchiefs found at the crime scene (a blue cloth) was not Regasamy's at all but rather Pope's. It was difficult, however, for the defense to counter the effect of the other kerchief (a red one), to which Weerasamy's key was attached. In addition, upon his arrest Velaithen had a neck laceration that investigators argued corresponded closely to the cord left at the place of the assault. Their contention was that in the course of Pope's desperate struggle with his attackers he had broken the cord from around Velaithen's neck.

The final gambit by the defense was to suggest that the best motive for killing Pope was not that nursed by the estate workers but rather the gang leader Kangay. According to that scenario from the defense, it was Kangay who was the real villain in the piece. Defense lawyers maintained that the police were not concentrating on Kangay because certain of their number were corrupt and the estate workers who had recent quarrels with Pope were easier targets. The police had hauled these Tamil workers into custody and manhandled them into incriminating themselves.

The prosecution presented a more straightforward case, although it was hampered by the difficulty of establishing that Velaithen's statement could be considered under the law. The Crown also had to step around the information that Weerasamy had given to police. The prosecution's theory of how and why the crime had occurred was, however, believable: Meaippen's friends had rushed to his defense by lying in wait for Pope near the factory on the night of May 9. Velaithen and Weerasamy had struck the fatal blows with a club and the iron pipe. The others had helped stop the car via the logs, turned off the car lights once Pope was struck down in order to avoid drawing attention to the scene, and helped the two main assailants escape and hide.

VERDICT

The jury, which the court record indicates were all English speakers, took just over an hour to deliberate. They found defendants nos. 1 and 2, Weerasamy and Velaithen, guilty of murder. The other accused men were declared not guilty. Justice Francis Soertsz released the four acquitted men with the statement that he concurred in the verdict. His comment to the convicted individuals was without bombast. He did note, though, that the murder of Pope had been more savage than any killing he had seen at bench or bar. He said that to impose the sentence of death was an easy decision for him. Soertsz respited the men's executions until the end of January 1942 to allow for the expected appeal.

The Court of Criminal Appeal found no grounds to consider an appeal from Weerasamy but took under serious consideration the argument of Velaithen's attorneys concerning Santiago's role in the case. After hearing several learned arguments about confessions and to whom they might be made, the three-judge appeals panel concluded that Santiago did not fit within any of the accepted categories of the law's determination of "persons in authority." The appeals court therefore dismissed Velaithen's appeal.

The men were executed on February 27 and 28, 1942. Velaithen's last recorded words were in a short note to his lawyer, B. G. S. David: "We thank you for all that you have done to try to save us from the hangman's rope. You tried your best, sir, but failed. The fault is in our stars. Long live the workers' raj!"

SIGNIFICANCE

Shortly after the executions of Weerasamy and Velaithen, prosecuting attorney Oswald de Kretser published a full record of the trial. World War II may have prohibited the volume from being well disseminated despite the fame of the case in the region. The Pope murder became better known only about 60 years later, with the 21st-century publication of a novel loosely grounded in the proceedings, by de Kretser's daughter.

Certain customs associated with English law such as oath swearing, ordeals, and even the insistence on technical precision in the wording of court documents were unexpectedly compatible with the native practices of Ceylon. Other aspects of criminal trials, such as the meaning of confessions, found English and Sinhalese people more at odds. The Pope case presented an opportunity for Anglo jurists to apply increasingly strict standards concerning confession, from the home country to the colonies.

This the colonial masters did with some attention to fairness. Did the Pope case represent a just decision? The language of both trial and appeals officials was moderate and very much in keeping with contemporary standards on the admissibility of confessions. Were the estate workers justified in being angry with Pope? He comes across in the case records as an inflexible, perhaps retributive man. Clearly he was the representative of a class of persons whom the workers had good reason to resent. The verdict in the trial of his six murderers reflected both British legal sensitivities and native sensibilities. It cast ultimate blame on the two men who rained blows onto Pope but exonerated those who merely supported the killing.

Further Reading

de Kretser, Oswald L. *The Pope Murder Case.* Colombo, Ceylon: Hamer Bros., 1942; de Kretser, Michelle. *The Hamilton Case: A Novel.* New York: Little, Brown, 2005; Ferdinands, Rodney. *Proud and Prejudiced: The Story of the Burghers of Sri Lanka.* Melbourne, Australia: R. Ferdinands, 1995; *The King v. Weerasamy, et al.* 56-M.C. Gampola, 2, 172 (1942). Available online. URL: http://www.lawnet.lk/docs/case_law/nlr/common/html/NLR43V207.htm. Accessed July 20, 2010; Rogers, John D. *Crime, Justice, and Society in Colonial Sri Lanka.* London: Curzon, 1987; Spittel, R. L. *Wild Ceylon.* Colombo, Ceylon: Colombo Apothecaries, 1933.

The trial of William Joyce

Also known as: *The King v. Joyce;* the trial of Lord Haw-Haw

Date: 1945

KEY ISSUES

William Joyce has the dubious distinction of being the last person executed in England on a charge of treason. Joyce was widely known during World War II as a voice in support of Germany. His sneering and pseudo-aristocratic speaking style—heard during German radio broadcasts aimed at the Allies—earned him the nickname "Lord Haw-Haw." Just after the conclusion of the war Joyce was tried, convicted, and hanged as a traitor. Vital

to his conviction was the fact that although he worked against British interests during the war, he held a British passport.

Joyce's trial and the unsuccessful legal appeals were well publicized in late 1945 and early 1946. Press attention was keen not just in Britain but all over the world, since his case was among the first treason prosecutions in Britain when the war ended. It would be easy to see Joyce's trial and execution simply as acts of catharsis for the British nation, but the case had longer-term implications.

That Joyce was tried in British courts at all became a point of objection by legal scholars, who on the grounds of Joyce's citizenship status considered the proceedings illegal. This view put them at odds with the general public, who were happy to see Joyce hang. Despite intellectuals' misgivings, courts around the world continued to cite the Joyce case when questions arose about national loyalty.

HISTORY OF THE CASE

Joyce's biographers concur that he was a complex and driven man who inspired loyalty among many who knew him. Biographers also agree on certain unsavory aspects of Joyce's life and character such as his penchant for street fighting, unflagging idolization of Adolf Hitler, and an abiding anti-Semitism.

It is of fundamental importance to note that William Joyce was born in New York City in 1906. His parents were native Britons who had immigrated to the United States. Joyce's father, Michael, was naturalized as a U.S. citizen in 1894. Thus, Joyce was a native-born citizen of the United States according to the laws of the time.

The Joyce family was disappointed with life in the United States and decided to return to the British Isles. From at least 1923, Joyce was an active participant in British fascist groups. About a year after Oswald Mosley began the British Union of Fascists (BUF), Joyce signed on, soon becoming propaganda director. He and Mosley fell out in 1937, with Joyce forming his own National Socialist League (NSL). Joyce was an impressive speaker. Even those who detested his message had to admit that he could be mesmerizing.

In the late spring or summer of 1939 evidence suggests that Joyce decided he could not continue to live in England. On August 24 he applied for a one-year renewal of his British passport, repeating an earlier affirmation from a previous passport that he was a British subject. It is likely that Joyce and his wife, Margaret, departed from England by boat on August 26.

Upon arrival in Germany Joyce quickly put himself at the service of the Nazi apparatus. Soon he secured a job with the Reichsrundfunk (RRF), the radio propaganda operation headed by Joseph Goebbels. Joyce proved a success in his adopted land. Joyce remained the Germans' favorite English-language radio broadcaster throughout the war. In addition, Joyce directed the process of recruiting British POWs as radio speakers.

What exactly did Joyce say over the radio? For the most part his broadcasts were exhortations about German racial, political, and military superiority and about Hitler himself. During the war Joyce was at his most dangerous not as a disseminator of news per se or even as a villifier of leaders such as Winston Churchill. Rather, Joyce was personally familiar with England and Ireland and could exploit that knowledge to spread disquiet. Joyce proved most memorable to the British, and most feared, as a person who was rumored to have intimate awareness of daily activities in individual localities.

Joyce did not possess such knowledge. It was his British connections and vaguely learned accent that gave him an air of authority not easily shaken off. The Allies captured Joyce in late May 1945, in a village near the Danish border. He was brought back to England to stand trial. By the time Joyce was required to enter a formal plea in court on June 21, 1945, both Joyce's lawyers and the press realized that Joyce's nationality was going to be an issue.

SUMMARY OF ARGUMENTS

The Joyce case involved vexing questions of law. Among the topics that had to be taken into account were rules on treason, passports, alien status, and citizenship. Despite the technicalities of the arguments the case attracted great press attention and even inspired some memorable writing. Journalist Rebecca West, for example, covered Joyce's trial in elegant detail.

The indictment against Joyce was comparatively straightforward; it listed three counts of treason. Within a couple of days after the commencement of the trial Judge Frederick James Tucker had heard convincing evidence that Joyce was an American and therefore could not be tried as a British citizen. The judge then asked the prosecution if they wished to challenge that evidence; they could not do so and thus the first two counts of the indictment—which hinged on his British citizenship—effectively were not applicable. The only count against Joyce that the court allowed the prosecution to use to any effect was count three, which was related to his owing allegiance to Britain. That count said he had committed treason between September 18, 1939, and July 2, 1940, the date of his first known employment at the RRF and the date that his last British passport expired. This count hinged on the matter of Joyce's possessing a British passport that was valid during a time when he was broadcasting for the Germans.

The dismissal of the first two counts was a major blow to the government's case in both legal and practical terms. On the day on which the judge's ruling came down, Attorney General Hartley Shawcross solicited the opinion of an expert in constitutional law, Professor J. H. Morgan: "Have we any chance?" asked Shawcross. Morgan's answer was discouraging: ". . . not unless the judge is prepared to make new law." Legally, the prosecution was backed against the wall because now it had to argue that Joyce owed allegiance "to our Lord the King" solely on the basis of his holding a British passport. The court had ruled that Joyce was an alien. Was Joyce, who was not a British citizen, to be required to submit to the authority of the British Crown at a time when he was not physically present within the country? The prosecution's only legal hope of winning the case consisted of convincing the court to answer "yes" to that query.

In a practical sense as well as in legal terms, the case was going poorly for the prosecution. The judge had narrowed the scope of the evidence that could be produced against Joyce. What the prosecution needed to do was to demonstrate that after Joyce's formal employment began with the RRF, but before his British passport expired, he had broadcast for Germany. The difficulty was that the Germans had confirmed Lord Haw-Haw's voice as being Joyce's only in the spring of 1940. So, unless the government produced a witness who could identify Joyce's voice, any broadcasts prior to the spring of 1940 could not be entered into evidence. There was one bit of good news for the prosecution, though: Due to a recent change in the law only one witness rather than two was required to provide evidence of an overt act of treason. Thus, if one person could identify Joyce as a broadcaster during that time, he might be convicted of treason.

The government made its argument based on the personal knowledge of one witness, Inspector Albert Hunt of Scotland Yard. Hunt had seen and heard Joyce when the Metropolitan Police followed him as a BUF official in the 1930s. Therefore, when Hunt was monitoring radio broadcasts during the fall of 1939, he was certain that he recognized Lord Haw-Haw's voice to be that of Joyce. Hunt recalled one particular broadcast that he was listening to at Folkstone in which Joyce claimed that a Luftwaffe bombing raid had destroyed Dover and Folkstone. Hunt could assess the report's veracity by simply looking out the window and seeing the town was still standing.

Before the prosecution could pursue its presentation of Hunt, however, the tenor of the trial changed very much to the detriment of Joyce. Justice Tucker instructed the jury in regard to the one count still under consideration. Tucker stated that from the renewal of the passport on August 24, 1939, until July 1940, "the prisoner undoubtedly owed allegiance to the Crown of this country." Tucker determined that Joyce, an alien who possessed a passport to which he was not entitled, by the mere fact of holding the passport was required to refrain from adhering to Britain's enemy. Thus, if the jury found that Joyce had "aided and comforted" Germany after the outbreak of formal hostilities on September 3, 1939, he could be convicted.

Most of the legal experts who watched the trial at that point thought Joyce as good as convicted. The testimony from Inspector Hunt was somewhat vague, and Joyce's counsel, Slade, did his best to weaken Hunt's impact. But still, it looked as though the judge was prepared to see this case as one that required some flexibility in interpreting past law. That leaning continued in Judge Tucker's summation to the jury. It was a lengthy statement.

Tucker seemed to be suggesting lines of argument that the defense might pursue in the event of an appeal. He reminded the jurors that Inspector Hunt's identification of Joyce in one particular broadcast was key evidence. If the jury believed Hunt, then they had to consider whether that broadcast had been with the intent of aiding Germany. If they thought Joyce had assisted the enemy knowingly, then they had to convict him of treason. It took the jurors 23 minutes to agree with the prosecution.

VERDICT

The conviction carried a mandatory death sentence. Appeal was automatic to the Court of Criminal Appeal. Joyce's lawyers argued for reversal on four grounds: 1) The court lacked jurisdiction to try an alien for crimes committed abroad; 2) the jury should not have been directed that Joyce owed allegiance to Britain between September 18, 1939, and July 2, 1940; 3) the passport issued on August 24, 1939, had not given Joyce any protection; and 4) the question of whether Joyce had been protected by the passport was for the jury rather than the judge to decide. Thomas Inskip, Viscount Caldecote, delivered the opinion of the court. It was a brisk affirmation of several of the decisions that Judge Tucker had made at trial, notably his jury instructions; Joyce's conviction should stand.

The attorney general then gave permission for Joyce's defense lawyers to appeal to the House of Lords sitting in its judicial capacity. Their decision in *Joyce v. Director of Public Prosecutions (Joyce v. DPP)* began by agreeing with the attorney general that the case was of unusual importance. Of the five "law lords" at the time, only Samuel Lord Porter had served in the British armed forces. He was decorated for front line service in World War I. Porter had gone on to become an expert in international law by the time he gained the peerage. Porter offered a dissent from the lords' affirmation of the death sentence. Porter's expertise gave his dissenting opinion in Joyce's final appeal a cachet that might not ordinarily have attached to a minority judicial view.

Porter maintained that the jury was entitled to consider whether Joyce had retained and used the passport that Joyce had obtained on August 24, 1939, at least through September 18, the date on which he was in the employ of German radio. Porter said that when Judge Tucker did not instruct the jury to consider that question at trial, Tucker had made such a serious error that the whole verdict should be thrown into doubt. Porter made it plain that he placed special responsibility on trial judges to take care that justice was done fairly when a case concerned the inflammatory matter of disloyalty. For a judge to usurp the functions of a jury, Porter implied, was more dangerous than to let a traitor go free. And yet, in certain respects Porter's dissent still was a rather narrow criticism of the previous decisions, for Porter did not dispute another point that was even more central to Joyce's case: the question of whether Joyce's passport carried with it the duty to give Britain allegiance.

The majority of the law lords noted that national loyalty was difficult for either the native born or the naturalized Briton to cast off and that the maxim *nemo potest exuere patriam* (no one can renounce his own country) had been moderated only in recent times. The judges admitted that aliens who once had claimed the protection of the monarch were a special case, though clearly they owed allegiance to Britain and the monarch while they were within the physical confines of the nation.

The judges who upheld Joyce's conviction in the House of Lords decided that allegiance was not completely dependent on the alien's physical location. An alien committed treason if he relied on the king's protection, even while operating against the nation abroad. Without evidence that Joyce had withdrawn his allegiance from Britain (for instance, by turning in his passport), the majority of the law lords believed that Joyce had come within the meaning of the words of an old but still operative treason regulation: According to the statute of Edward III (the Treason Act of 1351), Joyce had "adhered to the King's enemies."

Trying Joyce and letting him hang were very different matters, or so it was argued by many academics who examined Joyce's case. Few experts who wrote in the shadow of the Joyce case contended that Joyce should not have been charged

with something. Yet, most scholars argued that it was wrong to execute him.

Much of this opinion was expressed only in the abstract with regard to Joyce's fate, for he had been hanged in January 1946 even before the formal decision of the House of Lords on his final appeal had been published. One of the more curious aspects of the debate over Joyce was that it usually did not refer to his fascist colleague, Sir Oswald Mosley. While held in detention during most of the war, Mosley had not been (and would not ever be) charged with treason, despite the fact that in a personal sense he was quite friendly with Hitler. Joyce, meanwhile, had never met his and Mosley's hero.

SIGNIFICANCE

Joyce's fate continued to exert influence in courts all over the world where English law was applied. Courts that evoked the decisions of *R. v. Joyce* (his first appeal of conviction) and especially *Joyce v. DPP* (the decision of the final authority that rejected his appeal) usually did so approvingly. Joyce's conviction was applied to a surprising variety of areas of law.

The Joyce trial decision and subsequent appeals were cited in several postwar treason cases in the United States. The most important of those decisions, *Chandler v. U.S.,* in 1948, concerned the conviction of Douglas Chandler, an American broadcaster for the Nazis. Although Chandler got life in prison rather than the death penalty, his case had many similarities to Joyce's, certain of which were noted by the courts.

If the *Joyce* decisions remained widely known among Commonwealth nations and the United States, then one might expect them to be evoked within Britain, as well. Indeed, they appeared with some frequency with respect to cases involving national status. Judges as well as counsel cited *Joyce v. DPP* and *R. v. Joyce* in a number of cases well after the postwar treason trials, especially controversies concerning passports.

Who, besides a citizen, could be a traitor and under what circumstances? How could a person renounce national allegiance, especially during wartime? What duties did an alien owe to a host government? Those queries resonated long after the era of World War II. Particularly in the context of international travel, the Joyce case remained instructive because it spoke to the nature and responsibilities of citizenship.

Further Reading

Barnes, Thomas G. *The Trial of William Joyce, "Lord Haw-Haw."* Birmingham, Ala.: Legal Classics Library, 1987; *Chandler v. U.S.* 171 F. 2d 927 (1948). Available online. URL: http://libproxy.uta.edu:2156/hottopics/?. Accessed August 1, 2005; Cole, J. A. *Lord Haw-Haw and William Joyce, the Full Story.* New York: Farrar, Straus, & Giroux, 1964; Hall, J. W., ed. *The Trial of William Joyce.* London: W. Hodge, 1946; Joyce, William. *Twilight over England.* Berlin, Germany: Internationaler Verlag, 1940; *Joyce v. Director of Public Prosecutions* 1 All E.R. 186 (1946). Available online. URL: http://libproxy.uta.edu:2156/hottopics/?. Accessed July 27, 2005; Kenney, Mary. *Germany Calling.* Dublin, Ireland: New Island Books, 2003; Martland, Peter. *Lord Haw Haw: The English Voice of Nazi Germany.* London: National Archives, 2003; Simpson, A. W. Brian. *In the Highest Degree Odious: Detention without Trial in Wartime Britain.* Oxford, U.K.: Clarendon Press, 1992; West, Rebecca. *The Meaning of Treason.* London: Macmillan, 1949.

The Nuremberg War Crimes Trials

Date: 1945–1949

KEY ISSUES

Just as World War II was unprecedented in scope, the Nuremberg War Crimes Trials also were unique in addressing war's destruction through judicial procedures. Leaders among the vanquished stood accused of crimes that caused universal revulsion: the killing of millions of Jews and other groups, as well as opponents of Nazism; the forced relocations of Jews and other individuals and groups, and the drafting of defeated populations

into slave labor. Yet, when the trials began, the acts with which the Nuremberg defendants were charged were ill defined in international law.

Punishing the leaders of a defeated nation was nothing new in 1945, but such retribution almost always was not tied to a civilian judicial process. It was accomplished for example, through the actions of military commanders who simply dispatched their opponents or—more rarely—let them escape alive. Occasionally, as with the two examples of Napoleon Bonaparte's major defeats during the 1810s, nations might bargain among themselves diplomatically about a captured leader's fate. Sometimes they let justice run its course within each sovereign state. In the mid-20th century most international lawyers still maintained the traditional view that the legal treatment of persons accused of crimes connected with war lay with military authorities if the accused was a military person or civilian authorities in his or her home nation if he or she was a civilian.

Would international agreements such as the Kellogg-Briand Pact of 1928 bind signatories to stop using war as an instrument of aggrandizement? Such was the hope of the nations that had endured World War I in the 1910s. By signing the Covenant of the League of Nations, countries had pledged to view aggressive war as a criminal act. Yet, key definitions such as the meaning of *aggression* were missing from those international agreements. That made enforcement of the pacts difficult in a judicial setting. Courts among most of the leading powers of the world tried accused persons based on specific laws. Further, those laws had to be in force within the relevant countries before the crimes had taken place.

During World War II the Allied powers debated how they would proceed if they captured Axis leaders at the war's conclusion. At conferences during the war the "Big Three" mulled over several options for punishing their enemies. Great Britain, the Soviet Union, and the United States leaned toward swift retribution by military authorities. There were influential persons within Franklin Roosevelt's administration, notably U.S. secretary of the treasury Henry Morgenthau, who argued for decisive and punitive action against both the German nation and its leaders. Winston Churchill himself did not significantly differ with such an approach; indeed, the prevalent position among British bureaucrats was that war criminals should be "shot out of hand."

Beneath his bluster Joseph Stalin consistently maintained that enemy leaders should die only after sitting through a trial. Despite the other Allies' belief that Stalin was advocating only show proceedings such as he had put on in Moscow in the late 1930s, his public posturing posed a quandary for the Western Allies. How could the democratic powers argue against a trial for war criminals when Stalin advocated one?

Persuasive voices within the Roosevelt administration advocated a judicial hearing for war criminals. Secretary of War Henry Stimson supported the World Court and during the 1940s envisioned such a body presiding over justice for war criminals. Still, the Allied governments had limited resources during the war to undertake such plans because they were engaged in the conflict itself. They also were concerned that if they made plans for trials, it might spur enemy leaders to commit further atrocities to cover their tracks.

Public opinion during World War II played a role in altering the Allies' policy. Certain U.S. lawmakers maintained that war criminals should be accountable within their own nations for criminal acts, but then Americans saw evidence of concentration camp deaths and reprisals against Allied POWs late in the war. The electorate put pressure on U.S. leaders to charge Nazi leaders with crimes that had occurred in several nations—indeed, crimes that represented policies of transnational scope.

In London in October 1943 the Allies, excluding the Soviet Union, put together a general sketch for an international War Crimes Commission. At the end of the war, drawing a specific blueprint for war crimes trials was affected by the death of President Roosevelt in April 1945. Roosevelt's successor, Harry Truman, believed that a trial of Axis war leaders should be real rather than for show. Truman's view prevailed: He hoped that carefully planned and fairly administered war crimes proceedings would enhance the prestige of the victors.

HISTORY OF THE CASES

The four major powers that won World War II—the United States, the Soviet Union, France, and Great Britain—launched trials based on extensive negotiations among themselves that had picked up speed in the late spring of 1945. Separate trials were held concerning war crimes that had occurred in the Pacific theater. The proceedings converging Europe took place beginning in November 1945 and ran through 1949. The trials in Europe were before specially constructed military courts: the International Military Tribunal (IMT) and the U.S. Nuremberg Military Tribunals (NMT).

The Nuremberg War Crimes Trials were a hybrid of military and civilian justice. For example, the prosecutions occurred before tribunals, which were temporary judicial bodies rather than standing courts. Nuremberg featured participation by certain Allied military officials, such as the U.S. general Telford Taylor as chief counsel for war crimes. The Nuremberg trials, however, operated not according to principles of military law but rather under tenets of international law as well as elements from Continental and Anglo-American judicial systems.

The blending of Continental and English rules concerning trial procedures was the result of delicate negotiations among the Allies in mid-1945 concerning the tribunals' operation. In the Continental tradition, for example, testimony was heard before a panel of judges rather than by a judge and jury. Also familiar to Continental jurists was Nuremberg's admission of hearsay, a type of evidence not usually allowed in English and U.S. courtrooms.

Reminiscent of the principle in international law that war criminals generally were tried in their homelands, the proceedings took place in Germany. The trial site at Nuremberg had political implications. Nuremberg was the location of the greatest Nazi Party rally in the prewar period (1934), an event widely seen in filmmaker Leni Riefenstahl's *Triumph of the Will*. It also was the place where in 1935 Germany introduced the Nuremberg Race Laws that severely curtailed the civil rights of Jews and other minority groups.

According to modern English principles, the prosecution and defense were allowed equal time for a presentation of their cases, and counsel was permitted to the defendants. In the end, though, the tribunals operated in ways that seemed to hearken mostly to U.S. law; for instance, the tribunals' rules gave the right of cross-examination to defendants. In the most practical sense the Nuremberg trials had an American flavor, heavily peopled as they were with judges, military figures, and lawyers from the United States. The chief prosecutor at Nuremberg was a sitting justice on the U.S. Supreme Court, Robert H. Jackson. A particularly Anglo-American feature of the charges was the inclusion of counts of conspiracy.

The four judges overseeing the trials represented the greatest Allied powers. The judges made decisions by majority vote, with the chief judge (from Britain) having authority to break ties. Testimony and evidence were translated into the four languages of the key powers (English, French, and Russian, as well as German), and the defendants heard testimony in their own native languages. The difficulty of providing those translation services alone made the Nuremberg trials complicated and time consuming.

The most famous of the tribunals were the IMT's hearing of cases against well-known political and military figures such as Hermann Göring and Rudolf Hess in 1945–46, and the NMT's case concerning medical figures, the "Doctors' Trial" in 1946–47. The defendants all were accused of war crimes and crimes against humanity, although the precise statements of their alleged offenses varied. The IMT conducted 13 trials: an initial proceeding against 22 major figures that lasted about one year, followed by 12 separate trials called the Subsequent Nuremberg Proceedings. The trial of major figures was the highest-profile proceeding.

Summary of Arguments

The four major crimes with which the defendants at Nuremberg were charged were conspiracy, crimes against peace, war crimes, and crimes against humanity. Not every defendant was charged with every offense. Of the four categories of offenses war crimes were the type of charge most familiar in international and national laws. To commit a war crime was to maltreat enemy soldiers or POWs or to inflict violence on civilians.

The conspiracy charges meant that persons who belonged to certain political and military groups, most especially the Nazi Party, were prima facie liable to prosecution. Including conspiracy

counts at Nuremberg meant that any individual who had joined the Nazi Party at a time when that organization was not prohibited by German law later could have party membership used against him in court. According to the indictments in this case, the conspiracies alleged consisted of membership in organizations such as the Nazi Party that planned and oversaw policies of military aggression on an international scale.

To be charged with committing crimes against peace was tantamount to saying that a defendant had helped initiate World War II. The Nuremberg trials were the first major instance in world history of nations' leaders being prosecuted for starting a war. Similarly, the prosecutions for crimes against humanity were unique in 1945, and Nuremberg also was the first occasion on which defendants were charged with persecution that they had carried out on religious or racial grounds. These accusations were the charges connected with the killings and other acts against Jews and a number of groups that had been targeted before and during the war. Although the allegations necessarily concerned not only the period of declared hostilities in Europe but also the prewar era, the Nuremberg tribunals ruled that they were not trying defendants for acts that they had committed prior to the diplomatic breakdown between nations in 1939.

The evidence against the defendants consisted of their writings and other paper documentation and the testimony of eyewitnesses. Also certain information such as film footage that traditionally had not been a part of criminal proceedings was important at Nuremberg. The Allies had created a portion of that visual record in the last stages of the war, for instance, at the liberation of concentration camps. The alleged war criminals had produced many images for their own purposes, and those the prosecution also wielded to strong effect.

The German state and the Nazis had been unusually diligent record keepers, thus, during the Nuremberg prosecutions Allied prosecutors traced party membership using the Nazis' own materials. In addition, the Nazis were concerned about preserving a record of their actions for posterity. The German propaganda films and newspaper editorials that berated Jews and spoke more or less openly of the killing of persons with mental disabilities, came back to haunt defendants such as

Julius Streicher who were charged with spreading inflammatory ideas that culminated in genocide.

VERDICTS

In the first Nuremberg trial three persons were acquitted; four were sentenced to lengthy prison terms, and three, to life terms; and 12 were given the death penalty. But, even among those high-profile convicts, there were gaps because many key Nazis either were dead or missing. Adolf Hitler had died by his own hand as Berlin fell to Soviet troops. Likewise, the Nazi minister of propaganda, Joseph Goebbels, died in the Riechschancellory bunker, and Heinrich Himmler of the Gestapo and the SS committed suicide rather than be put on trial. It was likely that Martin Bormann, a leader in the Nazi Party and a close associate of Hitler, died while fleeing Berlin in the war's final days, but at Nuremberg he was tried and sentenced to death in absentia. Göring was the highest Nazi official who survived the war to be tried at Nuremberg.

Of those supposed to be punished with death, 11 actually were executed; Göring committed suicide after sentencing. Among those who garnered the death penalty was Joachim von Ribentropp, who had been Germany's foreign minister during the war. He had not only presided over German takeovers of much of central and western Europe but also advocated to local leaders the mass killing of Jews in those countries. Himmler's second in command in the SS, Ernst Kaltenbrunner, stood convicted of viewing deaths at the gas chambers in concentration camps; he had written of the need to kill prisoners who could not work. The former cabinet-level officer in charge of the eastern sector, Alfred Rosenberg, was convicted and executed for enforcing policies that led to the murders of thousands of Jewish persons. Wilhelm Frick, the former head of the Interior Ministry, was hanged for similar offenses in central Europe; he had worked closely with Himmler to eliminate supposed "security threats" and in the process had facilitated thousands of executions.

Wilhelm Keitel and Alfred Jodl were German military officials who had authorized the executions of military captives, sometimes recommending to Hitler that such actions occur en masse.

Both men admitted at Nuremberg that their actions were in contravention of the existing rules of conduct for war and were among the defendants sentenced to death. Streicher was unique among the major defendants in that he did not hold an official government or Nazi position. But, the Nuremberg tribunal found that, as a newspaper publisher, Streicher was able to foment hatred against Jews and other groups in pursuance of Nazi policies. Streicher's words, the court found, had led to many deaths; he was sentenced to hang.

The tribunal labored to make its punishments consistent with the severity of the crimes for which defendants were convicted. Yet, although all of the major defendants had key responsibilities for war and genocide, not all got the supreme penalty. Some of the differences in sentencing seemed to boil down to the accused persons' demeanor during trial.

Göring presented particular difficulties for prosecutors because he attempted to influence other prisoners, indeed, to manage the entire defense effort. He bantered with prosecutor Jackson during cross-examination, usually expressing contempt for the legitimacy of trials. The Allies tried to find ways to undercut Göring's self-confidence and lessen his effect on other prisoners. Finally, British attorney general Hartley Shawcross and prosecutor David Maxwell-Fyfe managed to deflate Göring on the stand with specific questions about reprisals against British POWs. Göring had maintained that there was a "code of honor" among "Teutonic" nations, but mass executions of enemy soldiers gave the lie to his supposed principles.

A quite different character was Albert Speer, the chief architect for the grand buildings either constructed or planned by Hitler and the Nazis. At trial Speer appeared cooperative in contrast to the egocentric Göring. Upon cross-examination Speer seemed ready to shoulder some individual blame for Nazi policies that included authorizing forced labor for his projects. Critics at the time and subsequently pondered whether Speer simply was acting in a manner that he expected would play well with his captors or he indeed suffered pangs of conscience for his actions.

Certain major figures who were indicted with the others did not suffer the death penalty for unusual reasons. The NMT ruled that German businessman Gustav Krupp was mentally unfit for trial. In effect, the court did the same for defendant Hess. Hess had been a close associate of the Fuhrer during Hitler's early years in power. He stood trial for serious offenses such as helping initiate hostilities in eastern Europe. Hess's behavior in the courtroom was bizarre, and his flight to England during the war also raised questions as to his mental competence. That Hess was handed a life sentence rather than death was widely viewed as an act of mercy by the court.

The Allies took special care to photograph the corpses of the executed criminals to counter rumors among Nazi admirers that the men somehow had escaped. After the prosecution of the major leaders, both the IMT and NMT heard additional cases of slightly less well-placed officials. In those subsequent trials at Nuremberg 177 persons were accused of war crimes, and 97 were convicted. The most famous set of trials among the subsequent cases were those concerning individuals who had conducted involuntary medical procedures on prisoners and other civilians during the war.

At the Doctors' Trial, 23 people, the majority of them physicians, were charged with the same four counts as the major defendants: belonging to criminal groups, engaging in conspiracy, committing war crimes, and perpetrating crimes against humanity. Most of the offenses had involved actions that the defendants called medical experimentation. A theme of the prosecution was that the so-called experiments in fact had limited or no medical value and were designed either to further military goals or simply to inflict pain. For example, the prosecution introduced evidence that the tests run on concentration camp inmates to chronicle their resistance to cold water were efforts to decide how long German sailors could survive after ocean immersion. In addition, the tribunal heard evidence that even their fellow Nazis scorned some of the procedures as unscientific. In the end the tribunal cared not whether any of the doctors' actions could be justified as scientifically valuable. The persons who had been the "subjects" in such procedures had not consented to the doctors' actions. The "patients" had therefore been the victims of assault and—in thousands of instances—murder.

The Doctors' Trial, which was officially termed *The U.S.A. v. Karl Brandt et al.*, ended with death sentences against seven defendants, nine other convictions carrying prison terms, and seven acquittals. That the prosecution could secure convictions was a tribute to its dedication in assembling evidence, for the alleged crimes usually had occurred in settings such as concentration camps where witnesses often no longer lived to tell the tale.

The Nuremberg War Crimes Trials involved vital figures in the Nazi hierarchy. Prosecutions occurred for lower-level officials such as camp guards, Nazi sympathizers in the press, and minor bureaucrats, among their home nations. For example, William Joyce and Iva Toguri, who had spoken words of encouragement over the radio during the war on behalf of the Axis powers, were charged with treason in proceedings in England and the United States, respectively. Pierre Laval, an architect of Vichy policy, and Robert Brassilach, an anti-Semitic writer, both were tried and executed in France as collaborators whose words had led to arrests and deaths at the hands of the German occupiers. Within the postwar Federal Republic of Germany (West Germany) and eventually a united Germany, more than 900 trials were held concerning World War II war criminals. Some of those trials transpired in the 21st century.

SIGNIFICANCE

Despite the sense among much of the world that the Nuremberg War Crimes Trials were necessary and carried out with due—indeed, some said excessive—regard for the niceties of justice, there were enduring criticisms. The charges of conspiracy on which certain Nuremberg defendants were convicted struck Continental and international lawyers at the time as unfair, since conspiracy was a feature of Anglo-American law but was not so usual in other legal systems. At Nuremberg the victors applied laws that were not in force within Germany at the time the war criminals' offenses took place—a violation of Anglo-American principles condemning ex post facto laws.

The Allies scrambled during the proceedings to ensure not only that they retained a united front but also that basic fairness prevailed. For example, at Nuremberg the Soviets proposed to prosecute defendants for a massacre of Polish officers in the Katyn Forest, but German lawyers responded that the allegations were trumped up. The other Allies had to threaten the Soviets in order to get them to retract the charges, which years later were found to have been a cover-up for atrocities by the Soviets themselves. The Allies were bruised—though not seriously deterred in their prosecutions—by the German argument that war crimes had been committed on all sides.

At Nuremberg individuals were held accountable for the collective actions of groups such as the Nazi Party. No longer could alleged war criminals claim they were immune from prosecution for acts they committed in wartime by justifying their actions with the argument that they were "just following orders" or were "simply a cog in a wheel."

In some quarters the Allies' decision not to try in absentia Hitler and other missing figures such as "Nazi death doctor" Josef Mengele made the proceedings seem unfinished. Indeed, the hunt for war criminals did continue well after the Nuremberg trials' conclusion, with high-profile prosecutions such as those of Adolf Eichmann and Ivan Demjanjuk occurring decades after the war's end. Courts within individual countries rather than an international tribunal, though, heard such later cases. Although a few powers—notably Israel—pursued war criminals diligently and punished them severely upon conviction, other nations smarted under the charge that they let defendants off lightly as time wore on.

In his initial speech to the tribunal at Nuremberg on November 21, 1945, Chief Prosecutor Jackson made a memorable plea to the court and the larger public that was watching the trials unfold. He argued that the Nuremberg proceedings, though they might prove flawed, were a vital step in establishing standards of conduct for nations and individuals:

> The real complaining party at your bar is Civilization. In all countries it is still a struggling and imperfect thing. It does not plead that the United States, or any other country, has been blameless of the conditions which made the German people easy victims to the blandishments and intimidations of the Nazi conspirators.

But it points to the dreadful sequence of aggressions and crimes I have recited, it points to the weariness of flesh, the exhaustion of resources and the destruction of all that was beautiful or useful in so much of the world, and to greater potentialities for destruction in the days to come. It is not necessary among the ruins of this ancient and beautiful city with untold members of its civilian habitants still buried in its rubble, to argue the proposition that to start or wage an aggressive war has the moral qualities of the worst of crimes. The refuge of the defendants can be only their hope that international law will lag so far behind the moral sense of mankind that conduct which is crime in the moral sense must be regarded as innocent in law.

Civilization asks whether law is so laggard as to be utterly helpless to deal with crimes of this magnitude by criminals of this order of importance.

However imperfect the Nuremberg trials were to be, he maintained, to do nothing in response to the war and the Holocaust would be infinitely worse. Perhaps civilization could find its bearings once again through the operation of a trial that not only exacted retribution but also modeled how justice should be carried out.

Further Reading

Avalon Project. "The Nuremberg War Crimes Trials." Available online. URL: http://www.yale.edu/lawweb/avalon/imt/imt.ht. Accessed September 9, 2009; Harvard Law School Library. "The Nuremberg Trials Project." Available online. URL: http://www.nuremberg.law.harvard.edu/. Accessed September 12, 2009; Jorgensen, Nina H. B. *The Responsibility of States for International Crimes.* Oxford: Oxford University Press, 2005; Lifton, Robert Jay. *The Nazi Doctors: Medical Killing and the Psychology of Genocide.* New York: Basic Books, 1986; Stave, Bruce M., et al. *Witnesses to Nuremberg: An Oral History of American Participants at the War Crimes Trials.* New York: Twayne Publishers and Prentice Hall International, 1998; Taylor, Telford. *The Anatomy of the Nuremberg Trials.* Boston: Little, Brown & Co., 1992; Tusa,

Ann, and Tusa, John. *The Nuremberg Trial.* London: Macmillan, 1983; United States Holocaust Memorial Museum. "The Holocaust." Available online. URL: http://www.ushmm.org/wlc/en/article.php?ModuleId=10005143. Accessed September 14, 2009.

The Tokyo War Crimes Trials

Also known as: The Japanese War Crimes Trials

Date: 1946–1948

KEY ISSUES

Just as there were war crimes trials at Nuremberg concerning the actions of German leaders during World War II, so were the actions of the leaders of Japan put before a judicial forum in a separate set of trials between May 1946 and November 1948. The Tokyo trials began shortly after the end of hostilities in the region, having been authorized by an international conference. A statement at Potsdam in July 1945 laid the basis for the Tokyo trials, just as the London Agreement of August 1945 set forth a diplomatic concurrence on the Nuremberg hearings.

Echoing Nuremberg's concentration on the higher-profile leaders among the Germans and their allies, the Tokyo proceedings identified several categories of war criminals, the most visible of whom were brought initially before a tribunal on charges of having committed "Class A" offenses—violations "against peace." The Allies prosecuted slightly less important defendants via the international tribunal at Tokyo on "Class B" or "Class C" charges. Those persons were charged with war crimes or crimes against humanity, for instance, for maltreatment of prisoners or atrocities against civilians, but unlike the class A defendants were not charged with actually directing the war effort. The class A defendants also faced other charges.

Those individuals without much influence in Japan's or the Axis leadership but rather Japanese and other persons who had been local apologists or administrators of the Japanese war effort were tried within individual nations all over Asia by regularly constituted courts. China, for example, held 10 separate war crimes trials. A few well-known war criminals were prosecuted in the United States, for example, the wartime broadcaster Iva Toguri d'Aquino, who was tried for treason in 1949 as "Tokyo Rose." D'Aquino, a native of the United States, was held at Sugamo Prison with the Japanese accused war criminals in 1945 and 1946; she was convicted of treason in San Francisco in 1949 in a trial bedeviled with charges of perjury on the part of the prosecution.

The trial and execution of Lieutenant General Tomoyuki Yamashita in the Philippines in the fall of 1945 presaged the Tokyo trials. It was an example of the local trial of a Japanese war leader. Pacific commander General Douglas MacArthur hoped that Yamashita's trial would be both a catharsis for the Filipino people and a precedent for the Tokyo proceedings. Yamashita had been in command of Japanese forces in the Philippines during the invasion and occupation of Malaya and Singapore, during which time notorious killings of POWs and hospital patients occurred. He also was in command during the February 1945 Manila Massacre, when more than 100,000 citizens died at the hands of Japanese troops. After his capture Yamashita expressed remorse for the atrocities, yet his defense counsel before a U.S. military tribunal argued that Yamashita should not be held responsible for actions such as "the rape of Manila" because he was away from the immediate area when the war crimes occurred.

Yamashita's controversial trial and conviction led to a key decision regarding military law on the part of the U.S. Supreme Court. The case of *in re Yamashita* (1946) established the "Yamashita standard," or the idea of "command responsibility"—the principle that commanders were required to address the actions of their subordinates who committed war crimes. It was ironic that Yamashita's case, which was held far away from the central war crimes trials in the Pacific, should have provided the most important U.S. legal standard on war crimes that came out of the World War II era.

HISTORY OF THE CASES

A key decision concerning the Tokyo War Crimes Trials was made in a military rather than a legal context. General MacArthur and the United States won an unconditional surrender from Japan in early September 1945. In that surrender the Japanese government accepted the authority of a future war crimes tribunal run by the Allies. The Allied nations that had been militarily arrayed against Japan in the war (the United States, Soviet Union, Great Britain, Australia, China, France, India, New Zealand, Philippines, and Netherlands) each were entitled to a judge on the panel of the International Military Tribunal for the Far East (IMTFE).

As at Nuremberg, U.S. authorities directed the trials in Tokyo. U.S. lawyers and judges had assistance from important allies in the region. The chief judge and pivotal members of the prosecution team at Nuremberg had been British; the person presiding at the tribunal in Tokyo was an Australian, William Webb. As at Nuremberg, where Supreme Court Justice Robert Jackson was chief prosecutor, at Tokyo, Joseph B. Keenan, who had served as the U.S. assistant attorney general, represented the United States as lead prosecutor. President Harry Truman chose Keenan for the task. There was a palpable difference, however, between the comportment of Keenan and the demeanor of Jackson. Keenan drew fire during the Tokyo trials and later as a person of some—perhaps excessive—sociability, while Jackson's mien was grave. Several of the judges had experience with military law. The member of the IMTFE bench from New Zealand, for example, Erima Harvey Northcroft, was the former judge advocate general of the army of his nation.

SUMMARY OF ARGUMENTS

It was not only the starting of "aggressive war" in the Pacific region that formed a basis for several charges against certain of the accused. In addition, the Allies alleged that the defendants who were architects of Japanese policy had pursued unconventional means of effecting aggression that were not strictly military. The prosecution at Tokyo presented evidence that Japanese arms of government actively fostered the opium trade in China in order to raise revenue for war making and to weaken civilian resistance to Japanese occupation.

Several of the persons on trial at Tokyo were charged in connection with notorious incidents that occurred before all of the Allies had entered the war. In particular, they were accused of participating in the atrocities toward Chinese soldiers and civilians at Nanjing (Nanking) in 1937, when perhaps 100,000 Chinese died and the Japanese perpetrated rape, enslavement, and forced relocation on a vast population of captives. The Nanjing offenses were called Class C crimes at Tokyo due to their involving mostly civilian victims.

Meanwhile, the acts such as the Japanese perpetrated during the "Bataan death march" of 1942 were termed Class B offenses because they involved combatants. Such charges against the defendants were fairly usual types of war crimes; they did not break new ground in international law. For example, as a general, Seishiro Itagaki held key commands in China, Korea, and Singapore during the late 1930s and early 1940s. At Tokyo he was convicted of overseeing prisoners' maltreatment in those posts. Other defendants had became notorious for supervising projects such as the building of railways in Burma with POW laborers.

The "Doctors' Trial" that was part of the Nuremberg proceedings took up the subject of medical testing among prisoners of war and civilian detainees. Several persons who had participated in such "death camp" experiments were executed as a result of the Doctors' Trial. Although rumors abounded at Tokyo about Unit 731, through which Japanese authorities allowed numerous biological tests on unwilling subjects, persons in charge of that department never were prosecuted as war criminals at Tokyo. U.S. prosecutors made quick reference to the Japanese unit that they called TAMA. Still, Japanese associated with biological experimentation on humans were tried not at Tokyo but rather by the Soviets in a small-scale prosecution in 1949.

The defenses that were put forward at Tokyo were complex because there were multiple defendants and various charges, but defense contentions had several key prongs. In part, the defense argued that the trial was mounted by parties who could not effect justice because they had been military enemies of the defendants. Eventually, one of the judges of the tribunal echoed this concern, stating that there should have been Japanese judges on the panel at Tokyo. Lawyers representing the defendants objected to the application of "command responsibility" in reference to episodes in which the accused persons were not physically present. The defense maintained that to say a defendant was in charge of military policy in a geographical area and thus should have known of atrocities being committed in the vicinity was to introduce a new principle into military and international law. The defense disputed the application of *waging aggressive war* as a novel charge before an international tribunal. The defense also stated that such a charge also was inapplicable to Japan's situation, for Japan had acted to defend itself against Western aggression. Certain defense lawyers suggested that the Allies had committed war crimes such as the bombings of civilians that ought to be addressed.

VERDICTS

It took the tribunal about six months to digest the testimony and arguments and compose a verdict. The 11 judges divided among themselves as to whether the prosecution had proven its case, with eight jurists voting for guilty verdicts against all of the accused, and three (from India, the Netherlands, and France) offering dissents from the majority. Several other judges contributed separate opinions, though they ultimately concurred with their peers in favor of conviction. A few concurring judges called for even sterner penalties or wider-scale prosecutions.

The dissent from French judge Henri Bernard was based on his view that Emperor Hirohito and members of the Japanese royal family had been excluded from prosecution. Bernard argued that the emperor's being omitted from the list of accused war criminals brought the whole proceeding into question. Bernard maintained that Hirohito had concurred in Japanese policy, indeed, directing it before and during the war. One of the few professors on the panel, Justice Bert Roling of the Netherlands, in his dissent expressed discomfort with the definition of *aggressive war* as put forward at Tokyo (as well as at Nuremberg). That concept had been the basis for charges against the

most high-profile defendants. The dissent from Judge Radhabinod Pal of India was the most comprehensive critique of the trial by one of its administrators. Pal noted that atrocities had occurred during the war and were directed by Japanese authorities, but his quite lengthy minority opinion called into disrepute the tribunal as merely the action of a victorious military power.

Of the 28 original defendants at Tokyo, two died before the trial ended and one, pan-Asian philosopher Shumei Okawa, was declared unfit for trial on grounds of mental incapacity early in the proceedings. (Okawa, bizarrely, had struck Japanese general Hideki Tojo in court.) A handful of persons who were sentenced to life terms died soon in prison, but the rest of those who were given life terms served fewer than 10 years before being paroled.

The seven defendants who were sentenced to death at Tokyo were the most elite among Japan's military establishment, with three of the men also having held extremely high-level state posts: Baron Koki Hirota, who served as foreign minister (a cabinet-level post) from 1933 to 1936 as well as prime minister for about a year from early 1936 into 1937; General Tojo, who had been Japan's prime minister from 1941 through 1944 while also serving in high offices concerning commerce, domestic affairs, foreign affairs, and education during the war; and General Itagaki, who was minister of war for some months in 1938 and 1939.

Tojo was the best-known defendant of all, certainly outside Japan. He had attempted to commit suicide rather than face trial. U.S. occupation forces in early September 1945 literally heard Tojo shoot himself in the chest as they rushed to detain him. Although a sympathetic Japanese doctor had assisted Tojo by drawing a diagram on Tojo's chest of where his heart was located, the bullet missed all major organs, and American medical personnel revived him to make him fit for trial. Tojo, unrepentant of the effects of his policies, nevertheless said that he accepted full responsibility for his actions.

SIGNIFICANCE

There was one parallel between Nuremberg and Tokyo that even the most casual observer could see: The supreme leaders of neither Germany nor

Japan were put on trial. Adolf Hitler (despite stray rumors that he somehow had escaped Berlin) certainly had died in the last days of the war in Europe. The emperor of Japan, Hirohito, went uncharged with war crimes at Tokyo. His absence, which undoubtedly was for political reasons, cast a long shadow over the proceedings.

In addition to the omission of the Japanese royal house, certain well-placed political figures such as Kishi Nobusuke were detained but not tried at Tokyo, thereby also casting doubts as to the consistency of the proceedings. Nobusuke, who before the war had assisted Tojo in the conquest of Manchuria and had been commerce minister at the time of Pearl Harbor, went on to become Japan's prime minister. Indeed, there were several such individuals who held high office in Japan in the postwar years. Their standing in Japan and abroad seemingly was untarnished by long detention at Sugamo Prison.

Some specific procedural similarities linked Nuremberg and Tokyo, as well. The court took the form of a specially created tribunal, the IMTFE. A multijudge panel heard the A, B, and C class cases without recourse to a jury. Translation issues bedeviled the running of the trials at times, just as they had with the multinational defendants and witnesses at Nuremberg. As had occurred at Nuremberg, too, a large percentage of the defendants in Tokyo were not only sentenced but were hanged or committed to long prison terms. Even the form of execution, hanging, was common to both venues. Although at Tokyo one defendant was ruled insane and there were a few deaths among the defendants before the trials ended, there were, however, no successful suicide attempts in the Asian trials and no acquittals.

There were certain major differences in the proceedings that assigned war crimes guilt in the Pacific versus the Atlantic theaters. The Tokyo trials were focused on military leaders and military actions as war crimes, whereas Nuremberg included military figures but also considered the actions of high-ranking bureaucrats and even nongovernment officials such as Nazi Party leaders, physicians, and propagandists. At Nuremberg there had been certain key prosecutors on behalf of the Allies but no one indispensable director. At Tokyo there was a single person who managed the entire postwar environment in the Far East: U.S. general MacArthur.

The Tokyo War Crimes Trials had a much lower profile among the general public than Nuremberg did. In part this was because the major European war criminals had been executed prior to the proceedings' getting well under way at Tokyo, and public interest had waned. Although the Japanese war leaders were of very high rank in their nation, they were not well known in the West, so their trials did not garner the same attention as the prosecutions of figures such as Hermann Göring, Rudolf Hess, and "Hitler's physician" Karl Brandt.

The full story of Japanese medical and scientific experiments on prisoners and civilians did not come out until the 1980s. Western journalists who broke such stories fed the beliefs of those who argued that the U.S. government had refused to prosecute such offenses at Tokyo in order to expropriate the data from such experimentation. In a parallel development right-wing forces within Japan insisted for many years after the war that the Allies had manufactured evidence concerning human rights abuses in Manchuria for political purposes. Indeed, it took another major legal case, the Ineaga textbook controversy, to force the Japanese government to admit publicly that Unit 731 had existed. Only at the very end of the 20th century did Japan as a nation make public acknowledgement of atrocities such as sexual bondage placed upon its own female citizens and large-scale sexual assaults within conquered populations.

The Tokyo War Crimes Trials were like the proceedings at Nuremberg in certain key respects. They served as a catharsis for many Allied citizens who had participated in war in the Pacific region. The trials also generated criticism among some legal experts who said that they were an exercise in "victors' justice." Recent scholarship on both Nuremberg and Tokyo has emphasized the care with which lawyers and judges at both of the post–World War II war crimes trials framed the prosecutions. Most of the experts associated with such multinational trials were concerned not to inflame racial or national prejudice, worked hard to comport with standards of international law, and even considered the precedents that they would pass along to future human rights lawyers.

Further Reading

Close, Frederick. *Tokyo Rose: An American Patriot.* Metuchen, N.J.: Scarecrow Press, 2010; Danner, Allison Marston. "Beyond the Geneva Convention: Lessons from the Tokyo Tribunal in Prosecuting War and Terrorism." *Virginia Journal of International Law* 26 (Fall 2005): 2–43; Frank, Richard. *Downfall: The End of the Imperial Japanese Empire.* New York: Random House, 1999; Harry S. Truman Library and Museum. "Tokyo War Crimes Trials." Available online. URL: http://www. trumanlibrary.org/whistlestop/study_collections/ nuremberg/tokyo.htm. Accessed May 15, 2009; *In re Yamashita* 327 U.S. 1 (1946); Laughland, John. *A History of Political Trials: From Charles I to Saddam Hussein.* Oxford, U.K.: Peter Lang, 2008; Maga, Timothy. *Judgment at Tokyo: The Japanese War Crimes Trials.* Lexington: University of Kentucky Press, 2001; Moghalu, Kingsley Chiedu. *Global Justice: The Politics of War Crimes Trials.* Westport, Conn.: Praeger, 2006; Oshima, Nagisa (dir.), *Merry Christmas Mr. Lawrence.* Recorded Pictures Company, 1983; Totani, Yuma. *The Tokyo War Crimes Trials: The Pursuit of Justice in the Wake of World War II.* Cambridge, Mass.: Harvard University Press, 2008; University of Canterbury. "Justice Erima Harvey Northcroft Tokyo War Crimes Trial Collection [MB1549]." Available online. URL: http://library. canterbury.ac.nz/mb/war_crimes/toc.shtml. Accessed May 14, 2009.

The trial of the Rosenbergs

Also known as: *U.S. v. Rosenberg, Rosenberg and Sobell*

Date: 1951

KEY ISSUES

Despite the later furor over Senator Joseph McCarthy's communist baiting, historical scholars recognize that spy rings existed in the United States during the cold war. Soviet espionage had a particular goal of finding out details of U.S. development of atomic weapons at sites such as Los Alamos Laboratory in New Mexico. Especially valuable to the Soviet Union were persons who could spy effectively from their position as U.S. citizens. Such operatives often agreed to work for the Soviets out of adherence to Communist ideology or disaffection with life in the United States.

The Western pursuit of Soviet spies became famous in not only historical but also cinematic and literary venues. The writing of John le Carré and Ian Fleming, for example, described espionage in vastly different ways. Le Carré in *The Spy Who Came in from the Cold* spoke of the mechanical, workaday, even boring business of undercover work. Fleming famously portrayed "secret agents" such as James Bond as dashing and dangerous. Fleming's agent "007" made an enduring screen hero. Commercial treatments of espionage emphasized that the Soviet spy network and its Western counterparts were active beyond the United States and the USSR. They also operated in Great Britain, for example, with its World War II legacy of code breaking. The composers of fictional portraits of spies agreed that the stakes of the contest were exceedingly high. No less than the safety of the world was at risk if atomic technology fell into the wrong hands.

The case of Julius and Ethel Rosenberg demonstrated that spying was neither as methodical nor as glamorous as the novelists would have it. The Rosenbergs' actions pointed to a network that stretched from Western Europe and the Soviet Union into New York City and far beyond in the United States. The uncovering of a Soviet spy ring involving the Rosenbergs underlined that the Soviets indeed had gotten classified information that assisted them in the cold war. The trial of the Rosenbergs was a rooting out of traitors. It also was an admission that U.S. security and intelligence were lacking.

The trial of the Rosenbergs was not a triumph for the legal values that the United States cherished. It involved the suborning of witnesses, perjury, a fatal plea bargain, and a standoff in which one defendant's life was forfeited. Historical scholars still disagree as to whether the goal of the government prosecutors—the exposure of communism—justified their tactics.

HISTORY OF THE CASE

The Rosenberg case included several memorable characters—not as worthy of the big screen, perhaps, as a Fleming novel, but still lending intrigue to the story. McCarthy, of course, just a bit later would give his name to the search for "reds." At the time that the net was tightening around the Rosenberg conspirators in the late 1940s, however, two other persons with national profiles were at least as important as Communist hunters: Federal Bureau of Investigation (FBI) director J. Edgar Hoover and lawyer and adviser to members of Congress Roy Cohn.

There were several other spies allegedly in league with the Rosenbergs, including Ethel Rosenberg's brother David Greenglass and his wife, Ruth. David Greenglass stole secrets from his position at Los Alamos in 1944 and 1945 during the development of the first atomic bomb. Ruth Greenglass was a courier in the same spy ring. David Greenglass drew crude sketches of a lens that scientists at the Manhattan Project were developing to detonate the atomic bomb. Greenglass handed that and other sensitive information to Harry Gold, who turned it over to a Soviet "diplomat" named Anatoly Yakovlev. Gold was the American contact to a German-born scientist named Klaus Fuchs. The physicist Fuchs was based in England. He was passing secrets from the Harwell nuclear research center, just as he had leaked information about the Manhattan Project to the Soviets during the war.

It was Fuchs who was caught first, trapped in January 1950 by the British domestic Military Intelligence service (MI5) in a protracted sting operation. British intelligence got word in 1945 from a Soviet defector named Igor Gouzenko that a high-level ring was stealing atomic secrets. Fuchs was tried quickly and sentenced to 14 years in prison, of which he served only about two-thirds before being exchanged to East Germany for political prisoners there. Also in 1945 the FBI had gotten word from American Communist Elizabeth Bentley that a number of individuals were spying as U.S. citizens for the Soviets. When Gold's name

cropped up again in 1950 during Fuch's interrogations, after having been on Bentley's list, the FBI pursued further questioning of Gold. Gold in turn named David Greenglass as the supplier of key information, and Greenglass then specified that his American "handler" was his brother-in-law, Julius Rosenberg.

The FBI and Hoover, specifically, perceived that a cluster of operatives worked under Rosenberg. Rosenberg was an engineer by training who had become interested in communism during his student days at City College of New York. He joined the Young Communist League and later became a full member of the Communist Party USA. Like many undergraduates in the 1930s, Rosenberg admired the "experiments" in collectivization taking place in the Soviet Union.

It took a die-hard ideologue, however, to ally with the Soviets once news of Stalin's purges got out in the late 1930s. Rosenberg was one of those who continued to profess admiration and support for Soviet communism in spite of Stalin's human rights atrocities. Like the moles in British intelligence during World War II, Rosenberg funneled classified information to the Soviets while he was employed as a civilian with the U.S. Army Signal Corps. Rosenberg and his peers later claimed that the United States and the Soviet Union were allies during the war and thus such sharing of information ought to have been legal.

When the FBI interrogated Rosenberg in the summer of 1950, he refused to provide the names of any associates, either Soviet or American. Although he acted on the belief that Ethel Rosenberg was a "simple housewife" who either did not know about or was not involved in Julius's activities for the Soviets, Hoover determined that Ethel Rosenberg might provide leverage against her husband. Her arrest took place in August 1950. The FBI informed both of the Rosenbergs that the agency and other authorities would recommend leniency for Ethel if either of the couple would list their colleagues in espionage.

Meanwhile, David Greenglass also got an offer from those preparing the prosecution of both the Greenglasses and the Rosenbergs, as well as a few other suspected spies. If Greenglass would turn state's evidence, he could expect a lesser sentence and Ruth Greenglass would not face charges.

Greenglass took the bargain, and 10 days before trial changed his story to implicate his sister, Ethel Rosenberg. In his initial statements to the FBI and before a grand jury in early 1951, Greenglass claimed that he and Julius Rosenberg always shared confidential information in "neutral territory," such as on the street. After being allowed to exchange his wife's and his fates for the Rosenbergs', Greenglass "recalled" that he and Julius got Ethel to type sensitive correspondence. Furthermore, Greenglass alleged that several incriminating conversations took place inside the Rosenbergs' small apartment.

Most damaging of all to Ethel Rosenberg was Greenglass's new claim, in August 1951, that Ethel Rosenberg and Ruth Greenglass had arranged a signal for Ruth to pass along to a Soviet contact. The sign was an item that—in typical spy style—was cut into halves so that the pieces could later be put together. This would demonstrate that those who now held the pieces were authentic members of the spy team. The everyday object that the sisters-in-law allegedly chose for that purpose was the most domestic of American products, a box of Jell-O.

SUMMARY OF ARGUMENTS

The Rosenbergs were charged under the provisions of the Espionage Act of 1917, which had been enacted by the U.S. Congress. The legislation originally aimed to curtail the expression of criticisms of World War I if those opinions interfered with enlistment. It also provided up to 20 years' imprisonment for passing along military or defense secrets. During and just after that war, U.S. attorney general A. Mitchell Palmer, assisted by a young Hoover, identified many dozens of U.S. citizens who were accused of being "reds," or Communists, and prosecuted them under either the Espionage Act or the Sedition Act of 1918. Those persons who were not legal citizens often were simply deported to their native lands. Such was the environment in which Nicola Sacco and Bartolomeo Vanzetti were condemned to death in the early 1920s.

According to the Espionage Act, persons convicted during wartime could find themselves facing the death penalty rather than a long jail term. Most of the famous cases carried forward during the Red Scare of the late 1910s and early 1920s involved "peacetime" espionage, and thus, those radicals faced incarceration or deportation only. The Rosenbergs had a grimmer prospect. While Greenglass had done some of his machinist's work at Los Alamos, World War II still was under way. Greenglass and his in-laws could be charged with espionage, not during the cold war, but during a hot conflict, so the death penalty might apply. Greenglass was tried earlier than the Rosenbergs and under the terms of his agreement with authorities got a relatively moderate sentence of 15 years. He served 10 years, going back into private life in 1960.

The prosecution in the Rosenbergs' case had framed its charges cleverly under the direction of the U.S. attorney for the Southern District of New York, Irving Saypol. Julius and Ethel Rosenberg were accused of "conspiracy to commit wartime espionage." They stood trial with Morton Sobell, an alleged associate who recently had gone to Mexico with his wife and was illegally captured by Mexican authorities in time for the proceedings in federal court in New York City. Whether Sobell had fled or simply was on vacation was a matter of some dispute. Proving a conspiracy was easier than demonstrating that a particular individual had committed espionage, because all that the state had to show was that the persons charged had acted in concert. Then, if one were guilty, all of his or her colleagues were equally culpable under the law.

The chief evidence against the Rosenbergs came from David Greenglass. It consisted of Greenglass's accounts of his own selling of secrets from Los Alamos to Julius Rosenberg. Upon Greenglass's proposing to testify for the prosecution about such sensitive matters, defense counsel Emanuel "Manny" Bloch requested that the courtroom be cleared on account of the secret nature of the information. It was a strategy designed to convince the court that the Rosenbergs preferred that official secrets should not be divulged. The request, however, had a different—and more negative—effect on the defendants: It seemed to impress upon the jury and Judge Irving Kaufman that information of a high order had been compromised. Some information that was suppressed from public reporting at trial was released only in 1966. A few details remained under wraps into the 21st century because of requests from interested parties, including David Greenglass, that they not be released.

Although several times during the trial defense counsel argued that "communism was not on trial," at certain junctures the defendants' political associations came in for close scrutiny. Often it was the bench that posed questions about the Rosenbergs' Communist Party affiliations. Despite the fact that the U.S. Constitution included a provision against self-incrimination, evoking that right proved to the Rosenbergs, as to many defendants, nearly an admission of guilt to the jury. Interestingly, Julius and Ethel Rosenberg used their Fifth Amendment privilege solely to answer questions about the Communist Party. They seemed to think that communism was more dangerous to them than their association with the convicted spy Greenglass. Again, it was a miscalculation by the defense, for the jury apparently read their refusal to answer as caginess.

The prosecution under lead attorney Saypol introduced a surprise witness at trial: a photographer who testified that the Rosenbergs had asked him to make passport pictures. The government contended this was evidence of the defendants' plan to flee the United States when they got wind of the spy ring being investigated in early 1950. The Greenglasses corroborated such a theory, saying that only Ruth Greenglass's refusal to leave the United States had kept the family from departing. The details of that photographers' story, however, did not hold up well under cross-examination. For example, he could not produce copies of the pictures he said he had taken. The defense vigorously objected to the introduction of evidence that was not mentioned in pretrial discovery documents, but the government argued that the photographer only just had been discovered.

Another of Saypol's tactics came under fire both during and after trial: his repeated reference to *treason* when speaking of the Rosenbergs. An experienced lawyer, Saypol had to know that treason was not the same as espionage, although, of course, the two offenses could be factually connected. His aim, though, seemed to be to ask the jury and Judge Kaufman to consider the actions of the Rosenbergs and Sobell as tantamount to treason. This was in order to justify a

capital sentence—which, though permissible under the 1917 legislation—was unusual.

The Rosenbergs' defense lawyers, led by the father-and-son team of Alexander and Manny Bloch, had a simple line of argument. They maintained that Greenglass was trying to save himself and his wife by making a deal with the U.S. government. The defense practically admitted that the Rosenbergs were Communists, despite the couple's unwillingness to acknowledge the affiliation on the stand. In his summation to the jury Manny Bloch begged the jury not to let communism be the deciding factor in the case. Bloch characterized the actions of David Greenglass as not just selfish but also inhuman. He reminded the jury that Greenglass himself was a convicted spy, although that point had not been one that the defense had emphasized during cross-examination:

> But we ask you now as we asked you before, please don't decide this case because you may have some bias or some prejudice against some political philosophy.
>
> If you want to convict these defendants because you think that they are Communists and you don't like communism and you don't like any member of the Communist Party, then, ladies and gentlemen, I can sit down now and there is absolutely no use in my talking. There was no use in going through this whole rigmarole of a three weeks' trial. That is not the crime.
>
> But believe me, ladies and gentlemen, I am not here, other defense counsel are not here as attorneys for the Communist Party and we are not here as attorneys for the Soviet Union. I can only speak for myself and my father. We are representing Julius and Ethel Rosenberg, two American citizens, who come to you as American citizens, charged with a specific crime, and ask you to judge them the way you would want to be judged if you were sitting over there before twelve other jurors. . . .
>
> Do you know what that man [Greenglass] did? He was assigned to one of the most important secret projects in this country, and by his own statements, by his own admissions, he told you that he stole information out of there and gave it to

strangers, and that it was going to the Soviet Government.

But one thing I think you do know, that any man who will testify against his own blood and flesh, his own sister, is repulsive, is revolting, who violates every code that any civilization has ever lived by. He is the lowest of the lowest animals that I have ever seen, and if you are honest with yourself, you will admit that he is lower than the lowest animal that you have ever seen.

Bloch trusted that the jurors would find a man who would betray his sister to be more repulsive than a Communist. He was wrong.

VERDICT

The public followed the Rosenberg-Sobell trial avidly. Many were alarmed at the close brush with disaster that the prosecution portrayed: What if the Soviets had gotten the bomb before the war's end? Had the actions of persons like these defendants hastened the Soviet development of atomic weaponry? (The USSR had detonated its first nuclear bomb in August 1949.) And yet, the prosecution of a couple with young children was tragic. If she were convicted and executed, Ethel Rosenberg would be but the second woman to have gotten a capital sentence for a federal crime in U.S. history. Only the "Lincoln conspirator" Mary Surratt had preceded her. In addition, these defendants seemed so ordinary—hardly the stereotypical secret agents of stage and screen. Could it be that the U.S. government was desperate to show its allies (and enemies) that it would be stern toward dissidents?

Not just during the trial but also in its aftermath the Rosenberg case was the story of the year for three years running. As was expected by those who followed the trial, the jury returned convictions for Julius and Ethel Rosenberg and Sobell. Judge Kaufman had a reputation as a tough sentencer and had appeared sympathetic to the government case during trial. Court watchers expected Kaufman to hand down a death sentence for Julius Rosenberg and hard time for Sobell, but what would he do about Ethel? Although prosecutor Saypol and his assistants, such as the zealous anti-Communist Cohn, had attempted to paint Ethel

Rosenberg as an equal partner in the conspiracy to commit espionage, prevailing mores were that a young mother should be left alive to care for her children. Ethel Rosenberg's gender, in other words, was widely perceived to be the reason that the court would show her mercy.

Judge Kaufman did not do so. On April 5, 1951, he sentenced Julius and Ethel Rosenberg to death and Sobell to 30 years in prison. Kaufman observed that the Rosenbergs had committed crimes that were worthy of the ultimate punishment:

Citizens of this country who betray their fellow-countrymen can be under none of the delusions about the benignity of Soviet power that they might have been prior to World War II. The nature of Russian terrorism is now self-evident. Idealism as a rationale dissolves. . . .

I consider your crime worse than murder. Plain deliberate contemplated murder is dwarfed in magnitude by comparison with the crime you have committed. In committing the act of murder, the criminal kills only his victim. The immediate family is brought to grief and when justice is meted out the chapter is closed. But in your case, I believe your conduct in putting into the hands of the Russians the A-bomb years before our best scientists predicted Russia would perfect the bomb has already caused, in my opinion, the Communist aggression in Korea, with the resultant casualties exceeding 50,000 and who knows but that millions more innocent people may pay the price of your treason. Indeed, by your betrayal you undoubtedly have altered the course of history to the disadvantage of our country.

The furor increased as supporters of the Rosenbergs joined critics of the trial in requesting either reversal of the verdict or clemency. Judge Kaufman's use of the offense of treason in sentencing came in for special criticism. The Rosenbergs were not on trial for that offense. The appeals process was exhausted in courts below the Supreme Court level in the winter of 1952. The highest court in the nation several times heard petitions on the case and seemed divided, with a bare majority at times favoring the carrying out of the executions. Although several Supreme Court justices were willing to issue stays of execution, those on the Court sympathetic to the defendants ultimately did not have the votes to win. Even on the day of the scheduled execution, several appeals court judges held out a slim possibility of issuing stays, but the Rosenbergs' lawyers labored in vain to get them to go against the Supreme Court's implicit condemnation.

The only real hope for a remission of sentence was executive clemency by the incoming U.S. president, Dwight Eisenhower. Eisenhower, though no rabid anti-Communist, listened to the intelligence given him by the FBI and the courts. Those details spoke to Ethel Rosenberg's substantive involvement in the espionage for which her husband and Sobell also had been convicted.

Amid scenes of protest of an intensity rivaled last in the Sacco and Vanzetti case, both of the Rosenbergs died by electrocution at Sing-Sing Prison in Ossining, New York. Due to concerns that the couple would expire on the Jewish Sabbath, the execution was moved forward to a summer Friday evening, June 19, 1953. Until the very end Cohn and Hoover seemed to expect one or the other of the couple to confess their crimes.

SIGNIFICANCE

To experts on the diplomatic and military history of the 20th century, the Rosenbergs' trial bore reexamination in light of newly discovered records at the end of the century. With the breakup of the Soviet Union came an opening of Russian files concerning the cold war. Former Soviet spies became willing and able to discuss their work in the West, including in connection with the Rosenberg case. Increasing access to American documents under legislation such as the Freedom of Information Act meant that researchers could gather details of the government's cases against Communists and Soviet agents. The information gleaned from such revelations in the 1990s and early 2000s pointed in interesting directions.

Although the newly available data was not of a single opinion, it generally exonerated Ethel Rosenberg and made clearer the depth of Julius Rosenberg's involvement in espionage. The freshly released details concerning the case also tended to underline the fact that several intelligence officials, certainly including Hoover, knew of Ethel Rosenberg's lack of complicity but allowed the case against her to go forward as a tool to get information from her and Julius about their associates. The government bet that the couple would not take secrets to their graves, but that wager was incorrect.

Among the many New Yorkers who watched demonstrations against the Rosenbergs' execution was a six-year-old boy named Sam Roberts. Roberts went on to become a *New York Times* reporter. Like many observers of the Rosenberg case, he was moved by the situation of the two children of the couple, boys who were orphaned by their parents' executions. These children were reared by relatives and took the names of their guardians, Meeropol. Roberts made it a personal quest to get answers from one of the survivors of the Rosenbergs' case who might have personal knowledge of the case: David Greenglass. When Roberts conducted a series of interviews with Greenglass in the mid-1990s, Greenglass and his wife, Ruth, were living in New York City under assumed names. Even as the case was being concluded, Greenglass had expressed a desire to retreat into obscurity, but he spoke freely, finally, with the late-20th-century interviewer.

Greenglass admitted to Roberts that he had lied at trial to save his wife so that she could be with their children, even at the expense of his sister, Ethel. Greenglass in 1996 said that Julius Rosenberg had had the documents in question typed, but he did not know by whom. He said that it even might have been Ruth Greenglass herself who did the typing. In response to Roberts's query as to whether David Greenglass would act differently toward the Rosenbergs if he had the chance, Greenglass stated that he would change nothing.

Further Reading

Meeropol, Robert, and Michael Meeropol. *We Are Your Sons*. New York: Houghton Mifflin, 1975; Neville, John. *The Press, the Rosenbergs, and the Cold War*. New York: Praeger, 1995; Radosh, Ronald, and Joyce Milton. *The Rosenberg File*. New York: Holt Rinehart & Winston, 1983;

Roberts, Sam. *The Brother.* New York: Random House, 2003; Sharlitt, Joseph. *Fatal Error.* New York: Scribner, 1989; Sobell, Morton. *On Doing Time.* New York: Charles Scribner's Sons, 1974.

The trial of Steven Truscott

Also known as: *The Crown v. Truscott;* the Lynne Harper case

Date: 1959

KEY ISSUES

The 20th century saw the rise of a most unlikely celebrity in the courtroom: the forensic pathologist. As expert witnesses in a series of notorious cases, several specialists in forensic pathology greatly enhanced the reputation of their field within the legal and medical professions. Forensic investigation came to a much wider public, as well, through the publications of those who admired professional pathologists.

One of the great literary characters of the late Victorian era was based on its creator's extensive experience in the courtroom. When Arthur Conan Doyle characterized Sherlock Holmes as a scientist, he was lionizing figures such as the extraordinarily popular forensic pathologist Dr. Bernard Spilsbury. Conan Doyle also was promoting a working alliance between science and the police.

In the late 1950s and early 1960s the trial of a young Canadian man named Steven Truscott for murder and the legal complexities that ensued brought medical evidence even more fully into courtrooms all over the world. The participation of several international teams of forensic specialists in the case proved troublesome, though, both legally and medically.

Several writers and journalists wrote extensively about the case during trial and afterward, for it involved difficult matters of evidence that in many observers' minds were unsatisfactorily resolved in court. The Truscott case included important legal issues that went beyond forensics; for example, it forced an anguished examination of the status of juveniles before courts as both accused persons and witnesses in capital cases.

HISTORY OF THE CASE

The facts of the case were puzzling and disturbing: After going missing about 48 hours earlier, 12-year-old Lynne Harper was found dead in a wooded area a few miles from her home in Ontario, Canada. She had been sexually assaulted and strangled. The medico-legal officer for the province, Dr. John Penistan, examined Harper's body where she lay. On the basis of his crime scene observation, as well as some laboratory work soon after, Penistan made what was to be a crucial determination in the case, the time of Harper's death.

Penistan had a vital piece of information from the police with which to determine a time of death. Although warm weather had hastened post mortem changes to such an extent that rigor mortis was not a very reliable guide in this instance, Harper's parents could recall exactly what and when Harper had consumed at recent meals. The rate of the emptying of the stomach was a factor that pathologists often employed to establish time of death. Having in mind that Harper finished her supper at 5:45 P.M., Dr. Penistan concluded that she had died within two hours of the meal. That finding changed the approach of the police toward the case.

Harper last had been seen riding on a bicycle with her schoolmate Truscott. In the hours when Harper was missing, the police considered Truscott only a witness in the case. They were loath to suspect a boy of 14 of committing a crime of the magnitude of murder or kidnapping. But, after the discovery of Harper's body Truscott became the prime suspect because he gave evasive answers to authorities about exactly when and where he last had seen Harper. The reports of other children who had been nearby also cast doubt on Truscott's account of events on the evening that Harper disappeared.

When the police got Dr. Penistan's estimate of a time of death, they looked at Truscott with even greater suspicion. By Truscott's own admission he was the only person near Harper for about 45 minutes, just after 7:00 P.M. on the day of her disappearance. Truscott claimed that after he and Lynne had chatted, he dropped her off of his bicycle. Truscott said he had seen her go hitchhiking, entering a car with a yellow license plate. But, Truscott was the only witness to Harper's movements on that evening who reported seeing such a vehicle.

The police investigated—the yellow plate would have indicated a Michigan motor vehicle registration—but never could find such a vehicle. They also established that from the vantage point where Truscott claimed to have seen the license plate, it would have been impossible to make out its color. Truscott had a solid alibi after about 7:45. In other words, if the killing occurred after that time, he could not have been the murderer. But, if Harper had died between 7:00 and 7:45, Truscott almost certainly was the perpetrator.

SUMMARY OF ARGUMENTS

Truscott was charged and tried as an adult for Harper's murder. The scientific case against Truscott turned mostly on the exact time of Harper's death. Other forensic issues arose during the case, some of which were much debated among the forensic medical community. For example, there was a divergence of opinion among physicians about abrasions that Truscott had on his penis, marks that were discovered about three days after Harper's death. Some medical authorities thought the marks had been caused in an effort to rape; others thought they merely indicated a preexisting rash; still others argued that Truscott could have had a skin condition that became inflamed during forceful sexual intercourse. Finally, the Crown prosecution accepted that third interpretation. But, it was the question of the stomach contents as the basis for the time of death estimate that was central.

Convicted of murder and given a death sentence but not executed because of his youth, Truscott spent eight years in prison. His situation spurred angry debates concerning the death penalty in Canada. Some argued that more than any other episode, Truscott's case led to reconsideration, and ultimately abolition, of capital punishment in the nation.

Truscott got a chance at what was in effect a retrial of his case. An author named Isabel Lebourdais wrote an extremely critical view of the conviction, which was published by Gollancz in 1966. Several well-known members of the medico-legal community in England, including Dr. Francis Camps, endorsed Lebourdais's arguments. Britain's leading forensic pathologist, Dr. Keith Simpson, was dismayed at the criticisms of the trial. He wrote a sharp review of the Lebourdais book for the *Medico Legal Journal*. He then consulted with experts on stomach emptying and commented again on Lebourdais's evidence at the behest of the Canadian director of public prosecutions. Eventually, Simpson traveled to Canada, first to examine evidence that had been preserved from the case in Toronto's crime lab, then to testify before a panel of judges who were reviewing Truscott's conviction.

That hearing in 1967 was a showdown about medical evidence. The judges listened to an array of medico-legal experts from Great Britain, Canada, and the United States. Certain experts, including Camps, Frederick Jaffe (a regional pathologist for Ontario), and Charles Petty of the Medical Examiner's Office in Maryland, tried to cast doubt on certain aspects of the science through which Truscott had been convicted.

Simpson, Dr. Milton Helpern of the New York City Medical Examiner's Office, Coroner Samuel Gerber of Cuyahoga County, Ohio, and other supporters of Penistan attested to the validity of Penistan's estimate about time of death. Simpson did not remember it until he met Pensitan in Canada after he already formed his opinion that Pensitan's conclusion were correct in the Truscott case, but Simpson had been one of Penistan's examiners when Pensitan was a premedical student at Oxford. Simpson answered the critics of Pensitan who thought him to be "merely" a provincial medico-legal officer. Simpson argued that Penistan's report on Harper's body was as thorough as any Simpson had seen, in 30 years of practice.

VERDICT

The high court judges themselves noted that they considered 467 pages of new testimony on appeal in 1967—most of it medical—in their effort to ascertain whether Truscott had been given a fair trial and an appropriate chance at appeal. They decided that the raft of questioning about Truscott's conviction was unjustified. The high court concluded that the medical evidence against the defendant had been applied justly. Truscott testified during the appeals process; he had not at the initial trial. This appeals court did not consider Truscott's testimony itself to be pivotal. According to the high court judges in 1967, Truscott had been duly tried and convicted in 1959.

Truscott had lost only in the short term. Seemingly worn down by the persistent criticism of its prosecution of Truscott, the government agreed to release Truscott on parole in 1969. He had served 10 years for the murder of Harper. The National Parole Board allowed his parole to lapse in 1974. Truscott took another name and lived a quiet life, rearing a family and working.

Simpson ended the chapter on the Truscott case in his autobiography with two observations: Truscott had evoked sympathy from conspiracy mongers that led to his being freed from custody. When asked whether he really thought Truscott could have been the murderer, especially given Truscott's collected behavior in the hours just after Harper had disappeared, Simpson assured his readers that several of the perpetrators of terrible crimes he had investigated had manifested remarkable poise afterward. But Dr. Penistan, Simpson's former pupil, had begun to have doubts about his setting such a narrow window for the time of Harper's death. At about the time of the 1967 review, Penistan wrote that the stomach contents might have supported a much longer window in which Harper could have been killed, a theory that would have taken focus away from Truscott as a suspect.

There persisted the opinion that the case had been incorrectly decided. Journalists from the Canadian Broadcast Corporation and writer Sher Julian argued that new evidence was available that would have changed the outcome of the original trial. The defenders of Truscott proposed that police had been too quick to home in on Truscott as a suspect while not looking carefully at the whereabouts of at least two other men in the vicinity who had records for sexual assault and who might have known the victim. Skeptics pointed to the fact that several children who had given evidence about seeing Truscott in 1959 now wished to alter their stories. Those critical of Truscott's conviction also included forensic pathologists who considered Penistan's stomach content analysis to be unsophisticated by more modern standards. It now was possible, also, to consider a forensic element that had not been well understood in 1959: entomological (insect) evidence that had been preserved from Harper's body. If 21st-century scientists could show that flies had laid larvae on the body only after a certain point, then it would be possible to expand the time of death, thus casting more doubt on Truscott's being the killer.

The Association in Defence of the Wrongly Convicted also pushed for a rehearing of the case. Investigations by provincial authorities included an exhumation of Harper's body to test for DNA evidence and reviews of evidence by retired judges. The Court of Appeal for Ontario formally heard the case once again. In August 2007 the judges on that panel ruled Truscott not guilty. Truscott's lawyers had pressed to obtain a verdict that would declare Truscott "factually innocent," that is, that he had not committed the crime alleged. The court refused, however, saying that they had not heard evidence sufficient to prove innocence, but only that Truscott should not have been convicted in 1959. The provincial government presented Truscott with compensation of more than $6 million and offered an official apology for the original prosecution. Harper's family bitterly objected to all of those official actions.

SIGNIFICANCE

During the 20th century courts in Britain, the United States, Canada, and other nations increasingly allowed the testimony of medical experts. Chief among those was the forensic pathologist in a murder trial. The Truscott case was a harbinger of medico-legal developments that are well known in the 21st century: the use of forensic science as a standard courtroom tool, for example, and the presence of forensic pathologists as trusted and frequent expert witnesses in courts. With regard to its social impact, the Truscott trial helped make forensic pathology newsworthy for a vast public. Indeed, persons throughout the world not only grew informed about forensic investigations; they looked to them as entertainment.

Like the fate of many other defendants in modern trials, Truscott's rested on medical and scientific evidence and its interpretation by specialists. When those experts disagreed, confusion resulted. If the science of medical detection changed over time, as it did in Truscott's case, what first had seemed a reasonable conclusion might come under fire again.

Further Reading

Erickson, Don L. *The Silent Courtroom*. Seagrave, Canada: D. L. Erickson, 1988; Jones, Carol. *Expert Witnesses: Science, Medicine, and the Practice of Law*. Oxford: Oxford University Press, 1993; Sher, Julian. *In the Matter of a Reference re: Steven Murray Truscott* 1 C.R.N.S. (1967). Available online. URL: http://libproxy.uta.edu.2156/hottopics/inacademic/?. Accessed May 17, 2004; *Until You Are Dead: Steven Truscott's Long Ride into History*. Toronto, Canada: Seal Books, 2008; Simpson, Keith. *Forty Years of Murder*. New York: Scribner, 1979; Trent, Bill. *Who Killed Lynne Harper?* Montreal, Canada: Optimum Publishing Co., 1979.

The trial of Adolf Eichmann

Also known as: *Israel v. Eichmann*

Date: 1961

KEY ISSUES

Adolf Eichmann's 1961 trial for crimes against humanity presented logistical, political, legal, and diplomatic challenges. The facts of the case were something of a nonissue, for there was much evidence of Eichmann's involvement in the Holocaust. According to Israel's law, he could be charged and convicted of offenses that first were defined at the Nuremberg War Crimes Trials. But, according to many experts in international law, the proceedings against Eichmann—though morally justified—were irregular.

HISTORY OF THE CASE

For Israelis who had survived the Nazi death camps, in 1961 there was a sense of urgency about apprehending war criminals who had fled Europe at the end of World War II. Those criminals and their accusers were aging, as were potential witnesses. The fugitives from war crimes prosecutions often got help from pro-Nazi organizations such as ODESSA, which was founded by SS agents specifically to assist in escapes from justice. The war criminals often resided in right-wing nations of South America. Such powers showed little interest in extraditing the former Nazis, and there was no momentum for prosecution in West Germany.

The Israeli secret service, the Mossad, kept track of the movements of Nazis who had fled abroad to avoid prosecution at Nuremberg. "Nazi hunters" such as Simon Wiesenthal were another force for the apprehension of missing war criminals, some of whom actually had been named in the Nuremberg proceedings as key figures. Although at Nuremberg the Allies discussed trying several people in absentia, Martin Bormann was the only major Nazi who got such treatment. Of the Nazis who had absconded and were suspected to be alive (for Bormann was thought to have died in the Allied capture of Berlin), there were two figures in whom the Israelis and the Nazi hunters were especially interested: Josef Mengele, the concentration camp "death doctor," and Eichmann.

Eichmann had worked within a division of the Gestapo called the Reichssicherheitshauptampt (RHSA) that focused on "enemies" of the Nazi regime. While other groups such as Romani (Gypsy) people, liberals, homosexuals, and Catholics were targets of the Nazis, the Jews came in for the most virulent treatment. Within the Gestapo, Eichmann was known as something of an expert on Jewish culture. He even spoke Yiddish. He therefore got assignments related to what the party called "the Jewish question," meaning the systematic deportation and then killing of Jews.

Eichmann ranked below both Reinhardt Heydrich, head of the RHSA until 1942, and Heinrich Müller, head of the Gestapo, who themselves reported to Heinrich Himmler of the SS, which was the military arm of the Nazi Party. The level of Eichmann's appointment within Nazi hierarchy and the nature of his everyday duties were to become important issues at his trial.

Eichmann's basic job description was clear. He was in charge of transporting persons by rail from several places in eastern Europe to the concentration camps. He supervised the running of the death trains, sometimes overseeing their operation in person but more usually working behind a desk. He coordinated efforts within German-occupied countries such as Hungary. Upon entering a conquered territory, Eichmann first assured Jewish community leaders that their cooperation would mean leniency. The Nazis did not want to risk civil strife until they were thoroughly in control in any nation. Within weeks or months the deportations of Jews and other "undesirables" would begin at Eichmann's order. His word to the local folk was that the Jews were being "resettled" or sent to work camps. In fact, the trains ended at such places as Auschwitz and Birkenau. There, individuals such as Mengele presided over the trains' occupants. Mengele earned his sobering nickname "the Angel of Death" because he literally stood at the train platform in his white medical jacket, arms outstretched. With one arm pointing to the gas chambers and the other toward murderous work assignments, he assigned the "deportees" to their fates.

Eichmann had been living in Argentina for more than 10 years when the Mossad agents located him in 1959; he had assumed the name "Richard Klement." Interestingly, it was a man who had been blinded by the Gestapo before the war who put together clues identifying Eichmann. He in turn alerted a prosecutor in West Germany, Fritz Bauer, who, finding his own government unresponsive, informally alerted the head of the Israeli mission in Bonn. That Israeli diplomat, Felix Shinar, passed along word to his superiors, including Israel's prime minister David Ben-Gurion.

Eichmann's kidnapping was authorized at the highest levels of the Israeli state in 1960. It was not an easy decision for Ben-Gurion to make, for he feared that capturing Eichmann and refusing to turn him over to German authorities might jeopardize the newly established diplomatic relationship between Germany and Israel. Ben-Gurion, however, finally decided that there were too many

Holocaust survivors in Israel who wished to try Eichmann there to turn Eichmann over to the Germans. A veteran security officer who had played a key intelligence role in Israel's independence movement, Isser Harel, was put personally in charge of the case. He sent an experienced operative, Zvi Aharoni, to Argentina to track down Eichmann.

Aharoni had only a small contingent of agents with whom to work in country, but he could rely on Jewish volunteers—*sayanim*—to be his discreet lookouts. It took months, but finally, the operatives confirmed to their own satisfaction that Richard Klement was Eichmann. They also learned his routine. As they expected, the former RHSA employee was meticulous in covering his tracks. His young adult children, for example, did not seem to know much of his past, although Eichmann did warn them to be circumspect owing to his current right-wing political views. Staking out Eichmann's home, they waited for him to return to his wife (he had a mistress and frequently was away) to celebrate their silver wedding anniversary. When Eichmann arrived with flowers, the kidnappers were certain that they had their man.

Why did Eichmann not summon help or make more of an effort to escape? No doubt his captors told him that their mission was to convey him to Israel but also that to them, it would make little difference if they shot him. Most of the operatives who were assigned to carry out the abduction were persons who either had suffered Nazi atrocities themselves or had lost family members in the Holocaust. After a week in a safe house in Argentina, Eichmann's captors flew him to Israel disguised as a crewmember on an El Al airliner. Eichmann was drugged to make him compliant but still able to walk with assistance. His "colleagues" told airport security they had drunk too much the night before. The flight to Israel was palpably tense. The real airline crew did not disguise their hatred for Eichmann.

As Harel had anticipated, the Eichmann family did not immediately raise a general alarm about Eichmann going missing. They checked with hospitals, for example, but did not report the disappearance to the police. Other ex-Nazis refused to assist the Eichmanns, so concerned were they with going into more secure hiding. When Mrs. Eichmann finally went before an Argentine judge to present a formal complaint that the Israelis had taken Eichmann out of the country, the judge dismissed her case with the observation that the kidnappers could not be identified.

Upon arrival in Israel Eichmann underwent a series of interviews, as requested by the authorities and to which he consented. Those sessions in the winter of 1960 provided a great deal of information that prosecutors used at Eichmann's trial. The criminal prosecution of Eichmann lasted from April until mid-December 1961. An appeal of the initial court's decision was finalized on May 29, 1962. The three judges who decided the lower court case were men of considerable legal training and experience. All were fluent in German. The bench consisted of Dr. Yitzhak Raveh of the Tel Aviv district court; Dr. Benjamin Halevy, the president of that court; and Justice Moshe Landau of the Israeli Supreme Court.

There were 15 counts laid against Eichmann, from forced deportation to confiscation of property, from imprisonment in vile conditions to enslavement and murder. Count one of the indictment charged that Eichmann had "ultimate" responsibility for the deaths of millions of Jews. During the four months of Eichmann's trial the people of Israel seemed to focus on nothing else.

SUMMARY OF ARGUMENTS

As Israel's attorney general, prosecutor Gideon Hausner and a small group of assistants represented the state. The legal basis of the case against Eichmann was threefold. Eichmann already had been named at Nuremberg as a perpetrator of war crimes; he simply was not available to be prosecuted there. Among other offenses, the Nuremberg charter had defined membership in the Nazi Party as a crime. Clearly, Eichmann was a party functionary who had been involved in key planning sessions such as the Wannsee Conference of 1942. This was, then, a kind of continuation of the Nuremberg proceedings. But, Hausner also grounded the prosecution in an Israeli policy of 1950 that was called the Nazi and Nazi Collaborators Punishment Law. That enactment made certain actions within Nazi territory in the past into present crimes in Israel. In other words, the state of Israel had passed an ex post facto law under

which Eichmann now would be tried. Israel was unapologetic about such a situation. The justification offered was that the Holocaust was unique. The formation of the nation in 1948 provided a chance thereafter to address the destruction of the Jews during the 1930s and 1940s.

The most compelling of Hausner's arguments at trial was his contention that the trial was best justified on moral grounds. Hausner told the court—and all of the people listening by radio and following along in newspaper dispatches—that as prosecutor he was a voice for millions of victims:

> When I stand before you, oh judges of Israel, to lead the prosecution of Adolf Eichmann, I do not stand alone. With me here are six million accusers. But they cannot rise to their feet and point their finger at the man in the dock with the cry "J'accuse!" on their lips. For they are now only ashes— ashes piled high on the hills of Auschwitz and the fields of Treblinka and strewn in the forests of Poland. Their graves are scattered throughout Europe. Their blood cries out, but their voice is stilled. Therefore will I be their spokesman. In their name will I unfold this terrible indictment.

At first, Hausner seemed to be discussing the Holocaust generally rather than Eichmann specifically:

> . . . The deeds of those classic figures of barbarism, Nero, Attila, Genghis Khan, pale into insignificance when set against the abominations, the murderous horrors, which will be presented to you in this trial. Only in our generation has an organized state set upon an entire defenceless and peaceful population—men, women, and children, greybeards and babies—incarcerated them behind electrified fences, imprisoned them in concentration camps, and resolved to destroy them utterly.

But Hausner rapidly came around to a consideration of why this bespectacled, middle-aged man was a terrible criminal, worthy of the most severe censure that a court could impose. Hausner skillfully confronted the observation that Eichmann looked too benign to be a mass killer. The prosecutor also began to take on the argument that he knew the defense would raise—the contention that Eichmann was a mere functionary:

> . . . In this trial, we shall encounter a new kind of killer, the kind that exercises his bloody craft behind a desk, and only occasionally does the deed with his own hands. . . . But it was his word that put gas chambers into action; he lifted the telephone, and railway trains left for the extermination centers; his signature it was that sealed the doom of tens of thousands. He had but to give the order, and troopers took off to rout Jews out of their homes, to beat and torture them and drive them into ghettos, to steal their property and, after brutality and pillage, after all had been wrung from them, when even their hair had been taken, to transport them en masse to their slaughter. Even their dead bodies were not immune. Gold teeth were extracted and wedding rings torn from fingers.
> . . . Eichmann was the one who planned, initiated and organized, who instructed others to spill this ocean of blood, and to use all the means of murder, theft and torture. He is responsible, therefore, as though he with his own hands had knotted the hangman's noose, lashed the victims into the gas chambers, shot and thrust into the open pits every single one of the millions who were murdered. Such is his responsibility in the eyes of the law. And such is his responsibility by every standard of morality.

Eichmann had several offers from lawyers who wished to represent him, but he preferred the services of Dr. Robert Servatius, a German attorney who had been a lead defense counsel at Nuremberg. The Israeli government paid Servatius's hefty fees.

Servatius's arguments for Eichmann included a contention that became notorious: Eichmann was "just following orders" from much more highly placed Nazis. Servatius's plan of defense for the trial, however, was not at all simplistic. He emphasized several points that were related to Eichmann's comparatively lower status within the

Nazi Party, including that Eichmann acted under compulsion and in fact evidenced some sympathy for Jews.

It was uncomplicated for the prosecution to undermine that series of factual propositions. The state marshaled dozens of Holocaust survivors and cited hundreds of pages of testimony from Nuremberg linking Eichmann personally with crimes against individuals and groups. The prosecution spent much time, in other words, establishing that being sent on the trains that Eichmann controlled was a death sentence for most and torture for those who managed to survive because of their "usefulness" to the Nazis in charge of the camps.

Witness Avraham Lindwasser was one of the Polish Jews Eichmann deported from Warsaw in August 1942. Lindwasser recalled that he was spared immediate execution when he arrived at Treblinka because the camp guards needed someone to extract the teeth of persons who had been gassed:

> After all I was a dentist. . . . He pulled me by the sleeve, seized me by the hand, by the sleeve, dragged me by force, again with blows, and he brought me to a well. Next to the well there were basins with gold teeth and also pairs of forceps for extracting teeth. He ordered me to take a pair of forceps and to extract the teeth from the bodies by the side of the cabins, next to the small gas chambers.
> I was occupied in this work for approximately one month, a month and a half, perhaps less, perhaps more, until once I recognised my sister's body. Then the commander of our group was Dr. Zimmerman, I asked him to take me back to the cabin, I could not continue with this. [Dr. Zimmerman was the Jewish head of the enslaved dentists.]
> . . . That he should take me off teeth extraction and put me on to cleaning the teeth in the cabin, inside the building where we were living.
> Each week two suitcases were sent off, each of them containing about eight to ten kilograms. [The "plunder" mostly consisted of gold fillings.] They were delivered again to this Matthias (Matthes), who was the chief of our camp—in fact, the chief of our

barracks, told us they were dispatching them to Berlin.

After I knew what my job was to be, I could not stand it. I tried to commit suicide. I was already hanging by my belt, when a bearded Jew—I do not know his name—took me down.

He began preaching to me, that while the work in which we were going to be engaged was contemptible and not the kind of thing one ought to do, nevertheless we should tolerate it and ought to make efforts, so that at least someone should survive who would be able to relate what was happening here, and this would be my duty, since I had light work and would be able to go on living and be of help to others.

Servatius declined to cross-examine the concentration camp survivors.

Servatius maintained that the judges, as German Jews displaced by the Nazis, could not be impartial. In this opinion he echoed several diplomats from other nations who called for Eichmann to be handled by a more neutral tribunal. Servatius challenged Israel's reliance on the 1950 legislation, which he argued was after the fact and outside the territorial jurisdiction of Israel. He called upon Israel to dismiss the charges and turn Eichmann over to either Argentina or West Germany for prosecution He contended that Israel could not prosecute Eichmann because Israel did not exist as a state at the time of the commission of the alleged offenses.

VERDICT

Between August and December 1962 the three judges deliberated and composed their verdict. They found Eichmann guilty on all 15 counts of the indictment; 12 of those charges carried a mandatory capital sentence. After appeals to the Israeli Supreme Court and a clemency request to President Itzhak Ben-Zvi failed, Eichmann's sentence was carried out on May 31, 1962. Eichmann's last words were exhortations to his fellow Nazis.

SIGNIFICANCE

Until the Eichmann trial some Israelis had not realized the magnitude of the Holocaust but only their

personal grief due to it. The courtroom proceedings brought back floods of memories for some family members and survivors that caused the judicial hearing to be extremely emotional. And yet, not everyone in Israel agreed that mounting a trial was the best course of action. Some offered the opinion that a trial was a waste of time, money, and energy; why had the Mossad not simply assassinated Eichmann? Others wished for a protracted punishment, contending that hanging was too quick a retribution for Eichmann. Still additional critics of the trial posited that Israel had reaped international displeasure by circumventing the extradition process, thereby lessening the nation's stature.

International controversy over the execution of Eichmann may have kept Israel from pursuing two other major Nazis who had landed in South America: Mengele and Klaus Barbie. The Mossad had Mengele under fairly close watch at the time of the Eichmann kidnapping but determined that to apprehend Mengele might compromise its escape with Eichmann. Meanwhile, attention to the Eichmann case allowed Mengele to slip away from Argentina. Mengele went first to Paraguay, where fascist president Alberto Stroessner protected him. He eventually moved to Brazil, where he died in 1979 in a swimming accident.

Barbie was not so lucky. He had murdered hundreds of persons, among them many children, in Nazi-occupied France during the war. The U.S. Counter-Intelligence Corps (CIC) recruited Barbie in 1947 to spy on Communists, first in Germany and later in Bolivia. After a regime change in Bolivia and an alteration in the leanings of the French administration in 1982–83, the Bolivians bargained with France to allow Barbie's extradition. Although the statute of limitations had run out on Barbie's convictions in France in the early 1950s for war crimes, he was convicted to a life term in 1987 for crimes against humanity. He died in jail several years later.

Eichmann's trial brought much criticism to Israel for acting seemingly without respect for international law. Israeli officials, though, were more concerned with the opinions of their own citizens. In general, the population of that nation supported the capture, trial, and execution of Eichmann. Moreover, for many Israelis the process of bringing Eichmann to justice caused a general consideration of the Holocaust that had not previously taken place. The Eichmann trial therefore not only made the world more aware of Nazi atrocities; it caused many Israelis to confront a sorrowful past and discuss the reasons for the existence of the present nation.

Further Reading

Aharoni, Zvi, and Wilhelm Dietl. *Operation Eichmann: The Truth about the Pursuit, Capture and Trial.* New York: Wiley, 1997; Arendt, Hannah. *Eichmann in Jerusalem, a Report on the Banality of Evil.* New York: Penguin Classics, 2006; Bascomb, Neal. *Hunting Eichmann.* Boston: Houghton Mifflin Harcourt, 2009; Harel, Isser. *The House on Garibaldi Street: The First Full Account of the Capture of Adolf Eichmann.* New York: Viking Press, 1975; Hausner, Gideon. *Justice in Jerusalem.* New York: Harper & Row, 1966; Yarnold, Barbara M. *International Fugitives: A New Role for the International Court of Justice.* New York: Praeger, 1991; Zertal, Idith. *Israel's Holocaust and the Politics of Nationhood.* Cambridge: Cambridge University Press, 2005.

The trial of Nelson Mandela

Also known as: *The State v. Mandela et al.,* the Rivonia trial

Date: 1963–1964

KEY ISSUES

Like several other parts of the British Empire, South Africa gained independence in the 20th century, but separation in 1910 did not mean that its political system accounted for self-determination among the citizenry. In spite of the persistent criticism of racist policies in South Africa, organized by leaders such as Mohandas Gandhi, there still was a discriminatory system in place that heavily favored persons who were defined by law as "whites."

Indeed, discrimination based on race and ethnicity got much worse in the years after World War II in South Africa. After 1948 the policy of apartheid found expression in a series of enactments by the National Party government. For example, the laws prohibited blacks from attending universities identified as all white and designated special curricula for black schools; resettled blacks in certain areas and forbade appeals against those relocations; segregated public amenities by race and declared that such separate facilities did not have to be equal; required blacks to carry extensive documentation at all times (the "pass laws"); created and enforced regulations against interracial marriage and intimacy; and vastly limited the rights of "coloureds" (who were neither black nor white) to vote. The creation of "homelands" for large numbers of black South Africans effectively denationalized them and denied them the right to vote for members of the South African parliament.

The laws had teeth. The minority white government of South Africa also passed revisions of the criminal law that underlined the ability of the authorities to impose states of emergency and enhanced courts' discretion in imposing penalties for disobedience. The police in South Africa were well known to use strong-arm tactics such as lengthy and violent interrogations, and the courts did little to stop protracted detentions. During states of emergency, which were frequently declared, the police were allowed to hold suspected criminals for up to 60 days without trial. During those episodes many suspects suffered torture and even death.

HISTORY OF THE CASE

Persons of Dutch and British descent in South Africa who supported apartheid backed policies that separated the races. Such segregation was complex in a multiracial society. Enforcement of the laws sometimes literally depended on whether an individual "looked white" to authorities such as police officers or what one's speech pattern was. Campaigns by leaders such as Gandhi in the years between the world wars had somewhat improved the situation of persons who were neither white nor black Africans, such as the many persons of

Indian heritage in the region. Still, apartheid threatened to worsen the status of all persons of color, including Indians. And so, many nonwhites joined in the effort to strike down segregation in South Africa.

But, what form should protest against apartheid take? Certain critics of the system envisioned that they could accomplish change gradually, through the electoral process or even by bringing moral pressure from abroad onto the South African government. Many who denounced apartheid, however, looked to more unconventional means. Those who organized themselves into political parties dedicated to the abolition of apartheid in the late 1940s adopted some of the methods of civil resistance that Gandhi had advocated. Large-scale work stoppages, for example, were designed to shut down the economy so as to draw attention to the grievances of black South Africans. The most important group that pursued such tactics was the African National Congress (ANC). That organization had been founded in 1912 to advocate for voting and civil rights for persons of color. The ANC was a group that was racially inclusive, nationalist, and oriented toward professionals. It did not have nearly the popularity among ordinary folk in its early years that it came to have during the later struggle against apartheid. Particularly with the participation of talented young organizers such as Oliver Tambo and Nelson Mandela in the late 1940s, the ANC gained a higher profile among the public. The ANC also got assistance from groups such as the Congress Alliance, which focused on improving the circumstances of its many Indian members.

After a series of nonviolent demonstrations in 1956 the government pursued treason prosecutions against a large group of ANC members and organizers. Those targeted included Mandela, Walter Sisulu, Albert Luthuli, Lionel Bernstein, and several Indian Congress Alliance leaders. That mass treason trial dragged on for several years. The trial ended in defeat for the government owing to shoddy presentations of evidence and, indeed, an overall impression that the authorities were overreacting to the ANC's activities.

In March 1961, in stopping the trial prior to a formal wrap-up, Justice F. L. Rumpff observed that the ANC was not engaged in violent means of overthrowing the government, only that its "Defiance Campaign" violated current laws. Still, the treason prosecution showed that those in charge in Pretoria considered the ANC a major threat and were working to suppress it. Despite the government's targeting of the ANC, there were factions that thought the ANC too moderate. The Pan African Congress (PAC), for example, split from the ANC in 1959 on a program of "Africanism" that focused on the goals of black Africans.

Facing a government crackdown on such groups and a series of reprisals against black protests beginning in 1960, some members of the ANC formed a militaristic branch of their organization called Umkhonto We Sizwe (MK, or "Spear of the Nation") that promised to take up arms to achieve the end of apartheid. MK had the support of South African Communists. It was an alliance that caused concern among more moderate ANC leaders. For certain higher-profile figures in the ANC, MK was a facet of the anti-apartheid movement that was tolerated but never fully embraced. Mandela argued that the ANC would only countenance acts of sabotage against property but not directly against persons. Meanwhile, MK was less squeamish about violence toward individuals. While Mandela did maintain that MK would pursue property damage, including bombings, as a means to destroy apartheid, he said that MK would resort to open warfare only if those intermediate methods failed. The precise nature of the relationship between the heads of the ANC and MK, and the preferred tactics of MK, would become a matter of legal importance.

The massacre of 69 black Africans by police on March 21, 1960, at Sharpeville township focused new international attention on South Africa's troubles. The Sharpeville massacre also pushed even those previously committed to nonviolence to consider increasingly risky methods. In 1961 and 1962 Mandela went underground and helped found several MK branches. MK operated out of a farm at Rivonia, near Johannesburg. Mandela also traveled to England and elsewhere abroad, raising funds for anti-apartheid activities. The U.S. Central Intelligence Agency (CIA) followed him closely. The U.S. security and intelligence agencies apprised the South African government of Mandela's whereabouts. Mandela was arrested on charges of fleeing the country in order to evade trial and sentencing on a variety of charges, such as instigating strikes.

At the same time police carried out raids on the Rivonia farm. The South African government's aim was to shut down not only the militant wing of the ANC but also the parent organization by prosecuting its leadership. The "Rivonia trial" represented the official effort to neutralize the ANC and other groups that opposed apartheid. In contrast to the earlier treason trial, at the Rivonia trial the government took care to pursue charges that would be easier to prove. At the proceedings, beginning in 1963, the state framed allegations of sedition. That offense meant inciting disaffection rather than actually plotting to overthrow the government, although sedition traditionally and in this case was viewed as being a step on the road to treason.

SUMMARY OF ARGUMENTS

Due to the government's concern that holding the trial in Johannesburg would inspire civil unrest, the proceedings took place in Pretoria. Dr. Quartus de Wet, the judge-president (chief judge) of the Transvaal, presided; there was no jury. De Wet was the son of another famous jurist who had served as the governor general of the region during World War II. The Rivonia judge was unquestionably experienced. He was widely thought to be progovernment.

The trial began on October 9, 1963, with the reading of the state's indictment of Mandela, Sisulu, Dennis Goldberg, Govan Mbeki, Elias Motsoaledi, Andrew Mlangeni, Ahmed Kathadra, and Bernstein. Immediately the defense lodged serious objections to the proceedings. First, lead attorney Bram Fischer contended that the defendants needed more time to confer with their lawyers. They had been held under severe conditions. Discussions with defense counsel were monitored and reported to the state.

In addition, the defense took issue with the indictment itself as vague and inaccurate in spots. Furthermore, it was made available for defense review only at the trial itself, a clear contravention of accepted practice in Anglo-inspired courts. Judge de Wet ordered the indictment quashed, although

the prisoners were held pending the refiling of an amended indictment. That new document proved more factually correct. The trial proceeded again in earnest in early December, despite repeated requests for more time to prepare a defense.

There were three main branches of the prosecution's case. The government charged that MK was setting up plans for armed insurrection in a scheme called Operation Mayibuye; the MK operated with the full knowledge of the ANC, and both were in the thrall of the Communist Party; and those organizations had connived with foreign powers to invade South Africa. The prosecution called dozens of witnesses to speak about the violent aims of MK. Those witnesses attested to intimidation and threats against MK saboteurs who balked at extreme measures or who simply wanted out of the movement. Many of those witnesses, however, had been detained. To critics of the Rivonia trial, such witnesses were compromised. They had extracted themselves from confinement, intimidation, pressure on their families, and perhaps torture, with the bargain that they would turn state's evidence.

Mandela, as the leading ANC-MK member among the defendants, took the initiative in deciding how to plead to the various counts alleged. He admitted planning sabotage, denied that the ANC and MK were synonymous, and vigorously contested consorting to encourage foreign invaders. The defendants made opening statements from the dock only once the trial had gotten well under way, in April 1964. Mandela's five-hour-long speech stood out. It was a straightforward admission of his involvement in both the ANC and MK. In that sense Mandela took a page from the experience in court of Gandhi in 1922. He openly acknowledged commission of many of the acts alleged by his critics. Mandela's statement also went further in a personal vein, serving as an explanation of his lifelong struggles for dignity for those he considered his compatriots:

> I hoped then that life might offer me the opportunity to serve my people and make my own humble contribution to their freedom struggle. This is what has motivated me in all that I have done in relation to the charges made against me in this case.

Having said this, I must deal immediately and at some length with the question of violence. Some of the things so far told to the Court are true and some are untrue. I do not, however, deny that I planned sabotage. I did not plan it in a spirit of recklessness, nor because I have any love of violence. I planned it as a result of a calm and sober assessment of the political situation that had arisen after many years of tyranny, exploitation, and oppression of my people by the Whites.

I admit immediately that I was one of the persons who helped to form Umkhonto we Sizwe, and that I played a prominent role in its affairs until I was arrested in August 1962.

Mandela garnered praise for his simple eloquence in stating that he was playing for high stakes. He recognized that the price of failure would be the forfeiture of his life, and he was prepared for that sacrifice. He argued for inclusion and racial harmony, yet Mandela did not shy away from the idea of black control of South African politics. His closing words became famous almost immediately:

Above all, we want equal political rights, because without them our disabilities will be permanent. I know this sounds revolutionary to the whites in this country, because the majority of voters will be Africans. This makes the white man fear democracy.

But this fear cannot be allowed to stand in the way of the only solution which will guarantee racial harmony and freedom for all. It is not true that the enfranchisement of all will result in racial domination. Political division, based on colour, is entirely artificial and, when it disappears, so will the domination of one colour group by another. The ANC has spent half a century fighting against racialism. When it triumphs it will not change that policy.

This then is what the ANC is fighting. Their struggle is a truly national one. It is a struggle of the African people, inspired by their own suffering and their own experience. It is a struggle for the right to live.

During my lifetime I have dedicated myself to this struggle of the African people. I have fought against white domination, and I have fought against black domination. I have cherished the ideal of a democratic and free society in which all persons live together in harmony and with equal opportunities. It is an ideal which I hope to live for and to achieve. But if need be, it is an ideal for which I am prepared to die.

Sisulu decided that he would state his own case as a witness so that he could show through cross-examination that he was not afraid to answer the prosecution's questions. Sisulu and his fellow defendants did note, however, that they were not prepared to involve persons who were not already on trial in legal difficulties. They refused, in other words, to "name names" in order to lessen their own responsibility. As Sisulu was undergoing cross-examination, he faced questioning not only from prosecutor Yutar but also Judge de Wet. The bench intervened at several junctures to the detriment of the defense position:

Yutar: What precautions were taken to avoid injury to persons?

Sisulu: The fact that this was to be avoided was stressed repeatedly, and the targets were chosen with this in view.

Yutar: If you remove a rail from a railway line you endanger human life, don't you?

Sisulu: This kind of sabotage was not encouraged by Umkhonto.

Yutar: What are the consequences if a bomb is hurled into a room?

Sisulu: It was not in the nature of Umkhonto to do that.

Yutar: What of the two children who were severely burnt in Port Elizabeth, and one of whom died?

Sisulu: Mbeki said that this had not been the work of Umkhonto.

Yutar: Then who was responsible, if not Umkhonto?

Sisulu: Mbeki did not say.

Mr. Justice de Wet: There was a trial during the last war that I remember in which a bomb was placed next to the Benoni post office. Some unfortunate passer-by came to post a letter; the bomb exploded and he was killed. If you are going to start bombing buildings is it possible to avoid that type of accident? Can you ever be sure that you have avoided killing or injuring people?'

Sisulu: My Lord, an accident is an accident. But the precaution in fact is in the intention, and the method used—for instance at night, when people are not there. These are some of the things we take into consideration, that it should not be done at any time in any manner, in order to avoid the loss of life.

Mr. Justice de Wet: Your argument is that as long as you have not got the intention to kill people, it does not matter if you kill people. Is that your argument?

Sisulu: No sir. I am saying that precautions are taken in order to avoid such a thing. I am not saying that it can't happen. But I am saying that precautions are taken that it should not happen. . . .

Yutar: Name me one responsible person in the whole [Umkhonto] organization?

Sisulu: I am not prepared to give names.

Yutar: Were your saboteurs required to possess any academic qualifications?

Sisulu: No.

Yutar: In other words, you were reckless in your choice of persons who handled explosives?

Sisulu: That is an exaggeration.

The less well-known defendants gave moving, though shorter justifications for their association with the ANC and MK. Those statements

amounted to the argument that they resorted to plans for sabotage only when the South African government launched ever-more-repressive policies. Black Africans, defendant Motsoaledi maintained, had become desperate. They felt they were fighting not only political authority but also the brutal tactics of the police:

My Lord, I am 39 years old. I was a clerk and canvasser. I am a married man and have seven small children. I joined the African National Congress in 1948 and remained a member until 1954 when I was banned from membership of this organization. Although I am a listed communist I did not join the Communist Party after it had been banned, but I do admit that I was on the technical committee of the Johannesburg Region and was recruited to Umkhonto we Sizwe during the end of 1962. . . .

There was nothing left for us to do except suffer [after the ANC was banned]. Then Umkhonto we Sizwe was formed. When I was asked to join it I did so. There was nothing else I could do. Any African who thought the way I did about my own life and the lives of my people would have done the same. There was nothing else. . . .

I did what I did because I wanted to help my people in their struggle for equal rights. When I was asked to join Umkhonto we Sizwe it was at the time when it was clear to me that all our years of peaceful struggle had been of no use. The government would not let us fight peacefully anymore and blocked all our legal acts by making them illegal. I thought a great deal about the matter. I could see no other way open to me. What I did brought me no personal gain. What I did, I did for my people and because I thought it was the only way left for me to help my people. That is all I have to say.

In addition, my Lord, I want to say that I was assaulted by the Security Branch in an attempt to make me make a statement. . . . More than three months ago they arrested my wife and detained her under 90-days. And when she finished her 90-days, she was re-arrested again. As it is she is still in jail. I consider this disgraceful on the part of the police, my Lord, that a woman with seven children should be punished, because of offences committed by me. That is all I have to say.

VERDICT

Judge de Wet noted in passing sentence that he remained unconvinced that the accused men had motives as altruistic as they claimed. He also indicated that the state had been merciful in not charging the defendants again with treason. Since they were accused only of conspiracy to commit sedition, he would impose a penalty one step short of a capital sentence. De Wet sentenced all but two of the defendants to life terms in prison. He acquitted Bernstein and imposed a short sentence on Kathrada, accepting the defense's contentions that they were not members of MK at all and certainly were not involved in its high command.

The defense called author and politician Alan Paton to speak on behalf of a reduced sentence. Paton had written the best-selling book *Cry, the Beloved Country*. The judge permitted Paton to begin but then allowed prosecutor Yutar to cross-examine Paton. Paton's appearance turned into a three-way discussion between de Wet, Paton, and Yutar, with Judge de Wet along the way reminding Paton that a certain case in English history provided a parallel to the Rivonia trial. It was not an analogy that served the defendants well:

> There are many, many examples, Mr. Paton, of people who have resisted and been convicted of high treason and executed, when they have done what the accused in the present case have done. I have in mind the famous gunpowder plot in England. In the light of subsequent history, the people had legitimate grievances, but they were not entitled to break the law by force and what happens to people like that, historically, is that they are convicted of high treason and condemned to death. That is what generally happens, is it not so?

While de Wet's words in sentencing were stern, historians have amassed evidence to indicate that the South African government during trial bowed to international pressure not to impose the death penalty. The United Nations discussed the Rivonia proceedings, taking votes strongly recommending remission of sentences and even the stopping of the case altogether. Despite some reluctance on the part of the United States and Great Britain to lean on Pretoria openly, those nations' emissaries worked behind the scenes. They hoped to impress upon the South African authorities that executing Mandela and his colleagues could prove disastrous to the nation's international reputation. By the time that de Wet handed down the sentence, diplomats were privately certain that the defendants' lives would be spared.

SIGNIFICANCE

In many eyes the defense team prevailed at the Rivonia trial because the defendants were not executed. It hardly seemed that the government would have countenanced an acquittal. De Wet was not the judge to have handed down such a verdict, anyway. But, a life at Robben Island—South Africa's maximum-security location for political prisoners—was no minor penalty. That Mandela and his colleagues were serving the punishing sentence was known inside and beyond South Africa. As they endured their arduous terms, the prisoners were in the eye of a storm: a worldwide effort to end apartheid.

During the late 1970s and early 1980s, the South African government took steps to moderate the conditions of incarceration of Mandela in particular. Those skeptical of the government's motives suspected that the move was not for the reasons officially given. (Mandela was undergoing treatment for prostate cancer, and the South African authorities said they were showing him compassion.) Mandela himself argued that a lessening of his restrictions came from Pretoria's desire to negotiate separately with him. Also, the government saw Mandela and the senior ANC leaders as coming into too much contact with younger agitators who had been imprisoned at Robben Island. They feared the prison was turning into "Mandela University" and training a future generation in resistance. The senior ANC-MK leadership was moved to Pollsmoor Prison in 1982. Mandela was taken to a third facility in 1988.

Mandela recounted that the authorities presented him with several offers of freedom on condition that he would renounce violent tactics. Mandela's response was widely reported: "Only free men can negotiate. A prisoner cannot enter into contracts." Change of leadership in South Africa in 1989 provided an opportunity for the government to release Mandela and his colleagues. International campaigns for the prisoners' release went on.

For the next few years after his gaining of freedom in 1990, Mandela's stature increased still further. He had the opportunity to put to the test his commitment to "peace and reconciliation" after a series of confrontations between the ANC and the police. He also spearheaded negotiations for democratic elections. In April 1994, those elections took place; Mandela was chosen as the nation's first nonwhite president. After his retirement from the presidency in 1999, Mandela continued his key role as a conciliator within the nation. In an effort to heal the centuries of South African racial division the former president got considerable support from another black African, Anglican archbishop Desmond Tutu. With Tutu, Mandela labored as an advocate for reconciliation worldwide. Mandela's winning of the Nobel Peace Prize in 1994 was a testimony to his long prominence in South African politics, his consistent message favoring a diverse South Africa, and his personal sacrifice in serving a quarter century in jail after the Rivonia trial.

Further Reading

Bernstein, Hilda. *The World That Was Ours: The Story of the Rivonia Trial.* London: Persephone, 2009; Carlin, John. *Invictus: Nelson Mandela and the Game That Made a Nation.* New York: Penguin, 2009; Joffe, Joel. *The People vs. Nelson Mandela: The Trial That Changed South Africa.* Oxford, U.K.: Oneworld, 2007; Lodge, Tom. *Mandela: A Critical Life.* New York: Oxford University Press, 2007; Mandela, Nelson. *Long Walk to Freedom.* Boston: Little, Brown & Co., 1994; Sampson, Anthony. *Mandela: The Authorized Biography.* New York: Vintage Books, 1999; Strydom, Lauritz. *Rivonia Unmasked!* London: Britons, 1965.

The Ienaga textbook trials

Also known as: *Ienaga Saburō v. the Ministry of Education*

Date: 1965–1997

KEY ISSUES

The Allied victory over Japan in World War II meant that certain aspects of the Japanese constitution would be remodeled on Western (especially United States) principles. Particularly in regard to civil liberties such as freedom of the press, the postwar Japanese constitution echoed the U.S. Bill of Rights. The government of Japan, however, was left somewhat intact after the war. The U.S. decision to allow the imperial family to remain in power indicated that older leaders and traditional values would remain influential in Japan. There existed the potential for tension, then, between those in Japan who adhered to American-influenced ideals about freedom of expression and those who held a more conservative outlook politically, socially, and culturally.

Ienaga Saburō represented groups in Japan who inveighed against traditionalism in the postwar world. As a historian and writer of textbooks for Japanese schoolchildren, Ienaga challenged his government's longstanding bureaucratic control over what was written about Japanese history in textbooks. Ienaga had written a historical account of the early to mid-20th century that he thought to be even handed. He ran up against the Ministry of Education's policy of approving textbooks before they could be made official for schools' use. Ienaga's suits against the government questioning the approval process instituted a legal conflict that stretched over three decades.

HISTORY OF THE CASE

After Japan began a system of public education in 1872, textbooks were the provenance of individual schools. Textbook publishers did not have to go through any authority to print or distribute their works. The educational reforms of that period were a part of the Meiji Restoration begun just a few years prior. They involved the inclusion of foreign teachers and methods. That comparative freedom of expression for writers and educators did not survive the buildup of Japanese imperial might and an increasingly centralized national bureaucracy in the late 19th and early 20th century.

Ienaga was of a generation that came of age during World War II. Although generally opposed to the government's policies, he did not protest as the nation prepared for and embarked upon a course of expansionism. Ienaga was trained as a historian. He first held jobs as a researcher, gaining employment during the war in the civilian sector as a high school instructor. Fragile health kept him from front line service. He began teaching at Tokyo University of Education in 1944, specializing in intellectual and artistic history and Buddhist thought.

Soon after the war ended, Ienaga compiled his writings on Japanese history. As a scholar he was turning his attention away from his previous focus on earlier time periods such as the 10th century. While a young man, Ienaga had been frustrated by his inability to combat government restrictions on historical interpretations; for example, he found it unsatisfactory to have to explain in writings and the classroom that the Japanese royal house was descended from deities, but did so to keep his job as a secondary school teacher.

After the war, newly freed from the oversight of the imperial government, Ienaga turned his attention toward the interwar era of the 20th century. He became convinced that he needed to comment on Japanese atrocities during the 1930s and 1940s, which he thought were severely underplayed in approved textbooks. Among the events on which Ienaga focused were the Japanese occupation of Nanjing (Nanking) in 1937 and the chemical and biological experiments carried out on prisoners during the war under the auspices of Unit 731. Those topics were the subject of a number of scholarly inquiries during the 1950s and 1960s. Ienaga applied for approval from the Ministry of Education for several textbooks he had composed. One was at a general level and one specifically for high school students. Over the course of several years, beginning in 1947, Ienaga authored various texts, submitted them for vetting, and considered corrections that the ministry required.

In 1962 Japan's Ministry of Education eliminated from a list of possible textbooks a work by Ienaga entitled *Shin nihonshi (New History of Japan)*. Ienaga launched a series of suits against the ministry, claiming psychological damages from the process of revisions he had to undertake. It was a struggle involving three major lawsuits and several rehearings. Ienaga only partially won in court, but he considered the battle itself worthwhile.

SUMMARY OF ARGUMENTS

By 1965 Ienaga had formulated his reasons for embarking on a suit that he expected would be expensive and protracted. He stated that for too long the citizens of Japan had been molded by what their government told them to believe, including with regard to their own history:

> Up to the defeat in 1945, the Japanese people received a uniform education from their textbooks, and in accordance with government policy, that education was permeated by an unscientific, undemocratic, and bellicose spirit. Before the war, the state had come to provide absolutely all the needs of the spirit for all the people. Most of the people cooperated in that senseless, illadvised war and, trapped in the tragedy, paid dearly for it.

In the legal action that was to become known as his Suit No. 1, Ienaga charged that the Ministry of Education had violated his right to freedom of expression as guaranteed in Article 21 of the Constitution of Japan. He also maintained that according to another document, the Fundamental Law of Education (promulgated in 1947 as a companion to the postwar constitution), education should not be "subject to unjust control." While the older regulations on education in Japan were grounded in Confucianism, the education law did show Western influences, for example, stating the importance of educational opportunity and equal access to education. In Suit No. 1 Ienaga was asking specifically for redress due to his anguish at the nonapproval of his textbooks.

In his autobiography Ienaga recalled that the courtroom experience contained a number of dramatic moments for him. He remembered, for example, that during the initial hearings of Suit No. 1 the Ministry of Education utilized right-wing gangs to threaten him in court and at his home, for example, making noise on his street in the night. This was a theme not only in Ienaga's comments on his trials but also in his textbooks. To Ienaga, Japan was becoming more conservative during the 1950s and 1960s, effectively abandoning the commitment the nation had made to democracy during the period just after the war.

In court there was disagreement among the parties as to what the ministry had communicated to Ienaga in rejecting his textbooks. Ienaga reported that the government criticized his material on the Pacific war. He said that the ministry had told him several photographs made the section as a whole "too grim." In court the government argued that it had objected to only a photograph of a veteran with a prosthetic limb; officials had told him that image was inappropriate for a textbook. Such arguments contributed to Ienaga's sense that the government was engaging in obfuscation about its position. He also was angry that the ministry's posture in court was different than in more informal discussions with him.

VERDICTS

The first significant victory for Ienaga was not until July 17, 1970. This ruling concerned a second suit (Suit No. 2) that Ienaga had begun in 1965 to require the Ministry of Education to reverse its rejection of his textbook. Civil court judge Sugimoto Ryokichi of Tokyo District Court, joined by cojudges Nakadaira Kenkichi and Iwai Shun, nullified the ministry's noncertification of Ienaga's work, saying that the denial had been in violation of several laws. The government's censorship interfered with Japan's constitutional provision for a right to receive an education, and it flew in the face of the Fundamental Law of Education. It was important that the court read the constitution as not only giving students a right to an education. The constitution, they said, also permitted teachers to conduct instruction in what they considered to be a "true" manner. The "Sugimoto decision" was

a verdict that went beyond what Ienaga had expected. It rested in an interpretation of the constitution rather than only the education law, as had earlier, lower decisions related to Suit No. 1.

In a higher court ruling on Suit No. 1 in 1974, Judge Takatsu Tamaki reached a decision separate from and somewhat contradictory to the decision about Suit No. 2. The judge also countered the Sugimoto decision, finding that the government of Japan could screen textbooks and yet remain respectful of the constitution's provisions for freedom of education. At what was in reality an appeal of the Takatsu decision in 1975, Ienaga faced a hostile judge—indeed, so obviously disdainful of the proceedings that he was replaced at mid-trial. Soon after taking the bench, the new judge, Azegami Eliji, somewhat precipitously ended the arguments and handed down a narrow verdict: The Ministry of Education had not followed proper procedures when it rejected the textbooks in question. Judge Azegami did not comment on the constitutional matters that the Sugimoto decision had broached, though he did hint that there was no need to bring in the constitution when it was not at issue—a swipe at that earlier, broader ruling.

Subsequent rulings echoed the more restricted reasoning. As Ienaga hoped for a sweeping declaration that the government could not interfere with the "content" of education, he pressed on. In 1997 the courts responded to Ienaga's Suit No. 3 and a portion of Suit No. 2 by awarding two judgments that proved a partial victory for him. In Suit No. 3 Ienaga had challenged a ministry ruling from 1982 that hinged on another rejection of a textbook draft. Though failing to establish that government oversight of educational materials was unconstitutional, the decisions of 1997 did specifically state that Ienaga's contentions about Unit 731 were valid. The ministry had to pay him some damages, but the sum was not punitively large.

SIGNIFICANCE

Ienaga had reopened old wounds, his detractors maintained, to the glee of individual foreigners and rival governments such as that of China. Some of the individuals who claimed to have been harmed by Japanese policies during World War II now came to Japan applying for reparations. The stories of the "comfort women" in occupied zones such as the Philippines, whom the Japanese military forced to work as sexual slaves, were particularly distressing and seemed to cry out for redress.

Running almost exactly contrary to Ienaga, a conservative group called the Society for the Creation of New History emerged in 1997, promoting its inexpensive texts as pro-Japanese and unapologetically militaristic. That group secured the approval of the Ministry of Education for a textbook on Japanese history; the book engendered diplomatic protests from China and Korea. In the years since the decisions of the 1990s, and particularly after Ienaga's death in 2002, a number of Japanese intellectuals have argued that it was counterproductive to continue to emphasize Japan's mistakes or to dwell upon the war era. Ienaga, in other words, failed to carry the field among Japanese academics as well as the public at large, which seemed to flock to the traditionalist textbooks.

Critics of Ienaga considered him self-aggrandizing at best and unpatriotic at worst. To conservatives, he was a person who rejected key portions of his nation's history in favor of "Western values." Those who stood with Ienaga countered that they desired Japan to confront its own past—especially the recent past. They deplored instances of Japan celebrating its conduct during World War II, and they perceived that such reactionary viewpoints were reemerging. Starting in 2001, Prime Minister Koizumi Junichiro made several visits to the Yasukuni Shrine to pay his respects to the war dead; it did not go unnoticed that those deceased persons included several class A war criminals who were executed in the Tokyo War Crimes Trials. In Japan and worldwide such actions were perceived as reflections of a burgeoning traditionalism and drew diplomatic and popular protest.

Ienaga had contended that a critical examination of Japan's actions just before and during World War II was key to Japan's being able to move forward. To him, it was necessary for Japan to admit its mistakes in order to be able to form effective relationships with world neighbors. Ienaga was not necessarily expecting to win his suits. Rather, he wished to bring such matters to the attention of the public, force a widespread debate, and shine light on how Japan's judicial process responded in such controversies. In those senses his quest was successful.

Further Reading

Caiger, John. "Ienaga Saburo and the First Postwar Japanese History Textbook." *Modern Asian Studies* 3 (1969); 1–16; Huntsberry, Randy. "'Suffering History': The Textbook Trial of Ienaga Saburo." *Journal of the American Academy of Religion*, 44 (1976): 239–254; Ienaga Saburō. *Japan's Past, Japan's Future: One Historian's Odyssey.* Translated by Richard Minear. Lanham, Md.: Rowman & Littlefield, 2001; Nozaki Yoshiko. *War Memory, Nationalism and Education in Postwar Japan: The Japanese History Controversy and Ienaga Saburo's Court Challenges.* London: Routledge, 2009; Watts, Jonathan. "Saburo Ienaga: One Man's Campaign against Japanese Censorship." *Guardian*, December 3, 2002, 22.

The trial of the Chicago Seven

Also known as: *U.S. v. Hoffman, Hayden, Rubin, Dellinger, Davis, Froine, Weiner, and Seale*

Date: 1969–1970

KEY ISSUES

By the time the Democratic National Convention was held in Chicago in the summer of 1968, it was apparent that a generation gap existed in United States society. In morals, manners, and political opinions many young people differed from their parents. Distrust between parents and children was not unprecedented. But, during the era of the Vietnam War and the Civil Rights movement, intergenerational disagreement somehow seemed more forceful than in the past.

The breakdown in communication between young people and their elders now involved the question of whether old political forms were serviceable to newly enfranchised youth. Would young people choose to effect change through the ballot box? Or did they prefer taking to the streets? If they acted apart from voting, would they employ civil resistance of the type preached by persons such as Dr. Martin Luther King, Jr.? Would they engage in violent protests as advocated by groups like the Weathermen? Or were there still other approaches to political speech, such as the burning of flags and draft cards that better expressed youthful anger at government? The youth movement in the United States in the 1960s was neither cohesive nor sure of its aims. Some observed that young persons were more interested in sexual freedom, music, and drug experimentation than in politics. It was the ruckus that enthralled them, rather than any particular policy result.

The gathering of the Democratic Party in Chicago to choose a presidential nominee in 1968 was, on its face, a contest among factions within the Democrats. Contenders for the nomination included party regulars such as U.S. vice president Hubert Humphrey. That portion of the party was closely associated with President Lyndon Johnson and the U.S. armed participation in Vietnam. In another wing of the party, the liberalism of George McGovern and Eugene McCarthy commended them to young voters. Still, some wondered if a candidate who was perceived as being on the left fringe of the Democratic Party possibly could win a general election.

Robert Kennedy had been a key factor in the race, but his assassination in June 1968 left many young people adrift about whom to support within the Democratic Party. The death of King in April 1968 also had robbed some Democrats of their idealism and hope. Instead, many of the youth who came to Chicago arrived with an agenda simply of making trouble.

Mayor Richard Daley was the longtime, old-style political boss of the city. He lobbied hard to locate the convention in his town. Daley reminded party leaders of his service in collecting Democratic voters during the election of John F. Kennedy in 1960. Daley hoped to burnish his city's reputation nationally and further secure his own control within Chicago. Meanwhile, the medium of television had matured considerably since the last fully contested presidential conventions, in

1960. The television cameras were ready to record everything.

HISTORY OF THE CASE

The convention began on August 26 and ran through August 29. At the outset there was tension over the presence in the city of several youth groups, including the Youth International Party, or "Yippies," and the Students for a Democratic Society (SDS), as well as several antiwar organizations and activists. Defendant David Dellinger was an example of such a protester at Chicago; at age 54, he had a long record of opposition to war. The simplest explanation for certain groups arriving in Chicago in time for the convention was that they aimed to draw attention to their own agendas. They wanted to influence the planks of the Democratic Party. Such seemed to be the hope of "visitors" in 1968 such as Tom Hayden, who had been a cofounder and ideological force within the SDS, and Rennie Davis, who was a key SDS strategist.

Some who journeyed to Chicago had a more ambitious but amorphous goal: to provide a counterpoint to the traditional political proceedings. Such people included the Yippies, founded by a group of well-educated antiwar activists, including Jerry Rubin and Abbie Hoffman, in 1967. The Yippies made frequent mention of pigs to symbolize the status quo and particularly to insult the police. Yet, still others prominent among the Chicago protesters had no particular plan at all besides providing an opportunity for what they called a "be-in." They wished merely to be present, in other words, and would see what transpired.

What developed was looting, demonstrations, police suppression of protesters and observers, and media attention to it all. There was a riot at Lincoln Park on August 28 that spilled out into the streets surrounding the area—precisely the plan envisioned by SDS organizer Hayden. The police and the National Guard (which Daley had summoned rather too quickly for some local tastes) responded. The forces of order answered catcalls, taunts, and thrown objects with mace and tear gas and broke some skulls as well. Occasionally, reporters were caught up in the mayhem. The chaos threatened to take over the convention floor. Daley declared that the city authorities would not be intimidated. When convention speakers inside the International Amphitheater referred in negative terms to the street violence, Daley was seen on camera cursing at them.

While some of the activities out of doors were generated with an eye toward pressuring the party to withdraw from Vietnam, much of the action had no particular object. It was, as Yippie organizers said, street theater. When the convention ended and the smoke cleared, Chicago officials joined federal prosecutors to charge eight men with conspiracy and incitement to riot. The grand jury that considered the case probably was influenced by a changing political mood in the fall and winter of 1968. Although at first the grand jury seemed to lean away from charging the protesters with anything, the new U.S. attorney general under President-elect Richard Nixon, John Mitchell, pressed hard for indictments. Prosecutors also got encouragement to be severe from an angry mayor Daley.

Due to the diversity among the Chicago protesters, the conspiracy charges would prove problematic. As Yippie leader Hoffman said later at trial, the alleged conspirators were far from a united front: "We couldn't agree on lunch." There had been dangerous discord on the streets of Chicago during the convention, however. That visitors to the city had exacerbated the tension was little in doubt.

It was ironic that the protesters were charged under a recent piece of federal legislation that was supposed to promote civil rights. In addition to its more famous guarantees of fair housing opportunities and other policies to advance civil equality, the Civil Rights Act of 1968 included a sop to those who resented "outsider agitators" that campaigned for racial equality. The act made it a federal crime to cross state lines to incite a riot.

SUMMARY OF ARGUMENTS

The most serious substantive issue at trial was the charge that the eight defendants had caused rioting. The persons charged were originally Hoffman, Rubin, and Hayden, along with Dellinger, Davis, John Froine, Lee Weiner, and Bobby Seale. But, before that could be the subject of argumentation, there were some major procedural matters to be gotten through, most important of which was the

provision of counsel for the defendants. On the first day of trial, September 24, 1969, prosecutor Thomas Foran noted that four of the attorneys for the defense had not come to the courtroom but rather had resigned by telegram. A stickler for courtroom decorum, Judge Julius Hoffman promptly charged two of the missing lawyers with contempt of court. The contempt citation was a weapon that Judge Hoffman would wield frequently.

Also early on, defendant Seale promised to be vociferous. Seale said that he distrusted the defense lawyers that still were in service, William Kunstler and Leonard Wineglass. He demanded that Judge Hoffman summon radical lawyer Charles Garry, who in the summer of 1968 had shown skill in defending Black Panther Huey Newton on a murder charge. Judge Hoffman responded sharply to Seale's insults and finally had him bound to a chair and gagged. It was an image that Kunstler protested as most objectionable. The spectacle had the effect of putting Judge Hoffman's courtroom demeanor under scrutiny.

Seale's outbursts caused Judge Hoffman to separate his case from the others, so while the initial publicity from within the protesters' camp had touted the "Chicago Eight," they later referred to themselves as the "Chicago Seven." Seale represented all of the defendants' attitudes toward the judicial system—scornful. The accused heaped ridicule on the trial. They used name calling, particularly of Judge Hoffman, as a tactic to try to unhinge the bench further. Like the demonstrations outside the Conrad Hilton Hotel and at Lincoln and Grant Parks, many of the defendants' actions at trial were staged for an audience far beyond the courtroom.

Judge Hoffman often commented that rather than exhibiting an orderly demeanor himself, Attorney Kunstler seemed quite in sympathy with the defendants' shows of derision. The appeal record noted a typically tense exchange between Judge Hoffman and Kunstler at trial:

> On January 22, [1970] after a ruling by the Court, there were loud groans from the defense table. Instead of attempting to aid the Court in keeping order, Mr. Kunstler indicated that he encouraged and approved

of such behavior by the defendants. The incident is reported in the record as follows:

(Groans)

The Court [Judge Hoffman]: Mr. Marshal, I wish you'd take care of that.

Mr. Kunstler: Your Honor, those groans are highly appropriate. I get no help from you, so a groan of a client once in a while at least keeps my spirit up.

The Court: I note that you approve of the groans of the client in open court.

Mr. Kunstler: I approve of those groans, your Honor, when your Honor does not admonish Mr. Schultz.

The Court: I note them. I note them, sir.

Mr. Kunstler: What can I do.

The Court: You may continue with your argument.

The defense sought to undercut the charge of incitement to riot by noting that the high ideals of at least some of the defendants precluded recourse to violence. The defense produced a number of well-known character witnesses such as Reverend Jesse Jackson, singer Judy Collins, and poet Allen Ginsberg. The defense's point was that the defendants were more concerned about presenting alternatives to traditional political discourse than destroying property or inflicting personal harm. Ginsberg, for example, recalled talking with Hoffman about Hoffman's vision for a "Festival of Life" in Chicago in the summer of 1968 to rival the Democratic convention:

He [Abbie Hoffman] said that politics had become theater and magic; that it was the manipulation of imagery through mass media that was confusing and hypnotizing the people in the United States and making them accept a war which they did not really believe in; that people were involved in a life style that was intolerable to young folks,

which involved brutality and police violence as well as a larger violence in Vietnam; and that ourselves might be able to get together in Chicago and invite teachers to present different ideas of what is wrong with the planet, what we can do to solve the pollution crisis, what we can do to solve the Vietnam war, to present different ideas for making the society more sacred and less commercial, less materialistic; what we could do to uplevel or improve the whole tone of the trap that we all felt ourselves in as the population grew and as politics became more and more violent and chaotic.

Prosecutor Foran objected and Judge Hoffman struck much of Ginsberg's response as unresponsive, but it made for courtroom drama to hear the Beat poet's characterization of the Yippees' aims.

VERDICT

After four days of deliberation, on February 18, 1970, the jury announced that they were acquitting Froines and Weiner (who had been accused of making stink bombs) but found the other five defendants guilty of incitement to riot. Weiner and Froines had been conspicuously quiet and even a bit aloof from the other defendants. The evidence that appeared to carry the most weight with the jury was reports from police and reporters who heard several defendants, such as Hayden, openly talking before the convention. Some of the accused men said that they hoped demonstrations would become riots; they planned to urge protesters in the direction of disorder. No one was convicted of conspiracy.

By the end of the case, somewhat unexpectedly, Judge Hoffman began to appear more at ease with his role in subduing the unruly proceeding. It would take all of his forbearance to maintain calm as he announced a sentence on February 20. He ordered the courtroom cleared of spectators, including the families of defendants. He did let certain members of the press stay. Abbie Hoffman's wife, Anita, voiced support for the lawyers and the defendants but uttered a threat to Judge Hoffman as she was being led out:

Anita Hoffman: The ten of you will be avenged. They will dance on your grave,

Julie [Julius Hoffman] and the grave of the pig empire.

Unidentified spectator: They are demonstrating all over the country for you.

Richard Schultz [a prosecutor]: I just might point out for the record that we have in the hallway now the same kind of screaming we had in the courtroom.

David Dellinger: That's my thirteen-year-old daughter they're beating on.

Abbie Hoffman: Why don't you bring your wife in, Dick, to watch it?

Dellinger: You ought to be a proud man.

Abbie Hoffman: She would like to hear it.

As expected, Judge Hoffman gave each convicted person the maximum penalty. Each was sentenced to serve five years in jail and pay a fine. But, Judge Hoffman saved his real ire for the contempt of court sentences that he imposed for actions during the trial.

Even the issuance of the contempt citations was an occasion for verbal struggle between Judge Hoffman and the defendants. Abbie Hoffman at trial had complained that he no longer wanted to be known by his last name due to its connection with this jurist. (The two men were unrelated, but their last names were spelled the same way.) Judge Hoffman appeared especially put out with the defendant Hoffman after Hoffman engineered a bit of courtroom theatrics: The defendants had entered court in judicial robes. When ordered to take them off, they stepped out of the robes, stomped on them, and showed themselves to be sporting mock police uniforms. Upon hearing the contempt decree, Abbie Hoffman continued to ridicule the judicial process and its administrator. Judge Hoffman replied that he had been moderate in response to great provocation:

Judge Hoffman: Mr. Clerk, the court finds the defendant Hoffman guilty of direct contempt in the presence of . . .

Abbie Hoffman: I didn't say—I might say that a lot of those statements I didn't say, but maybe some of the other people that said them said it, but it's O.K., it don't matter.

Judge Hoffman: Direct contempt—

Abbie Hoffman: We are proud of what we say.

Judge Hoffman: direct contempt of the court with respect to the specifications mentioned.

Abbie Hoffman: You forgot that I wiped my feet on the robes because I didn't see a black robe of justice. I saw a white robe with a hood on it.

Judge Hoffman: Will you sit down. Yes, I was kind to you. I said you put the robe on the floor.

Abbie Hoffman: You're kind to us. You said you were kind to Bobby Seale when you chained and gagged him. You said, "I am doing this for your own good, Mr. Seale, in order to insure a fair and proper trial for you and the other defendants."

Judge Hoffman: Mr. Marshal, have that man sit down.

Abbie Hoffman: Sure. I can say it seated.

Judge Hoffman: Mr. Clerk, as I said before, the court finds the defendant Hoffman guilty of direct contempt in the presence of the court and in respect to the specifications which I shall mention here and designate the punishment in connection with each item. . . .

It was not only the defendants who got jail time. Defense counsel Kunstler came to understand that Judge Hoffman remained bitter about his conduct during trial. Hoffman ordered Kunstler to serve a multiyear incarceration for contempt.

The guilty verdicts for incitement to riot as well as the contempt findings were sent up for review. In two separate appeals judgments in 1972 the contempt citations and the original sentences were overturned. The reversals were on various grounds but mostly were related to Judge Hoffman's conduct of the trial. The appellate courts found his courtroom management lacking in judicial impartiality. They also declared that Judge Hoffman had failed to protect the right of the defendants to have a racially diverse jury. In 1973 an effort to reinstitute four of the contempt citations ended in ambiguity; the citations were upheld, but the defendants were allowed to get credit for time served. Coincidentally, Seale benefited from a hung jury in an unrelated murder case in 1970; he got out of jail in 1972.

SIGNIFICANCE

Were the Chicago defendants creative defenders of free speech or merely crude young people? Opinion as to the importance of the defendants' arguments depended on one's political perspective, but popular judgments about the Chicago Seven (or Eight) did not simply break down between those critical of an "establishment" and persons who defended the status quo. Rather, the proceedings pointed up other divisions in the U.S. public in the late 1960s. Some persons of a decidedly liberal bent were dismayed at the lack of seriousness displayed by the Chicago Seven. Likewise, the Chicago protesters' willingness to embrace violence as a technique—or at least not to disavow it—was of concern to those who advocated passive resistance.

Conversely, even those who were respectful toward the police and judicial authority wondered, after watching Judge Hoffman, whether judges' powers to direct criminal proceedings were too broad. The frequent television portrayals of "police riots" at the convention of 1968 did little to reassure the public that the police and the National Guard would exercise restraint in heated situations.

Legal scholars point out that the judicial system eventually came down on the side of defendants' rights in the appeals process. Judge Hoffman, while never formally censured for his conduct, clearly had not displayed the ideal judicial temperament. Social historians note that none of the

defendants seemed scarred by his connection with the Chicago conspiracy trial. The diverse group split apart almost as rapidly as it had come together for the convention. The defendants each took very different paths in mid-life, from the politically mainstream approach of Hayden (later a state assemblyman in California) to the continuing social protest of Dellinger and the more academic pursuits of Froines.

The term *Chicago Seven trial* eventually became a catchphrase for a judicial proceeding that was disrupted by defendants' antics. Still, the episode was oddly productive. When the Chicago conspiracy prosecution put important ideas in the mouths of irreverent defendants, it forced citizens to examine their own views on speech, protest, and the meaning of a fair trial.

Further Reading

Epstein, Jason. *The Great Conspiracy Trial*. New York: Random House, 1970; Feiffer, Jules, ed. and illus. *Pictures at a Prosecution: Drawings and Texts from the Chicago Conspiracy Trial*. New York: Grove Press, 1971; Long, John Arthur, Chet Meyer, and Jamie Jameson. *Conspiracy*. Round Top, N.Y.: Vellum Publishing, 2009; Schultz, John. *The Chicago Conspiracy Trial*. Chicago: University of Chicago Press, 2009.

The trial of Charles Manson

Also known as: *California v. Manson, Atkins, Krenwinkle, Van Houten, and Watson*; the Manson "family" murder trial; Tate-LaBianca trial

Date: 1970–1971

KEY ISSUES

The crime scene on the morning of August 9, 1969, was horrific, even to veteran homicide investigators of the Los Angeles Police Department. A beautiful young woman pregnant with a nearly full-term baby had been murdered in her own home. Her blood was smeared on the walls. Three of the victim's friends also had been slaughtered, and there was a fifth body in a car on the property. The motive at first appeared to be economic, for the victims were either wealthy or well connected in Hollywood, or both.

The dead included Sharon Tate, the wife of film director Roman Polanski. Newspapers sometimes described Tate as a "Hollywood starlet," although she was 26 years old and had starred in one well-known film (*Valley of the Dolls*), along with appearing in minor movie and television roles. Other victims that night were Tate's friends Abigail Folger (the heir to a coffee-manufacturing fortune); Folger's lover, actor Wojciech (Voytek) Frykowski; and Jay Sebring, a well-known hair stylist. The last victim, Steven Parent, was a young man with no relation to the residents at the Tate-Polanski home on Cielo Drive; he knew the caretaker of the property and had happened to stop by to visit that night. Despite the fact that the murders initially appeared to have been a byproduct of robbery, the more the authorities looked into the case, the less it seemed to be a usual type of home invasion.

Those who sought to bring the perpetrators to justice eventually saw that it was an unusually disturbing set of killings. The slaying of Tate and the other people on Cielo Drive on August 8 turned out to be part of a plot masterminded by a peculiar criminal, Charles Manson. Manson had ordered not only the deaths of those in the Tate-Polanski household but also the murders the night afterward of another couple, Rosemary and Leno LaBianca. The LaBiancas had no obvious connection to the other victims.

Manson's trial for the Tate-LaBianca murders became one of the best-known courtroom dramas of the late 20th century in the United States. In part the trial was famous because of the courtroom theatrics of the central figure himself. The lengthy and convoluted testimony in the Tate-LaBianca case also uncovered a deeper unease in U.S. society. Manson's actions underlined nervousness among middle-class Americans concerning the youth movements of the late 1960s. Although Manson himself was a drifter with a long history of mental illness and petty crime, several of those

who carried out his violent directions either had more stable backgrounds or at least looked wholesome. Susan Atkins was one of Manson's female lovers; on August 8, 1969, she stabbed Tate. A few years prior Atkins had sung in the church choir. If an outsider like Manson could lead seemingly ordinary young people astray, what could their elders expect from more politically active or even hostile members of the new generation?

HISTORY OF THE CASE

Early on investigators connected the Tate and LaBianca murders to each other through the scrawled messages in blood at the crime scenes. Manson's involvement, however, became clear only over the course of several months. The police got key information from motorcycle gang members that Manson had tried to enlist them in his schemes. Manson and Atkins were incarcerated in the fall of 1969 on charges unrelated to the killings. Atkins began talking to a jailmate about the murders, while Manson's absence from his home emboldened others to speak about him in connection with a murder that had occurred at Spahn Ranch, the hideaway just outside Los Angeles for Manson and his "family."

The prosecution eventually theorized that Manson's plan was to cause panic through the commission of multiple gruesome crimes. Manson hoped to create chaos among the entertainment industry and the wealthy in Los Angeles in order to spark a race war in the nation as a whole. Manson called this anticipated unleashing of violence "Helter Skelter" after the title of a song by the Beatles. He began by directing his anger at individuals who had rejected his efforts to be a recording artist.

Other details about the nights of the murders came out only at trial, forcing prosecutor Vincent Bugliosi to shift his strategy even while testimony was ongoing. A key development in the case was the decision of Manson family member Linda Kasabian to turn state's evidence; Kasabian had ridden along in a car with the killers on both nights but had not entered either the Tate or the LaBianca residences.

The prosecution of Manson was made more complicated by the fact that while the state alleged him to be the instigator of the Tate-LaBianca murders, Manson was not on the scene of the first (Tate) killings. And, although he had tied up the LaBiancas, he did not wield the murder weapon in that instance, either, but rather went to the car where several of his "family" were waiting and gave them instructions on how to carry out the crime.

It also was a complex matter to try multiple defendants, linking them to multiple murders. Who was at which scene? Who was present (literally in the room) while the Tate-LaBianca killings were taking place? Who knew of the plans to murder beforehand? To add further difficulty to the case, one key defendant, Charles "Tex" Watson, contested extradition from Texas.

SUMMARY OF ARGUMENTS

Initially the state planned to charge Watson, Patricia Krenwinkel, Leslie Van Houten, Atkins, Kasabian, and Manson with the murders. Assistant District Attorney Bugliosi was reluctant to bargain with the defendants but finally decided to negotiate with Atkins and Kasabian. Kasabian would testify at trial against her former "family;" Bugliosi did insist, though, that California grant her immunity only after the testimony was concluded. In return for remission of a capital sentence Atkins spoke to the grand jury in some detail about the events of the nights of August 8 and 9, but at trial she refused to talk. Bugliosi believed that other family members had threatened Atkins.

He stood by the promise of the District Attorney's Office not to seek the death penalty against Atkins, although she was cold and unsympathetic as she told of taunting Tate before killing her. Watson, Krenwinkel, and Atkins (and for the time being Kasabian) were charged with the murders at both residences, while Van Houten stood trial in regard to the LaBiancas' deaths. Due to Watson's extradition fight, as the trial began in mid-June 1970, it was Krenwinkel, Atkins, Van Houten, and Manson who were defendants.

Perhaps the most important witness at the Manson trial was Kasabian. Kasabian was on the stand for 18 days. She maintained that she had been in the car with the killers, so, in a legal sense, she had been a part of conspiracies to commit murder. She said she had not known that the killings were going to take place. She was especially important in confirming Manson's words to the others before and after the homicides. Kasabian made clear that Manson had not only told Watson what to do but also where to go inside the LaBianca house and how to cover the killers' tracks afterward. As they left to go into Los Angeles on the night of August 8, Manson reportedly reminded the women to "leave something witchy" at the scene.

The prosecution made several arguments that went beyond Kasabian's account of what she had seen and heard on the nights of the murders. It was key that Manson once had stayed at a home very close to the LaBiancas' house; thus, the LaBianca residence was not chosen at random. Apparently, he associated that neighborhood with wealth that he resented. Manson's real target on Cielo Drive had been music producer Terry Melcher (the son of Doris Day). Months before, Manson had approached Melcher about a music project but was turned down. Manson had tried to appeal to Melcher but had ended up at Tate's doorstep instead and was turned away briskly while Tate watched.

Bugliosi described Manson's general influence over the young women who had gathered around him for some months or years. The prosecutor detailed Manson's fascination with the Beatles and failed efforts to emulate their success in the music industry, as well as Manson's interest in end-time prophecies such as those in the book of Revelation. Bugliosi sketched out Manson's theories that black people would rise up against white society after being emboldened by Manson's crimes, which "whitey" would blame on persons of color. Manson intended for his family to flee for safety while the race war raged on and then to regain power from blacks.

Bugliosi took an unusually active part in the investigation of the case in addition to directing the courtroom effort. His willingness to go along and watch crime scene experts reconstruct the order of events at the Tate residence, for example, allowed him at trial to sift through sometimes hazy accounts by family members of what had transpired on the nights of August 8 and 9. Several of those witnesses and accused criminals had taken hundreds of "trips" on LSD and other hallucinogenic agents during their time with Manson, so they did not always speak with clarity. Bugliosi later detailed his immersion in the case in the bestselling book *Helter Skelter*.

In contrast to Bugliosi's meticulous approach, lead defense attorney Irving Kanorek seemed intent on delaying and confusing the proceedings. Kanorek already was known as an "obstructionist" in the courtroom, meaning he relied on frequent objections to testimony and arguments against the inclusion of pieces of evidence. Though good defense attorneys did raise evidentiary concerns along with objections to points that might be raised on appeal, Kanarek went to the extreme in the Manson case. At times Judge Charles Older barely controlled his irritation with Kanarek. The major line of argument that Kanarek and other defense attorneys pursued was that Manson was being targeted because he was a "hippie" with alternative moral values that offended mainstream society.

A serious complication in the trial was Manson's frequent disagreement with the arguments put forward by the defense. Attorneys representing Van Houten had an especially difficult time satisfying their client, who was instructed by Manson. Ronald Hughes, the attorney speaking for Van Houten, went missing in November 1970. Hughes's absence never was explained during the trial, though rumor was that Manson had ordered him killed for not cooperating with Manson's own defense strategy. Hughes's body was discovered several months after he disappeared, but his murder remained unsolved.

President Richard Nixon, a former prosecutor himself, made a serious error in speaking about the case while the trial was in progress. He publicly referred to Manson "being guilty . . . of eight murders." When the press reported the remark, Manson somehow obtained a newspaper and waved it at the jury. Judge Older had to interview each juror to ascertain if any one of the panel admitted being influenced by the president's declaration; none said he or she was affected by the headline.

Among the other notable moments during the trial was Manson's appearance in court on July 24, with an "X" carved into his own skin. He announced that this symbolized that he had removed himself from the world of the proceedings. Later, when he made the x into a swastika, several of his female followers who were not on trial but were vocal spectators in court followed suit. Manson repeatedly made comments under his breath or even aloud in court, criticizing the judge, the lawyers (including his own), and society in general. Manson's admirers sat outside the courthouse and within the courtroom. They chanted, sang, and donned clothing or hairstyles that they said showed support of him.

A controversy emerged late in the trial over whether the female defendants would testify. At certain points they had wanted to take the stand, but defense attorneys discouraged their offering testimony. Finally, Judge Older decided that to deny the women time to speak would be prejudicial to a fair trial, despite the risk that they might try to shift blame from Manson onto themselves. Manson, however, then demanded to make his own statement. He offered a rambling set of remarks that shed little light on the crimes. The defense never called any witnesses of its own. Manson's diatribe occurred after the defense had rested.

In his summation to the jury on January 15, 1971, Bugliosi returned to the two central difficulties of the prosecution's case: Manson had not personally wielded a murder weapon, and Manson's motivation was hard for the average person to grasp:

> In all murder cases, ladies and gentlemen, evidence of motive is extremely powerful and extremely important evidence. Motive points toward the killer. There is always a motive for every murder; for instance, revenge, hatred, money, fear, passion, escape. People simply do not go around killing other human beings for no reason whatsoever. There is always a reason, there is always a motive.
>
> Likewise, there was a motive for these murders. The fact that the motive for these murders was not a typical motive does not make it any less of a motive. Charles Manson and Charles Manson alone had a motive for these barbaric murders. It was an incredibly bizarre motive. The motives that the codefendants, the actual killers, had, on the other hand, was a very simple motive. It was

not bizarre. They killed the people "Because Charlie told us to."

Bugliosi also laid particular emphasis on the extreme violence that had occurred at the Tate and LaBianca homes. In total the killers inflicted more than 100 stab wounds on the victims—signs of rage and cruelty that went far beyond what was necessary to deprive their prey of life. It was a masterful summing up because the prosecutor painted a stunning contrast between the horrific crime scenes and the defendants' casual—at times whimsical—courtroom demeanor.

VERDICT

The jury of seven men and five women sat for more than 200 days—an exceptionally long trial even by modern U.S. standards. They needed nine days of deliberation in January 1971 to reach a verdict about defendants Krenwinkel, Van Houten, Atkins, and Manson: guilty of first-degree murder. The sentence was death. Watson was convicted separately of being the triggerman (except he used a knife in four cases) in the deaths of Parent, Sebring, Frykowski, Folger, Tate, and Leno LaBianca. The convicted murderers' time on death row was short, however, because in 1972 the U.S. Supreme Court declared California's death penalty to be unconstitutional. The five then began serving life terms.

Freedom, though, remained theoretically possible for all of the Tate-LaBianca offenders, several of whom married, wrote books, and gave interviews while behind bars. Some of the Manson family who were not directly involved in the Tate-LaBianca killings remained in the public eye long after the case had been decided. Lynette "Squeaky" Fromme, one of the most vociferous defenders of Manson at trial, in 1975 had pointed a gun at President Gerald Ford. Convicted of attempted assassination, Fromme was released from federal prison in 2009.

The extended Manson family mounted campaigns for their convicted colleagues to gain parole or compassionate release. Atkins, for example, who was convicted of first-degree murder for stabbing Frykowski and Tate, died of brain cancer while still incarcerated. She was denied release despite the argument that she had been a model

prisoner and had undergone a religious conversion. The most active speaker before the California parole board, urging that the murderers remain behind bars, was one of Tate's sisters.

A corollary to the killings was the story of Tate's husband, Polanski. Although he long had had an eye for young women, Polanski's behavior grew more risqué after the death of his wife. Polanski's art, likewise, became darker. Critics could not but link the sinister themes in certain of his subsequent films with Polanski's trauma over the murders of Tate and their unborn son. Polanski fled to Europe in 1978 to avoid being sentenced for the rape of a 13-year-old girl. Some of the defenders of Polanski in the controversy over whether he should be extradited to the United States evidenced sympathy for him that reached as far back as the 1969 crime against Tate.

SIGNIFICANCE

The crimes for which Manson was convicted included two other murders besides the Tate-LaBianca deaths; he likely engineered the killing of defense attorney Hughes as well. Manson's bizarre antics while on trial and his refusal to show remorse afterward continued to make him a magnet for persons who expressed hatred of "the system." Manson may have taken some pleasure in the fact that in the wake of the legal episode, his notoriety gained exposure for his songs and ideas. The main impact of the Manson trial, though, was its disquieting window into the sinister side of "hippie culture." The fear that a sociopathic leader might induce drug-addled young people to break into one's house with murder in mind became an American nightmare.

Further Reading

Bardsley, Marilyn. "Charles Manson and the Manson Family." Available online. URL: http://www.trutv.com/library/crime/serial_killers/notorious/manson/bibli_10.html. Accessed May 19, 2009; Bugliosi, Vincent. *Helter Skelter.* New York: W. W. Norton, 1975; Gilmore, John, and Rod Kenner. *The Garbage People: The Trip to Helter-Skelter and Beyond with Charlie Manson and the Family.* Los Angeles: Amok Books, 1995; "Nation: The Other End of Society." *Time* (August 3, 1970). Available online. URL:

http://www.time.com/time/magazine/article/ 0,9171,876675,00.html. Accessed May 20, 2009; "Sharon Tate Biography." Available online. URL: http://www.sharontate.net/home.html. Accessed May 20, 2009.

The trial of William Calley

Also known as: The court-martial of William Calley; the My Lai massacre trial

Date: 1970–1971

KEY ISSUES

The defense that someone was "just following orders" has been raised in several famous cases. Such a justification for horrific crimes had particular weight in military proceedings because the obeying of commands from superiors was a cornerstone of military discipline. Was such obedience ever punishable, though, as a higher crime than rebellion against one's commander? In the prosecution of Lieutenant William Calley, the U.S. Army decided that Calley had a greater duty than to obey; it was to refrain from slaughtering civilians. And yet, the resolution of the larger case that had given rise to Calley's court-martial seemed incomplete. In part this was because Calley was the only person convicted for the events at the heart of the trial.

The fact that Calley was charged with murder after his leading of a massacre at Son My, in Vietnam, on March 16, 1968, conveyed official military revulsion at his actions. It was a sense of disapproval that was mirrored in some public opinion. Some citizens of the United States already thought their nation's participation in the Vietnam War to be ill advised. Thus, to certain people, to prosecute Calley was a metaphor for condemning the entire U.S. role in Vietnam. What Calley's court-martial did was to provide details about action on the ground in Vietnam. This case only strengthened antiwar views among those who already condemned the war.

On the other hand, some in the United States expressed the view that American soldiers had a difficult task. As late as 1967 the U.S. commander in Vietnam, General William Westmoreland, was confident that the National Liberation Front of South Vietnam (NLF, or Viet Cong) was about to be defeated. Westmoreland said as much to President Lyndon Johnson. Westmoreland believed that guerrilla warfare was going to fade from importance, replaced by more conventional tactics. There was some factual support for such a position. Anti-U.S. forces in Vietnam had mounted the Tet Offensive in January 1968, and the United States had answered that effort effectively in a military sense. Still, both military observers and the U.S. public expressed concern about the recent course of events. The Tet Offensive had proved costly to address in terms of U.S. resources and lives. Also, it appeared that guerrilla warfare was not ceasing on the part of the North Vietnamese.

In contrast to Westmoreland's view of how the war was going, many inside and outside the military began to opine that this was an unconventional conflict that required strenuous measures. Civilians very well might not be immune from harm in Vietnam. Traditional rules of engagement might not apply in a guerrilla war, particularly if the war was to be "won" by U.S. interests. It was not long after the Tet Offensive that Westmoreland himself began to advocate "search-and-destroy" operations in Vietnamese villages. Such a strategy allowed individual soldiers to determine whether Vietnamese civilians were affiliated with the NLF and to act accordingly. The search-and-destroy approach often fostered an antagonistic attitude by U.S. troops toward villagers.

The search-and-destroy mentality was in marked contrast to the orders given by the NLF, which emphasized respectful relations with rural folk. The NLF, for example, engaged in small-scale (sometimes nearly one-to-one) operations with those in the Vietnamese countryside. It focused on asking for the use of resources, rather than commandeering them, and promising that impoverished villagers would gain property under a Communist regime. By the time that Lieutenant Calley and about 100 soldiers in his Charlie Company entered the hamlet of Son My in March 1968, it appeared that the NLF was much more committed to a policy of winning hearts and minds than were the United States and its South Vietnamese allies.

HISTORY OF THE CASE

What happened at Son My? Even in the accounts most sympathetic to the persons who did the killing there, there was concurrence that the deaths were not in combat. Nor was there much argument that the inhabitants of the hamlet were of military age or gender. Rather, the civilians at Son My simply were, at worst, in enemy territory and presumed to be hostile to the United States. They were Communists, or "reds" or "pinks." The women and young people were thought to be setting land mines on behalf of the Viet Cong. Among the U.S. soldiers, the settlement was not known as Son My or even by the name that later became common in the U.S. press, My Lai. Rather, it was called "Pinkville" in ridicule of its supposed status as a Communist hideout. Captain Ernest Medina briefed the troops of Charlie Company on March 15 about an assault that they were to undertake against the village of Son My. He gave the impression that only combatants would be present, with all women and children having been already "cleared out."

The soldiers of Charlie Company seemed to go berserk in the village when they entered it around dawn on March 16. Led by Lieutenant Calley, the Americans shot everyone who moved. The residents were dragged from their beds and killed in their huts. Several women were sexually assaulted and raped before being shot. Some villagers had their tongues cut out before being killed. The dead included a number of children and infants. No one who was present said that any male combatants were at the hamlet that day. The army eventually claimed that casualties numbered 23. The total of dead was then revised to just over 100. Later it came out that between 300 and 500 persons had died in about four hours.

A few villagers survived. A few people who were among those lined up at ditches and shot happened to fall beneath the bodies of others and were missed by the killers. (The Americans generally continued to aim at any sign of life.) A few soldiers in Charlie Company refused to partici-

pate; at least one American apparently shot himself in the foot rather than follow Lieutenant Calley's directions to kill.

Midway through the morning of March 16, the occupants of several army helicopters who were supporting the takeover of Son My saw the action on the ground and went down to investigate. Told that a group of noncombatants were huddled in an underground bunker, the flyers got the shooters (whether by threats or mere request is unclear) to allow the civilians out. They called for additional choppers and evacuated a group of 10 or 12 villagers, all women and children. At least one small child was plucked from a ditch full of bodies by helicopter crewman Glenn Andreotta and carried to safety. Pilot Hugh Thompson said later that he thought at the time of his own son, who was the same age as the rescued child. Thompson also recalled that the shootings reminded him of a scene of Nazi executions of civilians in World War II.

Shortly after it occurred, the massacre at My Lai became an open secret among the troops. Thompson immediately reported the incident, protesting the killing of civilians. His colleagues said he nearly resigned in disgust. Captain Medina's superiors got wind of the talk that many civilians had died. They could not ascertain what Medina himself saw on scene. He did arrive several hours after the killing started but had Medina himself participated in the shooting? In any case it appeared that the operation at My Lai was at best sloppy. Word was that Medina was informally reprimanded within days of March 16.

Through the work of journalists such as Seymour Hersh, the U.S. mainstream press learned of the story and published details of civilian casualties at My Lai beginning in November 1969. Hersh had to do considerable investigation to locate soldiers who had been involved at My Lai. His biggest break was tracking down Paul Meadlo, who finally admitted that he had shot people alongside Lieutenant Calley. Meadlo was at home on a farm in Indiana when Hersh interviewed him. Meadlo had lost a foot to a land mine within two days after My Lai. As Meadlo was evacuated by helicopter, he shouted to Calley that this was divine retribution for the killings of the previous day. Although Hersh later wrote for the *New York*

Times and won a Pulitzer Prize for his story on My Lai, at the time his stories first broke he was not well known. Details about the events at My Lai circulated openly, but not among major news services.

Photographs by military photograp011er Ronald Haeberle provided stunning corroboration of the fact that many of the dead at My Lai were not merely noncombatants but children and even babies. Haeberle asked the shooters at My Lai to let him photograph a group of women and children. Haeberle's picture of the anguished group just seconds before the Americans opened fire with their M-16 rifles became one of the most famous images of the war. In November 1969, when Haeberle submitted his visual documentation to the Cleveland *Plain Dealer,* the newspaper attempted to confirm with the U.S. military that Haeberle's images were legitimate representations of action in Vietnam. Instead, the news outlet got pressure from the army not to print the gruesome photographs.

The army warned Haeberle that the photos were army property; he answered that the color shots were taken with his personal camera. He had turned over the official black-and-white photographs to his superiors because they contained nothing terribly controversial. Haeberle—who later was criticized for selling his images and for not apprising the army of his knowledge of My Lai—countered that he believed the army would have torn up his color images and suppressed his information had he come forward sooner. Among those who advised the Ohio newspaper not to print Haeberle's pictures was the eventual army prosecutor of Lieutenant Calley, Aubrey Daniel. The photos proved shocking to the public when they appeared in *Life* magazine in the fall of 1969.

Within a few months of the My Lai massacre an American soldier who had served in Vietnam, Ron Ridenhour, sent letters about My Lai to various politicians in the United States. Only one major official, Congressman Morris Udall of Arizona, decided to inquire further. Ridenhour had not been at My Lai but knew many soldiers who were present. He was newly deployed in Vietnam in the winter of 1968. The U.S. Defense Department discussed My Lai with various leaders in the administration of President Richard Nixon, includ-

ing National Security Advisor Henry Kissinger. The U.S. National Security Archive contains records of comments by Defense Secretary Melvin Laird to Kissinger about Haeberle's disturbing photos.

The U.S. Army launched internal investigations of My Lai in spring 1969. Initially, army investigators in Vietnam who were connected with the 11th Light Infantry Brigade (to which Charlie Company was attached) concluded that the operations at My Lai had been against the Viet Cong overall but that about 20 civilians had been killed accidentally on March 16. But then, investigation into Ridenhour's charges that an officer named "Kalley" had killed hundreds of civilians at My Lai was launched, headed by Colonel William Wilson. Wilson spoke directly to Ridenhour as well as several others who had been at My Lai. He began his inquiry unconvinced of the truth of the rumors, but soon he said that he found Ridenhour to be an "impressive" young man and the allegations "depressingly" real. When Wilson interviewed Warrant Officer Thompson, he grew even more alarmed, for he thought Thompson's account as the helicopter pilot also to be highly convincing.

Wilson's investigation fed into a higher-level inquiry headed by Lieutenant General William Peers. Peers's investigators literally went to the scene of the alleged massacre, examined bodies, and reconstructed a time line for the events of March 16. When the two reports—Peers's meticulous recreation and Wilson's exhaustive sessions with witnesses—were combined, the result was a terrible internal criticism of what had transpired at My Lai. Much blame, said the Peers Report, lay with Lieutenant Calley, but others (especially Medina) also were named as complicit in the atrocities.

It was when the army tendered its charges against Calley and the trial began in November 1970 that a rush of national media coverage occurred. At that time, My Lai began to be discussed on national television networks. Meadlo's interview by Mike Wallace of CBS News was broadcast on November 20, 1970, the first day of Calley's court-martial. It was in that conversation that Meadlo admitted his own part in the killings. Almost as shocking as that admission was Meadlo's demeanor. His account to Wallace was fatalistic and oddly calm.

SUMMARY OF ARGUMENTS

Calley had several advantages beyond the wish of the Nixon administration to quiet the controversy quickly. His defense lawyer, George Latimer, was an experienced military judge, while prosecutor Daniel was still in his 20s and considerably less seasoned. The military officers who made up Calley's jury had combat experience, and five of the six had served in Vietnam. Surely, the defense contended, Calley would earn sympathy considering the pressures of conducting operations in the difficult conditions of the spring of 1968 near Pinkville.

Lieutenant Calley and his defense lawyers originally argued that the carnage at My Lai was unintended, the result of airborne operations that missed their marks. The defense seemed to bank on the fact that other soldiers in Charlie Company would refuse to incriminate themselves in the actions at My Lai or simply would not want to go against one of their fellow fighting men. A major problem for the prosecution was that almost everyone on the ground had been a perpetrator or at least had failed to stop the slaughter.

Eventually, however, lead judge Reid Kennedy compelled Meadlo, under threat of a contempt citation, to repeat his televised remarks for the court. After getting a grant of immunity, Meadlo relented and told of standing with Calley and firing his own weapon. Judge Kennedy seemed barely able to contain his dislike of Meadlo during much of the proceeding. Whether that distaste was based on Meadlo's televised interview or Meadlo's initial refusal to testify was unclear.

Several potential witnesses declined to give their recollections of March 16, invoking the Fifth Amendment privilege against self-incrimination. But a few other men who had been at My Lai corroborated Meadlo's account. Soldier Dennis Conti, for example, was examined first by the prosecutor, Daniel, and then by another defense lawyer, Richard Kay:

> Conti: Calley told me and Meadlo to take the people off and push them in a rice paddy. We took them out there, pushed them off the trail and made them squat down and bunch up so they couldn't get up and run. We stayed there and guarded them.

> At this time, I see a young child running from a hootch [hut] toward us. He seen us and he took off. I dropped my gear and checked out a hootch with a woman and a child in it. There was an old woman in a under [tunnel]. I took her out and put her on the ground. Then I saw a man running away. I took the other woman and child to the group. The old woman wouldn't go, so I left her there.

> Daniel: What was Meadlo doing at this time?

> Conti: He was guarding the people.

> Daniel: Where was he?

> Conti: He was standing on the village side of the people.

> Daniel: Then what happened?

> Conti: Lieutenant Calley came out and said take care of these people. So we said, okay, so we stood there and watched them. He went away, then he came back and said, "I thought I told you to take care of these people." We said, "We are." He said, "I mean, kill them." I was a little stunned and I didn't know what to do. He said, "Come around this side. We'll get on line and we'll fire into them." I said, "No, I've got a grenade launcher. I'll watch the tree line." I stood behind them and they stood side by side. So they—Calley and Meadlo—got on line and fired directly into the people. There were bursts and single shots for two minutes. It was automatic. The people screamed and yelled and fell. I guess they tried to get up, too. They couldn't. That was it. The people were pretty well messed up. Lots of heads was shot off, pieces of heads and pieces of flesh flew off the sides and arms. They were all messed up. Meadlo fired a little bit and broke down. He was crying. He said he couldn't do any more. He couldn't kill anymore people. He couldn't fire into the people any more. He gave me his weapon into my hands. I said I wouldn't.

"If they're going to be killed, I'm not going to do it. Let Lieutenant Calley do it," I told him. So I gave Meadlo back his weapon. At that time there was only a few kids still alive. Lieutenant Calley killed them one-by-one. Then I saw a group of five women and six kids—eleven in all—going to a tree line. "Get 'em! Get 'em! Kill 'em!" Calley told me. I waited until they got to the line and fired off four or five grenades. I don't know what happened. . . .

The cross-examination by Kay brought up rumors that Conti was impaired by either marijuana or prescription medication. Kay also questioned Conti about whether he had bragged about raping women on the scene. But Kay failed to shake the stark testimony from Conti about the shootings led by Calley:

Kay: Did you see any dead bodies at My Lai?—How many?

Conti: Quite a few

Kay: Were they sleeping or did they appear to be dead?

Conti: Well, they had holes in 'em so I assumed they were dead. . . .

Calley then took the stand. He reverted to the old justification that he had gotten orders from his superior, Captain Medina, and simply was carrying them out. He was unapologetic about the bloodshed:

I was ordered to go in there and destroy the enemy. That was my job that day. That was the mission I was given. I did not sit down and think in terms of men, women and children. They were all classified as the same, and that's the classification that we dealt with over there, just as the enemy. I felt then and I still do that I acted as I was directed, and I carried out the order that I was given and I do not feel wrong in doing so.

Others in Charlie Company agreed that Captain Medina had described the village as hostile

and had ordered Calley to "destroy the enemy." Calley testified that his own interpretation of "enemy" was "everyone at My Lai." Captain Medina stated on the stand at Calley's trial that he had meant for only "enemy combatants" to be killed: "No, you do not kill women and children. You use common sense. If they have a weapon and they are trying to engage you, then you shoot back. . . ."

Lead prosecutor Daniel, in his summary to the court, addressed the defense argument that in war all bets were off as to which persons died. Daniel made short work of the contention that the fatalities at My Lai were civilians who simply happened to be in harm's way. He reminded the court of witness after witness who testified that Calley and the other shooters deliberately aimed at noncombatants, including a number of children and infants. Here, most persuasive was the testimony of the helicopter pilots and crewmen such as Jerry Gulverhouse and Thompson, who had tried to stop the carnage.

Daniel refused to grant to the defense the point that the pilots and other witnesses might have been mistaken about the number of casualties. He refreshed the court's memory about the fact that certain witnesses literally had stepped down into an irrigation ditch to rescue an injured baby. Those soldiers would have had a very good view of how many people had been shot. He reminded the court, too, that if even one person had been killed in the manner alleged, then Calley could be termed a murderer.

Daniel's most poignant point was that even in wartime there were some deaths that were not justifiable. He dealt head-on with the assertion that the villagers of My Lai were Viet Cong sympathizers whom the soldiers of Charlie Company had carte blanche to kill on sight:

This was a combat operation, gentleman, and the military judge will instruct you that the conduct of warfare is not wholly unregulated by law, and that nations, including this nation, have agreed to treaties which attempt to maintain certain fundamental humanitarian principles applicable in the conduct of warfare. And over a period of time these practices have dealt with the circumstances and the law concerning when human life may be justifiably taken as an act of war. The killing of [an] armed enemy in combat is certainly a justifiable act of war. It's the mission of the soldier to meet and close with and destroy the enemy. However, the law attempts to protect those persons who are noncombatants. Even those individuals who may actually have engaged in warfare, once they have surrendered. They are entitled to be treated humanely. They are entitled not to be summarily executed.

VERDICT

Calley had been charged with the premeditated murder of "109 Oriental human beings." On March 31, 1971, the six-judge panel convicted him on 22 counts of the charge. Although Calley might have been hanged for his offenses, he did not receive the death penalty. The court-martial tendered the next most severe sentence: life imprisonment. It was a surprisingly unpopular verdict.

Within 24 hours, President Nixon ordered Calley transferred from the prison at Fort Leavenworth to house arrest at Fort Benning. It was a clear signal that the commander in chief thought the sentence not only too stern but completely incorrect. The president continued to try to mitigate Calley's punishment, causing dissent even within his own administration. Certain members of Nixon's cabinet thought it wrong to undercut the decision of the court-martial. Nixon, along with several other political leaders such as Georgia governor Jimmy Carter, publicly professed support for Calley. After a complex series of hearings within Fort Benning, the U.S. Army, the Department of Defense, and federal courts, Calley got his freedom in 1974. It was only a conditional pardon, and his court-martial conviction remained valid, but he was a free man.

During the Calley court-martial, President Nixon was under fire from critics of the Vietnam War. In responding to the case, the president often appeared worried that the prosecution of Calley would affect negotiations with the North Vietnamese or would change U.S. citizens' perceptions of the war effort. Polls of the American public seemed to justify such concerns. In his memoirs

Nixon noted that comment to the White House was overwhelmingly in favor of a remission of punishment for Calley: "Public reaction to this announcement [the sentencing] was emotional and sharply divided. More than 5,000 telegrams arrived at the White House, running 100 to 1 in favor of clemency."

A poignant protest against the perceived interference of the administration in the Calley case came from Daniel, who wrote a lengthy letter to President Nixon about it:

Certainly, no one wanted to believe what occurred at My Lai, including the officers who sat in judgment of Lieutenant Calley. To believe, however, that any large percentage of the population could believe the evidence which was presented and approve of the conduct of Lieutenant Calley would be as shocking to my conscience as the conduct itself, since I believe that we are still a civilized nation.

If such be the case, then the war in Viet-Nam has brutalized us more than I care to believe, and it must cease. How shocking it is if so many people across the nation have failed to see the moral issue which was involved in the trial of Lieutenant Calley—that it is unlawful for an American soldier to summarily execute unarmed and unresisting men, women, children, and babies.

But how much more appalling it is to see so many of the political leaders of the nation who have failed to see the moral issue, or, having seen it, to compromise it for political motive in the face of apparent public displeasure with the verdict.

. . . Your intervention has, in my opinion, damaged the military judicial system and lessened any respect it may have gained as a result of the proceedings. You have subjected a judicial system of this country to the criticism that it is subject to political influence, when it is a fundamental precept of our judicial system that the legal processes of this country must be kept free from any outside influences. What will be the impact of your decision upon the future trials, particularly those within the military?

The majority of public opinion and within the army held that Calley was a scapegoat for deepening distrust of U.S. policy in Vietnam. Some, both inside and apart from the military, thought Calley had been targeted unfairly; they believed that higher officers had authorized the massacre of civilians. Calley was the only person convicted for his part in the massacre at My Lai. His superior, Captain Medina, won an acquittal in 1971. Legal historians frequently contend that the presence of celebrated attorney F. Lee Bailey on Medina's defense team was key to that exoneration.

In a speech to a Kiwanis club in 2009, Calley gave his first public statement about My Lai since the court-martial. He said that he regretted his role in the killings but also justified Charlie Company's actions as being motivated by fear that the village was "hot." He said he and his men believed that if they left anyone alive at My Lai, they would be shot at from behind as had occurred in the days previous to the massacre. Calley reiterated that he had orders from above to "take out" the inhabitants.

SIGNIFICANCE

More than 40 years after its occurrence, the My Lai massacre continued to serve as a bellwether of opinion about the Vietnam War. Some commentators viewed the tragedy as an example of poor commanding rather than a reflection on U.S. military policy in Vietnam. My Lai, in other words, was an isolated event. Those who served in Vietnam on behalf of the United States were neither drug-crazed nor mindless killers. The average soldier, so the argument went, did not perpetrate such atrocities. Few who held this view actually excused the actions of the killers. Rather, they noted that those who committed outrages ought to have been punished severely. Calley, such observers note, received a stiff sentence from the court, yet politics apparently influenced his situation such that he stayed in confinement only a comparatively short time.

What sometimes is lost in nonmilitary histories of the Calley case is the fact that some of the sternest criticism of Calley's actions came from within the military. At least a few of his peers at the scene tried to halt the massacre. Other soldiers turned him in, perhaps at the cost of their own safety from those who might resent such an action as they continued to serve in Vietnam. A few went so far as to testify against him while knowing that they might be implicated in wrongdoing for speaking out. The Peers Report expressed outrage for My Lai, and the court-martial handed down a strong sentence. Cynical views of the military proceedings saw the army as simply winnowing out a bad seed or, worse, pinning blame for every outrage in Vietnam on one perpetrator. Another perspective might paint the military's prosecution of Calley as a sincere effort to uphold American values, even under the duress of an unwinnable war.

Further Reading

Bilton, Michael, and Kevin Sim. *Four Hours in My Lai.* New York: Penguin, 1993; Oliver, Kendrick. *The My Lai Massacre in American History and Memory.* Manchester, U.K.: Manchester University Press, 2006; Olsen, James Stuart, and Randy Roberts. *My Lai: A Brief History with Documents.* New York: Bedford/St. Martin's, 1998; U.S. Department of the Army. *The My Lai Massacre and Its Cover-up: Beyond the Reach of Law? The Peers Commission Report.* New York: Free Press, 1976.

The thalidomide case

Also known as: *Attorney General v. Times Newspapers Ltd*; the *Sunday Times* case

Date: 1979

KEY ISSUES

The British long prided themselves on having the right of open discussion of public issues. In a case in the late 1970s, though, Great Britain got a wake-up call. The European Court of Human Rights declared that British law as it stood did not allow sufficient room for the publication of details of controversies that were of considerable public interest. The European authority ruled that British courts must allow discussion of cases in the press under certain circumstances. Most especially this was required when the legal proceedings were of long standing and when the discussion was serious and in the public interest.

The European court's ruling was a criticism of British laws on contempt of court and, more broadly, libel. In particular, it was a condemnation (legal experts disagreed as to whether it should be called an "overturning") of the decision of the House of Lords in the case of *Attorney General v. Times Newspapers Ltd* (1973). That decision of Britain's highest legal authority concerned a scandal that had received worldwide attention 10 or 12 years earlier. The controversy had international implications. It involved the broad distribution of a drug that had proven harmful to thousands of persons, chiefly infants born with physical problems resulting from the drug's administration to their mothers.

HISTORY OF THE CASE

In the late 1950s a German pharmaceuticals manufacturer, Grünenthal, through subsidiaries and licensees such as Distillers Biochemicals Ltd. of Britain, began the distribution of a drug marketed as a tranquilizer and sleep aid. Among the persons designated as a target market for the drug were pregnant women. Despite indications from its own human trials that the drug, thalidomide, caused a variety of side effects, Grünenthal pursued an aggressive strategy in encouraging physicians to distribute samples to their patients, sometimes (as in Australia) as an over-the-counter remedy for sleeplessness.

The company marketed the drug in at least 46 countries, though often using local licensees with different corporate monikers. In the United States one potential corporation, Smith-Kline Pharmaceuticals, rebuffed Grünenthal, saying that testing methods even in animal subjects were inadequate. Another company, Richardson-Merrill, in 1959 took up thalidomide as a possibility, offering to shepherd it through the Food and Drug Administration's (FDA) approval process. In Europe the drug was a success in financial terms for Grünenthal. Though it was not without

problems during its earliest wide uses, initial patient complaints seemed to be about side effects that were manageable.

In order to obtain FDA approval Richardson-Merrill not only had to cite examples of human trials in Germany. The company also had to obtain human data from the United States. Richardson-Merrill began sending out samples to more than 1,000 physicians with minimal instructions to be given to patients. More than 20,000 persons took thalidomide in the United States in that manner, a far greater number than ever had served as experimental subjects in any previous drug trial. Although very few pregnant women got samples of the drug in the United States, in other countries many did. Some were under the impression that thalidomide, which was marketed under different names in various countries, was a prenatal vitamin. At one major center for maternal health in Australia pregnant women were given thalidomide as a sedative, sleeplessness being a common condition during pregnancy.

During the summer of 1961 physicians and public health workers in several countries raised an alarm: They suspected that thalidomide had caused women to give birth to children with a severe set of birth defects known as phocomelia. Often the children had mental disabilities, blindness, and serious deformities of their limbs. Under intense public pressure Grünenthal and its related companies pulled thalidomide from distribution, but not before thousands of children had been born with disabilities. The best guess was that Germany, for example, saw 5,000 thalidomide births. The only reason that nations in South America and Africa did not report more victims was that there were few procedures in place to gather such information.

The number of children affected in the United States was fairly small, perhaps dozens, rather than hundreds or thousands. A few U.S. women who had taken thalidomide attempted to have abortions, which proved difficult given the American patchwork of state regulations. Several states prohibited the termination of pregnancy except when the life of the mother was at stake. The fact that several women made public their effort to secure abortions was well remembered during discussions on the liberalization of American state and federal abortion laws later in the 1960s.

In Britain it was estimated that 1,000 children were born as "thalidomide babies." They suffered from physical disabilities ranging from fairly mild to life threatening. About half of those infants died within their first year of life. Some guessed that there were as many as 100,000 fetal deaths due to the effects of thalidomide. Although abortion had been relatively widely available in Britain since the 1930s (via the *Bourne* judicial decision), legal abortions usually had required the concurrence of a physician and a psychiatrist. The thalidomide tragedy in Britain factored into discussions about making abortion more widely available through legislation; major abortion reform from Parliament occurred in 1967.

SUMMARY OF ARGUMENTS

In Britain families of affected children got a cold reception from the Ministry of Health and its head, Enoch Powell, who supervised the National Health Service. The families turned from seeking redress by the government to the courts. Grünenthal, the parent company, was loath to fund any claims to injured children's families directly, although its subsidiaries, such as Distillers in Britain, did make some payouts through group settlements. In certain nations, such as Spain, thalidomide victims got no money at all from Grünenthal licensees. A few families pursued remedies through civil suits. As years passed, those families who had not yet had their days in court charged that Grünenthal and Distillers were engaging in delay tactics in hopes that the afflicted children would die before their suits could be heard. On September 24, 1972, the *Sunday Times* began to run a series of articles concerning the thalidomide children, their families, and their legal situation. Distillers complained to Britain's attorney general that litigation against the company was still pending and that any publicity on the case would imperil the company's right to a fair trial.

The Attorney General's Office decided to ask for an injunction after informing the *Sunday Times'* editor of its intentions. The newspaper continued with its series of articles after notification from the attorney general. The Court of Queen's Bench eventually granted an injunction against publication of further articles in the series. Subsequent to that injunction the controversy was dis-

cussed in Parliament, and newspaper reports appeared of members' speeches. When a court of appeal (consisting of Lords Alfred Denning, Leslie Scarman, and Godfrey Phillimore) discharged the injunction, the attorney general appealed to the House of Lords, which upheld it and found that the *Sunday Times* could be held in contempt for subsequent articles related to the case.

The House of Lords' decision in *Attorney General v. Times Newspapers Ltd* examined not only the actions of the *Sunday Times'* editor and publisher but also the course taken by the attorney general in asking for an injunction based on the one article that had appeared on September 24. Most of the law lords agreed that the attorney general had been premature to seek to restrain accounts such as that relatively temperate initial article. They also said, though, that his effort to enjoin publication had been borne out by the stronger tone of the later articles in the series.

The judges in the House of Lords had in mind a comparatively narrow gauge of whether an alleged contempt imperiled justice. The law lords wanted the test of contempt to be whether the publication had posed toward a fair trial a danger that was "clear and present," that is, imminent rather than remote or probable. Such terminology in a test for contempt was reminiscent of the U.S. case of *Wood v. Georgia* (1962), in which a contempt citation had not been allowed to stand because it failed to meet a "clear and present danger" standard.

Lord John Morris of Borth-y-Gest carved out the permissible scope of the newspaper's comment on the matter. He would have allowed the *Sunday Times,* for example, to ponder whether the legal system was at fault for allowing the case to drag on. He also would have permitted a public appeal for funds for the injured children, even to the extent that such an appeal would have proved an embarrassment to Distillers while it was involved in litigation.

Lord James Reid found the decision difficult precisely because it involved the balancing of weighty concerns. He recalled "no better statement of the law on contempt" than that in *Ex parte Bread Manufacturers Ltd:* "It is of extreme public interest that no conduct should be permitted which is likely to prevent a litigant from having his case tried free from all matter of prejudice. But the administration of justice, important though it undoubtedly is, is not the only matter in which the public is vitally interested. . . ."

Both Lord Reid and Lord Kenneth Diplock, however, went on to confront their worst fear relevant to the case at hand: the "horror" of "trial by newspaper":

> Responsible "mass-media" will do their best to be fair, but there will also be ill-informed, slapdash, or prejudiced attempts to influence the public. If people are led to think that it is easy to find the truth, disrespect for the processes of law could follow, and if mass-media are allowed to judge, unpopular people and unpopular causes will fare very badly.
>
> . . . What I think is regarded as most objectionable is that a newspaper or television programme should seek to persuade the public, by discussing the issues and evidence in a case before the court, whether civil or criminal, that one side is right and the other wrong. If we ask the ordinary man or even a lawyer . . . why he has that feeling, I suspect that the first reply would be—"well, look at what happens in some other countries where that is permitted."

The reference to the United States could not have been clearer. Appearing as it did during a time when some constitutional lawyers in Britain were calling for their nation to adopt a more "American-style" enumeration of civil liberties as in the U.S. Bill of Rights, the judges' comments were a slap at that notion.

The United States had been seriously affrighted by thalidomide. Alarm rippled through several areas of U.S. law. For example, during the late 1950s Congress had been considering tighter regulations on drug approvals for the U.S. market. When Senator Estes Kefauver attempted to update laws from the 1930s that authorized the FDA to regulate drug testing and marketing, his effort had been stalled because of political infighting. It was looking as though legislative reform of drug testing would not occur.

Then, witnesses before congressional committees began relating the effects of thalidomide in other countries. Enhancement of the FDA's authority quickly gained political support. The Kefauver-Harris Amendment was passed in 1962. It gave the FDA more control over drug approval prior to a drug's coming to market for the general public, though it did not set up procedures to monitor drugs once they were for sale.

On July 15, 1962, U.S. newspapers carried the story of how one researcher at the FDA, Dr. Frances Kelsey, had braved her superiors' disapproval in order to voice her concern that Richardson-Merrill and Grünenthal were greatly misrepresenting the scientific evidence about human trials of thalidomide. Dr. Kelsey almost single-handedly held up authorization by the FDA for thalidomide to be distributed much more widely. The United States had had a very narrow escape. Many people who were alive in 1962 recalled vividly that President John F. Kennedy appeared on television and talked about the danger of thalidomide. He asked all Americans to empty their medicine cabinets and to discard any unmarked bottles.

Other countries reacted through their bureaucracies and legislatures. Part of the solution recommended by the World Health Organization, the tracking of drugs' effects upon consumers, was put into effect in Britain as a result of the thalidomide tragedy. A few nations such as Germany instituted even more thorough reforms. The German state promised to pay victims if it did not properly monitor drug approval or distribution in future.

VERDICT

Nations thus responded to the news of thalidomide's dangers quite differently. In Britain the controversy not only spurred greater roles for agencies that were to monitor drug safety. The leading judicial case concerning thalidomide (*Attorney General v. Times*) gave rise to a much larger discussion involving Britain's legal standing within the European community. After the *Sunday Times* investigative series on the protracted litigation against Distillers was censured by British courts for interfering with the fair trial of the cases brought by thalidomide victims, the newspaper appealed to the European Court of Human Rights. In an 11–9 decision, that court criticized Britain's contempt of court law. British legal rules on contempt seemed to forbid pretrial publicity or comment in many cases, even in situations where suits were very longstanding.

In 1979 the European court ruled British courts' contempt decisions to be an unacceptable limitation on free speech under Article 10 of the European Convention on Human Rights. Although the European tribunal said that Britain's laws on contempt were reasonable protections designed to ensure an impartial judiciary, the court in Strasbourg held that British contempt laws were not "justified by a pressing social need" and therefore were in violation of Europe's human rights standards.

SIGNIFICANCE

In the 1960s and 1970s children who were born with disabilities as a result of their mothers' exposure to thalidomide were not expected to live long. In Great Britain the settlements that thalidomide children's families reached with Distillers were small prior to the publication of the *Sunday Times* article, though Distillers upped its payments substantially in the wake of the public discussions about the victims' situation. Still, even those greater amounts failed to take into account that many more of the thalidomide children lived into adulthood than ever were predicted to survive. As they grew into middle age, those individuals required increasing care, especially as their parents died.

Although the Thalidomide Trust had been established in Britain with the donations inspired by the *Sunday Times* articles, at the 50th anniversary of the thalidomide scare trust payments were proving inadequate. Several victims worked to increase payouts to the survivors, taking their case to the corporate successor of Distillers, a company called Diageo. They approached Grünenthal, still based in Germany, although the company never had paid compensation to the thalidomide children. They also battled the British government, which under Chancellor of the Exchequer Gordon Brown in 2002 had tried to tax trust payouts. In late 2009 representatives of the surviving 466 thalidomide children in Britain worked out an arrangement with the British government for an increase in payments to survivors.

Thalidomide enjoyed resurgence in medical use in the early 1990s, being employed with some success among patients who had conditions such as leprosy and multiple myeloma. In the United States, FDA controls on thalidomide remained extremely tight, however, as were the conditions under which thalidomide might be prescribed in most other nations. Among the many effects of the thalidomide scare of the late 1950s and early 1960s were not simply human tragedies but also changed perceptions about governmental institutions. The FDA found its authority first enhanced as a watchdog regarding new drugs. Later that agency garnered criticism as being too slow to approve drugs for market; many of its regulations on new pharmaceuticals had been formed during the thalidomide controversy.

Further Reading

Attorney General v. Times Newspapers Ltd. (1974) Q.B. 710 (1973). Available online. URL: http://lib-proxy.uta.edu:2156/hottopics/?. Accessed June 20, 2009; Cawthon, Elisabeth. "Kefauver-Harris Amendment Signed during Thalidomide Controversy." In *Encyclopedia of Great Events in Business/Commerce*, edited by Frank Magill, 1,180. Pasadena, Calif.: Salem Press, (1994); Knightley, Phillip, et al. *Suffer the Children: The Story of Thalidomide.* New York: Viking Press, 1979; Mintz, Morton. *The Therapeutic Nightmare.* Boston: Houghton-Mifflin, 1965; The *Sunday Times* Case *(Times Newspapers Ltd v. UK)*, 2 European Human Rights Reports 402 (1979). Available online. URL: http://www.hrcr.org/safrica/limitations/sunday_times_uk.html. Accessed June 20, 2009.

The trial of the Gang of Four

Date: 1980

KEY ISSUES

The Cultural Revolution was a shocking upheaval in Chinese society. When Chairman Mao Zedong initiated that transformation in 1966, Mao said that he intended to shake up the bureaucracy and intellectuals in China. The Cultural Revolution was a reminder from an old campaigner that change must be ongoing. Mao enlisted young people, many of them students, to upbraid those who traditionally were held in high regard in Chinese society: artists, scholars, professionals, members of the civil service, middle-class folk. Led by the Red Guards, groups of young people berated their employers, professors, local governors, and progenitors. At worst, those displaced individuals were tortured to death or driven to suicide. At the mildest, their "rehabilitation" might consist of public humiliation and resettlement to cooperative farms, with consequent loss of family ties, property, and life's work.

Such inversion of customary deference was dislocating both to individuals and to Chinese society as a whole, and nowhere was the disruption greater than in halls of learning. Entire libraries were burned, faculties displaced or killed, curricula upended. Painting, building design, and opera, for example, now had to conform to the guidelines of these new revolutionaries. Those inside China brave enough to express their alarm, and many outside the country, argued that Mao's need to reinvent the revolution was more an effort to hold on to power as a person than to adhere to abstract principle. And yet, Mao was a revered figure in China in the middle of the 1960s.

It was not merely Mao's longevity that made him widely respected in the nation. Mao was also recognized as the dominant figure of the Communist revolution in China in the 1930s and 1940s; he was already a figure of historical importance. It mattered little, therefore, that the cultural revolution was extremely divisive and that it caused China criticism and even derision overseas. The fact that Mao directed it was enough to gain support.

But, was Mao as fully in charge as it appeared? During the 1960s and early 1970s fractures within the leadership of the Communist Party in China were growing apparent—certainly in political circles in China but also abroad. Rival Lin Biao attempted an overthrow of the Maoists in 1971. Lin died while trying to escape to the Soviet Union. In 1974 Mao himself openly warned a group of powerful individuals not to challenge him. Mao

characterized the ambitious clique as a "gang of four" that sought to manage China via their direction of the Cultural Revolution. The group included three men who had key roles in the Cultural Revolution: politburo leader Zhang Chunqiao, journalist turned propaganda minister Yao Wenyuan, and Red Guard commander Wang Hongwen. The fourth person so marked out for Mao's curious mixture of protection and jealousy was none other than his longtime confidante and wife, Jiang Qing. Although Jiang Qing had a far less public role than Mao for most of their relationship, during the Cultural Revolution the former actress showed special interest in altering traditional Chinese theater in line with Maoist principles.

HISTORY OF THE CASE

Mao died on September 9, 1976. Immediately, there was a struggle over who would succeed him—a tussle that, as the chairman had noted, had been preceded by years of plotting. As Mao had specified in his will, a relatively obscure leader from Mao's home province, Hua Guofeng, became politburo chief. Within a month of the demise of the "Great Helmsman," the members of the Gang of Four were placed under arrest. They were alleged to have committed offenses during the Cultural Revolution. Though the extremely lengthy indictment was vague as to the exact nature of many actions by the defendants, the charges spoke of 34,274 individuals being killed as a result of "excesses" between 1966 to 1976, with a total number of 727,420 Chinese having been "persecuted" in the same decade. The trial of the principals did not commence until November 20, 1980. Along with the original Gang of Four that Mao had indicated, several other individuals, some presumed dead, were accused of a variety of crimes.

In the interim the accused persons were detained with limited access to any outside contacts. If their appearance at trial was any guide, their incarceration was arduous. It would not have been unusual for the defendants to undergo torture to induce them to confess. Defendant Chen Boda (age 76), for example, was the longtime personal secretary to Mao and himself an influential architect of political theory. In the courtroom in 1980 both he and Zhang Chunqiao (age 63) appeared very weak, leaning on their guards at times. For many centuries Chinese legal authorities and the public considered it critical that accused persons should admit fault before and during trial. Those who refused to do so did not show proper respect for the legal process. The long delay before trial in fact may have been related to the obduracy of at least one of the defendants.

When the proceedings commenced in an air force facility in western Beijing, the assembly hall was crowded with members of the citizenry who were admitted on a random basis. A panel of 35 persons presided as judges. The vast majority of those in charge in court were politicians rather than persons grounded in the law. Snippets of the trial appeared on Chinese television each day, but the foreign press was barred, and any official transcript that may have been kept was not released. Those who wished to follow the trial had to glean what occurred from those who attended or from the tidbits released to the media by the state.

SUMMARY OF ARGUMENTS

The defendants were tried at the same time but on separate counts of the complex indictment. Wang, who at age 45 was not of Mao's generation, was the defendant who played his part most appropriately according to Chinese tradition. He appeared ashamed and contrite before the court. Specifically, he was alleged to have inspired riots in Shanghai in which there were hundreds of deaths. Wang further was charged with influencing Mao to perceive rivals Zhou Enlai and Deng Xiaoping as dangerous.

Although Zhou had died of cancer in January 1976, Deng had regained his footing prior to Mao's death and was in a position of high authority during the trial. Deng had been a moderate within the party for some time, but his fortunes rose and fell in connection with the waxing and waning of far leftist elements such as the Gang of Four. Deng was a popular figure in many Chinese, and he was well known among the West for his efforts at rapprochement with democratic nations. In addition to other charges the prosecution alleged that Wang tried to initiate a coup when the chairman lay on his deathbed.

Yao, who also was of a younger generation than Mao, like Wang, was charged with trying to discredit Deng and Zhou. Yao, who sometimes was called a "killer by pen," was accused of framing much of the vitriolic rhetoric of the Cultural Revolution. In court Yao's words came back to haunt him. He had ridiculed those who shrank from violent put-downs of counterrevolution, for example, saying "dictatorship is not like embroidering flowers." Yao's abilities as a literary and theater critic were put to use in an influential essay in 1965 that questioned whether current theatrical offerings were truly in the spirit of Maoism. Yao thus was credited with making an early foray in the Cultural Revolution. As that movement proceeded he was linked closely with Jiang's control over the arts. His origins in Shanghai were cited as another link between Yao and Jiang; she spent several formative years as an actress in that city in the 1930s before meeting Mao.

Some of Yao's fostering of disrespect for Zhou allegedly occurred in connection with Zhou's commemoration ceremony in early 1976. In China respect for the recently departed was still a key value. Yao's attitude in court was in contrast to Wang's deference, if not obsequiousness. Yao attempted to state his justification for holding leftist positions and argued that he was acting upon the wishes of Mao.

Although defendant Zhang appeared in poor health and spoke in low tones, he managed to state his lack of confidence in the proceedings by refusing to enter a plea. The judges declared that the court would apply a law passed just that year (1980) that read a failure to plead as an acceptance of evidence against a defendant. It was a ruling analogous to the medieval English presumption that not pleading was a defiance of a court's authority. In such a situation the defendant would be treated as though he or she had confessed.

The case against Jiang was somewhat separate from that of the other defendants. She obviously had more personal influence over Mao, particularly in his years of declining health. But, at the same time the prosecution wanted to treat her gingerly because of the fact that she was Mao's widow, indeed, his partner of many years' standing, although much of their relationship had been hidden from the public.

Jiang and Mao had met when he was still married to his second wife in the mid-1930s. Other Communist Party leaders thought their affair something of a scandal, or at least a distraction for Mao. When Mao divorced his mentally ill wife, his fellow Communists extracted from him and Jiang a promise that Jiang would stay in the background. This was something that Jiang did, at least until the 1950s, when she began to circulate in politics. It was ironic that Jiang's political and cultural impact grew at a time when she and Mao seemed to be moving apart personally.

In the next decade Jiang became known to the public through a series of speeches about the state of Chinese theater specifically and the arts generally. Jiang called for a purification of the stage in line with Maoist principles. She was credited with elevating the Red Guards to a position of great influence and dismantling ancient traditions and records related to the arts.

Jiang, however, was rumored to be uncomfortable with her own history as an actress. Perhaps in the climate of the 1960s in China her film roles looked too Western, or maybe she had visited a casting couch or two. At trial Jiang was charged with several counts of using the Red Guards to terrorize persons in Shanghai to give up old materials related to her residence there. Such allegations were in addition to counts concerning her attempting to influence Mao against Zhou and Deng.

Jiang was asked to reply to charges that she had helped oust Mao's more moderate rival in the 1960s, chief of state Liu Shaoqi. Liu was sent into internal exile in 1968, with Lin clearly usurping his position as Mao's heir. The prosecution insisted that Jiang had a special vendetta against Liu's wife. That woman, Wang Guangmei, appeared at the trial in Beijing in the role of an observer rather than a witness, though she might have had much to say on the stand.

The case against Jiang also made a closer link between her and Lin than between Lin and the others in the gang. The indictment referred, for example, to the "Jiang Qing–Lin Biao counterrevolutionary clique" that had sought to discredit comparative moderates such as Liu, Deng, and Zhou. While Jiang was not specifically cited in connection with a particular plot to assassinate Mao in 1971, her supposed clique was mentioned. Allegedly, the con-

spirators aimed to blow up a train on which Mao was riding. By whom and how the plot was foiled was not made clear at trial.

Although the proceedings against of the Gang of Four clearly were stage-managed, there were certain elements that the government could not completely control. Most apparent was Jiang's attitude. When she was led into the courtroom to listen to the extensive indictment being read, she showed both derision and boredom. Jiang began the proceedings on another defiant note: she said that she preferred to represent herself rather than relying on court-appointed counsel. She sometimes interrupted either the judges or witnesses with fierce interjections. Jiang also challenged the authority of the court to meet at all and was held in contempt as a result. She did not hesitate to remind the judges and spectators that she was a link with their beloved departed leader:

> Everything is a frame-up. I don't understand this trial. Everyone affronts Mao Zedong, me, and even the Cultural Revolution. I am the best one who understands Chairman Mao, as his wife for thirty-eight years. When Mao triumphed, I triumphed. I am the woman who accompanied him during the past.

On several occasions the cameras recorded Jiang being pulled away, screaming, from the courtroom. Indeed, the most compelling images of the entire trial were of Jiang pumping a fist while shouting defiance at the court.

VERDICT

Jiang and Zhang each received death sentences; Wang, a life term; and Yao, 20 years behind bars. The other persons who had been charged got jail time of 16 to 18 years. None of the convicted persons was executed, although their lives were drastically affected by their stiff sentences. In 1983 the capital sentences were commuted to life imprisonment. Jiang was the first to die. She allegedly committed suicide by hanging in 1991, while under house arrest. Wang died in 1992. Zhang and Yao passed away in 2005 and 2006, respectively. Yao, who had been released from custody in 1996, reportedly was compiling a memoir at the time of his death.

SIGNIFICANCE

Even while the trial of the Gang of Four was taking place, Western news outlets surmised that the proceedings were trying to effect a delicate balance. The trial represented a refutation of the Cultural Revolution, yet it was too soon to banish the memory of Chairman Mao completely. Thus, the trial of some who had surrounded Mao during the Cultural Revolution—especially Mao's wife, Jiang—served as notice that China was moving away from Maoism, while preserving a veneer of respect for Mao as the father of modern China. The official position of the political survivor Deng was that the Cultural Revolution caused "the most severe setback and the heaviest losses suffered by the party, the state, and the people since the founding of the People's Republic."

Further Reading

Bonavia, David. *Verdict in Peking: The Trial of the Gang of Four.* New York: Putnam, 1984; *A Great Trial in Chinese History: The Trial of Lin Biao and Jiang Qing Counter-revolutionary Cliques, Nov. 1980–Jan. 1981.* Elmsford, N.Y.: New World Press, 1981; Li Zhisui. *The Private Life of Chairman Mao.* London: Random House, 1996; Spence, Jonathan. *Mao Zedong: A Life.* New York: Penguin, 2006; Terrill, Ross. *The White-Boned Demon: A Biography of Madame Mao Zedong.* New York: Morrow, 1984.

The trials of Mehmet Ali Agca

Also known as: The trials of the assassins of Pope John Paul II; Bulgarian conspiracy trials

Date: 1981, 1986

KEY ISSUES

To attempt to assassinate a political leader has been a common enough action in history. To try to kill a religious figure, especially one with world-wide influence, has been more unusual. When a gunman attacked Pope John Paul II as he rode in an open-air vehicle at the Vatican on May 13, 1981, the assumption among most who heard the news was that the assailant was a deranged individual. Who else would want to harm such a charismatic religious leader? The story behind the assassination attempt, however, was more complex. In this case conspiracy theorists were proven correct; the attempt to assassinate the pontiff was a plot engineered and financed from abroad for political reasons. Particularly important in cracking the case were inquiries by journalists about possible Soviet and Bulgarian ties to the alleged assassin, Mehmet Ali Agca. Those journalistic queries informed official investigations of the case by Italian police and prosecutors.

HISTORY OF THE CASE

Karol Cardinal Wojtyla was elected pope in October 1978. He was the first person from Poland to serve as the head of the Catholic Church and the first non-Italian pope in more than 400 years. A man of great influence in his native country, he had close ties to the workers' union Solidarity, headed by Lech Walesa. Solidarity was known throughout the world for its anti-Soviet activities during the late 1970s, when the influence of the Soviet Union was declining in Eastern Europe. The Soviets, under Premier Leonid Breshnev, considered mounting an invasion in order to crush the labor movement in Poland.

The new pope was not without his critics; some accused him of being overly political and charged that he was too focused on Eastern European affairs. Others disparaged his particular religious positions such as a strong anti-abortion stance and accused the pontiff of being slow to reform the church in regard to the inclusion of women as clergy. John Paul II was a widely traveled church leader, however, whose language skills and personal warmth served him well with diverse audiences around the globe.

Agca was about 23 years old at the time of the shooting. He already had been convicted of a politically motivated murder in 1979 in his home country, Turkey, and had been implicated in smuggling between Turkey and Bulgaria. He was a member of a right-wing organization called the Grey Wolves. After being sentenced in Turkey to serve 10 years for the murder of a journalist, Agca escaped from prison and lived for a time in Bulgaria, traveling around Europe and finally to Italy in 1981.

At the shooting in St. Peter's Square in May 1981, two other persons were injured besides the pope. John Paul II suffered three serious wounds for which he was hospitalized for several weeks. The enormous crowds that always greeted the pope upon public appearances immediately pounced on Agca. He was apprehended and charged with an attempt on the life of the pope plus the injuring of bystanders. One of the first comments by John Paul II was a public statement of forgiveness for Agca, made from his hospital bed. Several years later (after Agca's initial trial), John Paul had a long visit to Agca's prison; the assassin and his quarry prayed together. John Paul II died of natural causes in 2005. Vatican observers argued that he never fully regained his usual vigor.

SUMMARY OF ARGUMENTS

Agca was the pivotal figure in two trials in Italy: one for his role in the shooting and a second as a participant in a conspiracy to commit the assassination. The first trial, in 1981, occurred before prosecutors had thoroughly considered the possibility that Agca had not acted alone. The second trial, in 1986, centered on the idea that Agca was not a lone gunman and that there was indeed both a "Bulgarian connection" and Soviet inspiration for the plot to kill the pope.

Journalists already were raising the possibility of a conspiracy before the first trial began. Within the week of the attempted murder, the Italian paper *Il Corriere della Sera* as well as the *Washington Post* posited that Agca had connections to the Bulgarian secret police. Still, the charges against Agca were straightforward in the 1981 prosecution: Agca had tried to kill the pope and had injured two others besides John Paul II; he had carried illegal firearms; and he had traveled while carrying false identification papers. The trial in Rome was succinct. It took the six-person jury only a few hours to convict Agca on all charges. He was sentenced to serve a 19-year term.

But, the judge at Agca's criminal trial, Severino Santiapichi, officially noted that rumors of a plot abounded. In a closing statement he promised that anyone with information to support a contention of conspiracy could forward the details to him so that authorities might conduct an investigation. Among the many nations interested in the case were Turkey and Germany. The Turkish government was angry that their NATO allies sometimes were slow to pursue and hand over suspected terrorists. West Germany faced criticism that lax immigration controls might have provided a place of hiding for Agca during his rambles after escaping from Turkish prison.

Journalists in several nations dug up more details of Agca's connections and motivations. Writers such as Claire Sterling published their findings in Western periodicals such as the *New York Times* and *Readers' Digest*. The authors got information, for example, from interviews with Italian and Vatican security officials who believed that the Soviet security agency the KGB planned to silence John Paul II. U.S. intelligence supported the view that the Bulgarians would have participated in such a plan willingly. But why would Agca be chosen as a gunman for hire? Perhaps the Soviets and Bulgarians thought he would not be suspected of aiding Communist powers due to his long association with right-wing groups. Italian prosecutors took the time to interview journalists who had published such theories in print and on television, but they initially concluded that the evidence was mostly circumstantial and would not add up to a winnable case.

Over the next couple of years, however, Italian official Antonio Albano assembled a dossier of more than 25,000 pages of evidence and finally did enter into a second prosecution that centered on the conspiracy itself. One of the central tasks that Albano faced in moving forward was trying to resolve Agca's shifting testimony. Why had Agca first insisted that he had comrades in arms and then refused to implicate them at trial in 1981? Albano theorized that Agca had planned on being rescued after arrest, just as co-conspirators had plucked him from a Turkish jail after his murder conviction in the late 1970s. Albano reasoned that by 1982 Agca had decided to retract his denial of a conspiracy because he desired to tell the truth in hopes of obtaining a remission of sentence.

Albano reckoned that Agca's version of events circa 1982—that the Bulgarians, seeking to ingratiate themselves with the Soviet Union, had engineered the assassination—was the truest account available. Under the plan, Agca was to be paid 3 million German marks and was to get help to escape. Unsurprisingly, the Bulgarians hotly denied that theory, sending out several officially prepared books that linked Agca not to them but to his old associates, the Grey Wolves. Although the prosecutor's report was only a recommendation rather than a mandate that another trial should be held concerning the conspiracy, such a trial did go forward.

VERDICT

At that second trial in 1986 Italian prosecutors tried to demonstrate that Bulgarian authorities had funded and directed Agca. They were unsuccessful in getting any convictions of co-conspirators (five Turks and three Bulgarians went on trial starting in 1985), especially because Agca gainsaid his earlier claim that Bulgarian operatives had paid him. A few of the defendants at that trial were prosecuted in absentia. Especially confounding was the absence of Oral Celik, who allegedly also was present with a gun at St. Peter's Square at the shooting. Celik had not been seen since the day of the assassination attempt. Agca repeatedly garbled the focus of that trial; he garnered more than a little attention by claiming to be Jesus Christ. Public interest in the case continued, in part because of the official wording of the verdict in the conspiracy trial; the charges against the conspirators were "not proven." No one, that is, was declared "not guilty." On appeal in 1987 a higher court reached the same conclusion: The charges of Bulgarian and Soviet funding and direction of the plot were tantalizing but unproven.

With the fracturing of the Soviet Union and the gradual opening up of Soviet archives to researchers, journalists and prosecutors hoped to find additional information on the Soviets' knowledge or direction of the conspiracy. A book co-authored by Carl Bernstein in 1996, for example, contained a key recollection from Zbigniew Brzezinski, secretary of state under the administration of U.S. president Jimmy Carter. Brzezinski asserted that the United States expected an invasion of Poland in December 1980 and had requested the pope's help to diffuse the situation. John Paul II decided at that time to speak with the Soviet leadership. He threatened that he would mobilize Solidarity against a Communist action. That, in turn, caused the Soviets to resolve to assassinate the pope.

Prosecutors continued their probe of the assassination attempt after the trial in 1986 but closed their official inquiries in 1997. The investigation began again in 2006 through action of Italy's parliament. Through new computer technology, Bulgarian Sergei Antonov was conclusively identified as having been present at the shooting of the pope. According to Italian law, he could not be prosecuted again, however, having been tried once in the 1986 conspiracy case; Antonov died in 2007.

Along with the question of the exact terms of Soviet and Bulgarian involvement in the plot to kill John Paul II, other mysteries remained: Had the KGB and Bulgarian police placed operatives inside the Vatican? Was Agca the lone gunman, or did he have help on the scene? Was Agca's trial tied to the kidnapping of the daughter of a Vatican official in 1983? Although several of those questions were unanswered in the 2006 probe, the inquiry concluded with a clear finding that the Soviet Union had orchestrated the shooting in 1981.

Italian authorities increasingly regarded Agca as an embarrassing reminder that they never had solved the complex case. They certainly had not secured from either Bulgarian or Soviet officials any statements admitting complicity. John Paul himself played down the Bulgarian links to Agca, although in his autobiography the pontiff argued that a larger power was behind the shooting. Spurred by statements from the pope that 2000 was to be an international "year of forgiveness," Italy arranged for Agca to be pardoned and extradited to Turkey to serve out the remainder of his 1979 sentence for murder. Turkish courts allowed Agca out on parole in 2006 but jailed him again as a result of criticisms of that action. Turkey released Agca permanently on January 18, 2010, as he had by then served the remainder of his original sentence from 1979. Preparatory to that release he made a long pro-American statement through his lawyers, promising to work against terrorism and to provide new details of his part in the assassination plot.

SIGNIFICANCE

The fourth estate (press) played a key role in unearthing the Soviet-led conspiracy to kill John Paul II, although even they could not provide enough details to completely clear up the complicated connections among Bulgaria, the KGB, and Soviet political leadership. Italian prosecutors eventually were frustrated by the presence of the press in Agca's continuing saga. Agca courted the media, giving prison interviews that were more self-promoting than revealing. For example, to the *Sunday Times* of London in 2000, he expressed a wish to be converted to Catholicism on the steps of St. Peter's. He later stated he wished to meet with Pope Benedict XVI. As he prepared to gain release from jail in Turkey in 2010, Agca openly negotiated with potential book publishers, hinting that he could tell a story reminiscent of *The Da Vinci Code,* of intrigue concerning the Vatican. The Italian judges and lawyers who had listened to Agca's changing stories over the 30 years since the attack on John Paul II worried that Agca again would fabricate tales for the highest bidder.

Further Reading

Bernstein, Carl, and Marco Politi. *His Holiness: John Paul II and the Hidden History of Our Time.* New York: Doubleday Publishers, 1996; John Paul II. *Memory and Identity: Conversations at the Dawn of the Millennium.* New York: Rizzoli International Publications, 2005; Sterling, Claire. *Time of the Assassins.* New York: Holt Rinehart, 1983.

The dingo baby trial

Also known as: *The Crown v. Lindy and Michael Chamberlain;* the dingo trial

Date: 1982

KEY ISSUES

The two possible scenarios in the "dingo baby" case were equally repellant: Either the young parents had collaborated to kill their infant and concoct a lie about her death, or a wild dog had snatched and eaten the child. With the child's body absent, establishing what had occurred was up to the courts. The justice system turned to experts on forensic evidence and animal behavior to point to one possibility over the other. Judicial determination of the case was harrowing and complex. In the meantime, the family of the victim were pitied, vilified, and finally redeemed (in many eyes at least). Australian justice came under scrutiny both within the nation and abroad as a result of the Chamberlain case. The most controversial aspect of the dingo baby episode, however, was the conflicting role of expert witnesses in the proceedings.

HISTORY OF THE CASE

In late summer 1980 the Chamberlain family had gone camping at Ayers Rock, a national park in the Northern Territory of Australia. The parents, Michael and Lindy, had three children with them: two young boys and a baby girl. The infant, a nine-week-old girl named Azaria, disappeared from a tent near where the other members of the group were having a meal. After she heard the baby cry, Lindy Chamberlain went to investigate. The mother later said she thought she saw a dingo (a native wild dog) running away from the tent with something in its mouth. The baby was never seen again, though some of her bloodstained clothing was found.

An initial coroner's inquest concluded that a dingo had carried off the baby. Animal researchers demonstrated at that December 1980 inquest that dingoes were ruthless and skilled scavengers. Of particular importance were the opinions of animal expert Les Harris, who had kept dingoes and observed them in the wild. He concluded that a dingo of an average weight of 20 pounds easily could have taken away a baby who weighed about 10 pounds. Noting that dingoes were "fastidious eaters," he also posited that a dingo might well have peeled back the baby's clothing. Finally, he noted that dingoes digested their food quickly and that anything they ingested would have been excreted within 24 hours. With the inquest finding of accidental death, Coroner Denis Barritt recommended that the case be closed to further criminal proceedings. There was no suggestion of negligence on the parents' part. Azaria's death, in other words, was not any person's fault.

Several persons disputed the findings of the coroner's inquiry. Among the loudest detractors of Lindy Chamberlain, in particular, was a forensic dentist named Kenneth Brown. Brown argued that the baby's clothes had been cut by a knife rather than torn by a dingo's teeth. Brown enlisted the services of James Cameron, an English forensic pathologist whom many regarded as the successor to Francis Camps. Camps had made an international name for himself in sensational cases such as the Steven Truscott trial. Cameron was a protégé of Camps, and he shared some of Camps's demonstrative—if not flashy—personality traits on the stand. Unlike Camps, however, Cameron worked not as a solo practitioner but rather with a group of forensic experts.

Certain members of the police who interviewed Lindy Chamberlain did not find her account of the events at Ayers' Rock to be credible. For example, Inspector Michael Gilroy of the Northern Territory police wrote a report emphasizing that just after the baby's birth, hospital staff had deemed Chamberlain to be an uncaring mother. Supposedly, Chamberlain had told them of folk remedies for ailments from which she insisted Azaria suffered, though the medical persons thought the baby "completely normal." He also mentioned the comment of a doctor who, thinking the name *Azaria* unusual, had consulted a book of name origins and had found it to represent "sacrifice in the wilderness." The implication of the report was that Chamberlain had killed the baby herself in some kind of fertility rite.

A second coroner's inquest was held in February 1982. At that time Coroner Gerry Galvin reached the conclusion that Lindy Chamberlain had killed the baby, perhaps inside the Chamberlains' tent, and transported the body in their car. Further, he argued that Michael Chamberlain had helped hide evidence of the crime, making him an accessory after the fact. Although that inquest credited dingoes with the scavenging behavior that experts had noted earlier, the 1982 coroner's verdict was based on other findings, especially testimony about Azaria's blood within the car and vegetation contamination on the baby's clothes that seemed inconsistent with an animal dragging the body. The second inquest jury indicted Lindy Chamberlain for murder of the baby and Michael Chamberlain as an accessory.

SUMMARY OF ARGUMENTS

The main prosecutor, Ian Barker, argued at trial that the British Crown would not attempt to provide a motive for the killing of Azaria. He did not engage in speculation, for example, about how Lindy Chamberlain had reacted at Azaria's birth. He simply emphasized that the forensic evidence pointed to the baby having been transported in the Chamberlains' car while bleeding profusely, which gave the lie to Chamberlain's story about seeing the dingo with the baby in its mouth.

The evidence that appeared to carry the most weight with jurors was technical testimony that implicated Lindy Chamberlain. Certain damaging evidence came from forensic pathologist Cameron, for one. He maintained that the cuts in the baby's clothes could not have come from a dingo. Other critical testimony came from police pathologist Joy Kuhl, who argued that she had found evidence of blood staining inside the Chamberlains' car. Kuhl contended that scatter marks that she said were baby's blood indicated that the baby had been killed elsewhere than the spot where her clothes were found buried. Lindy Chamberlain was sentenced to life in prison; Michael Chamberlain received a more lenient term and a small fine for his part in the baby's death.

A series of appeals on behalf of Lindy Chamberlain went to the Australian Supreme Court in 1982 and 1983. Those appeals failed. But in 1986, both the benighted mother and those who were critical of the handling of the evidence that led to Lindy Chamberlain's conviction had another day in court. Slowly, several forensic researchers who were much less well known than Cameron's team of witnesses from London built a case that assailed the science upon which Chamberlain's conviction had stood. Especially under scrutiny were the evidence about dingo behavior and the alleged bloodstains in the Chamberlains' car. In addition, a jacket that Chamberlain had said that Azaria had been wearing but had not yet been found was discovered at Ayers Rock near a dingo lair.

The argument that the forensic evidence at trial had been seriously flawed eventually grew overwhelming. The government of the Northern Territory first released Lindy Chamberlain from prison and then convened a royal commission to look into the episode. In 1987 a report by Justice Trevor Morling reviewed a raft of evidence in the case. Among the arguments in the report was a time line of the alleged murder that to Morling appeared improbable at best. Morling concluded that he was "far from being persuaded that Mrs. Chamberlain's account of having seen a dingo near the tent was false or that Mr. Chamberlain falsely denied that he knew his wife had murdered his daughter." Morling observed that inconsistencies in the Chamberlains' statements to police in the immediate aftermath of Azaria's disappearance could be explained by their emotional distress. On appeal in 1988 the convictions of Lindy and Michael Chamberlain were overturned.

In 1992 the Chamberlains were awarded compensation of $1.3 million for Lindy's time in jail. Among some of the public, though, they remained under suspicion. Opinion toward them moderated only when a series of incidents were brought to light in which babies were observed being snatched by dingoes. That these incidents were well known among native Australian peoples was important, for it pointed to the longstanding tension in Australia among the races. Aborigines had seen dingoes acting aggressively toward infants and children on many occasions, but either they tended not to report the episodes, or the authorities discounted such sightings.

Public opinion seemed to shift mostly toward sympathy for the Chamberlains and belief that the dingo had been the killer. Provincial authorities, however, were not quite finished with the case. At a third coroner's inquest in December 1995 Coroner John Lowndes returned an "open finding" in the death of Azaria. Lowndes was careful to note that such a ruling did not place the Chamberlains under suspicion again; indeed, he emphasized that they still were presumed innocent under the law. Still, the official finding was that the cause of the baby's death had not been determined. In 2010, on the 30th anniversary of the disappearance of

Azaria, Lindy Chamberlain, now divorced and remarried, called for a revision of the baby's death certificate to reflect that the child had bene killed by a dingo. Among those who supported the request was an Aboriginal tracker, Barbara Tjikatu, who had helped search on the night of the incident. Tjikatu affirmed that she had seen dingo tracks leading away from the Chamberlains' tent.

SIGNIFICANCE

The dingo baby case shows how internationally renowned forensic expertise tends to carry great weight with juries. The efforts of persons who called the damning forensic testimony from Lindy and Michael Chamberlain's trial into question were laborious and lengthy. Australian critics of Cameron, particularly, had an uphill battle to make themselves credible because of the sense among some Australians that homegrown forensic talent could not be as weighty as that from Great Britain.

The role of rumor in the Chamberlains' case also was key. In hindsight it was easy for detractors to characterize the Chamberlains as having beliefs outside the mainstream—though their critics never settled on whether they were New Age adherents or fundamentalist Christians. Nevertheless, that the Chamberlains' unusual ideas and behavior could land them in prison for murder became a national scandal.

Further Reading

Bryson, J. *Evil Angels*. New York: Summit Books, 1985; Chamberlain, Lindy. *Through My Eyes*. London: Heinemann, 1990; *Chamberlain v. The Queen* (No. 2) 153 Commonwealth Law Reports 521 (1984); Dan, Kathryn. "The Chamberlain and Mapo Papers: Case Studies of Personal Papers of National Symbolic Significance." National Library of Australia. Available online. URL: http://www.nla.gov.au/nla/staffpaper/acunning4.html. Accessed July 18, 2010; Gerber, P. "Some Aspects of the Appeals in *Chamberlain v. the Queen*." *Medical Journal of Australia* 141 (September 15, 1984): 351–35; Schepisi, Fred (dir.), *A Cry in the Dark*. Warner Brothers, 1988; Young, Norman H. *Innocence Regained: The Fight to Free Lindy*

Chamberlain. Annandale, Australia: Federation Press, 1989.

The trial of John Hinckley, Jr.

Also known as: *U.S. v. Hinckley;* the Reagan assassination trial

Date: 1982

Key Issues

Any defendant who tried to claim insanity faced difficulty in court in the 20th-century United States. Some such accused persons were widely unpopular because of the nature of the crimes they supposedly committed, including the assassinations of leaders and the killing of children. In addition, defendants encountered a patchwork of laws related to insanity. On a state-by-state basis the law might vary from a dim view of insanity defenses to a permissive attitude toward their use. Periodically, a famous case might spur state legislators to change the law on insanity, usually narrowing the scope of the insanity defense.

If the law was confusing, though, so was medical opinion. Professional organizations such as groups within the psychiatric profession issued opinions on the state of medical knowledge and the law. Still, there was little unanimity among medical experts as to what constituted mental illness so acute that it constituted a legal excuse. A single overriding set of principles, however, colored debates about insanity within medicine, politics, and the courts: The M'Naghten rules still were the beginning point for discussions on insanity.

In the United States many legal authorities, when discussing insanity, looked to what was occurring in the courts of the District of Columbia for a couple of key reasons. First, the district contained a major psychiatric hospital, St. Elizabeth's, at which many mentally ill offenders were placed. Also, if a national political leader were assassinated, the trial often occurred in D.C. courts. D.C.

courts took from the M'Naghten rules a central tenet: the requirement that a defendant must have been able to appreciate the difference between right and wrong in order to have been sane. That requirement was vital in insanity cases within the District of Columbia certainly since the Guiteau trial of 1881–82. Although at least two cases in the late 19th century would have allowed the courts in the district to relax the right-wrong test, the courts rejected liberalization of insanity law until a case in 1929. At that time the courts allowed presentation of evidence that a defendant had acted under an "irresistible impulse." Such evidence might allow an accused person to fall within the M'Naghten rules' prescription for insanity. The irresistible-impulse test, though applied only sporadically, did sometimes engender controversy in a few high-profile cases.

In 1954, for example, the Durham case presented a common scenario; it involved a defendant about whom medical and legal experts could not agree regarding insanity. Monte Durham was a petty criminal who had been hospitalized for mental illness at St. Elizabeth's throughout his young life. But was Durham mentally ill? Mental health experts argued that he certainly was. And yet, according to the M'Naghten rules, Durham was sane because at some points he was stable and usually could appreciate the difference between right and wrong. Frustrated with the disconnect between medical opinion and legal rules, a U.S. court of appeals decided that Durham's case should be retried. The appeals court declared that the M'Naghten rules were long overdue for revision. The court criticized the right-wrong test as simplistic and out of step with more modern medical opinion. It was time, the court declared, to allow jurors to make key decisions about defendants' mental states. The appeals court opinion that criticized the M'Naghten rules as outmoded harkened back to the mid-19th century ideas of Dr. Isaac Ray and the New Hampshire rule.

A D.C. case subsequent to Durham's made for further refinements in the law. Donald Currens was a small-time offender about whom medical and legal authorities disagreed. Was he unstable? Frequently. Did he abuse substances and further alter his mental ability in that way? Unquestionably.

Thus, many mental health experts would have called Curren ill. But, what was the nature of his mental illness? And, did his constellation of symptoms and behaviors allow him to fall within M'Naghten guidelines? Almost certainly not. Curren was a typical mentally ill criminal because he fell into a gray area of mental illness in which he was never critically ill but his function was impaired. In addition, he represented the vast majority of persons who came to the courts' attention in insanity cases; Curren had not assassinated a president nor committed particularly violent crimes.

In considering the situation of Curren, a U.S. court of appeals again found the M'Naghten rules outmoded. The court recommended that they be superseded by medical tests. The court proposed questions literally to be asked of doctors concerning a defendant's mental state at the time that an alleged crime was committed. It was politic, however, for the court to recognize how unpopular such a relaxing of the rules on an insanity defense might be with the general public. The court added that along with a de-emphasis on the M'Naghten rules there should be a requirement that defendants thus acquitted by reason of insanity should be locked away in an institution. When could they be released, and by whom should their release be determined? The court was less clear on such questions of application. It was those standards as slightly restated by the American Law Institute (ALI) in 1962 that about half of U.S. state courts applied after the early 1960s. Other states stuck more closely to language and principles that recalled the M'Naghten rules.

HISTORY OF THE CASE

The insanity defense came under discussion again in the early 1980s with the attempted assassination of the president of the United States, Ronald Reagan. As Charles Guiteau had done, this would-be assassin acted in Washington D.C., where the president appeared in public frequently. As Guiteau had, John Hinckley, Jr., shadowed his intended victim and was able to predict the president's movements through extensive press coverage of the president's schedule. As Guiteau had argued, Hinckley made the interesting contention that he

had nothing personal against his prey but rather a larger point to make.

Hinckley wanted to win the attention of a film star, Jodie Foster, whom he had watched in several movies including *Taxi Driver,* which also starred Robert DeNiro. Hinckley had gotten treatment for mental illness at certain points in his young life. His parents had ample resources and had made him visit psychiatrists, but with limited success. A young man, like Guiteau, who had had a college-level education, Hinckley experienced moments of lucidity and yet was also sometimes delusional. His parents eventually took the advice of one mental health professional to practice "tough love" on their son. They cut him loose financially until Hinckley took greater responsibility in his own treatment.

Hinckley got his opportunity to gain the attention of his parents, Foster, and a far wider audience on March 30, 1981. As President Reagan walked to a limousine at the Washington, D.C., Hilton hotel, Hinckley fired several shots. Although it appeared initially that the president was unhurt, at least one bullet had bounced off the vehicle, entering the president's lung. Secret Service agents hustled Reagan inside the vehicle and away from the scene. Only a split-second decision to divert the limo to a nearby hospital rather than going to the White House may have saved Reagan's life. Several others on the scene obviously were seriously hurt: Secret Service agent Timothy McCarthy, who literally "took a bullet" for the president by blocking Reagan from the line of fire; policeman Thomas Delahanty; and Press Secretary James Brady, who was gravely injured.

There had been a few other presidential assassinations and serious assassination attempts since the time of Guiteau. At the trial in 1901 of Leon Czolgosz for the killing of President William McKinley, the assassin's lawyers had employed the insanity defense but had not pressed the point far. When Joseph Zangara had tried to kill President-elect Franklin Roosevelt, and had in fact shot to death the mayor of Chicago, his defense team did not raise an insanity defense. Assassin Lee Harvey Oswald never was even tried for the killing of President John F. Kennedy in 1963 because Oswald himself was shot dead while in custody.

Hinckley's trial was the first sustained effort to argue insanity in a presidential assassination case since Guiteau's. Of special importance in Hinckley's case was the fact that his parents brought all of their considerable financial resources to bear in hiring a defense team. Hinckley, in other words, had the most effective counsel that money could buy. That made him and his family the object of much criticism.

The case also brought out arguments that had been simmering for decades about the continuing use of the M'Naghten rules. Should the rules be abolished altogether and replaced with more medical standards? Or, on the other side of the debate, should the insanity defense not be allowed at all? Perhaps its abolition would quiet the concerns of those, like Senator Dan Quayle (later the U.S. vice president), who argued that allowing accused persons to claim insanity "pamper[ed] criminals."

SUMMARY OF ARGUMENTS

Even Hinckley's pretrial incarceration, first at the marine base in Quantico, Virginia, and then at the federal prison in Butner, North Carolina, raised sensitive issues related to his mental state. How and by whom would the court require psychiatric evaluations of the accused? Did such an examination come under Hinckley's Sixth Amendment right to have a lawyer present during questioning? While Hinckley was being detained, could his diary be searched? The diary proved particularly important to the case against Hinckley, for it contained evidence of his stalking not only President Reagan but also his predecessor, Jimmy Carter. That in turn led to the question of Hinckley's ability to engage in complex planning of the crime.

When Judge Barrington Parker early on decided that the trial would proceed using federal rules on insanity rather than D.C. legal standards, it was a major victory for the defense. Federal requirements were consistent with the New Hampshire rules, which placed the burden of proof on the state. Once Hinckley pleaded insanity, in order to win a conviction prosecutors would have to demonstrate that he was sane. The facts of Hinckley having purchased and fired the bullets that

caused such injury to his victims were never in doubt; news outlets repeatedly had played videotapes of the attack and Hinckley's apprehension in the minutes afterward.

It came down to a discussion of Hinckley's mental state at the time of the shootings. Hinckley's lawyers argued that their client had a long and well-documented history of mental illness. They claimed he had given ample warning of his violent intentions to a number of individuals, including Foster. Foster's presence in the case created a dilemma. On the one hand, if she were to testify about her contacts with Hinckley, then Hinckley had a right to confront Foster as an "accuser." On the other hand, Foster had legitimate concerns that Hinckley still might do her harm and that at the least he wished to compel her testimony simply to gain contact with her. At a broader level the presiding judge feared that such a meeting between Foster and Hinckley in open court might create a media frenzy that would imperil the order of the proceedings. Both sides finally worked out an arrangement in which Foster would testify with Hinckley present, but the testimony would be videotaped rather than live. Hinckley, frustrated with Foster's reluctance to engage him directly, hurled a pen at her and promised to take revenge for her lack of responsiveness toward him.

Hinckley acted, prosecutors said, under a compulsion that amounted to an "irresistible impulse." According to the defense, Hinckley's parents had tried to help their son but found that he fell into the large middling category of persons who were too ill to get along well in society yet too highly functioning to need institutional care. The prosecution focused on Hinckley's many decisions leading up to the crime: his movements around the country in pursuit of Foster and the presidents, for example, his writing of letters explaining himself, his purchase of a particularly destructive type of bullet. Prosecution psychiatrist Dr. Park Dietz was especially outspoken in his opinion that Hinckley was more spoiled than mentally ill. That line of argument played well with the public, although it did not ultimately convince the jury that Hinckley should be found guilty.

Much was made of the composition of the jury. Reflecting the primarily African-American population of Washington, D.C., where the crime had occurred, the jury had a large majority of non-whites. Some critics of the trial contended that persons who were not Anglos were unsympathetic to President Reagan and therefore "sided" with Hinckley. No statements from jurors supported that claim of reverse racism.

VERDICT

Hinckley certainly had hurt his victims, but the jury decided he was "not guilty by reason of insanity." The trial ended with his being found not legally responsible for his violent actions on account of his mental state. The verdict proved most unpopular. It inspired a number of attempts to change laws at the federal and the state level. According to the ALI standards, which long had been applied in such cases, Hinckley could not go free. Rather, he was to be confined to a mental hospital until medical experts certified that he was no longer a danger to society. When could he be released, and would Hinckley be granted permission to move about outside St. Elizabeth's? In 2003 Hinckley was allowed to stay with his parents, but in 2007 a judge decided that those unsupervised visits had to be of limited duration.

SIGNIFICANCE

In the wake of the Hinckley trial Congress and most states began considering legislation that limited the use of the insanity defense or forbade the defense altogether. The congressional solution was the Insanity Defense Reform Act of 1984. Congress and about two-third of the states changed the federal and state standards for insanity, for example, by reversing the burden of proof. As revised, federal law stated that it fell to the defense to prove that the accused was insane. The new state and federal laws often limited the role of medical witnesses in insanity cases. States, however, usually allowed defendants to meet a lower standard of proof than did the federal courts; that is, it was easier to prove insanity in state court than at the federal level. Some states added a new verdict to those available in insanity trials: Juries could find that a defendant was "guilty but mentally ill" (GBMI). Defendants who were termed by courts

GBMI could obtain treatment for their mental illness and get credit for time served while in a mental institution, but when their symptoms abated, they then had to finish out the rest of their sentences in a regular penal setting.

Legal scholars observed that in the wake of the Hinckley trial most of the changes concerning the insanity defense made U.S. law reflective of the M'Naghten rules once again. The Hinckley trial had created a deep suspicion among the American public not only of wily defendants and expensive lawyers but also the psychiatric experts who argued for more medical expertise in insanity cases.

In at least two ways Hinckley's actions affected the law apart from the insanity defense: with respect to the responsibility of therapists for the criminal actions of their patients and in connection with gun control. When several of the victims of the shooting sued Dr. John Hopper, Hinckley's psychiatrist, they were rebuffed in Colorado court. In the case of *Brady v. Hopper* (1993), a court found that although Dr. Hopper had treated Hinckley for several months, he had not known of Hinckley's violent plans and therefore could not be held accountable for failing to warn potential victims. Secretary Brady, who suffered a devastating head injury from one of Hinckley's bullets, became dedicated to gun control. Brady, who gave his name to a federal law that made purchasing handguns more difficult in the United States, never fully recovered from the shooting.

Further Reading

Aaron, Benjamin L., and David S. Rockoff. "The Attempted Assassination of President Reagan: Medical Implications and Historical Perspective." *Journal of the American Medical Association* 272 (December 1994): 1,689–1,693; *Brady v. Hopper,* 570 F. Supp. 1333 (D. Colo. 1983); Caplan, Lincoln. *The Insanity Defense and Trial of John W. Hinckley, Jr.* Boston: D. R. Godine, 1984; Cawthon, Elisabeth. *Medicine on Trial.* Santa Barbara, Calif.: ABC-CLIO, 2004; Steadman, Henry J. *Before and After Hinckley: Evaluating Insanity Defense Reform.* New York: Guilford Press, 1993; *United States of America v. John W. Hinckley, Jr.* 525 F. Supp. 1342 (1981). Available online. URL: http://libproxy.uta.edu:2156/hottopics/?. Accessed June 3, 2004.

The Argentine junta trials

Date: 1985

KEY ISSUES

Between 1976 and 1983 a military dictatorship controlled Argentina. The government was a conglomeration of military officials, an alliance of rightists termed the *junta*. The new leaders declared that they were engaged in a process of national reorganization, often called simply *"el proceso."* They cited the threat of insurgency by the Left as a justification for crackdowns on anyone who criticized them. Such supposed enemies of order included clerics, labor organizers, journalists, students, and intellectuals. The regime referred to their actions as a "dirty war" on terrorism, and soon Argentines came to realize that that label was all too accurate. At the height of the government's paranoia, 1976–79, tens of thousands of persons simply vanished. Their fellow citizens called such individuals *"los desaparecidos"* (the disappeared).

Distraught family members undertook gestures that they hoped would not further antagonize the dictators but would indicate their distrust of the regime. In 1977 a group called Mothers of the Plaza de Mayo began holding silent vigils in front of the central government offices in Buenos Aires. They aimed to create shame in the nation as a whole for the disappearances. Soon after organizing their protests, several leaders among the mothers (such as founder Azucena Villaflor) and those who sympathized with them (such as nuns, including Sister Leonie Duquet) vanished.

Federal institutions including the judiciary and the legislature were cowed into quiescence or their operations suspended. The junta instituted censorship over political comment, even going so far as to proscribe certain rock songs. The police hauled citizens out of their vehicles seemingly at random and beat them, sometimes without a word. The military intelligence unit known as Battalion 601 was an instrument for secret repression.

Those who looked to the judicial process for redress were told that the regular courts had no jurisdiction over military operations. As the regular police said they had no record of missing persons' apprehensions, writs of habeas corpus could not be issued—such remedies were orders to specific persons who were known to have detained an individual illegally.

Foreign powers including the United States remained aloof, assured by the regime that it was resisting radicalism and communism. The U.S. government, acting through Secretary of State Henry Kissinger, advised the new rulers of Argentina to consolidate power quickly. The junta read that as encouragement. The regime got outright assistance from certain Latin American neighbors, such as Chile's secret police agency, DINA. Together with supporters—including either governments or agencies in Peru, Uruguay, Paraguay, Bolivia, Ecuador, and Brazil—the junta participated in Operation Condor, which tried to undercut socialist and communist influence in Latin America.

The junta had come to power promising to bring prosperity to Argentina, but by 1982 the country was in chaos. Political and social repression had fuelled instability in the domestic economy and apprehension among foreign investors. The regime looked to divert attention from its record. It manufactured a war with Great Britain related to the Falkland Islands. Only after the embarrassment of losing that conflict did the junta (actually a third incarnation of the military dictatorship) topple.

A transition government headed by General Reynaldo Bignone took over after the fall of President Leopoldo Galtieri in the summer of 1983. Bignone committed the nation to free elections, but he also declared amnesty for junta leaders and worked to destroy evidence of the disappearances. For the first time in 10 years Argentina went through a democratic election to choose its leaders. At the polls voters put, for the first time since 1943 (before the era of dictator Juan Perón), civilian leaders in control of the government. The winner of that contest, Raúl Alfonsín, had campaigned on a pledge to investigate *los desaparecidos* and to punish those responsible for what were assumed to be tortures and deaths among unaccounted-for individuals.

HISTORY OF THE CASE

The most obvious forum for inquiring about the actions of the junta was a military tribunal, for the puppet masters of Argentina in recent years had been officers in the nation's army, navy, and air force. Indeed, junta members such as General Jorge Videla, Admiral Emilio Massera, and General Orlando Agosti characterized themselves as military commanders while they governed, maintaining that the country was in crisis and had to be managed by draconian methods. Nine key members of the junta as well as the Buenos Aires police chief Ramón Campos faced a court-martial, charged with directing policies that led to the disappearances. The military court also had jurisdiction over hundreds of lower-level officers accused of carrying out tortures, rapes, and killings that their superiors had authorized.

At the same time that he instituted the military investigation, President Alfonsín created a civilian authority, the National Commission on Disappeared Persons (CONADEP), to look into what had occurred during the junta's era in power. Argentine writer Ernesto Sabato headed the commission. In September 1984 the two investigations—civilian and military—made their findings public. The military court declared it was unable to link the nine major defendants directly with specific crimes and thus hamstrung on how to proceed. Critics of that venue said that the military was unwilling to condemn its own.

CONADEP produced a catalog of atrocities that had proceeded from the highest levels of the junta. Its report was titled *Nunca Más,* or "Never again." The investigation connected Videla, Massera, Agosti, and Galtieri with grave crimes, including murder, torture, and robbery; other junta leaders accused of such activities were Generals Roberto Viola and Admiral Armando Lambruschini. Although Brigadier General Omar Graffigna was not accused of murder, he was implicated in the other crimes. General Basilio Lami Dozo and Admiral Jorge Anaya also were accused of facilitating arrests on behalf of the regime.

The president then moved prosecution of the nine major defendants into the civilian arena, a controversial decision in itself. The military resented the implication that it could not manage its own affairs. The Right protested the hearing of the case, convinced that it would embolden radical elements. Paramilitary groups at times threatened a violent disruption of the trial of the junta.

SUMMARY OF ARGUMENTS

The Palace of Justice in Buenos Aires was the site of the trial in the federal court of appeals (parallel to a criminal trial taking place before the U.S. Supreme Court in Washington, D.C.). Arguments began in April 1985 with the prosecution's revelations of evidence from the CONADEP investigation.

A major difficulty that the prosecution had faced was the identification of victims. Many Argentine forensic specialists either had cooperated with the police in the dirty war or were not well trained in the latest methods for identifying human remains. For the latter reason they received assistance from abroad. American anthropologist Clyde Snow went to Argentina in 1984 at the behest of the new government, heading an effort to identify bodies from mass graves. Snow trained students in the latest techniques of identification. Together his team formed the Argentine Team of Forensic Anthropology (Equipo Argentino de Antropología Forense, EAAF).

Using their findings, they helped prosecutors compile cases about specific individuals. For example, the EAAF had identified the remains of Liliana Pereyra, who had disappeared in 1976. Pereyra was five months pregnant when she last was seen; from the work of the forensic specialists, prosecutors could present evidence that she had been tortured, raped, and killed but had given birth to her child before her death. That infant was among many children who also went missing, his or her fate in the hands of those behind the dirty war.

The testimony by prosecution witnesses was gripping. Hundreds of witnesses, many of them family members of missing persons, recounted their efforts to locate those who had been taken away. The offenses charged were chilling; hundreds of secret prisons were described. In them thousands of "opponents" of the regime had been tortured. Many of the people considered threats to the junta were teenagers. The galleries were packed; so many Argentines had friends, family, or neighbors to mourn. The summation by lead prosecutor Julio Strassera was noteworthy, ending as it did with the exhortation *"¡Nunca más!"* By contrast, the efforts of defense lawyers to cast their clients' actions as purely military came across as heartless. It also was quite inaccurate, for many of those who had disappeared had no connection to any political group.

Among the arguments by those who confessed to crimes was that they already were being punished enough through their own memories of cruel acts. Higher-ranking officials charged with human rights abuses usually pleaded justification because they were "fighting terrorism." Lower-level functionaries became angry as they watched the trials because they had felt pressured to commit atrocities and now were being blamed by their superiors for the violence.

Meanwhile, a debate went on about whether prosecution of the junta was adequate to send a message that Argentina had moved past such atrocities. Some writers and politicians pointed to the Nuremberg War Crimes Trials as precedent. There, they said, only the highest-ranking members of the Nazi hierarchy were charged with war crimes, yet the Allies maintained that their execution might atone for Germany's acceptance of such flawed leadership. How far down the chain of command should the trial of the Argentine junta go?

VERDICT

Seven-and-a-half months after the trial commenced, the six-judge civilian panel that headed the Argentine court of appeals handed down its verdict. Those members of the junta who had been in power the longest, Videla and Massera, got life sentences; those who served fewer years at the head of government, Viola and Lambruschini, received shorter terms. As leader of the air force, Agosti was thought by the court to be not as culpable as the leaders of the army and navy; he received just four-and-a-half years' imprisonment. The remaining defendants had come on board as

leaders late. Although the court decommissioned them as officers, they received acquittals.

Did the convictions of five of the junta leaders serve as catharsis? In the years just after 1985 the Argentine government tended to take a conservative line about the need for additional trials or investigations. It maintained that this trial had satisfied justice—at least with regard to the actions of national leaders during the dirty war. President Alfonsín was accused of bowing to pressure from the military to stop the prosecutions. His government sponsored legislation in 1986 and 1987, the Full Stop Law and the Law of Due Obedience, that limited further trials and granted immunity against future proceedings.

Victims' rights groups argued that the sentences of 1985 were grossly inadequate and that not nearly enough individuals had been prosecuted in the first place. They contended that a focus on the events of the years 1976–79 was too narrow. Such a concentration, they said, had obscured later misdeeds by those who sympathized with the junta or sought to cover its tracks.

Subsequent to the trials of 1985, Argentina debated whether to prosecute persons other than those who initially had been named as offenders in 1983. Some in the public sphere characterized the trials as an unnecessary rehashing of events that, though regrettable, were past. Argentine president Carlos Saúl Menem (in office from 1989 to 1999) commented: "Publicly coming forward to give such testimony is a way of returning to a horrible past that we are trying to forget."

Those interested in pursuing further legal action pressed for additional trials. They contended, for example, that new evidence was turning up that would implicate additional perpetrators. The discovery of a security archive in Paraguay in 1992 brought to light records of Operation Condor. Those materials also made clear which governments had allowed South Americans involved in the dirty war to immigrate after 1983—among them France, Spain, and Canada. The efforts of EAAF, meanwhile, had confirmed that some among the disappeared, such as Duquet and Villaflor, whose bodies had not been located before the 1985 trials, indeed had been murdered.

Villaflor had been thrown out of a plane while alive, a common fate among the disappeared. The revelations of Adolfo Scilingo, who had worked at the notorious Naval Mechanics School, provided details of exactly how such victims died. Scilingo was one of the many enforcers of the junta's policies who had grown angry at the leaders' denials of responsibility for crimes. Argentine journalist Horacio Verbitsky, a human rights agitator, in 1995 published those details in an influential book titled *Confessions of an Argentine Dirty Warrior.* In turn, that book seemed to energize Argentines and foreign powers to pursue additional prosecutions.

Advocacy groups contended that certain individuals' actions had extended into arenas not first known to have been part of the repressions. For example, victims' groups such as the Grandmothers of the Plaza de Mayo accused naval doctor Norberto Atilio Bianco of selling the infants of missing persons. Although Bianco eventually was sentenced on charges of kidnapping and forgery, he was allowed to count his years at his vacation home in Paraguay—itself a known haven for political criminals—as time served. Victims' rights groups also took to task the Catholic Church in Argentina, both for its reluctance to condemn the junta from 1976 through 1983 and the church's alleged protection of priests who had facilitated crimes for the regime.

The amnesties provided to junta supporters during the transition of 1983 had allowed several to escape the country. It took until the first decade of the 21st century, for example, for Julio Alberto Poch to be extradited to Argentina to face trial. Poch had piloted many of the "death flights" over the Río de la Plata (River Plate) and the ocean. Some such extraditions were pushed along by decisions of countries where junta operatives had fled. Spurred on by guilt that they had sheltered human rights violators, nations such as Spain declared that they were ready to mount trials for perpetrators of the Argentine genocide.

With the turn of the century the courts of Argentina appeared more willing to strike down laws that protected dirty war perpetrators from prosecution or allowed their pardon. In 2009 the highest court of criminal appeals in Argentina reaffirmed the unconstitutionality of President Menem's 1990 pardon of Videla and Massera. The

court declared that those two former junta members, convicted in the 1985 proceedings, would have to continue serving life terms.

SIGNIFICANCE

Some in Argentina adopted the position of those in South Africa and elsewhere who argued that if repressors would come clean, then the nation could heal. The Inter-American Commission on Human Rights lobbied for "truth commissions" that would give answers to victims' families about their fates. "Truth trials," though, did not impose punishments.

Other families of victims pressed for "justice and punishment," in other words, the continuation of judicial trials. But the courtroom pursuit of human rights criminals in Argentina continued somewhat slowly, in part because of the sheer numbers of the victims and the difficulty of proving their identities or the names of their persecutors. The legal system in the nation, too, played a part in the deliberate quality of the prosecutions. Under Argentine law judges, rather than public officials (such as district attorneys in the U.S. system), were the key decision makers about how investigations should occur and whether trials should proceed.

In 2010 former president Bignone was convicted in federal court for his oversight of a military barracks near Buenos Aires where about 5,000 persons had been detained during the dirty war. His critics were able to show in court that Bignone was connected to crimes committed against 56 of those prisoners at the Campo de Mayo, a place from which only a few of the missing persons walked free. Two of Bignone's codefendants, also generals, were sentenced to join him in prison for 25 years. The sentence against Bignone was considered a severe one given Bignone's advanced age. Bignone had been defiant in court, declaring that he had acted to prevent terrorism and averring that the "urban guerrillas" he had opposed were not "tender students driven by ideology."

Furthermore, prosecutors secured new indictments against some of the original nine junta defendants. Videla, for instance, was now charged with 49 counts of murder, kidnapping, and torture, in addition to those at issue in the 1985 trial. Critics of the trials that occurred after 1985, though, lamented the fact that some individuals they considered reprehensible, such as naval intelligence director Acosta, still were on the lam. Certain widely suspected perpetrators such as Victor Hermes Brusa and Luis Abelardo Patti actually were elected to public office or appointed as judges, even after word of their connection to the junta surfaced. Nonetheless, trials such as that of Bignone were satisfying to victims' advocacy organizations. Argentina was imposing and upholding substantial verdicts, after a period of sweeping the dirty war under the rug.

Further Reading

Feitlowitz, Marguerite. *A Lexicon of Terror: Argentina and the Legacies of Torture.* Oxford: Oxford University Press, 1998; Ferguson, Sam. "The Unending War: Argentina's Quest for Justice." *Boston Review* (May–June 2008). Available online. URL: http://bostonreview.net/BR33.3/ferguson.php. Accessed April 13, 2010; Forero, Juan. "Argentina's Dirty War Still Haunts Youngest Victims." National Public Radio. Available online. URL: http://www.npr.org/templates/story/story.php?storyId=124125440. Accessed April 11, 2010; Lewis, Mark. *Guerrillas and Generals: The Dirty War in Argentina.* Westport, Conn.: Praeger, 2001; Osiel, Mark. "Ever Again: Legal Remembrance of Administrative Massacre." *University of Pennsylvania Law Review* 144 (December 1995): 463–565; Proyecto Desaparecidos. "Nunca más." Available online. URL: http://www.desaparecidos.org/arg/. Accessed April 10, 2010; Puenzo, Luis (dir.), *The Official Story.* Koch Lorder Films, 1985; Speck, Paula K. "The Trial of the Argentine Junta: Responsibilities and Realities." *University of Miami Inter-American Law Review* 18 (Spring 1987): 491–534; Thornton, Lawrence. *Imagining Argentina.* New York: Bantam, 1991; United States National Security Archive. "New Declassified Details on Repression and U.S. Support for Military Dictatorship." Available online. URL: http://www.gwu.edu/~nsarchiv/NSAEBB/NSAEBB185/index.htm. Accessed April 10, 2010.

The trial of Peter Wright

Also known as: *The Crown v. Wright and Heinemann;* the *Spycatcher* trial

Date: 1986–1987

KEY ISSUES

Peter Wright was an old cold warrior. Wright had worked for British intelligence during World War II and in the subsequent three decades, rising to the position of assistant director of the British domestic intelligence agency MI5. He retired to Australia in 1976 while there still was open hostility between the superpowers of the East and West.

Wright was fully aware of many breaches of trust that had occurred in the British intelligence service. Some of those lapses became open knowledge almost as they happened, while others were hushed up for decades. For example, the defections to the Soviet Union of Cambridge spy ring members Kim Philby, Guy Burgess, and Donald Mclean were well known among the public during the 1950s and 1960s. But, despite whispers within the intelligence community on both sides of the Atlantic that others within that ring still held high positions in British government, British agencies remained notoriously tight lipped about compromises in security.

Wright and his colleagues, who were dedicated anticommunists, viewed such refusal to confront moles and treachery on a systemic basis as being motivated by several factors. First, there were old-school ties that seemed to bind certain socially elite members of the government from admitting that former university mates were spies. There also was the argument that so many young people in the 1930s had flirted with communism while at university in the 1930s, that to harp on such former associations decades later was to suspect a large number of government servants of disloyalty.

Wright also perceived that the British government was impelled by a need to impress its NATO allies, particularly the United States, with its supposed command of security. To admit breaches within Britain was to jeopardize the peacetime U.S.-British partnership, a connection that was military, political, economic, and cultural. Domestic politics figured, too, in British officials' reluctance to confront instances of past espionage and to uncover ongoing problems. The prime minister as of 1979, Margaret Thatcher, considered herself and the Conservative government to be strongly positioned against communism. Wright's contentions that British intelligence was still riddled with pro-Soviet treachery meant that Thatcher was being outflanked on her right. The Thatcher government worked hard, then, to muzzle former intelligence agents who made allegations such as Wright did about the history and the present condition of British security.

Since the late 19th century British law had said that the government could define which information ought to be kept from the public. The presumption of the main Official Secrets Acts (1889 and 1911) was that unauthorized spreading of classified information was illegal, no matter what the purpose of that dissemination. So, for example, under provisions of the Official Secrets Act of 1911 a government worker who leaked classified data to a newspaper was acting illegally, as was a "whistle-blower" who complained of impropriety within his or her government agency. Although one such distributor of official secrets might argue that he wished the public to be better informed on an issue and the other that she aimed to expose government waste or corruption, the Official Secrets Act equated the disseminators with foreign spies. One could not justify one's actions, in other words, as acting in the public interest. In addition, not only present and former government servants but also journalists and even the distributors and publishers of writings that the government deemed secret might be hauled into court on charges of violating the Official Secrets Acts.

British courts often were inconsistent in enforcing regulations on official secrecy. Whether a former government employee could publish his memoirs without government efforts to either censure or prohibit disclosure sometimes seemed dependent on who the former employee was rather than the level or quality of information to be disclosed. Famously, for example, Winston Churchill had a cottage industry in publishing autobiographical accounts. The former prime minister often mentioned cabinet discussions of the highest importance. The fact that Churchill had a Nobel Prize in literature to his credit seemed to influence the government not to suppress his work, as apparently did the fact that the teller of tales was, well, Churchill.

The estate of former government official Richard Crossman, however, in 1975 ran into legal difficulty in putting out Crossman's memoirs. This was in spite of the fact that Crossman's ministerial oversight was of domestic matters during peacetime. Rather than evoking the Official Secrets Act, the government tried to stop the publication of the Crossman diaries on grounds that such attention to the inner workings of politics would hamper future discourse within the cabinet. Lord Chief Justice John Widgery ruled that Crossman's writings could be published. Although the decision could have been broader in scope, most legal scholars saw the resolution of the Crossman controversy as a signal of liberalism. It seemed that both bureaucrats and the courts were prepared to construe the law liberally—to allow freer comment on official secrets.

HISTORY OF THE CASE

Wright aimed his memoirs, called *Spycatcher: The Candid Autobiography of a Senior Intelligence Officer,* at an English-speaking audience. Obviously the Official Secrets Act was a concern, but Wright and his publisher, Heinemann, of Australia, thought that they could justify publication of Wright's autobiography on several grounds. First of all, Wright had been retired for several years. The interval between events described and publication sometimes was a factor in whether the British government objected to publication and whether courts granted government injunctions against publication.

Wright also knew that others had published on the same subjects as he had in his manuscript. In particular, Wright recalled that he had collaborated with journalist Chapman Pincher to provide material for Pincher's 1981 book *Their Trade Is Treachery.* When composing the book, Wright and Pincher worked through a very highly placed government intermediary to include information that the government had vetted first. Other information that Wright put into his autobiography also had appeared in print with no comment—certainly with no effort at suppression—from the British government.

Finally, Wright and Heinemann were banking on the fact that Australia was a nation with only the most formal constitutional ties to Great Britain. Surely English fears about state secrecy did not hold in Australia in the last quarter of the 20th century. Even if the British government objected to distribution on English soil, Heinemann and Wright depended on the government's not pressing the case in Australia. The writer and publishers of *Spycatcher* did not count on the intransigence of Prime Minister Thatcher, who was determined to press home Australia's historic links to Great Britain. On the flip side, the Iron Lady did not have a good feel for the independent spirit of the Australian courts.

SUMMARY OF ARGUMENTS

Beginning in the spring of 1985 the British government proceeded on several fronts—both geographical and argumentative—to shut down publication and then distribution of Wright's memoirs. Its efforts to forestall publication within Great Britain were fairly successful, but the usual tactic of asking for injunctions against distribution was only partially helpful in stopping dissemination of the completed book printed elsewhere. In addition, contempt-of-court citations were effective in persuading booksellers within Great Britain not to stock *Spycatcher*. The threat of summary contempt verdicts convinced English newspapers and magazines not even to detail the growing controversy either in regard to developments at home or abroad.

In terms of winning the war for public opinion in Great Britain, however, the government faced growing resistance. The *Economist,* for example, published in an otherwise blank space a brief notice that its nearly half million readers were being denied access to coverage of the fracas over Wright's memoirs, to say nothing of the book itself. The magazine's editors ridiculed the English judges who seemingly bowed to government pressure, quoting Charles Dickens's famous trenchant phrase that "the law is an ass." By printing the law

lords' photographs upside down, the *Daily Mirror* lampooned the legal experts in the House of Lords who had backed government policy in prohibiting publication. In late November 1987, while legal proceedings continued in Australia, Labor leader Neil Kinnock asked the prime minister searching questions about the effort to suppress *Spycatcher*. It proved one of the rare instances in which Thatcher was backed into a corner in an argument. She had to acknowledge the government's pursuit of Wright publicly. That meant that *Spycatcher* was mentioned in the papers as a matter discussed in the House of Commons.

The attack on Wright's book was carried out with special fervor in Australia. The British government filed a case in the Supreme Court of New South Wales in Sydney in spring 1985. The government contended that Wright was bound by the Official Secrets Act not to divulge information about his intelligence work without prior approval from British authorities. Materials were gathered for months prior to trial, and formal arguments in the case began in November 1986. Thatcher sent Sir Robert Armstrong, head of the British Civil Service, to represent the prosecution on behalf of the British government. Judge Philip Powell heard the case without a jury, making his ruling after about a month of arguments in court.

A cornerstone of the defense that Wright put forward through his and Heinemann's lead defense attorney, Malcolm Turnbull, was that *Spycatcher* provided information of benefit to the citizens of Great Britain. Wright's contention that British intelligence still contained Soviet spies would allow a cleanup to proceed, in other words, and that was in the public interest. Turnbull focused as well on prior publications of Wright's material, especially in Pincher's writing. He developed the point that the British were presumptuous to try to enforce their rules on freedom of speech in a separate nation, no matter how closely Australia and Great Britain had been linked in the past.

Turnbull was a young lawyer, but he made a vivid impression as a cross-examiner, even on those arrayed against him, and Wright recalled that Turnbull's questioning of Armstrong was masterful. For example, Turnbull homed in on the antiquated notion that although the British almost universally thought of themselves as having a

Secret Intelligence Service (SIS) that included MI5 and MI6, it operated without any statutory basis. Funding was channeled through other budgetary categories, and SIS leaders were never officially named as such. Turnbull was discussing the relationship between the Australian Secret Intelligence Service (ASIS) and that in Britain. That connection was a link that Armstrong argued was vital to preserve. Such cooperation, Armstrong maintained, might mean suppressing Wright's book.

In the courtroom Armstrong had to dance around the identity of Britain's SIS chief, Sir Richard White. Turnbull asked, if White was the head of the SIS, did that not mean that SIS existed? Armstrong's reply was typical of the verbal elusiveness that his awkward position in the case necessitated: "Oh well, I can't admit that SIS existed before Dick White became its head and I can't admit it existed after Dick White became its head."

There was one even more famous instance of Turnbull's acuity and Armstrong's lack thereof in the case. Turnbull asked how much of Pincher's 1981 manuscript (informed by Wright and Lord Rothschild) the government had read before the book was published. When it came out in the Australian courtroom that the British government knew full well what the book said prior to publication, the prosecution's contentions about Wright's book looked inconsistent. Furthermore, it sounded as though the government subsequently had lied—in writing—about its prior knowledge of Pincher's work. Turnbull's characterization seemed to cover not just that lie but the government's whole case:

Turnbull: So it contains a lie?

Armstrong: It was a misleading impression. It does not contain a lie, I don't think.

Turnbull: What is the difference between a misleading impression and a lie?

Armstrong: A lie is a straight untruth.

Turnbull: What is a misleading impression? A sort of bent untruth?

Armstrong: . . . It is perhaps being economical with the truth.

The Australian press and much of its public reacted with derision to such verbal shenanigans. Armstrong's unfortunate phrase entered the popular lexicon as a prime example of doublespeak.

VERDICT

Judge Powell decided to let the publication of *Spycatcher* go forward in Australia. His judgment from mid-March 1987 was less a ringing endorsement of Wright's position than recognition that the British government's stance was outmoded. The court refrained from calling Armstrong a perjurer on behalf of Thatcher and MI5 but implied that he had been economical with the truth. While British authorities appealed Judge Powell's ruling, there was a temporary ban on publication, but it was lifted once the Federal High Court in Canberra ruled in Wright's favor in October 1987.

Meanwhile newspapers, even in Britain, began to defy court orders not to publish the book by printing excerpts under the guise of covering the *Spycatcher* legal proceedings. The intense discussion probably had the effect of vastly increasing sales of the book. Wright, who admitted penning the memoir in part due to anger that his civil service pension was so low, became a millionaire.

SIGNIFICANCE

In 2009 Pincher (then aged 95) published another book arguing that Roger Hollis was the "fifth man" of the Cambridge spy ring. It was a contention that Wright had articulated in *Spycatcher* and had implied in his and Pincher's 1981 book. Among Pincher's specific allegations in the 21st-century work were that Hollis had given security clearance to Klaus Fuchs (a convicted spy who finally went to live in East Germany) for his work at the atomic weapons development center at Los Alamos, New Mexico. Fuchs was the physicist whose unmasking as a Soviet spy was at the heart of the cracking of the Rosenberg case. Likewise, Hollis kept showing up in MI5 records as the power within the intelligence service who authorized the handling of sensitive information by other defectors and spies, including Burgess, Maclean, and the fourth ring member, Anthony Blunt.

Pincher chose to publish the book in the United States. In large part remembering the *Spy-*

catcher case, Pincher declared that he was afraid that if he had tried to bring the book out on his home turf, the British government would have sought to delay its publication until the author died and the estate chose to give up the effort. Crossman's case had shown how costly and protracted such an effort could be. Among those who came in for Pincher's later criticism was Thatcher, whom Pincher argued was misled into defending MI5 moles such as Hollis during the *Spycatcher* case. Like Wright, Pincher maintained that the quality of information that Soviet moles had passed along during the war years and afterward was quite high. Although the anticommunists had worked assiduously, the treachery of superior officers undermined the spycatchers' work.

In another book published at about the same time as Pincher's latest tome, the authorized historian of MI5 took Pincher's and Wright's longstanding thesis to task. Cambridge professor Christopher Andrews argued that Hollis was one of the most consistently loyal servants of the British government and decidedly not a mole. Andrews, furthermore, ridiculed Wright's book as sloppy. Andrews had access to thousands of documents that he maintained Wright could have consulted. The professional historian considered Wright's pursuit of Hollis in *Spycatcher* to be either badly misinformed or motivated by bitterness.

Still, Andrews noted that the *Spycatcher* controversy was an episode for which British intelligence ought to have been grateful, because it led to a reexamination of how the British security services were spoken of among politicians. In part due to embarrassment at the farcical answers given by Armstrong at the Australian trial, the British government changed its old policy of refusing to acknowledge that the security agencies such as MI5 and MI6 existed. In 1989 a statute was passed officially authorizing funding for the intelligence community in Britain. Henceforth, the Secret Intelligence Service had a public face. The government, however, did move to close a main loophole left by the *Spycatcher* controversy. The Official Secrets Act of 1989 forbade the publication of any memoir by a working or retired British intelligence operative.

British officials' efforts to suppress *Spycatcher* had other enduring effects, but not in the direction that the Thatcher government had envisioned. Although litigated in the era prior to the Internet, the case demonstrated how difficult it was becoming to stop the printed word from crossing national boundaries. In addition, the controversy underlined the degree to which former British colonies no longer thought themselves legally beholden to their former rulers. In Scotland, a part of Great Britain, courts would not enjoin the publication of Wright's book. Finally, within even the conservative Australian legal community, the *Spycatcher* affair stirred pride in the independence of Australia.

Further Reading

Andrew, Christopher. *The Defence of the Realm: The Authorized History of MI5.* London: Allen Lane, 2009; "Burgess, MacLean, and Philby." Federal Bureau of Investigation. Available online. URL: http://foia.fbi.gov/foiaindex/philby.htm. Accessed March 26, 2010; Fysh, Michael, ed. *The* Spycatcher *Cases.* London: Sweet & Maxwell, 1989; Hall, Richard. *A Spy's Revenge.* New York: Penguin, 1987; Pincher, Chapman. *Their Trade Is Treachery.* New York: Bantam Books, 1982; ———. *Treachery: Betrayals, Blunders, and Cover-ups.* New York: Random House, 2009; ———. *A Web of Deception: The* Spycatcher *Affair.* London: Sidgwick & Jackson, 1987; Turnbull, Malcolm. *The* Spycatcher *Trial.* Richmond: Heinemann Australia, 1988.

The Bhopal trials

Also known as: *India v. Keshub Mahindra, et al.*

Date: 1987–2010

KEY ISSUES

Multinational corporations based in the West brought economic opportunity to other areas of the world, but they also brought risks. What if a company was engaged in dangerous practices? Could that entity be held accountable within the underdeveloped nation where it had production facilities? If the business changed hands either within a third world nation or its place of incorporation, then did subsequent incarnations of the corporation inherit responsibility for damages that previously may have occurred? What was the role of the government of the nation where an accident occurred at the hands of a multinational operation?

These were among the intricate questions that bedeviled a legal response to the Bhopal gas leak of 1984. The incident at Bhopal is often called the worst industrial disaster in world history. Its implications were long lasting in terms of the physical damage it caused to individuals, to say nothing of economic and psychological scars. For more than 20 years the legal systems of India and the United States struggled to assign liability for such grave harm.

HISTORY OF THE CASE

On December 3, 1984, the chemical methyl isocyanate (MIC) leaked into the atmosphere, poisoning air in the 30 square miles around the Union Carbide plant in Bhopal, India. The owner of the facility was Union Carbide India Limited (UCIL). That company was a local subsidiary of the Union Carbide Corporation, a multinational company headquartered in the United States. The Bhopal plant manufactured substances used in pesticides.

Approximately 4,000 people died immediately; most had been asleep at the time of the accident. Many thousands of others suffered illnesses, including respiratory distress, cancer, and heart problems, and injuries, particularly blindness, as a result of their exposure to the toxic substance. Within a few weeks between 15,000 and 18,000 persons died. More than 500,000 people in the vicinity suffered as a result of contaminated water and air.

The government of India in early 1985 introduced legislation that placed litigation in the hands of the state rather than the many U.S. tort attorneys who had appeared in Bhopal just after the disaster. That new law spurred arguments from several parties, for example U.S. and Indian legal

professionals, Union Carbide, and victims' groups, concerning whether claims from the incident were most appropriately resolved in India or in the United States. The debate about how to respond to the Bhopal tragedy included discussion of the accessibility of each nation's legal process to underserved populations, the role of the legal process in each society, and the pace at which complex litigation moved through Indian and U.S. courts. Lawyers for UCIL, for example, decried the Bhopal Gas Leak Disaster Act of 1985 as trying to shunt legal business to U.S. courts.

In 1989 Union Carbide Corporation paid a settlement to the government of India, to be distributed to those who were affected. The total amount remitted was $470 million, which in theory amounted to about $10,000 per person who had died in the incident. Critics of the settlement offered the opinion that not only had the Indian government brokered an arrangement in order to protect Union Carbide Corporation and its Indian affiliate from further legal damage. Skeptics also said that the very nation where the disaster had occurred had valued Indian lives as cheap. Defenders of the settlement, which was by order of India's supreme court, pointed out that if funds were not available to sufferers soon, then their distress would worsen.

The settlement of 1989 came in for criticism among victims' rights groups in India. The sums that eventually reached the hands of survivors and the family members of the dead were small—about $500 per person. Critics such as the International Campaign for Justice in Bhopal contended that that amount, while it went further in India because of a lower standard of living than in the United States, still was insufficient to compensate victims for their losses. In addition, those who disliked the settlement pointed out that it did not include many persons who were gravely injured and took little account of communities and individuals whose quality of life was seriously affected, for example, via contaminated water.

After the settlement of 1989 Union Carbide Corporation consistently argued against further payments. In part, the corporation said that it was not liable for damages because Indian courts did not have authority to hear cases against a company that was chartered in another nation. Its settlement, in other words, was a goodwill gesture and not an admission of liability. Union Carbide also maintained that the settlement's terms made it a final resolution of all claims that possibly could arise from the disaster.

The situation was complicated when ownership of UCIL changed hands. Ten years after the disaster, McLeod Russell Limited of India purchased Union Carbide India Limited and renamed it Eveready Industries India Limited. Adding another dimension to the controversy was the question of whether the facility where the disaster occurred—and where there may have been long-term contamination as a result—was the responsibility of the regional authorities in India or the industrial owners. In 1998 that question seemed to be resolved in favor of public control of the site by the state of Madhya Pradesh. This left the cleanup under the auspices of the state government but also imposed on local authorities certain costs associated with upkeep and decontamination.

SUMMARY OF ARGUMENTS

Originally, the state where the accident occurred charged eight executives of UCIL with culpable homicide. The Central Bureau of Investigation (CBI), an authority equivalent to the U.S. Office of the Attorney General, drew up the indictment. Among the business leaders charged was the man who had headed UCIL at the time of the incident, Keshub Mahindra. Other defendants included the plant's managing director, vice president, plant manager, production manager, plant superintendent, and a leading production assistant.

The prosecution contended that UCIL oversaw a production facility that was flawed in design and whose maintenance was substandard. The case was filed in 1987 with the Chief Judicial Magistrate's Court in Bhopal. Prosecutors alleged that the high-level UCIL executives were in a position to appreciate the disastrous consequences of a gas leak. They therefore were charged with culpable homicide, the highest level of accountability under the law short of murder. Solicitor Altaf Ahmed, arguing for the prosecution, stated that all of the defendants "shared a common criminal knowledge" and that the Bhopal facility under their control was "defective." The prosecution was spe-

cifically aimed at officials of UCIL, but it also necessarily involved accusations against Union Carbide Corporation as the international entity.

Many of the arguments on behalf of the defense were part of a legal strategy approved by the U.S.-based corporation. Early in the proceedings a main argument of the defense was that the incident was caused by a deliberate action. At first, the corporation maintained that the leak was the result of a plot by Sikh extremists through their arm called Black June. Then Union Carbide Corporation theorized that a disgruntled employee had committed an act of industrial sabotage.

Another line of argument by Union Carbide Corporation had to do with its corporate structure and relationship with affiliates in foreign countries. The U.S. headquarters sought to distance itself from UCIL, downplaying its oversight of everyday operations at Bhopal. At one juncture during the trial Union Carbide Corporation let it be known that it should not be described as a multinational corporation at all, for that implied that the parent company had control of what went on within subsidiaries.

The prosecution answered contentions that the Bhopal plant had been sabotaged and that Indian operations were less carefully managed than other Union Carbide facilities (such as in the United States). The CBI offered evidence that a worker at UCIL had protested to Union Carbide Corporation about gas being stored in tanks that were too large. The U.S. office sent word, however, that smaller tanks were not needed. Union Carbide Corporation also had contradicted persons on-scene in India who were concerned about the over-filling of the tanks and the temperature of the gas storage. At trial Union Carbide Corporation responded by contrasting mistakes in India with its "superior operations" at a similar plant in West Virginia, although the prosecution pointed out that that U.S. facility had had a number of gas leaks, one such leak a few months after 100 workers had been injured at the Bhopal plant.

A decisive moment in the trial was a ruling by the Supreme Court of India in 1996. By that time the case already had gone on for nine years. Speaking through Indian supreme court chief justice A. M. Ahmedi and justice S. B. Majumdar, the high court mandated that prosecutors charge the defendants under a different law than they originally had applied. The shift was from a charge of "culpable homicide not amounting to murder" to "causing death by negligence," charges which were referred to in shorthand by the section numbers in the law: Sections 304A, 336, 337, and 338 of the Indian Penal Code versus Section 304A (the lesser offense).

The basis of the high court's decision was a set of documents concerning the defendants' possible knowledge of dangers at the plant. The Supreme Court of India ruled that for the prosecution to be able to charge the defendants under the more severe sections, the state had to make a prima facie case of the accused persons' contribution to culpable homicide. The court went on to conclude that that standard had not been met. The newer charges carried a smaller potential sentence of only two years' imprisonment and a $2,000+ fine in contrast to the earlier possibility of a 10-year prison term. Prosecutors and activists in India referred to the Supreme Court decision as a "dilution" of the original case. Most observers concurred that the Supreme Court ruling assigned less blame to the UCIL executives, although it also made them more likely to be convicted.

Prosecutors pursued the case from 1996 until its resolution in 2010 with the conviction of the seven remaining defendants. A team of investigators and lawyers were involved on both sides. The prosecution had two key leaders: Shri P. K. Shukla and Shri C. Sahay.

Indian officials also tried the case in the court of world opinion, for example, putting forward the view that Union Carbide's responsibility for the incident continued. This argument was maintained even though Union Carbide Corporation in the United States had been sold to Dow Chemical Corporation in 2001. Dow responded that its contract to buy Union Carbide Corporation did not include assumption of liability for the Bhopal catastrophe. It also contended that whatever financial stake Union Carbide Corporation had in the disaster had been discharged when it made the lump-sum payment to the Indian government in 1989.

At least one major lawsuit was filed in U.S. courts as a result of the Bhopal event: *Bano v. Union Carbide*. That class-action suit, brought in 1999 in New York State, alleged that people who lived and worked near the Bhopal plant were harmed by water contamination. The suit was against Union Carbide Corporation and its former chief executive, Warren Anderson. From 2001 onward several appeals court rulings and a rehearing in the trial court limited the plaintiffs' options for recovery of costs for cleanup of their property, also diminishing their prospects for gaining punitive damages. Those rebuffs to Bhopal residents were not on the merits of the evidence but rather were based on factors such as whether the Bhopal plaintiffs owned the land to which they claimed damages and whether any U.S. court order mandating a cleanup could be enforced in Bhopal.

VERDICT

In 2010 the seven UCIL executives who had been charged first in 1984 and recharged in 1997 were convicted of negligence; one had died during the protracted hearing of the case. The case against one individual defendant, however, continued unresolved. Indian authorities considered former Union Carbide Corporation chairman Anderson to have avoided the judicial process; he had left many subpoenas unanswered. Long before the convictions in 2010 of the seven UCIL executives, Anderson was declared an "absconder." He remained a fugitive from justice in India, though extradition proceedings for Anderson were stalled. The U.S. government adopted the position that it would hold no further inquiries concerning the disaster, referring to the 2010 convictions as "closure" for victims and their families.

SIGNIFICANCE

Among legal experts, the Bhopal trials are known for their length and complexity. Nineteen separate judges presided over the case from 1987 onward. The prosecution named 240 witnesses over the course of the proceedings, with the state entering 3,009 documents into evidence. Even before the decision in 2010, Union Carbide Corporation had paid $50 million in legal costs—a sum greater than the disbursement it had made to that date in compensation to victims.

Scholars of industrial disasters and corporate negligence note that however limited the compensation to Bhopal victims, at least they received some financial acknowledgment of their loss via the action of their government. Persons who suffered grave loss in the Chernobyl nuclear accident in the Ukraine got little even in the way of apology from the government officials who ran that plant. On the other hand, the punishment levied against the executives of UCIL appears slight when set alongside the verdicts of death imposed in 2009 on Chinese executives whose negligence led to deaths and at least 300,000 illnesses among the public from tainted milk. That contrast with the response of other legal systems is especially vivid when considering the number of people injured and killed at Bhopal and the lingering impact of the incident upon the environment.

The legal handling of the Bhopal disaster in certain respects recalled the thalidomide cases, for while the legal response to the thalidomide tragedy was spread over many more nations, the thalidomide controversy also involved questions of the culpability of individuals, international corporations, and local affiliates for harm done in their search for profits. In regard to Bhopal, as with thalidomide, no one government or corporate entity seemed willing to shoulder responsibility for the human and environmental costs of the tragedies.

Further Reading

Cassells, Jamie. *Uncertain Promise of Law: Lessons from Bhopal.* Toronto, Canada: University of Toronto Press, 1994; Earth Rights International. "*Bano v. Union Carbide* Case History." Available online. URL: http://www.earthrights.org/legal/bano-v-union-carbide-case-history. Accessed May 2, 2010; Fortun, Kim. *Advocacy after Bhopal: Environmentalism, Disaster, New Global Orders.* Chicago: University of Chicago Press, 2001; Hanna, Bridget, Ward Morehouse, and Satinath Sarangi. *The Bhopal Reader: Remembering Twenty Years of the World's Worst Industrial Disaster.* Goa: Other India Press, 2005; International Campaign for Justice in Bhopal. "A Bhopal Timeline." Available online. URL: http://bhopal.net. Accessed May 2, 2010; Lapierre, Dominique, and Javier Moro. *Five Past Midnight in Bhopal.* New York: Warner Books, 2002; Schuck, Peter H. *Agent Orange on Trial: Mass Toxic Disasters in the Courts.* Cambridge, Mass.: Harvard University Press, 1987.

The trial of Orenthal James Simpson

Also known as: *California v. Simpson;* the O. J. Simpson murder case

Date: 1995

KEY ISSUES

The facts of the O. J. Simpson case were not exceptional. It concerned a murder that was all too typical. A man who was physically abusive during a relationship remained jealous even when estranged from his wife. Reluctant to see her independent of him, the former husband killed her, also savaging the male in whose company she happened to be. What made this situation unusual was that the jealous former spouse was well known already. The mass media built on that fame, parlaying the killings into material that lasted for years.

Orenthal James Simpson had gone from renown as a college and professional football player into success in other arenas. Simpson, who was called "O. J." or "the Juice," was typical of celebrities in the late 20th-century United States: He was a sports figure, an advertising pitchman, and a movie actor. In 1995 Simpson stood trial for the murders of his former wife Nicole Brown Simpson and an acquaintance of hers, Ronald Goldman. The trial added another layer of fame to Simpson; he became a representative of his race. Simpson emerged as an African-American man who had stared down the U.S. criminal justice system. His trial quickly turned into a forum for discussion of whether that entire system was racist.

In statistical terms murder was a rare crime in 20th-century Los Angeles. For a person of Simpson's high profile as an entertainer, to be charged with intentional killing was therefore unusual. Not since the Roscoe Arbuckle trials had such a successful Hollywood figure been accused of murder, though Arbuckle actually stood trial for only manslaughter. Making Simpson's indictment even more sensational was the fact that since the time of Arbuckle's case in the 1920s, media had greatly expanded. Simpson's case was covered on television and even via the Internet, while Arbuckle's legal troubles were chronicled only in print.

HISTORY OF THE CASE

Several times during their seven-year marriage Nicole Simpson reported to the police that O. J. Simpson had been physically abusive toward her. In a pattern typical of domestic conflicts the alleged victim usually had second thoughts about pressing charges, either due to further threats from the perpetrator or a genuine sense that the abuser would mend his ways. Nicole Simpson left a record of "911" calls and anguished conversations with friends and family concerning her fear of O. J. In 1989, while the couple was living separately, O. J. Simpson pleaded "no contest" to battering Nicole. The couple divorced in 1992 and began other relationships, although they remained in contact because they shared custody of their two young children.

Late on the night of June 12, 1994, a barking dog belonging to Nicole Simpson attracted the attention of neighbors in the Brentwood area of Los Angeles, where Nicole lived in a condominium. When the neighbors looked closely at the dog, they saw its fur was covered in blood; the dog led them to what turned out to be a crime scene. Just inside the condo gate were two bodies—those of Nicole Brown Simpson and a young man—apparently very recently killed. There was no question that the deaths had been killings rather than suicides or an accident. Both of the victims had been stabbed, and Simpson's throat had been cut. There was no murder weapon in sight. It was a savage scene; the male victim had fought back, apparently, but Simpson had been incapacitated very quickly.

Police arrived just after midnight and called for backup to investigate the situation. Officers found the Simpson children asleep inside the condo. A Los Angeles Police Department (LAPD) detective, Mark Fuhrman, who arrived at the scene

stated to his colleagues that O. J. Simpson had been the subject of domestic violence calls at the address. Fuhrman had been a patrol officer in the area when the Simpsons were married.

Initially the officers still regarded the situation as ongoing. They looked for O. J. Simpson not only as a potential perpetrator but also a possible victim and, certainly, the father to the children in Nicole Simpson's house. They went to O. J. Simpson's home nearby and were unable to get anyone to answer the door or the phone. During their attempt to ascertain whether O. J. Simpson himself was in danger, they noticed marks that appeared to be bloodstains on Simpson's vehicle. They finally went inside Simpson's residence and discovered, in separate guest areas, Simpson's young adult daughter from his first marriage and a houseguest named Kato Kaelin. Through these contacts the police established that O. J. Simpson had flown from Los Angeles to Chicago late the previous evening.

Realizing that the crime was going to be of interest to news organizations because of the connection with O. J. Simpson, the investigators worked quickly to inform Nicole Brown Simpson's next of kin of her death, to speak to O. J. Simpson about caring for his children, and to secure the scene from intrusion by the media. It took longer to learn the identity of the male victim, but he was found to be Ronald Goldman, a casual acquaintance of Nicole Simpson. Eventually the police theorized that Nicole Simpson had left a pair of glasses at a restaurant that evening; Goldman, a waiter, was returning them to her when he came upon Nicole and her assailant. The assumption by investigators was that Goldman died because the killer did not want to leave any witnesses to his attack on Nicole.

The officers and coroner's office workers did their jobs on the morning of June 13, 1994, according to established protocols. Logging in the times of collection, they placed evidence from both the death scene and O. J. Simpson's residence into marked containers so that it would be available for forensic analysis. That evidence included drops of blood at O. J. Simpson's house and fiber and hair samples from the place where the killings had taken place.

Detectives soon centered their suspicion on O. J. Simpson for several reasons, including his history of violence toward Nicole, his muted reaction upon hearing of her death from LAPD over the phone, and certain inconsistencies in his account of his whereabouts on the night of June 12. On June 17, the day after Nicole Brown Simpson's funeral, authorities were set to arrest O. J. Simpson, who had been apprised of that possibility. Rather than surrendering, however, Simpson led the police on a multihour, low-speed chase through Los Angeles.

Before taking that ride, Simpson had written a rambling note that read as though he was either going to commit suicide or flee the country, thus hinting at his guilt. The chase of a white Ford Bronco in which Simpson was riding gained widespread television viewing—a foreshadowing that public interest in the case already had been fanned by media coverage. Simpson finally gave himself up peacefully and was set for trial. The confessional note and the chase were bizarre aspects of a case that the media were beginning to promote as "the trial of the century."

The trial went on for longer than any other case in California history, surpassing the Charles Manson case in duration. More than 100 witnesses appeared, and the proceedings cost the state more than $15 million. The case further presented the terrible example of a sequestered jury (and an alternate panel) being forced to stay away from their families for about half a year. Legal experts warned that potential jurors in other cases would think hard about serving in such demanding circumstances. Judge Lance Ito had the unenviable task of managing media access and imposing some order on the complex proceedings.

SUMMARY OF ARGUMENTS

Absent a witness to the crime or a confession, the case for the prosecution was circumstantial. The state centered its arguments on evidence linking O. J. Simpson to the crime scene: fiber, hair, and blood. The coroner's office in Los Angeles was among the most sophisticated in the world in scientific terms and had a long history of working successfully with the police. Investigators had found a number of specific pieces of evidence to support the theory that O. J. Simpson had planned and carried out the killings; thus, first-degree mur-

der charges had been filed. The police had confidence in lead prosecutor Marsha Clarke, who seemed comfortable with the new science concerning DNA evidence.

The defense had a challenge to counter such seemingly incontrovertible details placing O. J. Simpson in a location—the site of a double homicide—where he swore he had not been. The defense also faced the difficulty of Simpson's enduring reputation as a sports hero; his speed and strength argued for Simpson being able to commit two ferocious killings and yet escape detection by quickly fleeing the scene. Rather weakly, the defense contended in opening statements that Simpson suffered from arthritis such that his physical prowess had been compromised.

Early on in the trial the defense decided upon a risky strategy. Simpson's lawyers would concentrate on discrediting the forensic evidence. First, they would allege sloppy police methods, but if necessary they also would "play the race card," in the words of defense attorney Johnnie Cochran. They would make the argument that the LAPD was not merely incautious but also that certain persons connected with the investigation had set out to frame Simpson. The supposed motive for that police conspiracy to plant evidence pointing to O. J. Simpson's guilt was racism. Specifically, the defense homed in on Detective Fuhrman, alleging that he had an agenda to incriminate O. J. Simpson on account of race. It did not take much digging by the defense to find examples of Fuhrman using racist terms in taped interviews. On the stand Fuhrman denied using prejudicial language, but then he found his credibility demolished by defense lawyer F. Lee Bailey. Fuhrman eventually was convicted of perjury.

The defense alleged that Fuhrman and his superiors and coworkers had gone so far as to place Simpson's blood (obtained legally) in strategic locations at Simpson's own house. That residence was the location to which the prosecution claimed Simpson had fled to change clothing after the commission of the crime. It was the place that the police had searched quickly and without a warrant early on the morning of June 13, 1994, saying they feared for Simpson's safety. In the hands of the defense that search became a more sinister matter.

The defense was assisted by several key mis-calculations on the part of the state. The first mis-take was the most crucial of all: Prosecutors filed charges in downtown Los Angeles instead of in the more affluent area where the crime had occurred. Conducting the trial downtown meant that jurors would be from a more ethnically diverse pool. Indeed, the jury was a cross-section of the popula-tion of Los Angeles instead of a sample of Nicole and O. J. Simpson's lighter-skinned neighbors. Experts on jury selection contended that a racially mixed jury would be more sympathetic to O. J. Simpson simply on account of his ethnic back-ground. Prosecutors, though, were concerned not to exacerbate racial tensions that had simmered in Los Angeles since rioting connected with the beat-ing of Rodney King in 1991.

The defense, meanwhile, adopted several tech-niques that played well. Perhaps their major suc-cess, beyond making race rather than the crime the issue at trial, was to refrain from putting O. J. Simp-son on the stand. They thereby avoided Simpson voicing any contradictions in his story as he had done with investigators. They played upon the repu-tation that Simpson had for amiability with the audiences, who enjoyed his commercials and films.

The prosecution, furthermore, seriously mis-judged Simpson's acting skills at a key juncture in the trial. The state was convinced that Simpson had discarded a pair of expensive gloves he had worn during the killings, gloves that were recovered and presented as evidence in court. Simpson denied wearing that pair of gloves; prosecutor Christopher Darden insisted he try them on. Simpson made a show of trying to pull them on, holding up his hands to demonstrate that the gloves were too small. Defense attorney Cochran delivered a memorable line to the jury: "If it doesn't fit, you must acquit."

The prosecution may also have relied too heav-ily on the weight of forensic evidence with jurors, for while many forensic details pointed to O. J. Simpson's guilt, that evidence still had to be pre-sented to the jury in a comprehensible manner. This trial, as complex legal proceedings increasingly did, seemed bound up with the skills of "competing experts" on the stand. In this instance the testi-mony of forensic pathologist Dr. Henry Lee blurred the vision of the jury. Dr. Lee, for example, was not convinced by footprint evidence and analysis of blood spatters that a single assailant had commit-ted the crimes. Several jurors commented later that Dr. Lee helped place doubt in their minds as to O. J. Simpson's guilt, and reasonable doubt was all that the defense needed to avoid conviction.

VERDICT

The verdict was delivered on October 3, 1995. The jury's decision was broadcast live on the three major television networks in the United States. More than 90 percent of television viewers at that moment were tuned in to the trial—beyond 150 million people in the United States alone. After only a few hours of deliberation, the jurors declared Simpson "not guilty" on all counts.

National television networks and major news outlets devoted extraordinary space and time to coverage of the case, and from so much exposure viewers had strong opinions as to the guilt (or not) of O. J. Simpson. Simpson's efforts to detail his actions on the night of the murders came in for ridicule, for example, in rhymes that circulated on the Internet. Unlike his skillful lawyers, Simpson was not known for his ability to extemporize. His explanations struck critics on the Web as positively childlike:

> I did not do it with a knife
> I did not, could not kill my wife
> I did not do this awful crime
> I could not, would not anytime.

Public opinion polls immediately after the trial showed that the vast majority of African Ameri-cans were unconvinced of Simpson's guilt, while persons identifying themselves as white over-whelmingly believed that Simpson had committed the murders. In other words, whites were upset about the trial's result, but black citizens were sat-isfied with the outcome. Defense lawyer Robert Shapiro condemned his colleagues for pushing race as a key issue in the case, while in their accounts of the trial several prosecution lawyers seemed less convinced of the value of the race card.

SIGNIFICANCE

The Goldman and Brown families pursued O. J. Simpson after the criminal trial ended. Not only did they remind him that he had promised to search for the murderer of the mother of his children. They also filed a civil suit against him for the wrongful death of Goldman and the battery of Nicole Brown Simpson. In 1997 a jury in Santa Monica, California, unanimously awarded a multimillion-dollar judgment against Simpson. There was difficulty in collecting the money, however, in part because California law protected pensions such as Simpson's $25,000 per month payment from the National Football League from being garnished. The Goldmans and Browns did succeed in prohibiting Simpson from publishing a book entitled *If I Did It.*

That piece of writing by Simpson was an extraordinary document. In the book Simpson coyly detailed what he said "might" have occurred on the night that Goldman and Nicole Brown Simpson died. His description of the crime, though supposedly imagined, struck most readers as authentic. After the trial Simpson's defense attorneys had been cautious to speak in general terms about the verdict, for example, saying "justice was done" or "the state did not prove its case" rather than "an innocent man has been freed." Simpson's stance in court, however, repeatedly had been that he had not committed the murders.

It was not without precedent for persons acquitted of murder to speak candidly after trial about what had occurred, either openly or obliquely admitting that they had committed the crimes for which they had been found not guilty. Such occurred, for example, when the white killers of a young African American, Emmett Till, gave an interview bragging about that racially motivated murder to *Look* magazine in 1956. In such a situation, of course, the U.S. Constitution's rule against double jeopardy prohibited retrial. Simpson's effort to reap money from telling about the crime promised to prove far more profitable than the words of Till's killers. The Goldman and Brown families went to court and obtained the rights to Simpson's manuscript. In 2007 they put out the book under the title *If I Did It: Confessions of the Killer.* Several of the lawyers on each side published recollections of the case, as did Fuhrman and various journalists who had covered the trial.

Simpson's brushes with the legal system continued. He was convicted and sent to prison in 2008 on several charges including kidnapping and robbery after an incident in Las Vegas when he attempted to retrieve stolen sports memorabilia. The toughness of the prosecution's pursuit of Simpson in this case may have been directly related to the widespread perception that he had gone free in spite of being guilty in 1995.

Further Reading

Bugliosi, Vincent. "Crimes of the Century: O. J. Simpson." Investigation Discovery. Available online. URL: http://investigation.discovery.com/videos/crimes-of-the-century-oj-simpson-videos/. Accessed December 12, 2009; Clark, Marcia. *Without a Doubt.* New York: Viking, 1997; Dunne, Dominick. "L.A. in the Age of O. J." *Vanity Fair* (February 1995). Available online. URL: http://www.vanityfair.com/culture/features/dunne. Accessed December 12, 2009; Enomoto, Carl. "Public Sympathy for O. J. Simpson: The Roles of Race, Age, Gender, Income, and Education." *American Journal of Economics and Sociology* (January 1999). Available online. URL: http://findarticles.com/p/articles/mi_m0254/is_1_58/ai_54019303/. Accessed December 12, 2009; Jones, Thomas. "The O. J. Simpson Murder Trial." TruTV Crime Library. Available online. URL: http://www.trutv.com/library/crime/notorious_murders/famous/simpson/index_1.html. Accessed December 12, 2009; Toobin, Jeffrey. *The Run of His Life: The People versus O. J. Simpson.* New York: Touchstone, 1997.

The trial of Jean-Paul Akayesu

Also known as: *International Criminal Tribunal for Rwanda v. Akayesu;* the Rwandan genocide trials

Date: 1996–1998

KEY ISSUES

Even in a region long characterized by ethnic reprisals, 1994 stood out as a particularly bloody year in eastern Africa. Of all the African nations affected by mass killings in 1994, none was more decimated than Rwanda. The troubles in Rwanda in 1994 lay against a backdrop of imperialism, although Rwanda had been an independent republic since the early 1960s. First German and then Belgian authorities had governed Rwanda during the 19th and early 20th centuries. In the division of former German lands after World War I, Belgium took control of the territory known as Ruanda-Urundi. European colonizers designated the native Tutsi people as a kind of superior caste among the African residents of Rwanda. The Belgians, particularly, repeatedly supported the Tutsi over other groups within the region—notably in preference to the Hutu people.

Whether the Hutu and the Tutsi were ethnically different from each other was a question that could not be completely sorted out. Still, colonial governors classified the Tutsi differently, for example, on identification cards, and there developed among the native peoples of the vicinity resentment of such preferential treatment for the Tutsi "aristocracy." Pan-African leaders such as Patrice Lumumba and Gregoire Kayibanda in the 1950s pointed out the educational and social advantages that the Tutsi enjoyed. The United Nations voiced concern that the Hutu were excluded from self-determination in Ruanda-Urundi.

Therefore, while Ruanda-Urundi participated in a movement to wrest itself from European control in the late 1950s and early 1960s, there were deadly tensions inside the region. The Hutu majority chafed at recent favoritism shown to the Tutsi by Europeans, although the Roman Catholic Church had pushed for more equality between the groups. The Hutu also noted that Tutsi guerrillas sometimes had led raids into Ruanda from Urundi. When independence for the two areas was granted by Belgium—with UN involvement—in 1962, Rwanda became a republic dominated by the Hutu, while Burundi emerged as a monarchist state with a heavy Tutsi influence in its politics. The area remained rife with violence, usually involving Hutu-Tutsi reprisals. Between the 1960s and the 1980s hundreds of thousands of persons died within each country, especially in border areas.

Leaders in Rwanda periodically reminded their nation that the Tutsi were the enemy—a notion reinforced when a Tutsi-led group called the Rwandan Patriotic Front invaded the northern portion of Rwanda in 1990, leading to a civil war. There emerged in Rwanda a radical pro-Hutu stance called "Hutu power," which undercut efforts to find a peaceful solution to the situation. Hutu power, especially its arm called the Akazu, worked through political parties such as the Interahamwe and the Impuzamugambi, which had militias. Among many Hutu people in Rwanda, the slang term for Tutsi was *cockroach*.

In April 1994 a crisis emerged because of the crash of a plane in which Rwandan president Juvénal Habyarimana and Burundian president Cyprien Ntaryamira were killed. Ntaryamira and his immediate predecessor in Burundi actually were Hutu, having gained office through a democratic election in 1993. Many in the area as well as international observers assumed that Hutu power elements arranged the assassinations because they opposed any moderate settlement.

Rwanda dissolved into violence in the aftermath of the assassinations. Perhaps 1 million (20 percent of the country's inhabitants)—mainly Tutsis and pro-peace Hutus—died during 1994. In a number of communities neighbors killed those they knew. Persons who sought refuge in schools or churches might be trapped as whole buildings were razed or burned. Such were the circumstances of the deaths of more than 1,000 persons in a Catholic church in Nyange at the hands of the Interahamwe. Many Tutsi individuals who were not killed outright were subjected to torture, severe threats, and sexual assault and rape. Sometimes the victims were publicly shamed—for example, through nudity—and then marched to mass graves and shot or killed by machete. It was common for persons who did not perpetrate violence to be accused of sympathy for Tutsis and to become victims themselves.

Many hundreds of thousands of Tutsis fled Rwanda, some to Burundi and others to Zaire, Uganda, and Tanzania. There they lived amid desperate conditions, wracked with disease. The United Nations organized a massive relief effort between May and November 1994, but still thousands died in the refugee camps. Although there were instances of heroism among the bloodshed—Hollywood made a movie about the efforts of hotelier Paul Rusesabagina to shelter Tutsi refugees—even those who initially were opposed to ethnic reprisals got swept up in the carnage. The killings and other violence were well documented, for example, when they occurred among Rwandan employees of international relief agencies. Many non-Rwandans were evacuated as soon as conditions deteriorated in April. It was apparent that most of the victims in Rwanda died because of their perceived ethnicity.

HISTORY OF THE CASE

The Rwandan genocides of 1994 gained the attention of world authorities not only at the time but also afterward, in the courts. Organizations that sought to punish war crimes found in Rwanda an unfortunately high number of cases, as they did in the former Yugoslavia in the same time period of the early 1990s. Among the most important of the trials overseen by the United Nations was the prosecution of Jean-Paul Akayesu. The trial took place in Arusha, Tanzania, beginning in 1996. The judgment in the case was delivered in September 1998, and the sentence was set in October 1998. The case was under the auspices of the International Criminal Tribunal for Rwanda, which was based in Arusha, hence its nickname as the Arusha Tribunal.

Akayesu was the mayor (bourgmestre) of Tabu, a rural settlement in Rwanda. When general violence broke out in Rwanda in April 1994, Akayesu at first argued publicly for cessation of violence against the Tutsi. Within a few days, however, he seemed to reverse his stance. It was the norm in Rwanda in the spring of 1994 for national government officials as well as local leaders to urge the rounding up and killing of Tutsis. Witnesses reported that Akayesu had made a speech in which he incited crowds to kill "the enemy"—the Tutsi.

Akayesu was accused of more than simply protecting himself, however. He was charged with personally witnessing killings and perpetrating sexual violence through his encouragement of troops to assault women; one witness reported that he taunted rioters to "see what a Tutsi tastes like." He also was alleged to have allowed army officers at the communal headquarters to commit atrocities against refugees—largely women and children—who had sought protection there.

Between the time that an indictment was filed against Akayesu and his trial, international and Rwandan groups concerned with human rights and women's legal status applied to prosecutors to amend the indictment. With the concurrence of prosecutor Louise Arbour and Judge Navanethem Pillay (the only woman among the three judges hearing the case), they succeeded in having Akayesu charged with rape and sexual violence, along with the war crimes of which he already was accused.

SUMMARY OF ARGUMENTS

There were three main categories in which Akayesu was charged under international law. He was accused of genocide, crimes against humanity, and violations of the Geneva Convention. The gist of his offenses, according to the 15-count indictment, was that during an "internal armed conflict" within Rwanda, Akayesu proceeded against persons who were noncombatants solely on the basis of their ethnic backgrounds. To commit genocide or war crimes against a group because of their national political, ethnic, or racial background was to be in violation of United Nations conventions. To be liable for his actions under the earlier rules of the Geneva Convention, Akayesu had to have held a position of political or military authority that required him to relieve the suffering of those with whose welfare he had been entrusted. He also was accused of failing to summon external aid once he knew he could not protect those in distress.

In addressing the acts alleged in Rwanda, as with the situation in the former Yugoslavia, prosecutors were confounded by the legal definition of *ethnicity.* Clearly in Rwanda, as in Yugoslavia, persons had been targeted for torture and murder due to their classification in or identification with a persecuted group. But was a persecutor's anger over the perceived ethnicity of a victim sufficient proof of a crime against humanity under international law? After the amendment of the indictment to make it include sexual assault and rape, the prosecution hoped to make it clear that not only the victims' ethnic status but also their gender had marked them out for particularly fierce reprisals. In other words, prosecutors maintained that in Rwanda rape and other sexual crimes amounted to genocide under international law.

Akayesu was represented by court-appointed counsel before the international judicial panel. Much testimony was conducted in the local language of Kinyarwanda, with translation into the court's two official languages, French and English. Akayesu's defense consisted of flat denials of any involvement in the acts alleged. The defense also presented rebuttal witnesses and evidence. The court was unmoved by requests for expert witnesses for the defense when those persons were themselves under suspicion or indictment for similar crimes. The court denied defense requests for access to forensic evidence at mass graves on the grounds that the defense had not established why exhumations beyond those already done were necessary.

The prosecution called 28 witnesses, many of them eyewitnesses and a few of them victims of alleged crimes by Akayesu. A number of those witnesses were shielded from identification in court except to the court officials, Akayesu, and his lawyers. The court referred to them by letters rather than name out of fear that they would be subject to reprisals. This, of course, was an implicit admission by the court that the situation in Rwanda still was not completely stable.

VERDICT

The trial record makes plain the thoroughness of the proceedings. The tribunal considered the credibility of witnesses for both the prosecution and defense. In assessing Akayesu's versions of incidents in which he allegedly was implicated, sometimes there was airtight evidence against him; in other episodes for which he was charged, he probably had eliminated any potential hostile witnesses.

In its decision the court addressed the complex question of how ethnicity played into the Rwandan genocide. This was crucial if the case was to be under the tribunal's authority. The trial record included a long discussion of the history of Hutu-Tutsi conflict. The court focused on the fact that foreign occupiers had exacerbated ethnic tensions in the region as a whole. In spite of the fact that ethnographers contended that the Hutu and the Tutsi had many—perhaps decisive—linguistic, cultural, and racial similarities, within recent memory they had been treated as different people legally and politically. Besides, the court argued, at the heart of the international law's definition of genocide was the "special intent" to destroy a group because of its difference from the oppressor's group. That a perception of difference motivated the defendants was what courts had to consider.

The sections of the testimony that had to do with rape and sexual assault appear to have been the most carefully considered by the court. In its decision the court did not rule that Akayesu had himself perpetrated the rapes or assaults, yet it found several instances in which Akayesu had known that rapes were taking place. Those crimes occurred literally in the compound that he supervised and where he was then present, and he either had not stopped them or seemed to collaborate with the victimizers. In fact, Akayesu usually did not deny the details of the victims' accounts—only his connection with the crimes. The judges put it this way:

> Witnesses JJ, OO, KK, NN and PP were questioned by the Defence with regard to their testimony of sexual violence, but the testimony itself was never challenged. Details such as where the rapes took place, how many rapists there were, how old they were, whether the Accused participated in the rapes, who was raped and which rapists used condoms were all elicited by the Defence, but at no point did the Defence suggest to the witnesses that the rapes had not taken place. The main line of questioning by the Defence with regard to the rapes and other sexual violence, other than to confirm the details of the testimony, related to whether the Accused had the authority to stop them. In cross-examination of the evidence presented by the Prosecution, specific incidents of sexual violence were never challenged by the Defence.

The testimony of the survivors of sexual assault and rape emphasized that the victims continued to feel great shame because of their experiences. Many women had been infected with HIV and other sexually transmitted diseases. Several of the women spoke of begging the assailants to kill them after they had been assaulted. An avowed purpose of the sexual attacks—degradation of the Tutsi—had been achieved.

The court finally decided that Akayesu had aided and abetted sexual violence and rape. Those were acts that in Rwanda beginning in spring 1994 very often preceded the killing of the female victims. For both reasons the court ruled that Akayesu had committed genocide according to the UN conventions on human rights. But, had Akayesu violated the Geneva protocols and the UN tribunal's rules concerning "command responsibility"? The rules about command responsibility set high standards for the protection of civilian populations by military leaders in time of war. Did such standards apply to civilian leaders such as Akayesu?

Although some witnesses recalled that Akayesu wore a military jacket and carried a rifle, the court did not accept such behaviors as constituting proof that he had acted in a military capacity. The judges at Akayesu's trial concluded that international law on the command responsibility of civilians was not as well determined as the law with respect to military commanders. They cited the key case that they thought applicable: the finding of guilt at the Tokyo War Crimes Trials of former Japanese foreign minister Koki Hirota in regard to the "rape of Nanjing" atrocities. And yet, Hirota's conviction included a strong dissenting opinion that courts should only sparingly make civilian authorities responsible for the actions of armies in the field. Thus, Akayesu's tribunal held that he could not be convicted of criminal negligence such as failing to control the actions of the police or the Interahamwe but only for the positive actions that he took to incite and continue the violence.

Akayesu was convicted on one count of genocide, three counts of crimes against humanity for murders, one count of crimes against humanity for extermination, another count of crimes against humanity for torture, and one count each of crimes against humanity for rape and "other inhumane acts," including public degradation and sexual assault. Within each count several persons' deaths or assaults usually were included, so the conviction was for numerous crimes. He was sentenced to three life terms in prison plus 80 years.

SIGNIFICANCE

When she was a law student, Judge Pillay had read the transcripts of the Nuremberg War Crimes Trials, galvanized by the idea that war criminals could be prosecuted outside their own homelands. She became a jurist who concentrated on human rights cases that spanned nations, leading her to the Rwandan War Crimes Trials. Nuremberg had established a powerful example in international law of powers banding together through multinational tribunals to condemn crimes against humanity. But, as Rwandans and Judge Pillay discovered, Nuremberg's precedents covered only major war criminals. Lesser criminals remained to be prosecuted within individual countries, indeed, if these offenders could be located at all.

In response to the Rwandan genocides the United Nation handled prosecutions of higher-level officials and those accused of the most serious offenses, while local tribunals within Rwanda managed many of the numerous other cases. The sheer numbers of cases awaiting local resolution led to a considerable backlog in Rwandan jails, and the international tribunal moved slowly. Those accused persons who appeared before *gacaca* (local) courts often mitigated their sentences with public admissions of guilt. Within Rwanda there was heavy support for the imposition of capital sentences for notorious offenders.

The United Nations, which handled the higher-profile cases, did not apply the death penalty. This created tension between local and world authorities and, until the abolition of the death penalty in Rwanda in 2007, made the United Nations reluctant to cede authority over certain cases to Rwanda. Meanwhile, some individuals accused of war crimes in Rwanda escaped the region and Africa. The U.S. agency charged with tracking down such fugitives was the Office of Special Investigations at the U.S. Justice Department, an authority that for decades had assumed responsibility for locating Nazi war criminals in the United States.

Trials stemming from the genocides of 1994 continued for years. U.S. immigration authorities pursued individuals such as Lazare Kobagaya, who hid his participation in the Rwandan killings when he entered the United States and subsequently gained citizenship. In 2010 Kobagaya was charged with lying about his involvement in Rwandan crimes. Aside from facing charges in Rwanda, Kobagaya risked deportation and a lengthy U.S. jail term.

In late 2008 the Arusha Tribunal reached a judgment against Theoneste Bagosora for his part in killing Agathe Uwilingiyimana, who was the prime minister of Rwanda and effectively the head of state in the immediate wake of President Habyarimana's death. The tribunal found that presidential guards had killed Uwilingiyimana (a moderate Hutu and Rwanda's first female national leader), who was supposed to have been under UN protection while she took refuge at the United Nations Development Programme compound. The UN troops charged with her guardianship were themselves killed. Like the victims of Akayesu, Uwilingiyimana had been protected neither by international peacekeepers nor local governors. But, in response to her death, as in the case against Akayesu, courts finally had the opportunity to condemn the perpetrators of Rwandan atrocities according to international law.

Further Reading

Amann, Diane Marie. "*Prosecutor v. Akayesu.* Case ICTR-96-4-T." *American Journal of International Law* 93 (January 1999): 195–199; George, Terry (dir.), *Hotel Rwanda.* United Artists, 2004; Harvard Law School. "A Child at the Time of the Nuremberg Trials, Navanethem Pillay Now Carries Their Legacy Forward." Available online. URL: http://www.law.harvard.edu/news/spotlight/ils/related/bus-driver.html. Accessed May 14, 2010; Ilibagiza, Immaculée. *Left to Tell: Discovering God Amidst the Rwandan Holocaust.* Carlsbad, Calif.: Hay House, 2006; "International Criminal Tribunal for Rwanda." Coalition on Women's Human Rights in Conflict Situations. Available online. URL: http://www.womensrights coalition.org/site/advocacyDossiers/rwanda/index_en.php. Accessed May 14, 2010; "The Prosecutor versus Jean-Paul Akayesu." United National International Criminal Tribunal for Rwanda. Available online. URL: http://69.94.11.53/ENGLISH/cases/Akayesu/judgement/akay001.htm. Accessed May 14, 2010.

The Oklahoma City bombing trials

Also known as: *U.S. v. McVeigh; U.S. v. Nichols; Oklahoma v. Nichols*

Date: 1997–2004

KEY ISSUES

The trials of the three principal conspirators in the Oklahoma City bombing case were surprisingly muted as compared to the shock of the crime. The destruction of the Alfred P. Murrah Federal Building in Oklahoma City, Oklahoma, on April 19, 1995, was a disturbing occurrence. It was the worst instance of terrorism in U.S. history to date. A total of 163 people, including 19 children in an on-site day-care center, died when explosives were detonated at the building. More than 500 individuals were injured, including persons with severe wounds such as missing limbs. The three men who were convicted in separate trials of masterminding the bombing, Timothy McVeigh, Terry Nichols, and Michael Fortier, were of U.S. birth rather than foreign terrorists. (A fourth potential defendant, who was female, worked out an arrangement to avoid prosecution.) The fact that the convicted mass murderers were native sons made their crimes difficult to comprehend for many Americans.

HISTORY OF THE CASE

McVeigh, Nichols, and Fortier met at Fort Benning, Georgia, when all three were in the U.S. Army. They shared an interest in guns, voiced distrust of persons of color, and discussed their sharp criticisms of the federal government. For a time after being discharged from the military, McVeigh and Nichols lived together on a farm in Nichols's home state of Michigan. They were angered by the actions of federal Alcohol, Tobacco, and Firearms (ATF) agents during the takeover and burning of a supposed religious compound in Waco, Texas, in 1993. The two decided to exact revenge on a federal facility and its employees. Nichols and McVeigh began to assemble guns and ammunition, making money through odd jobs such as reselling weapons at gun shows.

With Fortier and his wife, Lori Fortier, who assisted in forging a driver's license for McVeigh, the conspirators purchased and stole materials to make explosive devices. On April 18, 1995, Nichols helped McVeigh load a rental truck with ammonium nitrate and the materials to ignite it. The next day McVeigh drove the truck into Oklahoma City, lighted a five-minute fuse, parked the truck in front of the Murrah building, and then strolled away. McVeigh used earplugs to muffle the explosion, but the force of the bomb still lifted him off his feet.

Nichols had an alibi for April 19. He turned himself in two days later. At both his home in Kansas and the farm where he and McVeigh had stayed in Michigan, investigators seized numerous materials indicating Nichols's links with McVeigh, his assembling of explosive devices, and his anti-government views. Nichols's brother James was detained but later released.

As McVeigh drove away from Oklahoma City on an interstate highway, an Oklahoma state trooper noticed that McVeigh's car had no license plate. While he questioned McVeigh, policeman Charlie Hanger observed a bulge under the young man's jacket. McVeigh said that it was a gun but declared he had an out-of-state permit to carry a concealed weapon. The trooper put McVeigh under arrest. The detention was due to the lack of insurance papers and license and because the gun permit was not valid in Oklahoma.

As he left the Ryder rental truck in front of the Murrah building, McVeigh was wearing a favorite T-shirt: Juxtaposed over a portrait of Abraham Lincoln were the words that John Wilkes Booth had shouted when he landed on the stage after shooting the president, *Sic semper tyrannis.* When a sketch was circulated of the person who had rented the Ryder truck, Oklahoma sheriff's officers realized that they had McVeigh in custody already. Fortunately for the functioning of justice, McVeigh's release had been delayed. McVeigh and Nichols were charged almost simultaneously, although they came into the authorities' hands at different locations. McVeigh recognized that feeling was running quite high against him among

local citizens; he asked for a bulletproof vest so as not to become "another Oswald."

Federal investigators who were experts in criminal profiling had strongly considered the possibility—rife in the media—that the blast had been set by persons with ties to foreign powers. Especially under suspicion were radical Islamic groups. Some investigators in the hours after the explosion, however, maintained that the date of the catastrophe was no accident. It was exactly two years after the Branch Davidian compound had burned in Waco and was a date meaningful to extreme right-wing organizations in the United States for also being the anniversary of the Battles of Lexington and Concord (1775). In other words, it was Patriots' Day, revered by militia groups and white supremacist organizations.

SUMMARY OF ARGUMENTS

McVeigh was tried in federal district court in Colorado, beginning on April 24, 1997. (The defense did not need much argument to make the case for a change of venue from the location where the bombings had occurred.) The defense had successfully argued for separation of trials of the alleged conspirators hoping at least to distinguish Nichols and Fortier from McVeigh.

Order in the courtroom was threatened by mass media coverage. The lawyers for both sides had ample experience. Judge Robert Matsch aimed for the courtroom to be calm and the trial as focused as possible. Especially in the immediate wake of the O. J. Simpson case, he was well aware of the dangers of high-profile trials getting out of hand.

Lead prosecutor Joseph Hartzler concentrated on the "mountain" of circumstantial evidence that linked McVeigh to the bombing. Although no one conclusively could identify McVeigh at the scene, there were rental records with his fingerprints on them, traces of explosives materials on his clothing, and—as a result of a plea bargain involving Michael and Lori Fortier—the testimony of two of his co-plotters. The prosecution summoned approximately six times as many witnesses as did the defense. Many of those witnesses were persons to whom the jury was sympathetic because they were victims or relatives of victims of the blast.

McVeigh remained stone-faced throughout his trial. He said that he refused to "curl up into a fetal ball" and weep in response to tearful stories from injured victims and the families of the dead. It remained for the defense, led by experienced criminal defense attorneys Steven Jones and Robert Nigh, to construct a plausible justification for McVeigh's actions. McVeigh suggested that the defense paint him as fearing an "immediate" threat from the government. McVeigh hoped to hear it said that he was acting in self-defense by bombing the Murrah building. Nigh and Jones declined to pursue McVeigh's suggestion as an argument.

His lawyers' tack was instead to contend that McVeigh envisioned himself as defending the U.S. Constitution from overarching federal agents such as the authorities who had directed operations at Waco. The defense brought as many witnesses as it could to testify to McVeigh's being a decorated soldier in the Persian Gulf War. They emphasized the "normalcy" of McVeigh's childhood and his care for family members such as his sister. The enormity of McVeigh's offense, though, and the length and intensity of his dissatisfaction with the federal government, made any justification a very tough sell.

Although the evidence against McVeigh remained circumstantial, the prosecution showed convincing data—such as an FBI trace of one of the axles of the Ryder truck, eventually linked to McVeigh's rental of that truck under an assumed name—that connected him to the crime. The prosecution also advanced a strong argument that McVeigh's actions could be understood in terms of greed. His income source from sales at gun shows (an early passion) had been cut off by increased federal oversight of firearms. According to the prosecution, McVeigh was motivated far less by love of the Constitution than by personal vendettas. He was, simply, a frustrated gun fanatic who took out his rage on federal regulators.

Nichols, meanwhile, contended that although he had helped plan the bombing, he was not as culpable as McVeigh. Witnesses at his separate trial in federal district court disputed Nichols's line of argument. His former wife, Marife, gave evidence about Nichols's hatred of the federal government, his sneaking about, and his many years of association with McVeigh. There was indication—including from McVeigh himself—that Nichols and the Fortiers had gotten cold feet just hours before the bombing. According to McVeigh's statement at his trial, his codefendants "were men who liked to talk tough, but in the end their bitches and their kids ruled."

VERDICTS

On June 2, 1997, McVeigh's jury found him guilty of killing eight federal employees at the Murrah building. About two weeks later the same jury recommended a capital sentence, and the judge confirmed the death penalty. McVeigh had not been cited for the killing of the other victims because they were citizens of Oklahoma and the trial for their deaths had to be under the auspices of Oklahoma courts. Oklahoma declined to press charges against McVeigh once the capital sentence was handed down.

Nichols's federal jury agreed that he was guilty of conspiracy but found him not guilty on charges of detonating the explosives. Apparently, the fact that Nichols was not on-scene at the time of the bombing was decisive in the minds of several jurors. Nichols convinced the panel that he and McVeigh had fallen out over the extreme violence of the plan. His sentence, announced on June 4, 1998, was life in prison without parole.

When Nichols's jury in federal court failed to invoke the death penalty, Oklahomans pressed their state government to launch an investigation into the bombings. That inquiry recommended indictments against Nichols on state charges. Proceedings in Oklahoma state court began against Nichols in 1999. State officials contended that the motivation for their charges was not mere vindictiveness. Instead, they hoped for a full airing of the charge that Nichols had brought about the deaths of persons other than the federal employees whose deaths were under discussion in the federal trials. At issue in this trial were more than 160 deaths by arson, plus conspiracy charges.

The defense in Nichols's state case attempted to shift some blame onto additional conspirators who were as yet unidentified. Eventually, Nichols let out details about specific persons he claimed were involved. Among his more controversial allegations was the charge that an FBI agent, Larry

Potts, somehow was involved in the plot at Oklahoma City. Potts previously had earned the ire of violent critics of the U.S. government through his involvement as a law-enforcement officer at the 1993 shootout involving the Branch Davidian cult in Waco and in 1992 at the Ruby Ridge shootout in Idaho. Potts's mention by Nichols as a possible co-conspirator or director of the operation in Oklahoma City was merely one of the bizarre claims by Nichols.

Nichols's general position, as was McVeigh's, was that their act of terror represented only a sample of wide disaffection among Americans with their government. Such a line of argument was in response to the prosecution's claim, in state court and at Nichols's federal trial, that Nichols was less a political protester than a maladjusted individual. The state presented much evidence that for many years Nichols had refused to pay taxes or otherwise recognize the authority of the U.S. government.

The Oklahoma trial for Nichols ended in a guilty verdict on May 26, 2004, but again, this jury could not reach unanimity about a capital sentence. Some of the panel appeared moved to leniency by character witnesses attesting to Nichols's constancy toward his family and his recent conversion to Christianity. At the instruction of Judge Steven Taylor, Nichols was sent to a "super maximum" security jail in Colorado, where he was supposed to serve many consecutive life terms.

Michael and Lori Fortier turned state's evidence in exchange for Lori's immunity from prosecution and Michael's receiving a sentence of 12 years—considerably less than Nichols's—and a fine that was lowered from $200,000 to $75,000. The formal sentence cited Michael Fortier for failing to warn federal authorities about the plot. After his release from jail in January 2006, Fortier began to live under an assumed identity via the federal witness protection program.

SIGNIFICANCE

Having rejected the appeals process, McVeigh gave interviews and further justified his actions in a series of writings. Several of those musings reflected his growing disillusionment with the U.S. government during the Persian Gulf War. He expressed anger, for example, that the United States criticized Saddam Hussein as a mass murderer, when the United States also had bombed civilians during World War II. He selected a last meal and chose a poem (William Ernest Henley's "Invictus") as his last statement. That expression seemed to exemplify McVeigh's insistence that he still was in charge of his destiny:

> It matters not how strait the gate,
> How charged with punishments the scroll,
> I am the master of my fate:
> I am the captain of my soul.

In a more informal but equally grim vein, McVeigh had said that while he stood convicted and in forfeit of his life, the "score" still was "168 to 1." The only slight show of remorse that McVeigh evidenced was his brief reference to the presence of the day-care center at the Murrah building. He noted that he might have "changed targets" had he known that the nursery was open on the day of the bombing. His reference to the youngest victims of his actions as "collateral damage," though, proved more disturbing than exculpatory.

McVeigh was executed at a federal penitentiary in Terre Haute, Indiana, on June 11, 2001. His death was from lethal injection. Although several opponents of the death penalty demonstrated outside the prison, a larger crowd of watchers witnessed the execution via a closed-circuit television broadcast to a location in Oklahoma City. Many of those witnesses had lost family members in the blast six years before. McVeigh had no last words for the cameras, although he smiled at a few of his friends who were present. Several observers commented that McVeigh's passing appeared quiet and peaceful, in contrast to the deaths of the people in the Murrah building.

Further Reading

Crothers, Lane. *Rage on the Right: The American Militia Movement from Ruby Ridge to Homeland Security.* Lanham, Md.: Rowman & Littlefield, 2003; Hewitt, Christopher. *Understanding Terrorism in America: From the Klan to Al Qaeda.* London: Routledge, 2003; Linenthal, Edward. *The*

Unfinished Bombing: Oklahoma City in American Memory. New York: Oxford University Press, 2001; Michel, Lou, and Dan Herbeck. *American Terrorist.* New York: Regan Books, 2001; Wright, Stuart A. *Patriots, Politics, and the Oklahoma City Bombing.* Cambridge: Cambridge University Press, 2007.

The trials of Saddam Hussein

Date: 2005–2006

KEY ISSUES

The regime of Iraqi leader Saddam Hussein was brutal toward anyone who got in its way. Hussein's government fell at the hands of U.S. and other forces in 2003. After the removal of Hussein, further information came out about his efforts to purge Iraq of internal dissent and to strike out at foreign critics. A few powers insisted that the U.S.-led invasion of Iraq was the result of the anger of a vengeful George W. Bush administration toward all Muslims after the terrorist attacks of 2001. Still, most international observers supported the idea of holding Hussein to account for repeated human rights violations.

But who would prosecute Hussein and his lieutenants? Under which law were they answerable? Where would such proceedings take place? Were Iraqi courts—coopted by the regime during Hussein's tenure in power from 1979 until 2003—up to the task of bringing the former leader to justice? The trials were ultimately conducted with assistance from U.S. security forces and lawyers but largely run under the auspices of the Iraqi system of justice. Iraq's control of the legal process, while reassuring politically to the United States, raised concerns about the depth of Iraq's commitment to Western notions of fair trials.

HISTORY OF THE CASE

A leader of the Baath political party in Iraq since the 1960s, Hussein consolidated his power as the nation's key leader in 1979. In that year he staged both a takeover of power from other groups and a purge of Baathist ranks. He already had earned international notice for his development of Iraq's oil industry. Although a majority of Iraq's population was affiliated with the Shiite branch of Islam, his power base was the minority Sunni element who appreciated his advocacy of social welfare programs. Hussein also broke with other Muslim powers in the region in the matter of the legal system; he favored Western-style law rather than sharia (justice based on Islamic principles). Several Western nations, including the United States, for a time in the early 1980s took care to cultivate good relations with the Hussein government. The administration of President Ronald Reagan, for example, regarded Iraq under Hussein as a counterweight to Islamic extremism in general and Iran in particular.

The Hussein regime identified several groups and nations that it felt to be especially threatening, including Kurdish rebels and Iran. Soon after Hussein took power he used chemical weapons against the Kurds in northern Iraq. He also went after people in contested areas on the Iranian border. That deployment of controversial weapons went on for at least eight years, the duration of the debilitating and inconclusive war between Iraq and Iran. A low point of the engagement was toward the end, with Hussein's unleashing of a poison gas attack on the mostly civilian population of the Kurdish settlement of Halaba. The assault resulted in at least 5,000 dead and twice as many seriously injured.

Less than two years after the conflict with Iran was concluded, Hussein spearheaded an invasion of Kuwait. That led to U.S. military involvement in the region: the Persian Gulf War of 1990–91. The United States had by that time decided that the Hussein regime was more of a threat to stability in the region than a bulwark against Iran, and the U.S. position toward Hussein further hardened over the next presidential administrations as the Iraqi leader courted radical Muslim support in the Middle East. Relations broke down completely after September 11, 2001. In 2002 U.S. president Bush alleged that Hussein had stores of "weapons of mass destruction," including nuclear, chemical, and biological agents. A main goal of the U.S.

invasion of Iraq in the spring of 2003 was the capture or killing of Hussein.

It took until December of that year to locate the former leader, hiding in a basement near his place of birth. Hussein was cleaned up and relocated to a U.S. army base, where he faced questioning by U.S. intelligence officers. Two of Hussein's sons and a grandson had died during the U.S. invasion of Iraq, but several of his former associates, including certain powerful relatives, were alive and in U.S. custody.

It was important to U.S. policy that world opinion should see the Iraqis as proceeding against their former leader. Setting up a mechanism for trying Hussein took some months, even after he began to talk to interrogators. For one thing, the government of Iraq that had succeeded him had to be officially recognized by international organizations such as the United Nations. Iraq's Coalition Provisional Authority (CPA) got a stamp of approval from the United Nations in spring 2003. The CPA finalized plans for an Iraqi Special Tribunal (IST) about the time of Hussein's capture. By mid-summer 2004 the United States had handed over official control in Iraq to authorities in country. Prosecutors in Iraq had launched an investigation into possible charges against Hussein and others in late 2004. In February 2005 they announced that a criminal case would proceed against principal offenders against human rights, including Hussein.

Questions arose within and outside Iraq about the legitimacy of the CPA and its creation of the IST. The main complaint was that both had been set up while the United States still was occupying Iraq. On October 9, 2005, Iraq's interim government passed another law authorizing a tribunal very similar to the IST. The new iteration was named the Supreme Iraqi Criminal Tribunal (SICT). Hussein and seven other men were examined before the SICT beginning on October 19, 2005. The trial began with hearings under an investigative judge, who then recommended that the case go forward to a different criminal court judge.

There was no jury tradition in Iraq. The decision of guilt or innocence customarily was made at the same time and by the same judge or panel of judges who heard the evidence. Under the legislation of October 9, 2005, an appeals panel called

the Cassation Chamber was set up. This higher judicial body was vested with the power to hear new evidence discovered subsequent to trial, review applications of law during a criminal trial, consider whether proper procedure was followed in a trial, and order a new trial if there were severe irregularities.

In separate proceedings also under the new law, starting on August 21, 2006, Hussein and six others were charged and their trials begun with regard to a different set of crimes. The two trials concerned different crimes, and the courts hearing the cases were constituted by different legislation. Still, several of the offenses alleged were similar and certain codefendants besides Hussein were common to both trials.

The persons charged along with Hussein who had the highest international profiles were his half brother Barzan Ibrahim al-Tikriti; the former chief judicial figure in Iraq, Awad Hamed al-Bandar; Hussein's righthand man, Vice President Taha Ramadan; and leaders of the Baath Party, including Mohammed Azawi Ali, Abdullah Kazem Roueid, and Muzher Roueid. Several individuals who were well known inside Iraq were charged separately from these defendants and tried in still later proceedings (that is, after the second trial of Hussein).

The charges for the first trial were in connection with the actions that the Hussein government had taken against residents of al-Dujail, a Shiite town about 40 miles from Baghdad. The regime suspected that the community fostered a plot by the Islamic Dawa Party to assassinate Hussein while he rode through the vicinity in a motorcade on July 8, 1982. The authorities rounded up more than 600 suspects, sending most of the women and children to a brutal camp where they stayed for four years. They detained under even more arduous conditions 184 individuals, executing 143 outright. The rest died during detention, allegedly under torture. Al-Bandar was the sentencing judge in the al-Dujail trial.

Al-Tikriti was the head of the main intelligence agency in Iraq, the Mukhabarat. He was alleged to have been responsible for the torture and murder of a number of so-called enemies of the regime. He had represented Iraq at international organizations such as the United Nations and served in Geneva as a human rights delegate for about 10 years beginning in 1989. His critics charged that al-Tikriti was more involved in funneling money into Swiss bank accounts for Hussein than in serving on the UN rights panel.

In October 2005, just as the first trial began, the court stated that the charges against Hussein and several of his immediate inferiors in the case concerning the al-Dujail massacre had been enumerated in a recent Iraqi law. The allegations were classified as crimes against humanity in the Iraqi statute of 2005 that also had set up the SICT. The several relevant crimes were premeditated murder, false imprisonment, forced relocation, destruction of farms, and land confiscation. The definitions of crimes against humanity in the 2005 Iraqi law were modeled on similar statements in the Rome Statute of 1998, which set up the International Criminal Court. They were thus consistent with international standards. All of the accused pleaded not guilty.

Summary of Arguments

It was several months into the first trial (May 2006) before the presiding judge issued a public statement of the exact terms of the formal indictment. The defense maintained that this meant that the prosecution was changing the nature of the charges—in effect, amending its working indictment. Although some commentators outside Iraq observed that it was within the scope of Iraqi legal practice to add to or change an indictment after a trial had begun, most scholars of Iraqi law maintained that this was not the norm within Iraqi justice. In order to reestablish legal norms for Iraq after the fall of the Hussein regime, the laws of 2003–05 referred to accepted practices within Iraqi courts between 1962 and 1979. For example, in 1971 Iraq had ratified the International Covenant on Civil and Political Rights, which required that persons under arrest had to be informed of particular charges against them. Moreover, many who criticized the Hussein trial that began in 2005 contended that it was incompatible with Anglo-American principles of justice for defendants not to be fully apprised of the charges against them well before trial proceedings began.

The court, however, had something of an answer for such objections. It said that there was a misunderstanding of what had transpired when the judge had seemed to state precise charges in May 2006. That announcement was in keeping with the traditional Iraqi practice of "certifying" the indictment after a trial had gotten well under way. Thus, the contention by the Iraqi judiciary in charge of Hussein's first trial was that they actually were only repeating charges that already had been listed for the defendants at the outset of the case but not announced to the public at that time. This court contended, therefore, that it was being more rather than less protective of the defendants' rights to a fair trial.

The second trial of Hussein and his contemporaries concerned the persecution of Kurds in northern Iraq during what was termed Operation Anfal, or the al-Anfal campaign, during the years 1986 through 1989. The government gave its nickname to the campaign from a portion of a chapter in the Qur'an that detailed looting following a famous victory of Muslims against their enemies. In this second prosecution Hussein and others such as commander Ali Hassan al-Majid (Chemical Ali) were charged with committing genocide. Their objects were not only the Kurds but also other minority groups including Assyrians and Turks. Conservative estimates were that the Hussein government killed more than 50,000 persons in the lands of the Kurds in northern Iraq; some put the total at nearly 200,000.

Hundreds of villages were obliterated; in some areas all Kurdish people simply disappeared. The Iraqi military undertook bombings and used mustard gas and biological agents against civilians, and violently "relocated" many other people. A variety of international human rights organizations such as Amnesty International and Human Rights Watch condemned the official Iraqi actions while they were occurring and agreed once the campaign had ended that the campaign represented a systematic policy of extermination. There was much evidence that the al-Anfal campaign aimed at killing every adult male Kurd between 15 and 70 years of age.

There was international comment on both of the proceedings against Hussein, both from the perspective of legal experts in international and

Middle Eastern law and from a media standpoint. Amnesty International, for example, issued statements criticizing the censorship of information that came from Iraqi courtrooms. Statements by Hussein that print reporters heard in court often were not audible in videotaped versions of the trial. At times the Iraqi authorities also restricted access to the courtroom to U.S. media representatives.

The two long trials spotlighted the often forceful personalities of the multiple defendants. Al-Tikriti became known during the proceedings for frequently interrupting speakers with his heated comments. Hussein himself had opened the first trial on a defiant note, insulting the qualifications of a judge of Kurdish origin and stating that he, Hussein, could not be a defendant because he still was the president of Iraq. Such outbursts sometimes resulted in defendants' being ejected from the courtroom.

An even more serious problem than the behavior of the defendants was the danger faced by lawyers for both sides. In October and November 2005 two defense attorneys were killed and one wounded in attacks outside the court. Still worse was the killing of Hussein's leading defense attorney, Khamis al-Obeidi, in June 2006. At one point chief judge Rizgar Amin stepped down and was replaced. Amin had complained that political authorities were too involved in the case. There was evidence for such a view; for example, Iraqi president Jalal Talabani had made a public statement just prior to the first trial that he personally had interrogated Hussein, who had confessed to several crimes. Hussein quickly denied that he had admitted fault.

VERDICT

Judge Raouf Abdul-Rahman announced the court's decision in the al-Dujail trial on November 5, 2006. The verdict held the three main defendants—Hussein, Al-Tikriti, and al-Bandar—to be guilty. All three received death sentences, while the court sentenced codefendant Ramadan to life in prison and three others to terms of 15 years behind bars. In an action that had little parallel in Western law, an appeals court changed Ramadan's sentence into a capital one; he was executed in March 2007.

The only major defendant to be acquitted (on grounds of insufficient evidence) was the Baath Party leader Azawi Ali.

The trial in regard to the al-Anfal charges was scheduled to begin in August 2006, but Hussein did not see the courtroom in that case until December. While Hussein was a defendant in the second case, the Cassation Chamber '(a nine-judge panel) announced its decision affirming the convictions in the first (al-Dujail) trial. On December 26, Hussein's hopes for a legal victory ended. He was hanged at a U.S. army outpost in the suburbs of Baghdad on December 30, 2006. Al-Tikriti and al-Bandar were executed by hanging on January 15, 2007. Rumors circulated on the Internet that the Iraqi soldiers in charge of the former dictator's execution had taunted Hussein before his hanging or had slashed his dead body. The Iraqi troop leader responsible for the execution denied all such reports. Apparently, the decision to execute al-Tikriti and al-Bandar after Hussein was informed by American judgments that Saddam Hussein's death ought to be marked out as especially important.

After the sentence against Hussein was carried out, the United Nations, through its human rights commissioner Louise Arbour, issued an official statement condemning the execution as contrary to human rights standards. It was unclear whether the UN criticism was in reference to the imposition of the death penalty or the use of hanging. In either case, after Hussein's death international lawyers continued to argue about whether Iraqi law in 2006 sanctioned capital punishment. Some experts maintained that Iraq's being a signatory to conventions such as that at Rome in 1998 meant that it rejected the ultimate penalty. Historians of Iraq, however, pointed to the imposition of hanging for serious crimes in Iraq in the immediate pre-Hussein era. The political and legal status quo in that time period had been used as a point of reference for other aspects of Hussein's trials.

The al-Anfal trial was adjourned temporarily. When it reconvened, the deceased dictator's name was removed from courtroom documents. In June 2007 three of Hussein's codefendants received death sentences for having committed genocide against the Kurds, although one leading defendant was acquitted.

SIGNIFICANCE

In 2008 the last set of leading politicians associated with Hussein went on trial in Iraq. The most famous among that later group of defendants was former deputy prime minister Tariq Aziz. He was tried along with Hussein's cousin al-Majid (Chemical Ali) and Hussein's half brother Watban Ibrahim al-Hassan. These defendants were accused of rounding up and executing 42 merchants who the regime said had hoarded food during a time of UN-imposed trade sanctions. Aziz was an unexpected addition to the list of war criminals prosecuted by the new anti-Hussein regime, for he had many foreign ties (including at the Vatican). Like Hussein, Chemical Ali had faced serious charges on several occasions. Al-Majid's multiple encounters with the judicial system of the new Iraq ended on January 25, 2010, when he was hanged for crimes including his direction of the al-Anfal campaign.

Some critics of the trials of Hussein asserted that the former president of Iraq had been convicted because he had angered the United States. They perceived the United States as stage-managing the trial. Hussein's lawyer Khalil al-Dulaimi had said exactly that when he opined: "This court is a creature of U.S., and the Iraqi court is just a tool and a rubber stamp of the invaders."

For many Westerners the trials of Hussein became a gauge of the commitment of Iraq to the legal principles that other powers—notably the United States—cherished. In that regard, certain aspects of the prosecution of Hussein and his cohorts came up wanting. The proceedings were not as transparent as would have been ideal, for example. The issue of effective legal counsel for the defendants was thorny, given the grave safety concerns that they faced. In addition, the penalties imposed went against current trends within the international legal community, even in cases of gross human rights violations. Scholars familiar with international human rights courts noted that in the genocide trials that recently had occurred in Rwanda and the former Yugoslavia, the defendants were given noncapital sentences.

Politically, though, the case against Hussein held up well. He was shown at trial to be a repressive leader who had surrounded himself with henchmen perhaps more vindictive than himself.

Dispatching him through a courtroom verdict seemed an effective way for Iraq to break with its bloody recent past.

Further Reading

Balaghi, Shiva. *Saddam Hussein: A Biography.* Westport, Conn.: Greenwood, 2008; Maddox, Eric, and Davin Seay. *Capturing Saddam: The Hunt for Saddam Hussein—As Told by the Unlikely Interrogator Who Spearheaded the Mission.* New York: HarperCollins, 2009; McDowall, David. *A Modern History of the Kurds.* London: I. B. Tauris, 2004; Newton, Michael, and Michael Scharf. *Enemy of the State: The Trial and Execution of Saddam Hussein.* New York: St. Martin's, 2008; "Saddam Hussein Trial." Law Library of Congress. Available online. URL: http://www.loc.gov/law/help/hussein/. Accessed February 20, 2010; Sasson, Jean. *Mayada, Daughter of Iraq: One Woman's Survival under Saddam Hussein.* New York: New American Library, 2004.

The trial of Kaing Guek Eav

Also known as: The killing fields trials

Date: 2010

KEY ISSUES

Between 1975 and 1979 the regime that the rest of the world knew as the Khmer Rouge controlled Cambodia. The Khmer Rouge (Communist Party of Kampuchea) came to power after U.S. bombings in Cambodia had wiped out Vietnamese resistance to the local insurgent movement headed by Pol Pot. Calling the nation that it dominated Democratic Kampuchea (DK), the leaders of the new government aimed at a forced collectivization of agriculture and ideological supremacy within the region. Not unlike late 20th-century dictatorships in Rwanda and Guatemala, as well as Stalinist rule in the Soviet Union and the Nazis in

Germany, the Khmer Rouge backed its goals with extreme violence.

Pol Pot and his supporters used indicators such as possession of "Western technology" (wristwatches and glasses, for example), to identify those who supposedly opposed the regime. Coming in for marked ill treatment—often immediate execution—were urban dwellers, intellectuals, and skilled tradespeople. Toward its goal of collectivization the Khmer Rouge forcibly moved many city people to the countryside. The ideal Khmer Rouge citizens (in the regime's parlance "the old people") were rural peasants who were hardworking, illiterate, and unquestioning of authority. The DK government contrasted such folk with former town dwellers, who were French speaking or Buddhist, for example. While laboring to meet agricultural quotas in farming cooperatives, any resistance by "the new people" often meant summary execution on the very sites where crops were grown. Rural Cambodia became known as "the killing fields."

Beyond perceived enemies of the Khmer Rouge who were murdered without trial, many thousands more were executed after show trials, kept from proper medical treatment, denied food, tortured, or worked to death in labor camps in the country. The Khmer Rouge sent many so-called enemies of the state to a hidden detention facility called Tuol Sleng. A proportion of those detainees were family members that the regime had encouraged children to inform against. Also known to the regime as S-21, the location of the detention center was a converted school in Phnom Penh. The vast majority of the tens of thousands of persons who entered the place died there. The vernacular name for the site was "hill of the poison tree."

International observers put the death toll within the nation in the few years of the Khmer Rouge rule at between 1.5 and 2 million persons; in other words, between one-fifth and one-quarter of the country's population died during the Cambodian holocaust. When the DK regime fell in 1979, it was difficult to locate anyone in Cambodia who had not been scarred by the violence.

Pol Pot had contacts in Southeast Asia and support among world powers. In 1977, for example, he presented himself as an ally of the successors to Mao Zedong such as Hua Guofeng. Although the dictator sometimes painted capitalist

powers such the United States as his greatest enemy, it was forces closer to home that unseated him. In 1979 the Socialist Republic of Vietnam, the newly united North and South Vietnam after years of civil and international conflict, launched a takeover of Cambodia. The new government of the People's Republic of Kampuchea (PRK, also known as the State of Cambodia, or SOC) pushed the Khmer Rouge back into the hinterlands. Persons who had had high positions under the Khmer Rouge hid or fled abroad.

Although the Vietnamese recently had seen combat and privation, they were appalled by the desolation of the Cambodian countryside. It did not take much investigation to determine that the mounds of earth scattered throughout rural areas were mass graves that betokened the slaughter of hundreds of thousands.

From the jungle and occasionally a refuge in Thailand, guerrillas from the former regime still loyal to Pol Pot continued to harass the PRK government. The remnant of the Khmer Rouge was wracked by defections to the Vietnam-backed government in Phnom Penh along with internal rancor. In 1997, the still-defiant Khmer Rouge actually placed its former head on trial and imposed a life sentence upon him. International observers derided the trial as a show tribunal put on by the former lackeys of Pol Pot. At the time of that trial Pol Pot showed little sympathy for the victims of the killing fields:

> First, I want to let you know that I came to join the revolution, not to kill the Cambodian people, . . . Look at me now. Do you think . . . am I a violent person? No. So, as far as my conscience and my mission were concerned, there was no problem. This needs to be clarified. . . . Whoever wishes to blame or attack me is entitled to do so. I regret I didn't have enough experience to totally control the movement. On the other hand, with our constant struggle, this had to be done together with others in the communist world to stop Kampuchea becoming Vietnamese. . . . For the love of the nation and the people it was the right thing to do but in the course of our actions we made mistakes.

Pol Pot died within the year while under house arrest. His demise was frustrating to those who had hoped to bring him before a less biased tribunal to answer charges of gross violation of human rights.

HISTORY OF THE CASE

In the first years of the 21st century the United Nations began to consider formal proceedings against persons alleged to have been responsible for many deaths under the Khmer Rouge. That inquiry proceeded under the leadership of several coprosecutors who were human rights lawyers from Cambodia and other nations. The four main coprosecutors included two Cambodians, a Canadian, and a U.S. citizen. Largely from inside Cambodia the prosecutors gathered more than 14,000 pages of documents, heard more than 350 witnesses, and examined more than 40 "undisturbed mass graves."

In order to fund such a cooperative judicial venture between Cambodian and UN authorities, individuals and groups supporting trials for the Khmer Rouge leaders solicited donations from outside Cambodia, which came to total $78.4 million. Among the other efforts for the prosecution were compilations of records remaining from the regime. Scholars at Yale University's Genocide Studies Program, for example, collected and made available to researchers records from the Santebal, the security arm of the Khmer Rouge. The Yale genocide project was partially funded by the U.S. State Department.

In 2007 the prosecutorial team issued a statement that terrible crimes had been committed by the regime. Among the tactics that the prosecutors alleged the DK government had employed were ethnic division and religious persecution. The crimes listed as committed by the regime included torture, murder, and rape, often as individual acts but also within systematic programs of oppression. The prosecutors provided a list of the names of five key officials whom they thought should be tried in an initial set of proceedings for crimes against humanity.

The persons identified as worthy of immediate prosecution for human rights crimes included the Kampuchean foreign minister Ieng Sary; Pol Pot's righthand man, Nuon Chea, known as "Brother Number Two"; Pol Pot's in-law and expert in economics Khieu Samphan; army leader Chhit Choeun (better known as Ta Mok); and an ex-teacher named Kaing Guek Eav (Comrade Duch), who had served as the warden at Tuol Sleng. Except for Duch, the men were at the center of Khmer Rouge policies, an inner clique known in the 1970s as the "Angka."

The coprosecutors handed that list of prime suspects to a set of judges in the Extraordinary Chambers in the Courts of Cambodia (ECCC). The ECCC in effect was a special court authorized by Cambodian legislation in 1999 to bring the worst offenders of the killing fields to justice. The first case to be heard, beginning in early 2010, was against the head of Tuol Sleng. By his own admission at trial Duch had some responsibility for at least 16,000 deaths at the prison. It had been a detention center charged with suppressing the activities of the opponents most feared by the Khmer Rouge. The others on the prosecutors' list were to be brought to justice in a separate proceeding, called "Case No. 2," after Duch's trial.

Although Comrade Duch did not have high-level political authority like the group who surrounded Cambodian leader Pol Pot, he clearly was the regime's chief man on the ground in the criminal justice system. He had been a force within the secret police—some said its leader. In 1999, quite by accident, a British journalist found Duch and made his location known. That led to the prison commander being targeted by those who sought to prosecute crimes against humanity in reference to the Khmer Rouge.

SUMMARY OF ARGUMENTS

The trial was held in Phnom Penh. The bench in the trial chamber consisted of three Cambodian judges and two foreigners. Two of the Cambodian judges spoke English and the other was educated in law in Ukraine. The vice president of the court was from France, and its fifth judge was a distinguished jurist from New Zealand. There were two reserve (alternate) judges: one from Cambodia and the other from Austria. Similarly, the court that would hear any appeals in the case, the Supreme Court Chamber, was a multinational group. The

Cambodian judicial figures all had tried cases involving former Khmer Rouge defendants.

Most witnesses in Duch's trial who spoke about Tuol Sleng were not persons who had been locked up in the prison but rather people who lived in the neighborhood near it. It had a fearsome reputation as a place that detainees never left. Ironically, many of the persons singled out for incarceration at Duch's facility were targeted by the regime as internal threats. A number were former soldiers. Especially as collectivization in the countryside stalled, in 1978, the regime grew paranoid that moles were damaging its efforts. The purpose of sending individuals to Tuol Sleng was to torture them into implicating others in their allegedly anti-Kampuchean activities. The supposed confessions of those brought to Tuol Sleng gave credence to further persecutions.

The prison keepers' methods of extracting information were crude, usually involving electric shock. Though they preferred not to kill their victims outright but let them die of privation, the prison staff, headed by Kaing Guek Eav, did keep extensive records of certain people's deaths in order to satisfy the regime that its enemies were no longer living. Such documentation, including photographs of deceased persons with slit throats and other fatal wounds, became part of the trial record used in Duch's case. Three witnesses at trial were among the 14 persons known to have survived a stint in Tuol Sleng. Their testimony of drinking their own urine and eating insects that fell from the ceiling echoed reports from the rural areas of widespread starvation and other horrors perpetrated by the regime.

Before the court from March through July 2010, the defendant did not contest his pivotal role at Tuol Sleng. Comrade Duch said he was impelled to confess his role now, at his trial, because of two things: his conversion to Christianity and the claims of Pol Pot that Tuol Sleng was a figment of the imagination of the enemies of the Khmer Rouge. The former prison commander, however, maintained that he did not make political decisions as a part of Pol Pot's inner circle. He did not use Adolf Eichmann's famous phrase "just following orders," but Comrade Duch's defense amounted to a similar excuse.

As a defendant, Duch expressed a certain amount of remorse for the multitude of deaths that he had supervised. When he came face to face with the rare survivors of the prison such as witness Bou Meng, Kaing Guek Eav sobbed in court. Bou Meng's wife had died in the torture center. Duch personally had chosen Bou Meng for a work detail, an assignment that saved the husband's life. Those in court recounted the comment that the prison commandant made to his former charge upon first seeing him at trial: "I send my respects to the soul of your wife." Among other dramatic moments at trial was the playing of a video showing Kaing Guek Eav's 2008 visit to Tuol Sleng. The detention center had been turned into a museum dedicated to the victims of genocide. At that tour Duch had appeared emotionally overcome.

The main justification by the defense was that Comrade Duch faced death himself if he did not carry out the orders of his superiors. Kaing Guek Eav had remained in hiding for nearly 20 years, in large part to elude possible prosecutors. Still, his lawyers emphasized to the tribunal that he was offering detailed information that would benefit future proceedings against the Khmer Rouge leadership. Duch's French attorney, François Roux, apparently counseled his client to begin the proceedings on a note of contrition and yet did not carry through that theme consistently in the trial.

The defendant's demeanor was difficult to read. Some observers recalled him in court as impassive, while others noted his occasional shows of contrition. His attitude seemed to harden as the trial went along. Before trial he had offered to undergo a public stoning; at the end of his courtroom appearance he requested acquittal. He appeared well prepared for the questioning that he underwent, occasionally lecturing the judges and lawyers on courtroom procedures. He stated that even he did not accept as truthful many of the confessions that he and his subordinates at Tuol Sleng extracted: "I never believed that the confessions I received told the truth. At most, they were about 40 percent true." Comrade Duch commented that he understood how the forced confessions of prisoners fed the delusions of the regime: "The work expanded, people were arrested illegally, right or wrong. I considered it evil eating evil eating evil."

VERDICT

The court remarked that it had taken into consideration Duch's cooperation. The judges also said that they recognized the defendant's expressions of remorse, though those were not as expansive as might be hoped. The judges noted that although Duch was personally culpable in many deaths, he had not formed the policy that led to incarcerations at the notorious prison. Still, the court observed that he had been present at a number of interrogations and deaths.

The international panel imposed a 35-year sentence on Kaing Guek Eav. Since he was 67 at the time of trial, he had a theoretical possibility of outliving his sentence. In addition, the court gave the convicted man credit for time served, including a stint that it called an illegal detention. That meant that Kaing Guek Eav might be out of prison in 12 years. Such an outcome brought expressions of disbelief and anger from the family members of Khmer Rouge victims, many of whom attended Duch's 77-day trial.

The tribunal imposed the sentence within Cambodia's law. At that time of Duch's trial the nation did not allow the death penalty. The highest possible term available to the court in this instance was 40 years, and prosecutors and victims' advocates had hoped for that maximum penalty. The UN judges defended their decision as "balanced," saying that they were charged with objectivity. A key purpose of such a trial, said Judge Silvia Cartwright of New Zealand, was to avoid retribution by angry loved ones.

SIGNIFICANCE

Prosecutors appealed the sentence in the case of the former jailer, maintaining that the sentence was not stern enough. Public comment included the observation that Duch had been sentenced to 11 hours' incarceration for every person killed at Tuol Sleng. The prosecution argued that the charges against Duch had been improperly combined under the general rubric of "persecution" and "torture." They maintained that the prison commander had been shown to be guilty of separate crimes against humanity such as rape and enslavement that should have been specified singly. Finally, those seeking a stiffening of the sentence offered the view that Kaing Guek Eav was a "willing participant" in the persecution masterminded by the regime.

The court reminded critics that the case had provided a great deal of data that could be utilized against the four remaining major defendants. Those former Khmer Rouge officials were mounting a vigorous defense, in contrast to Duch's apparent decision not to seriously contest his prosecution. Still, some in Cambodia who had helped assemble details of Duch's activities expressed chagrin that the defendant's limited apologies seemed to be accepted at face value by members of the Cambodian public. The director of the Documentation Center of Cambodia, which supplied many of the details of life at the prison that were cited at trial, commented while the proceedings were ongoing: "He is winning the case, even though he will be convicted. He has managed not to let his brutality show."

Others who viewed the ECCC from abroad were skeptical that its inquiries would go very deep due to the connection between the leader of Cambodia at the time of Duch's conviction and the Khmer Rouge. Cambodian prime minister Hun Sen, the nation's de facto ruler, was a Khmer Rouge operative before escaping to Vietnam. He had a major role in the Vietnamese takeover of 1979 that displaced the Khmer Rouge. Human rights organizations such as Amnesty International repeatedly cited the pro-Vietnamese PRK for its own excesses toward perceived enemies. Prior to the trial of Kaing Guek Eav, Hun Sen lamented the role of the United Nations and "foreign judges and prosecutors" in Cambodia.

Further Reading

Becker, Elizabeth. *When the War Was Over.* New York: Public Affairs, 1998; Cambodian Genocide Program. "Khmer Rouge Genocide Tribunal." Yale University. Available online. URL: http://www.yale.edu/cgp/news.html. Accessed August 30, 2010; Chandler, David. *Voices from S-21: Terror and History in Pol Pot's Secret Prison.* Berkeley: University of California Press, 2000; Clymer, Kenton. *The United States and Cambodia, 1969–2000: A Troubled Relationship.* New York: Routledge, 2004; Haas, Michael. *Cambodia, Pol Pot, and the United States: The Faustian Pact.* New

York: Praeger, 1991; Joffe, Ronald (dir.) *The Killing Fields*. Warner Brothers, 1984; "Kaing Guek Eav (alias 'Duch'): Duch Judicial Investigation and Pre-Trial Proceedings Overview." Cambodia Tribunal Monitor. Available online. URL: http://www.cambodiatribunal.org/trial-proceedings/kaing-guek-eav.html. Accessed September 1, 2010; Kiernan, Ben, ed. *Genocide and Democracy in Cambodia: The Khmer Rouge, the United Nations, and the International Community*. New Haven, Conn.: Yale Council on Southeast Asia Studies, 1993; Ung, Loung. *First They Killed My Father: A Daughter of Cambodia Remembers*. New York: HarperCollins, 2000.

APPENDIXES

TRIALS BY TOPIC

435

The trial of William Calley

The Argentine junta trials

The trial of Saddam Hussein

Murder and Attempted Murder

The trial of Sextus Roscius

The trial of Flosi

The trial of the sow of Falaise

The trial of Bapaji

The Overbury poisoning trials

The trials of William Kidd

The Boston Massacre trials

The trial of Cho Chae-hang

The trial of William Burke and Helen McDougal

The trial of Marie Lafarge

The trial of Daniel M'Naghten

The trial of Ned Kelly

The trial of Charles Guiteau

The trials of Alfred Packer

The Haymarket trials

The trial of Lizzie Borden

The trial of Harry Thaw

The trials of Sinnisiak and Uluksuk

The trial of Bruno Richard Hauptmann

The trial of Weerasamy and Velaithen

The trial of Steven Truscott

The trial of Charles Manson

The trials of Mehmet Ali Agca

The dingo baby trial

The trial of Orenthal James Simpson

The Oklahoma City bombing trials

Piracy and Mutiny

The trials of William Kidd

The Bounty court-martial trial

The trial of the Amistad mutineers

Race and Ethnicity

The trial of Francisco Vásquez de Coronado

The trial of James Somerset

The trial of the Amistad mutineers

The trial of Bahadur Shah Zafar II

The trial of John Brown

The trial of Chief Langalibalele

The trial of Ned Kelly

The Dreyfus case

The trials of Sinnisiak and Uluksuk

The trial of Mohandas Gandhi

The Sacco-Vanzetti trials

The Scottsboro Boys' trials

The Reichstag fire trial

The trial of Weerasamy and Velaithen

The trial of Nelson Mandela

The trial of Orenthal James Simpson

Rape and Domestic Violence

The trial of Jacques Le Gris

The trial of the Mamluka bride

The trial of Cho Chae-hang

The trial of Harry Thaw

The trials of Roscoe Arbuckle

The Scottsboro Boys' trials

The trial of Aleck Bourne

The dingo baby trial

The trial of Orenthal James Simpson

Rebellion and Terrorism

The trial of William Wallace

The trial of Mary, Queen of Scots

The Gunpowder Conspiracy trial

The trial of Joaquim José da Silva Xavier

The trial of Wolfe Tone

The trial of John Brown

The Tokyo War Crimes Trials

The trial of Adolf Eichmann

The Ienaga textbook trials

The trial of William Calley

The Argentine junta trials

The trial of Jean-Paul Akayesu

The trial of Saddam Hussein

The trial of Kaing Guek Eav

SELECTED BIBLIOGRAPHY

Aymar, Brandt, and Edward Sagarin. *A Pictorial History of the World's Great Trials: From Socrates to Jean Harris.* New York: Random House, 1986.

Ball, Howard. *Prosecuting War Crimes and Genocide: The Twentieth Century Experience.* Lawrence: University of Kansas Press, 1999.

Belknap, Michal R., ed. *American Political Trials.* Westport, Conn.: Praeger, 1994.

Block, Brian P., and John Hostettler. *Famous Cases: Nine Trials That Changed the Law.* Winchester, U.K.: Waterside Press, 2002.

Cairns, David J. A. *Advocacy and the Making of the Adversarial Criminal Trial, 1800–1865.* New York: Oxford University Press, 1998.

Carlson, A. Cheree. *The Crimes of Womanhood: Defining Femininity in a Court of Law.* Urbana: University of Illinois Press, 2009.

Chermak, Steven M., and Frankie Y. Bailey. *Crimes and Trials of the Century.* Westport, Conn.: Greenwood Press, 2007.

Chiasson, Lloyd. *Illusive Shadows: Justice, Media, and Socially Significant American Trials.* Westport, Conn.: Praeger, 2003.

Christenson, Ron. *Political Trials in History: From Antiquity to the Present.* New Brunswick, N.J.: Transaction Publishers, 1991.

Dershowitz, Alan M. *America on Trial: Inside the Legal Battles That Transformed Our Nation.* New York: Warner Books, 2004.

Dickler, Gerald. *Man on Trial: History-Making Trials from Socrates to Oppenheimer.* Garden City, N.Y.: Doubleday & Co., 1962.

Felman, Shoshana. *The Juridical Unconscious: Trials and Traumas in the Twentieth Century.* Cambridge, Mass.: Harvard University Press, 2002.

Ferguson, Robert A. *The Trial in American Life.* Chicago: University of Chicago Press, 2007.

Gordon-Reed, Annette. *Race on Trial: Law and Justice in American History.* Oxford: Oxford University Press, 2002.

Grant, Robert, and Joseph Katz. *The Great Trials of the Twenties: The Watershed Decade in American Courtrooms.* Rockville Centre, N.Y.: Sarpedon, 1998.

Harris, Brian. *Injustice: State Trials from Socrates to Nuremberg.* Stroud, U.K.: Sutton Publishing, 2006.

———. *Intolerance: Divided Societies on Trial.* London: Wildy, Simmons & Hill Publishing, 2008.

Haynes, John Earl. *Early Cold War Spies: The Espionage Trials That Shaped American Politics.* Cambridge: Cambridge University Press, 2006.

Hitchcock, Tim, and Robert Shoemaker. *Tales from the Hanging Court.* London: Hodder Arnold, 2006.

Hostettler, John. *Fighting for Justice: The History and Origins of Adversary Trial.* Winchester, U.K.: Waterside Press, 2006.

Kadri, Sadakat. *The Trial: A History, from Socrates to O. J. Simpson.* New York: Random House, 2005.

Knappmann, Edward, ed. *Great World Trials.* Canton, Mich.: Visible Ink Press, 1997.

Langbein, John H. *The Origins of Adversary Criminal Trial.* Oxford: Oxford University Press, 2005.

Langbert, Enid W. *The Right to a Fair Trial.* Detroit, Mich.: Greenhaven Press, 2005.

Laughland, John. *A History of Political Trials: From Charles I to Saddam Hussein.* Oxford: Peter Lang, 2008.

Lief, Michael S., and Harry M. Caldwell. *The Devil's Advocates: Greatest Closing Arguments in Criminal Law.* New York: Scribner, 2006.

Maogoto, Jackson Nyamuya. *War Crimes and Realpolitik: International Justice from World War I to the 21st century.* Boulder, Colo.: Lynne Rienner Publishers, 2004.

Marcus, Robert D., and Anthony Marcus. *On Trial: American History Through Court Proceedings and Hearings.* St. James, N.Y.: Brandywine Press, 1998.

Margulies, Phillip. *The Devil on Trial: Witches, Anarchists, Atheists, Communists, and Terrorists in America's Courtrooms.* Boston: Houghton Mifflin, 2008.

May, Allyson N. *The Bar and the Old Bailey, 1750–1850.* Chapel Hill: University of North Carolina Press, 2003.

McLynn, Frank. *Famous Trials.* Pleasantville, N.Y.: Reader's Digest, 1995.

Melkian, R. A. *The Trial in History.* Manchester, U.K.: Manchester University Press, 2003.

Mulholland, Maureen, and Brian S. Pullan. *Judicial Tribunals in England and Europe, 1200–1700.* Manchester, U.K.: Manchester University Press, 2003.

Rapley, Robert. *Witch Hunts: From Salem to Guantanamo Bay.* Montreal, Canada: McGill-Queen's University Press, 2007.

Shriver, George H., ed. *American Religious Heretics: Formal and Informal Trials.* Nashville, Tenn.: Abingdon Press, 1966.

Thurston, Robert W. *The Witch Hunts: History of the Witch Persecutions in Europe and North America.* New York: Pearson Longman, 2007.

Whitman, James Q. *The Origins of Reasonable Doubt: Theological Roots of the Criminal Trial.* New Haven, Conn.: Yale University Press, 2008.

Zolo, Danillo. *Victors' Justice: From Nuremberg to Baghdad.* London: Verso, 2009.

INDEX